Information Systems Today

Canadian Edition

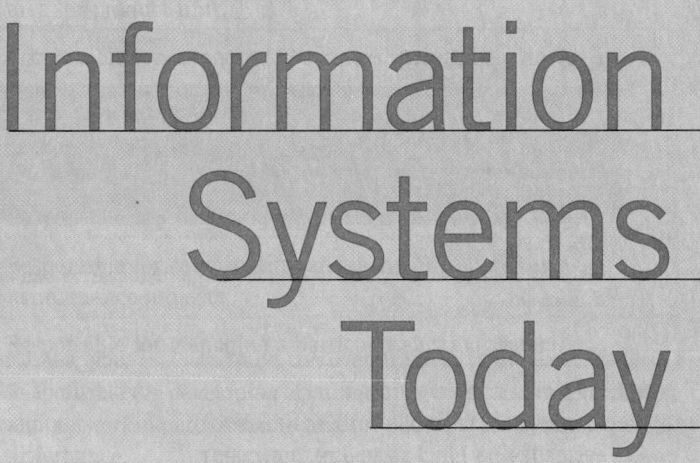

Information Systems Today

Canadian Edition

Leonard M. Jessup
Washington State University

Joseph S. Valacich
Washington State University

Michael R. Wade
Schulich School of Business, York University

Toronto

Library and Archives Canada Cataloguing in Publication

Jessup, Leonard M., 1961–
Information systems today/Leonard M. Jessup, Joseph S. Valacich, Michael R. Wade.—Canadian ed.

Includes index.
ISBN 0-13-109290-1

1. Information technology. 2. Information storage and retrieval systems—Business. I. Valacich, Joseph S., 1959– II. Wade, Michael, 1968– III. Title.

T58.5.J48 2006 658′.05 C2004-904477-X

0-13-109290-1

Vice President, Editorial Director: Michael J. Young
Acquisitions Editor: Laura Forbes
Marketing Manager: Jeff Clarke
Senior Developmental Editor: Paul Donnelly
Production Editor: Marisa D'Andrea
Copy Editor: Kelli Howey
Production Coordinator: Deborah Starks
Page Layout: Hermia Chung
Photo/Literary Permissions Researcher: Sandy Cooke
Art Director: Julia Hall
Interior and Cover Design: Anthony Leung
Cover Image: Masterfile

2 3 4 5 QPD 10 09 08 07 06

Printed and bound in the United States.

Dedication

To Joy, Jamie, and David, for your love and support.
—Len

To Jackie, Jordan, and James, for your sacrifices, encouragement, and support.
—Joe

To Heidi, Christopher, and Benjamin, for your patience and encouragement.
—Mike

Leonard M. Jessup is the Dean of the College of Business and Economics, and the Philip L. Kays Distinguished Professor of MIS, at Washington State University. Professor Jessup received his B.A. in information and communication studies in 1983 and his M.B.A. in 1985 from California State University, Chico, where he was voted "outstanding M.B.A student." He received his Ph.D. in organizational behaviour and management information systems from the University of Arizona in 1989. He is a member of the Association for Information Systems and Alpha Iota Delta; associate editor for the *Management Information Systems Quarterly;* a member of the editorial board for Small Group Research; a former program co-chair for the Association for Information Systems Americas Conference; and conference co-chair for the International Conference on Information Systems, which was hosted by WSU and held in Seattle in December 2003.

In addition, he has held administrative and/or reviewer responsibilities for a number of other research journals, research conferences, and book publishers. He teaches in various areas of management and management information systems and has published, presented, and consulted on electronic commerce, computer-supported collaborative work, technology-supported teaching and learning, and other related topics. With Joseph S. Valacich, he co-edited the book *Group Support Systems: New Perspectives* for Macmillan Publishing Company. With his wife, Joy L. Egbert, he won the Zenith Data Systems' annual Masters of Innovation award.

Joseph S. Valacich, the Marian E. Smith Presidential Endowed Chair and the George and Carolyn Hubman Distinguished Professor in MIS, joined the faculty at Washington State University in 1996. He received his Ph.D. from the University of Arizona in 1989, and his M.B.A. and B.S. from the University of Montana. His teaching interests include systems analysis and design, collaborative computing, and management information systems. Professor Valacich served on the national task forces to design "IS '97: The Model Curriculum and Guidelines for Undergraduate Degree Programs in Information Systems" and "MSIS 2000, the Master of Science in Information Systems" curriculum. He served on the executive committee, funded by the National Science Foundation, working to define IS program accreditation standards and is on the board of directors for the Computing Sciences Accreditation Board (CSAB), representing the Association for Information Systems (AIS). He was the general conference co-chair for the 2003 International Conference on Information Systems that was held in Seattle.

He has conducted numerous corporate training and executive development programs for organizations, including AT&T, Dow Chemical, EDS, Exxon, FedEx, General Motors, and Xerox. His research interests include technology-mediated collaboration and distance education. His past research has appeared in publications such as *MIS Quarterly*, *Information Systems Research*, *Management Science*, *Academy of Management Journal*, *Communications of the ACM*, *Decision Science*, *Organizational Behavior and Human Decision Processes*, *Journal of Applied Psychology*, and *Journal of Management Information Systems*. He is a co-author of the best-selling *Modern Systems Analysis and Design* (3rd edition) and *Essentials of Systems Analysis and Design* (2nd edition), both published by Pearson Education.

Michael R. Wade is Assistant Professor of Operations Management and Information Systems at the Schulich School of Business, York University. He received his Ph.D. in management information systems at the Richard Ivey School of Business, University of Western Ontario. Professor Wade is a co-author of the textbook *Cases in Electronic Commerce* (1st and 2nd editions), published by McGraw-Hill. His research has appeared in journals such as *MIS Quarterly*, the *Journal of Management Information Systems*, *DataBase*, and *Information & Management*. His current research focuses on the strategic use of information systems for sustainable competitive advantage. Professor Wade has worked extensively in the technology management field in Canada, Europe, and Asia.

Brief Table of Contents

Chapters:

Table of Contents

APPROACH

One of the greatest challenges that we face in teaching information systems courses is how to keep pace in the class with what is happening out in the real world. Hardware, software, telecommunications, and networking equipment—all of it continues to become faster, cheaper, and better, and business organizations in Canada and elsewhere continue to adopt and adapt these new technologies rapidly. In fact, whereas a decade ago large businesses would spend 2 or 3 percent of their revenues on information technology, today, spending on information technology for many large businesses can range from 7 to 10 percent of revenue. Most important, organizations are now relying on that technology as a fundamental part of their business strategy and their competitiveness.

As a result of this pervasiveness and the fast pace of technology change and use in organizations, teaching people about information systems has never been more valuable or challenging.

Given the dynamic nature of information systems, and given that it is difficult to find introductory information systems textbooks that are both up to date and student-friendly, we wrote *Information Systems Today,* Canadian Edition, with four primary goals in mind. First, we wanted readers not only to learn about information systems, but also to feel as excited as we do about the field and about the amazing opportunities available in this area. Second, we did not simply want to spoon-feed students with the technical terms and the history of information systems. Instead, we want students to understand exactly what innovative organizations are doing with contemporary information systems and, more important, where things are headed. Third, we wanted to empower students with the essential knowledge they need to be successful in the use and understanding of information technology in their careers.

Finally, we wanted to present a uniquely Canadian perspective on the field of information systems (IS). When it comes to information systems, Canada shares a great deal with other countries of the world. After all, a computer works in much the same way in Kamloops as it does in Kuala Lumpur. However, there are a number of important factors that set Canada apart from other countries, particularly the United States. Canada relies much more heavily on the small- and medium-sized enterprise (SME) sector than the United States. SMEs face a different set of challenges than large firms when it comes to the adoption and use of business information systems. As a large, sparsely populated nation, Canada must rely on a robust communications infrastructure. Partly for this reason, Canada has emerged as a world leader in networking technologies. Many of you reading this book will live and work in Canada, and so it is appropriate that you learn about information systems from a Canadian perspective.

To this end, we wrote *Information Systems Today,* Canadian Edition, so that it is contemporary, fun to read, and useful, and includes the essential body of knowledge regarding information systems in Canada.

AUDIENCE

Information Systems Today, Canadian Edition, is designed to be used in an undergraduate or graduate (MBA) introductory information systems course, as required by many schools of business. The introductory information systems course typically has a diverse audience of students with experience and expertise in many different areas, such as accounting, economics, finance, marketing, general management, human resource management, production and operations, international business, entrepreneurship, and information systems. Given the range of students taking this type of course, we have written this book so that it is a valuable guide to all business students and provides them with the essential information they need to know. Students majoring in areas outside of business may also attend the introductory information systems course. Therefore, this book has been written to appeal to a diverse audience.

KEY FEATURES

As authors, teachers, developers, and managers of information systems, we understand that in order for students to best learn about information systems with this book, they must be motivated to learn. To this end we have included a number of unique features to help students quickly and easily assess the true value of information systems and their impact on everyday life. We show how today's professionals are using information systems to help modern organizations become more efficient and competitive. Our focus is on the application of technology to real-world, contemporary situations in a Canadian context. Below, we describe each of the features that contribute to that focus.

Cases: A Multitiered Approach

Cases provide a useful bridge between theory and practice. They are designed to show students how the concepts in the book relate to problems and issues faced by real managers. Most of the cases in this book are written to reflect the challenges that firms face in a Canadian business environment.

Opening Scenario: Each chapter begins with an opening scenario describing a real-world Canadian company, technology, and/or issue to spark students' interest in the chapter topic. We have chosen engaging scenarios that relate to students' interests and concerns. A photo or illustration is included with each scenario.

Brief Case: Each chapter also includes several "Brief Cases" that are taken directly from the news and discuss contemporary companies and technologies. These are embedded right in the text of the chapter and highlight concepts from the surrounding chapter material. Each Brief Case is followed by two questions that relate the case to the surrounding text.

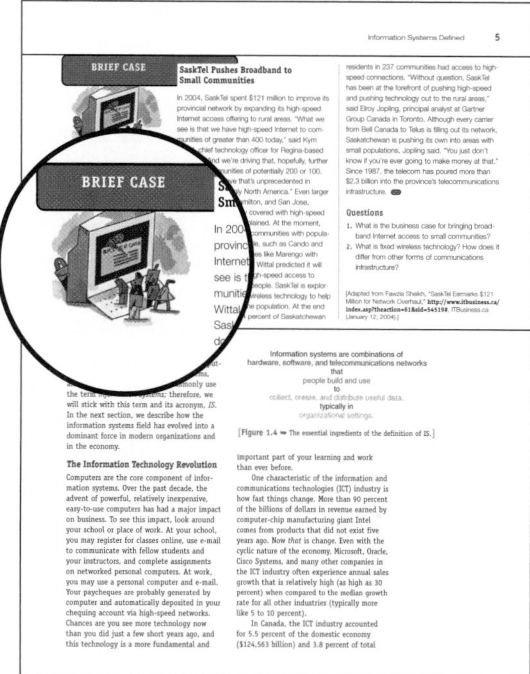
Information Systems Defined 5

BRIEF CASE

SaskTel Pushes Broadband to Small Communities

In 2004, SaskTel spent $121 million to improve its provincial network by expanding its high-speed Internet access offering to rural areas. "What we see is that we have high-speed Internet to communities of greater than 400 today," said Kym [illegible] chief technology officer for Regina-based [illegible] nd we're driving that, hopefully, further [illegible] unities of potentially 200 or 100. [illegible] e that's unprecedented in [illegible] ly North America." Even larger [illegible] milton, and San Jose, [illegible] covered with high-speed [illegible] lained. At the moment, [illegible] communities with population[illegible] e, such as Cando and [illegible] es like Marengo with [illegible] Wittal predicted it will [illegible] gh-speed access to [illegible] people. SaskTel is exploring [illegible] wireless technology to help [illegible] he population. At the end [illegible] percent of Saskatchewan residents in 237 communities had access to high-speed connections. "Without question, SaskTel has been at the forefront of pushing high-speed and pushing technology out to the rural areas," said Elroy Jopling, principal analyst at Gartner Group Canada in Toronto. Although every carrier from Bell Canada to Telus is filling out its network, Saskatchewan is pushing its own into areas with small populations, Jopling said. "You just don't know if you're ever going to make money at that." Since 1987, the telecom has poured more than $2.3 billion into the province's telecommunications infrastructure.

Questions

1. What is the business case for bringing broadband Internet access to small communities?
2. What is fixed wireless technology? How does it differ from other forms of communications infrastructure?

[Adapted from Fawzia Sheikh, "SaskTel Earmarks $121 Million for Network Overhaul," **http://www.itbusiness.ca/index.asp?theaction=61&sid=54519#**, ITBusiness.ca (January 12, 2004).]

[illegible] the term [illegible] systems; therefore, we will stick with this term and its acronym, *IS*. In the next section, we describe how the information systems field has evolved into a dominant force in modern organizations and in the economy.

The Information Technology Revolution

Computers are the core component of information systems. Over the past decade, the advent of powerful, relatively inexpensive, easy-to-use computers has had a major impact on business. To see this impact, look around your school or place of work. At your school, you may register for classes online, use e-mail to communicate with fellow students and your instructors, and complete assignments on networked personal computers. At work, you may use a personal computer and e-mail. Your paycheques are probably generated by computer and automatically deposited in your chequing account via high-speed networks. Chances are you see more technology now than you did just a few short years ago, and this technology is a more fundamental and important part of your learning and work than ever before.

One characteristic of the information and communications technologies (ICT) industry is how fast things change. More than 90 percent of the billions of dollars in revenue earned by computer-chip manufacturing giant Intel comes from products that did not exist five years ago. Now *that* is change. Even with the cyclic nature of the economy, Microsoft, Oracle, Cisco Systems, and many other companies in the ICT industry often experience annual sales growth that is relatively high (as high as 30 percent) when compared to the median growth rate for all other industries (typically more like 5 to 10 percent).

In Canada, the ICT industry accounted for 5.5 percent of the domestic economy ($124,563 billion) and 3.8 percent of total

[Figure 1.4 ➡ The essential ingredients of the definition of IS.]

End-of-Chapter Case: To test and reinforce chapter content, we present two real-world cases at the end of each chapter. Like the Brief Cases within the chapter, these are taken from the news and are contemporary. However, these are longer and more substantive than the Brief Cases and are followed by discussion questions that help the student apply and master the chapter.

Career Implications

To show students how the material from each chapter applies to their individual career tracks, we have created a "Career Implications" feature. This feature maps the material to the fields of accounting and finance, marketing, information systems, human resource management, and operations management in each chapter. That means there are five Career Implications in every chapter. For example, an aspiring accountant will find an explanation within every chapter of how that chapter's material applies to the field of accounting. Similarly, every chapter has such a feature for a marketing major, for an operations management major, and so on. This feature often

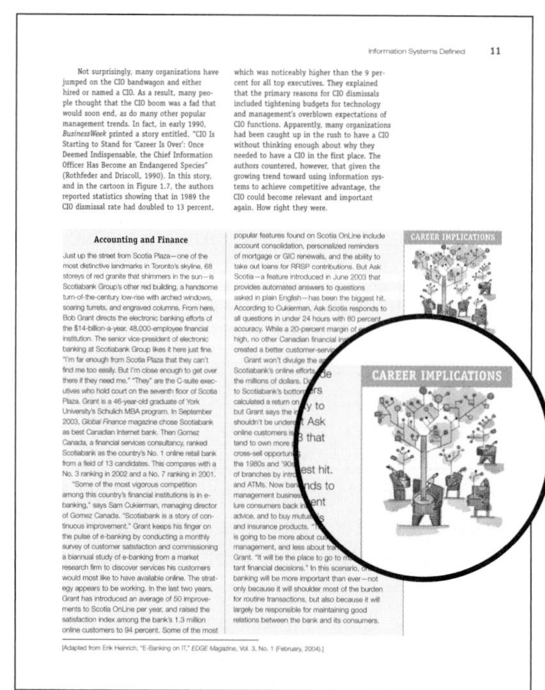
Information Systems Defined 11

Not surprisingly, many organizations have jumped on the CIO bandwagon and either hired or named a CIO. As a result, many people thought that the CIO boom was a fad that would soon end, as do many other popular management trends. In fact, in early 1990, *BusinessWeek* printed a story entitled, "CIO Is Starting to Stand for 'Career Is Over': Once Deemed Indispensable, the Chief Information Officer Has Become an Endangered Species" (Rothfeder and Driscoll, 1990). In this story, and in the cartoon in Figure 1.7, the authors reported statistics showing that in 1989 the CIO dismissal rate had doubled to 13 percent, which was noticeably higher than the 9 percent for all top executives. They explained that the primary reasons for CIO dismissals included tightening budgets for technology and management's overblown expectations of CIO functions. Apparently, many organizations had been caught up in the rush to have a CIO without thinking enough about why they needed to have a CIO in the first place. The authors countered, however, that given the growing trend toward using information systems to achieve competitive advantage, the CIO could become relevant and important again. How right they were.

CAREER IMPLICATIONS

Accounting and Finance

Just up the street from Scotia Plaza—one of the most distinctive landmarks in Toronto's skyline, 68 storeys of red granite that shimmers in the sun—is Scotiabank Group's other red building, a handsome turn-of-the-century low-rise with arched windows, soaring turrets, and engraved columns. From here, Bob Grant directs the electronic banking efforts of the $14-billion-a-year, 48,000-employee financial institution. The senior vice-president of electronic banking at Scotiabank Group likes it here just fine. "I'm far enough from Scotia Plaza that they can't find me too easily. But I'm close enough to get over there if they need me." "They" are the C-suite executives who hold court on the seventh floor of Scotia Plaza. Grant is a 46-year-old graduate of York University's Schulich MBA program. In September 2003, *Global Finance* magazine chose Scotiabank as best Canadian Internet bank. Then Gomez Canada, a financial services consultancy, ranked Scotiabank as the country's No. 1 online retail bank from a field of 13 candidates. This compares with a No. 3 ranking in 2002 and a No. 7 ranking in 2001.

"Some of the most vigorous competition among this country's financial institutions is in e-banking," says Sam Cukierman, managing director of Gomez Canada. "Scotiabank is a story of continuous improvement." Grant keeps his finger on the pulse of e-banking by conducting a monthly survey of customer satisfaction and commissioning a biannual study of e-banking from a market research firm to discover services his customers would most like to have available online. The strategy appears to be working. In the last two years, Grant has introduced an average of 50 improvements to Scotia OnLine per year, and raised the satisfaction index among the bank's 1.3 million online customers to 94 percent. Some of the most popular features found on Scotia OnLine include account consolidation, personalized reminders of mortgage or GIC renewals, and the ability to take out loans for RRSP contributions. But Ask Scotia—a feature introduced in June 2003 that provides automated answers to questions asked in plain English—has been the biggest hit. According to Cukierman, Ask Scotia responds to all questions in under 24 hours with 80 percent accuracy. While a 20-percent margin of [illegible] high, no other Canadian financial in[illegible] created a better customer-servic[illegible]

Grant won't divulge the [illegible] Scotiabank's online efforts [illegible] the millions of dollars. [illegible] to Scotiabank's bottom [illegible] calculated a return on [illegible] but Grant says the [illegible] shouldn't be under[illegible] online customers [illegible] tend to own more [illegible] cross-sell opportun[illegible] the 1980s and '90s [illegible] of branches by intr[illegible] and ATMs. Now ban[illegible] management busines[illegible] lure consumers back in[illegible] advice, and to buy mutua[illegible] and insurance products. "[illegible] is going to be more about cu[illegible] management, and less about tra[illegible] Grant. "It will be the place to go to m[illegible] tant financial decisions." In this scenario, o[illegible] banking will be more important than ever—not only because it will shoulder most of the burden for routine transactions, but also because it will largely be responsible for maintaining good relations between the bank and its consumers.

[Adapted from Erik Heinrich, "E-Banking on IT," *EDGE Magazine*, Vol. 3, No. 1 (February, 2004).]

includes real-world examples of how information systems are applied and used in other functional areas of the firm.

Coming Attractions

We worked hard to ensure that this book is contemporary. We cover literally hundreds of different emerging technologies throughout the book. In order to drive the point home, we also included a "Coming Attractions" feature in each chapter, which describes some specific new technology and how it is or will be used.

24 Chapter 1 Information Systems: The Big Picture

COMING ATTRACTIONS

A Bright Future for Organic Displays

A group of University of Toronto researchers say they are the first Canadians to produce a display technology that is as flexible as paper. The experimental technology is called an organic light-emit[illegible] device (or OLED). It's flexible, so it could fit [illegible] ctor or even mould itself to the shape [illegible] Figure 1.13). "What differentiates [illegible] ventional LEDs is that the [illegible] ble. You can make any [illegible] Zheng-Hong Lu, the [illegible] the University of [illegible] d up a whole potential [illegible] working with his [illegible] ve years and has [illegible] umber of flexible [illegible] film and reflective [illegible] epresent the next [illegible] cent years, liquid [illegible] le substantial [illegible] es (CRT) in the [illegible] Many experts con[illegible] display device replac[illegible] design, the OLED man[illegible] d be substantially different from the way conventional displays are produced today. "Like newspapers, you could print rolls and rolls of displays," said Lu. "With big companies willing to invest lots of money, I'm really optimistic about some sort of commercial device." Lu said he hopes to see commercially viable products in the market in five years. Further down the line, flexible laptops that could be rolled up and stuffed in a back pocket may be a reality. The commercial applications of OLED are very real and are already here, albeit in a much smaller-factor form. Kodak, which owns an OLED patent, has an Easy Share 633 digital camera with an embedded OLED display. Samsung is now shipping its E700 series cell phone with an external OLED screen. However, making the leap to full-size OLED for something the size of a computer monitor or TV is still a distant goal, according to IDC analyst Jennifer Gallo.

She conservatively estimates that it could be at least 2010 before such products are available. "It's been proven that it can be done, but not for large displays. There are a lot of people focusing on the production and the manufacturing process of OLED, such as DuPont, and they're still working on it. It's not easy," she said. The product has limitations that have yet to be overcome. Much like a break-and-shake glowstick that provides a light source only for a short time, OLED has some serious lifespan concerns, Gallo said. "It's a chemical and there's a lifetime to that chemical and how long it will emit light for." If that problem can be solved, the future for OLED looks bright. Aside from the inherent advantage of a flexible display, OLED produces an extremely clear image that can be viewed from multiple angles (an issue with colour-screen LCD is that the colour tends to fade when viewed from the side).

[Figure 1.13 ➡ An organic light-emitting device.]
Source: Zheng-Hong Lu, U of T, Department of Materials, Science and Engineering.

[Adapted from Neil Sutton, "U of T Lab Sees Potential in Organic Display Technology," **www.itbusiness.ca/index.asp?theaction=61&sid=54581#**, ITBusiness.ca (January 20, 2004).]

size and structure of organizations and for the size and structure of the IS function.

Career Prospects and Opportunities

Although technology at some levels continues to become easier to use, there is still and is likely to continue to be an acute need for people within an organization to have the responsibility of planning for, designing, developing, maintaining, and managing technologies. Much of this will happen within the business units and will be performed by those with primarily business duties and tasks, as opposed to systems duties and tasks. However, we are a long way from the day when technology is so easy to deploy that a need no longer exists for people with deep information systems knowledge and skills. In fact, many people believe that this day may never come. Although increasing numbers of people will incorporate systems responsibilities within their non-systems jobs, there will continue to be a need for people with primarily systems responsibilities. In short, IS staffs and departments will likely continue to exist and play an important role in the foreseeable future.

When Things Go Wrong

It is rare to find an information systems textbook that describes what not to do, but this can be very helpful to students. In each chapter we provide a feature called "When Things Go Wrong," which enables students to learn about a real-world situation in which information systems did not work or were not built or used well.

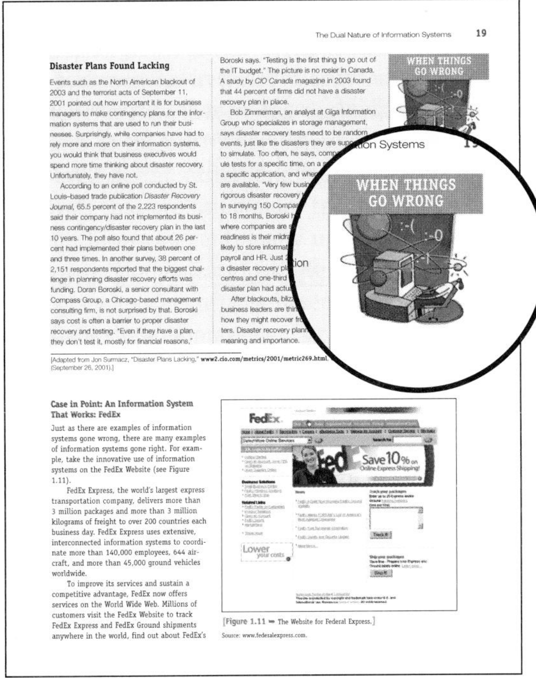

Global Perspective

In addition to scores of international issues and examples, we also provide a feature called "Global Perspective" in each chapter. With this feature, we show specifically how some aspect of the chapter applies to people, organizations, and technologies from around the world.

Web Search

In addition to end-of-chapter material, within each chapter we provide several opportunities for students to work alone or in teams to research topics on the Web that relate to chapter material.

Canadian Video Cases

Three video cases relate to Chapters 1, 3, and 9. Each case study focuses on a contemporary information systems–related issue faced by firms in Canada. The cases are accompanied by video segments from the

CBC programs *Venture* and *Marketplace*. Discussion questions are provided with each case study.

End-of-Chapter Material

Our end-of-chapter material is designed to accommodate various teaching and learning styles. It promotes learning beyond the book and the classroom. Elements include the following:

Key Terms Highlight key concepts within the chapter.

Review Questions Test students' understanding of basic content.

Self-Study Questions Enable students to assess whether they are ready for a test.

Matching Questions Check quickly to see if students understand basic terms.

Problems and Exercises Push students deeper into the material and encourage them to synthesize and apply it.

PEDAGOGY

In addition to our use of cases, chapter openers, and the other unique features described, we provide a list of learning objectives to lay the foundation for each chapter. At the end of the chapter, the "Key Points Review" repeats these learning objectives and describes how each objective was achieved.

A list of references is located at the end of the text, organized by chapter.

ORGANIZATION

The content and organization of this book are based on our own teaching, as well as on feedback from reviewers and colleagues throughout the field. Each chapter builds on the others to reinforce key concepts and allow for a seamless learning experience. Essentially, the book has been structured to answer four fundamental questions:

1. What are contemporary information systems, and how are they being used in innovative ways?
2. Why are information systems so important and interesting?
3. How best can we build, acquire, manage, and safeguard information systems?
4. How are information systems used in a Canadian business environment?

To answer these questions, we wrote and ordered the chapters in a specific way. To continually show you where you are in the book, we begin each chapter by describing "The Big Picture" and literally provide students with an image of The Big Picture that shows where the current chapter lies within the framework of the book.

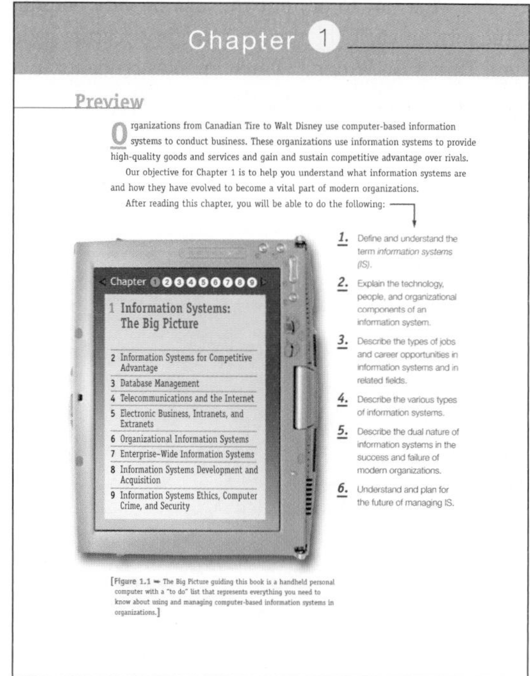
Chapter 1

Preview

Organizations from Canadian Tire to Walt Disney use computer-based information systems to conduct business. These organizations use information systems to provide high-quality goods and services and gain and sustain competitive advantage over rivals.

Our objective for Chapter 1 is to help you understand what information systems are and how they have evolved to become a vital part of modern organizations.

After reading this chapter, you will be able to do the following:

1. Define and understand the term *information systems* (IS).
2. Explain the technology, people, and organizational components of an information system.
3. Describe the types of jobs and career opportunities in information systems and in related fields.
4. Describe the various types of information systems.
5. Describe the dual nature of information systems in the success and failure of modern organizations.
6. Understand and plan for the future of managing IS.

[Figure 1.1 ➡ The Big Picture guiding this book is a handheld personal computer with a "to do" list that represents everything you need to know about using and managing computer-based information systems in organizations.]

The chapters are organized as follows:

- **Chapter 1: "Information Systems: The Big Picture"**—This chapter helps you understand what information systems are and how they have become a vital part of modern organizations. We walk the student through the technology, people, and organizational components of an information system, and we lay out types of jobs and career opportunities in information systems and in related fields. We use a number of cases and examples to show the student the types of systems being used in Canada and to point out common "best practices" in systems use and management.
- **Chapter 2: "Information Systems for Competitive Advantage"**—In this chapter we provide a number of business examples to show how to use information systems to support organizational strategy and enable competitive advantage. We also show the student how to formulate and present the business case for a system, and we explain why and how companies are continually looking for new ways to use technology to achieve and sustain competitive advantage.
- **Chapter 3: "Database Management"**—Databases have become the engine running underneath many information systems and business processes. In this chapter we use real-world examples to describe what databases and database management systems are and to show why they have become very important for successful, modern organizations.
- **Chapter 4: "Telecommunications and the Internet"**—Just as databases are the underlying engines, telecommunications and networks are the veins through which vital information flows in organizations. Here we show you how people use telecommunications and networking equipment effectively. We also focus on how the

Internet and the World Wide Web function and are used heavily by business organizations today.

- **Chapter 5: "Electronic Business, Intranets, and Extranets"**—Perhaps nothing has changed the landscape of business more than the use of the Internet for electronic business. In this chapter we describe how a number of firms, such as Chapters.ca, are using the Internet and Web to do business with customers, building intranets to support internal processes, and building extranets to interact with other firms.
- **Chapter 6: "Organizational Information Systems"**—Given how many different types of information systems organizations use, in this chapter we use examples from Canadian firms to describe the various types of systems. We provide ways to categorize the systems so that you can better make sense of them all.
- **Chapter 7: "Enterprise-Wide Information Systems"**—In this chapter we focus on enterprise systems, which are a popular type of information system used to integrate information and span organizations' boundaries to better connect a firm with customers, suppliers, and other partners. We show you examples of how firms compete by using enterprise resource planning, customer relationship management, and other popular types of software packages.
- **Chapter 8: "Information Systems Development and Acquisition"**—How are all these systems built? In this chapter we show you examples of how firms build and acquire new information systems. We walk you through the traditional systems development approach, as well as more contemporary approaches such as outsourcing, prototyping, rapid application development, and object-oriented analysis and design.
- **Chapter 9: "Information Systems Ethics, Computer Crime, and Security"**—In this chapter we describe the ethical dilemmas associated with information systems, as well as common forms of computer crime and various methods for providing computer security. We also highlight the importance of personal privacy protection in Canada. We show you how firms deal with hackers and ensure the safety and integrity of their critical systems.

In addition to these nine chapters, we include three appendices focusing on basic hardware, software, and networking concepts. By delivering this material as appendices, we provide instructors the greatest flexibility in how and when they can apply it.

SUPPLEMENTARY SUPPORT

Instructor's Resource CD-ROM

The convenient Instructor's CD-ROM includes all of the supplements: Instructor's Manual, Test Generator, PowerPoint Presentations, and Digital Image Gallery (text art). The Instructor's Manual includes answers to all review and discussion questions, exercises, and case questions. The Test Generator includes multiple-choice, true-false, and essay questions for each chapter. The PowerPoint Presentations highlight text learning objectives and key topics. They are also available on the text's Companion Website at **www.pearsoned.ca/jessup**. Finally, the Digital Image Gallery is a collection of the figures and tables from the text, supplied on the Instructor's Resource CD-ROM, for instructor use in PowerPoint slides and class lectures.

Companion Website

This text is supported by a Companion Website (**www.pearsoned.ca/jessup**) that features:

a. A password-protected faculty area where adopters can download the Instructor's Manual.

b. PowerPoint lecture notes (as described above).

c. An Interactive Study Guide that includes multiple-choice, true-false, and essay questions for each chapter. Each question includes a hint and coaching tip for students' reference. Students receive automatic feedback upon submitting each quiz.

d. Web Search exercises. All of the Web Search exercises from the text margins appear on the Website for convenient student use.

e. Chapter updates, posted periodically to help both students and instructors stay up to date with what is happening in information systems and how it relates to chapter material.

REVIEWERS

We wish to thank the following faculty who participated in reviews of the Canadian edition:

Boris Baran, Concordia University

Susan Birtwell, Kwantlen University College

Bill Bonner, University of Regina

Don Campbell, St. Francis Xavier University

Anthony Chan, Simon Fraser University

Danny Cho, Brock University

Albert Ersser, Mohawk College

Gregory Fleet, University of New Brunswick at Saint John

Franca Giacomelli, Humber College

Robert C. Goldstein, University of British Columbia

Jocelyn King, University of Alberta

Shirley Mauger, British Columbia Institute of Technology

Robert Riordan, Carleton University

ACKNOWLEDGMENTS

Although only our names are listed as the authors for this book, this was truly a team effort that went well beyond the three of us. A particular debt of thanks is owed to Michael Rutherford for his help in compiling the information on PIPEDA and IP laws in

Canada and elsewhere. Pearson Canada has been an outstanding publishing company to work with. They are innovative, have high standards, and are as competitive as we are.

Among the many amazingly helpful people at Pearson Canada, there are a few people we wish to thank specifically. Laura Forbes, Acquisitions Editor, helped us to strategize well for this book throughout the project. Paul Donnelly, Senior Developmental Editor, helped to whip this book into shape and get the manuscript finished on time. Finally, Marisa D'Andrea, Editorial Coordinator, skilfully oversaw the production of the text.

Most important, we thank our families for their patience and assistance in helping us to complete this book.

A Great Way to Learn and Instruct Online

The Pearson Education Canada Companion Website is easy to navigate and is organized to correspond to the chapters in this textbook. Whether you are a student in the classroom or a distance learner you will discover helpful resources for in-depth study and research that empower you in your quest for greater knowledge and maximize your potential for success in the course.

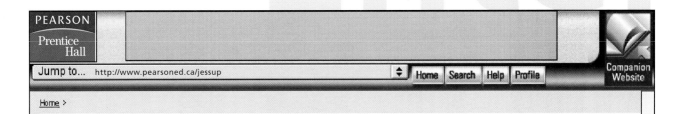

PEARSON Prentice Hall

Jump to... http://www.pearsoned.ca/jessup

Home Search Help Profile

Companion Website

Home >

PH Companion Website

Information Systems Today, Canadian Edition, by Jessup, Valacich, and Wade

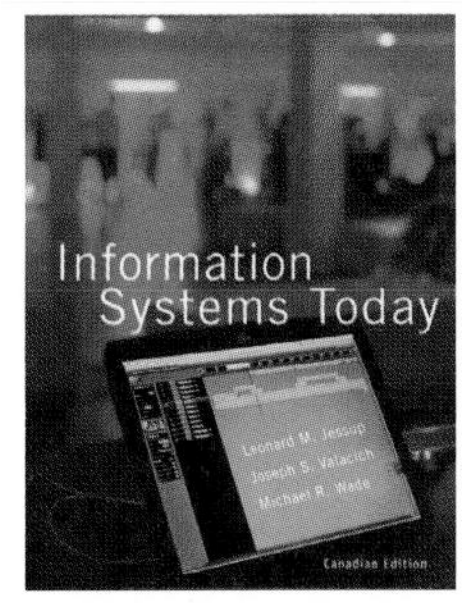

Student Resources

This online study guide provides students with tools for learning course material. Each chapter includes:

- Chapter Objectives
- Chapter Overview
- Quizzes
- Internet Exercises
- Weblinks

In the quiz modules students can send answers to the grader and receive instant feedback on their progress through the Results Reporter. Coaching comments and references to the textbook may be available to ensure that students take advantage of all available resources to enhance their learning experience.

Instructor Resources

A link to this book on the Pearson Education Canada online catalogue (www.pearsoned.ca) provides instructors with additional teaching tools. Downloadable PowerPoint Presentations and an Instructor's Manual are just some of the materials that may be available. The catalogue is password protected. To get a password, simply contact your Pearson Education Canada Representative or call Faculty Sales and Services at 1-800-850-5813.

Chapter 1

Preview

Organizations from Canadian Tire to Walt Disney use computer-based information systems to conduct business. These organizations use information systems to provide high-quality goods and services and gain and sustain competitive advantage over rivals.

Our objective for Chapter 1 is to help you understand what information systems are and how they have evolved to become a vital part of modern organizations.

After reading this chapter, you will be able to do the following:

1. Define and understand the term *information systems (IS)*.
2. Explain the technology, people, and organizational components of an information system.
3. Describe the types of jobs and career opportunities in information systems and in related fields.
4. Describe the various types of information systems.
5. Describe the dual nature of information systems in the success and failure of modern organizations.
6. Understand and plan for the future of managing IS.

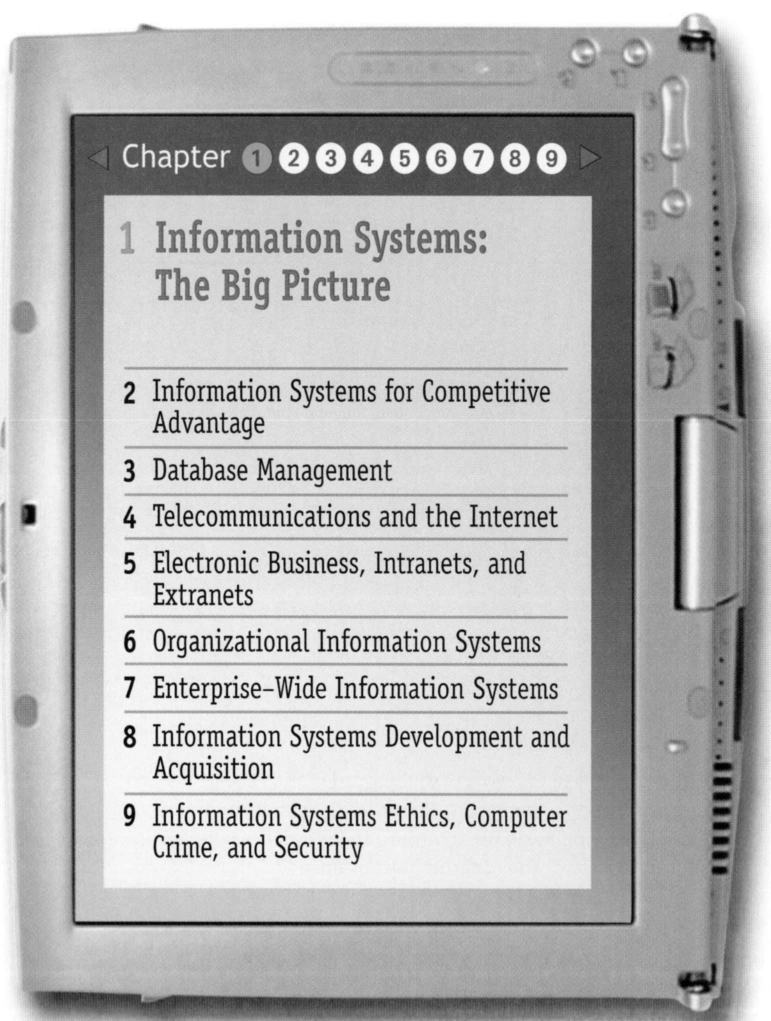

[**Figure 1.1** ➥ The Big Picture guiding this book is a handheld personal computer with a "to do" list that represents everything you need to know about using and managing computer-based information systems in organizations.]

Information Systems: The Big Picture

OPENING: Whistler.com Powers Up in Preparation for 2010

Vancouver still has time to prepare for the 2010 Winter Olympic Games, but a local online property company is taking steps now to prepare for a considerable increase in customer activity. Whistler.com has tapped Fusepoint Managed Services to handle its entire IT infrastructure, including hardware, operating systems, and database applications. Whistler.com provides reservations and resort information for visitors travelling to the popular vacation spot, located 115 km north of Vancouver. The company has already moved over its Web server, database, and e-mail server to Fusepoint's Vancouver data centre.

Chad Nantais, Whistler.com's IS manager, said he has studied other places that have hosted the Olympics in order to gauge the pressure on its IT infrastructure. "It's pretty much Wild West—we don't know what the traffic is going to be," he said. "We can project it all we want, but we need to know that the availability is going to be there."

Fusepoint president and CEO Robert Offley said his firm has hosted other customers planning major Webcasts or portals for the soccer World Cup, which has provided the necessary experience to assist Whistler.com. In some cases, Fusepoint has had to scale bandwidth 100 times within 24 hours' notice, he said. "The Olympics aren't until 2010, but we can actually help them try to size demand and build a scaleable infrastructure," he said. According to Nantais, Whistler.com will use its remaining in-house resources to focus on providing mobile services and extending the functionality of its booking engine. "We are going to extend our information services greatly, because we're pretty sure that's going to be a drawing point when the Olympics come," he said. "Digging deeper into information sources is the new direction."

The sudden surge in IT demands triggered by events like the Olympics may provide an interesting test case for on-demand services, Offley said. "Where we see the opportunity in this overall space is with people buying IT like it's electricity," he said. "I think with a company like Whistler.com—where there's a seasonal element and rapid growth—we enable them to match their costs to their business model."

[Adapted from Shane Schick, "Whistler.com in Training for Expected Increase in Traffic for 2010 Olympics," *Computing Canada*, Vol. 30, No. 3 (March 12, 2004).]

[**Figure 1.2** ➥ Whistler.com turned to Fusepoint to manage its IT infrastructure.]

Source: © Randy Lincks/Masterfile. www.masterfile.com.

THE BIG PICTURE

Figure 1.1 provides The Big Picture, which is the guiding framework for this book. The Big Picture is in the shape of a handheld personal computer illustrating the different parts of this book.

In this first chapter we introduce you to the field of information systems and help to prepare you for what you will learn throughout the rest of this book. In Chapter 2 we talk about why information systems are critical to creating a successful organization and how to use information systems to support organizational strategy and enable competitive advantage.

We then describe the essential elements of information systems. In Chapter 3 we describe databases and their management. Next, in Chapter 4, we discuss the growing importance of telecommunications and the Internet. For those who want to learn more about these essential information technology building blocks, we provide more detailed briefings on hardware, software, and networking in appendices at the end of this book.

We then describe information systems in practice in modern-day organizations. Building on what you learned in Chapter 4 about telecommunications and the Internet, in Chapter 5 we focus on electronic business and the use of intranets and extranets. In Chapter 6 we describe each of the various kinds of information systems that firms use. Then, in Chapter 7, we focus on enterprise-wide information systems, including enterprise resource planning, customer relationship management, and supply chain management systems, all relatively new, special types of information systems that help integrate the entire organization and help connect the firm to customers, suppliers, and partners.

Next, in Chapter 8, we describe how information systems are developed and/or acquired. Then, in Chapter 9, we discuss key issues in managing computer crime, security, privacy, and ethics. We will refer back to The Big Picture at the beginning of every chapter. That way you will know exactly what we will be talking about in each chapter and how it fits within The Big Picture.

INFORMATION SYSTEMS DEFINED

Information systems are combinations of ***hardware***, ***software***, and ***telecommunications networks*** that people build and use to collect, create, and distribute useful ***data***, typically in organizational settings. In Figure 1.3, we show the links among these IS components.

People in organizations use information systems to process sales transactions, manage loan applications, and help financial analysts decide where, when, and how to invest. Product managers also use them to help decide where, when, and how to market their products and related services, and production managers use them to help decide when and how to manufacture products. Information systems also enable us to get cash from ATMs, communicate by live video with people in other parts of the world, and buy concert tickets.

The term *information systems* is also used to describe the field comprising people who develop, use, manage, and study information systems in organizations. In Figure 1.4, we show the essential ingredients of the definition of IS.

Several terms are used to describe the field of information systems: management

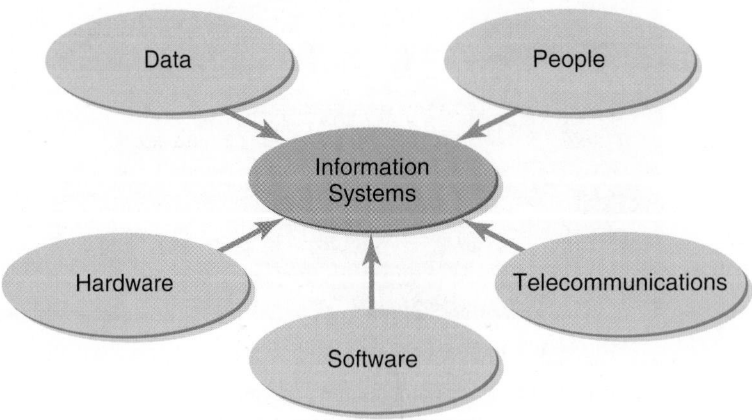

[**Figure 1.3** ➡ An information system is a combination of five key elements: people, hardware, software, data, and telecommunications networks.]

BRIEF CASE

SaskTel Pushes Broadband to Small Communities

In 2004, SaskTel spent $121 million to improve its provincial network by expanding its high-speed Internet access offering to rural areas. "What we see is that we have high-speed Internet to communities of greater than 400 today," said Kym Wittal, chief technology officer for Regina-based SaskTel. "And we're driving that, hopefully, further down to communities of potentially 200 or 100. And we just believe that's unprecedented in Canada and certainly North America." Even larger cities like Toronto, Hamilton, and San Jose, California, are not "fully covered with high-speed Internet access," he explained. At the moment, SaskTel is serving small communities with populations of 100 to 200 people, such as Cando and Christopher Lake, and ones like Marengo with fewer than 100 residents. Wittal predicted it will take three years to link high-speed access to centres of 200 or fewer people. SaskTel is exploring the viability of fixed wireless technology to help it reach 95 percent of the population. At the end of 2003, more than 74 percent of Saskatchewan residents in 237 communities had access to high-speed connections. "Without question, SaskTel has been at the forefront of pushing high-speed and pushing technology out to the rural areas," said Elroy Jopling, principal analyst at Gartner Group Canada in Toronto. Although every carrier from Bell Canada to Telus is filling out its network, Saskatchewan is pushing its own into areas with small populations, Jopling said. "You just don't know if you're ever going to make money at that." Since 1987, the telecom has poured more than $2.3 billion into the province's telecommunications infrastructure.

Questions

1. What is the business case for bringing broadband Internet access to small communities?
2. What is fixed wireless technology? How does it differ from other forms of communications infrastructure?

[Adapted from Fawzia Sheikh, "SaskTel Earmarks $121 Million for Network Overhaul," **http://www.itbusiness.ca/index.asp?theaction=61&sid=54519#**, ITBusiness.ca (January 12, 2004).]

information systems, data processing management, systems management, business computer systems, computer information systems, and just systems. People most commonly use the term *information systems;* therefore, we will stick with this term and its acronym, *IS*. In the next section, we describe how the information systems field has evolved into a dominant force in modern organizations and in the economy.

Information systems are combinations of
hardware, software, and telecommunications networks
that
people build and use
to
collect, create, and distribute useful data,
typically in
organizational settings.

[**Figure 1.4** ➡ The essential ingredients of the definition of IS.]

The Information Technology Revolution

Computers are the core component of information systems. Over the past decade, the advent of powerful, relatively inexpensive, easy-to-use computers has had a major impact on business. To see this impact, look around your school or place of work. At your school, you may register for classes online, use e-mail to communicate with fellow students and your instructors, and complete assignments on networked personal computers. At work, you may use a personal computer and e-mail. Your paycheques are probably generated by computer and automatically deposited in your chequing account via high-speed networks. Chances are you see more technology now than you did just a few short years ago, and this technology is a more fundamental and important part of your learning and work than ever before.

One characteristic of the information and communications technologies (ICT) industry is how fast things change. More than 90 percent of the billions of dollars in revenue earned by computer-chip manufacturing giant Intel comes from products that did not exist five years ago. Now *that* is change. Even with the cyclic nature of the economy, Microsoft, Oracle, Cisco Systems, and many other companies in the ICT industry often experience annual sales growth that is relatively high (as high as 30 percent) when compared to the median growth rate for all other industries (typically more like 5 to 10 percent).

In Canada, the ICT industry accounted for 5.5 percent of the domestic economy ($124,563 billion) and 3.8 percent of total

[**Figure 1.5** ➥ A popular business magazine featuring a cover story related to technology.]

Source: *Forbes* Magazine.

employment (579,000 jobs) in 2003. Sector revenues grew at a compound average growth rate (CAGR) of 6.8 percent between 1995 and 2002, and employment grew at a 5.2-percent CAGR. The software and computer industries were particularly robust, with a CAGR of 10.5 percent. Of course, the relevance of information technology is not only restricted to those companies in the ICT industry. IT is used extensively by all firms in all sectors.[1]

The information technology revolution has been chronicled in the popular business press. For example, the cover stories in many issues of *BusinessWeek, Forbes,* and other business magazines have focused on technology or a technology company or industry. Figure 1.5 shows a recent business magazines with a technology-related cover. These articles in the popular business press mirror what is happening in the real world. Information technology is pervasive in everything we do and strongly impacts business productivity and economic success. While stocks for technology companies are not as high as they were at their peak a few years ago, technology is still hot.

The Rise of the Knowledge Worker

In 1959, Peter Drucker predicted a rise in the importance of information and of information technology, and at that point over four decades ago he coined the term ***knowledge worker***. Knowledge workers are professionals who are relatively well educated and who create, modify, and/or synthesize knowledge as a fundamental part of their jobs.

Drucker's predictions about knowledge workers were very accurate. As he predicted, they are generally paid better than their prior agricultural and industrial counterparts; they rely on and are empowered by formal education, yet they often also possess valuable real-world skills; they are continually learning how to do their jobs better; they have much better career opportunities and far more bargaining power than workers ever had before; they make up about a quarter of the workforce in Canada and in other developed nations; and their numbers are rising quickly.

Drucker also predicted that, with the growth in the number of knowledge workers and with their rise in importance and leadership, a ***knowledge society*** would emerge. He reasoned that, given the importance of education and learning to knowledge workers and the firms that need them, education would become the cornerstone of the knowledge society. Possessing knowledge, he argued, would be as important as possessing property once was (if not more so). Indeed, research shows that people with a post-secondary education earn far more on average than people without a post-secondary education, and that gap is increasing (see, for example, Farrell et al., 1998).

People generally agree that Drucker was accurate about knowledge workers and the evolution of society. While people have settled on Drucker's term *knowledge worker*, there are many alternatives to the term *knowledge society*. For example, Manuel Castell has written that we now live in a network society. *Wired* magazine has published that we now live in a ***new economy***, and described it as follows:

> So what is the new economy? When we talk about the new economy, we're talking about a world in which people work with their brains instead of their hands. A world in which communications technology creates global competition—not just for running shoes and laptop computers, but also for bank loans and other services that can't be packed into a crate and shipped. A world in which innovation is more important than mass production. A world in which investment buys new concepts or the means to create them, rather than new machines. A world in which rapid change is a constant. A world at least as different from what came before it as the industrial age was from its agricultural predecessor. A world so different its emergence can only be described as a revolution.[2]

Others have referred to this phenomenon as the digital society, the network era, the Internet era, and by other names. All of these ideas have in common the premise that information and information technology have become very important to us and knowledge workers are vital.

Data: The Root and Purpose of Information Systems

Let us break down and discuss the definition of IS. Earlier we defined IS as combinations of hardware, software, and telecommunications networks that people build and use to collect, create, and distribute useful data, typically in organizational settings. We will begin by talking about data, the most basic element of any information system.

[1]Statistics from Industry Canada, **http://strategis.ic.gc.ca/epic/internet/inict-tic.nsf/en/h_it06155e.html**.

[2]Excerpt from *Wired* magazine's "Encyclopedia of the New Economy," 1998, a series published in the March, April, and May issues.

BRIEF CASE

What Should Rule the Day: Theory or Practice?

Most IT professionals have known for decades that hands-on experience counts when graduates head into the working world, but theoretical training is also important, particularly for the long-term development of graduates. Things are decidedly moving toward the practical at George Brown College in Toronto. "Everybody involved in this learning process, from the Ministry to college management to students to teachers, is pushing for hands-on experience," said Gerry Drappel, chair of the information technology department at George Brown. Stephen Mill, Toronto regional manager for recruiter Robert Half Technology, finds a potential hire's practical experience outweighs his or her theoretical, classroom experience. "It's always skill-driven in IT," said Mill. "If someone has a (computer science) background, that's great! They will have way more in-depth knowledge than someone who doesn't have that. But if they've never done anything practical with that, or relevant, or current, it doesn't matter."

While colleges are trying to keep in step with industry, universities are finding themselves in a different sort of predicament. Queen's University assistant professor of management information systems Kathryn Brohman says that at her school, theory remains the order of the day. "I think it's a challenge here in Canada because the university systems are very different (than in the U.S.). And it comes down to the age-old argument of, 'Is a business school a practitioner school?' or are we more of a true philosophical discipline where we should be evaluated more like the true sciences?" Though Queen's recently joined NCR Corp.'s Teradata University Network, an international learning portal that allows students hands-on access to valuable resources in the fields of data warehousing and database administration, Brohman thinks that it won't find as much use at Queen's as it might at more technical schools. "There's a more fuzzy line in the university system between hands-on training and college-level training. If it's going to be hands-on, then a lot of those skills should be able to be offered in outside seminars," said Brohman. "There's not a lot of place for that in university education, especially in a business school—we're teaching a more conceptual understanding of MIS in business. But the recruiters are coming in and wanting [a] technical student for MIS jobs." Brohman said there is a fundamental disconnect between what schools are trying to achieve in academia, their whole pedagogical vision, and what recruiters are coming in and looking for. "It always comes down to the same thing: how can you be strategic about finance and strategic about marketing if you don't know the tools that you're dealing with? If you don't know how a database is structured, how could you use that tool strategically?" she added.

Anthony Lucifero, a third-year student at George Brown, says that to him, theory and practice hold equal relevance toward his future. "I think that they're both essential to have, you need the theory part of the course as well as the hands-on, they're both very important."

Questions

1. Do you think business students need to learn about IS/IT? Why or why not?
2. What do you think is the right mix between theory and practice for an IS/IT course offered at a business school?

[Adapted from Liz Clayton, "IT Educators Grapple with Theory vs. Practice Debate," **http://www.itbusiness.ca/index.asp?theaction=61&sid=54861**, ITBusiness.ca, (February, 2004).]

Before you can understand how information systems work, it is important to distinguish between ***data*** and ***information***, terms that are often erroneously used interchangeably. Data is raw material—recorded, unformatted information, such as words and numbers. Data has no meaning in and of itself.

For example, if I asked you what 465889724 meant or stood for, you could not tell me. However, if I presented the same data as 465-889-724 and told you it was located in a certain database, in John Doe's file, in a field labelled "SIN," you might rightly surmise that the number was actually the social insurance number of someone named John Doe.

Data formatted with dashes or labels is more useful than unformatted data. It is transformed into information, which can be defined as a representation of reality. In the previous example, 465-889-724 was used to represent and identify an individual person, John Doe. Contextual cues, such as a label, are needed to turn data into information that is familiar to the reader. Think about your experience with ATMs. A list of all the transactions at a bank's ATMs over the course of a month would be fairly useless data. However, a table that divided ATM users into two categories—bank customers and non-bank customers—and compared the two groups' use of the machine—their purpose for using the ATM machines and the times and days on which they use them—would be incredibly useful information. A bank manager could use this information to create marketing mailings to attract new customers. Without information systems, it would be difficult to make data useful by turning it into information.

In addition to data and information, ***knowledge*** and ***wisdom*** are also important. Knowledge is needed to understand relationships between different pieces of information. For example, you must have knowledge to be aware that only one social insurance number can uniquely identify each individual. Knowledge is a body of governing procedures, such as guidelines or rules, which are used to organize or manipulate data to make it suitable for a given task.

Finally, wisdom is accumulated knowledge. Wisdom goes beyond knowledge in that it represents broader, more generalized rules and schemas for understanding a specific domain or domains. Wisdom allows you to understand how to apply concepts from one domain to new situations or problems. Understanding that a unique individual identifier, such as a social insurance number, can be applied in certain programming situations to single out an individual record in a database is the result of accumulated knowledge. Wisdom can be gained through a combination of academic study and personal experience.

Understanding the distinctions among data, information, knowledge, and wisdom is important because all are used in the study, development, and use of information systems.

The Technology Side of Information Systems

When we use the term *information system*, we are normally talking about ***computer-based information systems.*** Computer-based information systems are a type of ***technology***. Technology is any mechanical and/or electrical means to supplement, extend, or replace human, manual operations or devices. Sample machine technologies include the heating and cooling system for a building, the braking system for an automobile, and a laser used for surgery. In Figure 1.6, we show the relationship between technologies and computer-based information systems.

The term ***information technology*** refers to machine technology that is controlled by or uses information. One type of information technology is a programmable robot on the shop floor of a manufacturing firm that receives component specifications and operational instructions from a computer-based database.

We could argue that any technology makes use of information in some fundamental way, as does each of the three examples of basic technology listed earlier (a heating system, a braking system, and a laser). However, information technologies, such as programmable manufacturing robots, use more information and in a more sophisticated way. It may appear that we are splitting hairs by distinguishing among technologies and information technologies. While the distinction is subtle, it is important. Information technologies use machine technologies as building blocks and then combine them with computing and networking technologies. A technology such as a mechanical drill press is useful, but it is more useful when combined with a computer database that instructs that drill press when and how to act.

Information technologies and information systems are also similar. Information technology is the "boxes and wires," while an information system is a combination of hardware,

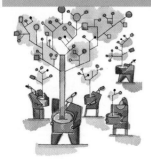

CAREER IMPLICATIONS

Operations Management

When it comes to just in time (JIT) manufacturing, a few minutes can mean thousands of dollars. For example, it costs about $100,000 per hour for an unscheduled shutdown of an automotive assembly line. Therefore, it is very important for large manufacturing firms to know the exact whereabouts of shipments at all times. Global positioning systems (GPS) use data from multiple satellites to pinpoint the location of compatible devices any place on Earth. However, GPS devices suffer from the same shortcoming as satellite phones—because they operate on a line-of-sight basis, they do not function well in buildings, in tunnels, under bridges, or even in poor weather. Bell Mobility, in conjunction with Sendum Corp. of Vancouver, has developed a new service that combines GPS technology with Bell's own cellular network to provide "Assisted GPS." When the Assisted GPS device loses touch with a satellite, it links up with the closest Bell Mobility cellular tower. GPS can normally pinpoint a user's location to within about 3 metres, while the cellular system is accurate to within 30 metres. Sendum Corp. has also developed a device that can track the location of valuable shipments such as fine art, money bags, and jewellery.

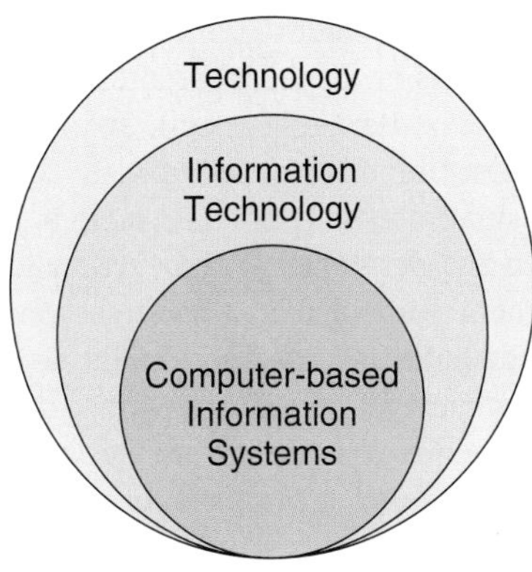

[Figure 1.6 ➥ Computer-based information systems are a subset of information technologies and of technologies in general.]

software, and telecommunications networks that people build and use to collect, create, and distribute data. The goal of an information system is to provide useful data to users. An example of an information system is the use of specialized software on a computer-controlled, mechanical machine used to produce compact discs (CDs), combined with other shop floor equipment that allows a person to monitor and control the production of each CD from a separate, possibly remote, computer.

Other examples of information systems include a series of integrated electronic spreadsheets used for a budget, an order fulfillment system for managing customers' purchases, or a set of linked pages on the World Wide Web. You may be asking, "Does my PC at work or school count as part of the company's or university's overall information system?" Our answer is yes. IS includes personal, group, organizational, inter-organizational, and even global computing systems.

The People Side of Information Systems

The information systems field includes a vast collection of people who develop, maintain, manage, and study information systems. The career opportunities for a person with IS training have never been better, and they are expected to continue to improve over the next 10 years. *Money* magazine recently reported that being a systems analyst—a common IS job—is one of the best jobs in the world today.

Canadian and U.S. statistics predict huge labour shortages over the next decade for people with skills in using, designing, developing, and managing information systems. Nearly every industry, not just computer hardware and software companies, relies heavily on IS professionals; therefore, the shortage in skilled technology workers may have a big impact on the economy if these jobs go unfilled. Industry Canada has reported that high demand for technology-related workers and escalating salaries could lead to inflation and lower corporate profits as companies scramble to offer competitive salaries to these people and, subsequently, have to drive up the prices of their goods and services.

Careers in IS

The field of IS includes those people in organizations who design and build systems, those who use these systems, and those responsible for managing these systems. In Table 1.1, we list careers in IS and the salaries you might earn in those positions. The variance in salary for each position reflects different levels of experience and education, as well as regional differences across Canada. The people who help develop and manage systems in organizations include

[Table 1.1] ***Careers and salaries in the information systems field.***

IS Activities	Typical Careers	Salary Ranges CDN$
Develop	Systems analyst	$40,000–$80,000+
	Systems programmer	$50,000–$80,000+
	Systems consultant	$50,000–$100,000+
Maintain	Database administrator	$75,000–$100,000+
	Webmaster	$40,000–$75,000+
Manage	IS director	$80,000–$120,000+
	Chief information officer	$125,000–$250,000+
Study	University professor	$60,000–$150,000+
	Government scientist	$60,000–$150,000+

Web Search

WEB SEARCH OPPORTUNITY
Visit Statistics Canada **www.statscan.ca** and Industry Canada **www.strategis.ic.gc.ca** to find information and publications about the effect of IT on the Canadian economy. Equivalent data from the U.S. can be found at the Department of Commerce **www.commerce.gov**.

systems analysts, systems programmers, systems operators, network administrators, database administrators, systems designers, systems managers, and chief information officers. In Canada, IT professionals have formed their own professional society, called the Canadian Information Processing Society (CIPS) **www.cips.ca**. The CIPS contains a wealth of information for those who wish to embark upon a career in the IT field in Canada. While the CIPS represents the people who work in IT, the IT industry itself is represented by another organization, the Information Technology Association of Canada (ITAC) **www.itac.ca**.

Another significant part of the IS field is the group of people who work in IS consulting firms such as IBM, CGI, and Accenture. These consultants advise organizations on how to build and manage their systems and sometimes actually build and run those systems. Companies such as IBM, which have traditionally been hardware/software companies, are now doing a lot of systems consulting and related work. Similarly, companies such as Accenture, which specialize in systems consulting, are very successful—hiring more people, opening new offices, taking on new business, generating lots of revenue, and so on.

University professors are another group of people in IS. These professors conduct research on the development, use, and management of information systems. Non-academic researchers who conduct research for government agencies or for large corporations such as IBM, Xerox, Hewlett-Packard, and AT&T face almost unlimited opportunities. These professionals generally conduct more applied research and development than academic researchers. For example, a researcher for a major computer manufacturer might develop a new computer product or examine ways to extend the life of a current product by integrating leading-edge components with the older architecture.

[**Figure 1.7** ➥ *BusinessWeek* cartoon showing the dangers of being a CIO.]

Source: © Dave Cutler.

The Advent of the Chief Information Officer

A number of important indications show that organizations are trying hard to manage information systems better. But perhaps nothing better demonstrates the growing importance of information systems in organizations than the advent of the ***chief information officer (CIO)*** and related positions in contemporary organizations.

Evolution of the CIO

In the early 1980s, the CIO position became popular as the new title given to executive-level individuals who were responsible for the information systems component within their organizations. The CIO was charged with integrating new technologies into the organization's business strategy. Traditionally, the responsibility for integrating technology and strategy had not officially rested with any one manager. Responsibility for managing the day-to-day information systems function had previously rested with a mid-level operations manager or, in some cases, with a vice-president of information systems. Ultimate responsibility for these activities would now rest with a high-level executive, the CIO. People began to realize that the information systems department was not simply a cost centre—a necessary evil that simply consumed resources. They realized that information systems could be of tremendous strategic value to the organization. As a result, this new IS executive would work much like other executives, sitting at the strategy table, working right alongside the chief executive officer, chief financial officer, chief operating officer, and other chief executives and key people in the organization. When strategic decisions were to be made, technology would play a major role, and the CIO needed to participate in the strategic decision-making process.

Not surprisingly, many organizations have jumped on the CIO bandwagon and either hired or named a CIO. As a result, many people thought that the CIO boom was a fad that would soon end, as do many other popular management trends. In fact, in early 1990, *BusinessWeek* printed a story entitled, "CIO Is Starting to Stand for 'Career Is Over': Once Deemed Indispensable, the Chief Information Officer Has Become an Endangered Species" (Rothfeder and Driscoll, 1990). In this story, and in the cartoon in Figure 1.7, the authors reported statistics showing that in 1989 the CIO dismissal rate had doubled to 13 percent, which was noticeably higher than the 9 percent for all top executives. They explained that the primary reasons for CIO dismissals included tightening budgets for technology and management's overblown expectations of CIO functions. Apparently, many organizations had been caught up in the rush to have a CIO without thinking enough about why they needed to have a CIO in the first place. The authors countered, however, that given the growing trend toward using information systems to achieve competitive advantage, the CIO could become relevant and important again. How right they were.

CAREER IMPLICATIONS

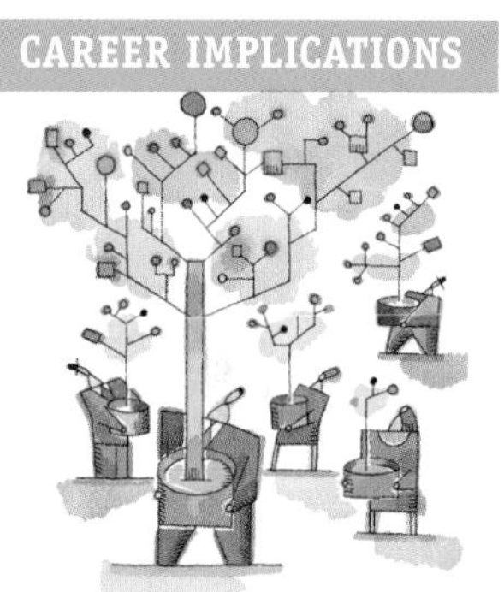

Accounting and Finance

Just up the street from Scotia Plaza—one of the most distinctive landmarks in Toronto's skyline, 68 storeys of red granite that shimmers in the sun—is Scotiabank Group's other red building, a handsome turn-of-the-century low-rise with arched windows, soaring turrets, and engraved columns. From here, Bob Grant directs the electronic banking efforts of the $14-billion-a-year, 48,000-employee financial institution. The senior vice-president of electronic banking at Scotiabank Group likes it here just fine. "I'm far enough from Scotia Plaza that they can't find me too easily. But I'm close enough to get over there if they need me." "They" are the C-suite executives who hold court on the seventh floor of Scotia Plaza. Grant is a 46-year-old graduate of York University's Schulich MBA program. In September 2003, *Global Finance* magazine chose Scotiabank as best Canadian Internet bank. Then Gomez Canada, a financial services consultancy, ranked Scotiabank as the country's No. 1 online retail bank from a field of 13 candidates. This compares with a No. 3 ranking in 2002 and a No. 7 ranking in 2001.

"Some of the most vigorous competition among this country's financial institutions is in e-banking," says Sam Cukierman, managing director of Gomez Canada. "Scotiabank is a story of continuous improvement." Grant keeps his finger on the pulse of e-banking by conducting a monthly survey of customer satisfaction and commissioning a biannual study of e-banking from a market research firm to discover services his customers would most like to have available online. The strategy appears to be working. In the last two years, Grant has introduced an average of 50 improvements to Scotia OnLine per year, and raised the satisfaction index among the bank's 1.3 million online customers to 94 percent. Some of the most popular features found on Scotia OnLine include account consolidation, personalized reminders of mortgage or GIC renewals, and the ability to take out loans for RRSP contributions. But Ask Scotia—a feature introduced in June 2003 that provides automated answers to questions asked in plain English—has been the biggest hit. According to Cukierman, Ask Scotia responds to all questions in under 24 hours with 80 percent accuracy. While a 20-percent margin of error is high, no other Canadian financial institution has created a better customer-service engine.

Grant won't divulge the annual cost of Scotiabank's online efforts, but says it runs into the millions of dollars. Does it make any difference to Scotiabank's bottom line? Scotiabank hasn't calculated a return on investment for Scotia OnLine, but Grant says the importance of e-banking shouldn't be underestimated. The retention of online customers is "huge," says Grant, and they tend to own more products and offer a better cross-sell opportunity than other customers. During the 1980s and '90s, banks pushed customers out of branches by introducing telephone banking and ATMs. Now banks want to be in the wealth management business, which means they must lure consumers back into the branches for financial advice, and to buy mutual funds, GICs, mortgages, and insurance products. "The branch of the future is going to be more about customer relationship management, and less about transactions," says Grant. "It will be the place to go to make important financial decisions." In this scenario, online banking will be more important than ever—not only because it will shoulder most of the burden for routine transactions, but also because it will largely be responsible for maintaining good relations between the bank and its consumers.

[Adapted from Erik Heinrich, "E-Banking on IT," *EDGE Magazine*, Vol. 3, No. 1 (February, 2004).]

CAREER IMPLICATIONS

Human Resource Management

Eugene Kaluzniacky, an instructor in the department of applied computer science and administrative studies at the University of Winnipeg, says there is a cultural and emotional difference between IT workers and, say, accountants. He says techies love to produce something that works and they get a high from that. What they are less concerned about, however, is whether the product serves the company's needs. "A lot of the time they say, 'Great, this system worked. I worked three months on it. How they use it, that's not my business.' And there's that disconnection, that they do not yet ultimately see the impact as being that important," says Kaluzniacky, the author of the book *Managing Psychological Factors in IT Work: An Orientation to Emotional Intelligence.* He blames part of this thinking on computer science programs at many colleges and universities. He says too few schools incorporate the business and marketing perspective of technology into the curriculum. Ideally, he says, the high that techies crave should come from meeting company goals rather than a system that never crashes, but this requires a leap of faith. "If they go into more uncharted and grey areas such as satisfying the management with their system, then maybe it's harder to get a high from that immediately because you have all kinds of human factors," Kaluzniacky says.

While part of the problem is a breakdown in communication, there is another dynamic at work. Lane says there is 40 times more project activity (tasks that have a start and end date and a deliverable) today than existed 20 years ago. "Whether the individual leaders are comfortable in technology may not be as significant as whether they understand the business case," says Greg Lane, president of the Canadian Information Processing Society. To maximize the effectiveness of a firm's IT operations, there needs to be a shared understanding between IT and non-IT personnel. People in IT need to gain a better appreciation of the objectives and pressures of non-IT managers. Non-IT managers, in turn, need to understand the challenges and motivations of IT workers.

[Adapted from Geoffrey Downey, "IT Workers: A World Apart," *Computing Canada,* Vol. 29, No. 22 (November 14, 2003).]

Web Search

WEB SEARCH OPPORTUNITY

You can investigate issues relevant to CIOs in Canada at **www.itworldcanada.com/Pages/Docbase/BrowsePublication.aspx?Publication=CIO**. Another site that contains information on issues that are important to CIOs can be found at **www.cio.com**.

The CIO Today

Today, most large organizations have a CIO or an equivalent position.[3] It is also now common for midsized and smaller organizations to have a CIO-like position within their organizations, although they may give this person a title such as Director of Information Systems. On the industry side, eight CIOs were named as "Chiefs of the Year" in December 2001 (the ranking has not been repeated since) by *InformationWeek* (see Figure 1.8), a magazine for business and technology managers. These CIOs were selected not only for their success in managing technology within their firms but also for the roles they played in leading their companies and staffs through the cataclysmic events of September 11, 2001. These and other CIOs are as critical to their organizations as the technologies that they manage.

IS Managerial Personnel

In large organizations, in addition to the CIO position there typically are many other different management positions within the IS function. In Table 1.2, we describe several such positions. This list is not exhaustive; rather, it is intended to provide a sampling of IS management positions. Furthermore, many firms will use the same job title, but each is likely to define it in a different way. As you can see from Table 1.2, the range of career opportunities for IS managers is very broad.

[3]Not to be confused with the chief technology officer, a post usually held by a person within a technology company who helps to chart the course for the company's technology products.

What Makes IS Personnel So Valuable?

In addition to the growing importance of people in the IS field, there have been changes in the nature of this type of work. No longer are IS departments in organizations filled only with nerdy men who wear pocket protectors. Many more women are in IS positions now. Also, it is now more common for an IS professional to be a polished, competent systems analyst who can talk fluently about both business and technology. Similarly, today's systems programmers are well-trained, highly skilled, valuable professionals who garner high wages and play a pivotal role in helping firms be successful. For example, good programmers with skills in hot software platforms such as SAP R/3 (Systems, Applications, and Products in Data Processing, Release 3) or Linux are so valuable that some organizations are willing to pay $150,000 a year or more to get them.

Many studies have been aimed at helping us understand what knowledge and skills are

[Table 1.2] ***Some IS management job titles and brief job descriptions.***

Job Title	Job Description
CIO	Highest-ranking IS manager. Responsible for strategic planning and IS use throughout the firm.
IS director	Responsible for managing all systems throughout the firm and the day-to-day operations of the entire IS unit.
Account executive	Responsible for managing the day-to-day operations of all aspects of IS within one particular division, plant, functional business area, or product unit.
Information centre manager	Responsible for managing IS services such as help desks, hot-lines, training, consulting, and so on.
Development manager	Responsible for coordinating and managing all new systems projects.
Project manager	Responsible for managing a particular new systems project.
Maintenance manager	Responsible for coordinating and managing all systems maintenance projects.
Systems manager	Responsible for managing a particular existing system.
IS planning manager	Responsible for developing an enterprise-wide hardware, software, and networking architecture and for planning for systems growth and change.
Operations manager	Responsible for supervising the day-to-day operations of the data and/or computer centre.
Programming manager	Responsible for coordinating all applications programming efforts.
Systems programming manager	Responsible for coordinating support for maintenance of all systems software (for example, operating systems, utilities, programming languages, and so on).
Manager of emerging technologies	Responsible for forecasting technology trends and for evaluating and experimenting with new technologies.
Telecommunications manager	Responsible for coordinating and managing the entire voice and data network.
Network manager	Responsible for managing one piece of the enterprise-wide network.
Database administrator	Responsible for managing database and database management software use.
Auditing or computer security manager	Responsible for managing ethical and legal use of information systems within the firm.
Quality assurance manager	Responsible for developing and monitoring standards and procedures to ensure that systems within the firm are accurate and of good quality.
Webmaster	Responsible for managing the firm's World Wide Website.

necessary for a person in the IS area to be successful (see, for example, Wade and Parent, 2002; and Todd, McKeen, and Gallupe, 1995). Interestingly, these studies also point out just what it is about IS personnel that makes them so valuable to their organizations. In a nutshell, good IS personnel possess valuable, integrated knowledge and skills in three areas—technical, business, and systems—as outlined in Table 1.3.

Technical Competency

These three areas of knowledge and skills—technical, business, and systems—are the core competencies that make IS professionals valuable to organizations. The technical

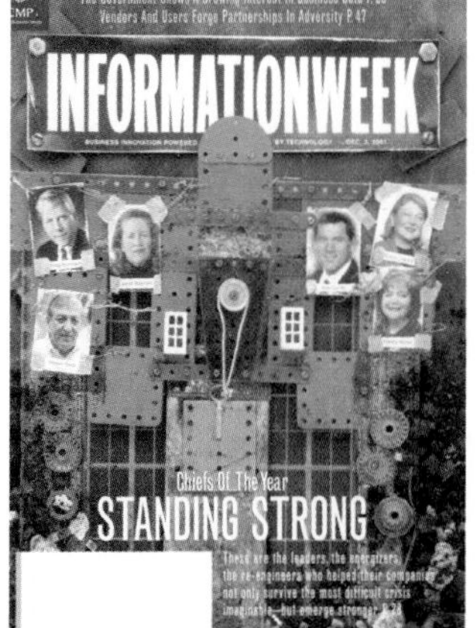

[Figure 1.8 ➥ *InformationWeek* cover with Chief Information Officers of the Year.]

Source: Copyright © 2001 by CMP Media Inc., 600 Community Drive, Manhasset, NY 11030. Reprinted from *InformationWeek* with permission.

[Table 1.3] ***IS professional core competencies.***

Domain	Description
Technical Knowledge and Skills	
Hardware	Hardware platforms, peripherals
Software	Operating systems, application software, drivers
Networking	Networking operating systems, cabling and networking interface cards, LANs, WANs, Internet
Business Knowledge and Skills	
Business	Business processes, functional areas of business and their integration, industry
Management	Planning, organizing, leading, controlling, managing, both people and projects
Social	Interpersonal, group dynamics, political
Communication	Verbal, written, and technological communication and presentation
Systems Knowledge and Skills	
Systems integration	Connectivity, compatibility, integrating subsystems and systems
Development methodologies	Steps in systems analysis and design, systems development life cycle, alternative development methodologies
Critical thinking	Challenging one's and others' assumptions and ideas
Problem solving	Information gathering and synthesis, problem identification, solution formulation, comparison, and choice

competency area includes knowledge and skills in hardware, software, and networking. In a sense, this is the "nuts and bolts" of IS. This is not to say that the IS professional must be a high-level technical expert in these areas. On the contrary, the IS professional must know just enough about these areas to understand how they work and how they can and should be applied. Typically, the IS professional manages or directs those who have deeper, more detailed technical knowledge.

The technical area of competency is, perhaps, the most difficult to maintain because the popularity of individual technologies is so fleeting. In Table 1.4, we list some technical skills areas that are currently popular. Many of these would not have appeared on this list a few years ago, and many will probably not appear on the list in a few years.

Business Competency

The business competency area is one that sets the IS professional apart from others who have only technical knowledge and skills. It is absolutely vital for IS professionals to understand the technical areas of the business and the technology/strategy fit. IS professionals must also be able to understand and manage people. These business skills propel IS professionals into project management and, ultimately, high-paying middle- and upper-level management positions.

Systems Competency

Systems competency is another area that sets the IS professional apart from others with only technical knowledge and skills. Those who understand how to build and integrate systems and how to solve problems will ultimately manage large, complex systems projects, as well as those in the firm who have only technical knowledge and skills.

Perhaps now you can see why IS professionals are so valuable to their organizations. These individuals have a solid foundation and integrated skills in technical, business, and systems knowledge. Perhaps most important, they also have the social skills to understand how to work well with and motivate others. It is these core competencies that make IS professionals a hot commodity.

Given how important technology is, what does this mean for your career? Technology is being used to radically change how business is

[Table 1.4] ***What technical skills are hot?***

Office/E-Mail	Languages and Data Formats	Applications
Microsoft Office	SmallTalk	Any enterprise resource planning package (e.g., those from SAP or Oracle)
MS Internet Explorer	C, C++, and C#	Any customer relationship management package (e.g., those from Siebel)
Netscape Navigator	Java and JavaScript	Any supply chain management package (e.g., those from I2, Ariba, or CommerceOne)
MS Project	HTML/CGI	PeopleSoft
Microsoft Exchange	Perl	SAS Enterprise Miner
Lotus Notes	ASP/VBScript	
POP mailers	PHP	
IMAP mailers	Python	
	Visual Basic	
	XML and UML	

RDBMS Administration	Development Tools	Internetworking
Sybase	Oracle Developer 2000 Uniface	Cisco
Oracle	Lotus Domino/Designer	Lucent
DB2	Microsoft Visual Studio	Juniper
MS SQL Server	Microsoft .NET platform	
MySQL	BEA Weblogic	
	IBM WebSphere	
	Sun's J2EE	

Operating Systems	NOS LAN Administration	Networking
Solaris	Windows 2000 Advanced Server	TCP/IP
HP-UX	Novell NetWare	IPX/SPX
AIX	SAMBA	SNMP
OS/2		IEEE 802.11a, b, & g (wireless Ethernet)
Windows XP		Frame Relay
Windows 2000 Professional		ATM
Windows CE		Voice over IP
Linux		VLANs
		VPNs
		Optical networking

conducted—from the way products and services are produced, distributed, and accounted for, to the ways they are marketed and sold. Whether you are majoring in information systems, finance, accounting, operations management, human resource management, business law, or marketing, knowledge of technology is critical to a successful career in business.

The Organizational Side of Information Systems

We have talked about data versus information, the technology side of IS, and the people side of IS. The last part of our IS definition is the term *organization*. People use information systems to help their organization to be more productive and profitable, to help their firm

CAREER IMPLICATIONS

Marketing

Ticketmaster, which was founded in 1976 by two Arizona college students, has grown to be the world's largest online ticketing company, serving more than 8,000 clients worldwide across multiple event categories. Headquartered in Los Angeles, California, Ticketmaster distributes tickets for sale using a mix of online services, cutting-edge technology, marketing, and traditional retail channels. As the ticketing service for hundreds of leading arenas, stadiums, performing arts venues, museums, and theatres, Ticketmaster sells 100 million tickets annually (year-ending 2003) through more than 3,300 retail ticket centre outlets, 19 worldwide telephone call centres, and online via ticketmaster.ca and Websites of the company's 10 international ticketing businesses. (See Figure 1.9 for Ticketmaster's site for Calgary and Southern Alberta.) Much of Ticketmaster's success is due to its superior capability to sell more tickets for its clients through a broad online and offline sales and marketing distribution network.

One important reason that Ticketmaster is able to maintain its leadership position in the increasingly competitive event ticketing industry is because the company is dedicated to constantly developing new and better ways to integrate cutting-edge information technologies and systems into its businesses. For example, Ticketmaster first introduced barcode printing on its event tickets in 1994 and then integrated that technology in 2000 to launch its online delivery service, ticketFast, enabling consumers to purchase, download, and print event tickets from their home or office. The barcode technology is now fully integrated with Ticketmaster's clients' on-site point-of-entry systems, whereby barcoded event tickets are scanned by wireless handheld devices at the point of entry to expedite the event-goer's arrival process. Through the continued development of barcoding and other ticketing technologies, Ticketmaster makes it easier and faster for consumers to buy, and clients to sell, tickets.

Ticketmaster is a great example of a company that uses computer-based information systems in innovative ways to make your life easier and better. You may be thinking to yourself, "I just want good tickets at low prices, and I want to get them quickly and easily. . . . I didn't know all of this computer stuff was going on in the background." Indeed, Ticketmaster does all the hard work behind the scenes to make it easier for you.

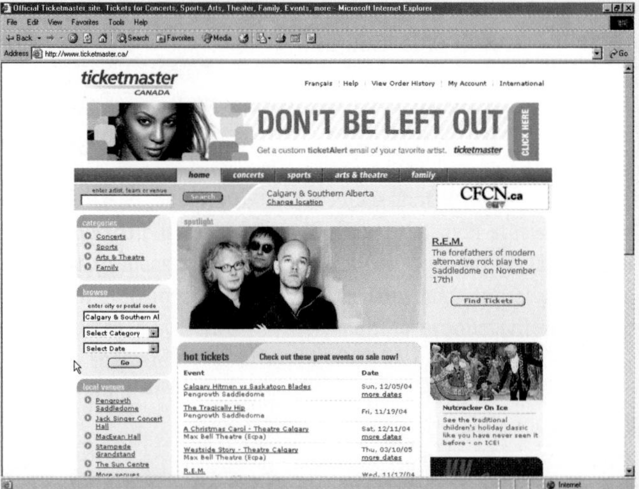

[**Figure 1.9** ➥ The Ticketmaster Website makes it easy to purchase tickets to a wide range of events.]

Source: Ticketmaster.

gain competitive advantage, to help their firm reach more customers, or to improve service to the customers their organization serves. This holds true for all types of organizations—professional, social, religious, educational, and governmental. In fact, not long ago the U.S. Internal Revenue Service launched its own site on the World Wide Web for the reasons just described. The IRS Website was so popular that approximately 220,000 users visited it during the first 24 hours and more than a million visited it in its first week—even before the Web address for the site was officially announced.

In Chapter 6 we will talk in detail about the types of information systems commonly

[Table 1.5] *Types of information systems used in organizations.*

Type of System	Designed To	Sample Application
Transaction Processing System	Process day-to-day business event data at the operational level of the organization	Grocery store checkout cash register with connection to network
Management Information System	Produce detailed information to help manage a firm or a part of a firm	Inventory management and planning system
Executive Information Update System	Provide very high-level, aggregate information to support executive-level decision making	News retrieval and stock information system
Decision Support System	Provide analysis tools and access to databases in order to support quantitative decision making	Product demand forecasting system
Expert System	Mimic human expert in a particular area and provide answers or advice	Automated system for analyzing bank loan applications
Functional Area Information System	Support the activities within a specific functional area of the firm	System for planning for personnel training and assignments
Office Automation System (a.k.a. Personal Productivity Software)	Support a wide range of predefined, day-to-day work activities of individuals and small groups	Word processor
Collaboration System	Enable people to communicate, collaborate, and coordinate with each other	Electronic mail system with automated, shared calendar
Customer Relationship Management System	Support interaction between the firm and its customers	Siebel's suite of e-business software products, including Siebel Sales
Electronic Business System	Enable customers to buy goods and services from a firm's Web-site	**www.amazon.ca**
Enterprise Resource Planning System	Support and integrate all facets of the business, including planning, manufacturing, sales, marketing, and so on	SAP R/3 (Systems, Applications, and Products in Data Processing, Release 3)

used in organizations. It makes sense, however, for us to describe briefly here the various types of systems used so that you will know exactly what we mean by the term *information system* as we use it throughout the rest of the book. Table 1.5 provides a list of the major types of information systems used in organizations.

Topping the list in the table are some of the more traditional, major categories that are used to describe information systems. These include ***transaction processing systems***, ***management information systems***, ***executive information systems***, ***decision support systems***, ***expert systems***, and ***functional area information systems***. Five to 10 years ago it would have been typical to see systems that fell cleanly into one of these categories. Today, with ***internetworking*** and ***systems integration***, it is difficult to say that any given information system fits into only one of these categories (i.e., that a system is a management information system only and nothing else). Modern-day information systems tend to span several of these categories of information systems, helping not only to collect data from throughout the firm and from customers, but also to integrate all that diverse data and present it to busy decision makers, along with tools to manipulate and analyze those data. ***Customer relationship management systems*** and ***enterprise resource planning systems*** are good examples of these types of systems that encompass

Information systems are combinations of
hardware, software, and telecommunications networks
that
people build and use
to
collect, create, and distribute useful data,
typically in
organizational settings.

[Figure 1.10 ➡ A representation of the definition of IS, as shown in Figure 1.4.]

many features and types of data and cannot easily be categorized.

Office automation systems and ***collaboration systems*** are typically bought "off-the-shelf" and enable people to 1) perform their own work, and 2) work with others. There are a handful of software packages that dominate this sector of the software industry and are commonly found on personal computers in people's homes and offices. Microsoft Office is an example of a very popular office automation system that provides word processing, spreadsheet, and other personal productivity tools. Microsoft's Exchange/Outlook and Lotus Notes are good examples of very popular collaboration systems that provide people with e-mail, automated calendaring, and online, threaded discussions.

Systems for ***electronic business***, such as corporate Websites, are also very popular and important. These systems are typically Internet-based and enable 1) consumers to find information about, and purchase, goods and services from each other and from business firms, and 2) business firms to electronically exchange products, services, and information. Given the pervasive use of the Internet to support electronic business, we devote a great deal of time to this topic in subsequent chapters. In Chapter 4 we talk about the nuts and bolts of how the Internet works. Then, in Chapter 5, we talk about how people are using the Internet to conduct electronic business.

While many modern-day information systems span several of these IS categories, it is still useful to understand each one. Doing so enables you to better understand the myriad approaches, goals, features, and functions of modern information systems.

We have talked about each of the parts of our definition of IS, shown again in Figure 1.10, and we have talked about different types of information systems. In the next section, we focus on how information systems can be applied within organizations.

THE DUAL NATURE OF INFORMATION SYSTEMS

Technology is like a sword—you can use it effectively as a competitive weapon, but as the old saying goes, those who live by the sword sometimes die by the sword. The two following cases illustrate this dual nature of information systems.

Case in Point: An Information System Gone Awry: The Denver International Airport

What happens when an information system is implemented poorly? Perhaps the most notable example of an information system gone wrong in recent years is the automated baggage-handling system for the US$4.2-billion Denver International Airport (DIA).

Like the newly constructed DIA, the new underground, automated baggage-handling system for the airport was intended to be amazing. This information system would not only coordinate the automated check-in and routing of all luggage for all customers throughout the airport, but it would also enable airport employees to monitor the flow of baggage and locate bags literally anywhere in the airport. The system, which cost US$200 million, included the following features:

- 33 km of steel track
- 4,000 independent "telecars" that route and deliver luggage among the counters, gates, and claim areas of 20 different airlines
- 100 networked computers
- 5,000 electric eyes
- 400 radio receivers
- 56 bar-code scanners

Due to problems in the software, the system opened, damaged, and misrouted cargo, forcing airport authorities to leave the system sitting idle for nearly a year. Because of this and other delays, the airport did not open and wasted US$1.1 million a day in interest and operating costs for quite some time.

The DIA story has a happy ending—or beginning, as it were. They fixed the software and the automated baggage system is now operational. The airport is now making money and winning awards. Indeed, the baggage-handling system is one of many ways that this organization is attempting to be innovative and to outdo the competition. However, the airport is still useful as an

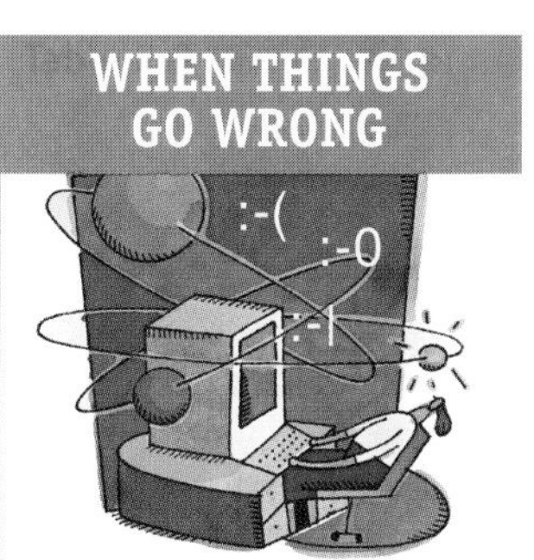

Disaster Plans Found Lacking

Events such as the North American blackout of 2003 and the terrorist acts of September 11, 2001 pointed out how important it is for business managers to make contingency plans for the information systems that are used to run their businesses. Surprisingly, while companies have had to rely more and more on their information systems, you would think that business executives would spend more time thinking about disaster recovery. Unfortunately, they have not.

According to an online poll conducted by St. Louis–based trade publication *Disaster Recovery Journal,* 65.5 percent of the 2,223 respondents said their company had not implemented its business contingency/disaster recovery plan in the last 10 years. The poll also found that about 26 percent had implemented their plans between one and three times. In another survey, 38 percent of 2,151 respondents reported that the biggest challenge in planning disaster recovery efforts was funding. Doran Boroski, a senior consultant with Compass Group, a Chicago-based management consulting firm, is not surprised by that. Boroski says cost is often a barrier to proper disaster recovery and testing. "Even if they have a plan, they don't test it, mostly for financial reasons," Boroski says. "Testing is the first thing to go out of the IT budget." The picture is no rosier in Canada. A study by *CIO Canada* magazine in 2003 found that 44 percent of firms did not have a disaster recovery plan in place.

Bob Zimmerman, an analyst at Giga Information Group who specializes in storage management, says disaster recovery tests need to be random events, just like the disasters they are supposed to simulate. Too often, he says, companies schedule tests for a specific time, on a specific day, on a specific application, and when specific personnel are available. "Very few businesses could pass a rigorous disaster recovery test," Zimmerman says. In surveying 150 Compass Group clients over 12 to 18 months, Boroski has found that one area where companies are sorely lacking in disaster readiness is their midrange data centres, which are likely to store information related to such things as payroll and HR. Just 25 percent of companies had a disaster recovery plan for their midrange data centres and one-third of the companies with a disaster plan had actually tested it.

After blackouts, blizzards, and terrorist acts, business leaders are thinking a lot more about how they might recover from unforeseen disasters. Disaster recovery planning has taken on new meaning and importance.

[Adapted from Jon Surmacz, "Disaster Plans Lacking," **www2.cio.com/metrics/2001/metric269.html**, *CIO Magazine* (September 26, 2001).]

example of how a problematic information system can adversely affect an organization's performance.

Case in Point: An Information System That Works: FedEx

Just as there are examples of information systems gone wrong, there are many examples of information systems gone right. For example, take the innovative use of information systems on the FedEx Website (see Figure 1.11).

FedEx Express, the world's largest express transportation company, delivers more than 3 million packages and more than 3 million kilograms of freight to over 200 countries each business day. FedEx Express uses extensive, interconnected information systems to coordinate more than 140,000 employees, 644 aircraft, and more than 45,000 ground vehicles worldwide.

To improve its services and sustain a competitive advantage, FedEx now offers

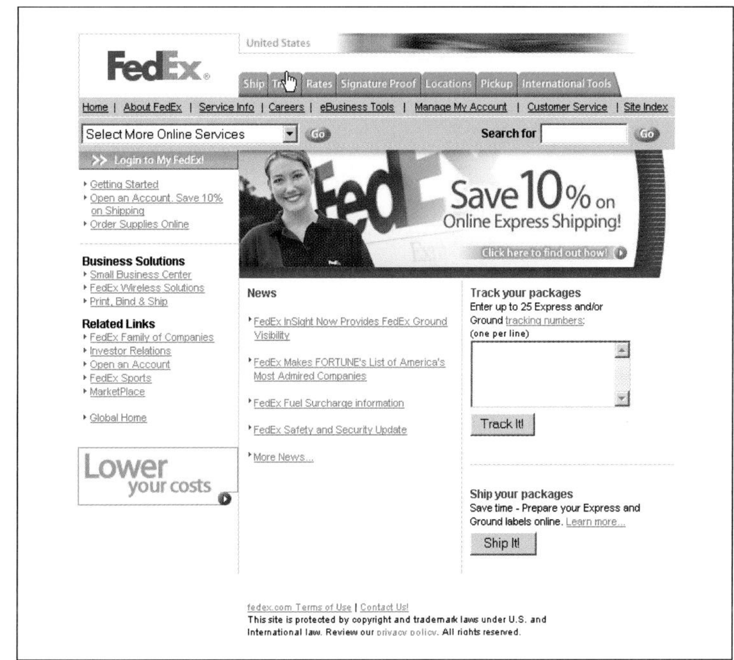

[Figure 1.11 ➥ The Website for Federal Express.]

Source: www.federalexpress.com.

GLOBAL PERSPECTIVE

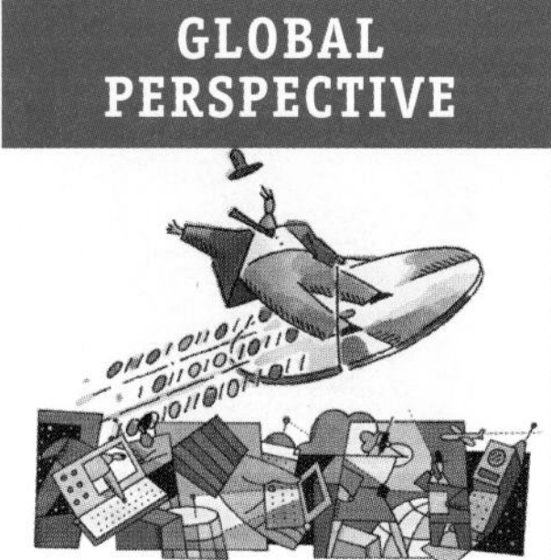

Businesses Look Overseas for IS Help

The growing demand for inexpensive yet competent programming talent is pushing the offshore-outsourcing market beyond its roots in India and encouraging North American and Western European IT service providers to increase their use of overseas workers.

"The technology skills needed to program in languages such as C++, .NET, and Java are available in China, the Philippines, Russia, and other countries, but offshore outsourcing is most mature in India, where the government has been supportive of IT for decades and has continued to improve on the solid educational systems built by the British," says Mukesh Mehta, VP of corporate systems for Metropolitan Life Insurance Company, which has an offshore-outsourcing contract with Cognizant Technology Solutions Corp. For instance, the Indian Parliament granted the Indian Institute of Technology its charter in 1961, and the school has evolved into a centre for teaching, research, and industrial consulting.

While India is the biggest resource for offshore programmers and project managers, Forrester Research predicts that demand for offshore workers will outstrip that country's supply in a few years. India has about 445,000 IT workers, a population that is expected to grow to 625,000 by 2006. But Forrester also predicts that demand for offshore IT workers will reach more than one million by 2006, compared with about 360,000 in 2002.

Executives are becoming increasingly comfortable with outsourcing projects to companies that do the work in remote locations at lower prices than can be found domestically. "A 25-percent cost savings on an outsourcing contract is a realistic goal when working with an offshore provider," Forrester analyst Christine Overby says. To mitigate risk, many offshore companies have management personnel in target countries who act as liaisons with overseas staff. The continued reliance on offshore talent by well-known service providers, such as Accenture, EDS, and IBM Global Services, also lends credence to the offshore model. Parts of Canada are even jumping into the act by promoting themselves as "near shore" outsourcing alternatives to more geographically and culturally remote locations (see Chapter 8 for an extensive discussion of IT outsourcing).

What began more than a decade ago as a cheap way to supplement overworked internal application developers with workers from India has grown into a worldwide search for the right mixture of talent, resources, and cost savings to create and manage today's most complex IT environments.

[Adapted from Larry Greenemeier, "Offshore Outsourcing Grows to Global Proportions," **www.informationweek.com/story/iwek20020207S0011**, *InformationWeek* (February 11, 2002).]

services on the World Wide Web. Millions of customers visit the FedEx Website to track FedEx Express and FedEx Ground shipments anywhere in the world, find out about FedEx's delivery options and costs, or use tools to prepare their own packages, verify them online, and print bar-coded shipping documents. These and other information systems ensure that FedEx has a dominant position in the shipping business.

Information Systems for Competitive Advantage

The Denver International Airport and FedEx information systems are typical of those used in large, complex organizations. These systems are so large in scale and scope that they are difficult to build. It is important to handle the development of such systems the right way the first time around.

Not only were these systems large and complicated, but they were, and continue to be, critical to the success of the firms that built them. The choices made in developing the new systems at both DIA and FedEx were strategic in their intent. These systems were not developed solely because managers in these organizations wanted to do things faster or because they wanted to have the latest, greatest technology. These organizations developed these systems strategically to help gain or sustain some competitive advantage (Porter, 1985; Porter and Millar, 1985) over their rivals. Let us not forget—technology should be strategic and can be a powerful enabler of competitive advantage.

Although we described information systems' uses at two relatively large organizations, firms of all types and sizes can use information systems to gain and sustain a competitive advantage over their rivals. Whether it is a small, mom-and-pop boutique or a large government agency, every organization can find a way to use information technology to beat its rivals. In the next chapter we will talk more about this opportunity to use information systems strategically.

THE FUTURE OF THE IS FUNCTION WITHIN THE FIRM

The current emphasis on the use of technology within businesses is not a fad. Indeed, all indicators point to the increased use of technology and organizations' continued awareness of the importance of technology, both as a tool for productivity and as a vehicle for achieving competitive advantage and organizational change. In this section, we briefly discuss some likely future trends.

From Ownership and Control to a Consulting and Service Mentality

Early IS departments typically had huge project backlogs, and IS personnel would often deliver systems that were over budget, were completed much too late, were difficult to use, and did not always work well. In addition, many of these old-school IS personnel believed they owned and controlled the computing resources, that they knew better than users did, and that they should tell users what they could and could not do with the computing resources. Needless to say, this was not a recipe for success and good relationships. Indeed, relations between IS personnel and users within a firm were often sour and were sometimes even bitter.

For a long time, users were forced to put up with the poor service and the poor attitude. Then technology started to become significantly better—faster, easier to build and use, and cheaper. As a result, end users began to develop their own computing applications. Disgruntled users simply said, "If the IS staff cannot or will not do this for us, then we will build our own systems." In many cases, they did just that, and they did it well, much to the dismay of some of the IS managers.

Business managers soon became more savvy about technology and the possibilities and opportunities that it offered, and they reasoned that the possibilities and opportunities were too great to let the IS function simply wither away as end-user development took over. In addition, smart, concerned IS personnel realized that they needed an attitude adjustment. Some people believe that the changes in the nature of technology forced people to cooperate more. For example, the shift from mainframes to a client-server model may have forced people within the IS function to improve their operations and their relationships with people in other units of the firm. The client-server model required a new kind of relationship between IS and other people throughout the firm (Stevens, 1994). As a result of these forces, in modern IS units that do a good job, the atmosphere, attitude, and culture are very different and much more sensitive and responsive than they used to be (see Figure 1.12).

In these more responsive IS units, the personnel have taken on more of a consulting relationship with their users. The IS personnel believe that, fundamentally, they are there to help the users solve problems and be more productive. Indeed, in many cases, the IS personnel do not even refer to the users as "users." They are "clients" or "customers." This new attitude is a major change from the old days, when IS personnel did not want to be bothered by users and thought that the techies knew better than users. It is unfortunate that this old-school mentality still exists in some organizations.

The same holds for IS units that have taken on this new ***service mentality***. The IS personnel do everything they can to ensure that they are satisfying their systems customers within the firm. They reach out to customers and proactively seek their input and needs, rather than waiting for customers to come in with systems complaints. They modify the systems at a moment's notice just to meet customer needs quickly and effectively. They celebrate the customer's new systems ideas

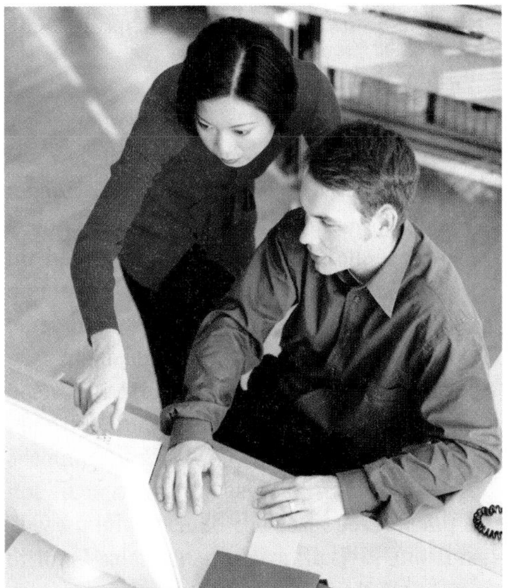

[**Figure 1.12** ➥ IS personnel are likely to be put out in the business unit, working directly with the people who will use the system being implemented.]

Source: © Getty Images, Inc.

BRIEF CASE

Developing a Consulting Mentality at Texas Instruments

The notion of a consulting mentality could not have been more appropriate than at Texas Instruments, the Dallas-based electronics manufacturer (Koch, 1998). When Pallab Chatterjee became CIO at Texas Instruments, the IT department had a very tight grip on decision making. Chatterjee soon realized that the control was so tight that the business units were literally scared to ask the IT department for anything, and they relied on "underground" IT projects without the help of the IT department. To combat this problem, Chatterjee has reorganized Texas Instruments' worldwide IT department and services into two subunits. The first, referred to as the worldwide utility, is responsible for the physical networks, the data centre, the numerous local LANs, and the global WAN. This group is mainly responsible for efficiency, control, and reliability. The second subunit, the consultants, is composed of all IT staff members who are not part of the utility group. These consultants work both at the central, corporate level and at the business-unit level. At the business-unit level, these consultants are able to work closely with the managers to develop and manage systems that do not require centralized control. The systems that do require more control are handled by the consultants at the corporate level. This model has proven to be very successful for Chatterjee and Texas Instruments because business units are no longer afraid to ask for corporate support and know that if they need corporate support, it will be there.

Questions

1. Can you foresee any problems that may arise from the way Texas Instruments has organized its IT function?
2. Why do areas of the firm circumvent the IT department? What can be done to reduce the incidence of "underground" IT projects?

rather than putting up roadblocks and giving reasons that the new ideas cannot or will not work. They fundamentally believe that the customers own the technology and the information and that the technology and information are there for the customers, not for the systems personnel. They create help desks, hotlines, information centres, and training centres to support customers. These service-oriented IS units structure the IS function so that it can better serve the customer.

The implications of this new service mentality for the IS function are staggering. It is simply amazing how unproductive it can be when the IS personnel and other people within the firm are at odds with one another. On the other hand, it is even more amazing how productive and fun work can be when people in the IS function work hand in hand with people throughout the organization. Technology is, potentially, the great lever, but it works best when people work together, not against each other, to use it.

The Spread of Technology in Organizations

Another phenomenon that shows how integral and vital information systems and their proper management have become to organizations is the extent to which the technology is firmly integrated and entrenched within the various business units (i.e., accounting, sales, marketing).

In many organizations today, you will find that the builders and managers of a particular information system or subsystem spend most of their time out in the business unit, along with the users of that particular system. Many times, these systems personnel are permanently placed—with an office, desk, phone, and personal computer—in the business unit along with the users.

In addition, it is not uncommon for systems personnel to have formal education, training, and work experience in information systems, as well as in the functional area that the system supports, such as finance. It is becoming increasingly difficult to separate the technology from the business or the systems staff from the other people in the organization. For this reason, how information systems are managed is important to you, no matter what career option you pursue.

As information systems are used more broadly throughout organizations, IS personnel often have dual reporting relationships—reporting to both the central IS group and the business function they serve. Therefore, at least some need for centralized IS planning, deployment, and management continues—particularly with respect to achieving economies of scale in systems acquisition and development and in optimizing systems integration, enterprise networking, and the like. Even in organizations that are decentralizing technology and related decisions, a need for coordination across the firm still persists. This coordination is likely to continue to happen through some form of a centralized (or, at least, centrally coordinated) IS staff. Organizations are likely to continue to want to reap the benefits of IS decentralization (flexibility, adaptability, and systems responsiveness), but it is equally likely that they will not want to—and will not be able to—forgo the benefits of IS centralization (coordination, economies of scale, compatibility, and connectivity).

Changing Skill Set and Human Resource Planning

Given the trend toward pushing people from the IS staff out into the various business units of the firm, and given the need for people within each of the functional areas of the business to have technology skills, there is clearly a need for people who know the technology side and the business side of the business well. We suspect that the need for people to play these boundary-spanning roles will continue. Many of these people will be hired into and located within the IS departments of firms, but they are likely to spend a lot of their time working out in the business unit with their clients (refer to Figure 1.12). Staffing the IS group with these kinds of boundary spanners is and will continue to be critical to the success of the IS group and to the success of the organization.

Downsizing of Organizations and IS Departments

Many organizations that are ***downsizing***, or rightsizing, as some call it, are looking toward the IS function and technology as the lever for simultaneously shrinking the organization and making it more productive. In short, they are using technology to streamline business functions and, in some cases, to slash costs and replace people. Although this approach may not be fair for the people who lose their jobs, many firms are forced to do this to remain competitive and, in some cases, to continue to exist. Such uses of information

CAREER IMPLICATIONS

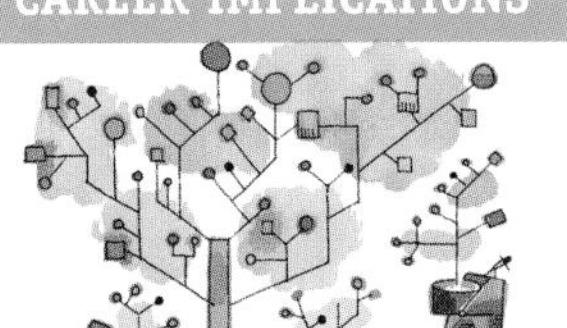

Information Systems

About 30 years ago, Greg Lane read a research report about how various employee groups view the importance of social and personal interaction in the workplace. He found IT workers near the bottom of the list, meaning they felt that interacting with the organization overall wasn't a priority. But that wasn't the most surprising part for the president of the Canadian Information Processing Society (CIPS). "One of the groups that still stands out in my mind that finished in front of IT workers was forest rangers," Lane says. "I think that is changing, but I think in our industry there's still that kind of preference for communicating electronically—or not at all."

Ironically, the people charged with ensuring a company can communicate aren't keen on it themselves. In terms of building links with other departments and raising their stature within the company, it is disastrous. In general, Lane says, there is a disconnect of varying severity between IT and the rest of the organization. Despite the mission-critical role technology plays in almost every business, techies are often viewed as second-class citizens, he says. "I think the CIO and IT people haven't had the right visibility or haven't had the right position within an organization and they're oftentimes an afterthought," says Lane, who is also the director of business development for Deloitte Consulting. "The reality is IT could and should be part of the strategic sessions, not an afterthought or not somebody trying to figure out how to incorporate them into your strategy. They should be baked into, and in fact leading, some of the discussions around how a technology is going to enable a corporation."

According to a survey of CIOs in April 2003 conducted by the Canadian Technology Human Resources Board (CTHRB), three out of five CIOs said selling their business case was getting harder. CTHRB executive director Bob Cook says the IT department, like human resources, is still viewed in some circles as a cost centre. According to a study by Athabasca University and *CIO Canada* magazine, only 47 percent of IT managers felt their CIO has a full role in determining corporate business strategy. As the importance of IT in organizations grows, Lane says the onus is on everyone to adapt—case in point being the power outage that hit most of the northeastern United States and Ontario. "As we move forward it's going to be very different," he says. "The power outage drove this home for a whole lot of people, 'Holy mackerel, if I'm off the air we're out of business.' That's not necessarily the way it was even 10 years ago, and I don't think it's going to get any easier or less technology intensive."

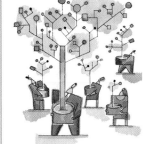

[Adapted from Geoffrey Downey, "IT Workers: A World Apart," *Computing Canada,* 29:22 (November 14, 2003).]

COMING ATTRACTIONS

A Bright Future for Organic Displays

A group of University of Toronto researchers say they are the first Canadians to produce a display technology that is as flexible as paper. The experimental technology is called an organic light-emitting device (or OLED). It's flexible, so it could fit any form factor or even mould itself to the shape of your lap (see Figure 1.13). "What differentiates this device from conventional LEDs is that the molecules are very flexible. You can make any substrate you want," said Zheng-Hong Lu, the project's lead researcher at the University of Toronto. "That's really opened up a whole potential display media." Lu has been working with his team on the project for about five years and has developed OLEDs made on a number of flexible materials, like transparent plastic film and reflective metal foil. Lu said OLED could represent the next wave of display technology. In recent years, liquid crystal displays (LCD) have made substantial inroads against cathode ray tubes (CRT) in the monitor and display markets. "Many experts consider [OLED] the next major display device replacing LCD," said Lu.

Because of its flexible design, the OLED manufacturing process would be substantially different from the way conventional displays are produced today. "Like newspapers, you could print rolls and rolls of displays," said Lu. "With big companies willing to invest lots of money, I'm really optimistic about some sort of commercial device." Lu said he hopes to see commercially viable products in the market in five years. Further down the line, flexible laptops that could be rolled up and stuffed in a back pocket may be a reality. The commercial applications of OLED are very real and are already here, albeit in a much smaller-factor form. Kodak, which owns an OLED patent, has an Easy Share 633 digital camera with an embedded OLED display. Samsung is now shipping its E700 series cell phone with an external OLED screen. However, making the leap to full-size OLED for something the size of a computer monitor or TV is still a distant goal, according to IDC analyst Jennifer Gallo.

She conservatively estimates that it could be at least 2010 before such products are available. "It's been proven that it can be done, but not for large displays. There are a lot of people focusing on the production and the manufacturing process of OLED, such as DuPont, and they're still working on it. It's not easy," she said. The product has limitations that have yet to be overcome. Much like a break-and-shake glowstick that provides a light source only for a short time, OLED has some serious lifespan concerns, Gallo said. "It's a chemical and there's a lifetime to that chemical and how long it will emit light for." If that problem can be solved, the future for OLED looks bright. Aside from the inherent advantage of a flexible display, OLED produces an extremely clear image that can be viewed from multiple angles (an issue with colour-screen LCD is that the colour tends to fade when viewed from the side).

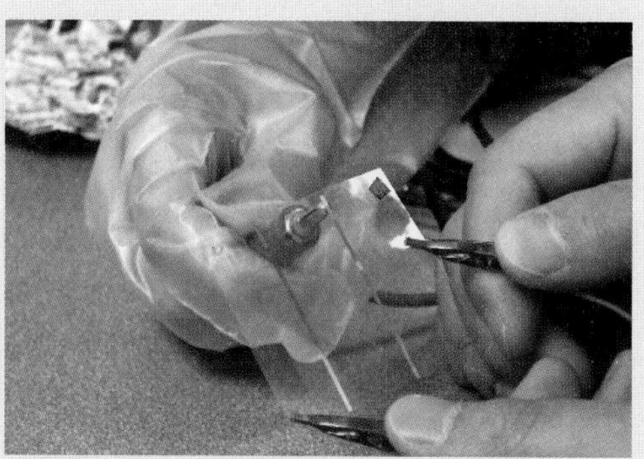

[**Figure 1.13** ➥ An organic light-emitting device.]

Source: Zheng-Hong Lu, U of T, Department of Materials, Science and Engineering.

[Adapted from Neil Sutton, "U of T Lab Sees Potential in Organic Display Technology," **www.itbusiness.ca/index.asp?theaction=61&sid=54581#**, ITBusiness.ca (January 20, 2004).]

systems have interesting implications for the size and structure of organizations and for the size and structure of the IS function.

Career Prospects and Opportunities

Although technology at some levels continues to become easier to use, there is still and is likely to continue to be an acute need for people within an organization to have the responsibility of planning for, designing, developing, maintaining, and managing technologies. Much of this will happen within the business units and will be performed by those with primarily business duties and tasks, as opposed to systems duties and tasks. However, we are a long way from the day when technology is so easy to deploy that a need no longer exists for people with deep information systems knowledge and skills. In fact, many people believe that this day may never come. Although increasing numbers of people will incorporate systems responsibilities within their non-systems jobs, there will continue to be a need for people with primarily systems responsibilities. In short, IS staffs and departments will likely continue to exist and play an important role in the foreseeable future.

While many organizations are downsizing, and while some are shrinking their IS staff, overall hiring within IS is growing. With hiring of systems personnel in a variety of positions at a fever pitch, and with the management of technology a critical business issue, it is not likely that IS departments will go away or even shrink significantly. Indeed, all projections are for growth of IS both in scale and scope.

The future opportunities in the IS field in Canada and elsewhere are likely to be found in a variety of areas, which is good news for everyone. You may want to pursue a career within a Canadian firm that specializes in developing, producing, or selling information systems. Many Canadian firms are world leaders in this area, as shown in Table 1.6. You may choose to work for a foreign IT company that operates in Canada, as shown in Table 1.7. Or you may choose to work for a firm far removed from the technology sector. All firms are affected in some way by information systems. The diversity in the technology area can embrace us all. It really does not matter much which area of IS you choose to pursue—there will likely be a promising future there for you. Even if your career interests are outside IS, being an informed and strong user of information technologies will greatly enhance your career prospects.

As we discuss throughout this book, the future of the IS field looks very promising by all accounts. All current growth indicators and forecasts for the future show that the use of information systems in organizations, the development of new technologies and systems, and, perhaps most important, the demand for IS personnel will continue to grow. If you had to choose a field to go into based on its growth potential and opportunities, you would most likely choose IS.

[Table 1.6] ***Top Canadian IT-sector firms in 2003.***

Company	Sales (CDN$ thousands)
Top 5 Canadian Hardware Companies	
Nortel Networks	14,451,360
Celestica	11,319,685
JDS Uniphase	1,502,887
ATI Technologies	1,398,227
Research In Motion	429,380
Top 5 Canadian Software Companies	
Cognos	754,053
Geac	623,667
Hummingbird	269,616
Open Text	248,815
Algorithmics	107,440
Top 5 Canadian Telecommunications Companies	
BCE	19,768,000
Telus	7,006,700
Rogers	4,323,045
Aliant	2,630,353
Shaw Communications	1,888,560
Top 5 Canadian IT Professional Services and Consulting Companies	
CGI	2,169,613
Nexinnovations	689,000
MacDonald, Dettwiler and Associates Ltd.	623,000
Softchoice	548,856
BCE Emergis	487,000

[Table 1.7] ***Top foreign IT-sector firms operating in Canada in 2003.***

Company	Sales (CDN$ thousands)
IBM Canada	5,300,000
HP Canada	3,000,000
Microsoft Canada	1,300,000
EDS Canada	1,120,000
Xerox Canada	1,064,000
Cisco Canada	1,000,000
Sun Microsystems	544,600
Cap, Gemini, Ernst and Young	356,056
Oracle Canada	350,000
SAP Canada	318,710

KEY POINTS REVIEW

1. **Define and understand the term *information systems (IS)*.** Information systems are combinations of hardware, software, and telecommunications networks that people build and use to collect, create, and distribute useful data, typically in organizational settings. When data are organized in a way that is useful to people, these data are defined as information. The term *information systems* is also used to represent the field in which people develop, use, manage, and study computer-based information systems in organizations. The field of IS is huge, diverse, and growing, and encompasses many different people, purposes, systems, and technologies.
2. **Explain the technology, people, and organizational components of an information system.** The technology part of information systems is the hardware, software, and telecommunications networks. The people who build, manage, use, and study information systems make up the people component. They include systems analysts, systems programmers, information systems professors, and many others. Finally, information systems typically reside and are used within organizations, so they are said to have an organizational component. Together, these three aspects form an information system.
3. **Describe the types of jobs and career opportunities in information systems and in related fields.** The people who help develop and manage systems in organizations include systems analysts, systems programmers, systems operators, network administrators, database administrators, systems designers, systems managers, and chief information officers. All of these types of people are in heavy demand and, as a result, salaries are high and continue to rise. The field of IS has changed such that IS personnel are now thought of as valuable business professionals rather than as "nerds" or "techies." The need for technology-related knowledge and skills has spread to other careers as well in fields such as finance, accounting, operations management, human resource management, business law, and marketing.
4. **Describe the various types of information systems.** Types of information systems include transaction processing systems, management information systems, executive information systems, decision support systems, expert systems, functional area information systems, customer relationship management systems, enterprise resource planning systems, office automation systems, collaboration systems, and systems for electronic commerce. While many modern-day information systems span several of these categories, it is still useful to understand each one. Doing so enables you to better understand the myriad approaches, goals, features, and functions of modern information systems.
5. **Describe the dual nature of information systems in the success and failure of modern organizations.** If information systems are conceived, designed, used, and managed effectively and strategically, they can enable organizations to be more effective, to be more productive, to expand their reach, and to gain or sustain competitive advantage over rivals. If information systems are not conceived, designed, used, or managed well, they can have negative effects on organizations, such as loss of money, loss of time, loss of customers' good will, and, ultimately, loss of customers. Modern organizations that embrace and manage information systems effectively and strategically tend to be the organizations that are successful and competitive.
6. **Understand and plan for the future of managing IS.** The future is difficult to predict. Nonetheless, we can expect that there will be broad and continued growth for IS applications, spread of technology and IS personnel throughout organizations, a new service mentality toward technology and IS personnel, and continued downsizing supported by IS. The career opportunities for IS professionals will increase at a rapid pace, making the management of the IS function and the IS human resources an important part of managing all modern organizations.

KEY TERMS

chief information officer (CIO) 10
collaboration system 18
computer-based information system 8
customer relationship management system 17
data 4, 7
decision support system 17
downsizing 23
electronic business 18
enterprise resource planning system 17
executive information system 17
expert system 17
functional area information system 17
hardware 4
information 7
information systems 4
information technology 8
internetworking 17
knowledge 8
knowledge society 6
knowledge worker 6
management information system 17
new economy 6
office automation system 18
service mentality 21
software 4
systems integration 17
technology 8
telecommunications network 4
transaction processing system 17
wisdom 8

REVIEW QUESTIONS

1. Define and understand the term *information systems (IS)*.
2. Explain the technology, people, and organizational components of an information system.
3. Define and list four business knowledge and/or skills core competencies.
4. Describe the three or four types of jobs and career opportunities in information systems and in related fields.
5. What are some reasons why the position of CIO has grown in importance?
6. Define the term *knowledge worker*. Who coined the term?
7. How does this textbook define technology? Give some basic examples.
8. List and define five types of information systems used in organizations.
9. Describe key factors in the future of the IS function within the firm.

SELF-STUDY QUESTIONS

Answers are at the end of the Problems and Exercises.

1. Information systems today are __________.
   A. slower than in the past
   B. continuing to evolve with improvements to the hardware and software
   C. utilized by only a few select individuals
   D. stable and should not change
2. Information systems are used in which of the following organizations?
   A. professional
   B. educational
   C. governmental
   D. all of the above
3. Whereas data are raw, unformatted pieces or lists of words or numbers, information is __________.
   A. data that have been organized in a form that is useful
   B. accumulated knowledge
   C. what you put in your computer
   D. what your computer prints out for you
4. Computer-based information systems are described in this chapter as __________.
   A. any complicated technology that requires expert use
   B. a combination of hardware, software, and telecommunications networks that people build and use to collect, create, and distribute data
   C. any technology (mechanical or electronic) used to supplement, extend, or replace human, manual labour
   D. any technology used to leverage human capital
5. In the 1980s, which of the following became a popular new title given to executives who were responsible for the information systems function?
   A. CFO
   B. CIO
   C. CEO
   D. CMA
6. Which of the following positions typically has the highest ranking in an IS department of a modern company?
   A. systems analyst
   B. systems programmer
   C. IS director
   D. networking professional

7. Which of the following IS job titles is used for a person whose primary responsibility is directly doing maintenance on an information system?
   A. IS director
   B. Webmaster
   C. systems analyst
   D. chief information officer
8. Which of the following is **not** classified as business knowledge and skills?
   A. management
   B. communication
   C. systems integration
   D. social
9. Which of the following is **not** discussed in this chapter as a common type, or category, of information system used in organizations?
   A. transaction processing
   B. decision support
   C. enterprise resource planning
   D. Web graphics
10. Which of the following is **not** an example of an information system?
   A. an accounting system in a business
   B. a concession stand
   C. a combination of different software packages in a company
   D. a database of customers

PROBLEMS AND EXERCISES

1. Match the following terms with the appropriate definitions
   _____ Transaction processing system
   _____ Systems competency
   _____ Information
   _____ Knowledge society
   _____ Electronic commerce
   _____ Customer relationship management
   _____ Systems analyst
   _____ Chief information officer
   _____ Information systems
   _____ Service mentality
   a. A society with a high proportion of knowledge workers who play an important, leadership role
   b. An executive-level individual who has overall responsibilities for the information systems component within the organization and is primarily concerned with the effective integration of technology and business strategy
   c. The use of typically Internet-based systems to enable consumers to find information about, and purchase, goods and services from business firms
   d. A system that processes day-to-day business event data at the operational level of the organization
   e. Data that have been formatted in a way that is useful
   f. Systems that enable employees to better manage interaction with customers
   g. A job title for a person who helps to develop information systems
   h. Ability to solve complex business problems and to build and integrate business systems
   i. The mindset that your goal is to enable others to be successful and that the "customer is always right"
   j. Combinations of hardware, software, and telecommunications networks that people build and use to collect, create, and distribute useful data, typically in organizational settings
2. How has Federal Express updated its information systems with current technology? Is the investment in technology a good one? How has this investment affected Federal Express' competitors? Visit FedEx's Website and look at how to track a package.
3. Peter Drucker has defined the knowledge worker and knowledge society. What are his definitions? Do you agree with them? What examples can you give to support or disprove these concepts?
4. List three major IS professional core competencies or general areas from the textbook. Do you agree or disagree that all three are needed to become a professional? Why? What competencies do you currently possess, and what do you need to improve on or acquire? What is your strategy to acquire new skills? Where and when will you acquire them?
5. Of the 10 information systems listed in the chapter, how many do you have experience with? What systems would you like to work with? What types of systems do you encounter at the university you are attending? Read the Brief Cases in this chapter and other chapters for applications of information systems. The World Wide Web is also a good source for additional information.
6. Consider an organization that you are familiar with, perhaps one that you have worked for or have done business with in the past. Describe the type of information systems that organization uses and whether or not they are useful or up-to-date. List specific examples for updating or installing information systems that improve productivity or efficiency.
7. Identify someone who works within the field of information systems as an information systems instructor, professor, or practitioner (for example, as a systems analyst or systems manager). Find out why this individual got into this field and what this person likes and dislikes about working within the field of IS. What advice can this person offer to someone entering the field?
8. The case of the Denver International Airport provides insight into the resources used to build large information systems. Is this problem unique to airlines, or do you think other companies have experienced similar problems? What are the tangible or observable costs and the hidden costs when a system takes time to get working as planned?
9. What type of information system do you use at the university you attend to register and add or drop courses? Are improvements to your current system planned?
10. Electronic business has changed purchasing over the Web. Have you ever bought anything over the Web? If you have not made any purchases, what is holding you back? Are you comfortable with the payment system of sending credit card information over the Internet?
11. What collaboration system are you using? Do you find that e-mail is a good communication method? What are the pros and

cons of having one or more e-mail accounts? How often do you check your e-mail? Do you consider e-mail time effective? How comfortable are you with e-mail?

12. Based on your previous work and/or professional experiences, describe your relationships with the personnel in the IS department. Was the IS department easy to work with? Why or why not? Were projects and requests completed on time and correctly? What was the organizational structure of this IS department? How do your answers compare with those of other classmates?

13. As a small group, conduct a search on the World Wide Web for job placement services. Pick at least four of these services and find as many IS job titles as you can. You may want to try the Monster Board at **www.monster.ca**. How many did you find? Were any of them different from those presented in this chapter? Could you determine the responsibilities of these positions based on the information given to you?

14. What aspect of information systems should be prioritized in an educational environment, theory or practice? Should the answer depend on the type of educational environment (i.e., colleges vs. universities, technical vs. managerial programs)?

15. In many companies, the value of the IS function is not reflected in the power that it wields. For example, IT is a strategic necessity for most firms, yet the CIO may not be involved in strategic decisions at the executive level, or may report to the CEO only through another C-level executive, such as a CFO. Do you think that this situation is reasonable and appropriate? Prepare an argument for and against the power/value balance of the IS function within organizations.

ANSWERS TO THE SELF-STUDY QUESTIONS

1. B 2. D 3. A 4. B 5. B 6. C 7. B 8. C 9. D 10. B

Case 1: *Canucks @ Microsoft, eh?*

Microsoft Corp. is not a Canadian company, but a strong Canuck presence at the U.S. high-tech behemoth continues to be a major influence on operations. With hundreds of Canada's best and brightest heading across the border each year, a covert northern takeover of the Washington-based company may already be taking place. "I can walk down the hallway here and I will always meet a Canadian," said Antoine Leblond, Microsoft's vice-president of office program management, who arrived at the company's Redmond, Washington, headquarters from Montreal in 1989. "We've often talked about stamping 'Made in Canada' on the products here," he added.

Accounting for 26,000 of its 36,000 U.S.-based workforce, Microsoft's main campus is the hub of the company's operations. While it won't publicly release figures on the number of its Canadian employees, the level of their influence is reflected in the internal code names of many major projects. "Windows XP was called Whistler and the next version was going to be Blackcomb, so we needed a name between the two for the version we're currently working on. The Longhorn Saloon is a bar between Whistler and Blackcomb mountains, so Longhorn became the code name," said Leblond. "There've been dozens of other Canadian code names like Toronto, Vancouver, and Halifax. I think this happens because we're the loudest group here."

Short of attaching maple leaf patches to their briefcases, Redmond's Team Canada makes no secret of its national roots, according to former Vancouverite Stephen Cawood, program manager in the content management server team. "There's a lively 'Canucks @ Microsoft' discussion group here, where hockey and politics seem to be the biggest topics. There are 40–50 messages on it every day and about 150 people in the group," said Cawood. "We also go to hockey games together, and there was even a Microsoft U.S. versus Microsoft Canada game recently."

It's this heightened level of opportunity that continues to attract the brightest Canadians, according to Peter Forsyth, professor and associate director in the School of Computer Science at the University of Waterloo, which traditionally fills more jobs at Microsoft than any other Canadian university. "The U.S. is an exciting place to work, and Microsoft's research is also very exciting," said Forsyth. "Generally, the big attraction for our students over staying and working in Canada is higher salaries, more opportunities, and more interesting research."

But it's not a simple a case of cross-border brain drain, according to Bruce Lumsden, Waterloo's director of co-operative education and career services, who has been sending co-op students to Microsoft since the first two were dispatched in 1987. "We don't look at it like that at all. We live in an international community, and this kind of opportunity gives our students valuable perspectives and much wider experiences," said Lumsden. Waterloo has sent 800 co-op students to Microsoft over a 16-year period, and 250 alumni—and at least one faculty member—have found permanent jobs at the company. One of its biggest computer science co-op partners, Microsoft continues to hire between 15 and 30 Waterloo students every term for co-op positions, predominantly at Redmond, but also in Vancouver, Ottawa, Mississauga, and Hong Kong.

"Microsoft is a model co-op employer because they know how to mentor, providing meaningful work rather than make-work projects. And they use co-op as part of their hiring strategy," said Lumsden. "The attraction for Microsoft is that our Canadian students are quick, nimble, and highly computer literate." "I don't know how long Canadians have been flocking to work at Microsoft, but we've had a fair number of them working here for a number of years. They work in all parts of the company in a variety of positions and they are a large group," said Microsoft human resources spokesperson Mara Hobler, who confirmed the widespread use of Canadian code names but was not aware of any U.S. place names being used in a similar fashion. "They [Canadians] are not taking over Microsoft, but they are certainly here in significant numbers," she added. Leblond and Cawood agree that while Microsoft's Canadian contingent is not planning an imminent Redmond coup, many of them still view Canada as home. "The second I left, Canadian things took on a more mythical gravitas. Poutine has become a delicacy," said Leblond. "I take French classes here in Redmond," added Cawood. "I wanted to learn another language and, as a Canadian, learning French made the most sense to me."

[Adapted from John Lee, "Microsoft, eh?" **www.itbusiness.ca/index.asp?theaction=61&sid=54242#**, ITBusiness.ca (November 28, 2004).]

Discussion Questions

1. Why do you think that Canada produces so many high-quality technologists?
2. Should Canada worry about *brain drain* when it comes to technology and technology management jobs?
3. Would you consider taking a job outside Canada? Why? Or why not?

Case 2: *High Tech, High Touch at Edward Jones*

Edward Jones is not your typical brokerage firm. Its average customer lives in a small town and is more likely to read *USA Today* than the *Financial Times*. In an industry that has gorged itself on virtually every technology fad and fashion, the St. Louis–based Jones stands out for its low-tech, no frills, relationship-focused approach to investing. Unlike nearly all of its competitors, Jones has yet to offer online trading to its clients. Instead, trades require a phone conversation or face-to-face meeting with a broker. In fact, customers cannot even contact brokers directly by e-mail; the Jones way dictates that customers wishing to e-mail must fill out a form on the company's Website. Those e-mail messages are then routed through the main office in St. Louis, sorted, and then dispatched to brokers via the corporate intranet, a two-day process.

Jones's refusal to trade online, its lack of direct e-mail, and its small-town focus have led many to label the company a technology dinosaur, trying to get by on a shoestring IT budget and Midwestern charm. Others would argue, however, that just the opposite is, in fact, the case. Jones invests a great deal of effort and money in technology (11 percent of its annual revenue is spent on IT, compared with an industry average of 9 percent). It recently made huge investments in two new data centres (a US$85-million one in Tempe, Arizona, and a US$30-million one in St. Louis in April 2002). The company has begun overhauling its satellite-based network and plans to implement digital document technologies that will cut down on the amount of paper travelling between almost 8,000 field offices and St. Louis headquarters. It also has not neglected the Internet: customers can check their account balances, pay bills, apply for mortgages, and view their statements on the company's Website.

Where the company draws the line is investing in a technology that might get between its customers and brokers. Jones believes that a relationship should be inviolate and that technology should support it but never replace it. As for Jones's behind-the-times image, managing partner John Bachmann shrugs it off, adding "We've never been hurt by being underestimated."

Jones caters to individual investors, many of whom are retirees and small-business owners in rural communities and suburban towns. "Their market is the mom-and-pop business with $10,000 to invest," says Heber Farnsworth, an assistant professor of finance at Washington University, based in St. Louis. "And the Jones model has been to try and take the level of service and attention that millionaires get and give it to those mom-and-pop investors."

The company provides that personal touch through its field offices in Canada, the United States, and the United Kingdom. Each new location is built from the ground up with investment reps going door to door to grow their clientele.

Keeping all of Jones's remote offices connected to the markets and to corporate headquarters is one of the company's biggest technical challenges. "We have only one profit centre: [the branches]," says CIO Rich Malone, "so the network is critical. It's how we get information back and forth, and it connects us to the exchanges. If the network doesn't work, we've got problems." Currently all the offices are connected by a satellite network, but during the past few years it has become clear to Malone and the rest of the management team that the current network will soon be insufficient for their growing technology needs. Bandwidth needs are rapidly outstripping what the satellite network can provide, and that problem is likely to get worse as the company begins digitally storing and sending the reams of paper it processes each day. Jones is also using an increasing number of Web applications, which tend to perform better on terrestrial networks (fibre-optic land-based cable).

Some analysts are doubtful that Jones can continue its present rate of growth without eventually offering online trading. "It puts them in the position of weakening the relationship, and when you add to that a little bit of poor performance or some other niggling problem, that's when you lose the relationship," says Jaime Punishill, a senior analyst at Cambridge, Massachusetts-based Forrester Research.

Jones has been incredibly successful in the last decade, and even in these times of economic stringency the company has managed to avoid the layoffs that have plagued so many of its competitors. In fact, though the company has instituted a hiring freeze at its St. Louis headquarters, the company is still hiring at a brisk clip of 200 new employees per month in the field offices.

Some analysts are still wondering, however, if the company will be able to keep up the brisk growth without bending a little on its no-online-trading policy—especially as its client base gets older and the need to lure younger, more tech-savvy customers increases. But Bachmann sees hope that the Edward Jones brand of conservative, relationship-focused investing will have some appeal for a younger audience. "Our fastest-growing segment is young people," he claims. "They know that Social Security will not be there for them, and they don't want to take the chance of putting their money into something that will blow up."

[Adapted from Daintry Duffy, "At Edward Jones, The Handshake Still Rules," **www.darwinmag.com/read/020102/rules.html**, *CIO Magazine* (February 1, 2002).]

Discussion Questions

1. Of the various categories of information systems described in this chapter, which types are talked about in this case?
2. What do you think of Edward Jones's use of information systems? Is the company on the right track?
3. Should the company move into online trading? Why or why not?

Spam and Workplace Productivity: The Canadian Connection

CBC

A professor received an e-mail message from her university's technical support department informing her that her e-mail account had been temporarily disabled due to suspicious activity. The message offered instructions on how to access a replacement account, contained within an attached file. The message was fake and the attachment contained a virus. An e-mail attachment containing a virus is not technically spam—it's not sent for commercial purposes—but it can be lumped in with the mass of irrelevant messages that clutter up most people's inboxes.

According to Ferris Research, U.S., Canadian, and European corporations spent US$11.5 billion on spam in 2002. The costs included "lost productivity, consumption of information technology, and help-desk support." Another study conducted by New York consultancy Basex found that the average firm lost between US$600 and US$1,000 per user in 2003 in terms of productivity and resources. All told, Basex said, U.S. and Canadian companies lose some US$20 billion each year because of spam. According to IDC, in May 2004 spam messages outnumbered legitimate messages in Canada for the first time.

Spam is annoying and fosters inefficiency, but what can be done? Broadly speaking, there are two strategies to reduce spam: an offensive strategy and a defensive strategy. The first strategy involves going after the spammers.

Interestingly, the number of hardcore spammers is relatively small. Experts estimate that 70 percent of spam comes from fewer than 200 sources. If these firms or individuals could be regulated or shut down, then the volume of spam cluttering up the world's networks could be reduced considerably. Of course, this is easier said than done. Spammers are using ever more sophisticated tools to protect their identities. They are not easy to find. Even if they are found and taken offline, there are others who are quick to jump into their place.

Spammers are also becoming more and more sophisticated. One of the latest techniques is to use "zombie spam armies"—groups of unwittingly compromised computers used as launch pads for spam attacks. The recent rash of zombie spam army attacks highlights why only whitelisting or blacklisting alone are insufficient means of fighting spam. Because domain name system (DNS)–based blacklists typically look only at the IP address of the sending machine, spammers are now using these zombie armies to attack from dozens of different machines, thereby increasing the likelihood of finding a machine that is not yet blacklisted.

Some of the U.S. industry's best-known ISPs have pursued an offensive strategy toward spammers by filing class-action lawsuits. These suits are based on the *Controlling the Assault of Non-Solicited Pornography and Marketing Act,* often referred to as the Can-Spam law, introduced in 2003. The law specifically penalizes spammers who send out e-mail from fraudulent addresses or with false information in the headers. It also requires users to opt out of any relationship with the source of the e-mail. Canadians are taking centre stage in the story. Among those who have been sued are Eric, Matthew, and Barry Head of Ontario, who Yahoo! has accused of sending 94 million spam messages to its e-mail customers since the beginning of 1994. In a 2004 settlement, the Heads agreed to pay Yahoo! US$100,000 and further agreed to cease sending unsolicited mail.

A recent study from security software provider Sophos estimated that Canada accounts for 6.8 percent of the world's unsolicited commercial e-mail—that puts it second only to the United States. This means the Heads will not be the last to become embroiled in legal disputes involving a law designed for Americans.

At the moment, Canada has a mishmash of legislation that can be used to fight spammers, including anti-fraud provisions in the *Criminal Code of Canada,* the *Personal Information Protection and Electronics Act* (PIPEDA), and the *Competition Act.* However, there is not yet any single piece of legislation that specifically targets spammers.

Governments can enact legislation, ISPs can launch lawsuits, but what can individuals do to attack spammers? Industry experts say that an effective strategy for individuals is to complain to their ISPs. If enough people complain, then the ISPs will act, as in the U.S. lawsuits.

An offensive strategy against spam and spammers may prove to be effective in the long term, but doesn't do much to unclutter our inboxes on a day-to-day basis. The second strategy to manage spam is defensive. Spam can be filtered at various points along a network—although no filter is perfect, and all filters eat up system resources.

Filtering spam is as much art as science, but technologies are improving, and once again Canada is playing a role. The Institute of Electrical and Electronic Engineers Inc., better known as the IEEE, has adopted Ottawa-based Roaring Penguin Software's CanIt-PRO software to filter spam from its 130,000 e-mail users around the globe. The IEEE, based in Piscataway, New Jersey, provides an alias service to its members whereby members are provided @ieee.org accounts that forward mail to an existing ISP. Matthew Persons, senior systems administrator for the IEEE, said that the organization considered a variety of spam-filtering tools, but "most of them were geared towards being centrally managed and didn't give us the capability to allow our members to do their own spam filtering or choose their own options." IEEE e-mail users can set their own preferred level of spam filtering—tagging incoming spam, filtering out the spam altogether, or opting out of the service. "We recommend tagging so they get an idea of how the software is working," said Persons.

Roaring Penguin is in the process of integrating its software with IEEE's Web portal so users can manage all their IEEE preferences, including spam settings, from one location instead of through a separate login. In 2003, 208 million messages were processed through the IEEE infrastructure. Persons said he has no hard and fast numbers on the level of spam reduction, but anecdotally members say it catches about 90 percent of unwanted messages. "Doing evaluations of the [anti-spam] software that's out there, we realized there's no solution that's 100 percent. But providing members with a tool that can help mitigate the amount of spam that we get was something that we were looking for," said Persons.

Filters are getting better at blocking spam, but increasingly the quest is also about making sure high-powered filters aren't preventing important messages from getting to their intended recipient. Spam was a problem that built over time at the Liquor Control Board of Ontario (LCBO). Feedback from individuals prompted investment in a filter product. "I would hear comments from other people who said they were getting tonnes of it. We estimated that 2,000 users received a total of 1,000 spam messages a day," says Vince Reynolds, manager of technical services at the LCBO. "They are no longer receiving that in the last couple of months since we put our filter in place, but one of the greatest challenges I'm finding with spam filtering is false positives. It's a fishing-net type of approach. It looks for certain contents, and you have to try and tune it all the time to make sure it's making the right decisions on what it allows through and what it doesn't. You can block 1,000 legitimate spams to somebody, but if they missed the one they wanted to get, it doesn't matter that you have blocked 1,000 objectionable ones; they didn't get the one they were expecting," says Reynolds.

By tweaking the filter at the LCBO, Reynolds says the false-positive problem has largely been addressed. Messages caught in the spam filter are held in quarantine for five days and a periodic spot check is done to see if there is anything that looks legitimate that has been filtered out.

The overall effect of spam on productivity is a serious problem for Canadian organizations, says Michael O'Neil, country manager at IDC Canada. "There's the cost of lost productivity and that's a fairly hairy one," he says. "If you get interrupted every time the e-mail lamp dings and half your messages are spam, that's a pretty meaningful cost. If you spend wisely on the intercept technology, fewer spams get through, and if you have well-trained users who know how to deal with spam, your costs diminish. They don't go to zero, but they get to be less than they might be."

Spam will never disappear completely—a mailing cost of $25 for 25 million e-mail addresses ensures that the business case for spam will always exist—but with a combination of offensive and defensive strategies, the impact of spam in business and personal users of e-mail will diminish considerably over time.

Questions

1. How many spam messages do you receive in the average day? Are these message merely an annoyance or do they affect your productivity in a substantial way?
2. The case is fairly optimistic about the future of spam. Do you share this view, or do you feel that the worst is yet to come?
3. Put yourself in the place of a senior IT executive. You have been asked by your CEO to develop a strategy to address spam in your workplace. What steps would you take to deal with spam? Would you pursue a defensive strategy, an offensive strategy, or both?
4. Do you think Canada should enact anti-spam legislation like in the U.S.? If so, how would you protect the rights of companies to market their products and services by electronic means?

Video Resource: "Life of the Spammed," *Venture* (January 18, 2004).

Sources: Shane Schick, "As ISPs Head to Court, It's Time to Argue the Case for a Canadian Spam Law," **http://www.itbusiness.ca/index.asp?theaction=61&sid=55015#**, ITBusiness.ca (March 10, 2004); Neil Sutton, "Engineering Association Responds to Member Complaints," **http://www.itbusiness.ca/index.asp?theaction=61&sid=55247#**, ITBusiness.ca (April 5, 2004); and Jennifer Brown, "Filtering Out the True Cost of Spam," *Computing Canada*, Vol. 30, No. 7 (May 14, 2004).

Chapter 2

Preview

The purpose of this chapter is to show you how information systems can be used strategically and how they can enable firms to gain and sustain a ***competitive advantage*** over their rivals. As described in Chapter 1, a firm has a competitive advantage over rival firms when it can do something better, faster, more cheaply, or uniquely when compared with its competitors. In addition, we will show why it is vital, but sometimes difficult, for people to determine the value of a new system. The same difficulties face those evaluating an existing system that is being considered for modification, continued support, scaling back, or elimination. Presenting the "case" for an information system is necessary for making good investment decisions.

After reading this chapter, you will be able to do the following:

1. Discuss how organizations can use information systems for automation, organizational learning, and strategic support.
2. Describe information systems' critical, strategic importance to the success of modern organizations.
3. Formulate and present the business case for a system and understand why it is sometimes difficult to do so.
4. Explain why and how companies are continually looking for new ways to use technology for competitive advantage.

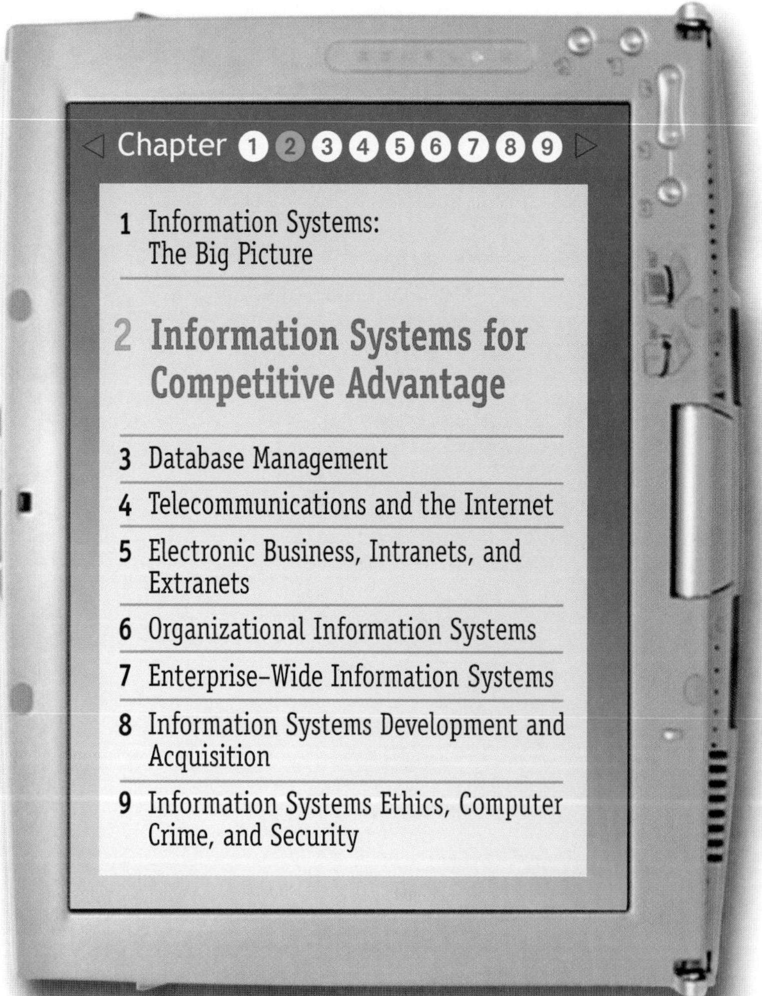

[**Figure 2.1** ➡ The Big Picture: focusing on information systems for competitive advantage.]

Information Systems for Competitive Advantage

OPENING: Aeroplan Leverages IT to Enhance Customer Service

Aeroplan spent 2004 developing its Web portal to replicate the kinds of customer service features it offers through its call centre. The company, which is trying to evolve from a frequent flier program to a more complex reward and loyalty firm, has already seen 30 percent of its reward redemptions move online since relaunching its site in May 2002. Right now the company only offers bookings for flights on Air Canada, but the site's functionality will be improved to allow bookings on Star Alliance partners like Lufthansa and United Airlines.

André Hébert, Aeroplan's vice-president of IT and Channels, said the company was approximately 75 percent of the way through the latest phase of its Website overhaul, which was prompted in part by Air Canada's decision to divest itself of Aeroplan during a 2001 restructuring process. Blast Radius, a Web design firm based in Vancouver and Toronto, helped Aeroplan rework its navigation, site architecture, and content, grouping topical data together. Hébert said the old site had about 20 pages, while the new portal has about 1,000 pages split between French and English content. "Obviously reward programs are a big part of an airline's success," said Brett Turner, executive vice-president of client relations at Blast Radius. "They've realized the Web can bring member services to life with the lowest possible investment."

Besides offering transactional capabilities, Hébert said Aeroplan is trying to make its portal a self-serve destination for travel research, account management, and problem resolutions. The company's busiest day of the year is January 2, when he said many people come back from the holiday season preparing their next vacation. Although Aeroplan employs about 1,200 people at its call centre, it doesn't nearly handle the load of potential inquiries from Aeroplan's 6 million members, according to Hébert. He said the portal has helped reduce wait times on the phone from 15 minutes to five.

The portal has also allowed call centre agents to focus on more complex customer requests, he added, since customers can usually handle simple bookings over the Web. It also means they can book on their own schedule. "You'd be surprised at the number of bookings that happen after midnight," Hébert said. "They're not people living in Asia or some either time zone, either. They're from Canada." So far, Aeroplan's Website has over 1.5 million customers and is being used to book 1,000 flights a day.

[Adapted from Shane Schick, "Aeroplan Overhauls Portal to Meet Call Centre Demand," **http://www.itbusiness.ca/index.asp?theaction=61&sid=54204#**, ITBusiness.ca (November 25, 2003).]

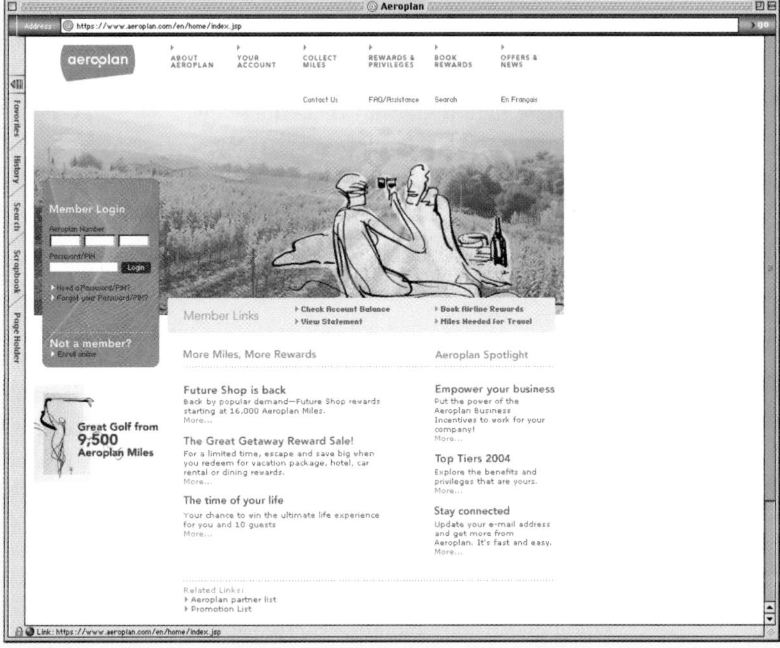

[**Figure 2.2** ➥ Aeroplan's Web portal supports its strategy to further improve customer service.]

Source: Courtesy of Aeroplan.

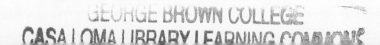

This chapter is the second piece of The Big Picture (see Figure 2.1). We begin by showing how and why a firm ought to use information systems to support its strategy and to enable it to gain and sustain a competitive advantage over rivals. We then describe what it means to make the business case for a system and discuss why it is important that the business cases for technology-related projects be carefully developed. Next, we describe the factors you must identify and consider when building a successful business case. We then illustrate important factors to keep in mind when presenting the business case to executives and other decision makers. Making the business case for a technology investment is a business decision that should be made in a way that helps your organization achieve its strategy. Finally, we talk about the continual need to find innovative ways to succeed with and through information systems.

WHY USE INFORMATION SYSTEMS?

In the first chapter we described the strategic importance of information systems developed for the Denver International Airport and Federal Express. These systems were developed strategically to help those organizations gain and sustain some competitive advantage over rivals. For example, Denver International Airport hopes that its state-of-the-art baggage management system not only will help to make baggage handling more efficient and subsequently lower operating costs and please passengers, but also that ultimately it will help to attract airlines, airline passengers, and other business vendors to that facility. This example highlights that there are many reasons for using an information system.

Next, we describe three ways to use an information system: for automating, for organizational learning, and for achieving strategy (see Figure 2.3). These three activities are not necessarily mutually exclusive, but we believe that each reason for using an information system is progressively more useful to the firm and, thus, adds more value to the business. The final category, strategizing, is the one in which you use information systems to support your firm's strategy and to enable your firm to gain and sustain competitive advantage over rivals.

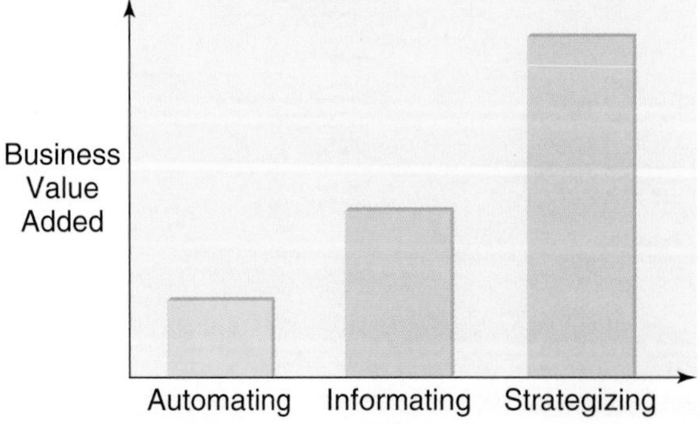

[**Figure 2.3** ➡ The business value added from automating, learning, and supporting strategy with IS.]

Information Systems for Automating: Doing Things Faster

Automating refers to using technology as a way to help complete a task within an organization faster, more cheaply, and perhaps with greater accuracy and/or consistency. Let us look at a typical example. A person with an automating mentality would take a loan application screening process and automate it by inputting the loan applications into a computer database so that those involved in decision making for the loans could process the applications faster, more easily, and with fewer errors. Such a system might also enable customers to complete the loan application online. A transition from a manual to an automated loan application process might enable the organization to deploy employees more efficiently, leading to further cost savings.

To illustrate the benefits of automating with an information system, in Table 2.1 we compare three different loan application processes. In the first example, everything is done by hand. In the second example, a technology-supported process, potential customers fill out applications by hand, and then an employee inputs them into a computer system. The third example is a completely automated process, whereby potential customers input loan applications directly online via the Web, and then the system automatically receives these applications into a database and processes them.

The real time savings with the fully automated system come into play with the applications for loans under $250,000, which typically make up the bulk of applications received. Conversely, one common thread across all three scenarios is that it takes the executive committee more than two full weeks to make decisions on applications for loans over $250,000. Automation can do only so much!

Although many significant gains from computing in organizations have come from automating previously manual processes, com-

[Table 2.1] *Activities involved under three different loan application processes and the average time for each activity.*

Primary Activities of Loan Processing	Manual Loan Process (Time)	Technology-Supported Process (Time)	Fully Automated Process (Time)
1. Complete and submit loan application	Customer takes the application home, completes it, returns it (1.5 days)	Customer takes the application home, completes it, returns it (1.5 days)	Customer fills out application from home via the Web (1 hour)
2. Check application for errors	Employee does this in batches (2.5 days)	Employee does this in batches (2.5 days)	Computer does this as it is being completed (3.5 seconds)
3. Input data from application into information system	Applications kept in paper form, although there is handling time involved (1 hour)	Employee does this in batches (2.5 days)	Done as part of the online application process (no extra time needed)
4. Assess loan applications under $250,000 to determine whether to fund them	Employee does this completely by hand (15 days)	Employee does with the help of the computer (1 hour)	Computer does this automatically (1 second)
5. Committee decides on any loan over $250,000	(15 days)	(15 days)	(15 days)
6. Applicant notified	Employee generates letters manually in batches (1 week)	Employee generates letters with the help of the computer (1 day)	System notifies applicant via e-mail (3.5 seconds)
Total Time:	Anywhere from **25 to 40 days**, depending on size of loan	Anywhere from **5 to 20 days**, depending on size of loan	Anywhere from **1 hour to 15 days**, depending on size of loan[1]

[1]Note that many online loan application services can now give you instant "tentative" approval pending verification of data you report in your online application.

puting solely for automation is a bit shortsighted. In the next section, we will explain how technology can be used more effectively.

Information Systems for Organizational Learning: Doing Things Better

We can also use information systems to learn and improve. This was described by Shoshana Zuboff (1988) as ***informating***.[2] Zuboff explained that a technology informates when it provides information about its operation and the underlying work process that it supports. The system helps us not only to automate a business process but also to learn to improve the day-to-day activities within that process.

The learning mentality builds on the automating mentality because it recognizes that information systems can be used as a vehicle for ***organizational learning*** and change, as well as for automation. In a 1993 *Harvard Business Review* article, David Garvin described a ***learning organization*** as one that is "skilled at creating, acquiring, and transferring knowledge, and at modifying its behavior to reflect new knowledge and insights."

To illustrate a learning mentality, let us think again about our loan processing example. Figure 2.4 shows how a computer-based loan processing system tracks types of loan applications by date, month, and season. The manager easily sees the trends and can plan for the timely ordering of blank application

Web Search

WEB SEARCH OPPORTUNITY
Visit the Website for the Society for Organizational Learning at **www.solonline.org** and investigate this phenomenon further. How did this organization first begin? What is the role of IS in organizational learning?

[2]The concept of informating is also very closely related to Argyris's term *double loop learning*, in which individuals learn and as a result subsequently change their thinking and/or behaviour (C. Argyris. 1993. *On Organizational Learning*. Cambridge, MA: Blackwell).

BRIEF CASE

Pitney Bowes Saves Costs with Two-Way Paging Solution

Pitney Bowes Canada chose ZIM's two-way short messaging service (SMS) paging system to deal with problems using one-way paging on standard pagers, and to move its field service staff toward wireless technologies. "The inherent problem with paging, of course, is you send a page out and you have no confirmation of whether the page was received by the technician or not," explained Doug Best, director of field service operations in Pitney Bowes' office in Richmond Hill, Ontario. ZIM's technology allows Pitney Bowes to track pages and receive proof that they have been received, and permits field staff to reply to specific messages, said Best. It also reduces customer inquiries about the status of work orders typically directed to the Pitney Bowes's call centre, he added.

The new dispatch system permits a single or distributed call centre using a Web-based application to communicate with 350 mobile technicians in real time across Canada, said Bill Parisi, vice-president, business development and implementation, at Ottawa-based ZIM Technologies International Inc. The difference between a one-way paging system and ZIM's product is huge, explained Parisi. Pitney Bowes is "spending half the money that they were on their traditional paging solution, and they're getting at least 10 times the functionality." Apart from confirming delivery, ZIM's SMS paging solution persists in sending a message over 78 hours if for some reason (for instance, if a phone is turned off or the receiver is not in a coverage area) the technician fails to answer it, Parisi said.

Another advantage is auto escalation, meaning the Web application will respond to a priority page gone unanswered for 30 minutes by contacting the technician's colleague and, failing that, will move up the company's hierarchy until finally the page "ends up on the phone of the vice-president" after four hours, he explained. On average, a company pays $5 to $15 per person each month using the ZIM dispatch system, said Parisi. In Pitney Bowes' case, adopting the technology allowed it to practically eliminate the need for pagers (priced at about $25 every month) and pay $10 for SMS messaging, said Best.

Pitney Bowes has also been able to use the SMS technology to find parts located in the field inventory, Best said. "It's eliminated a lot of phoning back and forth."

Questions

1. Now that mobile phones have SMS (two-way text) capabilities, is there still a business case for pagers?
2. Is the solution described here an example of automating, informating, or strategizing?

[Adapted from Fawzia Sheikh, "Pitney Bowes Canada Moves from Mailroom to SMS," **http://www.itbusiness.ca/index.asp?theaction=61&sid=54343#**, ITBusiness.ca (November 27, 2003).]

forms and the staffing and training of personnel in the loan department. The manager can also more efficiently manage the funds used to fulfill loans.

A learning approach allows people to track and learn about the types of applications filed by certain types of people at certain times of the year (e.g., more auto loan applications in the fall, mostly from men in their 20s and 30s), the patterns of the loan decisions made, or the subsequent performance of those loans. This new system creates data about the underlying business process that can be used to better monitor, control, and change that process. In other words, you learn from this information system about loan applications and approvals and, as a result, you can do a better job at evaluating loan applications.

A combined automating and learning approach, in the long run, is more effective than an automating approach alone. If the underlying business process supported by technology is inherently flawed, a learning use of the technology might help you detect the problems with the process and change it. For instance, in our loan processing example, a learning use of technology may help us uncover a pattern among the loans accepted that enables us to distinguish between low- and high-performing loans over their lives and, subsequently, change the criteria for loan acceptance.

If, however, the underlying business process is bad, and you are using technology only for automating (i.e., you would not uncover the data that would tell you this process is bad), you are more likely to continue with a flawed or less-than-optimal business process. In fact, such an automating use of the technology may mask the process problems.

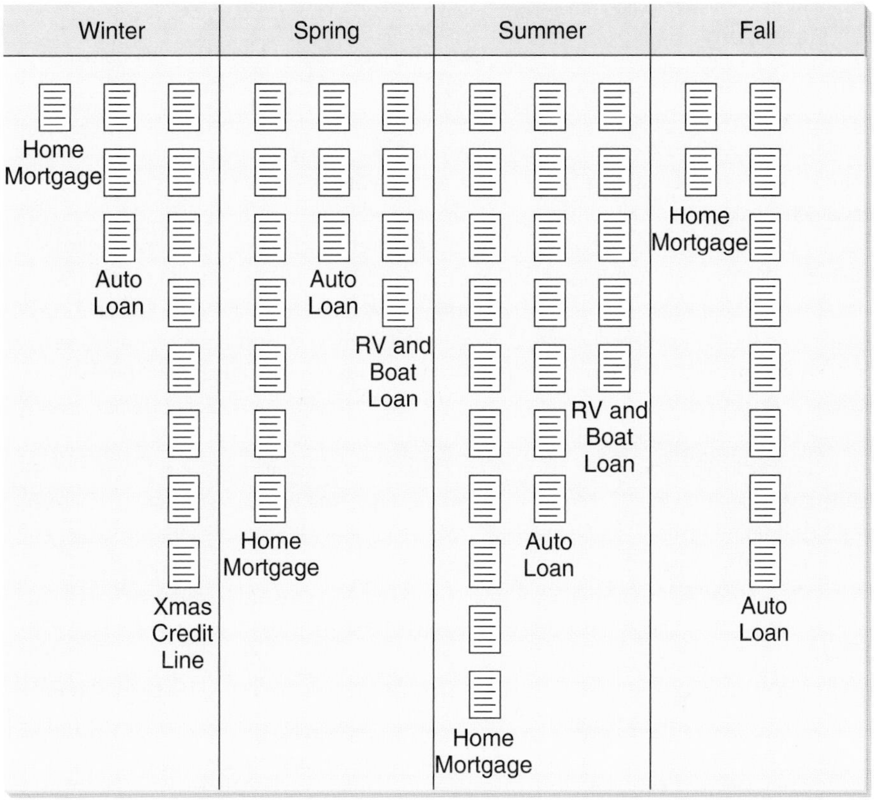

[**Figure 2.4** ➥ A computer-based loan processing system informs the bank manager of which types of loans are highest during each season.]

For example, with a bad underlying set of loan acceptance criteria (i.e., the rules would allow you to approve a loan for someone who had a high level of debt as long as they had not been late on any payments recently), a person might manually review four applications in a day and, because of the problematic criteria used, inadvertently accept two "bad" applications per week on average. If you automated the same faulty process, with no learning aspects built in, the system might help a person review 12 applications per day, with six "bad" applications accepted per week on average. The technology would serve only to magnify the existing business problems. Without learning, it is more difficult to uncover bad business processes underlying the information system.

Using Information Systems to Support Total Quality Management

Organizations that use information systems to support a ***total quality management (TQM)*** initiative are more than likely using these systems with a learning approach. As part of a TQM approach, people within the organization are constantly monitoring what they do to find ways to improve quality of operations, products, services, and everything else about the firm. Information systems might be used to accomplish this end through the use of computer-based statistical analysis to determine the exact procedures and materials to use in a manufacturing process in order to achieve the highest levels of quality output. In this way, people use an information system to understand a business process better and, as a result, make changes to improve that process.

Information Systems for Supporting Strategy: Doing Things Smarter

Using information systems to automate or improve processes has advantages, as described above. In most cases, however, the best way to use an information system is to support the organization's strategy in a way that enables the firm to gain and sustain competitive advantage over rivals. To understand why, think about ***organizational strategy*** and how it relates to information systems. When senior managers conduct ***strategic planning,*** they form a vision of where the organization needs to head, convert that vision into measurable objectives and performance targets,

CAREER IMPLICATIONS

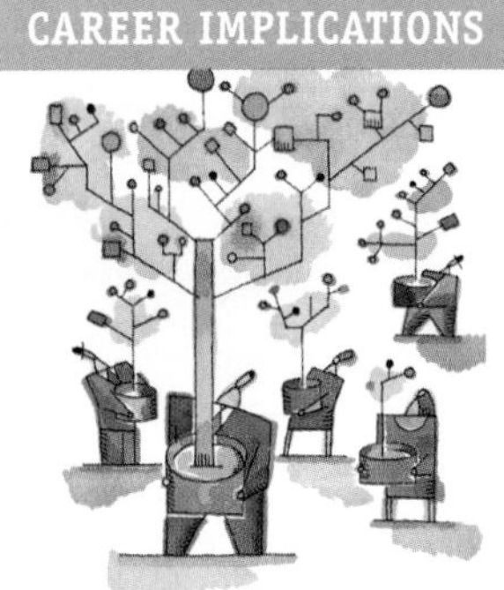

Marketing

Fewer than two-thirds of Canadian telecommunications providers respond to all online inquiries and more than a third share their customers' personal data without permission, according to a recent survey of carriers across the country. The survey, conducted by the Customer Respect Group Inc., of Bellevue, Washington, saw Rogers Communications Inc. score best, while Aliant Communications Inc. had the lowest overall score. In general, Canadian telecom firms did worse than their U.S. counterparts. Roger Fairchild, president of Customer Respect Group, said his firm did two surveys of U.S. telecommunications providers in 2003, in February and August, and the industry average improved slightly in that time. He said the telecommunications industry's overall ratings are slightly below the average for all the industries the firm surveys. The rankings are based on such factors as speed of response to online customer inquiries, the simplicity and ease of navigation of the companies' Websites, whether sites are customer-focused and friendly, and the companies' privacy policies. Customer Respect Group evaluates companies by studying their Websites and sending test inquiries to determine response time.

The Canadian survey included 11 companies. Rogers ranked first with nine points out of a possible 10, followed by Bell Canada with eight and Microcell Solutions Inc. with 6.8. The other eight companies in order of ranking were Cogeco Cable Inc. (6.2 points), Sprint Canada Inc. (6.0), Telus Corp. (5.7), Allstream Corp. (5.5), 360networks Corp. (5.2), Shaw Communications (4.9), Vidéotron Ltée (4.7), and Aliant Corp. (3.5). The Canadian companies averaged 6.0 points, while the average of the latest U.S. survey was 7.0. Fairchild said Rogers and Bell scored best on principles and transparency—including privacy issues—and Telus and 360networks were also strong in this area. The survey found that 73 percent of telecom firms post privacy policies on their Websites to explain how customers' personal data will be used. Of those, 25 percent do not collect data or use it only for internal purposes, 38 percent share it with affiliates or subsidiaries, and 37 percent share data without customer permission. It also found that 18 percent of the firms surveyed—that is, two of them—did not respond to any customer inquiries. Two others responded to only half of the inquiries received—one within 48 hours, the other after four days.

McKerlie said Rogers incorporated more than 700 customer suggestions in the last redesign of its Website, and is planning another redesign now. "It's not a perfect 10 yet," he said, "but we're still working on it." Lynn Coveyduck, public affairs manager at Aliant, said her company would look at the issues raised in the survey and try to use its advice in improving the carrier's Website. "This is one other tool that we'll be able to use to make our online experience better for customers," she said.

[Adapted from Grant Buckler, "Would Somebody PLEASE Answer the Phone?" **http://www.itbusiness.ca/index.asp?theaction=61&sid=54370#**, ITBusiness.ca (December 11, 2003).]

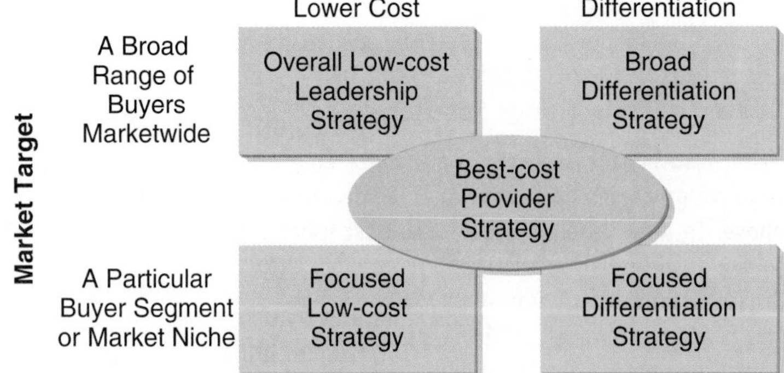

[**Figure 2.5** ➥ Five general types of organizational strategy: broad differentiation, focused differentiation, focused low-cost, overall low-cost leadership, and best-cost provider.]

Source: Courtesy Thompson, A. A. and Strickland, A. J. III, 1995. *Strategic Management: Concepts and Cases*, 8th ed., Homewood, IL: Richard D. Irwin.

and craft a strategy to achieve the desired results. In Figure 2.5, we show some common organizational strategies. An organization might decide to pursue a ***low-cost leadership strategy***, as do Zellers and Dell, by which it offers the best prices in its industry on its goods and/or services. Alternatively, an organization might decide to pursue a ***differentiation strategy***, whereby it tries to provide better products or services than its competitors, as do Porsche, Holt Renfrew, and IBM. A company might aim that differentiation broadly at many different types of consumers, or it might target a particular segment of consumers, as Apple did for many years with its focus on high-quality computers to home and educational markets. Still other organizations might pursue a middle-of-the-road strategy of being the ***best-cost provider***, offering products or services of reasonably good quality at competitive prices, as does the Bay.

A person with a strategic mentality toward information systems goes beyond mere automating and learning and instead tries to find ways to use information systems to achieve the organization's chosen strategy. This individual wants the benefits of automating and learning but also looks for some strategic, competitive advantage from the system.

INFORMATION SYSTEMS FOR COMPETITIVE ADVANTAGE

Sources of Competitive Advantage

How do firms typically achieve competitive advantage? An organization has competitive advantage whenever it has an edge over rivals in one or more key factors such as profitability, attracting customers, and/or defending against competitive forces (Porter, 1985; 2001). To be successful, a business must have a clear vision, one that focuses investments in resources such as information systems and technologies to help achieve competitive advantage. Some sources of competitive advantage include the following:

- Having the best-made product on the market
- Delivering superior customer service
- Achieving lower costs than rivals
- Having a proprietary manufacturing technology
- Having shorter lead times in developing and testing new products
- Having a well-known brand name and reputation
- Providing customers with more value for their money

Companies can gain and sustain each of these sources of competitive advantage through the effective use of information systems. For example, rental car agencies compete fiercely with each other to provide the best cars, the best service, and the best rates. Companies find it difficult to differentiate themselves, so they discover innovative ways to use information systems to improve customer service.

For an information system to become the source of a competitive advantage it must have two attributes: it must be valuable, and it must be rare. An ATM network, for example, is a valuable asset for a bank; but, in Canada at least, it is not rare. Thus, an ATM network is unlikely to become a source of competitive advantage for a Canadian bank. Information technology assets are often valuable, but since they are not rare, they become fragile sources of advantage. Even if a technology is both valuable and rare, it must resist imitation and substitution if it is to sustain a competitive advantage. The Avis example on page 42 describes a technology-based system that enhances customer service in a very important way—it reduces the time that customers need to spend picking up and dropping off rental vehicles. For the moment, this resource is both valuable and rare. But, given time, other rental car firms will recognize Avis's advantage and seek to imitate it. If the system is based primarily on imitable technologies, then the advantage is likely to be short lived. The key with information systems is to create a competitive advantage that is based on the *strategic use* of technology. The technology itself may be duplicated, but the usage of that technology may be much harder to copy. Think of Wal-Mart's logistics systems. The component parts of the systems, such as computers, networks, scanners, warehouses, and databases, are commercially available on open markets, but Wal-Mart's ability to combine and utilize those assets has been extremely hard for competitors, such as Kmart and Zellers, to duplicate.

Let us return to the computer-based loan application processing example. A person with a strategic view of information systems would choose a computer-based loan application process because it can help achieve the organization's strategic plan to process loan applications faster and better than rivals and to improve the selection criteria for loans. This process and the supporting information system add value to the organization *and* match the organization's strategy. It is, therefore, essential to the long-term survival of the organization. If, on the other hand, managers determine that the organization's strategy is to grow and generate new products and services, the computer-based loan application process and underlying system might not be an efficient, effective use of resources, even though the system could provide automating and learning benefits.

Information Systems and Value Chain Analysis

Managers use ***value chain analysis*** to identify opportunities to use information systems for competitive advantage (Porter, 1985, 2001;

BRIEF CASE

Avis Rent A Car

To gain a competitive advantage over rivals in the area of customer service, Avis Rent A Car customer service representatives wait for the customer out in the lot, armed with specially designed, handheld computers and printers either strapped around their waists or over their shoulders. With this "Avis Preferred" service (shown in Figure 2.6), the representative inputs the licence number of the car on the portable computer when he sees the customer driving in to return a car. Inputting this information brings up the customer's rental contract. As the customer gets out of the car, the representative inputs the mileage and the fuel level, while a second attendant retrieves the customer's luggage and places it on the curb. By the time the customer has gotten out of the car and stood next to her luggage, the representative has already printed a receipt. The service encounter for the customer is fast and pleasant. That is using technology for competitive advantage! In Table 2.2, we show how Avis's computer-supported process compares with the traditional rental car service encounter. Notice that the computer-based service encounter (in the right column) takes significantly less time than the traditional approach.

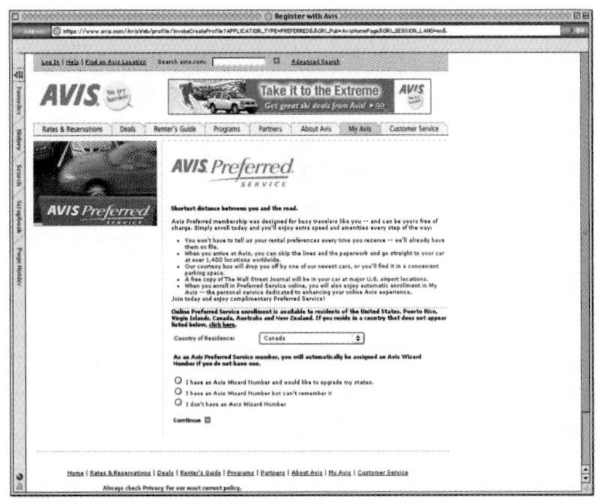

[Figure 2.6 ➡ Avis uses IT to reduce wait times.]

Source: Courtesy of Avis.

Questions

1. Is the competitive advantage achieved by Avis sustainable? If so, for how long?
2. Is it possible for an IT product or service to resist imitation and/or substitution? If yes, describe some real-world examples.

[Table 2.2] ***The Avis airport computer-supported service encounter versus the traditional airport rental car service encounter.***

	Traditional Rental Car Return Service Encounter	Avis' Computer-Based Service Encounter
	Return car to lot attendant, get bags from another attendant, walk inside and wait in line to settle contract with another attendant, walk out, and board a shuttle.	Return car to lot attendant, grab receipt and bags, and board shuttle.
Elapsed time	5–20 minutes	5–20 seconds
Number of people to interact with	2–3 people	1–2 people
Average number of footsteps customer takes	60–75 steps	5–10 steps
Relative efficiency	Low	High

Shank and Govindarajan, 1993). Think of an organization as a big input/output process. At one end, supplies are purchased and brought into the organization (see Figure 2.7 on page 44). The organization integrates those supplies to create products and services, which it markets, sells, and then distributes to customers. The organization provides customer service after the sale of these products and services. Throughout this process, there are opportunities for people to add value to the organization by acquiring supplies in a more effective manner, improving products, and selling more products. This process of adding value throughout the organization is known as the ***value chain*** within an organization.

Value chain analysis is the process of analyzing an organization's activities to determine where value is added to products and/or services and the costs that are

CAREER IMPLICATIONS

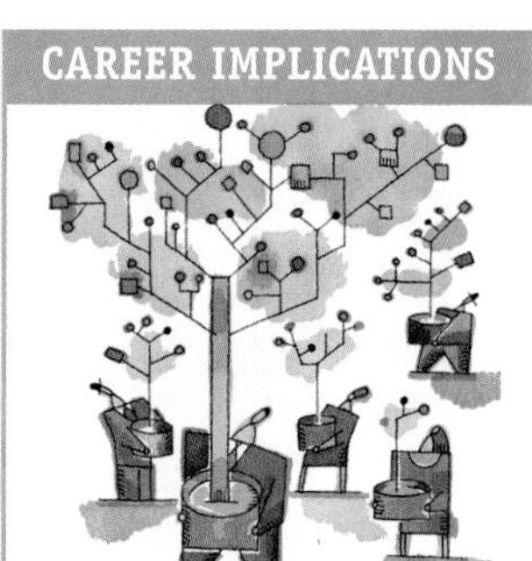

Human Resource Management

Without some understanding of objectives, IT professionals won't achieve long-term success in their careers, says Kevin Brown, vice-president and chief information officer at Edmonton-based utility company Epcor. Brown says the IT landscape has changed dramatically in the past few years; today, almost all IT projects need a solid business case before they move forward on the corporate agenda. "All IT employees that work at Epcor need to have a knowledge of the business... if you don't have a good appreciation for the business, you can miss why the initiative you're participating in is critical," he says. For example, says Brown, "if you put in those new servers, how is that going to impact our costs to our customers?"

At Epcor, and in other companies, IT workers are beginning to see this business focus sewn into the fabric of their annual performance review, says Brown. "We have an emphasis on making sure you can link your activities back to the goals of the business," he says. Performance reviews for Epcor's 150 IT employees focus on three areas—technical aptitudes, business knowledge, and behavioural skills—says Brown, because while technical excellence is important, the spotlight these days is on softer skills, such as the ability to work well in team environments. "Very little work gets done in isolation... if you're working in a team, you need to have those softer skills such as communication and teamwork," says Brown.

It's a sermon Brown preaches not only to his staff, but also to students when he's on the speaking circuit at universities and colleges. "I give them the same message: Even when you think you're going to produce a product on your own, you won't find very many opportunities in those highly technical jobs... you're going to have to sell the product, and those soft skills are going to be very important," he says. It's no surprise companies are encouraging their IT staffs to beef up their business knowledge, since business units are more and more driving IT projects. Industry research firm Gartner estimates that more than 60 percent of all IT projects are initiated by business units.

"If IT departments weren't already convinced of the need to factor business operations and goals into consolidation strategy, they should find this impetus to do so," states a recent report from Gartner. Although Epcor is a large national company with a large IT department, the same rules apply to IT workers across the board, says Stephen Mill, regional manager for IT staffing firm Robert Half Technology in Toronto. Mill says when the IT industry started to bleed a few years back, the demands placed on workers started to change. "I can remember when communication and presentation (skills) were not a barometer for success in IT," he says, adding those days are over.

Mill says if he had to choose just one soft skill for IT types to sharpen, it would be articulating technical issues to non-technical people, because the technical person has to be able to communicate the value proposition on an IT investment to people they "wouldn't normally interface with. Sometimes there is a condescending approach an IT person will use; it may not be conscious, but when you're in tech, you're talking technology all the time," he says. "You'll find a large percentage of people lacking in this area." Mill says those IT workers who take the initiative to broaden their knowledge of corporate objectives and develop their communication skills will be the long-term winners. Those who wait for their employers to lead the way are in for a rude awakening.

[Adapted from Patricia MacInnis, "Minding Business Is the New IT Imperative," *Computing Canada,* Vol. 30, No. 2 (February 6, 2004).]

incurred in doing so. Because IS can automate many activities along the value chain, value chain analysis has become a popular tool for applying IS for competitive advantage. In value chain analysis, you first draw the value chain for your organization by fleshing out each of the activities, functions, and processes where value is or should be added. Next, determine the costs—and the factors that drive costs or cause them to fluctuate—within each of the areas in your value chain diagram. You then benchmark (compare) your value chain and associated costs with those of your competitors. You can then make changes and improvements in your value chain to gain a competitive advantage. This advantage can be sustained by building in barriers to imitation, such as using proprietary technologies or locking partners into exclusive contracts.

The Role of Information Systems in Value Chain Analysis

The use of information systems has become one of the primary ways that organizations improve their value chains. In Figure 2.8 on

Web Search

WEB SEARCH OPPORTUNITY
Visit the Websites of Avis Canada
www.avis.ca
and Air Canada
www.aircanada.ca
and investigate ways that these companies are using technology to gain and sustain competitive advantages.

WHEN THINGS GO WRONG

Ouch . . . ! A Small Mistake Proves Costly

When can a $100 mistake cost $5 million? The answer is when the $100 is the cost of a hard drive that contains information on nearly one million people . . . and it goes missing. IBM Canada learned the hard way that a simple blunder can lead to a mountain of direct and indirect costs.

Information Systems Management (ISM), a division of IBM, was fulfilling a contract to refurbish computers storing data for clients when a 30 GB hard drive went missing. ISM first thought that the hard drive contained information on about 100,000 clients of several agencies of the Government of Saskatchewan. While this was problematic, it was later discovered that the small storage device also contained information on about 170,000 customers of the Co-operators Life Insurance Company, and 650,000 clients of Investors Group, a mutual fund company.

What happened to the hard drive? It was recovered by Regina city police at the home of an ISM employee. The employee had evidently brought the hard drive home and installed it in a personal computer to provide a little extra storage. Apparently, the employee had wiped the hard drive clean and none of the information had been compromised. The employee was charged with possession of stolen property under $5,000 and the hard drive was recovered.

However, the cost to ISM will be significantly more than $5,000. Direct costs, not including legal fees, have amounted to $500,000, and a class-action lawsuit has been launched claiming damages of $5 million. Since the "lost" information included names, addresses, social insurance numbers, and bank account information, more litigation is likely. In addition, a number of firms and government agencies have put existing contracts with ISM under review and refused to renew expiring contracts until the firm can demonstrate that it has improved its security practices.

page 45, we show a sample value chain and some ways that information systems can be used to improve productivity within it. For example, many organizations use the Internet to connect businesses with one another electronically so that they can exchange orders, invoices, and receipts online in real time. Using the Internet has become a popular method for improving the front end of the organizational value chain. In fact, many firms now use the Internet for such business-to-business interactions; these systems are called ***extranets*** (described in greater detail in Chapter 5).

An innovative way to use information systems to improve the back end of the value chain, the service after the sale, is to provide online customer service. For example, owners of McLaren's F1 Supercar (see Figure 2.9) plug a modem into the car and into a phone line and then let McLaren engineers diagnose the car and make adjustments to it over the phone lines in real time. That may sound exotic and restricted to those few individuals who can afford a million-dollar automobile, but computer companies such as IBM and Sun also use this method to diagnose and maintain their customers' products remotely and, in some cases, to download new software products.

The Technology/Strategy Fit

You might be asking yourself this: if an information system helps to do things faster and better and helps save money, who cares whether it matches the company's strategy?

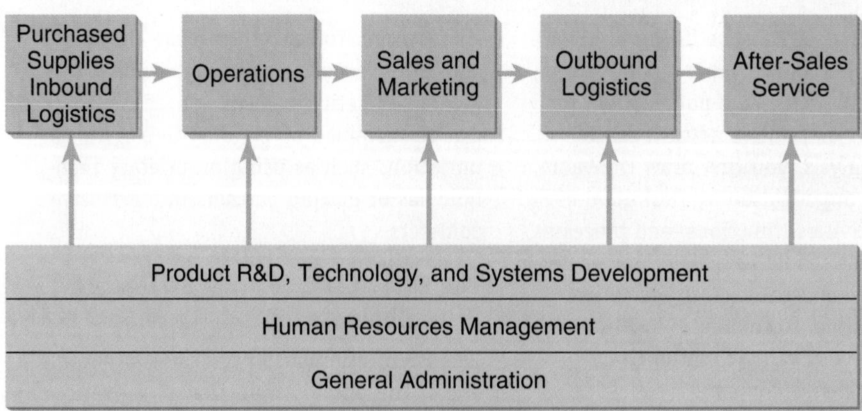

[Figure 2.7 ➡ A sample generic organizational value chain.]

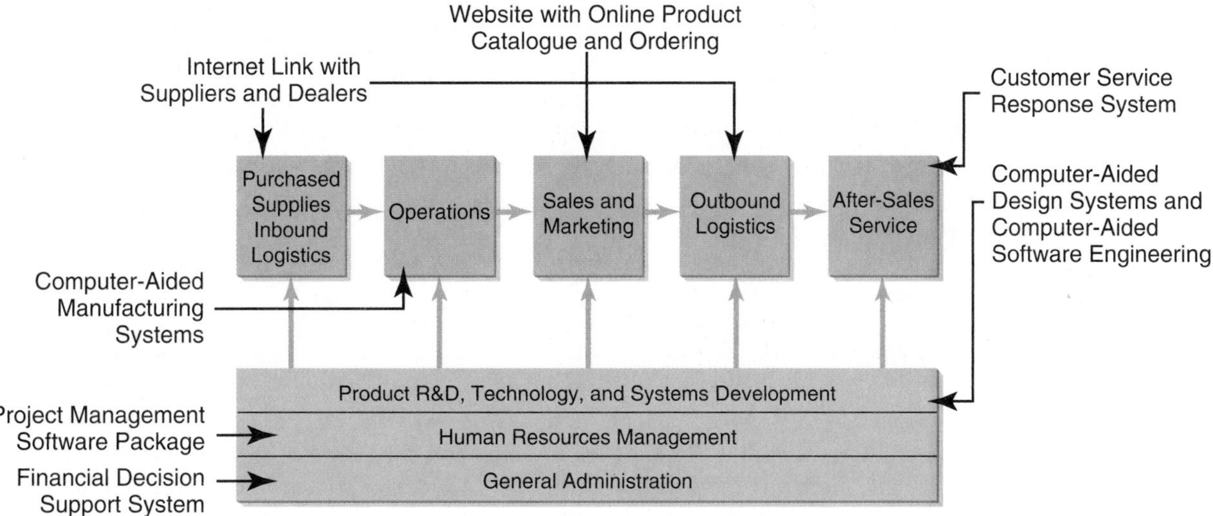

[**Figure 2.8** ➥ Sample value chain and corresponding sample uses of information systems to add value.]

Good question. If money grew on trees, you probably would build and use just about every information system you could imagine. Organizations could build many different, valuable systems but are constrained by time and money to build only those that add the most value: those that help automate and learn, as well as have strategic value. In most cases, you do not want systems that do not match the strategy, even if they offer automating and learning benefits.

You probably do not want a system that helps differentiate your products based on high quality when the organizational strategy is to be the overall industry low-cost leader. For example, if managers of a firm were trying to make the firm a low-cost leader, would they want to buy or build an expensive ***computer-aided design*** system that enabled them to use high-powered computers to design very state-of-the-art, high-quality products? They probably would not choose to do that, given that such a system would most likely add exorbitant costs to the design and manufacturing process and would likely defeat the strategy of spending less in the production of products and, subsequently, selling products at the lowest possible prices.

[**Figure 2.9** ➥ The McLaren F1 Supercar.]

Source: © Getty Images, Inc.

We should also caution that merely choosing and implementing an emerging information system is not sufficient to gain or sustain competitive advantage. In any significant information systems implementation, there must be commensurate, significant organizational change. Information systems are most effective in organizations when they work in a complementary way with a firm's existing assets and capabilities. This may come in the form of ***business process reengineering (BPR)*** and other similar methods of improving the functioning of the organization, as opposed to merely dropping in an information system with no attempts at changing and improving the organization. We will talk more in Chapter 7 about the role of BPR in enterprise-wide information systems implementations.

MAKING THE BUSINESS CASE FOR A SYSTEM

Given that money does not grow on trees, people in organizations are constantly trying to justify having to spend money on anything, especially information systems. Before people are willing to spend money to purchase or build a new information system or spend more money on an existing system, they want to be convinced that this will be a good investment. Will the system provide automating, learning, and/or strategic benefits? The phrase that is used to describe the process of identifying the value provided by an information system is ***making the business case***.

What does making the business case for an information system mean? Think for a moment about what defence lawyers do in court trials. They carefully build a strong, integrated set of arguments and evidence to prove that their clients are innocent. In short, they build and present their case to those who will pass judgment on their clients. In much the same way, people in business often have to build a strong, integrated set of arguments and evidence to prove that an information system is adding value to the organization or its constituents.

As a business professional, you will be called on to make the business case for systems and other capital investments. As a finance, accounting, marketing, or management professional, you are likely to be involved in this process and will need to know how to make the business case for a system effectively, as well as understand the relevant organizational issues involved. It will be in the organization's best interest, and in your own, to ferret out systems that are not adding value. In these cases, you will either need to improve the systems or replace them.

Making the business case is as important for proposed systems as it is for existing systems. For a proposed system, the case will be used to determine whether the new system is a "go" or a "no go." For an existing system, the case determines whether the company will continue to fund the system. Whether a new system or an existing one is being considered, your goal is to make sure that the system adds value, that it helps the firm to achieve its strategy and competitive advantage over its rivals.

The Productivity Paradox

Unfortunately, while it is easy to quantify the costs associated with developing an information system, it is often difficult to quantify tangible productivity gains from the use of an information system. Recently, the press has given a lot of attention to computer systems' impact or lack of impact on worker productivity. In many cases, IS expenditures, salaries, and the number of people on the IS staff have all been rising, but results from these investments have been disappointing. For example, it is estimated that technology-related spending by organizations increased fivefold from the 1980s to the 1990s (Hagendorf, 1998). As a result, justifying the costs for information technology has been a hot topic among senior managers at many firms. In particular, "white-collar" productivity, especially in the service sector, has not increased at the rate one might expect, given the billions of dollars spent on office information systems (Leibs and Carrillo, 1997).

Why has it been difficult to show that these vast expenditures on information technology have led to productivity gains? Have information systems somehow failed us, promising increases in performance and productivity and then failing to deliver on that promise? Determining the answer is not easy. Information systems may have increased productivity, but other forces may have simultaneously worked to reduce it, the end result being no visible change. Factors such as government regulation, more complex tax codes, more intense competition, and complex products can all have major impacts on a firm's productivity.

GLOBAL PERSPECTIVE

Using IS to Manage Global Customer Service at Unilever

Have you ever had a Lipton iced tea or used a bar of Dove soap? You might not realize it, but Unilever provides these and other everyday products for consumers all over the world (see Figure 2.10). With sales well into the billions of dollars annually, with nearly 300,000 employees worldwide, and with products sold in 150 countries in categories such as washing powder, shampoo and toothpaste, teas, ice cream, and oils and spreads, it is amazing that Unilever can keep track of it all.

Even more amazing is that, with millions of customers spread across 150 countries, Unilever's competitive advantage is based on providing excellent customer service. Unilever prides itself on not only responding to consumers' needs but also anticipating their future demands.

To provide the best customer service in its Philippines operation, in early 2002 Unilever successfully implemented mySAP™ customer relationship management software. The mySAP CRM software now helps improve Unilever's call centre capability and boosts the productivity of its customer service and consumer advisory representatives.

The implementation, dubbed "Project Polaris," automates the help desk processes of Unilever's two call centres: customer service and consumer advisory. Unilever Philippines commercial director Efren Samonte, who served as the project sponsor for the implementation, said, "mySAP CRM enabled faster response time to queries and needs raised by consumers, provided for effective maintenance of our customer database, and gave the company easy access to customer information for analysis and strategy development."

Samonte added that, "Prior to the implementation, our customer and consumer care officers browsed through thick books, brochures, various online databases, and reports to answer customer inquiries. Now, they can click on any Unilever product on their computer screen, and data about the particular item automatically comes up. This significantly enhances our agents' ability to respond to customer inquiries fast, accurately, and completely."

Easy data access resulted in substantial productivity gains, according to Samonte. "Previously, monthly calls peaked at 3,000," he said. "MySAP CRM increased the company's call centre capability immediately to 5,000 calls per month."

"The ability to access product information quickly and efficiently is the foundation for providing effective customer relationship management," said Carol Burch, senior vice-president, Global CRM, SAP AG. "Unilever Philippines is now in the position to provide their customers with superior service than in the past, and will be able to handle more customer inquiries than ever before."

[Adapted in part from "Unilever Goes Live with mySAP™ Customer Relationship Management," **www.sap.com/company/press** (April 1, 2002).]

[**Figure 2.10** ➡ Unilever uses information systems to provide the best global customer service possible for products such as iced tea and soap.]

Source: © Getty Images, Inc.

It is also true that information systems built with the best intentions may have had unintended consequences—employees spending excessive amounts of time surfing the Web to check sports scores on the TSN Website, volumes of electronic junk mail being sent by Internet marketing companies or from personal friends, and company PCs being used to download and play software games. In these situations, information technology can result in less efficient and effective communication among employees and less productive uses of employee time than before the IS was implemented. Does this kind of employee behaviour affect productivity figures? You bet it does. Still, in general, sound IS investments should increase organizational productivity. If this is so, why have organizations not been able to show this increased productivity? A number of reasons have been given for the apparent "productivity paradox" of IS investments.

Measurement Problems

In many cases, the benefits of information technology are difficult to pinpoint because firms may be measuring the wrong things. Often, the biggest increases in productivity result from increased ***system effectiveness.*** Unfortunately, many business metrics focus on ***system efficiency.*** Although information systems may have real benefits, those benefits may not be detected. Effectiveness improvements are sometimes difficult to measure. Also, expected benefits from IS are not always defined in advance, so they are never "seen." After all, in order to "see" something, you usually have to know what to look for. Measurement problems are not limited to traditional office information systems either. All types of systems have potential measurement problems. Consider the following:

End-user development. Because end-user-developed systems are often designed for individual users or individual needs, those individuals often do not meticulously track costs and benefits in order to measure impact. In addition, end users in one business unit may be tracking and analyzing a system's benefits and costs in ways that are quite different from the methods employed by end users in other units.

Decision support systems (DSSs). By definition, DSSs are designed to improve decision making. The problem is, how do we measure their impact? To quantify the results of a DSS, we would need to measure the differences between decisions made with the DSS and the decisions that would have been made if no DSS had been in place. This kind of comparison is difficult to make in a business setting. Furthermore, it is not clear what constitutes adding value in this context. Does adding value mean making decisions that result in better outcomes, improving the decision-making process, having the capability to make more decisions, being able to justify a decision more effectively, making people feel better about the decision outcomes and/or the decision-making process, or some combination of these and other factors? Until it becomes clearer how to measure the benefits of a DSS easily and effectively, making the business case for a DSS will continue to be difficult.

Strategic systems. Ideally, IS managers could point to strategic information systems as having a tremendous impact on the firm's financial performance. However, the intent of strategic systems is often to help the organization enter a new market, gain or maintain market share, better serve customers, and so on. As we have said, traditional financial measures of system benefits—time/money saved or return on investment—do not adequately indicate whether these strategic systems have been successful. Better serving customers may be vitally important in a competitive environment. However, this may not easily translate into impressive-looking productivity figures for an information system in the short run.

A good example of measurement problems associated with IS investment is the use of automated teller machines (ATMs). How much have ATMs contributed to banking productivity? Traditional statistics might look at the number of transactions or output as some multiple of the labour input needed to produce that output (for example, a transaction). However, such statistics do not work well for the ATM example. The number of cheques written may actually decrease with ATMs, making productivity statistics appear lower. On the other hand, can you imagine a bank staying competitive without offering ATM services? The value added for the customer in terms of improved delivery of services almost dictates that banks offer a wide range of ATM services in today's competitive market. As noted earlier, an ATM network is valuable, but not rare for a financial institution in Canada. Not having such a network would put a bank at a strategic disadvantage, but having one is merely enough to achieve competitive parity. In this respect, the ATM network has become a strategic necessity.

Time Lags

A second explanation for why productivity is difficult to demonstrate for IS investment is that a significant time lag may occur from when a company makes the IS investment until that investment is translated into improvement in the bottom line. Brynjolfsson (1993) reports that lags of two to three years are typical before strong organizational impacts of IS investment are felt.

The explanation for lags is fairly simple. At one level, it takes time for people to become proficient at using new technologies. Remember the first time you ever used a computer? It probably seemed difficult and cryptic to use. It may have taken you more time to figure out how to use the computer than it would have to complete the task manually. Nonetheless, the computer probably became easier to use as you became more proficient with it. If you multiply this learning curve over everyone in an organization who may be using a given technology, you can see that until a firm has some experience in using a technology, the benefits associated with using it may be deferred. Everyone must become proficient with that technology in order to gain the benefits from its use.

It may also take some time before the tangible benefits of a new information system can be felt. Let us return to our ATM example. It may take years from the first implementation of this new system before the benefits may be felt. The system must first be implemented, which could take years in a large, distributed financial institution. Then the system must be fine-tuned to operate optimally and must be tied into all of the necessary subsystems. Employees and customers must be trained in how to use the system properly, and it may take years before they truly become proficient and comfortable with using it.

When the system is working well, and people are using it efficiently, productivity gains may be measured. It takes time for the system to produce any labour savings within the organization and for customers' satisfaction levels to rise. Given that ATMs have become a strategic necessity, perhaps one of their benefits is that they enable banks to gain, or simply keep, customers. It can take years for a financial institution to feel the effects of its deployment of ATMs.

If time lags are the reason why IS investments do not show up in productivity figures, then eventually IS managers should be able to report some very good news about organizational return on IS investment. Still, for managers faced with the day-to-day pressures of coming up with a demonstrable impact on firm performance, the issue of time lags may not be very helpful or comforting.

Redistribution

A third possible explanation for why IS productivity figures are not easy to find is that IS may be beneficial for individual firms, but not for a particular industry or the economy as a whole. Particularly in competitive situations, IS may be used to redistribute the pieces of the pie rather than making the whole pie bigger. In other words, strategic information systems may help one firm to increase its market share; however, this may come at the expense of another firm, which loses its market share as consumers transfer to the first firm. The result for the industry or economy as a whole is a wash—that is, the same number of products is being sold and the same number of dollars is being spent across all the firms. The only difference is that now one firm is getting a larger share of the business, while another firm is getting a smaller share.

While such an explanation may be feasible for some markets and industries, it does not fully explain why productivity figures would be stagnant at the level of one individual firm. Shouldn't each organization be more productive than before? Part of the problem is that our expectations of performance are somewhat biased. We tend to take for granted that technology fundamentally enables people to do things that would otherwise be nearly impossible. In effect, we continue to "raise the bar" with our expectations of what people can accomplish when supported by technology. For example, you might wonder whether the electronic spreadsheet on the PC on your desk is really helping you do your job better. To best answer this, you should think back to what it was like to create a spreadsheet by hand. It was a much slower process, was far more likely to produce errors, and left people significantly less time to work on other, more important tasks.

Mismanagement

A fourth explanation is that IS has not been implemented and managed well. Some believe that people often simply build bad systems, implement them poorly, and rely on technology fixes when the organization has problems that require a joint technology/process solution. Rather than increasing outputs or profits, IS investments might merely be a Band-Aid solution and may serve to mask or even increase organizational slack and inefficiency.

Similarly, the rapid decrease in processing time enabled by IS can result in unanticipated bottlenecks. For example, if automation has increased the potential output of a system, but part of that system is reliant on human input, then the system can operate only as fast as the human can feed input into or through that system. Eli Goldratt very aptly showed how this happens in his best-selling book *The Goal*, in which he uses the format of a novel to show how people can think logically and consistently about organizational problems in order to determine true "cause and effect" relationships between their actions and the results. In the novel, the characters do this so well that they save their manufacturing plant and make it successful. Spending money on IS does not help increase the firm's productivity until all of the bottlenecks are addressed. From a management standpoint, this means that managers must be sure that they evaluate the entire process being automated, making changes as necessary to old processes in order to truly benefit from IS investment. If managers simply overlay new technology on old processes, sometimes known as "paving the cow path," then they will likely be disappointed in the meagre productivity gains reaped from their investment.

If it is so difficult to quantify the benefits of information systems for individual firms and for entire industries, why do managers continue to invest in information systems? There are two answers. First, competitive pressures force managers to invest in information systems whether they like it or not. Second, some managers are getting better at making the business case for information systems.

MAKING A SUCCESSFUL BUSINESS CASE

There are a number of types of arguments that people make in their business cases for information systems. When managers make the business case for an information system, they typically base their arguments on **f**aith, **f**ear, and/or **f**acts (Wheeler, 2002a).[3] Table 2.3 shows examples of these three types of arguments.

Do not assume that you must base your business case on facts only. It is entirely appropriate to base the business case on faith, fear, or facts. Indeed, the strongest and most comprehensive business case will include a little of each type of argument. In the following sections, we talk about each of these types of arguments for the business case.

Business Case Arguments Based on Faith

In some situations, arguments based on faith (or fear) are the most compelling and are what drive the decision to invest in an information system despite the lack of any data on system costs or even in the face of some data that say that the dollar costs for the system will be high. Arguments based on faith often hold that an information system *must* be implemented to achieve the organization's strategy effectively and to gain or sustain a competitive advantage over rivals, despite the dollar costs associated with that system. Given the power of modern information systems, their rapid evolution, and their pervasiveness in business today, information systems have become a common tool for enabling business strategy. Consequently, the business cases for systems are frequently grounded in strategic arguments.

An example would be that a firm has set as its strategy that it will be the dominant global force in its industry. As a result, this firm cannot escape that it will have to adopt a global telecommunications network and a variety of collaboration technologies, such as e-mail, desktop video conferencing, and groupware tools, to enable employees from different parts of the globe to work together effectively and efficiently. Similarly, a firm that has set as its strategy that it will have a broad scope—producing products and services across a wide range of consumer needs—cannot escape that it will have to adopt some form of an enterprise resource planning system to coordinate business activities across its diverse product lines. For example, Procter & Gamble produces dozens of household products that are consumed under various brand names—Noxzema, Folgers coffee, Tide laundry detergent, Cover Girl cosmetics, Crest toothpaste, and Pringles potato chips, to name a few. Integration across various product lines and divisions is a key goal for IS investments. Such integration allows Procter & Gamble to streamline inventory, thus improving efficiency. In short, successful business case arguments based on faith should clearly describe the firm's mission and objectives, the strategy for achieving them, and

[3] Wheeler also adds a fourth F, that being for **f**iction, and notes that, unfortunately, managers sometimes base their arguments on pure fiction, which not only is bad for their careers, but is not at all healthy for their firms either.

[Table 2.3] ***Three types of arguments commonly made in the business case for an information system.***

Type of Argument	Description	Example
Faith	Arguments based on beliefs about organizational strategy, competitive advantage, industry forces, customer perceptions, market share, and so on.	"I know I don't have good data to back this up, but I'm convinced that having this customer relationship management system will enable us to serve our customers significantly better than do our competitors and, as a result, we'll beat the competition . . . . You just have to take it on faith."
Fear	Arguments based on the notion that if the system is not implemented, the firm will lose out to the competition or, worse, go out of business.	"If we don't implement this enterprise resource planning system, we'll get killed by our competitors because they're all implementing these kinds of systems . . . . We either do this or we die."
Fact	Arguments based on data, quantitative analysis, and/or indisputable factors.	"This analysis shows that implementing the inventory control system will help us reduce errors by 50 percent, reduce operating costs by 15 percent a year, and increase production by 5 percent a year, and will pay for itself within 18 months."

the types of information systems that are needed to enact the strategy.

Business Case Arguments Based on Fear

There are several different factors to take into account when making a business case in which you will provide arguments based on fear. These include a number of factors involving competition and other elements of the industry in which the firm operates, which are shown in Figure 2.11 (Harris and Katz, 1991).

Industry Factors

The nature of the industry can often determine what types of information systems would be most effective. Furthermore, many different types of industry factors can affect the business value of different systems. A system that may have a very positive impact on a firm in one industry may have little or no impact on a firm in another industry.

Stage of maturity. The stage of maturity for a given industry can have an important influence on IS investment. For example, a mature and stable industry, such as the automotive industry, may need IS simply to maintain the current pace of operations. While having the newest IS available may be nice, it may not be needed to stay in business. However, a company in a newer, more volatile industry, such as the cellular phone industry, may find it more important to be on the leading edge of technology in order to compete effectively in the marketplace. In fact, it may be a strategic necessity in some industries to deploy newer technologies, even though the tangible benefits of deploying these technologies may be difficult to demonstrate.

Regulation. Some industries are more highly regulated than others. In some cases, companies can use IS to control processes and ensure compliance with appropriate regulations. For example, the aircraft industry is highly regulated. Information technology can provide sophisticated engineering and modelling tools to designers who can test various designs for reactions to gravity forces (G-forces) and turbulence before aircraft prototypes are built. The designer can then understand which designs may not comply with regulatory requirements. Similar applications exist (and are often mandated) across other highly regulated industries, such as the radio and television broadcasting industries. The argument for the business case here would be something like, "If we do not implement this information system, we run the risk of being sued or, worse, being thrown in jail."

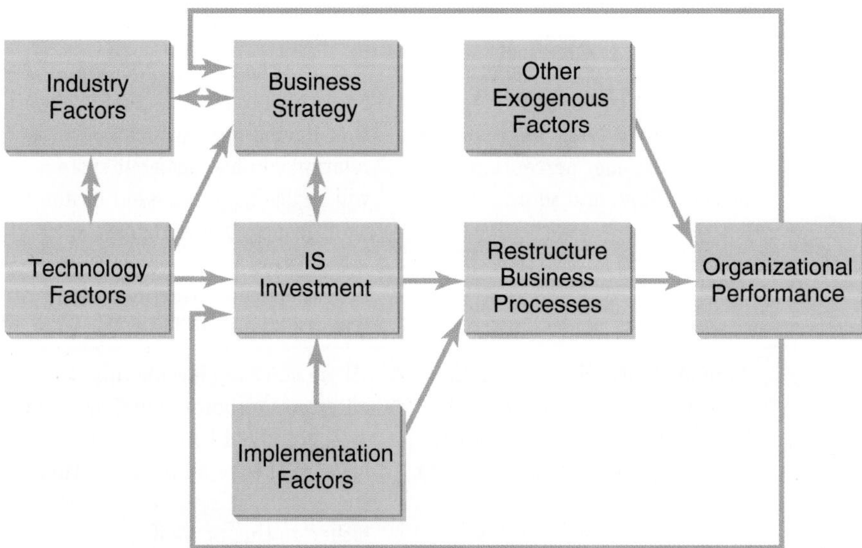

[**Figure 2.11** ➡ Factors in IS investment decisions.]

Nature of competition or rivalry. Probably the most important industry factor that can affect IS investment is the nature of competition or rivalry in the industry. For example, when competition in an industry is high and use of information systems is extensive, as it is in the personal computer industry, strategic necessity more than anything else forces firms to adopt information systems. Given how tight profit margins are in the PC industry, Dell and other manufacturers must use inventory control systems, Web-based purchasing and customer service, and a host of other systems that help them to be more effective and efficient. If they do not adopt these information systems, they will likely go out of business. One framework often used to analyze the competition within an industry is Porter's notion of the five primary competitive forces (Porter, 1979): 1) the rivalry among competing sellers in your industry, 2) the threat of potential new entrants into your industry, 3) the bargaining power that customers have within your industry, 4) the bargaining power that suppliers have within your industry, and 5) the potential for substitute products from other industries. Table 2.4 provides examples of how IS can have an impact on the various competitive forces in an industry.

Porter's Five Forces model of competition can be used in this way to help you determine which specific technologies will be more or less useful, depending on the nature of your industry. You can then use these as the bases for your arguments as to whether or not to invest in new or existing information systems. This kind of industry-based business case might not enable you to attach specific, monetary benefits to particular information systems, but it can be used to show you and others that specific uses of particular systems are necessary to compete in your markets. Business case arguments formulated this way sound something like, "If we do not implement this information system, our competitors are going to beat us on price, we will lose market share, and we will go out of business."

Business Case Arguments Based on Fact

Many people, including most chief financial officers, want to see a business case for an information system that is based on some convincing, quantitative analysis that proves beyond a shadow of doubt that the benefits of the system will outweigh the costs. The most common way to prove this is to provide a detailed cost–benefit analysis of the information system. Although this step is critical, the manager must remember that there are inherent limits to cost–benefit analysis for information systems, as described previously.

Cost–Benefit Analysis for a Web-Based System

In this section we are going to discuss the cost–benefit analysis for an information system and show how that analysis would be part of a business case based on fact. Let us consider the development of a Web-based order entry system for a relatively small firm.

In a cost–benefit analysis, costs can usually be divided into two categories: ***nonrecurring costs*** and ***recurring costs.*** Nonrecurring costs are one-time costs that are

[Table 2.4] ***IS impact on competitive forces.***

Competitive Force	Implication for Firm	Potential Use of IS to Combat Competitive Force
Traditional rivals within your industry	Competition in price, product distribution, and service	Implement enterprise resource planning system to reduce costs and be able to act and react more quickly Implement Website to offer better service to customers
Threat of new entrants into your market	Increased capacity in the industry Reduced prices Decreased market share	Better Website to reach customers and differentiate product Inventory control system to lower costs and better manage excess capacity
Customers' bargaining power	Reduced prices Increased quality Demand for more services	Implement customer relationship management system to serve customers better Implement computer-aided design and/or computer-aided manufacturing system to improve product quality
Suppliers' bargaining power	Prices raised Reduced quality	Use Internet to establish closer electronic ties with suppliers and to create relationships with new suppliers located far away
Threat of substitute products from other industries	Potential returns on products Decreased market share Losing customers for life	Use decision support system and customer purchase database to assess trends and customer needs better Use computer-aided design systems to redefine products

[Source: Adapted from Applegate and McFarlan, *Corporate Information Systems Management: Text and Cases*, 5th ed. (Columbus, OH: McGraw-Hill/Irwin, 1999).]

not expected to continue after the system is implemented. These include costs for things such as the Web server, telecommunications equipment, Web server software, HTML editors, Java, PhotoShop, and other tools. These one-time costs also include the costs of attracting and training a Webmaster, renovating some office space to serve as the location of the Web server, and paying analysts and programmers to develop the system.

Recurring costs are ongoing costs that occur throughout the life cycle of systems development, implementation, and maintenance. Recurring costs include the salary and benefits of the Webmaster and any other personnel assigned to maintain the system, upgrades and maintenance for the system components, monthly fees paid to a local Internet service provider, and the continuing costs for the space in which the Webmaster works and the server resides. Personnel costs are usually the largest recurring costs, and the Web-based system is no exception in this regard. These recurring expenses can go well beyond the Webmaster to include expenses for help desk personnel, maintenance programmers, IS management, and data entry personnel.

The sample costs described thus far have been fairly ***tangible costs,*** which are easy to identify. Some ***intangible costs*** ought to be accounted for as well, even though they will not fit neatly into the quantitative analysis. These might include the costs of reducing traditional sales (channel conflict), losing some customers that are not "Web ready," or losing customers if the Web application is poorly designed or not on par with competitors' sites. We can choose either to quantify these in some way (that is, determine the cost of losing a customer) or simply to reserve these as important costs to consider outside of, but

CAREER IMPLICATIONS

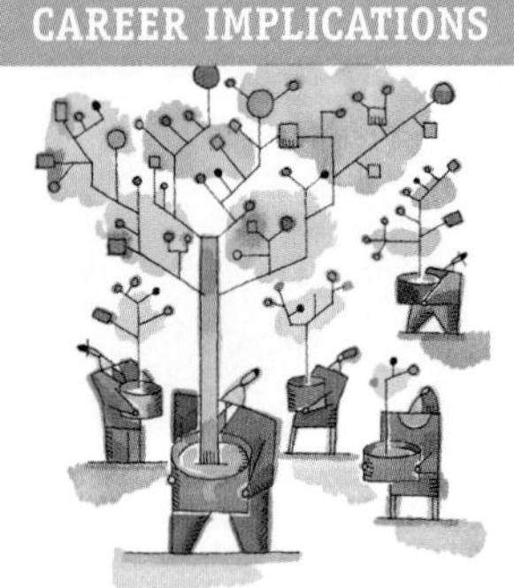

Operations Management

Trudeau International Airport in Montreal is the latest Canadian facility to move away from paper-based air traffic control towers to an all-electronic system. NAV Canada, the nation's privately owned provider of civil air navigation services, has spent approximately $1 billion to modernize towers in Canadian airports—$11 million of which was spent in Montreal. The newly designed and implemented extended computer display system (EXCDS) allows controllers to enter the flight information, such as type and size, altitude, and identification codes, of incoming aircraft on-screen. The information can be routed electronically among Trudeau's 32 air traffic controllers via touchscreen technology. "It was a system that we developed to ensure that controllers in different facilities, and even controllers in the same facility, are all looking at the same information. That's certainly a big safety issue for us," said vice-president of engineering Kim Troutman, referring to the removal of potential human error.

"We're providing upgraded technology to allow them to be more efficient in their job. Certainly we'll never get rid of the air traffic controller, but it allows them to be somewhat more efficient and provide the safeguards that we can put in, utilizing automation," he said. Previously, this information was printed out on paper flight progress strips and manually handed off to controllers. The fact that it is now available on-screen also cuts the amount of verbal communication required. "Voice communication [was] getting congested, and this is certainly a much more efficient way of passing information," said Troutman.

Every keystroke is recorded to provide a permanent record of each aircraft's flight information, he added. In the event of an incident, the information can be called up and played back. Play-backs can also be used for training purposes. The control centre at Trudeau has been completely refurbished over the course of a year, according to its general manager, Larry Lachance. The EXCDS system "requires a lot less real estate as compared to the old system where you had flight progress printers and so on," he said. "It allows for better real estate utilization, as well as bringing the controller closer to the glass of the tower [for a better view of the airport]." Lachance added that the control centre refurbishment has included other enhancements, such as a new voice communications system. Virtually every airport across Canada will receive the latest software. According to Troutman, about a dozen are already using it—there are a total of 700 workstations in place—and there are three or four new deployments a year. Toronto was the first facility to get the system back in 1999, and has since upgraded to a more recent version. Troutman said that paper-based flight strips are still the norm across most of the globe.

[Adapted from Neil Sutton, "NAV Canada Retools Industry's Air Traffic Control Systems," **http://www.itbusiness.ca/index.asp?theaction=61&sid=54498#**, ITBusiness.ca (January 8, 2004).]

along with, the quantitative cost-benefit analysis.

Next we determine both ***tangible benefits*** and ***intangible benefits.*** Some tangible benefits are relatively easy to determine. For example, we can estimate that the increased customer reach of the new Web-based system will result in at least a modest increase in sales. Based on evidence from similar projects, you might estimate, say, a 5-percent increase in sales in the first year, a 10-percent increase in the second year, and a 15-percent increase in the third year. In addition, we might also include as tangible benefits the reduction of order entry errors because orders will now be tracked electronically and shipped automatically. We could calculate the money previously lost on faulty and lost orders, along with the salaries and wages of personnel assigned to fix and find these orders, and then consider the reduction of these costs as a quantifiable benefit of the new system. Cost avoidance is a legitimate, quantifiable benefit of an information system. Similarly, the new system may enable the company to use fewer order entry clerks or redeploy these personnel to other, more important functions within the company. We could consider these cost reductions as benefits of the new system.

Our Web-based system has intangible benefits as well. Some intangible benefits of this new system might include faster turnaround on fulfilling orders and resulting improvements in customer service. These are real benefits, but they might be hard to quantify with confidence. Perhaps an even more intangible benefit would be the overall improved perception of the firm. Customers might consider it more progressive and customer-service–oriented than its rivals, and, in addition to attracting new customers, this might increase the value of the firm's stock if it were a publicly traded firm. Another intangible benefit might be simply that it was a strategic necessity to offer Web-based ordering to customers to keep pace with rivals. While these intangibles are difficult to quantify, they must be considered along with the more quantitative analysis of benefits. In fact, the intangible benefits of this Web-based system might be so important that they could carry the day despite an inconclusive or even negative cost–benefit analysis.

An example of a simplified cost–benefit analysis with tangible costs and benefits is presented in Figure 2.12. You will notice the fairly large investment up front, with another significant outlay in the fifth year for a system upgrade. We could now use the net costs/benefits for each year as the basis of our conclusion about this system. Alternatively, we could perform a break-even analysis (break even occurs early in the second year of the system's life) or a more formal net present value analysis of the relevant cash flow streams associated with the system. In any event, this cost–benefit analysis helps us make the business case for this proposed Web-based order fulfillment system. It clearly shows that the investment for this system is relatively small, and we can fairly quickly recapture the investment. In addition, there appear to be intangible, strategic benefits to deploying this system. This analysis, and the accompanying arguments and evidence, go a long way toward convincing senior managers in the firm that this new system makes sense.

		2005	2006	2007	2008	2009
Costs						
Non-recurring						
Hardware		$ 20,000				
Software		$ 7,500				
Networking		$ 4,500				
Infrastructure		$ 7,500				
Personnel		$100,000				
Recurring						
Hardware			$ 500	$ 1,000	$ 2,500	$ 15,000
Software			$ 500	$ 500	$ 1,000	$ 2,500
Networking			$ 250	$ 250	$ 500	$ 1,000
Service Fees			$ 250	$ 250	$ 250	$ 500
Infrastructure				$ 250	$ 500	$ 1,500
Personnel			$ 60,000	$ 62,500	$ 70,000	$ 90,000
Total Costs		$139,500	$ 61,500	$ 64,750	$ 74,750	$110,500
Benefits						
Increased Sales		$ 20,000	$ 50,000	$ 80,000	$115,000	$175,000
Error Reduction		$ 15,000	$ 15,000	$ 15,000	$ 15,000	$ 15,000
Cost Reduction		$100,000	$100,000	$100,000	$100,000	$100,000
Total Benefits		$135,000	$165,000	$195,000	$230,000	$290,000
Net Costs/Benefit		$ (4,500)	$103,500	$130,250	$155,250	$179,500

[**Figure 2.12** ➥ Worksheet showing simplified cost–benefit analysis for the Web-based order fulfillment system.]

CAREER IMPLICATIONS

Accounting and Finance

If you find yourself working in the field of accounting and/or finance, you will likely be asked to prepare or evaluate a proposal for an information system, given your expertise with numbers. As noted in this chapter, it will be relatively easy for you to determine and report the costs of the information system, but it will be more difficult for you to quantify the benefits of the system. In some cases, you will be able to quantify the benefits in terms of cost savings or increased sales, but in many cases, you will not be able to quantify clear, tangible benefits. Does that mean you should recommend against implementing such systems? Not necessarily. It means that there ought to be clear, compelling reasons for implementing these systems in the absence of hard numbers.

Measuring the value of IS and justifying that value to various stakeholders in the organization has become one of the most important aspects of information systems projects. In many cases, the value of IS has been justified if the CIO has been able to prove that a new information system will enable the company to cut costs and increase efficiency. Financial or tangible measures of return on investment thus have often been used as a measure of the value of an information systems project. However, such measures are useful only in the case of projects where the benefits are tangible, such as the implementation of a new processing system that will clearly decrease the time taken to process orders (and thus cut costs demonstrably). However, many other important IS projects have less tangible outcomes and return on investment (ROI), and hence ROI is becoming a controversial measure of the value of IS. For different types of IS projects, companies are switching to alternative measures of their value, including evaluating the strategic value of that project to the organization. For example, while justifying e-business projects, CEOs are evaluating how they may enhance the competitive edge of the organization, open up new marketing channels for the company, or lead to higher customer satisfaction, rather than focusing only on the dollar amount of the return the system will provide. Similarly, for intranet projects, factors such as increased employee morale and higher levels of collaboration are taking precedence over how much money the project will cost or will help save.

CAREER IMPLICATIONS

Information Systems

Keith Powell was chief information officer (CIO) at Nortel Networks for four years until June 2000. Today, he is a partner in a venture capital company called XPV Capital Corp., which invests in high-tech companies. He has also been coaching organizations on how to deliver leadership strategies to senior executives. Powell believes the changing role of the CIO demands that IT managers develop their leadership skills and business acumen or risk missing out on opportunities. "In dealing with many IT companies, I see IT professionals losing out on opportunities. That is because CEOs are looking for more business-oriented people to run their IT environments. The reason is that the CEO doesn't understand whether he is getting a return on investment. He is looking for someone who can translate all the technical stuff into something that is going to create business value and derive a return on investment as his business organization sees it, not as a bunch of technocrats perceive it. For many technical people, the result is that bright people who should be candidates for the CIO role are coming up against a glass ceiling. Consequently, it is absolutely necessary that IT managers start to understand the impact they can have on the business and then be able to translate that in the way they deal with their peers and be seen as business-oriented information technology professionals."

Companies that recognize the strategic value of IT and can translate IT value into business value have enjoyed sustained success. Powell cites Wal-Mart as an example of this type of company. "Wal-Mart is an organization that has truly taken information technology and made it a strategic underpinning for its success in the retail industry. It's not a retail company at all—it's an information technology company." Powell believes that IT will continue to provide strategic value for organizations in all lines of business. "People always talk about CRM and enterprise planning, and you often hear about it on the negative side, but I think we are on the thin edge of the wedge of significant change to the way business is conducted and it's because of that underpinning of information technology."

[Adapted from Jennifer Brown, "The Path to the CIO's Office," *Computing Canada,* Vol. 30, No. 1 (January 20, 2004).]

PRESENTING THE BUSINESS CASE

Up to this point, we have discussed the key issues to consider as you prepare to make the business case for a system. We have also shown you some tools for determining the value that a system adds to an organization. Now you are actually ready to make the case, to present your arguments and evidence to the decision makers in the firm. This task is much like that of a lawyer presenting a persuasive written and oral argument to win a judgment in her client's favour. You are simply trying to persuade the boss, steering committee, or board of directors to invest money in something you think is important to the business. Your job is to persuade them that you are right!

Know the Audience Matters!

Depending on the firm, a number of people might be involved in the decision-making process. In the following sections, we describe the typical decision makers and their perspectives when evaluating a business case.

The IS Manager

Obviously, as the head of the information systems department, the IS manager has overall responsibility for managing IS development, implementation, and maintenance. They should be in the best position to make recommendations to decision makers, given their expertise in applying IS to business problems. The IS manager may also rely on experts in particular areas within IS to help analyze and present useful information to decision makers. For example, a networking expert may provide detailed technical information about cost, speed, and installation procedures.

Company Executives (Vice-Presidents and Higher)

Often, executives act as the decision-making body for the firm's large investment projects. They typically represent various stakeholders or interest groups within the organization, and they may have their own agendas at stake when making decisions about expenses. For example, approving a large IS investment may mean that a new, expensive marketing idea gets delayed. Understanding the political

BRIEF CASE

Cisco and Microsoft Team Up to Offer SME Solutions

In an attempt to accelerate small- and medium-sized enterprises (SMEs) in the reseller channel, Cisco forged what the company is calling a "collaborative" partnership with Microsoft Corp. The two firms have already built two solutions that are ready for the channel. The first marries the Windows small business server with the Cisco router 831. The second combines Cisco IP communications with Microsoft's CRM software. Peter Alexander, vice-president of commercial marketing, said the products will reduce the integration burden on resellers working with SMEs. "This frees up resources for them to go after the higher-value services offerings for companies," he said. Dan McLean, lead networking analyst at IDC Canada, a technology research firm, agreed. "Both companies are being very strategic with SMEs. They want to be known as technology influencers. They are on the same page here. They want to be advisors of technology. They know more companies are interested in services and they want it to be on their products," McLean said.

McLean said he anticipates other vendors aligning themselves with Cisco as a "collaborative" partner. "Why not partner up with other vendors for SME solutions? It gives Cisco tighter integration with their products," he said. Companies such as IBM, Hewlett-Packard, and Oracle could potentially partner with Cisco in a collaborative way, McLean said. The upgraded program will be available only on the Cisco IP communications and Microsoft CRM package. Cisco and Microsoft will also create reference architecture blueprints for Microsoft's IT Solutions for SMEs. According to Alexander, this will enable resellers to provide Cisco-based secure networking infrastructures around Microsoft platforms.

Questions

1. Does this partnership between Microsoft and Cisco to target the SME sector make sense? Why or why not?
2. Why are more and more technology solution vendors targeting the SME sector?

[Adapted from Paolo Del Nibletto, "Cisco Constructs Programs around Partner Profitability," **http://www.itbusiness.ca/index.asp?theaction=61&sid=54799#**, ITBusiness.ca (February 12, 2004).]

implications of the approval process can be just as important as demonstrating a solid impact on the firm's bottom line.

Steering Committee
Sometimes, a firm uses a steering committee made up of representatives or managers from each of the functional areas within the firm. The IS manager may make her case on which projects should be pursued and why to this steering committee. The steering committee then makes its recommendation to the CEO or corporate staff. In other cases, the steering committee may have approval authority, depending on its makeup. It may, for example, include the CEO, senior vice-presidents, or other influential people in the organization. The goal of a steering committee is to get an organization's leaders, who have different interests and agendas, to share the responsibilities and risks that come with aligning IS initiatives with broader business aims. Many organizations utilize a steering committee for some aspect of their IS management.

Convert Benefits to Monetary Terms

Try to translate all benefits into monetary terms. For example, if a new system saves department managers an hour per day, try to quantify that savings in terms of dollars. Figure 2.13 shows how you might convert time savings into dollar figures. While merely explaining this benefit as "saving managers' time" makes it sound useful, managers may not consider it a significant enough inducement to warrant spending a significant amount of money. Justifying a $50,000 system because it will "save time" may not be persuasive enough. However, an annual savings of $90,000 is more likely to capture the attention of firm managers and is more likely to result in project approval. Senior managers can easily rationalize a $50,000 expense for a $90,000 savings and can easily see why they should approve such a request. They can also more easily rationalize their decision later on if something goes wrong with the system.

Devise Proxy Variables

The situation presented in Figure 2.13 is fairly straightforward. Anyone can see that the $50,000 investment is a good idea because the return on that investment is $90,000 in the first year. Unfortunately, not all cases are this clear-cut. In cases in which it is not as easy to quantify the impact of an investment, you can come up with ***proxy variables*** to help clarify what the impact on the firm will be. Proxy variables can be used to measure changes in terms of their perceived value to the organization. For example, if mundane administrative tasks are seen as a low value (perhaps a 1 on a 5-point scale) while direct contact with customers is seen as a high value (a 5), you can use these perceptions to indicate how new systems will add value to the organization. In this example, you can show that a new system will allow personnel to have more contact with customers, while at the same time reducing the administrative workload. Senior managers can quickly see that individual workload is being shifted from low-value to high-value activities.

Alternatively, you can create a customer contact scale from 1 to 5, with 1 representing very low customer contact and 5 representing very high customer contact. You can argue that currently your firm rates a 2 on the customer contact scale and that with the new information system, your firm will rate a significantly higher number on the scale.

You can communicate these differences using percentages, increases or decreases, and so on—whatever best conveys the idea that the new system is creating changes in work, in performance, and in the way people think about their work. This gives senior firm management some relatively solid data upon

Benefit:

New system saves at least one hour per day for 12 mid-level managers.

Quantified as:

Manager's salary (per hour)	$30.00
Number of managers affected	12
Daily savings (one hour saved × 12 managers)	$360.00
Weekly savings (daily savings × 5)	$1,800.00
Annual savings (weekly savings × 50)	$90,000.00

[**Figure 2.13** ➡ Converting time savings into dollar figures.]

which to base their decision. They typically like numbers. Why not make them happy?

Develop a Work Profile Matrix

Sassone and Schwartz (1986) have developed a model that has also been used to measure the benefits of information systems directly. As suggested earlier in the chapter, productivity gains have been notoriously difficult to measure with respect to information technology. Sassone and Schwartz use a two-step method to help quantify productivity benefits.

First, a ***work profile matrix*** is developed. The matrix, which consists of job categories and work categories, shows how much time is spent on each of the job categories and each of the different types of work. Figure 2.14 shows an example of a work profile matrix. To design a work profile matrix, you must first have participants fill out an activity log. Every two hours over several weeks, the activity log asks participants to indicate how much time they have spent in each category over the last two hours. This information is summarized and indicated on the matrix. The results provide you with a snapshot view of how human resources are being allocated.

Second, as in Figure 2.13, you calculate the amount of money each department is spending on each type of work, using salary figures. You compile this information into a "before system" figure. Then you make an estimate of how the new system will change the amount of time each job category spends on each type of activity. This can help quantify how a new system will change the balance of time spent by various workgroups on different activities and can make work shifts associated with the new system more salient to senior managers in terms of actual dollar savings or shifts.

Measure What Is Important to Management

One of the most important things you can do to show the benefits of a system is one of the simplest: measure what senior managers think is important. You may think this is trivial advice, but you would be surprised how often people calculate impressive-looking statistics in terms of downtime, reliability, and so on, only to find that senior managers disregard or only briefly skim over those figures. You should concentrate on the issues senior business managers care about. The "hot button" issues with senior firm managers should be easy to discover, and they are not always financial reports. Hot issues with senior managers could include cycle time (how long it takes to process an order), customer feedback, or employee morale. By focusing on what senior business managers believe to be important, you can make the business case for systems in a way that is more meaningful for those managers, which makes selling systems to decision makers much easier. Managers are more likely to buy in to the importance of systems if they can see the impact on areas that are important to them.

Case in Point: Making a Good Case at Conoco

Lloyd Belcher, manager of executive information systems (EIS) at Conoco, and Hugh Watson at the University of Georgia, outlined a methodology that was used to establish the value of Conoco's EIS (Belcher and Watson, 1993). Conoco, based in Houston, Texas, is a global energy company with oil and natural gas refineries, as well as retail gasoline outlets. The EIS at Conoco was initially developed in the early 1980s but has grown significantly to include thousands of users

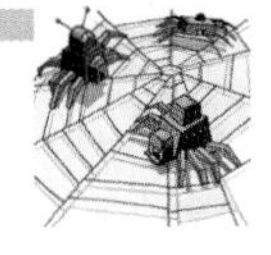

Web Search

WEB SEARCH OPPORTUNITY Visit **www.3m.com/meetingnetwork/presentations/delivering.html** and find tips on giving presentations. How can this Website help you find other ways to effectively make the business case for an information system?

Work Categories	Managers	Senior Professionals (or Senior Clerks)	Junior Professionals (or Junior Clerks)	Administrators & Technicians	Secretaries
Managerial	30%	2%	1%	0%	0%
Senior Professional	16	35	10	0	0
Junior Professional	13	26	50	1	0
Administrative	16	13	13	58	10
Clerical	7	12	14	27	76
Nonproductive*	18	12	12	14	14

*Necessary but not useful activities, such as walking to a meeting or waiting to use a photocopier or fax

[**Figure 2.14** ➥ A sample work profile matrix.]

worldwide. The IS group at Conoco was charged with conducting a complete review of the existing EIS in order to determine its value for the firm.

The IS group interviewed users of the current system from all departments, and they discussed the results with each of the respective department heads. The summaries included details about the amount of usage and which parts of the system were actually used by each department. They completed a review for each of these parts of the system to determine the purpose, costs, savings, and improvements in decision making for each department, as well as any intangible improvements gained. They combined costs and benefits of using the system into a single worksheet to show a bottom line for each part of the system (see Figure 2.15 for an example). When they completed these assessments for all applications and for all departments, they summarized the results across all departments into a single corporate report.

Using conservative assessments that focused primarily on tangible benefits and ignored most intangible benefits, Belcher and Watson were able to show that the benefits of Conoco's EIS were four to five times greater than the costs of the system. However, the analysis did show that parts of the system were not being used. As a result, these pieces of the system were eliminated while, overall, the system proved its worth and was kept.

Work to Change Mindsets about Information Systems

Perhaps the most significant change in the information systems field has been in mindsets about technology rather than in technology itself. The old way for managers to think about information systems was that information systems are a strategic necessity, or perhaps even a necessary evil. Managers cannot afford to think this way anymore. Many managers now think of information systems as a competitive asset to be nurtured and invested in. Does this mean that managers should not require a sound business case for every information systems investment? No! Does this mean that managers do not need to have facts as part of a business case for a system? No! This means that managers should stop thinking about systems as an expense and start thinking about systems as a strategic asset.

Canada's critical infrastructure (transportation; oil and gas; water; emergency services; continuity of government services; banking and finance; electrical power; and telecommunications) is largely operated through the use of computer networks, which makes protecting these networks increasingly

EIS Application Benefits Worksheets

Application: *Industry Statistical Data*

Improved Productivity	
A. Decreased information creation cost savings:	*$ 41,000*
B. New information creation cost savings:	*0*
C. Reduced information access time savings:	
(1) Average access time reduction: *1 Minute*	
(2) Average number of accesses: *108/Week*	
(3) Employee cost: *$1.00/Minute*	
(4) Savings per year: *1 * 108 * 1 * 52*	*$ 5,615*
Improved Decision Making	*0*
Information Distribution Cost Savings	
(1) Cost of document: *$2.00*	
(2) Average number of copies: *60/Week*	
(3) Savings per year: *2 * 60 * 52*	*$ 6,240*
Services Replacement Cost Savings	*0*
Total Tangible Benefits	*$ 52,856*

[**Figure 2.15** ➡ A sample EIS application benefits worksheet.]

a matter of national security. As a consequence of this concern, the Canadian Security Intelligence Service (CSIS) has applied a steadily increasing proportion of its resources to addressing this threat.

COMPETITIVE ADVANTAGE IN BEING AT THE CUTTING EDGE

To differentiate itself, an organization must utilize technologies in a way that is valuable and rare. This may involve the deployment of new, state-of-the-art technologies to do things even better, faster, and more cheaply than rivals that are using older technologies. Although firms can continually upgrade contemporary organizational information systems, such as mainframe-based transaction processing, these improvements can at best give only a short-lived competitive edge. To gain and sustain significant competitive advantage, firms must create barriers to duplication and imitation, such as by deploying new or existing technologies in clever, new ways.

Imagine, for example, that a manager decides to implement a local area network within a department to automate the operations of the office workers and to enable them to share peripheral devices, such as laser printers. This local area network is implemented using a personal computer with a Pentium 4® microprocessor with 512 MB of RAM as a server for the network. This may seem like state-of-the-art computing to the office workers, but it is likely that rival firms have already been doing this for years. The manager might upgrade the server to an Itanium 2® microprocessor with a gigabyte of RAM. Chances are that this would make the

Using Information Systems in the Military

Perhaps nothing demonstrates better the ability to use information systems for competitive advantage than the uses of modern information technologies in the military. We all know that soldiers now use high-tech equipment and weapons (see Figure 2.16). However, these types of uses of technology in war are fast becoming less important than the use of sophisticated information systems in what is being called "information warfare." Information warfare was a significant part of the U.S. military strategy in Afghanistan and Iraq. For example, prior to entering Iraq, the U.S. military bombarded Iraqi leaders with e-mails containing inducements, misinformation, and calls for surrender.

Information warfare involves the use of information systems to eavesdrop on, confuse, or subvert the enemy and other stakeholders in an attempt to either win or avoid a war. Information warfare is not new—Sun Tzu extolled its virtues in 500 BC—but advances in computing and networking technologies have increased its reach and range. One example is intercepting enemy communication in order to know what they are thinking and doing. This is known as "signals intelligence" and is a huge part of the armed forces of every developed country.

Another example of information warfare is feeding the enemy false information that would cause them to take a misstep such as being at the wrong place at the wrong time or bombing the wrong targets. On electronic networks, it becomes difficult to tell the good guys from the bad. A subtler alternative is the use of information systems to destabilize the economies and governments of enemy countries by spreading false information.

One thing is clear: information warfare is on the rise. Indeed, as a result of this reliance on technology, the all-important first step in battle has now become to take out the enemies' communications and networking infrastructure. Ironically, as information warfare becomes more prevalent, it will appear to us that there are fewer "wars." Think about it. In conventional warfare it is painfully obvious that there has been an attack when a bomb has been dropped. On the other hand, with information warfare it will be very difficult for us to see the various forms of digital attack that occur. Chances are that even the enemy that is being attacked will not notice it, or will pass it off as a systems error!

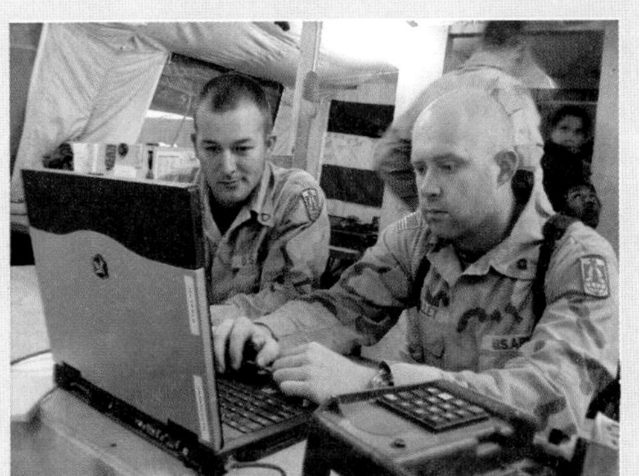

[Figure 2.16 ➡ Use of high-tech equipment has become a first step in warfare.]
Source: © AP/Wide World Photos.

COMING ATTRACTIONS

local area network run a bit faster, but would this necessarily give the firm a clear advantage over rivals? What would be the result of rivals upgrading their own networks with faster, more powerful servers? As mentioned before, these technologies are valuable, but not rare.

Consider another example. A firm implements a relational database management system for sales and inventory, giving it an edge over rivals in fulfilling orders faster and more accurately. Competitors soon do the same thing, and it becomes necessary to improve to stay ahead. The firm could improve the system and gain a relatively small, short-lived advantage over rivals. Even better, the firm could extend this idea and implement similar database applications for all of its business processes and then integrate these applications with one another. Perhaps the firm could go one step further and enable customers and suppliers to access these systems directly. There is nearly always a better way to do things, along with new technologies to help you do these things better. Clearly, if you choose to use information technology as a source of competitive advantage, you must choose to use emerging technologies in innovative ways. As they say, the best never rest.

But with the plethora of new information technologies and systems being developed, how can you possibly choose winners? Indeed, how can you even keep track of all the new breakthroughs, new products, new versions, and new ways of using technologies? For example, in Figure 2.17 we present a small subset of some new information technologies and systems, ranging from some that are here now and currently being used to some that are easily a decade away from being a reality. Which one is important for you? Which one will make or break your business? Does this list even include the one that you need to be concerned about?

The Need for Constant IS Innovation

Sir John Maddox, a physicist and for 22 years the editor of the influential scientific journal *Nature*, was quoted in *Scientific American* in 1999 as saying, "The most important discoveries of the next 50 years are likely to be ones of which we cannot now even conceive." Think about that for a moment. Most of the important discoveries of the next 50 years are likely to be things that, at present, we have no clue about. To illustrate that point, think back to the state of the Internet just 15 years ago. That is difficult to do because the Internet as we now know it did not even exist then, and certainly the Internet was not on the radar screens of business organizations back at that point. Yet, look now at how the Internet has transformed modern business. How could something so transformational as the Internet not have been easier for businesses to imagine or predict a decade ago? Well, it is difficult to see these things coming. You have to work at it.

Executives today who are serious about using information technology in innovative ways have made it a point to have their people be continually on the lookout for new information technologies that will have a significant impact on their business. Wheeler (2002b) has summarized this process nicely as the ***E-Business Innovation Cycle*** (see Figure 2.18). Like the term *electronic commerce*, ***electronic business*** refers to the use of information technologies and systems to support the business. Whereas the term *electronic commerce* is generally used to mean the use of

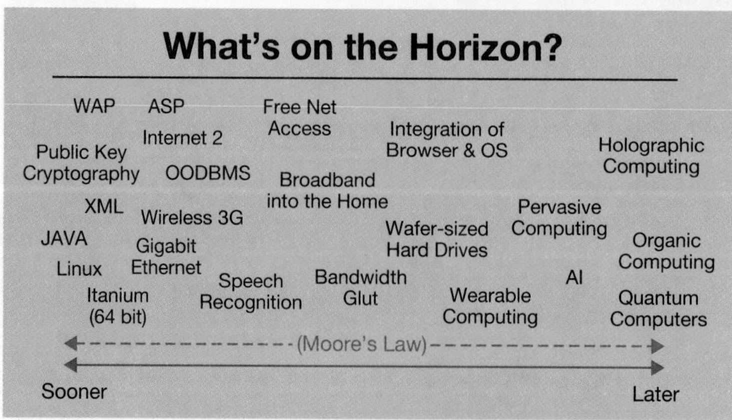

[Figure 2.17 ➡ Some new information technologies on the horizon.]

the Internet and related technologies to support commerce, the term *electronic business* includes everything having to do with the application of information and communication technologies (ICT) to the conduct of business between organizations or from company to consumer. The model essentially holds that the key to success for modern organizations is the extent to which they use information technologies and systems in timely, innovative ways.

On the vertical dimension of the E-Business Innovation Cycle is the extent to which an organization derives value from a particular information technology, and on the horizontal dimension is time. The first bubble in the lower left of the graph shows that successful organizations first create jobs, groups, and processes that are all devoted to scanning the environment for new emerging and ***enabling technologies*** that appear to be relevant for the organization. For example, an organization might designate a small group within the MIS unit as the "emerging technologies" unit and charge it with looking out for new technologies that will have an impact on the business. As part of its job, this group will pore over current technology magazines, participate in Internet discussion forums on technology topics, go to technology conferences and conventions, and have strong, active relationships with technology researchers at universities and technology companies.

Next, in the second bubble, the organization matches the most promising new technologies with current ***economic opportunities***. For example, the "emerging technologies" group might have identified advances in database management systems (and a dramatic drop in data storage costs) as a key emerging technology that now enables a massive data warehouse to be feasible. In addition, managers within the marketing function of the firm have recognized that competitors have really dropped the ball in terms of customer service and that there is an opportunity to gain customers and market share by serving customers better.

The third bubble represents the process of selecting, among myriad opportunities, to take advantage of the database and data storage advances, and addressing the current opportunity to grab customers and market share. The organization decides to implement an enterprise-wide data warehouse that

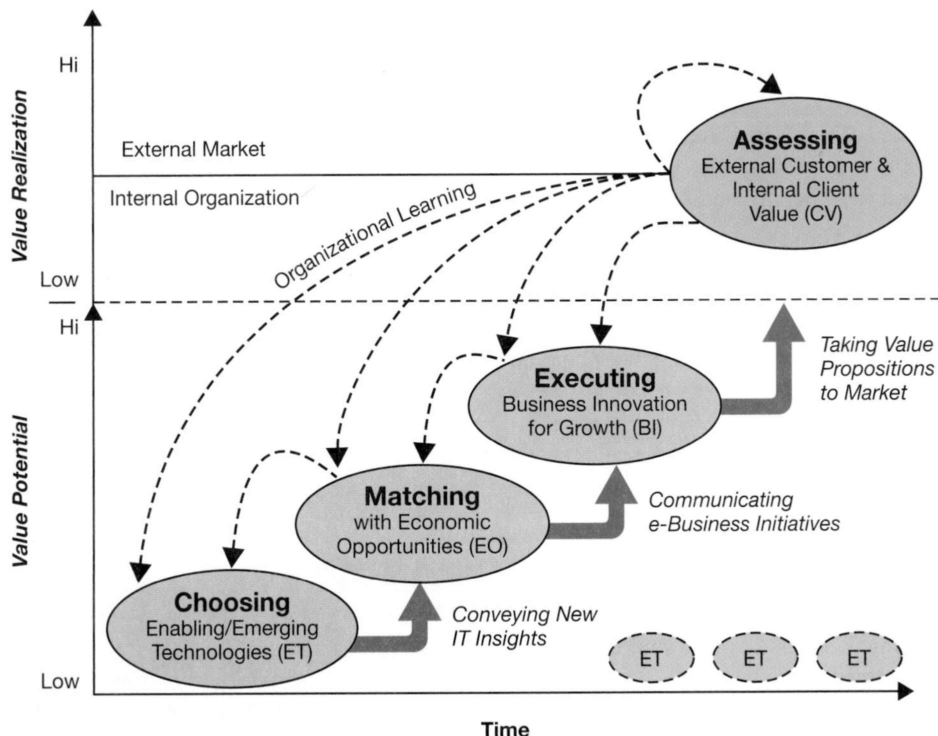

[Figure 2.18 ➡ The E-Business Innovation Cycle.[4]**]**

[4]B. C. Wheeler, "NEBIC: A Dynamic Capabilities Theory for Assessing Net-Enablement," *Information Systems Research*, Vol. 13, No. 2, pp. 125–146 (2002).

enables its employees to have at their fingertips integrated corporate-wide data and an unparalleled capability to understand, react to, and better serve customers. The fourth bubble represents the process of assessing the value of that use of technology not only to customers but also to internal clients (i.e., sales representatives, marketing managers, senior executives, etc.).

So, what is new about this way of thinking about information technology? First, this approach says that technology is important to strategy. Notice that the first bubble involves understanding, identifying, and choosing technologies that are important. The first bubble does not begin with strategy, as a traditional approach to running a business organization would suggest. In fact, many would argue that given the importance of technology today and how fast it changes, if you start with a strategy and then try to retrofit technology into your aging strategy, then you are doomed. This approach argues that you begin by understanding technology and develop a strategy from there. This approach is admittedly very uncomfortable for people who think in traditional ways and/or who are not comfortable with technology. We believe, however, that for many modern organizations, thinking about technology in this way is key.

The second way that this approach turns conventional wisdom on its head is that, like strategy, marketing takes a back seat to the technology. Think about it carefully and you will see that marketing does not come into play until later in this model. A very traditional marketing-oriented approach would be to go first to your customers and find out from them what their needs are and what you ought to be doing with technology. The trouble with this approach is that, given the rapid evolution of technology, your customers are not likely to know about new technologies and their capabilities. In some sense, they are the last place you ought to be looking for ideas about new technologies and their impact on your business. Indeed, if they know about the new technology, then chances are your competitors already do too, and that technology is not one to rest your competitive advantage on.

The third way that this approach is interesting, and potentially troubling, is that the process has to be ongoing. As shown along the time dimension along the bottom of the graph, the first bubble repeats over and over again as the "emerging technologies" group is constantly on the lookout for the "next new thing" that will revolutionize the business. The rate of information technology evolution is not likely to slow down, and innovative organizations truly cannot, and do not, ever rest.

The Cutting Edge versus the Bleeding Edge

As we hinted at above, there are limits to using emerging information systems to gain or sustain a competitive advantage. Information systems are often bought from, or built by, someone else. They are often either purchased from a vendor or developed by a consultant or outsourcing partner. In these situations, the information systems are usually not proprietary technologies owned by the organization. For example, although a soft drink company can patent the formula for a cola, or a pharmaceutical company can patent a new drug, an organization typically cannot patent its use of an information system, particularly if someone else developed it. The data in the system may be proprietary, but the information system typically is not.

Even in situations where an organization has developed an information system in-house, it usually does so with hardware, software, and networking components others can purchase. In short, rivals can copy emerging information systems, so this form of competitive advantage can be short-lived. Indeed, if use of the new system causes one organization to gain a significant advantage over others, smart rivals are quick to duplicate or improve on that use of the system.

Using emerging information systems always entails a risk. The classic example from consumer electronics is the choice of a VCR in the early days of that technology and the competing Betamax and VHS designs (see Figure 2.19). Most experts agreed that the Betamax had superior recording and playback quality, but VHS ultimately won the battle in the marketplace. People who made the "smart" choice at the time probably would have chosen a VCR with the Betamax design. Ultimately, however, that turned out to be an unfortunate choice. Other examples in the field of consumer electronics abound today. For example, when buying a stereo, should you invest in traditional compact disc technology (such as the read-only CD-ROM), recordable compact discs, digital audiotape, an MP3 device, or some other technology? Many people have been stuck with huge collections of vinyl records, cassette tapes, or (gulp!) 8-track tapes. It is easy to make poor choices in consumer electronics, or to make choices that are good at the time but soon turn out to be poor choices.

Choosing among emerging information systems is just as difficult as choosing consumer electronics. In fact, choosing emerging systems may be far more difficult, given that the evolution of many consumer electronic technologies has stabilized, whereas the evolution of emerging information systems is just beginning to heat up. Furthermore, it is far more devastating to choose a poor information system due to the size of the investment and the mission-critical nature of the system. On the other hand, choosing a suboptimal home stereo, although disappointing, is usually not devastating.

Choosing new technologies in the information systems area is like trying to hit one of several equally attractive fast-moving targets. You can find examples of the difficulty of forecasting emerging technologies in the experiences that many organizations have had in forecasting the growth, use, and importance of the Internet. The 1994 Technology Forecast prepared by the major consulting firm Price Waterhouse mentioned the word "Internet" on only five pages of the 750-page document. The next year, more than 75 pages addressed the Internet. In the 1997 briefing, the Internet is a pervasive topic. Back in 1994 it would have been difficult, perhaps even foolish, to forecast such pervasive, rapidly growing business use of the Internet today. Table 2.5 illustrates how many people and organizations have had difficulty making technology-related predictions.

[Figure 2.19 ➡ Betamax tapes required different technology inside the VCR than did VHS tapes.]

Source: © Getty Images, Inc.

Given the pace of research and development in the information systems and components area, staying current has been nearly impossible. Probably one of the most famous metrics of computer evolution has been "Moore's Law." Intel founder Gordon Moore predicted that the number of transistors that could be squeezed onto a silicon chip would double every 18 months, and this prediction has proven itself over the past 20 years. In fact, some computer hardware and software firms roll out new versions of their products every three months. Keeping up with this pace of change can be difficult for any organization.

[Table 2.5] ***Some predictions about technology that were not quite correct.***

Year	Source	Quote
1876	Western Union, internal memo	"This 'telephone' has too many shortcomings to be seriously considered as a means of communication. The device is inherently of no value to us."
1895	Lord Kelvin, president, Royal Society	"Heavier-than-air flying machines are impossible."
1899	C. H. Duell, commissioner, U.S. Office of Patents	"Everything that can be invented has been invented."
1927	H. M. Warner, Warner Bros.	"Who the hell wants to hear actors talk?"
1943	Thomas Watson, chairman, IBM	"I think there is a world market for maybe five computers."
1977	Ken Olsen, president, Digital Equipment Corp.	"There is no reason for any individuals to have a computer in their home."

Source: "The Past Imperfect," *Time Magazine* (July 15, 1996): 54.

Requirements for Being at the Cutting Edge

Certain types of competitive environments require that organizations remain at the cutting edge in their use of information systems. For example, consider an organization that operates within an environment with strong competitive forces (Porter, 1979). The organization has competitive pressures coming from existing rival firms or from the threat of entry of new rivals. It is critical for these organizations to do things better, faster, and more cheaply than rivals. These organizations are driven to deploy emerging information systems.

These environmental characteristics alone, however, are not enough to determine whether an organization should deploy emerging information systems. Before an organization can deploy new systems well, its people, structure, and processes must be capable of adapting well to change. An organization that has, say, a 10-month approval process for new information systems will probably have difficulty keeping up in an environment that forces organizations to decide on and deploy emerging information systems within a matter of weeks.

To deploy emerging systems well, people in the organization must be willing to do whatever they can to bypass and eliminate internal bureaucracy, set aside political squabbles, and pull together for the common good. Can you imagine, for example, a firm trying to deploy a Web-based order entry system that enables customers to access inventory information directly, when people in that firm do not even share such information with each other?

Organizations deploying emerging systems must also have the human capital necessary to deploy the new systems. The organization must have enough employees available with the proper systems knowledge, skills, time, and other resources to deploy these systems. Alternatively, the organization must have resources and able systems partners available to outsource the development of such systems.

The last characteristic of an organization ready for the deployment of emerging systems is that its members must have the appropriate tolerance of risk, uncertainty, and problems to be willing to deploy and use emerging information systems that may not be as proven and pervasive as more traditional technologies. If people within the organization desire low risk in their use of information systems, then gambling on cutting-edge systems will probably not be desirable or tolerable for them.

Predicting the New, New Thing

As you can see, using information systems toward a strategic end will be difficult to sustain. As Bakos and Treacy (1986) and others have argued, if you are using information systems to gain a competitive advantage in the area of operating efficiencies, it is likely that your rivals can just as easily adopt the same types of information systems and achieve the same gains. For example, you might set up a Website that enables customers to check on the status of their order without requiring help from a customer service representative, and this might enable you to cut costs. Rivals could, however, easily copy this approach and match your cost reductions. The competitive advantage thus turns into strategic necessity for anyone in this industry.

On the other hand, there are ways to use information systems to gain a competitive advantage in a way that is easier to sustain. For example, Bakos and Treacy argued that if you can use information systems to make your products or services rare or unique, or to cause your customers to invest heavily in you so that their switching costs are high, then you are better able to develop competitive advantage that is sustainable over the long haul. For example, you might combine heavy investments in computer-aided design systems with very bright engineers in order to perfect your product and make it unique, something relatively difficult to copy. Alternatively, you might use a customer relationship management system to build an extensive database containing the entire history of your interaction with each of your customers, and then use that system to provide very high-quality, intimate, rapid, customized service that would convince customers that if they switched to a rival, it would take them years to build up that kind of relationship with the other firm.

How can you possibly predict the next wave of emerging information systems? Well, you have help. Michael Lewis wrote the best-selling book *The New, New Thing: A Silicon Valley Story* (W. W. Norton, 2000), which tells the story of Jim Clark, a noted high-tech entrepreneur who is famous for the unprecedented business "hat trick" of creating three separate billion-dollar technology companies—

Silicon Graphics, Netscape, and Healtheon. As a result, Jim Clark is known as someone who is very good at knowing what the next new major information technology breakthrough will be. Most of us do not have that same level of business or technology acumen. Fortunately, we can take our cue from Jim Clark and others like him.

In any event, while using information systems for competitive advantage has become a given for modern organizations, it can be difficult to achieve and sustain, and it can be expensive. Go forth and conquer, but do so with your eyes wide open!

KEY POINTS REVIEW

1. **Discuss how organizations can use information systems for automation, organizational learning, and strategic support.** Automating business activities occurs when information systems are used to do a business activity faster or more cheaply. IS can be used to help automate. It can also be used to improve aspects of an operation in order to gain dramatic improvements in the operation as a whole. When this occurs, technology is said to help us learn because it provides information about its operation and the underlying work process that it supports. Using information systems strategically occurs when the technology is used to enable organizational strategy and to help the firm gain or sustain competitive advantage over rivals
2. **Describe information systems' critical, strategic importance to the success of modern organizations.** Using information systems to automate and learn about business processes is a good start. However, information systems can add even more value to an organization if they are conceived, designed, used, and managed with a strategic approach. To apply information systems strategically, you must understand the organization's value chain and be able to identify opportunities in which you can use information systems to make changes or improvements in the value chain to gain or sustain a competitive advantage. In order to create a competitive advantage, the system needs to be rare and valuable. In order to create an advantage that is sustainable, the system needs to resist imitation and duplication. This requires a change in mindset from thinking about information systems as an expense to be minimized to thinking of information systems as an asset to be invested in.
3. **Formulate and present the business case for a system and understand why it is sometimes difficult to do so.** Making the business case is the process of building and presenting the set of arguments that show that an information system is adding value to the organization and/or its constituents. It is often difficult to quantify the value that an information system provides. To formulate a business case for an information system, you must understand the nature of the industry—its stage of maturity, its regulation, and the nature of its competition or rivalry. You must also understand the particular business strategy of your organization in order to make an effective business case for systems. In short, technology investments should be closely linked to the business strategy of the organization because these investments are becoming one of the major vehicles by which organizations can achieve their strategy. After you gain an understanding of your organization's position in the marketplace, its strategy for investing in systems that add value, and firm-level implementation factors, you can quantify the relative costs and benefits of the system. Considering all of these factors simultaneously will help you formulate an effective business case. In order to make a convincing presentation, you should be specific about the benefits this investment will provide for the organization. To do this, you must convert the benefits into monetary terms, such as the amount of money saved or revenue generated. If you have difficulty identifying specific monetary measures, you should devise some proxy measures to demonstrate the benefits of the system. Alternatively, you could develop a work profile matrix to help build the business case for a system. Finally, make sure that you measure things that are important to the decision makers of the organizations. Choosing the wrong measures can yield a negative decision about a beneficial system.
4. **Explain why and how companies are continually looking for new ways to use technology for competitive advantage.** Organizations are finding clever ways to use new technologies to help them do things faster, better, and more cheaply than rivals. Being at the technological cutting edge has its disadvantages. Given that new technologies are not as stable as traditional ones, relying on emerging systems can be problematic. Because constantly upgrading to newer and better systems is expensive, relying on emerging systems can hurt a firm financially. In addition, using emerging information systems for competitive advantage can be short-lived; competitors can quickly jump on the technological bandwagon and easily mimic the same system. As a result, many organizations find themselves on the technological bleeding edge rather than the cutting edge. Not every organization should deploy emerging information systems. Those organizations that find themselves in highly competitive environments are probably most in need of deploying new technologies to stay ahead of rivals. To best deploy these new technologies, organizations must be ready for the changes that will ensue, have the resources necessary to deploy new technologies successfully, and be tolerant of the risk and problems involved in being at the cutting edge. Deploying emerging information systems is essentially a risk/return gamble: the risks are relatively high, but the potential rewards are great. Firms today have people, and in some cases special units, that scan the environment, looking out for emerging and enabling technologies that can help their firm. They then narrow down the list to technologies that match with or create economic opportunities the firm faces. Next, they choose a particular technology, or set of technologies, and implement them in

a way that enables them to gain or sustain competitive advantage. Finally, they assess these technology projects in terms of their value not only to internal people and groups but also to external clients and partners. This process is ongoing, as information technologies and systems continually evolve.

KEY TERMS

automating 36
best-cost provider 40
business process reengineering (BPR) 46
competitive advantage 34
computer-aided design 45
differentiation strategy 40
electronic business 62
E-Business Innovation Cycle 62
economic opportunities 63
enabling technologies 63
extranet 44
informating 37
intangible benefits 54
intangible costs 53
learning organization 37
low-cost leadership strategy 40
making the business case 46
nonrecurring costs 52
organizational learning 37
organizational strategy 39
proxy variables 58
recurring costs 52
strategic planning 39
system effectiveness 48
system efficiency 48
tangible benefits 54
tangible costs 53
total quality management (TQM) 39
value chain 42
value chain analysis 41
work profile matrix 59

REVIEW QUESTIONS

1. Describe six ways companies can achieve a competitive advantage.
2. Compare and contrast automating and learning.
3. Describe the attributes of a learning organization.
4. List five general types of organizational strategy.
5. What are some of the problems in measuring productivity changes?
6. List the three factors you should consider when making the business case for an information system.
7. Who might be on a steering committee, and what is the purpose of the committee?
8. Define a proxy variable and give an example.
9. Describe the productivity paradox.
10. Compare and contrast tangible and intangible benefits and costs.

SELF-STUDY QUESTIONS

Answers are at the end of the Problems and Exercises.

1. ________ is using technology as a way to help complete a task within an organization faster and, perhaps, more cheaply.
   A. Automating
   B. Learning
   C. Strategizing
   D. Processing
2. Which of the following is an intangible benefit?
   A. negative benefits
   B. qualitative benefits
   C. quantitative costs
   D. positive cash flows
3. Which of the following is **not** improving the value chain?
   A. improving procurement processes
   B. increasing operating costs
   C. minimizing marketing expenditures
   D. selling more products
4. Which of the following is **not** one of the three types of arguments commonly made in the business case for an information system?
   A. Fear
   B. Fact
   C. Faith
   D. Fun
5. A company is said to have ________ when it has gained an edge over its rivals.
   A. a monopoly
   B. profitability
   C. competitive advantage
   D. computer advantage
6. The IS manager has the overall responsibility for the ________ of the information systems.
   A. management, development, implementation, and maintenance
   B. development, implementation, and maintenance
   C. management, development, and maintenance
   D. management, development, and implementation

7. Many firms now use the Internet for business-to-business interactions, and these systems are called ________.
   A. Internets
   B. extranets
   C. intranets
   D. infonets

8. A ________ consists of job and work categories, along with how time is spent in each of those categories.
   A. budget
   B. work budget
   C. work profile matrix
   D. professional matrix

9. Making the ________ is the process of building and presenting the set of arguments that show that an information system is adding value to the organization.
   A. organizational chart
   B. organizational case
   C. law case
   D. business case

10. Besides business industry and strategic factors, other implementation-related factors must be considered when making the business case for systems, including the type of ________.
   A. organization
   B. culture
   C. political environment
   D. all of the above

PROBLEMS AND EXERCISES

1. Match the following terms with the appropriate definitions:
   ____ Value chain analysis
   ____ Tangible costs
   ____ Extranet
   ____ Competitive advantage
   ____ Business case
   ____ Learning organization
   ____ Total quality management
   ____ Value chain
   ____ Work profile matrix
   ____ Proxy variable
   a. An approach in which people within an organization are constantly monitoring what they do to find ways to improve quality of operations, products, services, and everything else about the firm
   b. Costs that are quantifiable or have physical substance
   c. The set of arguments that illustrate that an information system is adding value to the organization and/or its constituents
   d. The use of the Internet by firms for business-to-business interactions
   e. A substitute variable (such as customer contact) expressed on a 5-point scale from low to high that is used in place of an information system's intangible benefit, which is difficult to quantify
   f. The edge a firm has over its rivals
   g. An organization that is able to learn, grow, and manage its knowledge well
   h. A matrix consisting of job and work categories that is used to show how much time is spent by each of the job categories on different types of work
   i. Identification of opportunities to use information systems for competitive advantage
   j. The process of adding value to products and/or services throughout the organization

2. After reading this chapter, it should be fairly obvious why an IS professional should be able to make a business case for a given system. Why, however, is it just as important for non–IS professionals? How are they involved in this process? What is their role in information systems planning?

3. Search the World Wide Web for items related to end-user development. What information did you find? Why is end-user development difficult to track in terms of productivity? What are some of the measurement problems associated with end-user development? How can these problems be eliminated? Prepare a 10-minute presentation of your findings to the rest of the class.

4. Why is it important to look at industry factors when making a business case? What effect might strong competition have on IS investment and use? What effect might weak competition have on IS investment and use? Why?

5. Argue for or against the following statement: "When making the business case, you should concentrate on the 'hot buttons' of the decision makers and gloss over some of the other details."

6. What role does the organizational culture play in IS investments? Is this something that can be easily adjusted when necessary? Why or why not? Who is in control of a firm's organizational culture? Do you have personal experiences with this issue?

7. Why can it be difficult to develop an accurate cost–benefit analysis? What factors may be difficult to quantify? How can this be handled? Is this something that should just be avoided altogether? What are the consequences of that approach?

8. Have you ever rented a car over the Web? Research car rentals, including Avis Rent A Car, over the Web, and then telephone the car agency to find the following answers. What types of vehicles are available for what price and for how long? Is there a minimum age required to rent a vehicle? Is insurance a consideration? Is it difficult to rent a car in a particular area of Canada or it is easy? How do you make a rental reservation?

9. Within a small group of classmates, describe any involvement you have had with making the business case for a system. To whom were you making the case? Was it a difficult sell? Why? Did you follow the guidelines set forth in this chapter? How did your business case differ from those of others in your group? Were you successful? Why or why not? Were they successful? Why or why not?

10. Choose one of the Brief Cases in this chapter or a firm that is familiar to you. Of the five industry factors presented in the chapter (Porter's model), which is the most significant for this

organization in terms of IS investment and development? Why? Which is the least significant? Why?

11. Discuss the following in a small group of classmates or with a friend. Describe a situation from your own experience in which a system's cost–benefit analysis showed a negative result when based on tangible factors but the system was still implemented. Was the implementation decision based on intangible factors? Have these intangible factors proven themselves to be worth the investment in this system? Was it a harder sell because of these intangible factors?

12. Choose one of the Brief Cases in this or another chapter or a firm that is familiar to you. Determine the length of time it has taken for various information systems to show their productivity improvements. Was it a long time? Why did it take so long? Was it longer than expected? Why or why not? Search the Internet to find additional anecdotes about IS productivity improvements. You may want to search through *CIO Canada* magazine online at **www.itworldcanada.com/Pages/Docbase/BrowsePublication.aspx?Publication=CIO** to get started. Summarize one of these articles for the rest of the class.

13. Why shouldn't every organization deploy cutting-edge emerging information systems? What are some of the recommended characteristics of an organization that are necessary for that organization to successfully deploy emerging information systems?

ANSWERS TO THE SELF-STUDY QUESTIONS

1. A 2. B 3. B 4. D 5. C 6. A 7. B 8. C 9. D 10. D

Case 1: *Using IS for Efficiency, Effectiveness, and Competitive Advantage*

No one can imagine a successful business organization of today not using information systems. IS is being seen as the driving force for most companies, and the primary means through which strategic advantage can be gained or sustained. Teradyne Inc. is a manufacturing company that specializes in building equipment that tests computer chips. In its zeal to stay ahead of its competitors, the company has focused on the use of IS to lower its costs and increase its efficiency. The company installed a new virtual private network (VPN) that allows its employees to log in through its firewall, irrespective of their location in the world, by entering six digits from small palm tokens that they carry with them. These tokens generate certain random numbers, which are matched with another set of numbers generated by a computer located behind the company's firewall. Once the numbers match, Teradyne employees from any part of the world can log in to the system and perform a variety of functions, such as conducting performance evaluations with their supervisors, who may be located in another city or country, or modifying their benefit packages. The company also installed some new software that enables it to service the equipment of its customers by remotely logging in to the customer's server and conducting repairs.

Staples Inc. has also focused on using information systems to enhance its customer service. New software now enables Staples' customer service representatives to chat directly with shoppers using an online chat tool. The company is also installing kiosks in each of its stores, which will enable customers to go directly to the Staples Website and browse through its large inventory if they cannot find a certain product in store.

L.L. Bean, on the other hand, is focusing on using IS for increasing its Internet sales. It has recently acquired software to track who visits its site and which banners or links on its site are most commonly clicked on. The ultimate goal of L.L. Bean is to transform the "clicks to sales."

Kompass has shown that in addition to adopting a new information system, firms also have to undergo other corresponding changes as well. Kompass is a mid-sized company in Ireland whose primary business is to provide a directory of Irish businesses. Its primary purpose is to link buyers and sellers. Kompass links buyers accurately to the products of their choice and helps sellers to target their potential clients. Initially, the company published its directory on paper, but with the advent of new technology, it now offers a fully developed search engine over the Web. In the late 1990s, the company realized that the Web technology may provide it with the opportunity to deliver its directory of Irish businesses to a global market. Unlike many other companies, Kompass realized that in order to adopt this new technology, the company would have to go through significant remodelling and repositioning. At first, the company conducted a detailed evaluation of the strategic opportunities that the Internet provided. The firm's business model, along with its position, staffing, and so on, were also evaluated. The evaluation revealed that the adoption of the new technology would help the company to position itself in a new marketplace (the digital marketplace) and would help it to increase its market share. The company executives also realized through their detailed surveys that in order to succeed, the company would have to align its new use of the Internet with the existing business strategy and structure. The alignment of this new technology took place at three levels.

At the first level, the firm aligned its Internet strategy with its business strategy. The firm decided that the Internet would become core to its business and would help it to enhance its relationship with its customers and deliver better options to them. At the second level, the firm aligned the new technology with its existing marketing approach. The firm's executives realized that in order to gain from this new technology, the Internet could not be treated just as a delivery channel, but it had to form the foundation of the organization's products. As a result, they made attempts to make the Internet central to the product development process. Finally, the firm also aligned the new technology with its human resource management processes. They decided that new human resources, specialized training, tools, and technical skills would be required to make this new venture a success. Thus, they formed a new division called Kompass Internet, whose primary responsibility was to oversee all aspects of this new business of the company.

While many other companies have attempted to use information systems to experience quick gains, such as lowered costs or increased market share, Kompass has focused on integrating the new technology into its existing business processes in order to gain long-term benefits. This is probably why today Kompass' Internet strategy is seen as one of the success stories of the business use of the Internet.

[Adapted from E. Medina, "N.E. Companies Focus on Creative Use of Technology: It's Vital to Boost Efficiency, Competitive Edge," *Boston Globe* (June 11, 2001): C2; C. O'Kelley, "Electronic Commerce: A Case Study in Competitive Advantage," *Accountancy Ireland* 31 No. 4 (August 1999): 39–40; **www.kompass.ie**.]

Discussion Questions

1. Do you think that the companies mentioned in the first part of the case (Teradyne, Staples, etc.) will experience significant gains from their implementation of the new information technologies?
2. What did Kompass do differently that made the adoption of the Internet technology a success in its organization?
3. In order to gain strategically, what should an organization focus on while implementing a new information technology?

Case 2: *Are Desktops the Weakest Link?*

An exasperated executive stares helplessly at the hourglass icon on her computer screen while a program crashes. Urgent e-mails linger in an inaccessible in-box, while a harried technician sets aside other tasks to investigate the glitch. The speed of e-business slackens as precious moments of productivity are lost. This is a familiar scenario in the corporate world, where few people can do their jobs without access to e-mail, the Internet, and all the data stored on their personal computers. In fact, managing and operating desktop computers and other indispensable technology is a huge expense and a major headache for both small and large businesses, yet it's an issue that many organizations are only now coming to grips with.

After investing millions of dollars to integrate enterprise-wide software and connect with customers and suppliers, companies are finding that the technology on their employees' desktops has become "the weakest link," according to Bill Dupley, business solutions manager at Hewlett-Packard (Canada) Co. HP is one of many vendors offering new ways for companies to manage their technology. The company claims that it can save businesses 50 percent in technology costs over four years with a solution that involves powerful backroom servers performing many of the functions now carried out by desktop PCs. Because this involves a considerable investment in new equipment, it makes the most sense for organizations with more than 1,000 end users.

International Business Machines Corp., purveyors of on-demand service for managing the desktop environment, calls end-user systems the next frontier in the quest for lower tech costs. IBM's approach is different from HP's: it involves the use of standard desktop technology and helps enterprises of all sizes buy hardware as and when they need it. At the same time, it reduces the need for support staff by taking advantage of self-healing and automation tools. According to Eric Johnson, head of wireless and pervasive computing at IBM Global Services, companies can realize 30-percent savings by reducing support costs.

At Accenture Inc., partner Michael Sivo says his firm can offer SMEs an effective desktop management solution whose focus is to keep a tight lid on which technologies are available to employees, while being flexible enough to let workers choose from a list of software deemed appropriate for their job functions. It also uses self-help applications, automation software, and a call-centre help desk model to reduce labour costs. Without this kind of approach, "The status quo support costs are exhausting the budgets that these companies have, and that's preventing them from adding new capabilities," Sivo says.

One way to cut costs is to extend the number of years each computer is used before being replaced. In the 1990s, it was generally believed that personal computers would prove useful for a maximum of three years, by which time new hardware and the demands of software upgrades would render them virtually useless. But both desktops and laptops are now powerful enough to last four years, according to technology research firm Gartner Inc. There is, of course, a downside: as aging computers wear out, they require more and more technical support.

Augie Onesi, vice-president of PC-LAN at RBC Financial Group, has found ways of cutting the costs associated with his company's 50,000 desktops without compromising productivity. Onesi claims the key to stretching the refresh cycle to four years is to adopt a centralized strategy that provides everyone with similar and compatible hardware, and software that can be upgraded and maintained in a standardized way. One potential problem with this approach is that end users often want the latest gadgets and productivity tools. "We took the approach that we'll give you what the bank feels is required for you to do your job," he says, though it's necessary to "stay ahead of the curve" in selecting technology for employees; otherwise, they bring their own devices to work, creating a potentially disruptive situation and placing additional demands on support staff.

Onesi notes that the time spent by workmates trying to solve problems when systems are down does not show up on any expense line. "If you don't manage the environment, your costs will get out of control and the reality is you won't know where those costs are going."

[Adapted from Kevin Marron, "End-user Friendly," *Report on Business Magazine* (January 30, 2004).]

Discussion Questions

1. Do you think that office-based data, applications, and computing power should mainly reside on desktops or servers? What are the strategic implications of each approach?
2. How much authority should employees have to configure office computers? What are the advantages and disadvantages of end-user–managed systems?
3. How often do you upgrade your computer? What approaches might firms take to lengthen this cycle?

Chapter 3

Preview

In the last chapter, you learned how organizations are using information systems for competitive advantage. In this chapter, we will discuss how a very important category of information system, databases and database management systems, allow organizations to store and manipulate their key information easily.

People in organizations rely on information about customers, products, invoices, suppliers, markets, transactions, and competitors. In large organizations, this information is stored in databases that can be billions (giga-) or trillions (tera-) of bytes in size. If an organization lost this data, it would have difficulty pricing and selling its products or services, cutting payroll cheques for its employees, and even sending out mail.

After reading this chapter, you will be able to do the following:

1. Describe why databases have become so important to modern organizations.
2. Describe what databases and database management systems are and how they work.
3. Explain how organizations are getting the most from their investment in database technologies.

[Figure 3.1 ➥ The Big Picture: focusing on database management.]

Database Management

OPENING: Fire Marshal Helps to Develop a Province-Wide Database

Ontario's Office of the Fire Marshal (OFM) is a partner in an effort to construct an online database so that important information about fire loss, emergency response, fire prevention, and public education can be shared and analyzed by the province's 500-plus municipal fire departments. A key objective of the project is to make this information available to each department, said Carol-Lynn Chambers, operations manager of field fire protection services at the Office of the Fire Marshal. The database allows a fire chief to access his or her own statistics, analyze trends, and make comparisons with peers. This information can positively affect decision making, aid risk assessments, and bolster business cases for more resources when chiefs go before local councils, said Chambers.

Often, the big challenge is that fire services are "data rich" and "information poor," added Chambers. "How we pull that information together and make sense of it to tell the story is really critical. And it's difficult to do that without a common language. Having some electronic tool that's easy to use is really a balancing act because as soon as we move to a technology solution, we need to balance functionality with something that's going to be friendly to all users." Chambers emphasized that the database would need to be Internet-based so all departments, including those in remote northern communities, can easily access it.

At the same time, the quality of data and the need to respect confidentiality cannot be compromised, said Chambers, adding that this factor played a large role in the final decision. The group decided to adopt a Web-based tool that did not require any third-party software beyond a Web browser. The system was built around an Oracle database and incorporated standardized data based on XML specifications. The database was constructed so that users could see different "views" of the data, depending on what they were searching for. Users could then "drill-down" into the database to find specific items of interest. Benchmarking tools were also available to evaluate performance against organizational and/or time-dependent targets.

Lou Agosta, industry analyst with Forrester Research, said the OFM's approach is definitely the right one. Taking incident-related figures and using them to measure risks is especially important, he said. "If you can't measure it, how can you manage it? This is a principle to be guided by." Agosta added that the undertaking will likely produce "a complex, yet important and useful, database."

[Adapted from Scott Foster, "Ontario Begins Search for Fire-fighting Database," ITBusiness.ca **http://www.itbusiness.ca/index.asp?theaction=61&sid=54211#** (November 25, 2003).]

[**Figure 3.2** ➥ The OFM uses a province-wide database to increase fire safety and awareness.]

Source: © Robert Landan/CORBIS/MAGMA.

In terms of our guiding framework—The Big Picture—this chapter focuses on one of the essential elements of "information" systems (see Figure 3.1). We begin by discussing the importance of database technology for the success of organizations. The chapter continues by describing the key activities involved in designing and using modern databases. We conclude by examining how organizations are utilizing this stored information for competitive advantage.

DATABASE MANAGEMENT FOR STRATEGIC ADVANTAGE

Database technology, a collection of related data organized in a way to facilitate data searches, is vital to an organization's success. Increasingly, we are living in an Information Age. Information once taken for granted or never collected at all is now used to make organizations more productive and competitive. Stock prices in the market, potential customers who meet a company's criteria for its products' target audience, and the credit rating of wholesalers and customers are all types of information. Think about this book you are reading, which is in itself information. The publisher had to know available authors capable of writing this book. The publisher also had to have information on you, the target audience, to determine that writing this book was worthwhile and to suggest a writing style and collection of topics. The publisher had to use market information to set a price for the book, along with information on reliable wholesalers and distribution partners to get the books from the publisher to you, the consumer.

In addition to using databases to create this book, the publisher also uses databases to keep track of the book's sales, to determine royalties for the authors, to set salaries and wages for employees, to pay employees, to prospect for new book opportunities, to pay bills, and to perform nearly every other function in the business. For example, to determine royalties for authors on books sold, the publisher must collect information from hundreds of bookstores and consolidate it into a single report. Large publishers, such as Prentice Hall/Pearson Education, rely on computer databases to perform these tasks.

Other organizations also make use of the database process used to create and sell this book. For example, Lands' End uses databases to design and produce its clothing catalogue and market and sell products. Companies such as Lands' End also use databases to gather and store information about customers and their purchasing behaviour. Sears and Eddie Bauer produce tailor-made catalogues and other mailings for specific individuals based on the purchasing information stored in corporate databases. In addition, all transactional Websites rely on databases to manage inventory, store and manipulate customer information, process financial transactions, and so on. A large component of e-business is built on the productive use of databases.

Given these examples, it should be no surprise that database management systems have become an integral part of the total information systems solution for many organizations. Database management systems allow organizations to retrieve, store, and analyze information easily. Failure to properly build, populate, and manage databases can lead to organizational problems, such as increased costs or reduced levels of customer service. For example, difficulties with database development and administration contributed to the massive cost overruns with the Canadian Firearms Centre's gun registry.

Next we examine some basic concepts, advantages of the database approach, and how databases are managed.

The Database Approach: Foundation Concepts

The database approach now dominates nearly all of the computer-based information systems used today. To understand databases, we must familiarize ourselves with some terminology.

In Figure 3.3, we compare database terminology (middle column) with equivalents in a library (left column) and a business office (right column). We use ***database management systems (DBMSs)*** to interact with the data in databases. A DBMS is a software application with which you create, store, organize, and retrieve data from a single database or several databases. FileMaker Pro is an example of a popular DBMS for personal computers; another is Microsoft Access. In the DBMS, the individual database is a collection of related attributes about entities. An ***entity*** is something you collect data about, such as people or classes (see Figure 3.4). We often think of entities as ***tables,*** where each row is a ***record*** and each column is an ***attribute*** (also referred to as a field). A record is a collection of related attributes about a single entity. Each record typically consists of many attributes, which are individual pieces of information. For

BRIEF CASE

A Centralized Global Database for Major Drilling

Major Drilling Group International Inc., based in Moncton, New Brunswick, is a contractor to mining companies around the world for drilling work and core sampling. Major Drilling was using a software package that ran on client-server architecture, which proved problematic for a global company. "We were running into issues with it, architecturally as well as performance, as well as maintenance issues," said CIO Stephane Godbout. "The company that built it has actually gone under. From a risk management perspective, we needed to look at alternatives." The company required a system that could interface with its financial tools and handle contracts, invoicing, and employee time management. "It was actually a challenging project for us," said Mounir Hilal, director of professional services for Tenrox, based in Montreal. "Terminology [played] a big role there. There's a lot of things that they use in their industry that obviously we had to get familiarized with.... It was a challenging project but definitely very interesting at the same time."

Tenrox's Web-based solution was chosen so the company's offices across the world could share data from a central pool in Moncton. "No matter if you're in South America, U.S., Canada, Australia, Mongolia—they'll be connecting here," said Godbout. Under the old system, each office had to maintain a copy of the company database and update it independently. Data was shared across the organization, but often too late for management to act on it. "The information does roll up... but usually after the fact. We find out about it kind of late in the game if there was a performance issue or if there's something wrong going on," said Godbout.

Another issue for Godbout was compliance with the *Personal Information Protection and Electronic Documents Act* (see Chapter 9 for more information). Tenrox users could see only as much information as was necessary to perform their jobs, he said. "It was also one of my requirements that the product give me the ability to control data access at the micro level. I truly believe that people should only see what they're required to see from a business perspective."

Questions

1. What are some advantages of adopting a centralized database?
2. What are some disadvantages?

[Adapted from Neil Sutton, "Major Drilling Group Bores into Global Software Project," **http://www.itbusiness.ca/index.asp?theaction=61&sid=54895**, ITBusiness.ca (February 23, 2004).]

example, a name and social insurance number are attributes about a person.

Advantages of the Database Approach

Before there were DBMSs, organizations used the file-processing approach to store and manipulate data electronically. Data were usually kept in a long, sequential computer file, which was often stored on tape. Information about entities often appeared in several different places throughout the information system, and the data was often stored along with, and sometimes embedded within, the programming code that used the data. People had not yet envisioned the concept of separately storing information about entities in nonredundant databases, so files often had repetitive data about a customer, supplier, or another entity. When someone's address changed, it had to be changed in every file where that information occurred, an often tedious process. Similarly, if programmers changed the code, they typically had to change the corresponding data along with it.

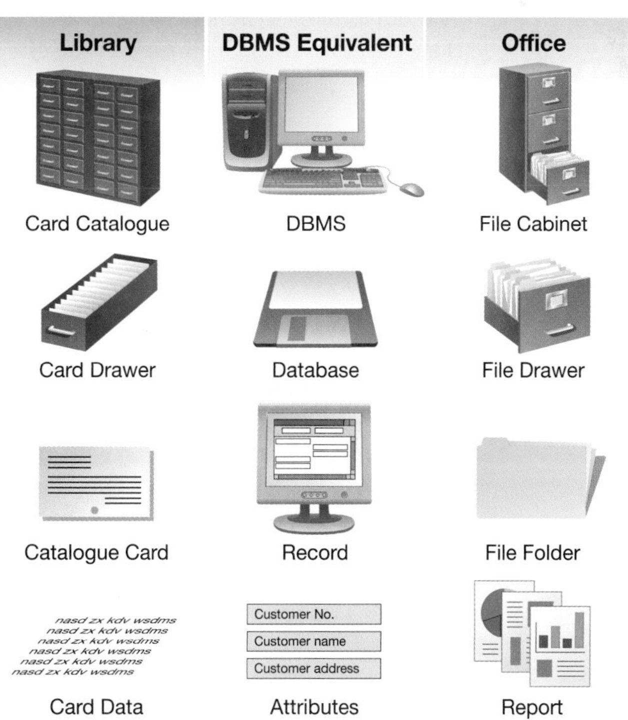

[Figure 3.3 ➥ Computers make the process of storing and managing data much easier.]

ID Number	Last Name	First Name	Street Address	City	Province	Postal Code	Major
209345	Jung	Judy	1242 N. Maple	Kingston	Ontario	K7L 3N9	Recreation
213009	Beaubien	Louis	3400 E. Longvi	Kingston	Ontario	K7L 3P4	Business Management
345987	Fleury	Monika	367 Ridge Roa	Kingston	Ontario	K7L 4L1	Aeronautical Engineering
457838	Wade	Benjamin	12 Long Lake	Kingston	Ontario	K7L 2S2	Computer Science
459987	Angel	Rita	8009 Walnut	Kingston	Ontario	K7L 6N1	Sociology
466711	Park	Charles	234 Jamie Lan	Kingston	Ontario	K7L 2N7	Pre-Medicine
512678	Stone	Brian	3837 Wood's E	Kingston	Ontario	K7L 1P6	Law
691112	Clark	Andrew	988 Woodbridg	Kingston	Ontario	K7L 1B0	Political Science
910234	Singh	Parv	1234 S. Grant	Kingston	Ontario	K7L 3P4	Civil Engineering
979776	Gilmore	Doug	109 Hoosier Av	Kingston	Ontario	K7L 3N8	Psychology
983445	Huff	Sid	989 College	Kingston	Ontario	K7L 2N7	Sports Science

[**Figure 3.4** ➥ This sample data table for the entity Student includes 8 attributes and 11 records.]

It is possible for a database to consist of only a single file or table. However, most databases managed under a DBMS consist of several files, tables, or entities. A DBMS can manage hundreds, or even thousands, of tables simultaneously by linking the tables as part of a single system. The DBMS helps us manage the tremendous volume and complexity of interrelated data so that we can be sure that a change is automatically made for every instance of that data. For example, if a student or customer address is changed, that change is made through all parts of the system where that data might occur. Using the DBMS prevents unnecessary and problematic redundancies of the data, and the data are kept separate from the programming code in applications. The database need not be changed if a change is made to the code in any of the applications. Consequently, there are numerous advantages to using a database approach to managing organizational data, and these are summarized in Table 3.1. Of course, moving to the database approach comes with some costs and risks that must be recognized and managed (see Table 3.2).

[Table 3.1] ***Advantages of the database approach.***

Advantages	Description
Program–data independence	Much easier to evolve and alter software to changing business needs when data and programs are independent.
Minimal data redundancy	Single copy of data ensures that data storage is minimized.
Improved data consistency	Eliminating redundancy greatly reduces the opportunities for inconsistency.
Improved data sharing	Easier to deploy and control data access using a centralized system.
Increased productivity of application development	Data standards make it easier to build and modify applications.
Enforcement of standards	A centralized system makes it much easier to enforce standards and rules for data creation, modification, naming, and deletion.
Improved data quality	Centralized control, minimized redundancy, and improved data consistency help to enhance the quality of data.
Improved data accessibility	Centralized system makes it easier to provide access for new personnel within or outside organizational boundaries.
Reduced program maintenance	Information changed in the central database is replicated seamlessly throughout all applications.

[Table 3.2] ***Costs and risks of the database approach.***

Cost or Risk	Description
New, specialized personnel	Conversion to the database approach may require hiring additional personnel.
Installation and management cost and complexity	Database approach has higher up-front costs and complexity in order to gain long-term benefits.
Conversion costs	Extensive costs are common when converting existing systems, often referred to as *legacy systems,* to the database approach.
Need for explicit backup and recovery	A shared corporate data resource must be accurate and available at all times.
Organizational conflict	Ownership—creation, naming, modification, and deletion—of data can cause organizational conflict.

Nonetheless, most organizations have embraced the database approach because most feel that the advantages far exceed the risks or costs.

Effective Management of Databases

Now that we have outlined why databases are important to organizations, we can talk about how organizational databases can be managed effectively. The ***database administrator (DBA)*** is responsible for the development and management of the organization's databases. The DBA works with the systems analysts (described in Chapter 8) and programmers to design and implement the database. The DBA must also work with users and managers of the firm to establish policies for managing an organization's databases. The DBA implements security features for the database, such as designating who can look at the database and who is authorized to make changes. The DBA should not make these decisions unilaterally; rather, the DBA merely implements the business decisions made by organizational managers. A good DBA is fundamental to adequately leveraging the investment in database technology.

WHEN THINGS GO WRONG

Royal Bank Screens Data for Illegal Activity

RBC Financial implemented a tool from software firm SAS to help it comply with anti-terrorism and anti–money laundering regulations that went into effect after September 11, 2001. Canadian federal authorities, such as the Financial Transactions and Report Analysis Centre of Canada (FINTRAC), the nation's financial intelligence unit, require that banks review their customer records to search for suspected terrorists. Until recently, RBC had conducted those searches manually. "We've been using some technology—basic SQL queries and stuff like that—but essentially it's been a manual process," said the bank's anti–money laundering officer, Karim Rajwani. RBC has bought data cleansing and data matching tools from SAS subsidiary Dataflux to automate that process. "If you're looking for a terrorist's name in your data source records, variations on that name can be matched," explained Gary Love, head of risk management strategy for SAS Canada.

"These tools that RBC has taken from SAS are key to ensure information and the intelligence they service within Royal Bank are in fact highly accurate, as opposed to receiving a lot of false positives, as they did previous to this," he added. "We feed in our client data and we feed in the various control lists provided by the regulators, and the tool matches the client name with the terrorist name," said Rajwani. "If there's a potential match, it kicks it out as an alert." The lists that RBC matches names against include FINTRAC's registry of known terrorists. A positive result must be reported to FINTRAC. The *Personal Information Protection and Electronic Documents Act* (PIPEDA), which came into effect for all Canadian companies on January 1, 2004, is a piece of legislation designed to regulate the way companies collect and use personal data. (See Chapter 9 for more information on PIPEDA.) Like all other Canadian businesses, RBC will have to comply with that legislation, but "the reporting obligations under the terrorism regulations... supersede privacy," said Rajwani. He added, however, "From our perspective, privacy is obviously paramount to our business and we will not automatically report a client until [we go] through the process. We must have reasonable grounds to suspect before we can report."

[Adapted from Neil Sutton, "RBC Tracks Potential Terrorists with SAS Tools," *Computing Canada,* Vol. 29, No. 23 (December 8, 2003).]

KEY DATABASE ACTIVITIES

In this section, we describe the key activities involved in the design, creation, use, and management of databases (for more information, see Hoffer, Prescott, and McFadden, 2002). We start by describing how people use databases, beginning with the entry of data.

There are literally thousands of databases available on the Internet for you to query to find information. Most of these databases are maintained by businesses trying to sell products; however, there are many other interesting databases that you might not be aware of. For example, if you go to **www.agso.gov.au/oracle/nukexp_query.html**, you can query about nuclear explosions; the database includes information about the location, time, and size of explosions around the world since 1945. Another interesting database is CanLII **www.canlii.org**, maintained by the Federation of Law Societies of Canada. CanLII makes practically all federal and provincial statutes and regulations available in electronic format. Go to one of these sites and report back to your class on what you found when you queried the database.

Entering and Querying Data

DBMS software enables end users to create and manage their own database applications. At some point, data must be entered into the database.

A clerk or other data entry professional creates records in the database by entering data. This data may come from telephone conversations, preprinted forms that must be filled out, historical records, or electronic files (see Figure 3.5A). Most applications enable us to use a graphical user interface (GUI) (see Figure 3.5B) to create a ***form***, which typically has blanks where the user can enter the information or make choices, each of which represents an attribute within a database record. This form presents the information to the user in an intuitive way so the user can easily see and enter the data. The form might be online or printed, and the data could even be entered directly by the customer rather

Application For Employment — Pine Valley Furniture

Personal Information

Name: Date:

Social Insurance Number:

Home Address:

City, Province, Postal Code

Home Phone: Business Phone:

Citizenship:

Position Applying For

Title: Salary Desired:

Referred By: Date Available:

Education

High School (Name, City, Province):

Graduation Date:

Business or Technical School:

Dates Attended: Degree, Major:

Undergraduate University:

Dates Attended: Degree, Major:

Graduate University:

Dates Attended: Degree, Major:

Pine Valley Furniture

References

Form #2019
Last Revised:9/15/04

(a)

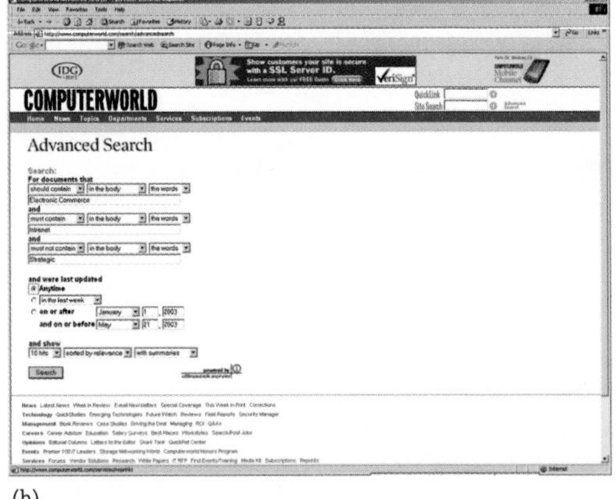

(b)

[**Figure 3.5** ➥ (a) A preprinted form used for gathering information that could be stored in a database. (b) A computer-based form used for gathering information that could be stored in a database.]

Source: Benjamin/Cummings Pub. [3.5A] **www.computerworld.com** [3.5B].

than by a data entry clerk. Forms can be used to add, modify, and delete data from the database.

To retrieve information from a database, we use a ***query***. ***Structured Query Language (SQL)*** is the most common language used to interface with databases. Figure 3.6 is an example of an SQL statement used to find students who earned an "A" in a particular course. These grades are sorted by student ID number.

Writing SQL statements requires time and practice, especially when you are dealing with complex databases with many entities or when you are writing complex queries with multiple integrated criteria—such as adding numbers while sorting on two different attributes. Many DBMS packages have a simpler way of interfacing with the databases—using a concept called ***query by example (QBE)***. QBE capabilities in a database enable us to fill out a grid, or template, in order to construct a sample or description of the data we would like to see. Modern DBMS packages, such as Microsoft Access, let us take advantage of the drag-and-drop features of a GUI to create a query quickly and easily. Conducting queries in this manner is much easier than typing the corresponding SQL commands. In Figure 3.7, we provide an example of the QBE grid from Microsoft Access' desktop DBMS package.

```
SELECT DISTINCTROW STUDENT_ID, GRADE
FROM GRADES
WHERE GRADE="A"
ORDER BY STUDENT_ID;
```

[**Figure 3.6** ➡ This sample SQL statement would be used to find students who earned an "A" in a particular course and to sort that information by student ID number.]

Creating Database Reports

DBMS packages include a report generation feature. A ***report*** is a compilation of data from the database that is organized and produced in printed format. Reports are typically produced on paper, but they can be presented to users on-screen as well. ***Report generators*** retrieve data from the database and manipulate (aggregate, transform, or group) and display it in a useful format.

An example of a report is a quarterly sales report for a restaurant. Adding the daily sales totals, grouping them into quarterly totals, and displaying the results in a table of totals creates a quarterly sales report. Reports are not limited to text and numbers. Report writers enable us to create reports using any data in the databases at whatever level we choose. For example, we could add to the

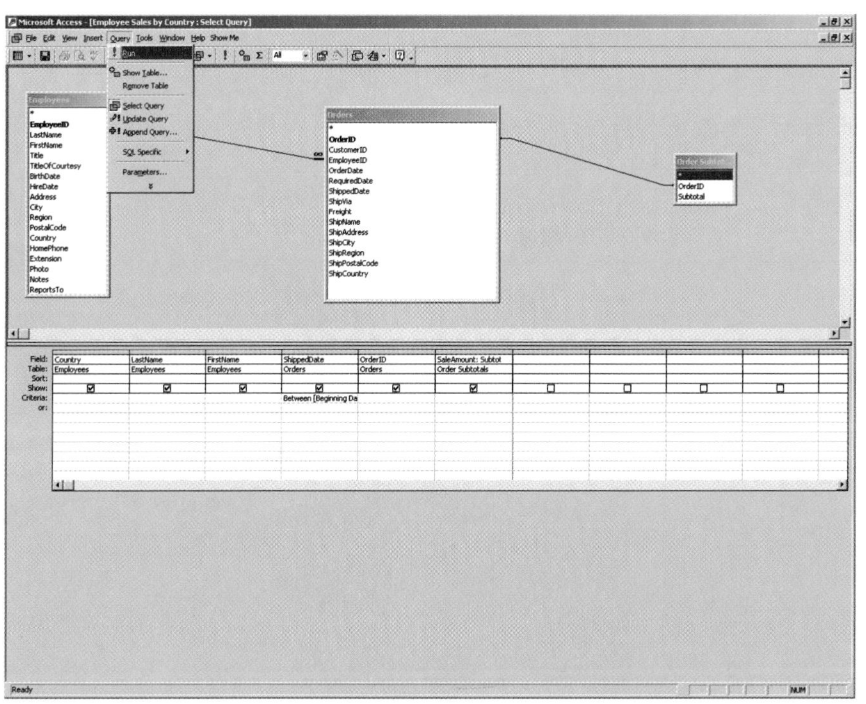

[**Figure 3.7** ➡ Query by example allows you to fill out a form to define what information you want to see.]

Source: Microsoft.

CAREER IMPLICATIONS

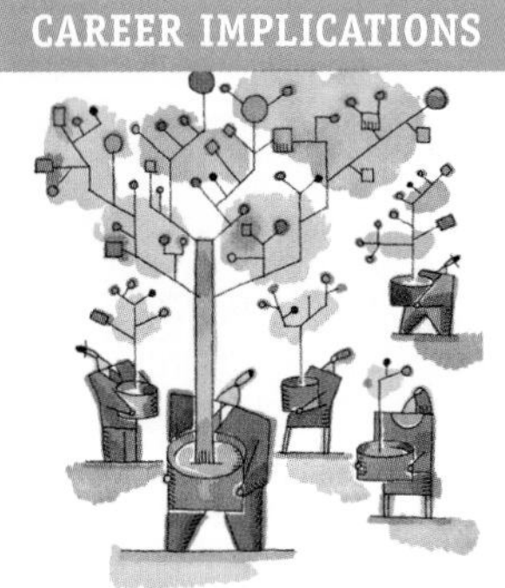

Accounting and Finance

Gesco was born in 1938 when George Shnier moved from Manitoba to Toronto to sell rubber products for two American manufacturers. In time, Shnier focused his energies on a new product, sponge rubber, and as he prospered, he was joined in the business by his five brothers. The Shnier brothers built their company into a giant in the floor covering industry, selling everything from carpeting and no-wax vinyl to Italian-made ceramic tiles—and, of course, sponge rubber cushioning. Mark Shnier is Gesco's vice-president for customer service and logistics. "Gesco is a complicated company," he says, "because we have a huge geography, an extensive line of products, and over 3,000 active customers ranging from 'mom and pop' stores to Home Depot." With a hundred sales reps, sales managers, and sales support staff, thousands of customers, and a territory 5,600 km across, Gesco needed a way to see and share the account data gathered daily by each of Gesco's field reps. Mark knew that such data, gathered and analyzed, could be a crucial corporate asset. "It shouldn't just be in the sales rep's head," he says. "If we lose a sales rep, we don't want to lose all the information about that territory." In turn, Gesco wanted a better way to send data to its sales reps. "They are constantly bombarded with product information from us: pricing, promotions, policies and procedures. Most would use a combination of three-ring binders, filing, and e-mail inboxes to keep track." Quips Mark, "We would blast something out to our reps and most of them would immediately lose it." Gesco adopted an online database solution from Intuit, called QuickBase. Field reps could log on to the Web and input data into the database, which would then become instantly available to sales managers and head office. Once the reps had captured the info, QuickBase summarized all the accounts, and sales managers could designate a certain number per region as "key accounts" to focus on for growth. Documents can also be posted to the database for use instantly by reps in the field.

restaurant report breakdowns of the data that show the average daily sales totals by days of the week. We could also show the quarterly sales totals in a bar chart, as shown in Figure 3.8. Each of these reports could be presented to the user either on paper or online. We could create automatic links between the underlying sales data located in the database and the attributes on the report in which the underlying data is used so the reports could be updated automatically.

Database Design

The best database in the world is no better than the data it holds. Conversely, all the data in the world will do you no good if it is not organized in a manner in which there are few or no redundancies and in which you can retrieve, analyze, and understand it. The two key elements of an organizational database are the data and the structure of that data.

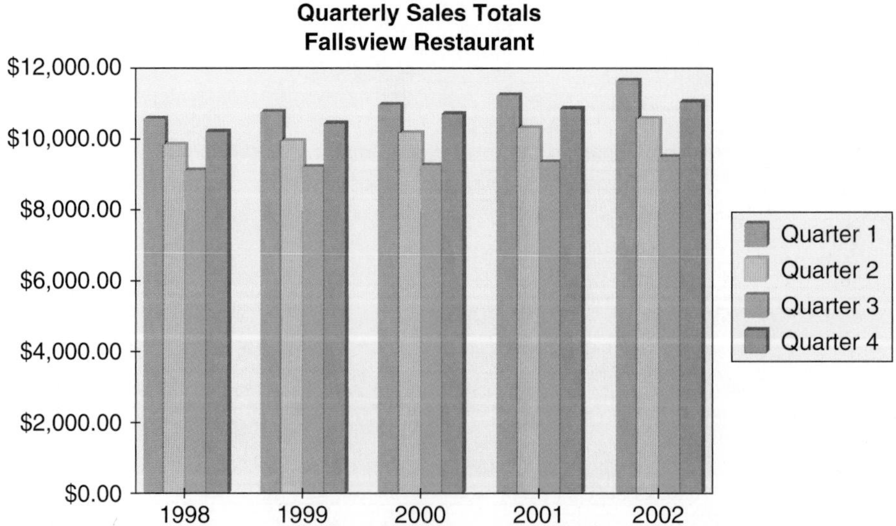

[**Figure 3.8** ➡ The quarterly sales report could show either text and numbers or a bar chart and could include the level of detail captured by the database data.]

Let us refer back to the library example in Figure 3.3 to understand the structure of data. We know that we can find books in the library by using the card catalogue. The card catalogue is a structure for finding books. Each book has three cards, one each for the title, the author, and the subject. These classifications—title, author, subject—are a model, or representation, of the data in this system. Likewise, we must have a data model for databases. A ***data model*** is a map or diagram that represents entities and their relationships.

Much of the work of creating an effective organizational database is in the modelling. If the model is not accurate, the database will not be effective. A poor data model will result in data that is inaccurate, redundant, or difficult to search. If the database is relatively small, the effects of a poor design might not be too severe. In a corporate database, however, there are many entities, perhaps hundreds or thousands. In this case, the implications of a poor data model can be catastrophic. A poorly organized database is difficult to maintain and process—thus defeating the purpose of having a database management system in the first place. Undoubtedly, your school maintains databases with a variety of entity types—for example, students and grades—with both of these entities having several attributes. Attributes of a Student entity might be Student ID, Name, Campus Address, Major, and Phone. Attributes of a Grades entity might include Student ID, Course ID, Section Number, Term, and Grade (see Figure 3.9).

For the DBMS to distinguish among records correctly, each instance of an entity must have one unique identifier. For example, each student has a unique Student ID. Note that using the student name, or most other attributes, would not be adequate because students may have the exact same name, live at the same address, or have the same phone number. Consequently, when designing a database, we must always create and use a unique identifier called a ***primary key*** for each type of entity, in order to store and retrieve data accurately. In some instances, the primary key can also be a combination of two or more attributes, in which case it is called a ***combination primary key***. An example of this is the Grades entity shown in Figure 3.9, where the combination of Student ID, Course ID, Section Number, and Term uniquely refers to the grade of an individual student, in a particular class (section number), from a particular term.

Attributes not used as the primary key can be referred to as ***secondary keys*** when they are used to identify one or more records within a table that share a common value. For example, a secondary key in the Student entity shown in Figure 3.9 would be Major when used to find all students who share a particular major.

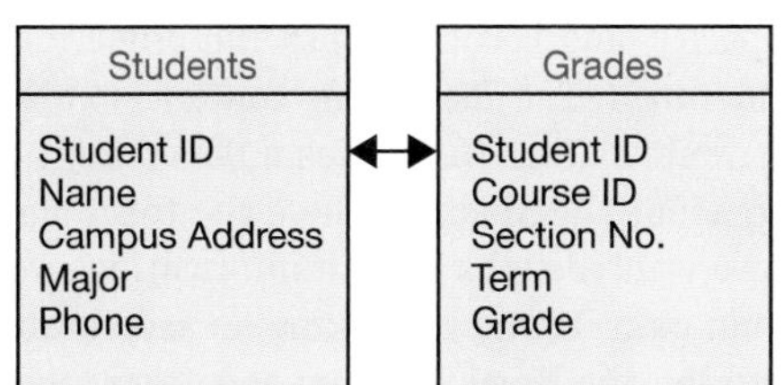

Students

Student ID	Name	Campus Address	Major	Phone
100261	Hae Yung Yim	123 Any Avenue	Finance	335-2211
210312	Peter Tingling	1200 Wolf Street #12	Marketing	335-8702

Grades

Student ID	Course ID	Section No.	Term	Grade
100261	MIS 5110	2	F'04	D+
100261	MIS 5110	1	F'04	A–
210312	MIS 5110	3	S'05	B+

[**Figure 3.9** ➥ The attributes for and links between two entities—students and grades.]

CAREER IMPLICATIONS

Operations Management

B.C. Assessment spent 2004 expanding its nascent online property database by offering municipalities access to older records and opening it up to the private sector. The provincial Crown agency, which classifies and assesses the market value of all property in B.C., launched Assessment LinkBC in June 2003. The online tool allows any B.C. municipality to access a server containing several years' worth of property data via a secure Website. A local government might want to identify all the properties in a specific area for mapping purposes, for example. Until recently, municipalities would either have to dig this information out through a legacy system called Data Advice or send a request to B.C. Assessment, which could take up to five days to fulfill.

Assessment LinkBC, which is based on Cognos' EBI Series, allows users not only to access the information but also to compare it with the property data of other areas. "The sky's the limit," said Peter Barber, B.C. Assessment's marketing manager. "They can just slice and dice however they want." The organization had initially planned Assessment LinkBC as a tool for internal use only, Barber said, but later realized it would make sense to offer it to the province's 200 local governments as well. Right now the database goes back four years but Barber said future enhancements could see B.C. Assessment offer data stretching back 10 years. "We'll also look at more specific information—around bedrooms, bathrooms, square footage," he said.

Ontario's Municipal Property and Assessment Corp. (MPAC) offers its own online service, MyProperty, which allows users to access basic property information. Ontario and B.C. are the only provinces to conduct market value assessments at the provincial level, which is why there are few systems like Assessment LinkBC available elsewhere. "The rest of [the country] is still doing assessment by city," he said. "It makes it difficult to build systems like this." The value, he said, comes when the information becomes more efficiently delivered to the users being served. "When somebody dies in Ontario, the family has to register that death in three different places," he said by way of example. "What e-government is trying to do is to represent a single face—to businesses, to constituents or other departments—so they only have to go to one place."

[Adapted from Shane Schick, "B.C. Assessment to Open Doors to Property Database," **http://www.itbusiness.ca/index.asp?theaction=61&sid=54547#**, ITBusiness.ca (January 15, 2004).]

Associations

To retrieve information from a database, it is necessary to associate, or relate, information from separate tables. The three types of associations among entities are one-to-one, one-to-many, and many-to-many. Table 3.3 summarizes each of these three associations and how they should be handled in database design for a basketball league.

To understand how associations work, consider Figure 3.10, which shows four tables—Home Stadium, Team, Player, and Games—for keeping track of the information for a basketball league. The Home Stadium table lists the Stadium ID, Stadium Name, Capacity, and Location, with the primary key underlined. The Team table contains two attributes, Team ID and Team Name, but nothing about the Stadium where the team plays. If we wanted to have such information, we could gain it only by making an association between the Home Stadium and Team tables.

[Table 3.3] ***Rules for expressing associations among entities and their corresponding data structures.***

Relationship	Example	Instructions
One-to-One	Each team has only one home stadium, and each home stadium has only one team.	Place the primary key from each table in the table for the other entity as a foreign key.
One-to-Many	Each player is on only one team, but each team has many players.	Place the primary key from the entity on the one side of the relationship as a foreign key in the table for the entity on the many side of the relationship.
Many-to-Many	Each player participates in games, and each game has many players.	Create a third entity/table and place the primary keys from each of the original entities together in the third table as a combination primary key.

Home Stadium

Stadium ID	Stadium Name	Capacity	Location

Team

Team ID	Team Name

Player

Player ID	Player Name	Position

Games

Team ID (1)	Team ID (2)	Date	Final Score

[**Figure 3.10** ➥ Tables used for storing information about several basketball teams, with *no* attributes added so that associations cannot be made.]

For example, if each team has only one home stadium, and each home stadium has only one team, we have a one-to-one relationship between the team and the home stadium entities. In situations in which we have one-to-one relationships between entities, we place the primary key from one table in the table for the other entity and refer to this attribute as a foreign key. In other words, a ***foreign key*** refers to an attribute that appears as a non-primary key attribute in one entity and as a primary key attribute (or part of a primary key) in another entity. By sharing this common—but unique—value, entities can be linked, or associated, together. We can choose in which of these tables to place the foreign key of the other. After adding the primary key of the Home Stadium entity to the Team entity, we can identify which stadium is the home for a particular team and find all the details about that stadium (see section A in Figure 3.11).

When we find a one-to-many relationship—for example, each player plays for only one team, but each team has many players—we place the primary key from the entity on the one side of the relationship, the team entity, as a foreign key in the table for the entity on the many side of the relationship, the player entity (see section B in Figure 3.11). In essence, we take from the one and give to the many, a Robin Hood strategy.

When we find a many-to-many relationship (for example, each player plays in many games, and each game has many players), we create a third, new entity—in this case, the Player Statistics entity and corresponding table. We then place the primary keys from each of the original entities together into the third, new table as a new, combination primary key (see section C in Figure 3.11).

You may have noticed that by placing the primary key from one entity in the table of another entity, we are creating a bit of redundancy. We are repeating the data in different places. We are willing to live with this bit of redundancy, however, because it enables us to keep track of the interrelationships among the many pieces of important organizational data that are stored in different tables. By keeping track of these relationships, we can quickly answer questions such as, "Which players on the Raptors played in the game on February 16 and scored more than 10 points?" In a business setting, the question might be, "Which customers purchased the 2005 forest green Ford Escape from Heidi Bjerkan at the Keltic Motors Ford dealership in Antigonish, Nova Scotia, during the first quarter of 2005, and how much did

A. One-to-one relationship: Each team has only one home stadium, and each home stadium has only one team.

Team

Team ID	Team Name	*Stadium ID*

B. One-to-many relationship: Each player is on only one team, but each team has many players.

Player

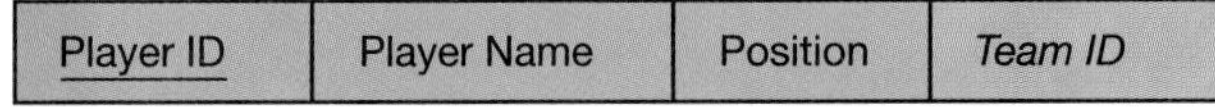

Player ID	Player Name	Position	*Team ID*

C. Many-to-many relationship: Each player participates in many games, and each game has many players.

Player Statistics

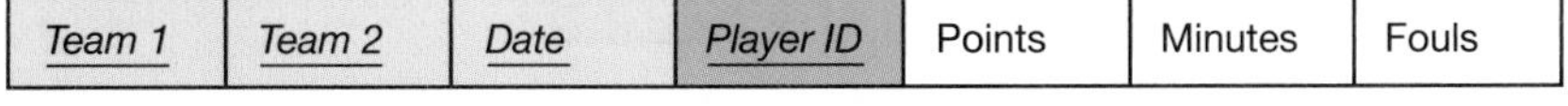

Team 1	*Team 2*	*Date*	*Player ID*	Points	Minutes	Fouls

[**Figure 3.11** ➥ Tables used for storing information about several basketball teams, with attributes added in order to make associations.]

BRIEF CASE

How to Cross the U.S. Border in 15 Seconds

A unified system for Canadian–U.S. commuters is one step closer, as the NEXUS program continues to grow—this time in Quebec. NEXUS, a fast-clearance crossing program operated jointly by the Canada Customs and Revenue Agency (CCRA), Citizenship and Immigration Canada (CIC), and the United States Bureau of Customs and Border Protection (CBP), has operated on the Ontario/Michigan and B.C./Washington borders since mid-2001. New crossings between St.-Bernard-de-Lacolle, Quebec, and Champlain, New York, and between Saint-Armand/Philipsburg, Quebec, and Highgate Springs, Vermont, opened in 2004, marking the first time the program has come to Quebec or Vermont.

NEXUS allows regular border-crossers express entry through customs checkpoints on both sides of the border via special lanes designated for cardholders only (see Figure 3.12). The program costs $80 (US$50) for a five-year membership. Admission to the program requires screening by both Canadian and U.S. authorities, as well as an in-person interview. "Once the client is really deemed by both countries to be low-risk, then the client is invited to an appointment for an interview. If the interview goes well, then a card is printed out right there on the spot," said Dominique McNeely of the CCRA. Fingerprints are also taken as part of the biometric screening process sometimes used at secondary border checkpoints.

At the moment, the card works somewhat differently on different sides of the border. The cards themselves, manufactured by Intermec, contain RF transmitters, which, in the U.S., broadcast to proximity sensors as the cardholder's vehicle approaches a checkpoint. "The antenna captures the particular signal unique to that card, sends a search into the NEXUS database, and a digital photo of the person and various biographical data (citizenship, name, documents that are needed, etc.) are presented on a monitor in the inspection booth," said George St. Clair of the CBP. From that point, the U.S. inspector will make a visual identification between the driver and the cardholder's picture on the screen, ask if the individual has anything to declare, and release him or her. Should a further identification be required, the driver will be sent to secondary screening for a fingerprint ID check. Individuals entering Canada may not yet take advantage of the card's radio technology, and instead simply hand their card to an inspector as one might normally hand over a passport. However, the time saved for NEXUS

Web Search

WEB SEARCH OPPORTUNITY Using one or more search engines, research the origins of the entity-relationship diagramming notation. Who invented this notation and when? See if you can find an answer to this question at **www.peterchen.com**. How many different versions of the notation can you find? If you search on entity relationship or variations of it, you will likely find URLs to many class lecture notes. See how many different ways instructors draw ERDs. Why are there several notations rather than one international standard notation? Write a report of your findings to submit to your instructor.

each pay?" This kind of question would be useful in calculating the bonus money Heidi should receive for that quarter or in recalling those specific vehicles in the event of a recall by the manufacturer.

Entity-Relationship Diagramming

A diagramming technique called an ***entity-relationship diagram (ERD)*** is commonly used when designing databases, especially when showing associations among entities. To create an ERD, you draw entities as boxes and draw lines between entities to show relationships. Each relationship can be labelled on the diagram to give additional meaning to the diagram. For example, Figure 3.13 shows an ERD for the basketball league data previously discussed. From this diagram, you can see the following associations:

- Each Home Stadium has a Team.
- Each Team has Players.
- Each Team participates in Games.
- For each Player and Game there are Game Statistics.

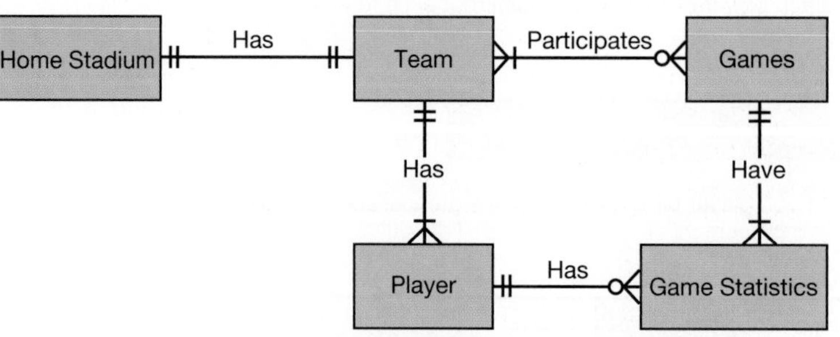

[**Figure 3.13** ➡ An entity-relationship diagram showing the relationships among entities in a basketball league database.]

cardholders is not so much in the actual interview process, but in their ability to utilize special NEXUS lanes that have far shorter lineups than the regular lanes. St. Clair noted that while border wait times are different at different crossings, the time saved by using a NEXUS lane can be significant, depending on where you are. "Waits at the Peace Arch [on the B.C./Washington] border in the summertime can average two hours or more. Cars at the end of the line at 2:00 p.m. on a Wednesday were waiting an hour and 45 minutes. Cars in the NEXUS lane were waiting 15 seconds."

Construction of special approach lanes at sites such as the Peace Arch has further aided NEXUS commuters in staying out of checkpoint gridlock. At present, the NEXUS system is not nationally integrated in the United States, and each checkpoint draws on its own NEXUS member database for that specific site. In 2004, however, both the U.S. and Canada plan to launch national enrollment databases that will allow NEXUS members to cross with ease at any NEXUS lane, whether they signed up in Detroit, Michigan, or Fort Erie, Ontario. "NEXUS was designed originally as a commuter system. As a commuter lane, we figured everyone was local. We're realizing now they're not, and we're making amends," said St. Clair. On the

[Figure 3.12]

Source: Hugh Conroy—Whatcom Council of Governments.

Canadian side, plans to roll out a national NEXUS enrollment database will be paired with existing licence plate photography technology.

Questions

1. Does NEXUS sound to you like a good idea? Could it also work for cross-border air traffic?
2. Can you think of other examples of how IT-enabled solutions can facilitate international trade?

[Adapted from Liz Clayton, "All Roads Meet at the NEXUS," **http://www.itbusiness.ca/index.asp?theaction=61&sid=54397#**, ITBusiness.ca (December 17, 2003).]

When designing a complex database with numerous entities and relationships, ERDs are very useful. They allow the designer to talk with people throughout the organization to make sure that all entities and relationships have been found.

The Relational Model

Now that we have discussed data, data models, and the storage of data, we need a mechanism for joining entities that have natural relationships with one another. For example, there are several relationships among the four entities we described previously—students, instructors, classes, and grades. Students are enrolled in classes. Likewise, instructors teach multiple classes and have many students in their classes in a semester. It is important to keep track of these relationships. We might, for example, want to know which courses a student is enrolled in so that we can notify her instructors that she will miss courses because of an illness. The primary DBMS approach, or model, for keeping track of these relationships among data entities is the relational model. Other models are also used to join entities with commercial DBMSs—the hierarchical, network, and object-oriented models—but this is beyond the scope of our discussion (see Hoffer, Prescott, and McFadden, 2002).

The most common DBMS approach in use today is the ***relational database model***. A DBMS package using this approach is referred to as a relational DBMS, or RDBMS. With this approach, the DBMS views and presents entities as two-dimensional tables, with records as rows and attributes as columns. Tables can be joined when there are common columns in the tables. The uniqueness of the primary key, as mentioned earlier, tells the DBMS which records should be joined with others in the corresponding tables. This structure supports very powerful data manipulation capabilities and linking of interrelated data. Database files in the relational model are three-dimensional: a database has rows (one dimension) and columns (a second dimension), and can contain a row of data in common with another file (a third dimension). This three-dimensional

Web Search

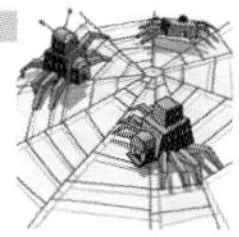

WEB SEARCH OPPORTUNITY
Search the Web and digital libraries to discover the origins of the relational database model. Who invented this data modelling notation? When did it first appear? What roles have E. F. Codd and C. J. Date played in the development of the relational database model? What database management products use this model of data today? Are there any special programming languages for these products? Is there a standard programming language for relational database management products? A very important standards organization for information technology is the American National Standards Institute, whose Website is **www.ansi.org**—check them out. What is the relationship of this organization to the relational database model? Summarize your results in a brief report to submit to your instructor.

Department Records

Department No.	Dept Name	Location	Dean
Dept A			
Dept B			
Dept C			

Instructor Records

Instructor No.	Inst Name	Title	Salary	Dept No.
Inst 1				
Inst 2				
Inst 3				
Inst 4				

[**Figure 3.14** ➡ With the relational model, we represent these two entities, department and instructor, as two separate tables and capture the relationship between them with a common column in each table.]

database is potentially much more powerful and useful than traditional, two-dimensional, "flat file" databases (see Figure 3.14).

A good relational database design eliminates unnecessary data duplications and is easy to maintain. To design a database with clear, nonredundant relationships, you perform a process called normalization.

Normalization

To be effective, databases must be efficient. Developed in the 1970s, ***normalization*** is a technique to make complex databases more efficient and more easily handled by the DBMS (Date, 1995). To understand the normalization process, let us return to the scenario in the beginning of this chapter. Think about your report card. It looks like nearly any other form or invoice. Your personal information is usually at the top, and each of your classes is listed, along with an instructor, a class day and time, the number of credit hours, and a location. Now think about how this data is stored in a database. Imagine that this database is organized so that in each row of the database, the student's identification

Student ID#	Student Name	Campus Address	Major	Phone	Course ID	Course Title	Instructor Name	Instructor Location	Instructor Phone	Term	Grade
A121	Joy Egbert	100 N. River Street	MIS	555-7771	MIS 350	Intro. MIS	Van Deventer	T240C	555-2222	F'05	A
A121	Joy Egbert	100 N. River Street	MIS	555-7771	MIS 372	Database	Hann	T240F	555-2224	F'05	B
A121	Joy Egbert	100 N. River Street	MIS	555-7771	MIS 375	Elec. Comm.	Chatterjee	T240D	555-2228	F'05	B+
A121	Joy Egbert	100 N. River Street	MIS	555-7771	MIS 448	Strategic MIS	Chatterjee	T240D	555-2228	F'05	A-
A121	Joy Egbert	100 N. River Street	MIS	555-7771	MIS 474	Telecomm	Gilson	T240E	555-2226	F'05	C+
A123	Larry Mueller	123 S. River Street	MIS	555-1235	MIS 350	Intro. MIS	Van Deventer	T240C	555-2222	F'05	A
A123	Larry Mueller	123 S. River Street	MIS	555-1235	MIS 372	Database	Hann	T240F	555-2224	F'05	B-
A123	Larry Mueller	123 S. River Street	MIS	555-1235	MIS 375	Elec. Comm.	Chatterjee	T240D	555-2228	F'05	A-
A123	Larry Mueller	123 S. River Street	MIS	555-1235	MIS 448	Strategic MIS	Chatterjee	T240D	555-2228	F'05	C+
A124	Mike Guon	125 S. Elm	MGT	555-2214	MIS 350	Intro. MIS	Van Deventer	T240C	555-2222	F'05	A-
A124	Mike Guon	125 S. Elm	MGT	555-2214	MIS 372	Database	Hann	T240F	555-2224	F'05	A-
A124	Mike Guon	125 S. Elm	MGT	555-2214	MIS 375	Elec. Comm.	Chatterjee	T240D	555-2228	F'05	B+
A124	Mike Guon	125 S. Elm	MGT	555-2214	MIS 474	Telecomm	Gilson	T240E	555-2226	F'05	B
A126	Jackie Judson	224 S. Sixth Street	MKT	555-1245	MIS 350	Intro. MIS	Van Deventer	T240C	555-2222	F'05	A
A126	Jackie Judson	224 S. Sixth Street	MKT	555-1245	MIS 372	Database	Hann	T240F	555-2224	F'05	B+
A126	Jackie Judson	224 S. Sixth Street	MKT	555-1245	MIS 375	Elec. Comm.	Chatterjee	T240D	555-2228	F'05	B+
A126	Jackie Judson	224 S. Sixth Street	MKT	555-1245	MIS 474	Telecomm	Gilson	T240E	555-2226	F'05	A-
...	...	...	...	...	...	...	...	...	...	...	...

[**Figure 3.15** ➡ Database of students, courses, instructors, and grades with redundant data.]

number is listed on the far left. To the right of the student ID are the student's name, local address, major, phone number, course and instructor information, and a final course grade (see Figure 3.15). Notice that there is redundant data for students, courses, and instructors in each row of this database. This redundancy means that this database is not well organized. If, for example, we want to change the phone number of an instructor who has hundreds of students, we have to change this number hundreds of times.

Elimination of data redundancy is a major goal and benefit of using data normalization techniques. After the normalization process, the student data is organized into five separate tables (see Figure 3.16). This reorganization helps simplify the ongoing use and maintenance of the database and any associated analysis programs.

Data Dictionary

Each attribute in the database needs to be of a certain type. For example, an attribute may contain text, numbers, or dates. This ***data type*** helps the DBMS organize and sort the data, complete calculations, and allocate storage space.

Once the data model is created, a format is needed to enter the data in the database. A

Student Table

Student ID#	Student Name	Campus Address	Major	Phone
A121	Joy Egbert	100 N. River Street	MIS	555-7771
A123	Larry Mueller	123 S. River Street	MIS	555-1235
A124	Mike Guon	125 S. Elm	MGT	555-2214
A126	Jackie Judson	224 S. Sixth Street	MKT	555-1245
...	...	...	...	...

Class Table

Course ID	Course Title
MIS 350	Intro. MIS
MIS 372	Database
MIS 375	Elec. Comm.
MIS 448	Strategic MIS
MIS 474	Telecomm
...	...

Teaching Assignment

Course ID	Term	Instructor Name
MIS 350	F'05	Van Deventer
MIS 372	F'05	Hann
MIS 375	F'05	Chatterjee
MIS 448	F'05	Chatterjee
MIS 474	F'05	Gilson
...	...	...

Instructor Table

Instructor Name	Instructor Location	Instructor Phone
Chatterjee	T240D	555-2228
Gilson	T240E	555-2226
Hann	T240F	555-2224
Van Deventer	T240C	555-2222

Enrolled Table

Student ID#	Course ID	Term	Grade
A121	MIS 350	F'05	A
A121	MIS 372	F'05	B
A121	MIS 375	F'05	B+
A121	MIS 448	F'05	A-
A121	MIS 474	F'05	C+
A123	MIS 350	F'05	A
A123	MIS 372	F'05	B-
A123	MIS 375	F'05	A-
A123	MIS 448	F'05	C+
A124	MIS 350	F'05	A-
A124	MIS 372	F'05	A-
A124	MIS 375	F'05	B+
A124	MIS 474	F'05	B
A126	MIS 350	F'05	A
A126	MIS 372	F'05	B+
A126	MIS 375	F'05	B+
A126	MIS 474	F'05	A-
...	...	...	...

[**Figure 3.16** ➥ Organization of information on students, courses, instructors, and grades after normalization.]

CAREER IMPLICATIONS

Marketing

Pizza Hut's customer relationship management programs are built on a data warehouse of millions of customer records gleaned from point-of-sale transactions at its restaurants. They know your favourite toppings, what you ordered last, and whether you like salad with your meat lover's pie. Much of that has to do with data mining, a technology that converts details from customer data into competitive intelligence that companies use to predict trends and behaviours. Pizza Hut installed Teradata Warehouse Miner, and after a year of using it to better manage direct mail campaigns, the chain and its parent company, Yum Brands (Pizza Hut is one of eight restaurants in the group that includes Kentucky Fried Chicken and Taco Bell), are starting to see results.

Pizza Hut claims to have the largest fast food customer data warehouse in the world with 40 million households or between 40 and 50 percent of the North American market, according to Keith Jones, the man responsible for analysis and management of direct marketing analytics for Pizza Hut International. For about six years the company did analysis on a small sampling of the 40 million households it knew about, but nothing it could really call data mining, says Jones. "There was no prediction or analysis, really," he said. "There was a lot of error in the data because people moved around a lot and the phone numbers weren't correct. We had to clean up the data." The existence of duplicate households in the warehouse (same family, different phone number) made it difficult to target successful direct mail campaigns.

In the first year of using the Teradata Warehouse Miner product, Jones said Pizza Hut was able to recover the cost of licensing and integrating and training staff to use the product, and it made money for the company in the first quarter of use. "We made so much money this year, we're afraid our competition will start using it," said Jones. Using Warehouse Miner meant an improvement in "household uniqueness" from 80 percent to 95 percent. While direct mail has traditionally been a break-even cost centre, Pizza Hut has turned it into a profit centre. "We use it to do target marketing and find the best coupon offer for that household. We can segment customer households for groupings according to patterns of past buying behaviours, offer preferences and price points," he said. "We can also use it to predict the success of a campaign."

Pizza Hut now tracks not only phone orders, but online orders, too. Keith Gonzales, president of El Paso, Texas–based The Focus Group, Ltd., a firm that offers clients information on managing data warehouses, says data mining is good for medium and large data volumes, as it eliminates the cost of data movement and allows for a collaborative environment. He said database vendors are pushing mining into the warehouse and they are doing it so companies can exploit all the technology of data mining from the database. "Pizza Hut is taking advantage of this," he said. The added benefits of data mining include minimizing data redundancy, reduced proprietary data structures, and simplified data and system management.

[Adapted from Jennifer Brown, "Pizza Hut Delivers Hot Results Using Data Warehouse," *Computing Canada,* Vol. 29, No. 20 (October 17, 2003).]

data dictionary is a document prepared by the database designers to help individuals enter data. The data dictionary explains several pieces of information for each attribute, such as its name, whether or not it is a key or part of a key, the type of data expected (dates, alphanumeric, numbers, and so on), and valid values. Data dictionaries can include information such as why the data item is needed, how often it should be updated, and on which forms and reports the data appears.

Data dictionaries can be used to enforce business rules. ***Business rules,*** such as who has authority to update a piece of data, are captured by the designers of the database and included in the data dictionary to prevent illegal or illogical entries from entering the database. For example, designers of a warehouse database could capture a rule in the data dictionary to prevent invalid ship dates from being entered into the database.

HOW ORGANIZATIONS GET THE MOST FROM THEIR DATA

Many organizations, like the fire marshal's office in the opening case, are said to be data rich and information poor. The advent of Internet-based electronic commerce has resulted in the collection of an enormous amount of customer and transactional data. How this data is collected, stored, and manipulated is a significant factor influencing the success of a commercial Internet Website. In this section we discuss how organizations are getting the most from their data.

Linking Website Applications to Organizational Databases

A recent database development is the creation of links between sites on the Web and organizational databases. For example, many companies are enabling users of their Website to view product catalogues, check inventory, and place orders—all actions that ultimately read and write to the organizations' databases.

Some Internet electronic commerce applications can receive and process millions of transactions per day. To gain the greatest understanding of customer behaviour and to ensure adequate system performance for customers, you must manage online data effectively. For example, Amazon.com is the world's largest bookstore, with more than 2.5 million titles, and is open 24 hours a day, 365 days a year with customers all over the world ordering books and a broad range of other products. Amazon's servers log millions of transactions per day. Amazon is a vast departure from a traditional physical bookstore. In fact, the largest physical bookstore carries "only" about 170,000 titles, and it would not be economically feasible to build a physical bookstore the size of Amazon; a physical bookstore that carried Amazon's 2.5 million titles would need to be the size of nearly 25 football fields! The key to effectively designing an online electronic commerce business is clearly the effective management of online data.

Data Mining

To support more effective information management, many large organizations such as Bank of Montreal and Canadian Tire are using data mining. ***Data mining*** is a method used by companies to sort and analyze information to better understand their customers, products, markets, or any other phase of their business for which data has been captured. With data mining tools, you can graphically drill down from summary data to more detailed data, sort or extract data based on certain conditions, and perform a variety of statistical analyses, such as trend analysis, correlation analysis, forecasting, and analysis of variance. The next section describes how data mining is being implemented.

Online Transaction Processing (OLTP)

Fast customer response is fundamental to having a successful Internet-based business. ***Online transaction processing (OLTP)*** refers to immediate automated responses to the requests of users. OLTP systems are designed specifically to handle multiple concurrent transactions from customers. Typically, these transactions have a fixed number of inputs, such as customer name and address, and a specified output, such as total order price or order tracking number. Common transactions include receiving user information, processing orders, and generating sales receipts. Consequently, OLTP is a big part of interactive electronic commerce applications on the Internet. Since customers can be located virtually anywhere in the world, it is critical that transactions be processed efficiently (see Figure 3.17). The speed with which database management systems can process transactions is, therefore, an important design decision when building Internet systems. In addition

BRIEF CASE

Database Technology Powers CNN Interactive

CNN Interactive presents an example of the successful linking of a large corporate database with a Web interface. CNN Interactive provides a free, online custom news service to hundreds of thousands of subscribers around the world. Using the World Wide Web, the site delivers up-to-the-minute news from over 100 sources and offers more than 2,000 categories of customized news options, ranging from sports and health to recreation, pop culture, crime, and consumer issues. In a typical week, 20,000 new articles are stored. CNN Interactive uses an Oracle database to dynamically build personalized news pages for hundreds of thousands of daily users. These pages are updated every 15 minutes to deliver the most current information. This application is made possible only by the sophisticated database system, which manages the vast amount of changing information and automatically builds the customized Web pages.

Questions

1. Think of your favourite Websites. How do these sites use databases?
2. Who are the major players in the corporate database market?

[Adapted from **www.oracle.com**.]

GLOBAL PERSPECTIVE

Transborder Data Security and Privacy

Apart from technical and human resource–related challenges, some cultural issues also pose significant challenges for organizations. The most important of these issues is that of the general rules and regulations existing in different nations regarding information systems and transborder data flow. One of the most prominent examples of rules and regulations on transborder data flow is the European Union Data Protection Directive, which went into effect in October 1998. The data protection laws according to this directive limit how personal data may be used within Europe. While some European countries, such as France, have had data protection laws for a long time, the laws passed by the directive are stricter. The *Personal Information Protection and Electronic Documents Act* (PIPEDA) in Canada contains a set of standards similar to the European directive. However, regulations in the United States fall short of the European directive and PIPEDA in a number of respects. For example, unlike the U.S., personal data collected in Europe and Canada may be used only for the purposes for which they were collected. For all other purposes, a consent form needs to be obtained from the consumer. Frequent-flyer rewards information, for example, can be associated with a passenger's name but cannot include other information about the passenger. This directive has had severe implications for the airline industry in Europe. Moreover, Article 25 of the directive argues that no personal data can be transferred from Europe to countries that have less stringent privacy policies, including the United States but not Canada. This article has posed challenges for U.S. organizations that conduct business with European companies. There is hope that a single unified treaty on data security and privacy might be developed. In the meantime, organizations will expend considerable resources complying with the different rules in different countries. Refer to Chapter 9 for more extensive coverage of this issue.

to which technology is chosen to process the transactions, how the data is organized is also a major factor in determining system performance. Although the database operations behind most transactions are relatively simple, designers often spend considerable time making adjustments to the database design in order to "tune" processing for optimal system performance. Once an organization has all this data, it must design ways to gain the greatest value from its collection; online analytical processing is one method being used to analyze these vast amounts of data.

Online Analytical Processing (OLAP)

Online analytical processing (OLAP) refers to graphical software tools that provide complex analysis of data stored in a database (note: in the case of OLAP, online is taken to mean "real time," and does not necessarily mean "on the Internet"). The chief component of an OLAP system is the ***OLAP server***, which understands how data is organized in the database and has special functions for analyzing the data. OLAP tools enable users to analyze different dimensions of data, beyond data summary and data aggregations of normal database queries. For example, OLAP can provide time series and trend analysis views of data, data drill-downs to deeper levels of consolidation, and the ability to answer "what if" and "why" questions. An OLAP query for Amazon.com might be: "What would be the effect on profits if wholesale book prices

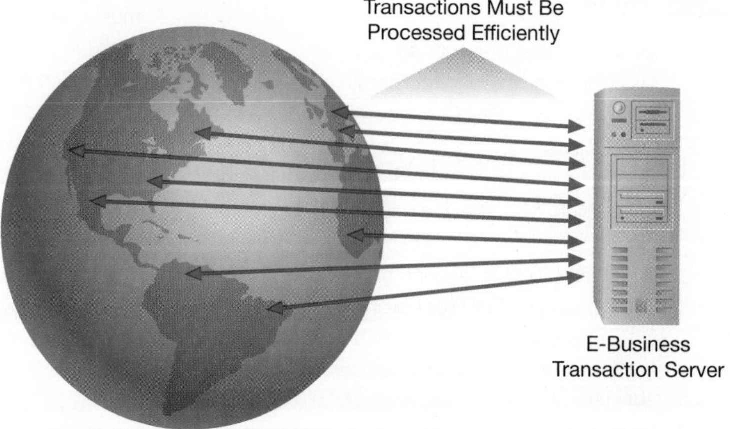

[Figure 3.17 ➡ Global customers require that online transactions be processed efficiently.]

increased by 10 percent and transportation costs decreased by five percent?" Managers use the complex query capabilities of an OLAP system to answer questions within executive information systems (EISs), decision support systems (DSSs), and enterprise resource planning (ERP) systems (each of these systems is described in a later chapter). Given the high volume of transactions within Internet-based systems, analysts must provide extensive OLAP capabilities to managers in order to gain the greatest business value.

Merging Transaction and Analytical Processing

The requirements for designing and supporting transactional and analytical systems are quite different. In a distributed online environment, performing real-time analytical processing diminishes the performance of transaction processing. For example, complex analytical queries from an OLAP system require the locking of data resources for extended periods of execution time, whereas transactional events—data insertions and simple queries from customers—are fast and can often occur simultaneously. Thus, a well-tuned and responsive transaction system may have uneven performance for customers while analytical processing occurs. As a result, many organizations replicate all transactions on a second database server so that analytical processing does not slow customer transaction processing performance. This replication typically occurs in batches during off-peak hours when site traffic volumes are at a minimum.

The systems that are used to interact with customers and run a business in real time are called the ***operational systems.*** Examples of operational systems are sales order processing and reservations systems. The systems designed to support decision making based on stable point-in-time or historical data are called ***informational systems.*** The key differences between operational and informational systems are shown in Table 3.4. Increasingly, data from informational systems is being consolidated with other organizational data into a comprehensive data warehouse, where OLAP tools can be used to extract the greatest and broadest understanding from the data.

Data Warehousing

Organizations such as Wal-Mart, Best Buy, and Canadian Tire have built ***data warehouses,*** which integrate multiple large databases and other information sources into a single repository. This repository is suitable for direct querying, analysis, or processing. Much like a physical warehouse for products and components, the data warehouse stores and distributes data on computer-based information systems. The data warehouse is a user's virtual storehouse of valuable data from the organization's disparate information systems and external sources. It supports the online analysis of sales, inventory, and other vital business data that has been culled from operational systems. The purpose of a data warehouse is to put key business information into the hands of more decision makers. Table 3.5 lists sample industry uses of data warehouses. Data warehouses can take up hundreds of gigabytes, even terabytes, of data. They usually run on fairly powerful mainframe computers and can cost millions of dollars.

CAREER IMPLICATIONS

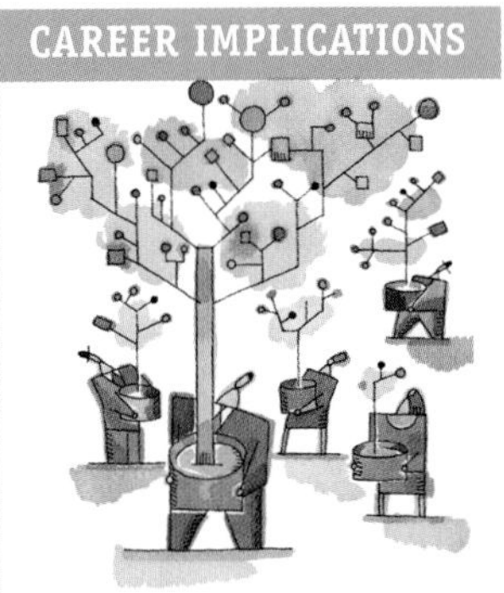

Human Resource Management

The consultants at Accenture, one of the leading global consulting firms, depend on a knowledge management system on a regular basis. This system, known as Knowledge Xchange, is an online system, and consultants are required to be connected to the network in order to access it. Due to the fact that most of the consultants spend much of their time on planes and at hotels, they often run into difficulty connecting and thus fail to access the knowledge management (KM) system. To add to the complexity, the KM system had grown to over 100 gigabytes of data, and accessing the database easily and quickly had become a problem. To ease these problems, Accenture's IT staff designed and developed a new application system called Pocket Xchange, which operates on a Microsoft SQL server database and is installed on Microsoft Windows NT server. Pocket Xchange accesses data from a Microsoft Access database using data access objects (DAO) and displays the data in a document view. The Access database is populated with data retrieved from a set of Lotus Notes databases. This application is loaded on the consultants' machines and enables them to access the data without being connected to the network. Some Accenture consultants have reported that the new software has saved them at least as much time as one day a week.

[Adapted from **www.microsoft.com/business/casestudies/bi/accenture.asp**.]

[Table 3.4] *Comparison of operational and informational systems.*

Characteristic	Operational System	Informational System
Primary purpose	Run the business on a current basis	Support managerial decision making
Type of data	Current representation of state of the business	Historical or point in time (snapshot)
Primary users	Online customers, clerks, salespersons, administrators	Managers, business analysts, customers (checking status, history)
Scope of usage	Narrow vs. simple updates and queries	Broad vs. complex queries and analysis
Design goal	Performance	Ease of access and use

Data warehouses represent more than just big databases. An organization that successfully deploys a data warehouse has committed to pulling together, integrating, and sharing critical corporate data throughout the firm.

Data Marts

Rather than storing all enterprise data in one data warehouse, many organizations have created multiple data marts, each containing a subset of the data for a single aspect of a company's business—for example, finance, inventory, or personnel. A ***data mart*** is a data warehouse that is limited in scope. It contains selected information from the data warehouse, such that each separate data mart is customized for the decision support applications of a particular end-user group. For

[Table 3.5] *Sample industry uses of data warehousing (adapted from Boar, 1998).*

Uses of Data Warehousing	Representative Companies
Retail	
Analysis of scanner checkout data	Loblaws
Tracking, analysis, and tuning of sales	Canadian Tire
promotions and coupons	Sears
Inventory analysis and redeployment	Osco/Savon Drugs
Price reduction modelling to "move" the product	Grocery Gateway
Negotiating leverage with suppliers	Chapters/Indigo
Frequent-buyer program management	Air Canada
Profitability analysis	Purolator
Product selections or granular market segmentation	Scotiabank
Telecommunications	
Analysis of the following:	AT&T
Call volumes	Telus
Equipment sales	Nortel
Customer profitability	Bell Canada
Costs	Microcell
Inventory	Telecom Ireland
Purchasing leverage with suppliers	Telecom Italia
Frequent-buyer program management	Primus
Banking and Financing	
Relationship banking	Royal Bank
Cross-segment marketing	Scotiabank
Risk and credit analysis	Bank of Montreal
Merger and acquisition analysis	CIBC
Customer profiles	TD Canada Trust
Branch performance	

Source: Copyright © 1998, NCR Corporation. Used with permission.

Using Databases to Stop Telemarketers

Very few people enjoy receiving calls from telemarketers. As a result, the United States Congress implemented a "do not call" database that made it illegal for telemarketers to call anyone on the list. The database, which is administered by the Federal Communications Commission (FCC), was officially launched on October 1, 2003 at **www.donotcall.gov**. Not surprisingly, the telemarketing industry was (and is) greatly opposed to this plan because of the increased costs associated with maintaining accurate databases and the fear that a large part of the population would want to be listed in the database. Indeed, in the first five months of operation, 55 million Americans registered with the service, which is free of charge. In that same time period, the FCC received 10,000 complaints from consumers and issued eight citations.

Canada has yet to enact similar legislation. For the moment, the only recourse available to Canadians is to register with a "do not contact" service offered by the Canadian Marketing Association (CMA). The CMA is a trade organization for direct marketers in Canada, covering about 80 percent of the industry. Canadians can register for free with the service at **www.cmaconsumersense.org/marketing_lists.cfm**. The CMA distributes the list to its members, who are encouraged to remove registrants from their new-contact databases. The service works for telephone, fax, and mail solicitations. However, since there is no law in place, the effectiveness of this system in Canada is lower than in the United States. Canadian legislators are closely watching the development of the "do not call" list south of the border, so do not be surprised if similar legislation surfaces here.

COMING ATTRACTIONS

example, an organization may have several data marts that are customized for a particular type of user, such as a marketing data mart or a finance data mart. Data marts have been popular among small- and medium-sized businesses and among departments within larger organizations, all of which were previously prohibited from developing their own data warehouses due to the high costs involved.

Data marts typically contain tens of gigabytes of data, as opposed to the hundreds of gigabytes in data warehouses. Therefore, data marts can be deployed on less powerful hardware. The differences in costs between different types of data marts and data warehouses can be significant. The cost to develop a data mart is typically less than $1 million, while the cost for a data warehouse can exceed $10 million. Clearly, organizations committed to getting the most out of their data must make a large investment in database technology.

DATABASE CHALLENGES

This chapter has shown that databases are a key component of information systems. When utilized successfully, databases can propel a firm to a position of competitive advantage. However, databases can also present numerous challenges to firms. For example, firms often contain multiple databases and the data contained within these systems may be incompatible. This is often the case when new systems are connected to older, legacy systems. There are more than a few sophisticated Websites where data has had to be re-entered manually behind the scenes! The problem of multiple systems and data incompatibility spurred the growth of enterprise systems in the 1990s. Enterprise systems will be discussed in depth in Chapter 7.

Another challenge with databases that has come to light recently is data security and privacy. Databases were developed primarily to ensure that data can be stored and retrieved accurately and efficiently. Recent legislation in Canada and elsewhere has placed a priority on keeping data secure and private. With many older systems, the process of redesigning the database to bring it into line with new standards and regulations is very complex, time consuming, and expensive. Even newer databases may require changes to ensure that the data contained within them is protected from unauthorized access, yet available to legitimate users. The existence of multiple databases within some firms complicates this process considerably. More information on data security and privacy is contained in Chapter 9.

CAREER IMPLICATIONS

Information Systems

Mike Barron has his sights set on the Holy Grail of health care: a comprehensive electronic patient record for each of Newfoundland and Labrador's 530,000 citizens. Barron is the health information network project leader for the Newfoundland and Labrador Centre for Health Information, an organization that represents 13 regional health authorities in the province and works with government, service providers, researchers, and the private sector to develop health information systems. In 1998, Barron and his team created a business case for the $3.6-million Unique Personal Identifier/Client Registry system, the first building block of a comprehensive electronic health record. After the system went live in 2001, Health Canada expressed interest in using it as the template for a Canadian electronic health record. "The Feds got serious and created Canada's Health Infoway and invested an additional $5.4 million in the project," says Barron. "That took it from a Chevy to a Cadillac."

He says the biggest challenge was getting people to buy into his vision. "We have no authority," he says with a chuckle, "but we have a mandate to represent the health system. That means we need to get people involved, not just push things down their throats." The next phase Barron will tackle is the provincial Pharmacy Network, which will link the province's 170 pharmacies and 1,000 physician offices. Barron says the system will cut down on fraud and give physicians all the information they need to write prescriptions. The Pharmacy Network patient record will contain information on prescription medication a patient is taking and over-the-counter remedies. This will help reduce hospital admissions due to adverse reactions to medication.

[Adapted from Patricia MacInnis, "A Passion for Engineering a Healthy Network," *Computing Canada*, Vol. 29, No. 24 (December 12, 2003).]

KEY POINTS REVIEW

1. **Describe why databases have become so important to modern organizations.** Databases often house mission-critical organizational data, so proper design and management of the databases is critical. If they are designed and managed well, the databases can be used to transform raw data into information that helps people do their jobs faster, better, and more cheaply, which ultimately helps customers and makes the firm more competitive.
2. **Describe what databases and database management systems are and how they work.** A database is a collection of related data organized in a way that facilitates data searches. A database contains entities, attributes, records, and tables. Entities are things about which we collect data, such as people, courses, customers, or products. Attributes are the individual pieces of information about an entity, such as a person's last name or social insurance number, that are stored in a database record. A record is the collection of related attributes about an entity; usually, a record is displayed as a database row. A table is a collection of related records about an entity type; each row in the table is a record, and each column is an attribute. A database management system is a software application with which you create, store, organize, and retrieve data from a single database or several databases. Data is typically entered into a database through the use of a specially formatted form. Data is retrieved from a data base through the use of queries and reports. The data within a database must be adequately organized so that it is possible to store and retrieve information effectively. The main approach for structuring the relationships among data entities is the relational database model. Normalization is a technique to transform complex databases into a more efficient form, allowing them to be more easily maintained and manipulated.
3. **Explain how organizations are getting the most from their investment in database technologies.** Many organizations are allowing employees and customers to access corporate database management systems via the World Wide Web. This capability allows greater flexibility and innovative products and services. Data mining is a popular application of database technologies in which information stored in organizational databases, data warehouses, or data marts is sorted and analyzed to improve organizational decision making and performance. A data warehouse is the integration of multiple large databases and other information sources into a single repository or access point that is suitable for direct querying, analysis, or processing. A data mart is a small-scale data warehouse that contains a subset of the data for a single aspect of a company's business—for example, finance, inventory, or personnel.

KEY TERMS

attribute 74
business rules 88
combination primary key 81
data dictionary 88
data mart 92
data mining 88
data model 81
data type 87
data warehouse 91
database 74
database administrator (DBA) 77
database management system (DBMS) 74
entity 74
entity-relationship diagram (ERD) 84
form 78
foreign key 83
informational system 91
normalization 86
online analytical processing (OLAP) 90
online transaction processing (OLTP) 89
OLAP server 90
operational systems 91
primary key 81
query 79
query by example (QBE) 79
record 74
relational database model 85
report 79
report generator 79
secondary key 81
Structured Query Language (SQL) 79
table 74

REVIEW QUESTIONS

1. Explain the difference between a database and a database management system.
2. List some reasons why record keeping with physical filing systems is less efficient than using a database on a computer.
3. Describe how the following terms are related: entity, attribute, record, and table.
4. Compare and contrast the primary key, combination key, and foreign key within an entity.
5. How do Structured Query Language (SQL) and query by example (QBE) relate to each other?
6. What is the purpose of normalization?
7. Explain how organizations are getting the most from their investment in database technologies.
8. How are databases used with a World Wide Web interface? Who has access to the database?
9. Compare and contrast a data warehouse and a data mart.
10. Describe why databases have become so important to modern organizations.

SELF-STUDY QUESTIONS

Answers are at the end of the Problems and Exercises.

1. A database comprises __________.
   A. attributes
   B. records
   C. organized data for querying
   D. all of the above
2. A database is used to collect, organize, and query information. Which of the following people is least likely to use a database as a fundamental part of their job?
   A. airline reservations agent
   B. university registrar
   C. Canada Pension Plan administrator
   D. security guard
3. A(n) __________ is a unique identifier that can be a combination of two or more attributes.
   A. secondary key
   B. primary key
   C. tertiary key
   D. elementary key
4. Which of the following is not true in regard to the relational database model?
   A. Entities are viewed as tables, with records as rows and attributes as columns.
   B. Tables use keys and redundant data in different tables in order to link interrelated data.
   C. Entities are viewed as children of higher-level attributes.
   D. A properly designed table has a unique identifier that may be one or more attributes.
5. Each team has only one home stadium, and each home stadium has only one team. This is an example of which of the following relationships?
   A. one-to-one
   B. one-to-many
   C. many-to-many
   D. many-to-one
6. Data warehousing refers to ______________.
   A. the secure storage of corporate data in a fireproof vault
   B. the integration of multiple large databases into a single repository
   C. a concept that is no longer practical due to the pace of technological change
   D. none of the above
7. Which of the following statements about databases is false?
   A. Databases are becoming more popular.
   B. Minimal planning is required since the software is so advanced.
   C. A data warehouse utilizes a database.
   D. A database administrator is responsible for the development and management of a database.

8. Databases are used for ________.
   - A. data mining
   - B. data marts
   - C. expert systems
   - D. all of the above

9. ________ is a technique to make a complex database more efficient by eliminating redundancy.
   - A. Data depository
   - B. Associating
   - C. Normalization
   - D. Standardization

10. Which of the following is a document, sometimes published as an online interactive application, prepared by the designers of the database to aid individuals in data entry?
    - A. data dictionary
    - B. database
    - C. normalization
    - D. data model

PROBLEMS AND EXERCISES

1. Match the following terms with the appropriate definitions:
   - ____ Database
   - ____ Database management system
   - ____ Data mart
   - ____ Query by example
   - ____ Data mining
   - ____ Data warehouse
   - ____ Data dictionary
   - ____ Relational model
   - ____ Normalization
   - ____ Entity-relationship diagram

   a. A data warehouse that is limited in scope and contains selected information that is customized for the decision support applications of a particular end-user group
   b. A diagramming technique commonly used when designing databases, especially when showing associations among entities
   c. A collection of related data organized in a way that facilitates data searches
   d. A method used to sort and analyze information to better understand data captured in normal business activities
   e. A software application with which you can create, store, organize, and retrieve data for one or many databases
   f. A technique used to simplify complex databases so that they are more efficient and easier to maintain
   g. The capability of a DBMS to enable us to request data by simply providing a sample or a description of the types of data we would like to see
   h. A DBMS approach in which entities are presented as two-dimensional tables that can be joined together with common columns
   i. A single repository that integrates multiple large databases and other information sources
   j. A document, sometimes published as an online interactive application, prepared by the designers of the database to aid individuals in data entry

2. You see an announcement for a job as a database administrator for a large corporation but are unclear about what this title means. Research this on the World Wide Web and obtain a specific job announcement.

3. How and why are organizations without extensive databases falling behind in competitiveness and growth? Is this simply a database problem that can be fixed easily with some software purchases? Search the World Wide Web for stories or news articles that deal with the issue of staying competitive by successfully managing data. How are these stories similar to each other? How are they different? Prepare a 10-minute presentation to the class on your findings.

4. What are six advantages of databases and three costs or risks of a database system? Why are databases becoming more popular?

5. Why would it matter what data type is used for the attributes within a database? How does this relate to programming? How does this relate to queries and calculations? Does the size of the database matter?

6. Discuss the issue of data accuracy, based on what you have learned from this chapter. Does a computer database handle accuracy issues better than a filing system? Who (or what) is ultimately responsible for data accuracy?

7. List three different database software applications. Compare and contrast the advantages and disadvantages, including price, program size, and other pertinent factors.

8. Have several classmates interview database administrators within organizations with which they are familiar. To whom do these people report? How many employees report to these people? Is there a big variance in the responsibilities across organizations? Why or why not?

9. On the World Wide Web, find data warehouses and data marts. What companies are currently using them? How do they differ in size, implementation time, scope, cost, and so on?

10. Based on your current understanding of a primary key and the following sample grades table, determine the best choice of attribute(s) for a primary key.

STUDENT ID	COURSE	GRADE
100013	Marketing	A–
000117	Finance	A
000117	Introduction to MIS	A

11. In the Brief Case about NEXUS, what are some of the challenges in developing and implementing an appropriate database? Which challenges are technical, which are behavioural, and which are political?

12. Search the World Wide Web for an organization with a Website that utilizes a link between the site and the organization's database. Describe the data that the browser enters and the organization's possible uses for this data. Can you retrieve company

information, or can you only send information to the company? How is the data displayed on the site?

13. Select an organization with which you are familiar that utilizes flat file databases for their database management. Determine whether the organization should move to a relational database. Why would you make this recommendation? Is it feasible to do so? Why or why not?

14. What databases are used at your educational institution? Have you filled out a lot of paperwork that was then entered by someone else? Did you actually do some of the data entry for your account? What kind of information were you able to retrieve about your account? From where was the database administered? Were you able to access it online?

ANSWERS TO THE SELF-STUDY QUESTIONS

1. D 2. D 3. B 4. C 5. A 6. C 7. B 8. D 9. C 10. A

Case 1: *RBC's Use of Analytics to Mine Data Goes Straight to the Bottom Line*

Jay Slade is up to his ears in data. As RBC Investments' manager of customer intelligence and analytics, he has millions of data items about the brokerage's clients at his disposal, from their portfolio size to the length of time they have dealt with the company. Together, massaged by analytic tools, these data paint a picture of RBC's clients that allows it to accurately segment and serve diverse groups more profitably. "This is what happens when you get segmentation, customer profitability, the ability to slice and dice at a detailed level right down to granular transactions, in a common environment," he says. "If you can put all that into one analytical environment, it gives you a lot of flexibility to target who you want to target for whatever purposes, whether that be a predictive model for one particular product or some sort of value-based segmentation for some sort of pricing or fee arrangement."

The analytical environment that RBC uses costs comparatively little, Slade notes, yet in conjunction with marketing, its impact has been significant. The worldwide analytics software market, according to technology research firm IDC, will reach over US$4.8 billion in 2007, with compound annual growth rates in its three subsectors (customer relationship management analytics, financial analytics/business performance management, and operations analytics) of between 7.4 and 12.9 percent. CRM analytics are leading the charge. "Analytic applications are the best means of navigating from data to decision making and action," says Bob Blumstein, research director for IDC's CRM analytics and marketing applications research. "As companies adopt these applications to enhance the effect of finance, customer relationship management (CRM), and operations, they will gain a distinct competitive advantage over those companies that tolerate traditional inefficiencies."

Almost 40 percent of North American companies surveyed by IDC have already installed business intelligence (BI) analytic tools, and another 11 percent are planning to do so within the next year. Nearly two-thirds of large enterprises have, or are planning, these solutions. "End-user organizations are implementing BI solutions to consolidate and analyze raw data and transform them into conclusive, actionable information," says Lucie Draper, IDC program manager for enterprise technology trends. "BI implementations allow companies to spot trends, enhance relationships, and create new sales opportunities for their business."

Slade's use of analytics reaches right into RBC's operations, helping investment advisors set fees for services and develop new marketing campaigns. But is the return on investment quantifiable? It is, according to Slade, who says, "I have an exact number, but I can't tell you." Forty-three other companies in a 2002 IDC study could and would quantify their ROI. Ranging from under 20 percent to more than 2,000 percent, their average ROI from analytics was a whopping 431 percent. And one of Slade's competitors, CIBC, achieved an estimated 300-percent return on its analytic investment on one project alone. "I've heard the phrase used in a lot of ways," she said. "Business analytics can be used to talk about data warehousing types of tools, where you have a huge set of information about customers and you're trolling through it to detect buying patterns: you know, whether the colour green is popular this year so we should make everything green."

That's probably the functionality most people associate with BI analytics, but Noel sees a wider scope. "Then there is business analytics in terms of, how do I measure what I'm doing internally? Are my processes working the way they should be working? Is my IT infrastructure aligned with my business goals? How do we measure that?" How indeed. She says it's something IT is still struggling with. "That's a really, really new area for IT and for IT vendors. People I talk to are trying to build tools from the bottom up, monitor everything in the universe and dump it into some sort of database, and try and do some reporting on how it's being used and what their resources are, where they're being used."

It's something of a sledgehammer approach, but important because, says Noel, "It's looking at IT as if it is a business. Getting at that kind of question, that's how you get the ROI. If we can actually get the information on our IT resources at that kind of level, we would see costs go down dramatically. Analytics are getting people to the point where they can get that type of information so they can make better decisions at a corporate level."

Analytics continue to make their way into a broad variety of companies. The Dow Chemical Company, for example, has implemented analytics to help it get a handle on its operational costs. This, says Mike Costa, the company's senior director of information systems, lets the company streamline and manage its resources. In a more concrete operational example, the United States Postal Service employed analytics to look at usage of its point-of-sale terminals. It discovered 1,500 terminals, with a cost of about US$9 million, had not been turned on, even during the busy holiday season. Instead of buying new terminals for other locations, it redeployed these units.

[Adapted from Lynn Greiner, "Analytics Unlock the Secrets to ROI," *Computing Canada*, Vol. 29, No. 23 (November 28, 2003).]

Discussion Questions

1. What are analytics, and how can they benefit organizations?
2. How does the phrase "we are data rich and information poor" from the opening case relate to analytics in this case?
3. Lew Platt, ex-CEO of HP, once said, "If only HP knew what HP knows, we could be three times more productive." What do you think he meant, and how does this relate to analytics and business intelligence?
4. Can business intelligence tools, such as those in the examples above, become sources of sustainable competitive advantage for firms?

Case 2: *Data Warehouse Project Failure at Close Call Corp.*

Close Call Corp. is a teleservices company that was founded about three decades ago. Over the years, the company has grown steadily and has a current net worth of approximately $100 million. The founder and CEO of the company realized that it was time to make some significant changes to the organization, especially on the technology front. Close Call still relied on some antiquated information systems, which were extremely ill equipped to handle the company's recent growth and expansion. The thought of a major technological change became even more deeply ingrained in the CEO's mind when he met a software vendor at a social event. The vendor promised him some customized solutions that would help integrate the company's data.

Close Call had two primary units: an outbound telemarketing unit and an inbound catalogue sales unit. Both these units operated independently of each other. Recently, however, the company was working toward integrating them, which required a significant amount of integration of the relevant data and information. In addition, the company was also planning some significant growth strategies whereby its number of call centres would be increased from six to 116. There were also plans to implement new open switching systems in the call centres that would enable automatic dialling and call forwarding. Plans were also in place to implement new human resources and ledger software. The vendor assured the CEO that the building of a data warehouse would be the company's solution for effectively managing its expansion plans and the new software. Convinced by the vendor, the CEO decided to go forward with the idea. He allocated a budget of $250,000, and the plan was to implement a 500GB data warehouse. Since most of the internal IS staff were not comfortable in handling a data warehouse and were already swamped with other IS projects, some new personnel, such as a manager of the data warehousing project and an MIS director, were hired from outside the company. The time span given for this project was approximately four months.

An initial project team was assembled, consisting of the MIS director, the project manager, and a couple of users, among others. The project manager attempted to push back the deadlines to make the project more realistic, but the CEO was insistent on staying with the original plan. Ultimately, the CEO agreed to the implementation of a pilot project after five months, before the rollout of the actual data warehouse. Although it was envisioned by the CEO that the data warehouse would serve the needs of multiple departments, the project team members were at a loss to understand the real importance of the data warehouse. In fact, because the company had never felt the need for a data warehouse in the past, the business objectives of this project were unclear to the team. Nonetheless, the project team remained optimistic and started the second phase of the project; namely, the collection of user requirements. The team scheduled lengthy interviews with potential users throughout the organization and asked them to talk in depth about their job requirements, day-to-day activities, technology needs, and so on. Hence, the user requirement phase was relatively long (about three months).

The project team members also focused on defining the business dimensions, attributes, relationships, and so on, for the design of the data warehouse. Since there were multiple departments, there were many conflicting needs and definitions, all of which needed to be integrated. At the end of this stage, the project team realized that the business requirements of each of the units were too inconsistent. All of the business managers had their own customized spreadsheets, which they used to create their respective reports. These individual spreadsheets were based on the managers' own set of assumptions and had no synergy with each other. The project team had to spend an enormous amount of time just sorting through these inconsistent definitions to find some coherence among them, which ended up delaying the project time frame to a great extent (which was not anticipated earlier). To add to the existing troubles of the data warehousing project team, roughly around this time the team also realized that there were no appropriate data to enter into the data warehouse. Some of the data was captured in the company's old proprietary systems, and extraction of the data from those systems would become costly and time consuming. The only solution was to upgrade the systems of the six existing call centres to open technology. The existing IS department refused to cooperate with the team, since they were threatened by the data warehousing project and viewed it as reducing their importance to the organization.

The data warehousing project team attempted to salvage the situation by gathering some data from the existing reports and manually entering them into the pilot data warehouse. However, they still knew that, without significant changes to the existing systems, the actual data warehouse could not be implemented. Yet plans for the pilot went ahead as scheduled. When the pilot data warehouse was finally installed, the situation became even worse. The users refused to use it, claiming that it did not add anything to their existing capabilities and was difficult to use. Instead of the originally planned five months, the pilot development and installation had taken over eight months. In addition, it incurred an estimated cost of US$750,000, significantly over the CEO's budget.

At the time the pilot failed, there were some structural changes in the organization as well, including new directors of MIS and technology. The data warehousing project manager built a new plan that estimated that the data warehousing project could be delivered within two years. However, by this time most of the company executives, including the CEO, had grown tired of it, and the project was officially closed within a short period of time.

[Adapted from Lauren Gibbons Paul, "Anatomy of Failure," **www.cio.com**, *CIO Enterprise Magazine* (November 15, 1997).]

Discussion Questions

1. Based on your knowledge of the information systems development process, what would you consider to be the factors that contributed to the failure of the data warehousing project at Close Call Corp.?
2. What would you do differently if you were the CEO of Close Call?
3. What would you do differently if you were the project manager of the data warehousing project?
4. Briefly describe five lessons that you learned from this case. Include both technology-related lessons and other social issues-related lessons.

Biometrics: Security That's in You to Give

CBC

Here is a short quiz. Be honest.

1. Do you use the same password across multiple applications?
2. Do you rotate three or fewer passwords for all your log-in accounts?
3. Is your password either a derivative of a pet's name or a place where you once lived?
4. Are you still using the default password for at least one application?
5. Have you kept the same password for more than one year?
6. Have you written down your password on a Post-it note, or saved it on a computer?

If you answered yes to three or more of these questions . . . you fail! That is, you are failing to maintain good security practices. We all know that we should alter our behaviour to maintain better security, but it is not always straightforward or practical. Here is another question. For those who keep different passwords for each application, and change them often, have you ever forgotten your password? The answer to this last question, unfortunately, is probably yes.

Most security systems consist of either something you *know* (a password, PIN, etc.) or something you *have* (a key, access card, etc.). Good security systems use both, like ATM machines that require a bank card and a PIN. Nevertheless, both these approaches are less effective than using something you *are;* that is, biometrics.

Biometrics is the science of using biological properties (fingerprints, face scans, and voice recognition) to identify individuals. Biometrics has a lot to offer. Everyone on Earth is biologically unique, we are hard to copy, and we bring our biometric information everywhere we go. Technology is now sufficiently advanced that we can harness biometric information for everyday purposes. For example, a number of vendors now produce biometric mice and keyboards that require users to provide a fingerprint scan before the unit will function.

Despite their many benefits, biometrics are not perfect. Over time, changes in our appearance can affect the accuracy of biometric information. For example, beards and tans confuse face scanning systems, contact lenses can affect iris scans, colds can confuse voice recognition systems, and cuts can ruin a fingerprint. Some biometrics, like fingerprints, can be lifted relatively easily—from a drinking glass, for instance.

Perhaps the largest problem with biometrics is that information on users must be stored in a central database, which could itself be compromised. Could you imagine if someone had access to your fingerprints, or a scan of your iris? You cannot cancel these like you would a credit card! The privacy concerns related to biometrics are extensive. Should people have a right to know what biometric information various organizations have on them, and when they are being scanned?

Despite these shortcomings, and the fact that they tend to be quite expensive, biometric systems are effective at verifying that someone is who he or she claims to be. Businesses are turning to biometrics for identification verification purposes. For example, airport workers across Canada are now required to supply fingerprint identification to access restricted areas. The Canadian Air Transport Security Authority (CATSA), the agency responsible for managing the initiative, has deployed biometric scanners in four airports to start with as part of a pilot project. If the pilot goes well, the nation's major airports, including 29 locations covering 92 percent of Canadian air traffic, will be equipped with scanners by the end of 2006. CATSA's pilot program will affect 40,000 Canadian airport workers, but a full rollout would increase that number to 150,000.

The restricted area of an airport refers to any area beyond the passenger security screening points. Workers affected by the move to biometric security measures include "anyone who has access to the restricted area and has a pass giving them access to that area," said Renée Fairweather, a spokesperson for CATSA. "That includes flight crews, caterers, refuellers, baggage handlers, even the people working in the concession stands."

A critical part of all biometric systems is the database that will be used to store the information. According to CATSA, the airport database contains only the document numbers employees are assigned when they are first hired and the biometric signature generated by the fingerprint—not an image of the fingerprint itself or any other personal information like names or addresses.

Law enforcement agencies are also turning to biometrics in the fight against terrorism. For this purpose, however, they are less effective. Biometric systems are very good at identity verification, as the airport example above illustrates, but matching someone with a database full of possible matches is a trickier problem.

Imagine an airport security system that takes pictures of passengers as they check in and then runs those pictures through a database of known terrorists. Then further imagine that such a system is 99.9-percent accurate, in that an actual terrorist will be flagged as such 99.9 percent of the time. Pretty good system, right?

Wrong. If we assume that there is one terrorist for every one million flyers (probably a high estimate), then for every terrorist that the system identifies, it would also identify 9,999 false positives. So even with 99.9-percent accuracy, 2,000 innocent passengers per month would be flagged as terrorists at an airport the size of Pearson in Toronto. Thus, while the system may ultimately be effective, it would not be practical.

Several Canadian companies are in the business of providing biometric equipment, including Mississauga, Ontario-based Bioscrypt Inc. Colin Soutar, chief technology officer at the firm, said an airport in Kelowna, B.C., is using the technology, as well as several airports in the U.S. Other airports have tried their own versions of biometric security to monitor employees. Thunder Bay International Airport, for example, ran a pilot program two years ago using facial recognition software.

Biometrics simplify the process of ensuring secured access. Many firms and government agencies use biometrics today to control access to restricted areas. In the not too distant future, we may be using biometrics to access ATMs, or as an alternative to student cards. However, the use of biometrics raises a number of tricky ethical questions. These questions relate both to the technology itself and to the data that result from use of the technology.

Questions

1. What are some strengths and weaknesses of biometrics in the workplace?
2. Should there be limits on the use of biometrics by firms? with employees? with customers?
3. Imagine you are the CIO of a large Canadian bank. Build a business case for the use of biometrics at the bank. Imagine where biometrics would add value and where they may not add value.
4. Try to predict how biometrics might be used in 15 years' time. What are the limits to the use of biometrics?

Video Resource: "Biometrics," *Marketplace* (October 31, 2001).

[Adapted from Neil Sutton, "Airport Biometrics: A Big Thumbs Up for Secure Skies," *EDGE Magazine,* Vol. 3, No. 4 (May 2004).]

Chapter 4

Preview

Organizations need to bring products to a global market quickly and be closely integrated with their customers and suppliers. These and related demands have driven the rapid development of telecommunications technologies. These technologies enable people and enterprises to share information across time and distance, and they can lower boundaries between markets and cultures. The telecommunications revolution is changing the way we live and work, and how we communicate with each other. This chapter introduces key telecommunications concepts, technologies, and applications, including how the Internet works and is being used in and across business organizations. This discussion provides you with a solid foundation for understanding how computers are connected across a room or across the world.

After reading this chapter, you will be able to do the following:

1. Understand the role of telecommunications in organizations.
2. Describe the evolution of and types of computer networks.
3. Describe the Internet and how it works.
4. Describe the basic Internet services and the use of the World Wide Web.

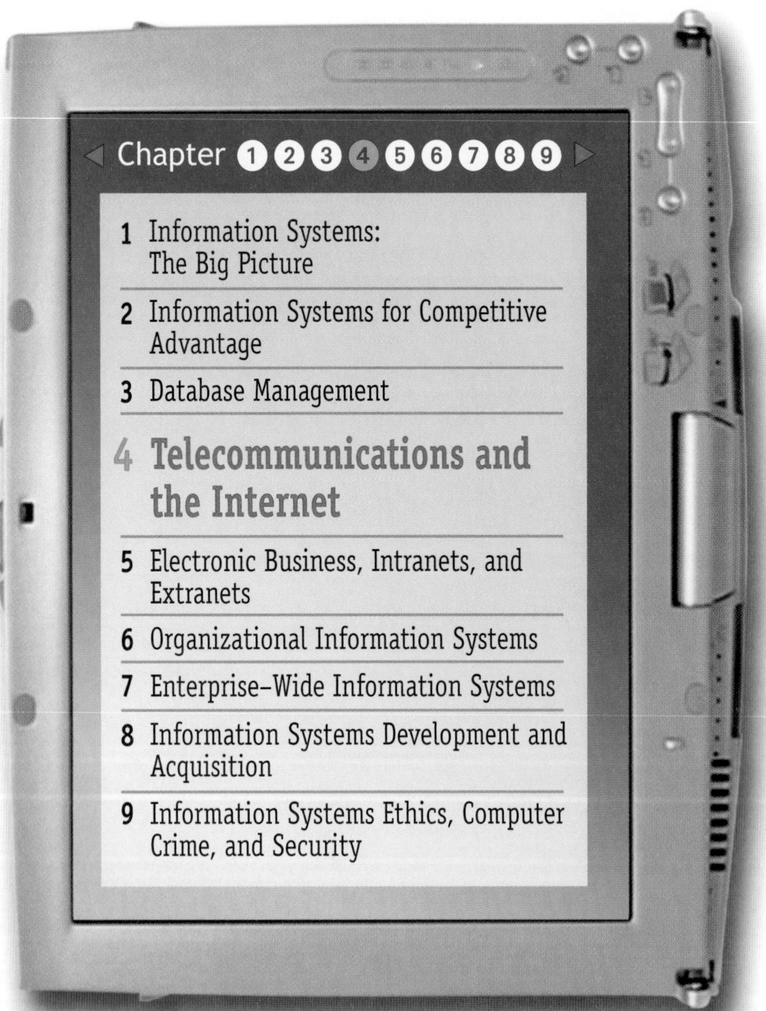

[Figure 4.1 ➡ The Big Picture: focusing on telecommunications.]

Telecommunications and the Internet

OPENING: Canada Confronts the Dark Side of Global Telecommunications

Have you been promised millions of dollars by the ex-finance minister of an African country lately? Tens of thousands of Canadian e-mail recipients have. This type of scam is typical of the problem facing both Canadian Internet users and law enforcement officials, said Constable Patrick Boismenu, an investigator with the RCMP's Integrated Technological Crime Unit in Montreal. "Foreign fraud [artists] have been attacking Canada for a long time. There is little we can do about it. Why? Because they're not operating from within the country. They can bypass borders using the phone or letters or e-mail to [trick] people into giving money or bank account numbers. They can circumvent any security feature that we implement on the borders," he said.

Similarly, many viruses, worms, and Trojans originate from the U.S., Russia, China, and other Far Eastern countries. "You can't touch anybody outside the country for that type of offence," Boismenu said. "Viruses come from around the world. Unfortunately, developing countries such as China have weak legislation and sometimes not enough police expertise to enforce the legislation that does exist."

The very nature of technology guarantees a continuing battle, said Gary Bouchard, head of the technology law group at Fogler, Rubinoff, Barristers and Solicitors, in Toronto. "You've got people from all over the world developing cutting-edge technology. It's the old one-upmanship problem—good guys keeping up with bad guys and bad guys keeping ahead of good guys—making for constant struggle."

For the international spy set, mi2g Ltd., a British security company, predicts an increase in politically motivated digital attacks, although this has not yet been a factor in Canada. "We don't see much of this as politically motivated," said Mark Fernandes, manager of the security services group at Deloitte & Touche in Toronto. Shortly after Fernandes predicted more attacks would come in the near future, Microsoft issued an alert about a new-found vulnerability in its Windows system, followed by dire warnings from security companies of possible damage.

Microsoft tacitly admitted the continuing struggle in a statement. "Microsoft understands that consumers are increasingly faced with a variety of cyber threats and [is] doing an unprecedented level of outreach to PC users with our 'Protect your PC' campaign to help raise awareness of the need for computer users to take steps, and ensure that those steps are as easy to understand and as easy to implement as possible."

[Adapted from Al Emid, "Cheats, Vandals, Spys and Villians," *Backbone* (January/February 2004).]

[**Figure 4.2** ➥ Global telecommunications link Canada to the world, but also threaten its security.]

Source: Courtesy of Amperion, Inc.

Telecommunications technologies are becoming more and more important in our lives. Understanding how these technologies work and can be leveraged for success is essential to your overall understanding of The Big Picture (see Figure 4.1). This chapter begins with a discussion of the expanding role that telecommunications is playing in organizations.

THE ROLE OF TELECOMMUNICATIONS AND NETWORKS IN ORGANIZATIONS

WEB SEARCH OPPORTUNITY
Check your Internet connection speed at **http://webservices.cnet.com/bandwidth**.

People in organizations around the world are finding that telecommunications and networks are highly effective tools for communication, coordination, and collaboration across and among enterprises and people. ***Telecommunications*** refers to the transmission of all forms of information, including digital data, voice, fax, sound, and video, from one location to another over some type of network. A ***network*** is a group of computers and associated peripheral devices connected by a communication channel capable of sharing information and other resources (e.g., a printer) among users. ***Bandwidth,*** or the carrying capacity of telecommunications networks, has increased to the point that any digitized data, from photographs, to art, to movies, to complicated business records, can be quickly transmitted via a network.

Powerful new technologies are giving networks the bandwidth needed to handle rich content, such as movies, medical records, or great works of art. These networks also work at speeds great enough to support interaction between users. In the next section, we offer some examples of how digital content and high-powered networks are changing interpersonal communication and business applications.

Interpersonal Communication Applications

The most remarkable feature of networking computers is not that computers can speak to each other, but that the people who use the computers can communicate with each other through their machines. Just as telephones let users communicate over long and short distances, networked computers allow users to send messages across the office, across town, across the country, or around the world.

Electronic Mail (E-mail)

One of the most pervasive uses of networks is sending ***electronic mail,*** or e-mail. The benefits of e-mail are that it nearly eliminates "telephone tag" and that it enables widespread work groups to ignore time zones and office hours. The greater the number of people in an organization who use e-mail, with its ability to store information and deliver it when a recipient is ready to receive it, the less they are controlled by the constraints of real-time communication.

Later in this chapter we will describe in more detail how the Internet works. For now, realize that people everywhere use the Internet to easily exchange information using a variety of tools. ***Newsgroups,*** also called computer-based discussion groups, allow individuals and organizations to participate in discussions on almost any subject. There are now thousands of newsgroups, on every topic imaginable. Companies are using discussion groups as an easy way to share information with customers who want to discuss topics such as product applications or customer support.

Mailing lists, also known as listservs, let you use e-mail to participate in discussion groups on topics of special interest to you. Lists can be small and regional, or they can include participants from all over the world. Companies often create mailing lists for customers in order to send a single e-mail message to thousands of customers simultaneously.

Instant Messaging

Instant messaging (IM) (also referred to as Internet Relay Chat or real-time messaging) lets you have conversations with others in real time on the Internet. The process is somewhat like talking on the telephone, although you must type your comments instead of speaking them. You can converse with others as long as they are online and using the same messaging service you are using. Companies are using IM as a way to have interactive conversations with colleagues and customers throughout the world.

Facsimile (Fax)

Facsimile or ***fax machines*** digitize images, such as letters, memos, newspaper and magazine articles, photos, contracts, even handwritten notes, so that they can be transmitted to other fax machines over telephone lines. The receiving fax machine translates the material from digital data back to the original image. Facsimile machines are stand-alone desktop peripherals that send and receive printed information. More and more, organizations are using a PC as a fax machine, where the fax is sent and received like an e-mail message.

Voice Mail

In addition to e-mail, you may also have access to a voice mail system, either at work or through your PC at home or school, since many PC fax applications allow users to set up a voice mail system. ***Voice mail*** allows callers to leave voice messages in a voice mailbox, much like leaving a message on an answering machine. Unlike an answering machine, however, voice mail digitizes voice messages so that they can be stored on the computer.

Videoconferencing

Videoconferencing lets groups of people in the same office or at diverse locations meet online, rather than gathering together in one meeting room or travelling across the country to see one another in person (see Figure 4.3). A combination of software and hardware, including video cameras, microphones, and speakers, allows people in diverse locations to get together online to share information, discuss projects, and otherwise conduct business. Some videoconferencing systems let remote participants share applications and data and jointly make changes to documents and other information shown on-screen.

[**Figure 4.3** ➥ Videoconferencing allows people to see each other, to talk, and to collaborate on the same document from two or more different locations.]

Source: Courtesy of Microsoft Corporation.

Common Business Applications

Today, companies around the world consider networks to be essential tools for daily business communication. In addition to supporting interpersonal communication, networks support other types of telecommunication used to exchange business information, including electronic business, electronic data interchange, telecommuting, and electronic fund transfer. In this section, we will briefly describe these and other business examples.

Electronic Business

Electronic business (EB, or e-business) refers to the use of the Internet to support a variety of business activities, such as streamlining operations, selling products and providing customer support, connecting to suppliers, and many other business-related activities. E-business has become such an important aspect of business communication that most organizations—both small and large—now have a presence on the World Wide Web and many use the Internet to conduct day-to-day business.

Business ***Websites*** range from simple, just-the-facts pages that resemble printed brochures or data sheets to more sophisticated, interactive productions where customers can do everything from ordering products to taking a virtual tour through manufacturing facilities. Chapter 5, "Electronic Business, Intranets, and Extranets," describes in more detail how companies utilize electronic business.

Electronic Data Interchange (EDI)

Electronic data interchange (EDI) is another form of electronic business. It involves the use of telecommunications technology to transfer business information between organizations, thus cutting down on paperwork. With computers linked via a network, businesses using EDI can quickly transfer purchase orders to a supplier or invoices to affiliated stores, as well as other information that would take much longer to reach destinations if sent through regular mail services and that would require paperwork at both ends of the transaction. For example, a company such as General Motors or Dow Chemicals may use EDI to send an electronic purchase order to a supplier, rather than a paper request. Some businesses use private proprietary networks that are not subject to the traffic and security problems common with Internet use. Other firms use the Internet but use encryption software to keep financial data private.

Home Depot first began implementing an electronic data interchange network in 1992; today, 85 percent of all the company's dealings with suppliers—from ordering to invoicing—are conducted electronically. Home Depot is working with suppliers to bring consumers into an electronic network, thereby completing the loop among supplier, retailer, and customer. For instance, the company is linking its e-commerce engine to marketing sites operated by manufacturers. Shoppers browsing small-engine manufacturer Briggs & Stratton Corp.'s Website, for example, are dropped directly into Home Depot's checkout page if they click the "Find a merchant" button; they can buy from the site if there is a store in their area. We will describe EDI in more detail in Chapter 5.

Telecommuting

Telecommuting is the act of working at home or from another remote location and "commuting" to the office via computing and networking technologies (see Figure 4.4). Many recent television advertisements tout the advantages of doing business online by showing a home worker dressed for a teleconference in a no-nonsense business suit—from the waist up. Below the waist, the happy telecommuter wears pajama bottoms and bunny slippers. Other ads show the at-home worker cheerfully bouncing a small child while at the same time performing routine workday business at the computer. Telecommuting can let workers live where

---

BRIEF CASE

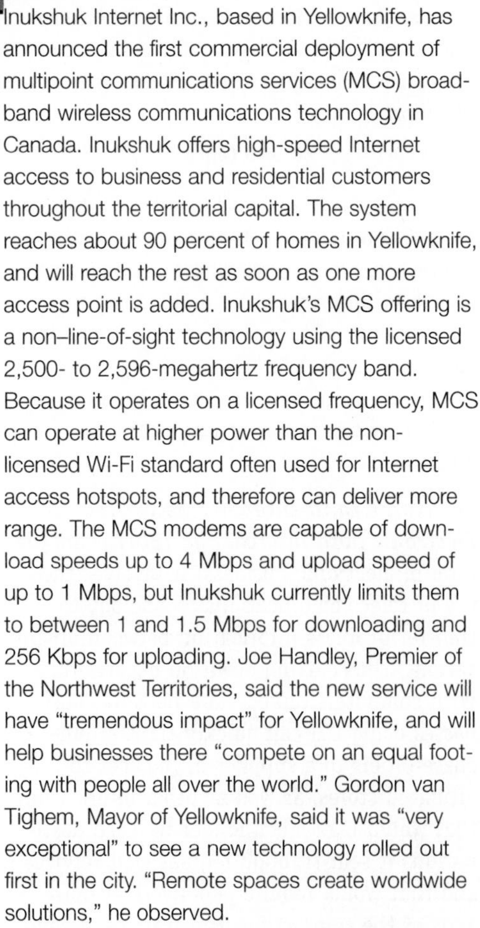

Fixed Wireless Connects the Far North

Inukshuk Internet Inc., based in Yellowknife, has announced the first commercial deployment of multipoint communications services (MCS) broadband wireless communications technology in Canada. Inukshuk offers high-speed Internet access to business and residential customers throughout the territorial capital. The system reaches about 90 percent of homes in Yellowknife, and will reach the rest as soon as one more access point is added. Inukshuk's MCS offering is a non–line-of-sight technology using the licensed 2,500- to 2,596-megahertz frequency band. Because it operates on a licensed frequency, MCS can operate at higher power than the non-licensed Wi-Fi standard often used for Internet access hotspots, and therefore can deliver more range. The MCS modems are capable of download speeds up to 4 Mbps and upload speed of up to 1 Mbps, but Inukshuk currently limits them to between 1 and 1.5 Mbps for downloading and 256 Kbps for uploading. Joe Handley, Premier of the Northwest Territories, said the new service will have "tremendous impact" for Yellowknife, and will help businesses there "compete on an equal footing with people all over the world." Gordon van Tighem, Mayor of Yellowknife, said it was "very exceptional" to see a new technology rolled out first in the city. "Remote spaces create worldwide solutions," he observed.

Tom Elliott, vice-president of consulting at Strategy Analytics, a Newton, Massachusetts, research firm, said there is renewed interest in fixed wireless technology for corporate networking and Internet access. He attributed the resurgence to several factors including declining costs and better non–line-of-sight technology. Not to mention ease of implementation in inhospitable environments; the people of Brandon, Manitoba, are used to the cold, but for Charlie Clark, President of I-Netlink Wireless, the cold can mean broken systems. I-Netlink runs 14 outdoor, fixed-link wireless devices for high-speed data transfer to the 20 communities and hundreds of subscribers served by the Brandon-based ISP. "With temperatures approaching the –40 Celsius level many times during the winter, I kept a vigilant eye on the network, wondering if the gear would hold up in such extreme weather," Clark explained. "So far, the units performed without a hitch." I-Netlink uses equipment manufactured by Markham, Ontario–based Redline Communications.

Questions

1. What is the business case for fixed wireless solutions? What are their advantages? Disadvantages?
2. What systems currently compete with fixed wireless? What systems might compete with them in the future?

[Adapted from Grant Buckler, "Yellowknife Gets High-Speed Access Through MCS," **http://www.itbusiness.ca/index.asp?theaction=61&sid=54796#**, ITBusiness.ca (February 11, 2004).]

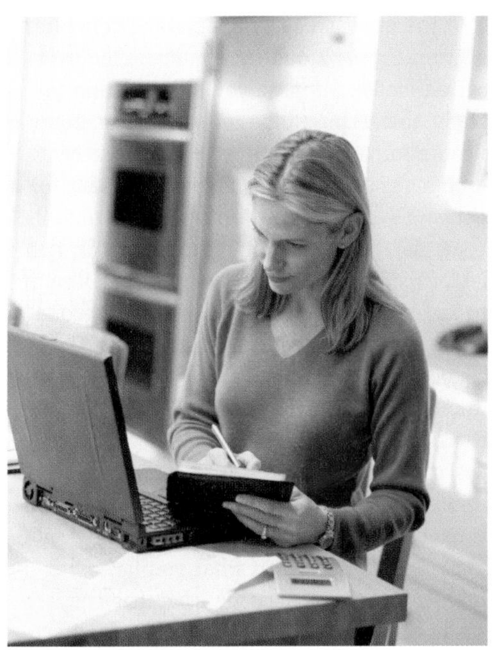

[**Figure 4.4** ➡ Telecommuting allows people to work from home using computing and networking technologies.]

Source: © Getty Images, Inc.

they choose, while being employed by a company in a distant location. The advantages of such an arrangement are obvious for disabled and ill employees, as well. Benefits for employers include increased worker satisfaction and productivity and decreased travel and on-site office maintenance costs.

Electronic Fund Transfer (EFT)

Electronic fund transfer (EFT) is another aspect of e-business. It involves transferring funds from one financial account to another via computer. For example, instead of receiving paycheques in the mail and depositing them in the bank, many people have such cheques sent directly from the source to their bank accounts. No money or paper changes hands, and the transfer occurs in the same day because cheques do not have to be mailed from one destination to another.

Many people also authorize the paying of bills electronically from their bank accounts. Automated teller machines (ATMs) are another visible means of electronic fund transfer that allow ATM card users to make deposits or withdraw cash quickly from machines placed in handy locations (see Figure 4.5). Companies, banks, and other financial institutions worldwide also use EFT to transfer funds among themselves. Unfortunately, these systems can be quite inefficient from a Canadian point of view. If a Canadian company wishes to wire

[**Figure 4.5** ➡ Automated teller machines are connected to networks, allowing people to access their bank accounts throughout the world.]

Source: © CORBIS.

funds to a vendor in Europe, for example, the transaction typically must go through a fixed set of intermediate financial institutions based in the United States.

Distance Learning

Distance learning is the process of providing instruction to students who are physically separated from instructors through the use of some sort of communication technologies including videoconferencing, Internet chatting, and various Web-based tools. As computer literacy and the availability of high-speed Internet access continue to increase, distance learning is gaining in popularity, and teaching methods are rapidly improving. Alberta-based Athabasca University runs a large online MBA program targeted at working professionals (see Figure 4.6).

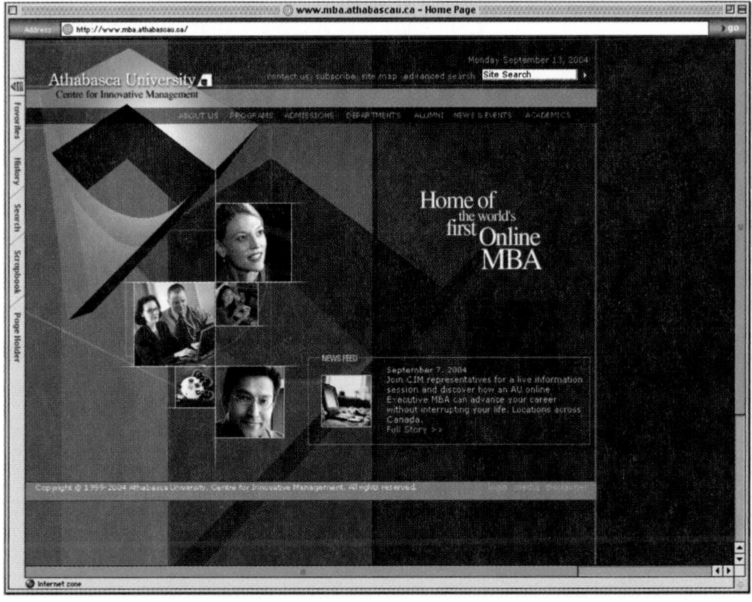

[**Figure 4.6** ➡ Athabasca University runs a large online MBA program.]

Source: Courtesy of Athabasca University's Centre for Innovative Management.

Telemedicine

Telemedicine is the exchange of medical information from one location to another via a computer network. This allows remote patients to be examined by the best medical doctors, regardless of where the doctors are located. When doctors are connected to a remote location, they can examine medical images and monitor patients effectively.

Now that you have seen some sample uses of telecommunications and networks, we will next describe how these technologies work and how they have evolved.

EVOLUTION OF COMPUTER NETWORKING

Human communication involves the sharing of information and messages between senders and receivers. The sender of a message forms the message in his brain and codes the message into a form that can be communicated to the receiver—through voice, for example. The message is then transmitted along a communication pathway to the receiver. The receiver, using her ears and brain, then attempts to decode the message, as shown in Figure 4.7. This basic model of human communication helps us to understand telecommunications or computer networking.

Messages, Senders, and Receivers

Computer networking is the sharing of information or services. As with human communication, all computer networks require three things:

- Senders and receivers that have something to share
- A pathway or transmission medium, such as a cable, to send the message
- Rules or protocols dictating communication between senders and receivers

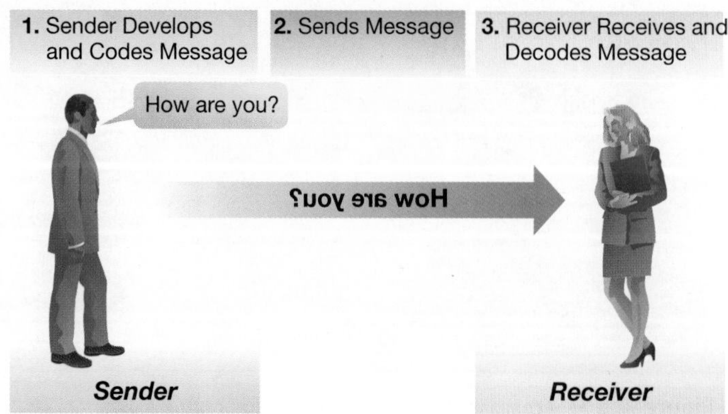

[Figure 4.7 ➥ Communication requires senders and receivers.]

The easiest way to understand computer networking is through the human communication model. Suppose you are planning to study abroad in Europe for a semester. You need information about schools that accept exchange students. The first requirement for a network—information to share—has now been met. You start your search by writing a letter (coding your message) and e-mailing it to several schools. You have met the second requirement—a means of transmitting the coded message. The e-mail system is the pathway or transmission medium used to contact the receiver. ***Transmission media*** refers to the physical cable(s) used to carry network information. At this point, you may run into some difficulties. Not all the receivers of your e-mail may understand what you have written—decode your message—because they speak other languages. Although you have contacted the receiver, you and the receiver of your message must meet the third requirement for a successful network: you must establish a language of communication—the rules or protocols governing your communication. ***Protocols*** define the procedures that different computers follow when they transmit and receive data. You both might decide that one communication protocol will be that you communicate in English. This communication session is illustrated in Figure 4.8.

Computer Networks

A fundamental difference between human and computer communication is that human communication consists of words, whereas computer communication consists of bits, the fundamental information units of computers, as depicted in Figure 4.9. Virtually all types of information can be transmitted on a computer network—documents, art, music, film—although each type of information has vastly different requirements for effective transmission. For example, a single screen of text is approximately 10 kilobytes of data, whereas an uncompressed photograph-quality picture could be larger than 200 megabytes of data (see Table 4.1). The process of converting a photograph or a song into digital information, or bits, is called ***digitizing.*** Note that when data is stored in a location, like a file on your hard drive, its size is measured in *bytes*. However, when data is being transferred from one place to another, it is measured in *bits*. There are eight bits in a byte. After information is converted into bits, it can travel across a network. To transmit either the screen of

[Figure 4.8 ➥ Coding, sending, and decoding a message.]

text or the picture in a timely manner from one location to another, adequate bandwidth is needed. For example, using a 56 Kbps ***modem***—a device that transmits approximately 56 kilobits of data in a second—a single screen of text would be transferred in under one second, while a digital image could take more than four seconds. Hence, different types of information have different communication bandwidth requirements.

Now that you understand the basic elements of networks, we will talk about how they have evolved. Since the beginning of the Information Age in the 1950s, people and enterprises have used computers to process data and information. Over the years, however, computer networks have become better and better.

Centralized Computing

Centralized computing, depicted in Figure 4.10, remained largely unchanged through the 1970s. In this model, large centralized computers, called mainframes, were used to process and store data. During the mainframe era (beginning in the 1940s), people entered data on mainframes through the use of local input devices called ***terminals.*** These devices were called "dumb" terminals because they did not conduct any processing or "smart"

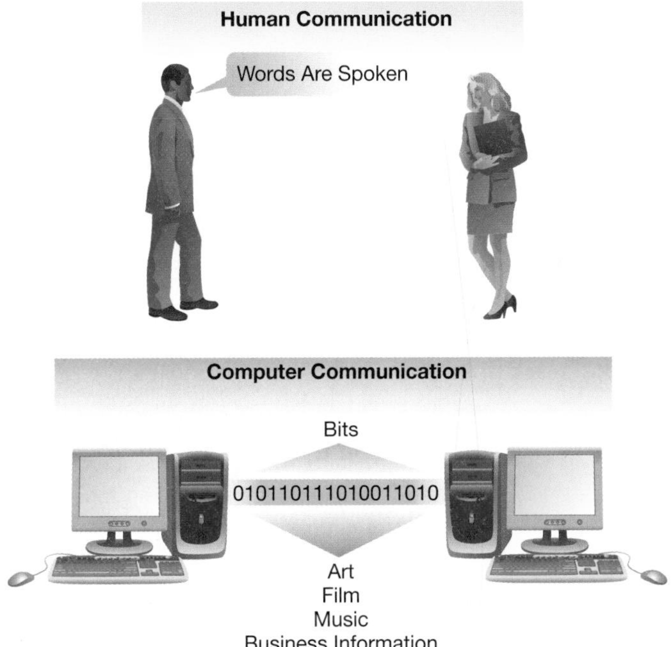

[Figure 4.9 ➥ In human communication, words are spoken and transmitted in the air. In computer communication, digital data is transmitted over some type of communication medium.]

[Table 4.1] ***Communication and storage/bandwidth requirements for different types of information.***

Type of Information	Raw Size	Compressed Size
Voice		
Telephone	64 Kbps	16–32 Kbps
Teleconference	96 Kbps	32–64 Kbps
Compact disc	1.41 Mbps	63–128 Kbps
Data		
Single screen of text	14.4 KB	4.8–7.2 KB
Typed page, single-spaced	28.8 KB	9.6–14.4 KB
Faxed page (low to high resolution)	1.68–3.36 MB	130–336 KB
Super VGA screen image	6.3 MB	315–630 KB
Digital X-ray	50.3 MB	16.8–25.1 MB
Publication-quality photograph	230.4 MB	23–46 MB
Video		
Video telephony	9.3 Mbps	64–384 Kbps
Video teleconferencing	37.3 Mbps	384 Kbps–1.92 Mbps
CCITT multimedia	166 Mbps	1.7 Mbps
High-definition television	1.33 Gbps	20–50 Mbps

Note: KB = kilobytes, Kbps = kilobits per second; MB = megabyte; Mbps = megabits per second; Gbps = gigabits per second.

Source: Table adapted from *Business Data Communications*, Second Edition by Stallings/VanSlyke. © 1997. Reprinted by permission of Prentice-Hall, Inc., Upper Saddle River, NJ.

activities. The centralized computing model is not a true network because there is no sharing of information and capabilities. The mainframe provides all the capabilities, and the terminals are only input/output devices. Computer networks evolved in the 1980s when organizations needed separate, independent computers to communicate with each other.

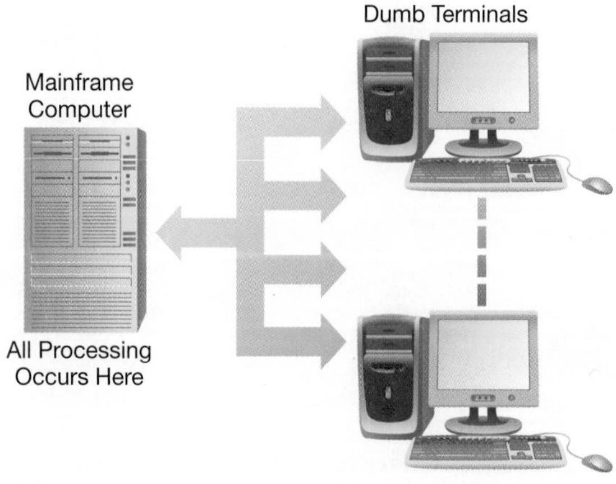

[Figure 4.10 ➥ In the centralized computing model, all processing occurs in one central mainframe.]

Distributed Computing

The introduction of personal computers in the late 1970s and early 1980s gave individuals control over their own computing. Organizations also realized that they could use multiple small computers to achieve many of the same processing goals of a single large computer. People could work on subsets of tasks on separate computers rather than using one mainframe to perform all the processing. Achieving the goal of separate processing required computer networks so that information and services could be easily shared between these distributed computers. The 1980s were characterized by an evolution to a computing model called ***distributed computing*** (shown in Figure 4.11), in which multiple types of computers are networked together to share information and services.

Collaborative Computing

In the 1990s, a new computing model, called ***collaborative computing,*** emerged. Collaborative computing is a synergistic form of distributed computing, in which two or

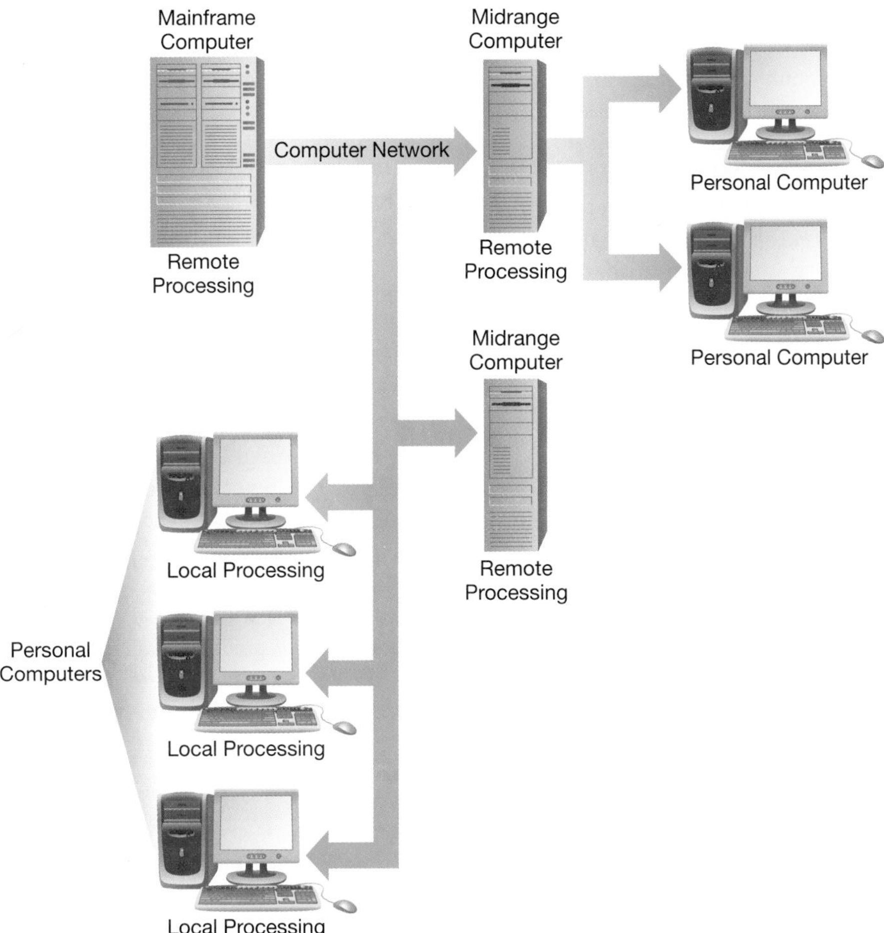

[**Figure 4.11** ➡ In the distributed computing model, separate computers work on subsets of tasks and then pool their results by communicating over a network.]

more networked computers are used to accomplish a common processing task. That is, in this model of computing, computers are not simply communicating data but are sharing processing capabilities. For example, one computer may be used to store a large employee database. A second computer may be used to process and update individual employee records selected from this database. The two computers collaborate to keep the company's employee records current, as depicted in Figure 4.12.

Types of Networks

Computing networks today include all three computing models: centralized, distributed, and collaborative. The emergence of new computing models did not mean that organizations completely discarded older technologies. Rather, a typical computer network includes

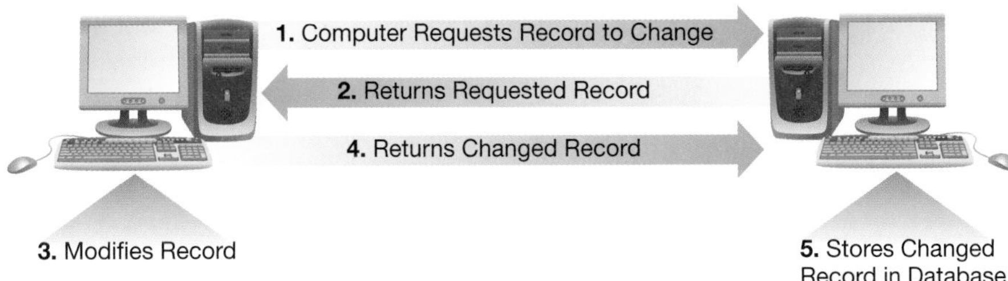

[**Figure 4.12** ➡ In the collaborative computing model, two or more networked computers are used to accomplish a common processing task.]

mainframes, minicomputers, personal computers, and a variety of other devices. Computer networks are commonly classified by size, distance covered, and structure. The most commonly used classifications are a private branch exchange (PBX), local area network (LAN), wide area network (WAN), metropolitan area network (MAN), and personal area network (PAN). Each is described in the following sections.

Private Branch Exchange (PBX)

A ***private branch exchange (PBX)*** is a telephone system that serves a particular location, such as a business (see Figure 4.13). It connects one telephone extension to another within the system and connects the PBX to the outside telephone network. It can also connect computers within the system to other PBX systems, to an outside network, or to various office devices such as fax machines or photocopiers. Since they use ordinary telephone lines, PBX systems have limited bandwidth. This prevents them from transmitting such forms of information as interactive video, digital music, or high-resolution photos. Using PBX technology, a business requires few outside phone lines but has to purchase or lease the PBX equipment. Many PBX systems are now being converted to Voice over Internet Protocol (VoIP) systems, which are better able to integrate voice and data traffic. Telus, for example, is moving all of its business telecommunications products to IP-based systems.

Local Area Network (LAN)

A ***local area network (LAN),*** shown in Figure 4.14, is a computer network that spans a relatively small area, allowing all computer users to connect with each other to share information and peripheral devices, such as a printer. LAN-based communications may involve the sharing of data, software applications, or other resources among several users. LANs typically do not exceed tens of kilometres in size, and are typically contained within a single building or a limited geographical area. They typically use only one kind of transmission medium or cabling, such as twisted-pair wire or coaxial cable. There are also ***wireless local area network*** products available. These are very popular because they are relatively easy to set up and enable you to have a network without any network cables strewn around your home or office.

Wide Area Network (WAN)

A ***wide area network (WAN)*** is a computer network that spans a relatively large geographical area. WANs are typically used to connect two or more LANs. Different hardware

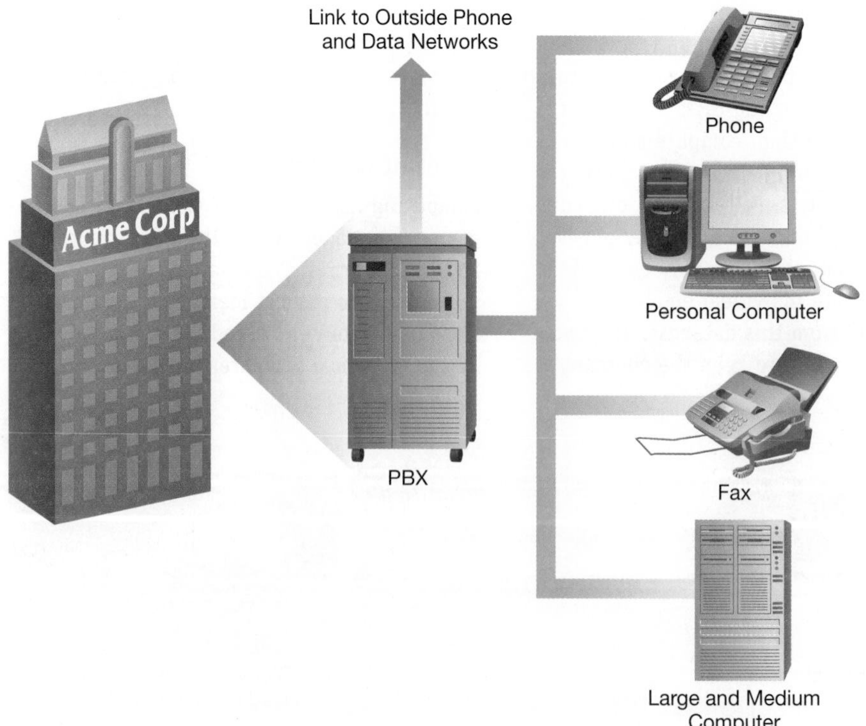

[**Figure 4.13** ➥ A private branch exchange (PBX) supports local phone and data communications, as well as links to outside phone and data networks.]

[Figure 4.14 ➡ A local area network (LAN) allows multiple computers located near each other to communicate directly with each other and to share peripheral devices, such as a printer.]

and transmission media are often used in WANs because they must cover large distances efficiently. Used by multinational companies, WANs transmit and receive information across cities and countries. Four specific types of WANs—global networks, enterprise networks, value-added networks, and metropolitan area networks—are discussed below.

Global Networks A ***global network*** spans multiple countries and may include the networks of several organizations. The Internet is

WHEN THINGS GO WRONG

VoIP Users May Be Lost to Emergency Services

Flexibility and portability, the very things that make Voice over Internet Protocol (VoIP) services attractive to enterprise users, are hampering efforts to track emergency 911 calls. VoIP devices are tracked back to an IP address rather than to a single physical location, which makes it hard for emergency services to locate callers. Providers of 911 solutions are holding their breath as industry and government bodies square off over how to regulate the transmission of voice over the Internet. "There's a great tug of war going on," says John Thompson, vice-president of marketing and product management at Gatineau, Quebec–based CML Emergency Services Inc. "One side is saying, 'Governments should mandate a solution so VoIP is carrier-grade, and as reliable as a legacy phone system,' while others believe private industry will solve the problem through the free market."

A big question regarding the use of residential VoIP is whether a 24/7, 911 service can be offered through an IP network. Since IP phones are so mobile, it's possible that an emergency response team would not be able to locate a 911 caller, subsequently putting users' lives at risk. Yet companies aren't exactly "rushing forward with any radical new technology" to solve the problem until regulators decide whether to mandate a solution or to leave it up to industry, says Thompson. "You could push something forward, but if the regulatory body wins, your investment could be lost."

Nonetheless, it seems CML is prepared to take some chances. The company's lab is currently working on a solution that allows a VoIP user to send a call into an IT-enabled answering point through end-to-end IP calls. CML is ready to conduct trials with such technology and is prepared to release test products by the end of 2004, says Thompson. "We're looking to provide a bulletproof solution. We're pushing this forward as fast as we possibly can, but the market's going to take a while to mature."

Some solutions that already exist include an attempt by New Jersey–based Vonage Holdings Corp. The company introduced its residential VoIP plan last December and announced its 911 scheme last April. Vonage tries to solve the 911 problem by recording the location of all users in a database, giving them the option of changing their information if they move temporarily. However, that information becomes erroneous if the user moves for a day or two and doesn't provide an information update, says Thompson. Even a Vonage spokeswoman calls the system "very rudimentary." "If you need [traditional 911] capability, we encourage you to maintain a land line. We're... months away from a solution," says Brooke Schulz.

[Adapted from Scott Foster, "Do You Know Where Your VoIP User Is?," **http://www.itbusiness.ca/index.asp?theaction=61&sid=54750#**, ITBusiness.ca (February 9, 2004).]

an example of a global network. The Internet is the world's largest computer network, consisting of thousands of individual networks supporting millions of computers and users in more than 160 countries. Later in this chapter we will provide a more detailed discussion of the Internet.

Enterprise Networks An ***enterprise network*** is a WAN that is the result of connecting disparate networks of a single organization into a single network (see Figure 4.15).

Value-Added Networks Medium-speed WANs, called ***value-added networks (VANs)***, are private, third-party–managed networks that are economical because they are shared by multiple organizations. Customers lease communication lines rather than investing in dedicated network equipment. The "added value" provided by VANs can include network management, e-mail, EDI, security, and other special capabilities. Consequently, VANs can be more expensive than generic communication lines leased from a common telecommunication company like Bell Canada or Aliant, but they provide valuable services for customers.

Metropolitan Area Networks A ***metropolitan area network (MAN)*** is a computer network of limited geographic scope, typically a citywide area, that combines both LAN and high-speed fibre-optic technologies. MANs are attractive to organizations that need high-speed data transmission within a limited geographic area.

BRIEF CASE

Maritime Steel Expands VoIP System

As president of Maritime Steel and Foundries Ltd. of Halifax, Don Cameron conducts a great deal of business by phone. So when his company—a manufacturer of bridges and steel supports—decided to replace an aging private branch exchange (PBX) with a Voice over IP (VoIP) platform in 2000, quality of service, convenience, and reliability were just a few of his top concerns. Four years later, there's no question his company made the right decision, he says. "I don't see a bit of difference—the quality is every bit as good and my phone has never been down," says Cameron. "I've never had an ounce of problem with it."

Maritime Steel recently expanded its VoIP platform—the NBX 100 phone system from 3Com Corp.—to provide long-distance service between its structural steel division in Dartmouth, Nova Scotia, and a foundry division in New Glasgow, Nova Scotia. Employees in either location can reach each other by dialling a three-digit extension, whether they're calling someone across the hall or two hours away, without incurring long-distance charges. Sean Green, Maritime Steel's manager of information systems, says the sites are taking advantage of the NBX 100's virtual tie line, which creates an open line between the NBX in Halifax and the second NBX recently installed in New Glasgow. "Basically, you pick up your set, hit three digits, and you're talking to a co-worker over our network routers," said Green.

Unlike the old phone system, which was costly to maintain and required constant servicing from a third party located more than two hours away, the VoIP platform is administered solely by Green. If a new employee requires a phone, he simply plugs it into the existing category five cabling, he says, and if there's no handset available, he sets up a "soft set," allowing a PC to be used to make and receive calls via a headpiece attached through the USB port. In addition to saving on long-distance costs between divisions, Green has also configured the phone system to save voice mail messages as .wav files that can be forwarded as e-mail. When executives are away on business, they use their laptops to retrieve voice mail, eliminating the need to dial in for messages. Incoming calls can also be forwarded to "hunt groups" so that if an extension isn't answered after a specified number of rings, the call will automatically be sent to a different device. "A user has the flexibility of moving around quite easily," says Jerry Gushue, 3Com's regional account manager for Atlantic Canada. "As long as you plug into the network, the network will find you."

Questions

1. What advantages do VoIP systems have over traditional PBX systems?
2. VoIP systems have received a good deal of positive spin in the media, yet their adoption by businesses in Canada has been disappointing. Why do you think this has been the case?

[Adapted from Dianne Daniel, "Halifax-based Steel Manufacturer Cuts Long-Distance Costs with VoIP," *Communications & Networking,* Vol. 6, No. 9 (September 2003).]

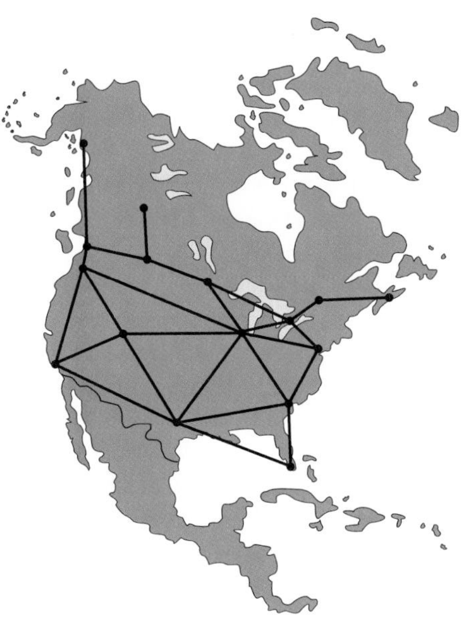

[**Figure 4.15** ➡ An enterprise network allows an organization to connect distributed locations into a single network.]

Personal Area Network (PAN)

A final type of computer network, called a ***personal area network (PAN)***, is an emerging technology that uses wireless communication to exchange data between computing devices using short-range radio communication, typically within an area of 10 metres. The enabling technology for PAN is called ***Bluetooth***, a specification for personal networking of desktop computers, peripheral devices, mobile phones, pagers, portable stereos, and other handheld devices. Bluetooth's founding members include Ericsson, IBM, Intel, Nokia, and Toshiba.

Although there are many different types of networks, all networks are very similar in how they are designed and function. In the next section, we examine in more detail the Internet, one of the largest and most widely used networks.

Web Search

WEB SEARCH OPPORTUNITY
To find out more about Bluetooth technologies and applications, see **www.bluetooth.com.**

CAREER IMPLICATIONS

Information Systems

Despite the recent growth spurt in Voice over IP (VoIP) adoption, not all companies are going to completely dispense with time division multiplexing (TDM) technologies for phone service. Three years ago, VoIP was touted as a technology that could supplant TDM in corporate networks, said Tracy Fleming, a convergence specialist with Markham, Ontario–based Avaya Canada Corp. But now, companies installing VoIP are using it only in select areas, such as wide area connections.

"We're actually seeing customers rip out pure-play Voice over IP systems," replacing them with hybrid VoIP and TDM systems, which allow certain advantages, such as redundancy. The whole concept of Voice over IP at one time was toll avoidance—'We're going to rip off the phone company,'" he said.

In order to make VoIP work well over a wide area network, Fleming said, users discovered they would need to add service-level guarantees, which cost more money. "And guess where you buy the wide area network service from? The same guys you buy your phone service from." Telecommunications carriers are now selling—and making profits from—IP services that include quality-of-service provisions. In some cases, Fleming said, VoIP has become more expensive than traditional services. "We now see a lot of people adopting the revolutionary new technology called voice over the telephone network!" he quipped.

Some companies use VoIP only to route calls between far-flung offices, and continue to use TDM for voice traffic within their offices. Elevator manufacturer ThyssenKrupp AG, for example, routes its customer calls between its Canadian offices over Bell Canada's frame relay network but uses TDM to route calls within its offices.

Calculating the ROI on VoIP is not an exact science, and varies from industry to industry, said Ronald Gruia, enterprise communications program leader for research firm Frost & Sullivan's Canadian office. Gruia agrees that toll bypass has become a less compelling selling point of VoIP. The big question now is what will drive future growth. Although VoIP will let companies use applications that could not be used with TDM, it is difficult to convince business managers to make the investment, he said, adding that companies that don't install VoIP now will do so eventually because they will discover competitors who are using VoIP have certain advantages.

The U.S. Federal Communications Commission (FCC) voted against subjecting voice calls between computers to the same regulations as telephony services. The Canadian Radio-television and Telecommunications Commission (CRTC) has yet to rule on the issue.

[Adapted from Greg Meckbach, "The Tenacity of TDM," **http://www.itbusiness.ca/index.asp?theaction=61&sid=54807#**, ITBusiness.ca (February 9, 2004).]

BRIEF CASE

Earls Restaurants Serves Wi-Fi on the Side

A restaurant chain hopes to provide its employees and customers greater access to the Internet throughout Western Canada through the installation of wireless access points. Vancouver-based Earls Restaurants, which has more than 50 locations in British Columbia, Alberta, and Saskatchewan, completed a Wi-Fi project with FatPort Inc. of Vancouver. Earls offers wireless Internet access to corporate customers, who regularly book business lunches, but a key driver for the initiative was to support its own executives, according to director of IT services Brad Brooks. Each restaurant has its own office but they're often quite small, and district managers, for example, travel regularly to various locations with laptops in tow. "There's no place for them to go into the back and check e-mail," he said.

Brooks said Earls needed to provide Internet access without creating an additional strain on his IT department. The company had also been watching Wi-Fi deployments at Fairmont Hotels, Coastal Resorts, and fast food giant McDonald's, he said. "If I knew that Earls had wireless access as a traveller or as a guy making sales calls—like I did in my previous life—I would eat in a restaurant that had that," he said. "It's one more way that we can service our customer."

FatPort marketing manager Malcolm McDonald said Wi-Fi could be particularly attractive during the mid-afternoons, which tend to be a quiet time at restaurants like Earls. "We are definitely seeing more and more restaurants jumping on this Wi-Fi bandwagon," he said. "Especially in lunch, there's a big drive towards business lunch meetings, and they need something to be able to attract their customers." Earls has been using DSL high-speed Internet access for several years and already had much of the necessary infrastructure in place, Brooks said. FatPort simply had to install a microwave transmitter at each location. A number of other Canadian restaurant chains have also started to offer Wi-Fi Internet access over the last year, including Lone Star Texas Grill and Big Daddy's Crab Shack & Oyster Bar.

Questions

1. Wi-Fi–based Internet access is being offered at an increasing number of locations across Canada. Describe some places where you have seen or used a Wi-Fi network.
2. Would you pay extra to eat in a restaurant that offered Wi-Fi Internet access? How much would you be prepared to pay?

[Adapted from Shane Schick, "B.C. Restaurant Chain Offers Wi-Fi with Power Lunch," **http://www.itbusiness.ca/index.asp?theaction=61&sid=54773#**, ITBusiness.ca (February 10, 2004).]

THE INTERNET

The name ***Internet*** is derived from the concept of ***internetworking***, which means connecting host computers and their networks together to form even larger networks. The Internet is a large worldwide collection of networks that use a common protocol to communicate with each other.

How Did the Internet Get Started?

You can trace the roots of the Internet back to the late 1960s, when the U.S. ***Defense Advanced Research Projects Agency (DARPA)*** began to study ways to interconnect networks of various kinds. This research effort produced ***ARPANET*** (Advanced Research Projects Agency Network), a large wide area network that linked many universities and research centres. The first two nodes on ARPANET were UCLA and the Stanford Research Institute, followed by the University of Utah.

ARPANET quickly evolved and was combined with other networks. For example, in 1986, the U.S. ***National Science Foundation (NSF)*** initiated the development of the ***NSFNET (National Science Foundation Network)***, which became a major component of the Internet. Other networks throughout the United States and the rest of the world were interconnected and/or morphed into the growing "Internet." Among these were BITNET, CSNET, NSINET, ESNET, and NORDUNET. Throughout the world, support for the Internet has come from a combination of federal and state governments, universities, national and international research organizations, and industry.

The Internet Uses Packet-Switching Technology

The Internet relies on ***packet-switching*** technology to deliver data and information across networks. Packet switching enables millions of users to send large and small chunks of data across the Internet concurrently. Packet switching is based on the concept of turn taking. To minimize delays, network technologies limit the amount of data that a computer can transfer on each turn. Consider a conveyor belt as a comparison. Suppose that the conveyor belt connects a warehouse and customer storeroom. When a customer places an order, it is sent to the warehouse, where a clerk assembles the items in the order. The items are placed on the conveyor belt and delivered to the storeroom. In most situations, clerks finish sending items from one order before proceeding to send items from another order. This process works well when orders are small, but when a large order with many items is placed, sharing a conveyor belt can introduce delays for others. Consider waiting in the storeroom for your one item while another order with 50 items is being filled.

LANs, WANs, and the Internet all use packet-switching technologies so that users can share the communication channel and minimize delivery delays. Figure 4.16 illustrates how computers use packet switching. Computer A wants to send a message to computer C; similarly, computer B wants to send a message to computer D. For example, computer A is trying to send an e-mail message to computer C, while computer B is trying to send a word processing file to computer D. The outgoing messages are divided into smaller packets of data, and then each sending computer (A and B) takes turns sending the packets over the transmission media. The incoming packets are reassembled at their respective destinations using previously identified packet sequence numbers.

For packet switching to work, each packet being sent across a network must be labelled with a header. This header contains the network address of the source (sending computer) and the network address of the destination (receiving computer). Each computer attached to a network has a unique network address. As packets are sent, network hardware detects whether a particular packet is destined for a local machine. Packet-switching systems adapt instantly to changes in network traffic. If only one computer needs to use the network, it can send data continuously. As soon as another computer needs to send data, packet switching, or turn taking, begins. Now, let us see how the Internet handles this packet switching.

Transmission Control Protocol/ Internet Protocol (TCP/IP)

Organizations use diverse network technologies that may or may not be compatible with the technologies of other organizations. Because so many different networks are interconnected nowadays, they must have a common language, or protocol, to communicate. The protocol of the Internet is called ***TCP/IP (transmission control protocol/Internet protocol).*** The first part, TCP, breaks information into small chunks called data packets and manages the transfer of those packets from computer to computer (via packet switching, as described above). For example, a single document may be broken into several packets, each containing several hundred characters, as well as a destination address, which is the IP part of the protocol. The IP defines how a data packet must be formed and to where a router must forward each packet. Packets travel independently to their destination, sometimes following different paths and arriving out of order. The destination computer reassembles all the packets based on their identification and sequencing information. Together, TCP and IP provide a reliable and efficient way to send data across the Internet.

A data packet that conforms to the IP specification is called an ***IP datagram.***

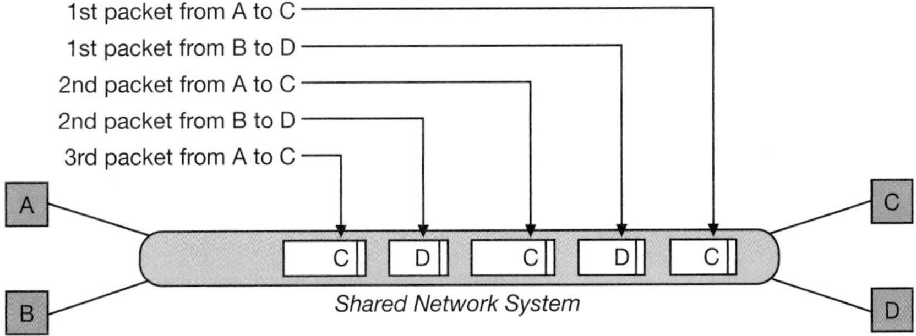

[**Figure 4.16** ➥ Using packet switching to send messages from files on computers A and B to computers C and D.]

Source: Comer, Douglas E., *The Internet Book*, 2/e, Prentice Hall, 1997.

Datagram routing and delivery are possible because, as previously mentioned, every computer and router connected to the Internet is assigned a unique IP address. When an organization connects to the Internet, it obtains a set of IP addresses that it can assign to its computers. TCP helps IP guarantee delivery of datagrams by performing three main tasks. First, it automatically checks for datagrams that may have been lost en route from their source to their destination. Second, TCP collects the incoming datagrams and puts them in the correct order to recreate the original message. Finally, TCP discards any duplicate copies of datagrams that may have been created by network hardware.

Connecting Independent Networks

Now that you understand how computers share a transmission path, we can examine how packet-switching networks are interconnected to form the Internet. The Internet uses special-purpose computers, called ***routers,*** to interconnect independent networks. For example, Figure 4.17 illustrates a router that connects Network 1 and Network 2. A router, like a conventional computer, has a central processor, memory, and network interfaces. However, routers do not use conventional software, nor are they used to run applications. Their only job is to interconnect networks and forward data packets from one network to another. For example, in Figure 4.17, computers A and F are connected to independent networks. If computer A generates a data packet destined for computer F, the packet is sent to the router that interconnects the two networks. The router forwards the packet onto Network 2, where it is delivered to its destination at computer F.

Routers are the fundamental building blocks of the Internet because they connect thousands of LANs and WANs. LANs are connected to backbone WANs, as depicted in Figure 4.18. A ***backbone network*** manages the bulk of network traffic and typically uses a higher-speed protocol than the individual LAN segments. For example, a backbone network might use fibre-optic cabling, which can transfer data at a rate of 3 Gbps, whereas a LAN connected to the backbone may use ethernet cabling, transferring data at a rate of 100 Mbps. To gain access to the Internet, an organization connects a router between one of its own networks and the closest Internet site. Business organizations typically connect to the Internet not only with personal computers but also with Web servers, or hosts.

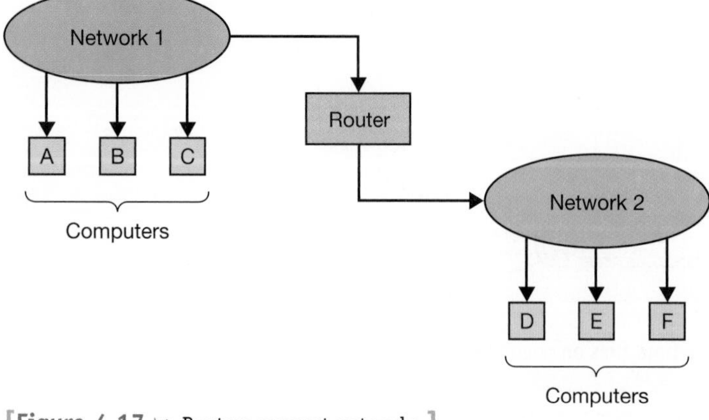

[**Figure 4.17** ➡ Routers connect networks.]

Web Domain Names and Addresses

Each of the hosts or Websites that you visit on the Internet is assigned a ***domain name.*** Domain names are used in ***Uniform Resource Locators (URLs)*** to identify particular ***Web pages.*** For example, in the URL **www.pcWebopedia.com/index.html**, the domain name is pcWebopedia.com.

The prefix of every domain name is a term that helps people recognize the company or person that domain name represents. For example, Microsoft's domain name is microsoft.com. The prefix, microsoft, lets you know that it is very likely that this domain name will lead you to the Website of Microsoft Corporation. Domain names also have a suffix that indicates which ***top-level domain*** they belong to. For example the "com" suffix is reserved for commercial organizations.

- edu—educational institutions
- org—organizations (nonprofit)
- mil—military
- com—commercial businesses
- net—network organizations
- ca—Canada

Domain names ending with .com, .net, or .org can be registered through many different companies (known as "registrars") that compete with one another. An alphabetical listing of these registrars is provided in the InterNIC Registrar Directory on the InterNIC site at **www.internic.net/regist.html**. In Canada, the registration process for the ".ca" domain is overseen by the Canadian Internet Registration Authority (CIRA) **www.cira.ca/en/register.html**. Organizations or individuals wanting to register a .ca domain must provide proof of residence in Canada. Once this proof has been provided, the registration process

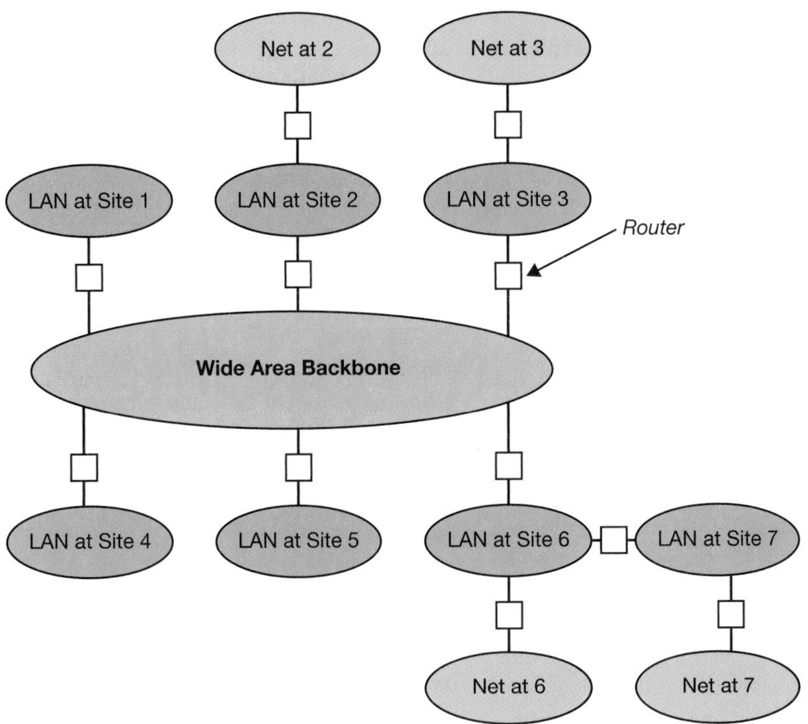

[**Figure 4.18** ➡ LANs connect to wide area backbones.]

Source: Comer, Douglas, E., *The Internet Book*, 2/e, Prentice Hall, 1997.

CAREER IMPLICATIONS

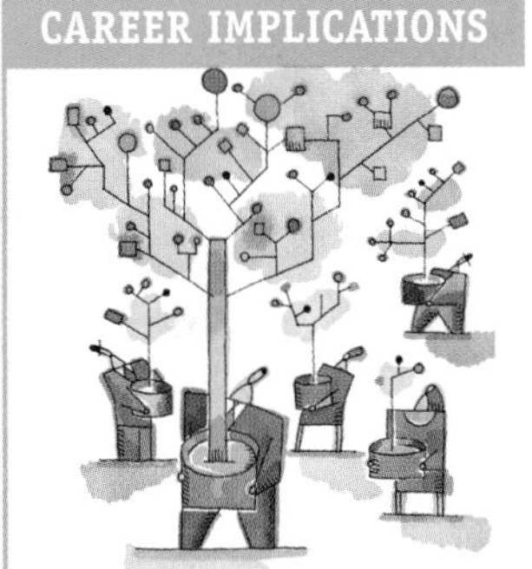

Accounting and Finance

Moneris Solutions Corp., the company that handles the bulk of Canada's transaction processing traffic for merchants, is moving away from a legacy pipeline to a private IP network platform. The company handled about 1.9 billion credit and debit card transactions in 2003 and predicts that half of those will move to its IP network by 2006. The new system will lower processing costs for merchants, while increasing point-of-sale (POS) functionality.

The IP network is cheaper to operate and faster than its legacy predecessor, said Moneris vice-president of product development Amer Matar. "The legacy networks are becoming more and more expensive. They're also getting outdated and the skills of supporting these networks are basically dwindling. Most of the skills in the sector today are geared towards IP," he said. Some of Moneris's larger clients, like Future Shop and Staples, are already IP-enabled and have a direct link to Moneris using their own corporate networks as a pipeline. "All of these guys have IP into their stores," said Matar. "For the smaller merchant, we have deployed a solution that goes all the way into the store," he added. "It's business to DSL, but it's a lot more... in the sense that it's a private offering, so these transactions do not ride over the public Internet." The advantage of using private IP that is dedicated to transaction processing is that it does not compete with any other traffic for bandwidth, he said.

Bell Canada's enterprise division, which provisioned Moneris's network, began offering private IP networks several years ago, and the payments industry in Canada is gravitating towards it, said director of new business development Herb Underhill. "We are on the cusp of a mass migration from an old architecture for payments in this country... to a new one," said Underhill. Moneris will continue to support dial-up technology, which some smaller merchants log on to every time they conduct a customer card transaction. Moneris's IP network, by contrast, is an always-on network.

With the addition of IP services, Matar noted that Moneris now often deals with CIOs in addition to the CFOs the company dealt with in the past. "We used to sell more to the CFO," he said. "With IP, as we make our applications richer in functionality, that is shifting a bit more into a technical discussion."

[Adapted from Neil Sutton, "Moneris Moves with Merchants to IP Networks," **http://www.itbusiness.ca/index.asp?theaction=61&sid=54737#**, (February 5, 2004); and Michael Martin, "Payment Processor Unveils IP Options," *IT World Canada* (February 5, 2004).]

can be undertaken through a number of licensed registrars, including **www.internic.ca** and **www.canreg.ca**. Just over 400,000 .ca domains had been registered as of August 2004.

Each of these domain names is associated with one or more ***IP addresses.*** For example, the domain name microsoft.com represents about a dozen underlying IP addresses. IP addresses serve to identify all the computers or devices on the Internet (or on any TCP/IP network). The IP address serves as the destination address of that computer or device and enables the network to route messages to the proper destination. The format of an IP address is a 32-bit numeric address written as four numbers separated by periods. Each of the four numbers can be any number between zero and 255. For example, 1.160.10.240 could be an IP address. You could set up a private network using the TCP/IP protocol and assign your own domain names and IP addresses for computers and other devices on that network. On the other hand, if you wish to connect to the Internet, you must use registered IP addresses.

Who Manages the Internet?

So, who keeps track of these IP addresses on the Internet? A number of national and international standing committees and task forces have been used to manage the development and use of the Internet. Among these is the Coordinating Committee for Intercontinental Networks (CCIRN), which has helped to coordinate government-sponsored research in this area. The Internet Society (ISOC) is a professional membership society, with more than 150 organizational and 6,000 individual members around the world, that helps to shape the future of the Internet and is home for the Internet Engineering Task Force (IETF) and the Internet Architecture Board (IAB). These groups help manage Internet standards. For example, the IAB has guided the evolution of the TCP/IP Protocol Suite. The Internet Assigned Numbers Authority (IANA) has provided the recording of system identifiers on the Internet and has helped to manage an ***Internet Registry*** that acts as a central repository for Internet-related information and provides central allocation of network system identifiers. The Internet Registry also provides central maintenance of the ***domain name system (DNS)*** root database, which points to distributed DNS servers replicated throughout the Internet. This database is used to associate Internet host names with their Internet IP addresses.

In 1993 the NSF created ***InterNIC,*** a government–industry collaboration, to manage directory and database services, domain registration services, and other information services on the Internet. In the late 1990s, this Internet oversight was transitioned more fully out into industry when InterNIC morphed into the ***Internet Corporation for Assigned Names and Numbers (ICANN),*** a nonprofit corporation that assumed responsibility for managing IP addresses, domain names, and root server system management. Specifically, the ***InterNIC Registration Service*** now assigns Internet addresses. The number of unassigned Internet addresses is running out, so new classes of addresses are being added as we adopt ***IPv6,*** the latest version of the Internet Protocol.

How Do You Connect to the Internet?

Now you can see how the Internet works and how it is managed. How do you connect to the Internet? For personal use (i.e., from home) we typically connect to the Internet through ***Internet service providers (ISPs),*** also called Internet access providers. For a monthly fee, these ISPs will give you a username, password, and an access gateway (and in some cases specialized access software). With your personal computer and a modem (phone, cable, or ADSL), you can then log on through the ISP's servers to access the Internet, browse the World Wide Web and Usenet, and send and receive e-mail. ISPs serve not only individuals but also large companies by providing them with a direct connection from the company's networks to the Internet.

ISPs connect to one another through ***network access points (NAPs).*** Much like railway stations, these NAPs serve as access points for ISPs and are an exchange point for Internet traffic. They determine how traffic is routed and are often the points of most Internet congestion. NAPs are a key component of the ***Internet backbone,*** which is the collection of main network connections and telecommunications lines making up the Internet (see Figure 4.19).

The Internet follows a hierarchical structure, similar to the national highway system. High-speed central network lines are like provincial highways, enabling traffic from midlevel networks to get on and off. Think of midlevel networks as city streets, which in

CAREER IMPLICATIONS

Human Resource Management

February 6, 2004, marked the first Stop Commuting Day in Barrie, Ontario. A bedroom community about 100 kilometres north of Toronto, Barrie was chosen by SuiteWorks Inc. as the site of its first telework centre, a 2,200 square-foot, 120-seat facility that will offer Barrie's 31,500 commuters a local workplace alternative. John Cameron, president of SuiteWorks, said the first clients are scheduled to move in by late summer, 2004. SuiteWorks plans to open other centres in Canada and the U.S. next year—it's particularly looking at locations surrounding Vancouver and Montreal.

Cameron said the building will have a "fully technology-enhanced boardroom with videoconferencing and smart board technology, Web and audio conferencing, and it will be available for individuals outside of our clientele." He added that SuiteWorks is having "conversations with many technology companies about who the final providers will be" for everything from PCs to communications technology. Systems integrator Compugen was chosen to set things up on the technological side. Compugen president Harry Zarek said his firm will "design and architect from the technology point of view all of the requirements. Everything will be state of the art, high speed and secure, and high quality, not only on the networking side, but also on the PC, printing, and faxing side."

Voice over IP will provide local calling into Toronto, as well as other features like call conferencing and forwarding. The building will have both SuiteWorks office managers and Compugen technicians onsite to provide assistance with configuration, Zarek said. Cameron said SuiteWorks has put a lot of thought into security, both on the physical and technological side. Employees will have access cards to enter the building and the turnstile entrance will allow only one person in at time; all guests will be badged, managed, and escorted. To provide workers a safe way to connect to their company networks, Compugen will set up virtual LAN technology. "No one will be able to see what is going through that connection outside of that party . . . . We're trying to replicate the experience of being at their desk at the office with all the connectivity that one would expect," said Zarek.

SuiteWorks expects the majority of clients will use full-time dedicated offices where workers will travel to their current office one day a week or two, and otherwise the SuiteWorks office will be their office. Leasing costs will range from $400 to $1,000 per month, depending on the office space, but the average cost will be on the higher end—$800 to $1,000, Cameron said. The costs are comparable to, if not lower than, having an employee work onsite, he added. "Organizations need to put a bit of thinking around their program, look at the ROI and answer for themselves questions like 'What's in it for us?' and 'Is it worth it financially?'" For example, research will help the company know exactly how much it is saving on things like office space or emergency preparedness. A formal telecommunications strategy will help reduce the risks of employees getting injured in their remote locations by things like a poor ergonomic setup. Digital risk is another area that can be addressed within the company's existing IT strategy, and managerial risk, which includes the inability to properly manage remote workers, resulting in poor performance, can be mitigated by including teleworking stipulations in the HR policy.

[Adapted from Patricia Pickett, "SuiteWorks Pushes Teleworking in Barrie," *IT World Canada* (February 6, 2004).]

turn accept traffic from their neighbourhood streets or member networks. However, you cannot just get on a provincial highway or city street whenever you want to. You have to share the highway and follow traffic control signs to arrive safely at your destination. The same holds true for traffic on the Internet.

How Fast Is Your Connection to the Internet?

There are a number of ways that people can connect to the Internet. In addition to traditional connections through plain old telephones and modems, there are a number of high-speed alternatives. This section briefly describes several different ways that people connect to the Internet from home, office, and beyond.

Plain Old Telephone Service

Many people, particularly in rural areas, connect to the Internet through a telephone line at home or work. The term we use for standard telephone lines is ***plain old telephone service (POTS).*** The speed, or bandwidth, of POTS is generally about 52 Kbps (52,000 bits per second). The POTS system is also called the ***public switched telephone network (PSTN).***

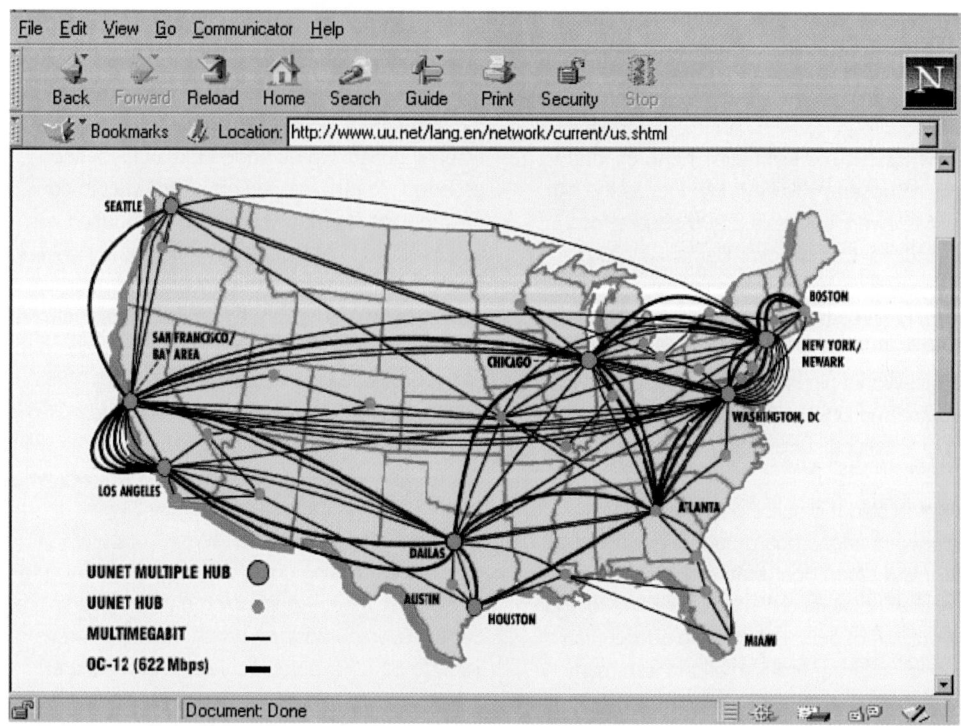

[**Figure 4.19** ➡ The Internet backbone.]

Source: UUNet Technologies.

Digital Subscriber Line (DSL)

One popular alternative now available from telephone service providers around the world is the use of ***digital subscriber lines (DSL).*** DSL uses special modulation schemes to fit more data onto copper wires. In Canada, DSL is quickly supplanting another digital telephone-based service called ISDN. DSL is referred to as a "last-mile" solution because it is used only for connections from a telephone switching station to a home or office, and is generally not used between telephone switching stations. DSL uses existing copper telephone lines and requires relatively short runs to a central telephone office (typically less than five kilometres). DSL has relatively high speeds of up to 32 Mbps when receiving data (i.e., for downstream traffic), and from 32 Kbps to more than 1 Mbps when sending data (i.e., for upstream traffic).

The acronym DSL is used to refer collectively to ADSL, SDSL, and other forms of DSL. ADSL and SDSL enable more data to be sent over existing copper telephone lines. ADSL is short for ***asymmetric digital subscriber line.*** ADSL speeds range from 1.5 to 9 Mbps downstream and from 16 to 640 Kbps upstream. ADSL requires a special ADSL modem-like device. SDSL is short for ***symmetric digital subscriber line.*** SDSL is said to be symmetric because it supports the same data rates for upstream and downstream traffic. SDSL supports data rates up to 3 Mbps and works by sending digital pulses in the high-frequency area of telephone wires. Given that these high frequencies are not used by normal voice communications, SDSL enables your computer to operate simultaneously with voice connections over the same wires. Like ADSL, SDSL requires a special modem-like device. ADSL is most popular in North America, whereas SDSL is being developed primarily in Europe.

Cable Modems

In many parts of Canada, the company that provides cable television service also provides Internet service. With this type of service, a special ***cable modem*** is designed to operate over cable TV lines. Coaxial cable used for cable TV provides much greater bandwidth than telephone lines, and millions of homes in Canada are already wired for cable TV, so cable modems are a fast, popular method for accessing the Internet. Cable modems offer speeds up to 2 Mbps.

Satellite Connections

In many regions of the world, people can now access the Internet via ***satellite,*** referred to as ***Internet over Satellite (IoS).*** IoS technologies allow users to access the Internet via satellites that are placed in fixed positions above the Earth's surface in what is known as a ***geostationary*** or ***geosynchronous*** orbit (i.e., the satellite moves along with the Earth). With these services, your PC is connected to a satellite dish hanging out on the side of your home or placed out on a pole (much like satellite services for your television) and is able to maintain a reliable connection to the satellite in the sky because the satellite orbits the Earth at the exact speed of the Earth's rotation. Given the vast distance that signals must travel from the Earth up to the satellite and back again, IoS is slower than high-speed terrestrial (i.e., land-based) connections to the Internet over copper or fibre-optic cables. In remote regions of the world, IoS is the only option available because installing the cables necessary for Internet connection is not economically feasible or in many cases is just not physically possible.

In addition to these ***fixed wireless*** approaches for connecting to the Internet, there are also many new ***mobile wireless*** approaches for connecting to the Internet. For example, there are Internet-enabled ***cellular phones*** from Telus and others, and small palm-top computers from Research In Motion and others, that give you Internet access nearly anywhere. With a special network adapter card you can use your notebook computer, tablet PC, or personal digital assistant and enjoy the freedom of wireless mobility. The beauty of these systems is that as long as you are in the coverage area you have access to the Internet (much like coverage with cellular phones). One other option for wireless access to the Internet is to use a wireless ethernet network adapter card in any of these computing devices, but with this type of equipment you would have to be located near a transceiver on the network. You would be free to roam around your office or building, but that would be it. With these other technologies you would be able to wander freely around your network, or cellular, coverage area.

Up until now we have talked about ways that individuals rather than organizations access the Internet. In the following sections we talk more about ways that organizations typically access the Internet—although an individual with high amounts of discretionary income could certainly access the Internet in these same ways!

T1 Lines

To gain adequate access to the Internet, organizations are turning to long-distance carriers to lease a dedicated ***T1 line*** for digital transmissions. The T1 line was developed by AT&T as a dedicated digital transmission line that can carry 1.544 Mbps of information. In the United States, companies such as BrandX that sell long-distance services are called interexchange carriers because their circuits carry service between the major telephone exchanges. As previously mentioned, a T1 line can carry 1.544 Mbps and usually traverses hundreds or thousands of kilometres over leased long-distance facilities.

Bell Canada and other carriers charge anywhere from $500 to several thousands of dollars per month for a dedicated T1 circuit spanning 1,000 kilometres. If you need an even faster link, you might choose a ***T3 line.*** T3 provides about 45 Mbps of service at about 10 times the cost of leasing a T1 line. Alternatively, organizations often choose to use two or more T1 lines simultaneously rather than jump to the more expensive T3 line. Higher speeds than the T3 are also available but are not typically used for normal business activity. See Table 4.2 for a summary of communication line capacities.

Asynchronous Transfer Mode (ATM)

Asynchronous transfer mode (ATM) is a method of transmitting voice, video, and data over high-speed LANs at speeds of up to 2.2 Gbps (gigabits per second). ATM has found wide acceptance in the LAN and WAN arenas as a solution to integrating disparate networks over large geographic distances. ATM uses a form of packet transmission in which data is sent over a packet-switched network in a fixed-length, 53-byte cell. Although it is based on packet-switching technology, ATM has the potential to do away with routers, allocated bandwidth, and contention for communications media. Organizations in the movie and entertainment industries that need

Type of Line	Data Rate (Mbps)	Equivalent Number of Voice Lines
T1	1.544	24
T3	44.736	672

[Table 4.2] *Capacity of communication lines.*

to deliver synchronized video and sound, for example, are particularly interested in ATM.

Security in the Internet Age

As use of the Internet and other types of technologies and systems has become more pervasive, the need for security has increased dramatically. Concerns have risen over the accuracy and privacy of personal data, and organizations now demand that their information systems be reliable and secure. A number of techniques have arisen to secure systems that are Internet-related. ***Encryption*** is a technique whereby key data are encoded with a special secret key when being stored or transmitted. ***Firewalls,*** consisting of specialized hardware and software, keep unwanted users out of a system, or let users in with restricted access and privileges. A variety of means of ***authentication*** are used to verify who users are and what they are allowed to do once they are inside a system or a database. These and other security tools and issues will be covered in detail in Chapter 9, which is devoted to the topic.

State of the Internet

The Internet is now the most prominent global network. More than a billion people worldwide have access to the Internet. One study found that the profile of the average U.S. Internet user now mirrors that of the average adult (InsightExpress, 2001). For example, today 51 percent of Internet users are female, as are 51 percent of adults. The average household income of Internet users has dropped from $62,700 in 1996 to $49,800, which is much closer to the overall average household income of $40,816. Back in 1996, 88 percent of Internet users were between

CAREER IMPLICATIONS

Operations Management

PUC Telecom in Sault Ste. Marie, Ontario, says it's the first Canadian service provider to use electrical power lines for high-speed Internet connectivity. PUC Telecom is building a broadband power-line (BPL) network that should allow the firm to extend its data offerings, and provide local businesses with an alternative to DSL or high-speed cable. BPL products take data signals running through fibre-optic lines and injects them into the power grid. Data packets are caught by special devices and reamplified or repackaged before signals can break apart and are then sent out again. According to Martin Wyant, PUC Telecom's general manager, the service provider already offers dedicated, commercial-grade Internet connections via its fibre-optic network. But the firm wanted to offer an Internet service outside of the fibre-optic network's reach—a service suitable for small- and medium-sized enterprises (SMEs).

It would have been too expensive to extend the optical infrastructure into the suburbs. And although PUC Telecom considered reselling other telcos' DSL offerings, that option had a profit problem: "There's no profit," Wyant said. The company opted for a BPL platform from Amperion Inc., based in Andover, Massachusetts. Amperion's platform marries wireless and BPL. The wired part of the network, the power line, terminates not inside businesses, but at hydro poles along Sault Ste. Marie's streets. Atop the poles are boxes that transmit Wi-Fi (802.11b) signals to customers' premises. The users need only have PUC Telecom subscriptions and Wi-Fi cards in their PCs to connect to the Web. PUC Telecom's product provides throughput rates of between 3 Mbps and 5 Mbps, comparable to DSL or cable modems.

The Wi-Fi part of the network means PUC Telecom can operate a city-wide hotspot, so people roving Sault Ste. Marie's streets with Wi-Fi–enabled laptops or PDAs can get online. PUC Telecom's field workers can use the wireless network to connect with headquarters and garner work-site data when they're out on the job. Wyant said his company might license the programs to other utility firms.

The Wi-Fi component also helps PUC Telecom sidestep certain regulatory concerns over BPL technology. In the U.S., the Federal Communications Commission (FCC) is investigating complaints that BPL interferes with licensed wireless devices like ham radios. But Jeff Tolnar from Amperion said the Wi-Fi last-mile connection means data-live wires are safely separated from customers' premises, where people might use ham radios and other interference-sensitive devices. The architecture addresses safety, too, he said. "Something that carries 35,000 volts—you really don't want a line running from that directly into a home or office."

[Adapted from Stefan Dubowski, "Broadband Power-Line Web Service Comes to Canada," *IT World Canada* (February 5, 2004); and Shane Schick, "Sault Ste. Marie Telco Puts Broadband over Power Lines," **http://www.itbusiness.ca/index.asp?theaction=61&sid=54730#**, ITBusiness.ca (February 5, 2004).]

ages 18 and 49, but that has dropped to 76 percent, much closer to the overall average of 63 percent. Finally, the number of people online over 50 years of age has increased in the past five years from 12 percent to 24 percent, which is much closer to the overall population figure of 37 percent. The Internet is clearly being used by more people and by a more diverse audience. It is becoming more a part of the mainstream.[1]

There is little doubt that Canadians have embraced the Internet like few other nations of the world. Ipsos-Insight recently discovered that Canadians are the leading users of the Internet in the world. More than 71 percent of Canadians accessed the Internet in 2003, compared with 70 percent in South Korea, 68 percent in the United States, and 65 percent in Japan.[2]

One other way to measure the rapid growth of the Internet, in addition to the number of users, is to examine the growth in the number of Internet hosts; that is, computers working as servers on the Internet, as shown in Figure 4.20.

What Are People Doing on the Internet?

The Internet enables people to access a wide range of data, including text, video, audio, graphics, databases, maps, and other data types. The Internet is more, however, than just access to data. The Internet enables people not only to access data but also to connect with each other. In the last couple of years, with increases in bandwidth and decreases in prices for computers and Internet access, there have been substantial changes in the ways people are using the Internet. For example, recent advancements in communication technologies and increasingly high transmission speeds have made interactivity—real-time collaboration between people—possible over the Internet.

A range of ways that people use, and have used, the Internet are summarized in Table 4.3. Essentially, these involve ways to access data and to communicate with other people via text. Perhaps the most significant use of the Internet has been for electronic mail.

Electronic Mail

As described earlier in this chapter, ***electronic mail***, or e-mail, is the transmission of messages over computer networks. Most organizations now use ***gateways*** to connect their internal computer systems and networks to the Internet, enabling people to send electronic mail over the Internet to and from nearly anywhere in the world.

All Internet service providers offer e-mail, and nearly all of them provide gateways so that you can exchange mail across the Internet with users of other systems. In business organizations, some popular e-mail systems include Microsoft Exchange, Lotus Notes, and Novell GroupWise. Hotmail is a free, Web-based e-mail system that requires only access to the Internet and use of a Web browser. Companies typically use e-mail

Web Search

WEB SEARCH OPPORTUNITY
Investigate the American National Standards Institute at **www.ansi.org**, and then investigate the International Organization for Standardization at **www.iso.ch/iso/en/ISOOnline.frontpage**. See what you can learn about these organizations and their interaction.

[1] See InsightExpress, "Net Population Mirrors Overall Population," July 23, 2001, at **Web.insightexpress.com/news/index.asp**.

[2] Mark Evans, "Canada Leads Global Pack in Internet Use: Number of People Using the Net Rose 7% in 2003," *Financial Post* (January 22, 2004). **http://www.canada.com/technology/story.html?id=FBFE274E-FC33-4240-B720-80276612AD7D**.

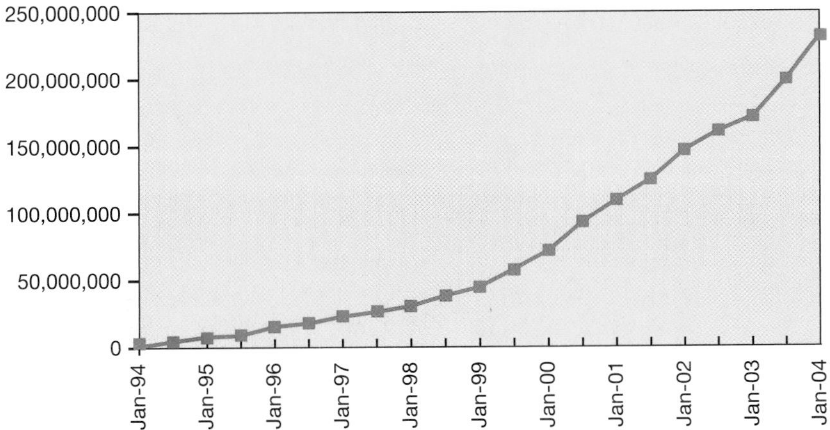

[**Figure 4.20** ➡ Growth in Internet servers (hosts).]

Source: Internet Software Consortium (**www.isc.org**).

[Table 4.3] *Internet tools past and present.*

Internet Tool	Description
E-mail	Enables users to send messages to each other.
Instant messaging	Enables users to send messages to each other synchronously, or in real time.
Telnet	Enables users to connect, or log in, to any computer on the Internet.
File transfer	Enables users to connect to a remote computer solely for the purpose of transferring files; either uploading (sending to the remote machine) or downloading (obtaining from the remote machine) files and data; using file transfer protocol (FTP).
***Listserv*, short for "mailing list server"**	Enables groups of people with common interests to send messages to each other. Interested people subscribe to a discussion group, which is essentially a mailing list. When a subscriber sends a message to the list, the message is sent to all other subscribers.
Usenet	Enables groups of people with common interests to send messages or other binary information to each other. Unlike listserv, Usenet has no master list of subscribers. Rather, anyone with access to Usenet may use a newsreader program to post and read articles from the group.
WAIS (wide area information server)	Enables users to locate information by indexing electronic data using standard keywords.
Voice over IP	A collection of hardware and software that enables the use of the Internet as the transmission medium for telephone calls.

GLOBAL PERSPECTIVE

Technology-Related Challenges for Global Telecommunications

The primary technological challenges faced by organizations when operating across national boundaries are related to telecommunications infrastructure. The price, quality, and speed of telecommunications support can vary from country to country. For example, in Greece only half of the telecommunication networks are digital, whereas the networks in Finland are 100-percent digital. You cannot assume you will find the same kind of telecommunications infrastructure and performance when you move from one country to the next.

In some cases, the differences are merely in terms of performance (e.g., one country has a faster telecommunications infrastructure for businesses than does another country). Worse, however, are situations in which one country uses a different telecommunications standard than does another country, because then businesses may face compatibility and other problems as they move from one country to the next. For example, a company headquartered in Hong Kong recently expanded its operations to Thailand, only to realize that the manufacturing facilities were located in an area that had no telecommunications connections available using the X.25 standard. As a result, given the network infrastructure that the parent firm was using, the subsidiary was not easily able to interact electronically with its headquarters located in Hong Kong (Sarker and Sarker, 2000).

Differences in telecommunications standards across the planet pose serious challenges for organizations, and these differences are more the norm than the exception. For example, in the United States, most people prefer to use network standards produced by the American National Standards Institute (e.g., ANSI X.12), whereas in Europe people more commonly use network standards produced by the International Organization for Standardization (e.g., the OSI model for networks). Moreover, within Europe itself one can witness a variety of different standards due to the lack of political unification.

Similarly, the hardware platforms used in different countries also vary, causing further, significant integration problems. For example, the United States has seen a predominance of the use of IBM mainframes and Windows-based servers and PCs, whereas in Europe UNIX is much more popular. The preferences for software are also different. European nations, such as Norway, prefer to use "pdf" files, whereas in the United States there is a predominance of files created using Microsoft Office software products. This, too, causes serious problems in data sharing and data transfer.

The proliferation of the Internet and platform-independent programming languages such as Java has helped, but it is still very difficult to develop a seamless global telecommunications infrastructure for an organization.

extensively because it is a fast, flexible, reliable, and relatively inexpensive way for people to communicate with each other.

Although different e-mail systems look and behave differently, there are some emerging standards that enable users on different systems to exchange messages. MAPI, IMAP, POP, MIME, and SMTP are all examples of standards used to manage the exchange of e-mail across different systems. Given how popular e-mail systems have become, estimates are that billions and billions of e-mail messages are sent each year.

While the Internet is an amazing collection of technologies, the real power of the Internet was not realized until the early 1990s with the invention of the World Wide Web and the Web browser. The Web and the Web browser have essentially given us a graphical user interface with which to use the Internet and, as a result, have made the Internet much more accessible and easy to use, and opened the door for some very innovative uses of the Internet.

What Is Next for the Internet?

In the mid-1990s, many researchers at universities became frustrated with the increased personal and business use of the Internet. The Internet had previously been a network primarily for researchers from universities and other organizations, and all of a sudden, shortly after 1995 (note that this is the year Netscape went public and Microsoft turned its attention squarely to the Internet), the Internet was quickly being overrun with all types of non–research-oriented traffic. As a result, in 1996, 34 U.S. research universities began working on ***Internet2,*** a faster, private alternative to the public Internet (**www.internet2.edu**). In 1997, the University Corporation for Advanced Internet Development (UCAID) was created to help manage Internet2. Researchers now use Internet2 as a testing-ground network to develop advanced Internet technologies and applications. Internet2 requires state-of-the-art infrastructure, so Internet2 universities are connected to the ***Abilene network backbone,*** which uses regional network aggregation points called ***gigaPoPs*** and very high-speed network equipment and facilities.

The term gigaPoP is short for *gigabit Point of Presence,* a network access point that supports data transfer rates of at least 1 Gbps. Each university that connects to Internet2 must do so through a gigaPoP, which connects the university's networks with Internet2. For comparison, the point-of-presence facilities maintained by regular ISPs are designed to allow low-speed modems to connect to the Internet, while these gigaPoPs are designed for fast access to a high-speed network like Internet2. There are over 180 Internet2 member universities and over 60 participating companies. Internet2 operates at speeds up to 2.4 gigabits per second, 45,000 times faster than a typical modem.

Canada has a high-speed network similar to Internet2 called ***CA*net 4,*** funded by the

CAREER IMPLICATIONS

Marketing

Applying for a mortgage is often a tiresome experience for customers. It includes filling out lengthy forms with a wide array of financial and credit information, multiple trips to the bank, and long waiting periods to get approval. All of this often results in frustration for customers and diminished profits for the mortgage companies. Chris Larsen and Janina Pawlowski, who owned a small brokerage firm in Palo Alto, California, realized this problem and wanted to do something about it. In their quest to make customers more satisfied and cut down on loan agents (who act as intermediaries and add to the time required to get an approval) and related fees, they realized that they could use the Internet to ease their problems. With the technical expertise they had gained at NASA and Xerox, they designed an online loan application system that enabled customers to search for more than 50,000 mortgage products from 70 lenders and then allowed them to submit and track loan applications online. They also transformed their physical organization to a virtual one (naming it E-Loan), thus providing more flexibility and access to customers. One of the pioneers in the online mortgage industry, today the company is the leader of online mortgages, just ahead of Quicken Loans. The company is now working toward adding two more features to its online system: 1) an ability to provide human customer service, a feature that most mortgage consumers desire, and 2) an ability to provide home equity loans, which are not yet offered by E-Loan Inc. Whether you go to work for one of these entrepreneurial Internet firms or for a more traditional bank or other financial institution, you will likely be working with just such an online system.

[Adapted from Constantin Von Hoffman, "Mouse-Click Mortgages," *CIO Web Business Magazine* (October 1, 1999).]

federal government and designed, deployed, and operated by CANARIE (**www.canarie.ca**). CA*net 4 connects provincial research networks, universities, research centres, government research laboratories, schools, and other eligible sites.

THE WORLD WIDE WEB

One of the most powerful uses of the Internet is something that you have no doubt heard a great deal about—the ***World Wide Web.*** More than likely, you have browsed the Web using Netscape Navigator, Microsoft's Internet Explorer, or some other popular ***Web browser,*** as shown in Figure 4.21. A Web browser is a software application that can be used to locate and display Web pages including text, graphics, and multimedia content. Browsers are fast becoming a standard Internet tool. As previously mentioned, the Web is a graphical user interface to the Internet and provides users with a simple, consistent interface to a wide variety of information.

Prior to the invention of the Web by Tim Berners-Lee in 1991, content posted on the Internet could be accessed through an Internet tool called ***Gopher***. Gopher provided a menu-driven, hierarchical interface to organize files stored on servers, providing a way to tie together related files from different Internet servers across the world. The Web took Gopher one step further by introducing ***hypertext.*** A hypertext document, otherwise known as a Web page, contains not only information, but also references or links to other documents that contain related information. These links are known as ***hyperlinks.*** The Web also introduced the ***Hypertext Markup Language (HTML),*** which is the standard method of specifying the format of Web pages. Specific content within each Web page is enclosed within codes, or markup tags, which stipulate how the content should appear to the user. Web pages are stored on ***Web servers,*** which process user requests for pages using the ***Hypertext Transfer Protocol (HTTP)***. Web servers typically host a collection of interlinked Web pages created by the same author, which is known as a Website. Websites and specific Web pages within those sites have a unique Internet address called a URL, or ***Uniform Resource Locator.*** A user who wants to access a Website enters the URL, and the Web server hosting the Website retrieves the desired page and delivers it to the user.

The introduction of the Web was the first of three events that led to its proliferation. The second event was the *Information Infrastructure Act,* passed by the U.S. government in 1992, which opened the Web for commercial purposes. Prior to this legislation, universities and governmental agencies were the Web's predominant users. The third event was the arrival of a graphical Web browser, Mosaic, which quickly transcended Gopher by adding a graphical front end to the Web. Mosaic's graphical interface allowed Web pages

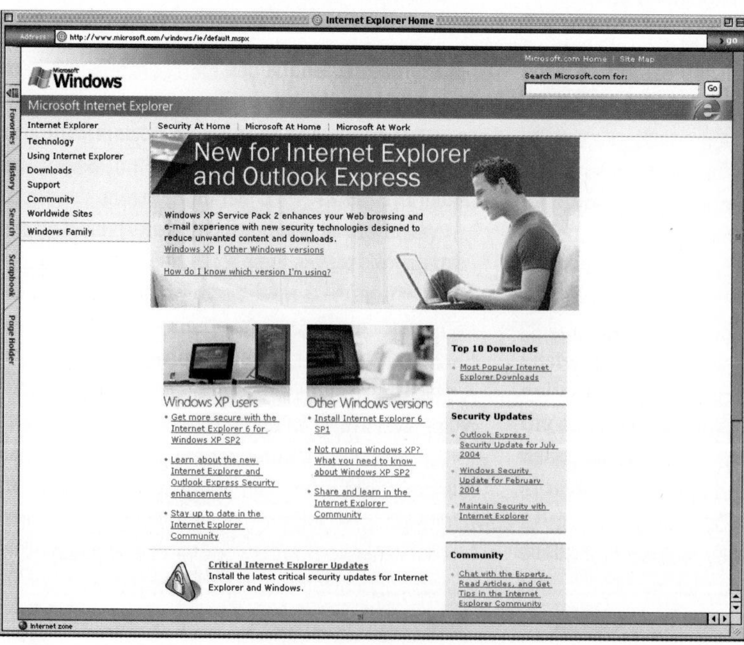

[**Figure 4.21** ➥ Microsoft's Internet Explorer Web browser.]

Source: Screen shot reprinted by permission from Microsoft Corporation.

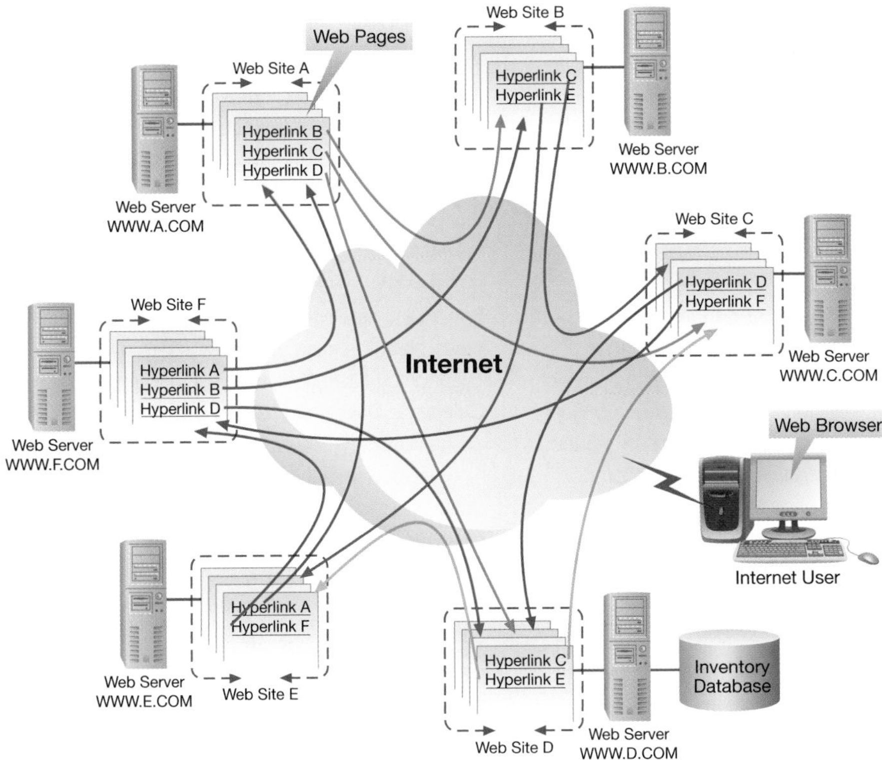

[**Figure 4.22** ➡ World Wide Web architecture.]

to be constructed to deliver an extended range of content, including images, audio, video, and other multimedia, all of which could be included and displayed within the same Web page. Mosaic was the predecessor to Netscape's Navigator.

World Wide Web Architecture

The Web uses Web browsers, Web servers, and the TCP/IP networking protocol to facilitate the transmission of Web pages over the Internet. Figure 4.22 depicts the architecture of the Web. To access information on the Web, a Web browser, as well as the TCP/IP protocol, must be installed on a user's computer. Users can access Web pages by entering into their Web browser the URL of the Web page. Once the user enters the URL in the Web browser, TCP/IP breaks the request into packets and routes them over the Internet to the Web server where the requested Web page is stored. When the packets reach their destination, TCP/IP reassembles them and passes the request to the Web server. The Web server understands that the user is requesting a Web page (indicated by the http://prefix in the URL) and retrieves the page, which is packetized by TCP/IP and transmitted over the Internet back to the Web browser. TCP/IP reassembles the packets at the destination and delivers the Web page to the Web browser. In turn, the Web browser translates the HTML code contained in the Web page, formats its physical appearance, and displays the results. If the Web page contains a hyperlink, the user can click on it and the process repeats itself.

World Wide Web Applications

Considering that the powerful and relatively inexpensive Web platform is extremely well suited for disseminating information on a global basis, organizations are constantly trying to devise innovative applications for the Web. Over the years, many organizations have become very sophisticated users of Web technologies. The first wave of Web-based commerce occurred around 1994, when new businesses brought product marketing to the Web, pioneering an explosion of commercial activity that will continue into the foreseeable future.

There are a number of ways in which companies can utilize the Web to support business activities. For example, very many companies use the Web to at least disseminate sales and marketing information—what is referred to as the ***electronic brochure.*** Many companies also now use the Web for ***online ordering,*** which means that they enable customers to order and, in many cases, actually

COMING ATTRACTIONS

"Fill 'Er Up with Wireless Data, Please!"

Imagine filling up your car not with fuel but with data, and doing it without stopping the vehicle! Well, the folks in the research division of Mercedes-Benz have built a C320 sedan equipped with what many people believe will be the "next big thing" in technology for vehicles. This car uses next-generation high-speed wireless LAN technology that can send and receive large amounts of data in spurts.

The equipment in the Mercedes test car, which is part of its DriveBy InfoFueling project, is based on the 802.11a wireless LAN standard. Mercedes USA gave a demonstration at a recent Comdex convention. The Mercedes system sent and received data from a moving vehicle at 54 Mbps in tests—many times faster than the data-transfer rates of cell-phone frequencies or even standard wireless local area networks. The 802.11a standard has the potential to accommodate wireless LANs at speeds up to 100 Mbps.

The DriveBy InfoFueling system involves sending data in bursts as vehicles pass transceiver sites with limited range. For example, a car would send and receive data as it sped past a transceiver and would not be able to send or receive again until it passed another base station.

"We've set up a network that has wireless hotspots the car can use to download large amounts of data as it drives by at highway speeds," says Wieland Holfelder, manager of smart vehicles research at DaimlerChrysler Research and Technology North America Inc. in Palo Alto, California. DaimlerChrysler is Mercedes-Benz USA's parent.

Potential uses include downloading maps, traffic data, and digital music or video without stopping or slowing down, Holfelder says. It could also be used to send data from a moving car to another vehicle or to a person connected to a conventional LAN or the Internet.

[Adapted from John Rendleman, "Fill 'Er Up with Wireless Data, Please," *InformationWeek* (November 19, 2001).]

pay for products and services online. Still other firms, such as eBay, create ***electronic marketplaces***, bringing multiple sellers and multiple buyers together and providing a vehicle for them to trade with each other online. Many firms also use the Web to provide ***online customer service***, or at least to enhance their traditional customer service. We will talk about each of these uses of the Web in detail in Chapter 5, "Electronic Business, Intranets, and Extranets."

KEY POINTS REVIEW

1. **Understand the role of telecommunications in organizations.** Applications such as electronic mail, instant messaging, newsgroups, mailing lists (listservs), facsimile, voice mail, and videoconferencing are rapidly changing business and interpersonal communication. Global computer networks allow organizations to streamline business operations in ways never before possible. Telecommunications technologies are becoming fundamental, not only for supporting day-to-day activities within most organizations, but also for playing a growing role in the competitive strategy of more and more organizations. Business applications that are particularly important include electronic business, electronic data interchange, telecommuting, electronic fund transfers, distance learning, and telemedicine. More than ever before, managers must understand these technologies to ride the information systems wave and to apply the right solutions to the right problems.
2. **Describe the evolution of and types of computer networks.** Since the 1950s, three models of computing have been used. First, from the 1950s until the 1970s, the centralized computing model was dominant. In the centralized computing model, all processing occurs at a large central computer, and users interact with the system through the use of terminals. From the late 1970s until the late 1980s, a distributed computing model was dominant. In this model, separate computers work on subsets of tasks and then pool their results by communicating via a network. In the 1990s, the collaborative computing model emerged. In this model, two or more networked computers work together to accomplish a common processing task. There are several types of computer networks. A private branch exchange (PBX) is a private telephone exchange, located in a single facility, which provides both voice and data communication. A local area network (LAN) is a group of computers at one location that share hardware and software resources. A wide area network (WAN) refers to two or more LANs from different locations that are linked together. There are four general types of WANs: global networks, enterprise networks, value-added networks (VANs), and metropolitan area networks (MANs). A global network is a WAN that spans multiple countries and may include the networks of several organizations. An enterprise network is a WAN that connects all the LANs of a single location. Value-added networks are private, third-party–managed networks that are shared by multiple organizations. Metropolitan area networks span a limited geographic scope, typically a city-wide area with both LAN and high-speed fibre-optic technologies. A final type of computer network, called

a personal area network (PAN), is an emerging technology that uses wireless communication to exchange data between computing devices using short-range radio communication, typically within an area of 10 metres.

3. **Describe the Internet and how it works.** The Internet is composed of networks that are developed and maintained by many different entities, and follows a hierarchical structure, similar to the national highway system. High-speed central networks called backbones are like provincial highways, enabling traffic from midlevel networks to get on and off. The Internet relies on packet-switching technology to deliver data and information across networks. Routers are used to interconnect independent networks. Because so many different networks are connected to the Internet, they use a common communication protocol (TCP/IP). TCP/IP is divided into two parts. TCP breaks information into small chunks, called data packets, which are transferred from computer to computer. IP defines how a data packet must be formed and how a router must forward each packet. All computers, including routers, are assigned unique IP addresses. Data routing and delivery are possible due to the unique addressing of every computer attached to the Internet. Together, TCP and IP provide a reliable and efficient way to send data across the Internet.

4. **Describe the basic Internet services and the use of the World Wide Web.** A collection of Internet tools enables you to exchange messages, share information, or connect to remote computers. These tools include electronic mail, Telnet, file transfer protocol, listserv, Usenet, WAIS, Gopher, and Voice over IP. The most powerful tool today is the World Wide Web, which binds together the various tools used on the Internet, providing users with a simple, consistent interface to a wide variety of information through the use of Web browsers.

KEY TERMS

Abilene network backbone 127
ARPANET 116
asymmetric digital subscriber line (ADSL) 122
asynchronous transfer mode (ATM) 123
authentication 124
backbone network 118
bandwidth 104
Bluetooth 115
cable modem 122
CA*net 4 127
cellular phone 123
centralized computing 109
collaborative computing 110
Defense Advanced Research Projects Agency (DARPA) 116
digital subscriber line (DSL) 122
digitizing 108
distance learning 107
distributed computing 110
domain name 118
domain name system (DNS) 120
electronic brochure 129
electronic business (EB) 105
electronic data interchange (EDI) 105
electronic fund transfer (EFT) 107
electronic mail 104, 125
electronic marketplace 130
encryption 124
enterprise network 114
facsimile, or fax, machine 104
file transfer 126
firewall 124
fixed wireless 123
gateway 125
geostationary 123
geosynchronous 123
gigaPoP 127
global network 113
Gopher 128
Hypertext Markup Language (HTML) 128
Hypertext Transfer Protocol (HTTP) 128
hyperlink 128
hypertext 128
instant messaging (IM) 104
Internet 116
Internet backbone 120
Internet Corporation for Assigned Names and Numbers (ICANN) 120
Internet over Satellite (IoS) 123
Internet Registry 120
Internet Service Provider (ISPs) 120
Internet2 127
internetworking 116
InterNIC 120
InterNIC Registration Service 120
IP address 120
IP datagram 117
IPv6 120
listserv 126
local area network (LAN) 112
mailing lists 104
metropolitan area network (MAN) 114
mobile wireless 123
modem 109
Nnational Science Foundation (NSF) 116
network 104
network access point 120
newsgroups 104
NSFNET (National Science Foundation Network) 116
online customer service 130
online ordering 129
packet switching 116
personal area network (PAN) 115
plain old telephone service (POTS) 121
private branch exchange (PBX) 112
protocols 108
public switched telephone network (PSTN) 121
router 118
satellite 122
symmetric digital subscriber line (SDSL) 122
T1 line 123
T3 line 123
(TCP/IP) transmission control protocol/ Internet protocol 117
telecommunications 104
telecommuting 106
telemedicine 108
Telnet 126
terminals 109
top-level domain 118
transmission media 108
Uniform Resource Locator (URL) 118, 128
Usenet 126
value-added network (VAN) 114
videoconferencing 105
voice mail 105
voice over IP (VoIP) 126
WAIS 126
Web browser 128
Web page 118
Web server 128
Website 105
wide area network (WAN) 112
wireless local area network 112
World Wide Web (the Web) 128

REVIEW QUESTIONS

1. List and describe three types of interpersonal communication applications for telecommunications.
2. List and describe three common business applications of telecommunications.
3. Compare and contrast centralized, distributed, and collaborative computing.
4. How are local area networks, wide area networks, enterprise networks, and global networks related to each other?
5. What is the Internet, and why was it created?
6. What are packet switching and TCP/IP?
7. What organization is responsible for managing IP addresses, domain names, and root server systems?
8. Other than the telephone, what are three alternatives for connecting to the Internet?
9. List and describe five major tools for and/or uses of the Internet.
10. What is the World Wide Web, and what is its relationship to the Internet?

SELF-STUDY QUESTIONS

Answers are at the end of the Problems and Exercises.

1. Telecommunications refers to the transmission of all forms of information, including ___________, from one location to another over a network.
   A. digital data
   B. voice and sound
   C. fax and video
   D. all of the above
2. ________ allow(s) conversations with others in real time on the Internet.
   A. Voice mail
   B. Newsgroups
   C. E-mail
   D. Instant messaging
3. All of the following are applications of telecommunications **except** _________.
   A. electronic business
   B. telemedicine
   C. distance learning
   D. transmission media
4. The process of converting a photograph or a song into digital information, or bits, is called __________. After information is converted into bits, it can travel across a network.
   A. digitizing
   B. analyzing
   C. converting
   D. importing
5. A _________ is a private, third-party-managed network that can be shared by multiple organizations.
   A. local area network
   B. wide area network
   C. value-added network
   D. personal area network
6. All of the following are correct domain suffix pairs **except** ________.
   A. edu—educational institutions
   B. mil—military
   C. neto—network organizations
   D. com—commercial businesses
7. Which of the following is faster and becoming more popular than the standard telephone as a way to connect to the Internet?
   A. SDSL
   B. ADSL
   C. cable
   D. all of the above
8. The Internet is being used by _________.
   A. more users than ever before
   B. young and old people
   C. companies and universities
   D. all of the above
9. __________ enables a person to send one e-mail message and have it simultaneously reach a group of people.
   A. Gopher
   B. Listserv
   C. Usenet
   D. WAIS
10. Websites and specific Web pages within those sites have a unique Internet address called a URL, or __________.
    A. Universal Resource Login
    B. Universal Router Locator
    C. Uniform Resource Locator
    D. Uniform Resource Language

PROBLEMS AND EXERCISES

1. Match the following terms to the appropriate definitions:
   ____ Distributed computing
   ____ Instant messaging
   ____ Router
   ____ Internet service provider
   ____ Web browser
   ____ Telecommuting
   ____ Desktop videoconferencing

____ Domain name
____ Firewall
____ Hypertext

a. Specialized hardware and software that are used to keep unwanted users out of a system, or to let users in with restricted access and privileges
b. Used in Uniform Resource Locators (URLs) to identify a source or host entity on the Internet
c. Text in a Web document that is highlighted and, when clicked on by the user, evokes an embedded command that goes to another specified file or location and brings up that file or location on the user's screen
d. A software application that can be used to locate and display Web pages including text, graphics, and multimedia content
e. A computing model in which computers are networked together to share information and services
f. The process of working at home or at another remote location and "commuting" to the office via computing and networking technologies
g. An application that allows conversations with others in real time on the Internet
h. An intelligent device used to connect and route data traffic across two or more individual networks
i. Allows people to use their desktop computers, together with specialized software and hardware (including cameras), to speak with and see other people online
j. An individual or organization who enables other individuals and organizations to connect to the Internet

2. Discuss the differences between PBX networks and LANs. What are the advantages of each? What are possible disadvantages of each? When would you recommend one over the other?

3. Have you taken a distance or online course at your university? What did you like and dislike? If you have not taken a course in this medium, investigate a course that you would be interested in taking. What are the pros and cons of a course without a regular classroom time?

4. How many types of communication tools do you use each day, such as e-mail, voice mail, fax, desktop videoconferencing, electronic fund transfers, pagers, and cellular phones? What is happening to the speed of communication today?

5. Do you feel that desktop videoconferencing, as described in the opening to this chapter, will continue to rise in popularity? Why or why not? What about the face-to-face, in-person meetings that have existed for centuries? Are certain industries or products more conducive to desktop videoconferencing?

6. Do you know of anyone telecommuting full- or part-time? What are the positive and the negative aspects of this type of commuting?

7. Scan the popular press and search the World Wide Web for clues concerning emerging technologies for telecommunications. This may include new uses for current technologies or new technologies altogether. Discuss as a group the "hot" issues. Do you feel they will become a reality in the near future? Why or why not? Prepare a 10-minute presentation to the class of your findings.

8. Explain in simple language how the Internet works. Be sure to talk about backbones, packet switching, networks, routers, TCP/IP, and Internet services. What technologies, hardware, and software do you utilize when using the Internet? What else is available?

9. How long, on average, are you willing to wait for a Web page to load in your browser on your computer? Under what conditions would you be willing to wait longer for a page to come up in your browser? Based on your answers, what are the implications for Website design? Do you wait longer if you know what you will be seeing (that is, if you are loading a page at a site you have been to in the past)?

10. Search through recent articles in your favourite IS publication—whether print or online. What are some of the issues being discussed that relate to the Internet and/or the World Wide Web in particular? Have you experienced any of these technologies or applications? What is your opinion about them? How will they affect your life and career? Prepare a 10-minute presentation to the class of your findings.

11. Research projects can now be accomplished by using the Internet as the sole source of information. Conduct such a research project using solely the Internet for source information, and answer the following questions: 1) what is the history of the Internet, 2) what are the demographics of the users of the Internet, and 3) what are the historical growth and the projected growth of the Internet? Remember, use only the Internet itself to research and write this short paper.

ANSWERS TO THE SELF-STUDY QUESTIONS

1. D 2. D 3. D 4. A 5. C 6. C 7. D 8. D 9. B 10. C

Case 1: *Telemedicine*

Telemedicine is quickly becoming a viable option for residents who are located in remote areas. This new form of providing state-of-the-art and timely medical help to underserved areas has a significant potential for reducing some of the health-care disparities that exist in remote locations. Many parts of Canada have large rural populations spread over huge areas, creating a significant challenge to offer leading-edge health care to all residents.

Bell Canada's virtual private networking enterprise (VPNe) service has been used to conduct surgeries over distances of nearly 400 km using a 10 Mbps link. At St. Joseph's Healthcare centre in Hamilton, Ontario, Dr.

Mehran Anvari used the Zeus Surgical system to control a robot carrying an endoscopic camera in the abdomen of a patient undergoing acid reflux surgery at the North Bay General Hospital (NBGH). Bell's VPNe network then carried Anvari's hand, wrist, and finger movements to the system's robotic arms residing in NBGH's operating room, where Dr. Craig McKinley was performing the surgery. "It was as if Dr. Anvari was in the room with me performing the procedure," McKinley said.

The network delivered information over 10 to 12 Mbps of bandwidth, Bell said. It ensured that the delay between Anvari's movements and the robotic arms' movements controlling the endoscopic camera in the patient's abdomen was no longer than 150 milliseconds. The VPNe, which is built over Cisco Systems Inc.'s Gigabit Switching Routing 12000 series and 7500 series routers, is suited for use in a surgical environment, Bell executives said. The network is protected against both fibre cuts and laser failures and has the ability to self-heal against failure within 50 milliseconds. Patients in remote areas do not generally have access to new surgical methods, like minimal-access surgeries, that are much less invasive than traditional procedures and cut down recovery time significantly.

One of North America's leaders in telemedicine is Arizona—a state with a large rural population and few big hospitals. After lobbying by multiple groups and organizations, legislation for telemedicine was passed in Arizona in 1996, which resulted in the creation of the Arizona Rural Telecommunications Network (ARTN). The leaders of the telemedicine program wanted to set up a network such that specialists at the University of Arizona's medical centres could be easily connected with the small rural hospitals. They could consult with the local physicians or the patients directly, depending on the need. The vision was to enable teleradiology as well, such that local physicians could send reports such as CT scans and x-rays over the network for referral by a specialist located at the university centres. The project leaders also wanted to ensure that the network to be built had sufficient bandwidth, such that it would be able to support a large volume of users and their communication.

After the initial plan was formulated, the next phase involved the building and the development of the network that would support the telemedicine program. The architects considered ISDN lines, but many of the participating locations throughout the state did not have access to high-speed phone services such as ISDN. They deployed an ATM network because they determined that it was the most cost effective. In addition to cost benefits, the ATM network also ensured high quality, reliability, and the ability to send multiple types of information (e.g., text, voice, pictures, etc.) quickly. They developed a distributed backbone network with switches located at Northern Arizona University and two other sites. After a lot of evaluation, they selected for the backbone the ASX-1000 switches from a company called Marconi, based in Pittsburgh. Each of the rural sites would then link to its nearest backbone switch.

Since the initial implementation of the network, the network architecture has gone through some significant changes. ATM inverse multiplexing was installed to support the increasing traffic on certain routes. This new technology has significantly reduced the work of many network administrators. They no longer have to assign traffic flows to specific connections. This is now done automatically. Four new ISDN circuits have also been added to the ARTN network. This now enables smoother videoconferencing over the Internet between some of the remote locations and the central offices. The next step is to implement IP video, which would enable the use of Internet technologies to provide videoconferencing facilities to a larger group of users at a significantly lower cost. Today, more than 90 physicians from various areas such as radiology, neurology, psychiatry, and cardiology have seen more than 11,000 patients through the telemedicine program. The program has also helped in reducing risky travel for patients with unstable conditions. The average cost of a rural patient's visit to an urban medical centre has gone from $500 down to about $100.

Telemedicine is not a new idea, but recent advances in telecommunications have made it a viable option for many surgical and nonsurgical procedures. Hamilton surgeon Dr. Anvari points out that thanks to telerobotics-assisted surgeries, the choice between a more invasive surgery and travelling to a large city may no longer be necessary.

[Adapted from Monika Rola, "Bell Canada's MPLS Virtual Private Network Used for Surgery from Remote Site Using Telerobotics," *Communications & Networking*, Vol. 6, No. 4 (April 2003); and Ronald S. Weinstein and Kevin M. McNeill, "Powering the Arizona Telemedicine Program," *Health Management Technology* 22(6): 46–47.]

Discussion Questions

1. Do you think that the telemedicine programs in Ontario and Arizona can be considered a success? Why or why not?
2. Do you think that something as important as medical care can be provided successfully through a telecommunications network? What do these systems lack?
3. Currently, telemedicine programs enable patient consultancy and routine surgical procedures. What other related capabilities could be included?
4. Predict what health care might look like in the future if we used more telecommunications and computer networks.

Case 2: *Convergence in Canada*

Depending on whom you talk to, telecommunications competition in Canada either needs regulatory first aid or is unfolding as intended. Not surprisingly, many competitors take the first view, while major incumbent carriers tend toward the second. In either case, the '90s buzzword "convergence" is becoming a reality in many Canadian communities as the distinction between telephone, TV, and Internet services is becoming blurred. The latest battleground is local telephone service.

"The incumbents are still leveraging their position," says Michael Stephens, vice-president of marketing for competitive local carrier Group Telecom Inc. "The regulatory system the Canadian Radio-television and Telecommunications Commission [CRTC] has adopted is the right model to promote sustained long-term competition," says Lawson Hunter, executive vice-president of Bell Canada parent BCE Inc. Local telephone service has been open to competition for more than five years, but most of the competitive local exchange carriers (CLECs) that sprang up in the late 1990s are history now. One significant survivor, Group Telecom, emerged from bankruptcy in early 2003 to be bought by Vancouver-based 360networks Corp.

Along with Group Telecom, competitors in local business telephony include the major competitive long-distance carriers, Allstream Corp. (formerly AT&T Canada), Call-Net Enterprises Inc. (Sprint Canada) and Telus Corp. Residential local service is even less competitive. Call-Net is the only sizeable non-incumbent in the market; Allstream abandoned it several years ago, and most CLECs have focused on business customers. A few cable companies and electrical utilities have taken advantage of existing networks and rights-of-way to get into local service. For instance, the Halifax-based Eastlink group of companies competes with incumbent Aliant Inc. in parts of Nova Scotia and Prince Edward Island. Some local hydro companies have subsidiaries offering phone service. Yet the incumbents—Aliant, Bell Canada, MTS, SaskTel, and Telus—carry well over 90 percent of local traffic.

Competitive startups in the telecom field have had a rough time in the years since local competition began, admits Lawrence Surtees, senior telecom and Internet research analyst at IDC Canada Ltd. in Toronto. "If we think that those are the only competitors, we get a pretty horrific picture in our minds." But Surtees contends the real competition in local service will come from companies that are new entrants in telecom but well-heeled incumbents in their own industries. Those would be cable companies, electrical utilities, and possibly IT service firms. Commercial service based on Internet protocol (IP) could be a reality by 2006. Add to that the fact that the largest incumbents—Bell Canada and Telus—are making cautious forays into each other's home territories, and some say you have a recipe for healthy competition in time.

Incumbents like to add that wireless service already competes with traditional local service. "In the not-too-distant future, perhaps a year or a little bit longer, there will be more wireless phones in Alberta and B.C. than there are wireline phones," predicts Willie Grieve, vice-president of public policy and regulatory affairs at Telus. Most Canadians have a choice of wireless carriers. As their volumes rise and their costs decline, Grieve says, wireless carriers will become more competitive.

The telecom ventures of electrical utilities, while small potatoes so far, could lead to bigger things. "You can laugh off little local companies," Surtees says, but municipal operations in Quebec are banding together, buying in bulk and targeting the telecom market. Such alliances could become significant competitors to the incumbent telcos.

The major cable companies are clearly interested in the local market, and would probably play primarily in residential service. Ken Engelhart, vice-president of regulatory at Rogers Communications Inc., says a few technological pieces still need to be put in place for his company to compete in telephony, but they will be there soon. Rogers has raised regulatory issues the company feels would put it at a disadvantage, and Engelhart says its future plans depend partly on the CRTC's response to those concerns.

While electrical utilities and cable companies are widely talked about as potential local phone competitors, Surtees suggests there is another dark horse in the race. Major computer services companies like IBM Canada Ltd. and Electronic Data Systems Corp. are increasingly providing communications services to large corporate customers.

Analysts and some competitors say the CRTC is moving to promote competition more aggressively. For years, the commission made rules but paid little attention to policing them, says Robert Yates, co-president of Montreal-based LeMay-Yates Associates Inc. Recently, the CRTC has taken a more activist role in enforcing its rules, but competitors want more. "We need more change, and we would like that change faster," says Chris Peirce, senior vice-president of regulatory and government affairs at Allstream. In particular, CLECs have asked for restrictions on bundling services, limits on the steps incumbents can take to lure back customers, and a better deal on facilities the competitors lease from incumbents.

Competitive carriers won a victory in July 2003, when the CRTC ordered incumbent carriers to unbundle digital subscriber line (DSL) Internet access from residential phone service. Both Rogers and Eastlink have asked the commission to stop incumbents from bundling local service with other services, arguing such bundles hurt competition in both local service and other areas. With three or four services bundled together, says Engelhart, "it just gets more complicated if you want to go to another competitor."

Call-Net alleged incumbent carriers are not equitable in handling cutovers from their services to the competitors. For instance, incumbent carriers will do residential installations for their own customers on Saturdays but won't do the same for customers switching to Call-Net. And cutovers don't always happen as quickly and smoothly as they might—for which the customer inevitably blames the competitive carrier. Ted Chislett, president of competitive carrier Primus Canada, adds that charges for cutovers vary widely across the country. Call-Net also wants a two-year reduction in charges for services CLECs must buy from incumbents and for a public-education campaign to make consumers more aware that competitive local service exists.

With all these claims and counterclaims, one could forgive regulators for feeling overwhelmed. The solution, Yates says, is to look at the whole picture and develop a blueprint for making competition work. "The reaction of the CRTC should be to have a proceeding on competition," he says. A very Canadian solution.

[Adapted from Grant Buckler, "Can You See the Difference?" *Communications & Networking,* Vol. 6, No. 9 (September 2003).]

Discussion Questions

1. Have you ever switched local phone companies? Have you ever switched long distance phone companies or wireless phone companies? If you answered yes to one question and no to the other, how do you explain the difference?
2. Do incumbents have an unfair advantage in local telephone services? Why or why not?
3. Who do you think will be the winners in the battle for the telecommunications market in Canada?
4. How far can information technology convergence go? Predict how a home or business will send and receive information in 2015.

Chapter 5

Preview

This chapter focuses on how companies are conducting business electronically with their customers, business partners, and suppliers, which is referred to as electronic business (e-business, or EB). The Internet and World Wide Web are extremely well suited for conducting business electronically on a global basis. Web-based EB has introduced unprecedented opportunities for the marketing of products, accompanied by features, functionality, and innovative methods to serve and support consumers.

After reading this chapter, you will be able to do the following:

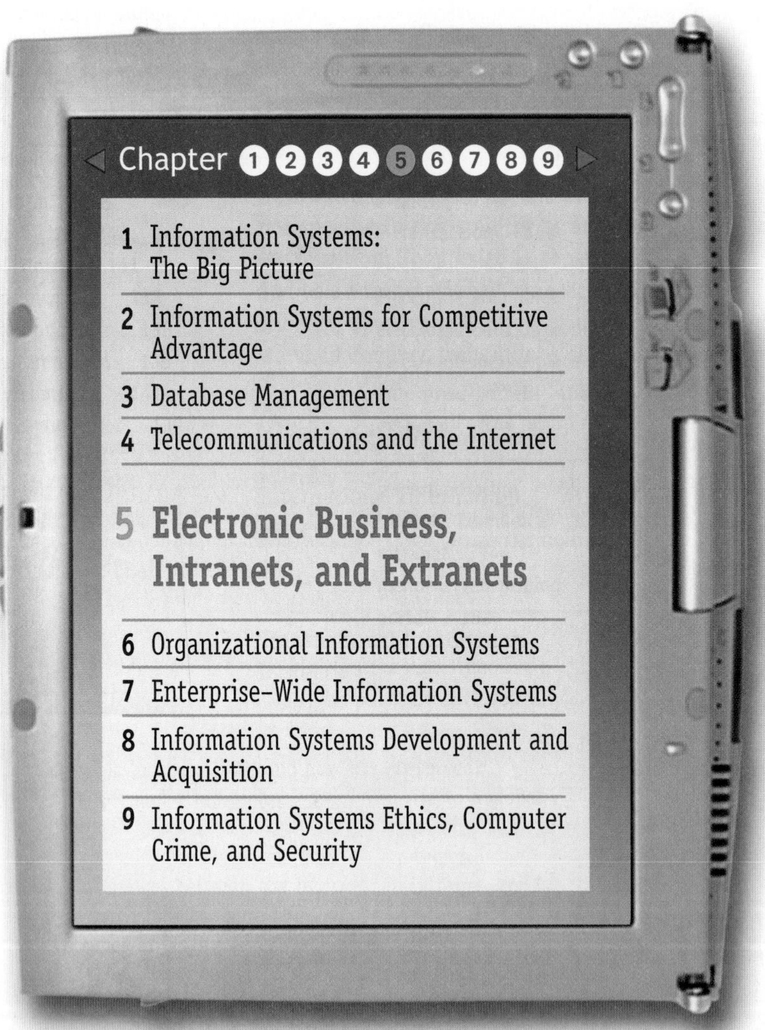

[**Figure 5.1** ➥ The Big Picture: focusing on electronic business, intranets, and extranets.]

1. Describe electronic business and how it has evolved.
2. Describe the strategies that companies are adopting to compete in cyberspace.
3. Explain the differences between intranets and extranets.
4. Describe the difference between consumer-focused and business-focused electronic business.
5. Understand the keys to successful electronic business applications.

Electronic Business, Intranets, and Extranets

OPENING: Clash of the Titans: Amazon.ca vs. Indigo.Chapters.ca

When Chapters and Indigo books merged in 2001, a Canadian powerhouse was born. The combined company accounted for more than half of retail book sales across the country. Prior to the merger, Chapters.ca was the leading online Canadian book seller, substantially ahead of Indigo.ca. After the merger, Chapters.Indigo.ca quickly became the dominant domestic online book and music retailer. Canadians could order books from U.S.-based online retailers such as Amazon.com and Barnesandnoble.com, but were faced with shipping delays, import duties, and shifting exchange rates.

In June 2002, Amazon.com "officially" entered the Canadian marketplace with Amazon.ca. Canadians could order in Canadian dollars and shipping was provided by Canada Post. Almost immediately, Amazon.ca cut the prices of its 40 best sellers by 40 percent in a bid to topple Chapters.Indigo.ca as Canada's dominant online book retailer. "We run our business based on what customers tell us they want. We have yet to meet a customer who doesn't like lower prices," Amazon's Kristin Schaefer said in an interview with the *Toronto Star.* "That's our corporate strategy." Chapters.Indigo.ca countered with a 30-percent discount on its best-selling books. Both firms offered free shipping on orders greater than $39.

Chapters.Indigo.ca then lodged a complaint with the Canadian Heritage Department complaining that Amazon.ca was violating rules that prohibited foreign-owned bookstores from setting up in Canada. However, Amazon.ca replied that the company had no Canadian place of business and the complaint was dismissed.

In 2003, Amazon.ca teamed up with HMV Canada to relaunch HMV.com. The company also unveiled a program with Canada Post to place its logo on mail delivery trucks. Chapters.Indigo.ca increased its sponsorship of Canadian literary festivals and broadened its product offerings to include gifts and jewellery. Although both firms claim double-digit sales increases, it is doubtful that either company is making any money in the Canadian marketplace. This battle has a few more rounds to go . . .

[**Figure 5.2** ➡ Chapters.Indigo.ca and Amazon.ca fight a costly battle for the Canadian marketplace.]

Source: CP Photo—Steve White.

Web Search

WEB SEARCH OPPORTUNITY
Ever wondered about starting your own e-business? The Government of Canada has created a Website designed to help Internet entrepreneurs get started. The site is called ebiz.enable and can be found at **strategis.ic.gc.ca/epic/internet/inee-ef.nsf/en/home/.**

Chapter 5's place within The Big Picture is shown in Figure 5.1. While the financial markets have risen and fallen over the last 10 years, online consumer and business spending have grown steadily in Canada and elsewhere. According to Statistics Canada, the size of the average online purchase jumped to $876 in 2002, up from $146 in 2000. People with EB skills are in high demand in the marketplace and, therefore, the more you know about EB, the more valuable you will become!

ELECTRONIC BUSINESS DEFINED

The growth of electronic business has given rise to a plethora of new terminology. Figure 5.3 illustrates the relationship among a number of the new economy terms. The largest oval is labelled ***electronic business.*** Simply put, this includes everything having to do with the application of information and communication technologies (ICT) to the conduct of business between organizations or from company to consumer. Within the electronic business oval is a smaller oval labelled ***electronic commerce.*** This highlights the fact that there are numerous forms of business-related ICT-based interactions that can occur between businesses, or between a business and an end consumer, which do not directly concern buying and selling (i.e., "commerce"). Only those forms of interaction having to do with commerce are included in the electronic commerce oval. This includes advertising of products or services, electronic shopping, and direct after-sales support. It would not include such things as interorganizational collaboration using ICT-based collaboration systems for the development of a new product.

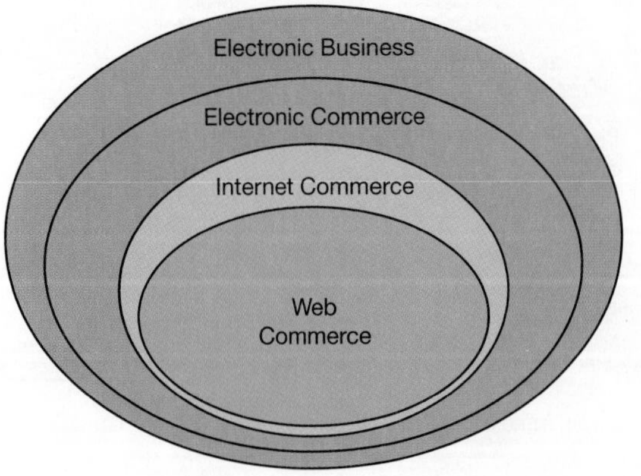

[Figure 5.3 ➥ The relationship among e-business terms and concepts.]

Source: S. L. Huff, M. Wade, and S. Schneberger, *Cases in Electronic Commerce*, 2nd ed. (Irwin/McGraw-Hill, 2002).

Within the electronic commerce oval is a smaller oval labelled ***Internet commerce.*** This reflects the fact that electronic commerce need not be conducted only over the Internet. In fact, a great deal of business-to-business electronic commerce today is still conducted over private networks, using primarily traditional electronic data interchange (EDI) channels and value-added network (VAN) service providers. This is changing, as more and more companies adopt the Internet for some or all of their business-to-business electronic commerce, but it will be many years before the Internet totally displaces the VANs.

Within the Internet commerce domain lies an even smaller subset, termed ***Web commerce.*** This is the component of Internet commerce conducted strictly over the World Wide Web. The WWW is not the only way of using the Internet for commercial interactions. Electronic mail, for example, serves well for certain forms of commerce. As another example, software may be conveniently sold over the Internet using the file transfer protocol (FTP) for product distribution. Nevertheless, the Web is clearly the dominant medium for the large majority of Internet commerce today. Furthermore, since modern Web browsers incorporate other Internet applications, including electronic mail and file transfer via FTP, all under one "hood," users today have the perception that they are relying solely on the Web even as they send and receive e-mail, transfer files, and conduct other forms of Internet applications that used to be conducted using separate application programs.

Contrary to popular belief, EB goes beyond merely buying and selling products online. EB can involve the events leading up to the purchase of a product, as well as customer service after the sale. Furthermore, EB is not limited to transactions between businesses and consumers, which is known as ***business-to-consumer*** (B2C) EB and vice versa. EB is also used to conduct business with business partners such as suppliers and intermediaries. This form of EB is commonly referred to as ***business-to-business*** (B2B) EB. Some companies choose to operate in both arenas, such as the clothing and home furnishing retailer Eddie Bauer, while other firms concentrate solely in B2C or B2B. Some forms of EB happen between businesses and their employees and are referred to as ***business-to-employee*** (B2E). Some forms of EB do not even involve business firms, as would be the case with an online textbook exchange service for students at a university or an online trading Website such as eBay.ca; these forms of EB are referred to as ***consumer-to-consumer*** (C2C).

Furthermore, there is a wide variety of ways to conduct business in each arena. In the following section, we examine the reasons that Web-based EB is revolutionizing the way business is being done. This is followed by an in-depth analysis of how companies are utilizing EB in their daily operations.

Internet and World Wide Web Capabilities

Technological forces are driving business, and the Internet and Web emerged as a strong new agent of change. The resulting technological revolution has essentially broken down the barriers to entry, levelled the playing field, and propelled commerce into the electronic domain. Companies are exploiting one or more of the capabilities of the Web to reach a wider customer base, offer a broader range of products, and develop closer relationships with customers by striving to meet their unique needs. These wide-ranging capabilities include global information dissemination, integration, mass customization, interactive communication, collaboration, and transactional support (Looney and Chatterjee, 2002; Chatterjee and Sambamurthy, 1999).

The powerful combination of Internet and Web technologies has given rise to a global platform where firms from across the world can effectively compete for customers and gain access to new markets. EB has wide geographical potential given that many countries have at least some type of Internet access. The global connectivity of the Internet provides a relatively economical medium for marketing products over vast distances. This increased geographical reach has been facilitated by storefronts located on every Web-enabled computer in the world. Unlike traditional storefronts, time limitations are not a factor, allowing firms to sell and service products seven days a week, 24 hours a day, 365 days a year to anyone, anywhere. A larger customer base creates increased sales volumes, which ultimately saves consumers money since firms can offer their products at lower prices (Christensen and Tedlow, 2000). In addition, parking for customers is no problem, and firms can deliver the goods right to the customer's door.

Web technologies also allow integration of information via Websites, which can be linked to corporate databases to provide real-time access to information. No longer must customers rely on old information from printed catalogues or account statements that arrive in the mail once a month. For example, when Air Canada (**www.aircanada.ca**) updates fare information in its corporate database, customers can access the revisions as they occur simply by browsing the company's Website. As with nearly every other major airline, the Web allows Air Canada to disseminate real-time fare pricing. This is particularly important for companies operating in highly competitive environments such as the airline industry. Furthermore, Aeroplan offers Air Canada's valued customers the ability to check the balances of their frequent-flyer accounts at its site, **www.aeroplan.com** (see Figure 5.4). Customers do not have to wait for monthly statements to see if they are eligible for travel benefits and awards.

Web technologies are also helping firms realize their goal of mass customization. Mass customization helps firms tailor their products and services to meet a customer's particular needs. For instance, clothing retailer Lands' End (**www.landsend.com**) has developed an application called My Virtual Model^{TM}, which allows customers to create a virtual person to model clothing for them (see Figure 5.5). Customers can configure the virtual model based on a number of criteria such as gender, height, weight, build, complexion, and hair colour. Once customers have created a virtual model, they can dress the model in clothing to see how it will look on them. The virtual model application also assists Lands' End in tracking customers' preferred clothing styles and colours, allowing them to target marketing efforts to individual customers.

Interactive communication via the Web enables firms to build customer loyalty by providing immediate communication and feedback to and from customers, which can dramatically improve the firm's image through demonstrated responsiveness. Many firms are augmenting telephone-based ordering and customer support with Web-based applications and electronic mail. In some cases, online chat applications are provided to allow customers to communicate with a customer service representative in real time through the corporate Website. The online brokerage firm E*Trade Canada (**www.etrade.ca**) has implemented such a feature. Should a question arise during the placing of an order, customers can click a button that opens a chat application, connecting them in real time to a customer

[**Figure 5.4** ➥ Aeroplan's rewards Website.]

Source: Courtesy of Aeroplan.

service representative. The customer can type questions into a window and receive immediate responses from the representative. This feature allows the customer service agent to walk the customer through the ordering process step by step while the customer is entering the transaction. Customers never have to leave E*Trade Canada's Website or terminate their Internet connection to get their business done. This customer-driven approach far out-distances traditional, nonelectronic means in terms of tailoring and timeliness.

Web technologies can also enable collaboration. As an example, E*Trade Canada maintains a community for investors, who regularly share opinions concerning companies, news, rumours, and investment strategies through an E*Trade Canada–sponsored forum. The community exposes investors to a wide array of information that would otherwise be unavailable through traditional channels. IBM Microelectronics uses the Web to collaborate with its custom-logic chip customers. A Java-enabled Web browser allows users to share

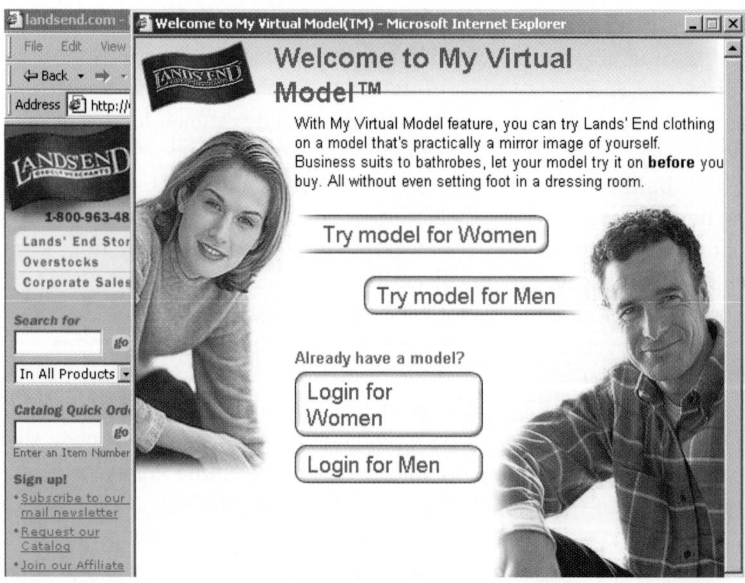

[**Figure 5.5** ➥ Lands' End's *My Virtual Model*™ application.]

Source: **www.landsend.com.**

product information, access design specifications, and download software tools from the Website. The application provides interactive, or two-way, communications, helping IBM engineers to pinpoint design issues and provide personalized support to better serve customers (Alexander, 2001).

By providing ways for clients and firms to conduct business online without human assistance, the Internet and Web have greatly reduced transaction costs while enhancing operational efficiency. Many companies, such as Dell Computer Corporation, are utilizing the Web to provide automated transaction support. Dell began selling computers on the Web in mid-1996. By early 1998, Dell was making around $3 million in online sales per day. Dell derives about 90 percent of its overall revenues from sales to medium and large businesses, yet more than half of its Web-based sales have been to individuals and small businesses, who typically buy one computer at a time. As a result, Dell is experiencing significant cost savings per sale by reducing the demand for phone representatives on the smaller purchases. Individual customers can access product information at any time from anywhere, empowering customers to service themselves. This benefits not only the end consumer but Dell as well. Customer service representatives can focus on lucrative corporate customers, reducing labour costs involved in servicing small-ticket items. By streamlining operations and greatly increasing sales through both online and traditional channels, Dell has grown into one of the world's largest personal computer manufacturers, with sales well in excess of $10 billion annually. This phenomenon of cutting out the intermediary and reaching customers more directly and efficiently is known as ***disintermediation***.

Electronic Business Strategies

The Web has transformed traditional business operations into a hyper-competitive electronic marketplace. Companies must strategically position themselves to compete in the EB environment. At one extreme, companies following a ***bricks-and-mortar*** approach choose to operate solely in the traditional, physical markets. These companies approach business activities in a traditional manner by operating physical locations such as department stores, business offices, and manufacturing plants. In other words, the bricks-and-mortar business strategy does not include EB. In contrast, ***clicks-only companies*** (also referred to as ***virtual,*** or "pure play," ***companies***) conduct business electronically in cyberspace. These firms have no physical locations, allowing them to focus purely on EB. One of the few remaining examples of a clicks-only company

Software Flaws Can Threaten Electronic Business

An Internet user who goes by the name ThePull reported an alleged flaw in Internet Explorer to Microsoft Corporation. ThePull is an example of a "White Hat," a hacker who uncovers problems in software and then reports those problems to the software's manufacturer. White Hats are the "good" version of Black Hats, who exploit software vulnerabilities for malicious purposes. The alleged flaw in Internet Explorer could potentially allow hackers to enter Websites undercover and steal cookies and related information from those Websites, or even from the computers of individual browser users. Rain Forest Puppy, another White Hat, found a vulnerability in Microsoft's Internet Information Services (IIS) server. If unchecked, hackers could use the vulnerability to gain access to the computers running IIS software and make any changes they wanted, including modifying or stealing content and erasing the hard drive. Every few weeks, it seems, another critical security flaw is uncovered in a piece of widely used software.

Microsoft has responded to these threats by launching the Microsoft Security Response Center (MSRC). The goal of the MSRC is to protect users by eliminating security vulnerabilities whenever they are found in a Microsoft product or service. Since its creation, the MSRC has eliminated more than 250 vulnerabilities affecting roughly 60 Microsoft products. In 2003, the MSRC replied to over 10,000 e-mails. Most of these potential problems, in turned out, were not security vulnerabilities at all, but occurred as a result of user error. According to Scott Culp, ex-manager of the MSRC and now senior security strategist for Microsoft's Trustworthy Computing Team, fewer than 1 percent of potential vulnerabilities actually turn out to be verified problems requiring action from Microsoft. Culp adds that software security vulnerabilities occur at about the same rate in software from all manufacturers. The economic consequence of software security vulnerabilities is hard to measure, but one can assume that it is significant.

For up-to-date information on security issues at Microsoft, check TechNet at **www.microsoft.com/technet/default.asp.**

WHEN THINGS GO WRONG

is the popular eBay trading and exchange Website, which does not have a physical storefront in the classic sense. Other firms choose to straddle the two environments, operating in both physical and virtual arenas. These firms operate under the ***bricks-and-clicks*** business model. The three general business models are depicted in Figure 5.6.

The greatest impact of the Web-based EB revolution has occurred in companies adopting the bricks-and-clicks approach. Bricks-and-clicks companies continue to operate their physical locations and have added the EB component to their business activities. With transactions occurring in both physical and virtual environments, it is imperative that bricks-and-clicks companies learn how to fully maximize commercial opportunities in both domains. Conducting physical and virtual operations presents special challenges for these firms, as business activities must be tailored to each of these different environments if the firms are to compete effectively.

Another challenge for bricks-and-clicks companies involves increasing information system complexity. Design and development of complex computing systems are required to support each aspect of the bricks-and-clicks approach (Looney and Chatterjee, 2002). Furthermore, different skills are necessary to support Web-based computing, requiring substantial resource investments. Companies must design, develop, and deploy systems and applications to accommodate an open computing architecture that must be globally and persistently available. For instance, over the course of 18 months, the bricks-and-clicks brokerage firm Charles Schwab increased its full-time IS staff by more than 50 percent, or 700 employees. In addition, the organization could no longer accurately predict usage trends of computing resources. Schwab experienced increased volatility in online transactions as compared with offline transactions, prompting the need to increase computing capacity to 32 mainframe computers in order to handle the increased volume (Tempest, 1999).

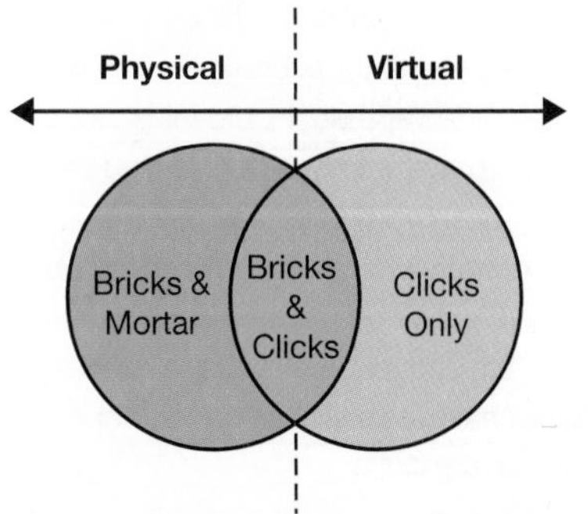

[**Figure 5.6** ➡ General approaches to electronic business.]

Source: Modified from Looney and Chatterjee, 2002.

Clicks-only companies often have a price advantage since they do not need to support the physical aspects of the bricks-and-clicks approach. Thus, these companies can reduce prices to rock-bottom levels. On the other hand, a relatively small clicks-only firm may not sell enough products and/or may not order enough from suppliers to be able to realize economies of scale and thus reduce prices. Clicks-only firms also tend to be highly adept with technology and can innovate very rapidly as new technologies become available. This can enable them to stay one step ahead of their competition. However, conducting business in cyberspace can be problematic in some respects. For example, it is much more difficult for a customer to return a product to a purely online company than simply to return it to a local department store. In addition, some consumers may not be comfortable making purchases online. Individuals may be leery about the security of giving credit card numbers to a virtual company.

As you can see, there is a variety of ways that firms can and have conducted EB. In the next section we describe in greater detail how firms have evolved toward using the Internet and Web to support internal operations and to interact with each other.

BUSINESS-TO-BUSINESS ELECTRONIC BUSINESS

Prior to the introduction of the Internet and Web, business-to-business EB was facilitated using electronic data interchange (EDI). These systems are generally limited to large corporations that can afford the associated expenses. The Internet and Web have provided an economical medium over which information can be transmitted, enabling small- to medium-sized enterprises (SMEs) to participate in B2B markets. Companies have devised a number of innovative ways to facilitate B2B transactions using these technologies. Web-based B2B systems range from simple extranet applications to complex trading exchanges where multiple buyers and sellers come together to conduct business. In the following sections, we examine the stages under which modern B2B EB is done, shedding light on the different approaches and their suitability for different business requirements. Figure 5.7 provides a high-level overview of how B2B architectures typically evolve.

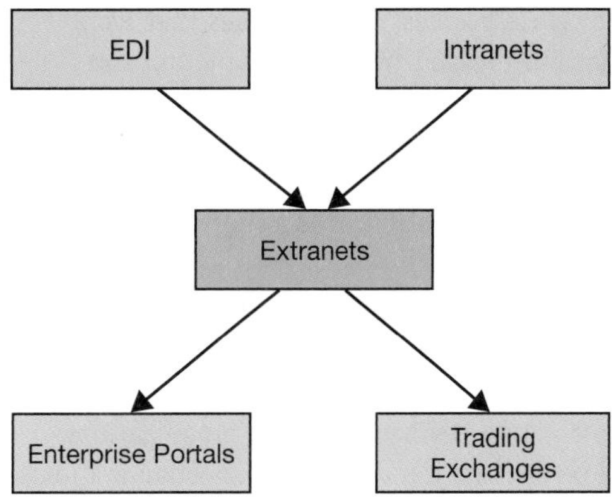

[**Figure 5.7** ➥ Stages of B2B electronic business.]

How Electronic Data Interchange Works

Electronic data interchange (EDI) is the forefather of modern B2B EB and continues to maintain a stronghold in B2B computing. Giga Information Group estimates that Canadian and U.S. companies buy about $500 billion worth of goods and services electronically each year via EDI networks. EDI refers to the digital, or electronic, transmission of business documents and related data between organizations via telecommunications networks. More specifically, these telecommunications networks commonly take the form of ***value-added networks (VANs)***, which provide a direct link over which data can be transmitted. VANs are telephone lines that are leased from telecommunications providers, creating a secure, dedicated circuit between a company and its business partners. Figure 5.8 depicts a typical EDI system architecture using VANs to connect a company with its suppliers and customers.

Companies use EDI to exchange a wide variety of business documents, including purchase orders, invoices, shipping manifests, delivery schedules, and electronic payments. Currently, over 100,000 U.S. and Canadian companies conduct business via EDI. EDI began in the mid-1960s as an initiative to reduce paperwork. Although EDI has never totally eliminated paper, it does help reduce the number of times business documents need to be handled. EDI provides many efficiencies because it helps to streamline business processes.

EDI enabled RJR Nabisco to reduce the cost of processing a paper-based purchase order from $70 to less than $1. However, the cost associated with EDI-based systems has limited its usefulness to large companies. EDI is costly to implement and maintain. Software and hardware required to enable EDI can cost upwards of $100,000, and monthly telecommunications charges associated with VANs can approach several thousand dollars per month, depending upon the number of communication lines necessary to connect the company with its business partners.

Large enterprises can afford the costs associated with EDI. They can justify the costs since EDI has created such dramatic efficiencies for their organizations. Yet EDI has proved to be beyond the reach of SMEs. Before the introduction of the Internet and Web, a viable, economical alternative to EDI was unavailable, preventing small to midsized firms from participating in B2B markets. To make matters worse, some large corporations and government agencies had gone so far as

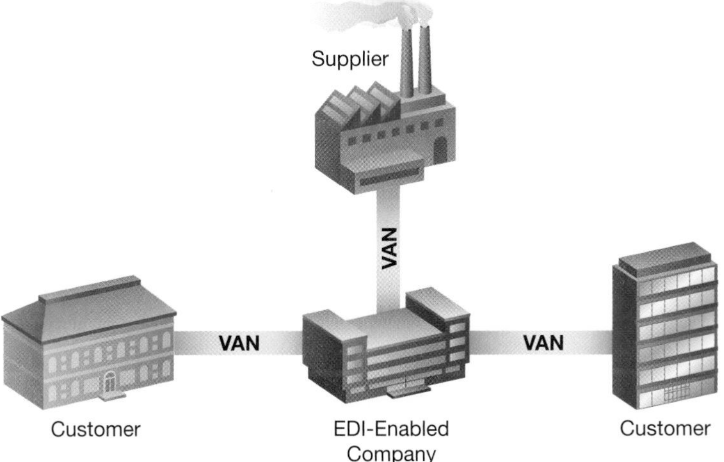

[**Figure 5.8** ➥ A typical EDI system architecture.]

to refuse business to companies that were not EDI-enabled. What small and midsized companies needed was a technology that would level the playing field, making B2B affordable and accessible. This leads us to the next generation of Internet-based B2B architectures.

How the Internet Changed Everything

EDI has been used for more than four decades to conduct business between organizations. However, the trend in business today is to use the public Internet and Web as the vehicle for business-to-business EB. The global accessibility and economics afforded by the Internet and Web have enabled SMEs to participate in B2B markets once reserved for large corporations. With the entrance of buyers and suppliers of all shapes and sizes, the mass adoption of these technologies has propelled B2B into the forefront of modern commerce.

By late 1997, Cisco Systems, a leading producer of networking technologies such as routers, had shifted nearly 40 percent of its B2B sales from bricks-and-mortar markets to the Web. That amounts to almost $9 million per day, or more than $3 billion per year. Cisco has continued its trend toward a clicks-only approach, selling more than 50 percent of its products online in 1998, and 60 percent in 1999. Additionally, Cisco is letting its biggest customers, such as Qwest Communications and Sprint, connect directly into its online inventory and product ordering system through Web-based applications. Cisco's B2B initiatives have enabled customers to service themselves, resulting in a redeployment of customer service representatives to other critical areas within the company. As a result, Cisco is saving about $20 million per year related to sales transactions. These cost savings are being invested into the company's research and development (R&D) program—far exceeding the R&D investment of Cisco's nearest competitors, such as Nortel Networks and Foundry Networks. Cisco's savings are passed on to its customers. For example, a six-person department at Sprint Communications buys approximately 40 routers per week for its customers. Using Cisco's B2B applications, Sprint estimates it will save as much as $200,000 per year in order processing costs.

Using the Internet for Intranets and Extranets

Once organizations realize the advantage of using the Internet and Web to communicate public information outside corporate boundaries, Web-based technologies can also be leveraged to support proprietary, internal communications within an organization through the implementation of an ***intranet.***[1] An intranet consists of an internal, private network using Web technologies to facilitate the secured transmission of proprietary information within the organization. An intranet can be considered a private, internal Web, which limits viewing access to authorized users within the organization. Intranets take advantage of standard Internet and Web protocols to communicate information to and from authorized employees. As they do on the Web, employees access information on the intranet through a Web browser. However, this information cannot be viewed by users outside the organization and, thus, is separated from the visible, publicly accessible Web.

In order to communicate proprietary information with authorized users outside organizational boundaries, a company can implement an extended intranet, or ***extranet.*** An extranet enables two or more firms to use the Internet to do business together. Table 5.1 provides a comparison of characteristics between the Internet, intranet, and extranet environments.

Intranets and extranets are the fastest growing segment of Web-based technologies, and the Web, whether it be Internet-, intranet-, or extranet-based, has become the predominant method of conducting business. The Canadian federal government operates an intranet containing more than 300,000 pages. The intranet has become pervasive, impacting every department within the government.

Aerospace giant Boeing has launched an extranet that can be accessed by more than 1,000 authorized business partners. One of Boeing's business partners, aluminum supplier Alcoa, accesses the extranet to coordinate its shipments to Boeing, as well as to check Boeing's raw materials supply to ensure appropriate inventory levels. Customers such as the United States Department of Defense log in to Boeing's extranet to receive status updates on the projects Boeing is working on for them (Sullivan, 1999). Overall B2B results mirror those of Boeing. B2B conducted via extranets in 1998 surpassed $35 billion and doubled in

[1]It can be argued that, on a technological level, intranets and extranets are variants of the same thing in that both employ firewalls to cordon off a select group of users. However, given that intranets and extranets have very different purposes from a business point of view, we choose to distinguish between the two.

CAREER IMPLICATIONS

Accounting and Finance

The TSX Group has become an early adopter of a Web-based specification that could improve the sharing of financial information in stock exchanges around the world. Toronto-based TSX said it had published its year-end results in extensible business reporting language (XBRL), a framework for handling data based on extensible markup language, or XML. The TSX is one of more than 40 Canadian organizations, which also include Export Development Canada, the Royal Bank of Canada, and Public Works and Government Services Canada, to join an international consortium working to bring the language to market.

XBRL reduces the time it takes to extract important data from financial statements or annual reports through the use of metadata tags. The development of Canadian-specific XBRL classifications has accelerated the development of the standard since the consortium took shape about five years ago. TSX Group CFO Michael Ptasznik said the company wanted to bolster its reputation as an IT pioneer. The Toronto Stock Exchange was the first to introduce electronic trading, for example. The project involved going through the TSX results and tagging things that are very common. If something unique to the TSX or an exchange came up, the taxonomy had to be modified. In the United States, XBRL working groups are creating industry-specific taxonomies for the financial services, forestry, oil and gas, and other sectors. The TSX project is the first step to create an exchange taxonomy.

Ptasznik said the business case for XBRL lies in its potential to help reduce the information overload often prevalent in financial reporting. "It's the simplicity with which, eventually, analysts and investors will be able to take down our data, compare with others, and then use it in their models," he said. "It goes along with our philosophy of better disclosure, and the easier it is for people to access and utilize your information, that's another means of increasing the disclosure capability."

[Adapted from Shane Schick, "TSX Pioneers New Standard for Financial Reporting," **http://www.itbusiness.ca/index.asp?theaction=61&sid=54689#**, ITBusiness.ca (February 9, 2004).]

2001. A survey conducted in 1998 with Fortune 1000 companies found that 68 percent of these companies had implemented an extranet for B2B, up 24 percent from the preceding year (Kalakota, Oliva, and Donath, 1999).

Intranets and extranets benefit corporations in a number of ways, so it is no surprise that firms have readily and rapidly adopted these technologies. First and foremost, intranets and extranets can dramatically improve the timeliness and accuracy of communications, reducing the number of misunderstandings within the organization, as well as with business partners and customers. In the business world, very little information is static and, therefore, information must be continually updated and disseminated as it changes. Intranets and extranets facilitate this process by providing a cost-effective, global medium over which proprietary information can be distributed. Furthermore, they allow central management of documents, thus reducing the number of versions and amount of out-of-date information that may be stored throughout the organization. While security is still thought to be better on proprietary networks, the Internet can be made to be a relatively secure medium for business.

Web-based technologies are cross-platform, meaning that disparate computing systems can communicate with each other, provided that standard Web protocols have been implemented. For example, an Apple Macintosh can request Web pages from a UNIX Web server. Even though the computers are running under different operating systems, they can

[Table 5.1] ***Characteristics of the Internet, intranet, and extranet (Szuprowicz, 1998; Turban et al., 2000).***

Focus	Type of Information	Users	Access	
The Internet	External communications	General, public, and "advertorial"	Any user with an Internet connection	Public and not restricted
Intranet	Internal communications	Specific, corporate, and proprietary	Authorized employees	Private and restricted
Extranet	External communications	Communications between business partners	Authorized business partners	Private and restricted

communicate with each other over the Internet, provided that TCP/IP is being used by each machine. The cross-platform nature of the Web makes implementing intranets and extranets extremely attractive as a way to connect disparate computing environments.

In addition, intranets and extranets do not require large expenditures to train users on the technologies. Since many employees, customers, and business partners are familiar with the tools associated with the Internet and Web, they do not require special training to familiarize them with intranet and extranet interfaces. In other words, intranets and extranets look and act just like public Websites and Web pages. As long as users are familiar with a Web browser, they can utilize intranets and extranets with little difficulty.

Above all, intranets and extranets impact the company's bottom line. A company can use them to automate business transactions, reducing processing costs and achieving shortened cycle times. Intranets and extranets can also reduce errors by providing a single point of data entry, from which the information can be updated on disparate corporate computing platforms without having to re-key the data. Management can then obtain real-time information to track and analyze business activities. Intranets and extranets are incredibly powerful and intensely popular. We describe in the following sections how they work and how they are being used best (beginning with intranets).

Intranet System Architecture

An intranet looks and acts just like a publicly accessible Website and uses the same software, hardware, and networking technologies to communicate information. However, intranets use ***firewalls*** to secure proprietary information stored within the corporate LAN and/or WAN. Firewalls are hardware devices with special software that are placed between the organization's LAN or WAN and the Internet, preventing unauthorized access to the proprietary information stored on the intranet. In the simplest form of an intranet, communications take place within the confines of organizational boundaries and do not travel across the Internet. Figure 5.9 depicts a typical intranet system architecture.

To enable access to an intranet, Web browsers are installed on each employee's workstation, and the TCP/IP protocol must be implemented on top of the protocols existing on the corporate LAN/WAN. An intranet Web server is placed behind the firewall and connected to the LAN/WAN to facilitate user requests for information. Employees may access intranet content through a Web browser by entering the URL of the main intranet Web page. Once the user enters the URL in the Web browser, TCP/IP breaks the request into data packets and routes the transmission over the LAN/WAN to the intranet Web server. When the packets reach their destination, they are reassembled and passed to the Web server. The Web server understands that the

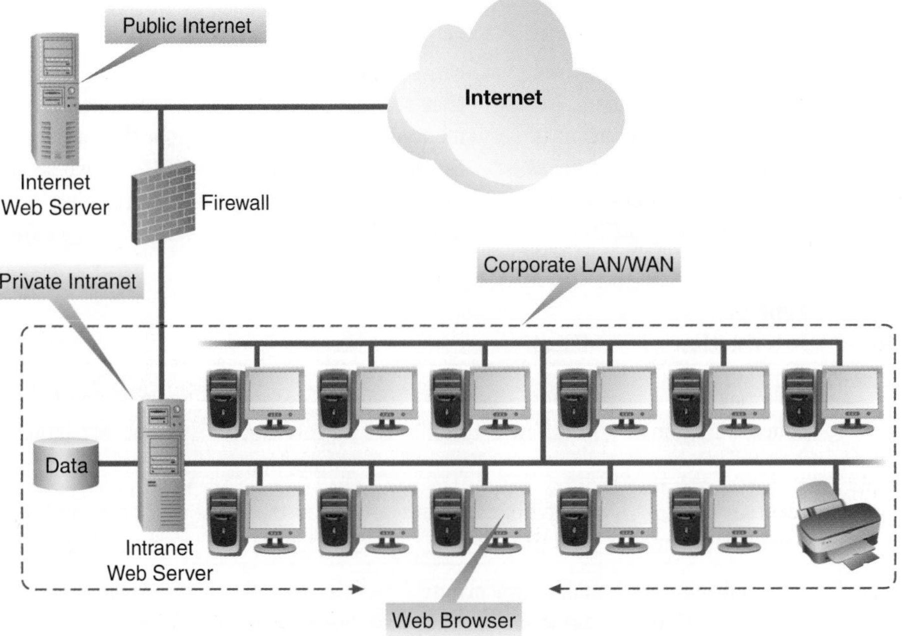

[**Figure 5.9** ➥ Intranet architecture.]

user is requesting a Web page and retrieves the information, which TCP/IP breaks into packets and transmits back to the Web browser. TCP/IP reassembles the Web page at the destination and delivers it to the Web browser. In turn, the Web browser processes the HTML code, formats the physical appearance of the Web page, and displays the results in the Web browser. It should be noted that during the intranet transaction, packets are never routed outside the corporate firewall. All transmissions travel within the bounds of the organization's private network rather than over the public Internet, eliminating potential security risks such as unauthorized access to corporate information.

Intranet Applications

Training

The Boeing Company offers training to more than 200,000 employees via the Center for Leadership and Training (CLT) intranet site. Delivering training over Boeing's intranet opens up courses and training opportunities for employees worldwide. By using the CLT intranet, employees can choose from a wide range of course offerings, including educational programs, supervisor training, and techniques to improve quality control. CLT contains an online catalogue summarizing course offerings and provides a feature that allows employees to register for courses using their Web browsers. Once registered for a course, users can access multimedia content including video lectures, presentation slides, and other course materials directly from their desktops.

Boeing's intranet-based training initiative has led to dramatic business improvements and cost reductions. The intranet helped eliminate redundant courses and standardize course material. It virtually eliminated travel costs associated with sending employees to training sites. In addition, employees can take courses on a time-permitting basis, meaning that they can learn at a pace that accommodates their work schedule.

Application Integration

Many organizations have invested substantial sums of money and resources in a variety of software applications such as enterprise resource planning (ERP), customer relationship management (CRM), sales force automation (SFA), and various other packages to support internal operations. Often these disparate applications are installed on different computing platforms, where each may be running under a different operating system, using a different database management system, and/or providing a different user interface. Due to these disparate environments, it may be difficult for a user to consolidate information from these different systems into a single screen that can display all the information the user needs to make a business decision. Intranets can be used to alleviate this problem by providing application integration.

For example, salespeople may need information about the sales calls they need to make for the upcoming day, as well as information related to customers that they currently support. Data related to sales calls may be located in an SFA application running on a UNIX server, whereas the CRM application may be running on an IBM mainframe. Prior to the emergence of intranets, the workstation that a salesperson used to access the information would need to be loaded with the appropriate network operating systems and user interfaces necessary to retrieve the information from each of the disparate systems. In addition, the salesperson would need to toggle back and forth between the applications to access all the necessary information from the SFA and CRM systems.

By installing a product such as DataChannel's Enterprise Information Portal (EIP) on the intranet Web server, information from the SFA and CRM applications can be consolidated and presented to the user through a single Web browser interface (see Figure 5.10). Now, when the salesperson needs information related to sales calls and customer support activities, the request is routed to the intranet Web server running EIP, which accesses the relevant data from the SFA and CRM applications. The intranet server consolidates the information and delivers it to the salesperson, displaying all the information necessary to make business decisions in a single Web page.

Online Entry of Information

Companies can use intranets to streamline routine business processes because an intranet provides a Web browser interface to facilitate online entry of information. Microsoft has implemented an intranet-based expense reporting application, called MSExpense, that allows employees from across the world to submit expense reports online, dramatically reducing the inefficiencies and expenses associated with paper-based expense report processing.

Prior to MSExpense, 136 different expense report templates existed within the

WEB SEARCH OPPORTUNITY
Visit the *Intranet Journal* online at **www.intranetjournal.com** to further your exploration of intranets.

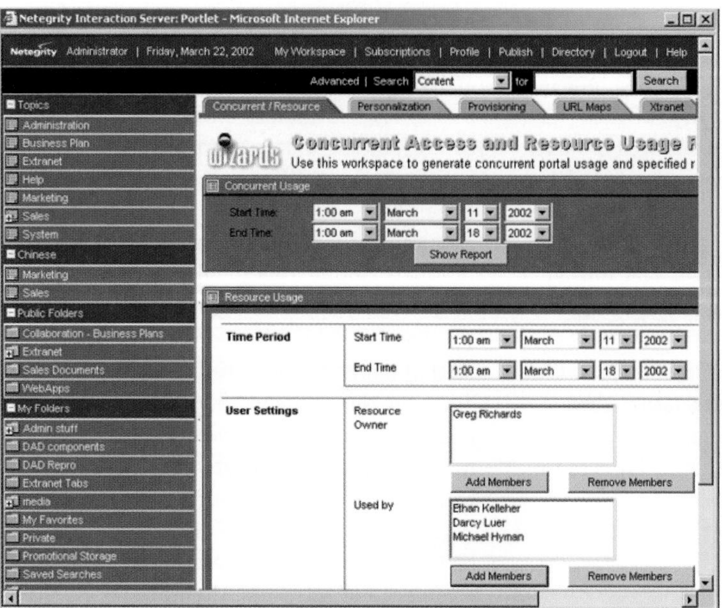

[**Figure 5.10** ➥ Application integration using DataChannel's EIP.]

Source: **www.datachannel.com**.

corporation, and information such as mileage rates were often outdated. These issues cost Microsoft employees precious time and effort in locating the appropriate template and ensuring that the expenses they were submitting were accurate. With MSExpense, expense report templates and expense rates are centrally managed on the intranet Web server, where modifications can be made instantaneously as conditions change. Now, Microsoft employees submit the appropriate template electronically with the assurance that they have used the correct version and up-to-date expense rates.

The implementation of the MSExpense intranet application reduced the cost of processing employee expense reports by over $3.3 million per year, shortened expense reimbursements from three weeks to three days, and dramatically reduced error rates by providing a single point of entry (Microsoft, 2001). Furthermore, applications such as MSExpense provide management with accurate, up-to-date information to track and analyze the costs associated with key business activities, as well as a way to enforce business policies to take advantage of reduced corporate rates offered by airlines, rental car companies, and hotels.

Real-Time Access to Information

Unlike paper-based documents, which need to be continually updated and distributed to employees when changes occur, intranets make it less complicated to manage, update, distribute, and access corporate information. Boeing disseminates corporate news using multimedia files distributed over the company's intranet. Formerly, news releases were produced on videotape, duplicated, and distributed via surface mail to each corporate office around the world. With the intranet-based solution, the company has eliminated the videotape reproduction process by allowing employees to monitor company news releases as they occur, from the convenience of their desktops. Boeing can now disseminate news in a more timely fashion while, in the process, saving millions annually in distribution costs. Intranets allow companies to become more flexible with resources required to create, maintain, and distribute corporate documents, while in the process employees become more knowledgeable and current about the information that is important to them.

Collaboration

One of the most common problems in large corporations relates to the communication of business activities in a timely fashion across divisional areas of the organization. For instance, a product engineer located at a branch office in Sydney, Australia, may need to access information from product marketing personnel located in Vancouver to ensure the product will meet the needs of the market. These individuals may need to share technical information such as CAD/CAM drawings, project management reports, and information related to prevailing industry and market conditions.

In other words, employees must be able to collaborate across departmental and geographical boundaries to complete project requirements in an efficient and timely manner.

Boeing uses its intranet to facilitate these collaborative efforts. Project managers disseminate daily project progress reports over the intranet to members of the project team, who may be located in any of its offices in 60 countries. Companies can also use multimedia technologies such as videoconferencing or Microsoft NetMeeting to facilitate team meetings over the intranet. Intranet-based collaboration alleviates the need for costly travel and use of less user-friendly media such as conference calling. Furthermore, three-dimensional modelling of aircraft designs can be shared among aerospace engineers. For example, an engineer can send a drawing across the intranet to another engineer at a remote location, who revises the drawing as necessary and returns the updated drawing using the intranet. The Boeing intranet provides the company with the capability of reducing product development cycles, as well as the ability to stay abreast of current project, corporate, and market conditions.

Extranet System Architecture

An extranet looks and acts just like an intranet and uses the same software, hardware, and networking technologies to communicate information (see Figure 5.11). However, an extranet connects the intranets of two or more business partners and, thus, requires an additional component. Intranets can be connected together using a ***virtual private network (VPN)*** to facilitate the secured transmission of proprietary information between business partners. VPNs take advantage of the public nature of the Internet and its standardized protocols to communicate information by combining the global connectivity of the Internet with the security of a closed, private network. When intranets are connected via a VPN, they act as if they are directly connected as a single LAN/WAN, but in reality they are not. As the name implies,

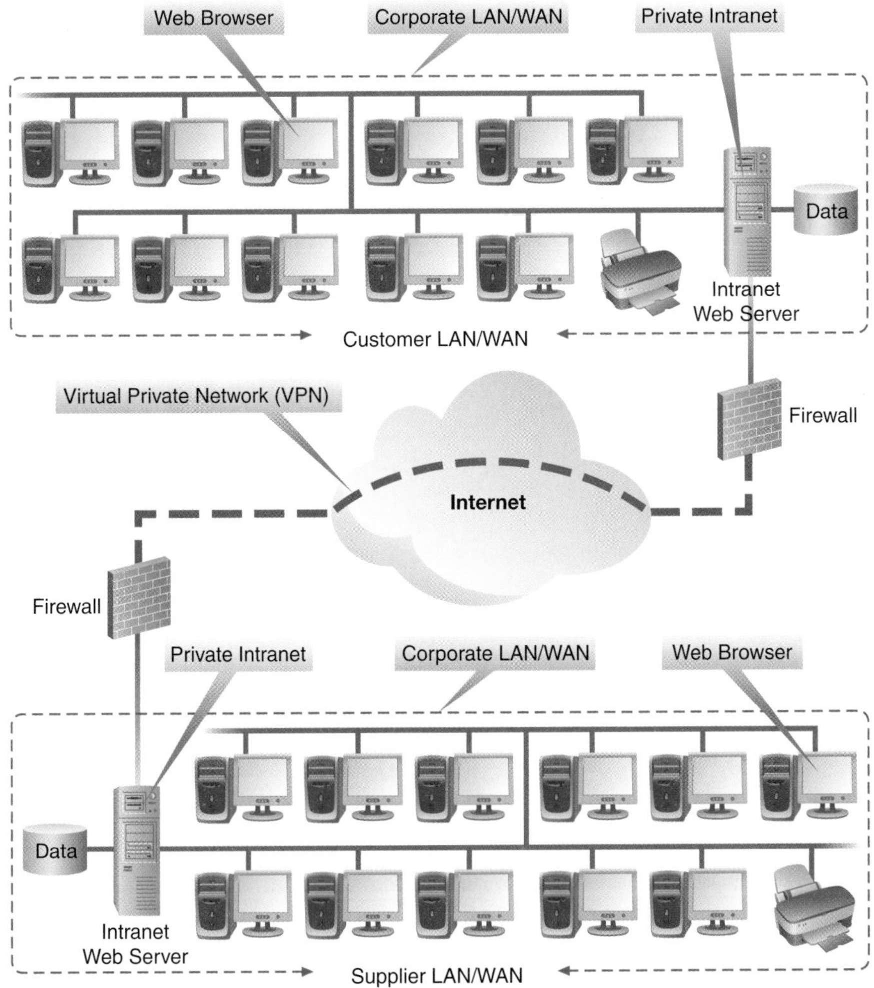

[**Figure 5.11** ➡ Typical extranet system architecture.]

virtual private networks are virtual in the sense that a connection is created between the intranets when a transmission needs to take place and terminated once the transmission has been completed. In other words, the VPN exists only when it is needed. Further, a VPN is backed by the telephone service provider, which adds an increased level of trust in the network. In addition, this approach enables you to scale bandwidth up and down as needed.

To access information on an extranet, Web browsers are installed on the workstations within each intranet and the TCP/IP protocol must be implemented on top of existing network protocols. Authorized business partners

CAREER IMPLICATIONS

Marketing

Clearwater Fine Foods, a vertically integrated seafood company based in Bedford, Nova Scotia, wanted to expand its market base beyond the usual mix of wholesalers and a few high-end restaurants (see Figure 5.12). James Davison, director of e-business at Clearwater, knew that because his company had never really stressed the consumer side of the business, there was a whole new market of untapped seafood lovers out there in cyberspace. "E-business brought Clearwater face to face with an entirely new market, and consumers seem very pleased that we've taken this step to reach out to them via the Internet," he said. Until its move into the e-business arena, Clearwater's Website was fundamentally an online brochure, which brought in the occasional e-mail order. "But there was never any real push to tap this market," Davison said.

"I was pretty confident in selling our e-business plan because we had done our homework, we already had some Web experience, upper management was very aware of e-business opportunities, and we knew we had superior products to offer the public," said Davison. Prior to the physical development of the site, Davison and his team did a good deal of research to find the right partners to help ensure the success of clearwater.ca. Davison says when considering how to structure an e-business site, every business is different. Some want to develop and host the site themselves, others prefer to outsource. Clearwater chose to outsource for scalability reasons. Development was done by Halifax-based Icom Alliance, and hosting was handled by Aliant. In setting up an e-business site, key costs to be aware of include site development, site hosting fees if that job is outsourced or equipment costs if it's done in-house, as well as ongoing maintenance and upgrades as required. Davison stressed that Clearwater's strategy involved much more than selling products online. "Of course, our key objective was to encourage people to purchase our products, but the site is also an educational and communication tool to help customers and potential customers learn about lobsters, to learn about the seafood business and to feel, when they leave our site, that they are indeed dealing with the seafood experts." With that in mind, the site included a section called "Lobster University," designed by Clearwater's biologists and offering interesting facts about lobster biology, along with advice on the care and handling of live lobsters.

[**Figure 5.12** ➡ Clearwater Fine Foods Inc.]

Source: David Murray © Dorling Kindersley.

[Adapted from *Clearwater Fine Foods Inc.—A Case Study,* Information Technology Association of Canada, **www.itac.ca** (2002).]

can access extranet content through a Web browser by entering the URL of their business partner's main extranet Web page. Once the user enters the URL in the Web browser, TCP/IP breaks the request into packets and routes the packets over the internal LAN/WAN to the firewall.

VPNs use a technology known as ***tunnelling*** to encapsulate, encrypt, and transmit data over the Internet infrastructure, enabling business partners to exchange information in a secured, private manner between organizational firewalls. Before information can be transmitted from one intranet to the other, the VPN connecting the two firewalls is established, and a secured tunnel is created over the VPN. TCP/IP routes the encrypted packets through the firewall and through the tunnel en route to their destination. When the packets reach the business partner's firewall, each packet is verified to ensure it has been sent from an authorized business partner. After packet verification, the packets are decrypted, and TCP/IP reassembles the packets and delivers them to the intranet Web server for processing.

Extranet Web servers perform an additional security measure through a process called ***authentication.*** Authentication confirms the identity of the remote user who is attempting to access information from the Web server. The authentication process forces the remote user to supply a valid username and password before the Web server fulfills requests. Great-West Life has implemented authentication through the Web page depicted in Figure 5.13.

After the remote user has been authenticated, the Web server retrieves the requested information, which is packetized by TCP/IP and sent back to the firewall. At the firewall, the packets are encapsulated and encrypted and sent via TCP/IP through the tunnel across the VPN. When the packets reach the business partner's firewall, each packet is verified to ensure it has been sent from an authorized business partner. After verification, the packets are decrypted, and TCP/IP reassembles the packets and delivers them to the Web browser that originally requested the information. The Web browser processes the HTML code, formats the physical appearance of the Web page, and displays the results in the Web browser. Once the transmission has been completed, the tunnel is discarded and the VPN is disconnected.

Extranet Applications

Supply Chain Management

The Big Three U.S. automobile manufacturers, Ford, General Motors, and Chrysler, teamed up in 1997 to implement an industry-wide extranet to exchange supply and manufacturing information between customers and suppliers. Although it may seem outlandish that major competitors within an industry are teaming up for ***supply chain management,*** the results have benefited everyone in the

WEB SEARCH OPPORTUNITY

Visit Aventail, a leading extranet service provider, at **www.extranet-strategist.com** to further your exploration of extranets.

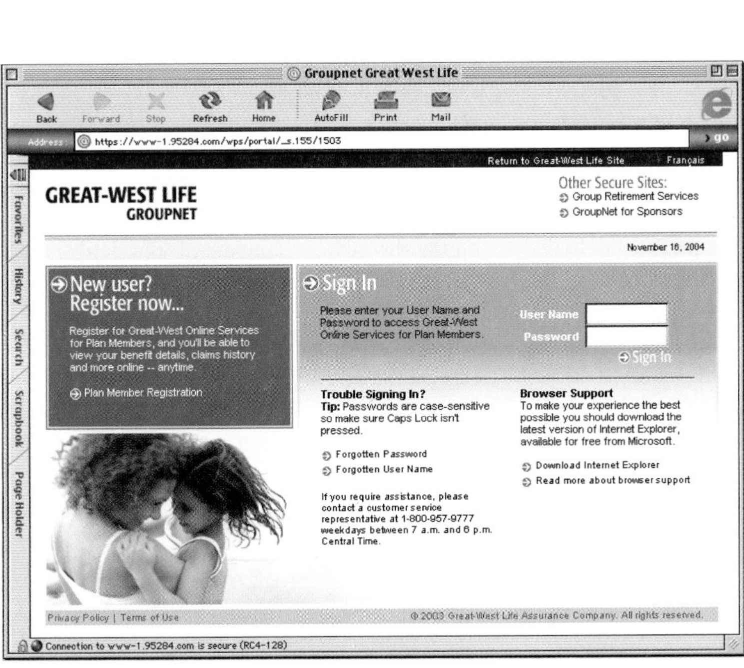

[Figure 5.13 ➡ Great-West Life's Extranet authentication page.]

Source: Great-West Life.

industry (Turban et al., 2000). The extranet includes features that allow participants to make online purchases, check supplier inventory levels, and transfer design specifications, as well as perform a variety of related tasks involved in business transactions. The extranet has helped reduce product manufacturing time, enabled inventory to arrive on a just-in-time basis, and compressed the turnaround time on work orders from three weeks to as little as five minutes. Overall, the extranet has achieved an industry-wide savings exceeding $1 billion per year (Turban et al., 2000).

Dell Computers has used an extranet to streamline its supply chain, reducing its number of suppliers from more than 1,000 to approximately 100. Dell's suppliers are able to predict upcoming demand by accessing data from the extranet and can pass these forecasts and orders along to their suppliers, in turn, to ensure they can meet Dell's orders. This trickle-down effect introduced by Dell's use of extranet technologies has resulted in operational efficiencies throughout its supply chain (McDougall, 2000).

Real-Time Access to Information

CSX, one of the largest railroad companies in North America, leverages extranet technologies to facilitate real-time information access by customers and business partners. CSX developed an application, originally implemented as an intranet-based tool for the company's customer service agents, that can track train shipments from coast to coast, providing real-time status updates. CSX now offers this service to its customers and business partners through an extranet. CSX has connected its extranet with more than 200 business partners, including freight shippers and forwarders, who act as intermediaries between CSX and its customers. These business partners deliver customer shipments to the railroad and deliver arriving shipments to customers on the company's behalf. CSX's business partners use the extranet's real-time information to streamline their business operations, enabling them to pick up and deliver goods at the yard on a just-in-time basis.

CSX customers can log in to see where their shipments are in transit (down to the individual package level), allowing them to identify unanticipated delays and respond to them in a timely manner. Customers also use the extranet to calculate expected shipping rates, which CSX keeps updated on a regular basis. Customers can enter purchase orders online and receive confirmations nearly instantaneously, creating great efficiencies in the order processing cycle for both companies (Turban et al., 2000).

Collaboration

Collaboration via extranets allows companies to respond proactively to the changing marketplace by working directly with their business partners, suppliers, and customers. These applications provide companies with the ability to develop products that will soon be in demand, giving them an understanding of what will be needed and when. Through extranet-based collaboration, the product development cycle can be initiated and completed faster. Companies can plan for the necessary components and communicate information with suppliers well in advance of the product coming to market. Companies can also deploy purchasing resources more effectively, transforming traditional procurement personnel into supplier relationship managers rather than transaction processors.

Caterpillar, a global manufacturer of heavy machinery, implemented an extranet to assist with customer requests for customizations to its products. Prior to the extranet, salespeople, managers, and technical staff would need to wade through a plethora of paperwork to process a request, resulting in poor response times and unsatisfactory customer service levels. With the extranet, customers can request customized components online, and the request can be forwarded to Caterpillar's product engineers and component suppliers, who can securely share the required information, such as CAD/CAM drawings. In some cases, Caterpillar gains process efficiencies by acting as an intermediary between the end customer and supplier. Caterpillar can redirect requests directly to the supplier, who builds the custom component and delivers it directly to the customer (Turban et al., 2000).

Enterprise Portals

Many companies operate multiple extranets, each designed to service particular business partners with particular business requirements. A desire to integrate these stand-alone extranets has prompted the evolution of a more powerful class of extranets known as ***enterprise portals***. ***Portals***, in the context of B2B EB, can be defined as access points (or front doors) through which a business partner accesses secured, proprietary information from an organization. Enterprise portals provide a single point of access to this type of

BRIEF CASE

Labatt's Puts the Pub on Tap

In 2001, Labatt launched an ambitious corporate intranet project called The Pub. Since its debut, The Pub has changed the beer company's approach to business intelligence and knowledge management, and made it possible for teams to effectively collaborate online. Labatt implemented an enterprise portal that improved overall communications between employees and eliminated silos of information between business units. Early on, Labatt was faced with the problem of convincing 3,800 employees, from Newfoundland to British Columbia—many of whom did not own computers—that The Pub was a better source of corporate information than traditional meetings, newsletters, and bulletin boards. In order to overcome this problem, Labatt installed information kiosks to give employees easy access to The Pub, and it ran the intranet like a news wire. "We provide national, regional, and local news," says Sharon Mackay, director of public affairs at Labatt. "We provide frequent updates, sometimes twice a day." Those frequent updates were the key to The Pub's early acceptance.

Over time, the intranet's ability to break down information silos and create an open business intelligence environment has been at least as important. For example, if anyone in marketing wanted to review brand positioning data, a recent presentation made to a corporate client, or a particular Blue commercial from the 1960s, they could find what they were searching for in The Pub's multidimensional database.

In terms of online collaboration, The Pub reduced confusion over document versions and eliminated instances where two people were working on the same document at the same time. Once used primarily as communication and knowledge management tools, intranets are now used to improve workforce performance and link that performance to business value. To improve performance, intranets must align to processes and roles in specific industries, and ensure that knowledge can support decision making—factors that have become critical in the competitive brewing industry.

Questions

1. A primary function of an intranet is to spread knowledge across the firm, as the above example illustrates. What are other functions of corporate intranets?
2. One problem with data repositories like The Pub is that employees do not tend to use them. Can you think of approaches that firms can take to improve the usage of corporate intranets?

[Adapted from "Heard It at The Pub," *EDGE Magazine*, Vol. 2, No. 12 (December 2003/January 2004).]

[**Figure 5.14** ➡ Labatt's intranet changes its approach to collaboration.]

Source: Labatt Breweries of Canada.

information, which may be dispersed throughout an organization. Enterprise portals can provide substantial productivity gains by combining multiple extranet applications to create a single point of access where the company can conduct business with any number of business partners. This can help reduce the maintenance costs associated with supporting

Web Search

WEB SEARCH OPPORTUNITY

Visit the home page for Strategis, the federal government's electronic business portal, **www.strategis.gc.ca**, to see what types of information and services can be found there.

multiple extranets and can simplify the process for end users since all the information they need to carry out business is available from a single source.

Enterprise portals come in two basic forms, *distribution portals* and *procurement portals*. Distribution portals automate the business processes involved in selling, or distributing, products from a single supplier to multiple buyers. On the other end of the spectrum, procurement portals automate the business processes involved in purchasing, or procuring, products between a single buyer and multiple suppliers (see Figure 5.15). Distribution and procurement portals can vary based on the number of buyers and suppliers that utilize the portal. For example, automotive industry giants Ford Motor Company, DaimlerChrysler, and General Motors have teamed up to create a procurement portal that suppliers to the Big Three can access. Similarly, a few companies can share distribution portals to purchase products from many suppliers. When the balance between buyers and sellers nears a point of equilibrium, these systems are classified as ***trading exchanges.***

Distribution portals, procurement portals, and trading exchanges commonly service specific industries or groups of firms that rely on similar products or services. Tailoring products and services to particular companies creates a ***vertical market,*** or a market that services the needs of a specific sector. Vertical markets can create tremendous efficiencies for companies since they can take advantage of existing applications that already meet the requirements of other companies in their industry, eliminating the need to develop proprietary systems of their own.

Distribution Portals

Distribution portals are designed to automate the business processes that occur before, during, and after sales have been transacted between a supplier and multiple customers.

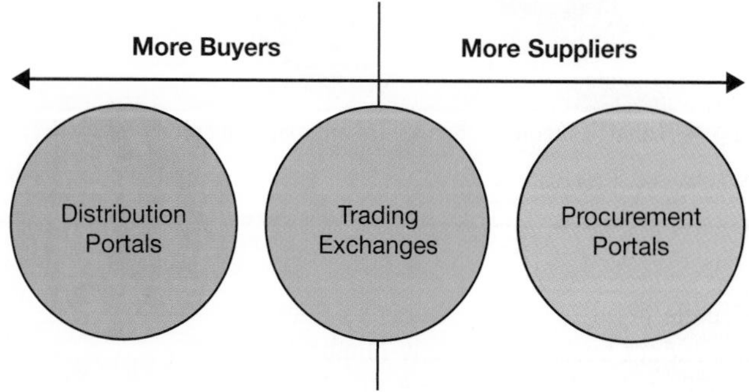

[Figure 5.15 ➥ Distribution portals, trading exchanges, and procurement portals.]

In other words, distribution portals provide efficient tools for customers to manage all phases of the purchasing cycle, including product information, order entry, and customer service. Dell Computers services business customers through its distribution portal Premier Dell.com.

Premier Dell.com goes well beyond providing its business customers with order-entry and status updates. The distribution portal helps companies keep track of and manage their computing equipment through a series of online reporting tools. Need to know when a particular piece of equipment was ordered? Premier Dell.com can search Dell's corporate database and produce a report tracing the equipment purchase to a particular transaction, purchase order, and/or order number.

Customers can also obtain customized, system-specific technical information about the products they have purchased. HelpTech, an application available on Premier Dell.com, provides help desk personnel with the same information available to Dell technicians. This information includes a troubleshooting toolkit, a library of documents containing manuals and technical specifications, and a knowledge base containing searchable documentation from technicians and end users.

When placing orders, customers are taken to a personalized storefront where discounted prices are calculated depending upon rates negotiated with Dell. The system immediately informs customers exactly how much an order will cost. Customers can utilize an application called E-Quote to build a purchase order online and send a copy of the quote via e-mail to a purchasing manager for approval. Once the quote has been received by the customer's purchasing department, an approved purchasing agent uses E-Quote to review the quote, approve it, and place the order with one click of the mouse. An application called ImageWatch informs Dell's customers of technological trends and changes before they impact Dell's products. This enables customers to make more educated purchasing decisions and plan ahead for technical innovations that can benefit the customer. Premier.Dell.com allows Dell's business customers to take control of business needs, saving them time and money while creating management efficiencies (Dell, 2001).

Procurement Portals

Procurement portals are designed to automate the business processes that occur before, during, and after sales have been transacted

CAREER IMPLICATIONS

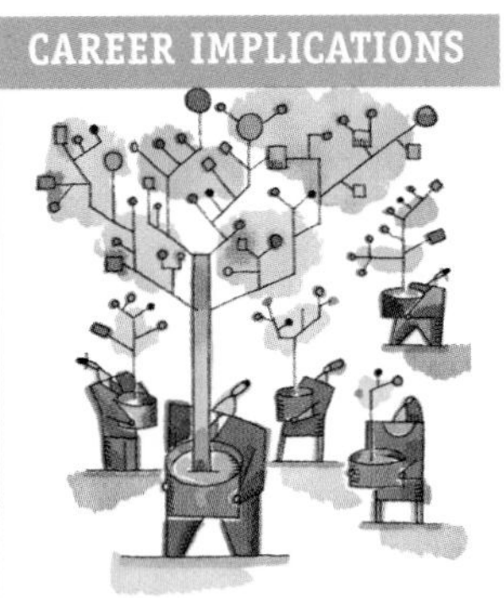

Information Systems

A new feature added to SAS Institute's Human Capital Management software promises to identify employees scoping out other opportunities. According to SAS, the Web-based software uses data mining techniques to calculate the groups of employees most likely to leave an organization. It determines which organizational and employee characteristics, such as salary, level of education and training, or length of service, contribute to turnover. Employees are ranked and assigned individual probabilities for voluntarily leaving within a specific time frame. The software is intended to help public- and private-sector organizations deal with the predicted skills shortage over the next decade. According to Statistics Canada, almost 20 percent of Canadians will be at least 61 by 2011, leading to thousands of retirements and ensuring staffing shortages. Gary J. Love, senior program manager at SAS Canada, said the software is especially important for the public sector in helping to retain long-time, highly skilled employees, who are difficult to replace. "They have found they cannot afford to lose people of that experience without training other people to come in and backfill them," said Love. "But it's applicable across industries and departments." Love said the software works by gathering information on employees across multiple data systems, such as financial, human resources, and payroll. "It accesses that data and turns that information into intelligence through the use of analytics," said Love. "It analyzes it and looks for trends and it can run certain scenarios given past behaviours." The software is being used at several Canadian government agencies that have insisted on non-disclosure agreements, due to the potentially negative view some employees might have of the tool.

[Adapted from Kathleen Sibley, "Canadian Government Moves to Predictive HR," **http://www.itbusiness.ca/index.asp?theaction=61&sid=54473#**, ITBusiness.ca (February 9, 2004).]

between a buyer and multiple suppliers. Procurement portals provide efficient tools for suppliers to manage all phases of the distribution cycle, including dissemination of product information, purchase order processing, and customer service. Ford Motor Company has implemented a procurement portal called Ford Supplier Network (FSN: **www.Ford.com** [word search Ford Supplier Network]), where suppliers come to share information and conduct business with Ford (see Figure 5.16).

The FSN portal consists of a variety of applications addressing such issues as customer support, quality control, purchase order management, and product development. DEALIS (Distribution, Export, and Logistics Information System) is a real-time tracking application built for FSN that provides up-to-the-minute sales and shipping information to suppliers and shippers. These business partners use DEALIS to receive updates on shipments in transit and allow users to view information

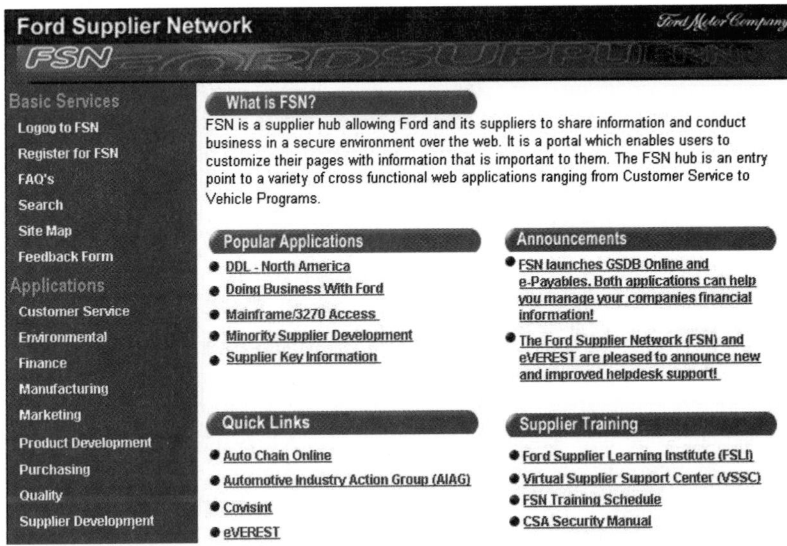

[Figure 5.16 ➥ Ford Supplier Network procurement portal.]

Source: **www.Ford.com**.

based on containers, packages, or even down to specific parts. If you are a Ford supplier and need to know where that shipment of bumpers is located, DEALIS can help you find out.

An FSN application called Supplier Direct Data Links (SDDL) provides real-time information internally as well as to suppliers concerning parts shortages. When inventory levels reach a critical or potentially critical stage, the application notifies suppliers, who can respond immediately to the issue. Suppliers can inform Ford that they are investigating the shortage and revise promised delivery dates through SDDL.

FSN is also a learning and information site. Included in the portal are applications that enable suppliers to take courses online. The FORDSTAR program helps Ford certify its dealerships, employees, and suppliers. Here, users can access training materials, online courses, and developmental resources that will help Ford and its suppliers remain competitive in the ever-changing automotive industry. The interactive system helps suppliers determine which learning opportunities would be most beneficial to the organization.

FSN also provides suppliers with information concerning Ford's key business processes and plans for the future, as well as an online tutorial to teach suppliers how to conduct business with Ford. From a supplier perspective, one of the key attractions of FSN lies in its distribution of competitive intelligence. Being aware of market trends and the activities of competitors enables Ford's suppliers to stay one step ahead of the competition.

Trading Exchanges

Enterprise portals tend to be beyond the reach of SMEs due to the costs involved in designing, developing, and maintaining this type of system. Many of these firms do not have the necessary monetary resources or skilled personnel to develop EB applications on their own. To service this market niche, a number of ***trading exchanges***, or electronic marketplaces, have sprung up. Trading exchanges are operated by third-party vendors, meaning that they are built and maintained by a particular company. These companies generate revenue by taking a small commission for each transaction that occurs, by charging usage fees, by charging association fees, and/or by generating advertising revenues. Unlike distribution and procurement portals, trading exchanges allow many buyers and many sellers to come together, offering firms access to real-time trading with other companies in their vertical markets. This can be accomplished at a reasonable cost, making trading exchanges a competitive reality.

Trading exchanges provide companies not only with transaction processing, but also with information pertinent to their industries, procurement resources to compare products from various sellers, and invoicing services. Some examples of trading exchanges include E-Steel.com (steel), Citadon.com (building and construction), PaperExchange.com (pulp and paper), and neoforma.com (medical equipment).

SciQuest Corporation (**www.SciQuest.com**) has developed a trading exchange to service the laboratory products and scientific supply industry, which represents a $36-billion vertical market (SciQuest, 2001). With industry globalization rapidly occurring, the industry had become increasingly fragmented, producing inefficiencies in distribution and procurement processes. Many customers purchased products from a multitude of suppliers based on outdated information in paper-based catalogues. As a result, firms were wasting time in product/supplier research and managing relationships with many more suppliers than necessary. To exacerbate matters, outside influences were exerting pressure on the industry to become more cost-conscious, bring new products to market at a faster pace, and adhere to environmental legislation mandated by government agencies.

SciQuest supports the particular needs of the laboratory products and scientific supply industry in six ways, as depicted in Figure 5.18 on page 158. Other trading exchanges, such as E-Steel, which services the steel industry, have different support strategies since different industries have unique business requirements that the exchanges need to support. SciQuest's SciCentral application provides a centralized repository for research articles relevant to the industry. SciCentral allows users to search thousands of scientific journals by keyword and also offers the capability to order and download research online. Trading exchange participants can also search for innovations that assist in the development of new products such as pharmaceuticals.

Once customers locate the product they are interested in, they need to source the product. Sourcing refers to finding the supplier that can provide the highest-quality product at the lowest price. SciQuest's SelectSite

GLOBAL PERSPECTIVE

Cisco Systems Online—The World's Most Successful Distribution Portal

Cisco Systems is the worldwide leader in networking for the Internet. The Cisco Website for online ordering (**www.cisco.com/en/US/ordering/index.shtml**) is considered by many to be one of the most successful global distribution portals on the planet (see Figure 5.17). Cisco Ordering is a global portal for all of Cisco's e-business tools.

With the processing of well over $2 billion of customer orders over the Web since October 1996, Cisco has entered into a new business model that takes complete advantage of the Internet. This raises a serious question: has this global electronic marketplace actually delivered on the promise of the Internet—a new way of making money—or is it merely a clever marketing ploy by the largest vendor in the Internet-working industry to showcase what can be done on the Internet without giving much thought to its real implications? This question is important to Cisco because the company has been promoting its online sales channel as the archetypical example of what EB should become.

The site offers Cisco's 45,000 global business customers real-time information on price, availability, configuration requirements, ordering, invoice status and validation, and shipping information over the Web. Regardless of which country the customer lives in, if she can get an Internet connection, then she can check out her Cisco orders and products. Cisco also uses the site to forward procurement information to its own employees for possible modifications and approvals via e-mail. It used to take days or weeks for a salesperson to complete an order; now it takes only 15 minutes to an hour. Customers are able to join discussion forums, receive bug alerts, and download software patches directly from the Internet. The site currently claims 80,000 registered users and 3.5 million hits per day, and handles about 40 percent of Cisco's multiple billions of dollars in sales. John Chambers, CEO, states that the annualized savings to the company of $270 million is due to taking advantage of the Internet, intranet, and extranet technologies.

One analyst suggests that it is difficult to measure the actual savings on the bottom line. It is not possible to put an accurate price tag on what it would have cost Cisco to implement a physical, global sales, marketing, and distribution infrastructure. Cisco has avoided these costs while at the same time increasing revenue globally, and the site is credited for increased customer satisfaction. But efficiency does not always translate into a stronger business relationship or higher demand for products. Thus, Cisco has made it a point to carefully manage the account relationship with its customers beyond what can be done on the Website.

As if operating one of the most successful online, global distribution portals were not enough, Cisco has also implemented the Cisco Networking Academy Program, a partnership between Cisco Systems, education, business, government, and community organizations around the world. The Networking Academy curriculum teaches students around the globe to design, build, and maintain computer networks. There are currently more than 8,400 academies enrolling nearly a quarter-million students in over 130 countries.

Source: **www.cisco.com**.

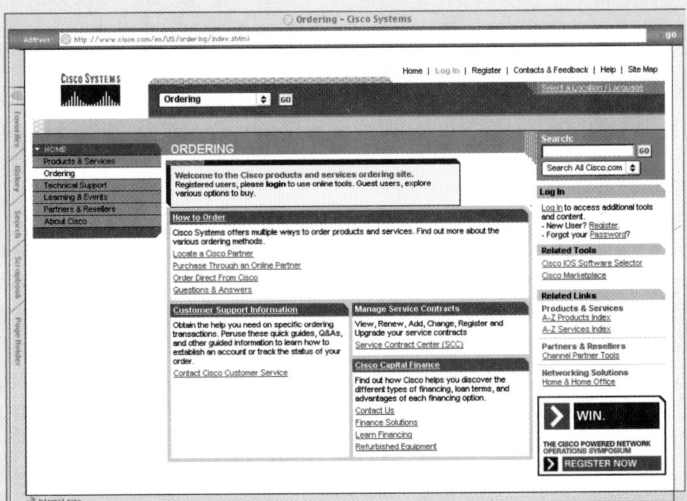

[**Figure 5.17** ➡ Website for Cisco Ordering, one of the most successful global distribution portals.]

Source: Cisco Canada.

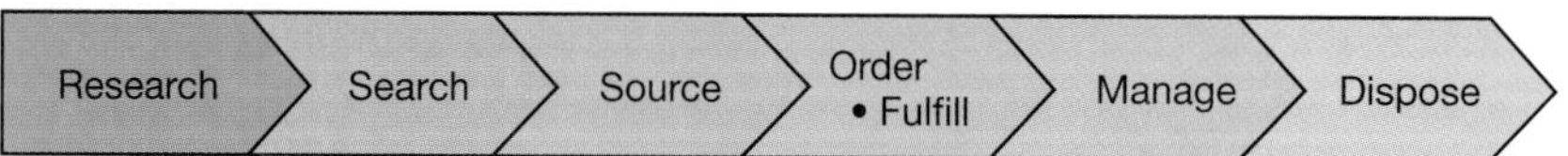

[**Figure 5.18** ➥ SciQuest supports its vertical market in six ways.]

Source: **www.SciQuest.com**.

APA (Advanced Procurement Application) takes the customer's request and matches it with the most appropriate supplier. This eliminates the time customers spend in searching for the best supplier, since the application does it for them. Customers review the results from the sourcing application and choose to place the order automatically with one mouse click, or reject the transaction.

SciQuest also supports the customer service aspects of the transaction by providing functions for coordinating shipping, receiving products, and tracking customer and supplier inventory levels. Furthermore, there can be a great deal of managerial overhead involved with transactions in the laboratory products and scientific supply industry. For example, certain chemical compounds must be cleared through government agencies. SciQuest can assist companies in coordinating government approvals. Other chemicals must be tracked and monitored as they move throughout an organization, and SciQuest's EMAX application can perform bar-code tracking functions to locate sensitive materials. Trading exchanges like SciQuest allow SMEs to conduct business as if they were industry heavyweights.

BUSINESS-TO-CONSUMER ELECTRONIC BUSINESS

The Internet and Web have evolved with mind-boggling quickness, achieving mass acceptance faster than any other technology in modern history. The widespread availability and adoption of the Internet and Web, which are based on an economical, open, ubiquitous computing platform, have made Internet access affordable and practical, allowing consumers to participate in Web-based commerce. In addition, a great number of businesses have similarly benefited from the revolution and have implemented Web-based systems in their daily operations. This heightened level of participation by both consumers and producers has made the emergence of business-to-consumer (B2C) EB economically feasible. Unlike B2B, which concentrates on business-to-business relationships at the wholesale level, B2C focuses on retail transactions between a company and end consumers.

B2C revenues are expected to be approximately $1 billion in Canada in 2004. The major portion of B2C focuses on electronic retailing, or ***e-tailing***, which provides many advantages over bricks-and-mortar retailing in terms of product, place, and price. Websites can offer a virtually unlimited number and variety of products since e-tailing is not limited by physical space restrictions. For instance, in 1999 clicks-only book e-tailer Amazon.com offered over four million book titles on the Web, compared with the bricks-and-clicks book retailer Barnes & Noble, which could offer only 200,000 items due to the restricted space of its physical stores. Place proves advantageous in the e-tailing environment because company storefronts exist on every computer that is connected to the Web, enabling e-tailers to compete more effectively for customers. Whereas traditional retailing can be accessed only at physical store locations during open hours, e-tailers can conduct business anywhere, at any time. E-tailers can also compete on price effectively since they can turn their inventory more often due to the sheer volume of products and customers who purchase them. In theory, companies can sell more products, reducing prices for consumers while at the same time enhancing profits for the company (Christensen and Tedlow, 2000).

Despite all the hype associated with e-tailing, there are some downsides to this approach. Barring products that you can download directly, such as music or an electronic magazine, e-tailing requires additional time for products to be delivered. If you have run out of ink for your printer and your research paper is due this afternoon, chances are that you will drive to your local office supply store to purchase a new ink cartridge rather than ordering it online. The ink cartridge purchased electronically needs to be packaged and shipped, delaying use of the product until it is delivered. Other issues can also arise. The credit card information that you provide online may not be approved, or the shipper may try to deliver the package when you are not home.

Another problem associated with e-tailing relates to a lack of sensory information such as taste, smell, and feel. When trying on clothes with your virtual model at Lands' End, how can you be sure that you will like the feel of the material? Or what if you discover that the pair of 9 EE inline skates you just purchased online fits you like an 8 D? Other products such as fragrances and foods can also be difficult for consumers to assess via the Web. Does the strawberry cheesecake offered online actually taste as good as it looks? How do you know if you will really like the smell of a perfume without actually sampling it? Finally, e-tailing eliminates the social aspects of the purchase. Some e-tailers are having a hard time competing with shopping malls since going to the mall with some friends is a lot more fun for most people than buying online! As with B2B procurement, comparison shopping can be difficult since vendors provide product information in different ways. However, a number of comparison shopping services that focus on aggregating content are available to consumers. Some companies fulfilling this niche are BestBookBuys.com, Bizrate (**www.bizrate.com**), and My Simon (**www.mysimon.com**). These comparison shopping sites can literally force sellers to focus on relatively low prices in order to be successful. Either that or sellers must be able to offer better quality, better service, or some other advantage if they do not have the lowest

Operations Management

Can a company be heavily involved in e-business without having a Website? Sherbrooke, Quebec–based Mesotec, a company that designs, manufactures, and markets high-precision parts and tools for the aeronautics and electronics industries, suggests that the answer may be yes. Mesotec is a medium-sized company with 90 employees and sales of $10 million. Most of its customers are located in North America: 70 percent in Quebec and 30 percent in the United States. French is the main language used in the company and is spoken by all of its employees, only one-quarter of whom are bilingual. Most of the transactions occur in French, since most of the customers are located in Quebec. The market for precision aeronautical equipment is quite small and therefore very few players are involved. Because of this, no particular effort is needed on the company's part to make itself known among principal customers—all of whom are large companies like General Electric (GE), IBM, Pratt & Whitney, and Bombardier. Further, most of Mesotec's products are tailor-made to suit each customer's needs. At first glance, one might question the value of electronic business to a company like Mesotec.

Yet Mesotec, like many firms, was pushed into adopting forms of e-business by its key customers. Mesotec implemented an intranet system that served the dual purpose of fostering collaboration among employees and linking up to its customers' extranet sites. The intranet significantly streamlined Mesotec's interaction with its customers, most of which had previously been conducted by hand. For example, through the intranet, Mesotec gained access to GE's online marketplace. Mesotec received an invitation by e-mail to bid for a given product; the invitation included a password giving Mesotec access to the bidding (done through a Website) and specified the date of the event. Mesotec also had access to other bidding-related information via a secure extranet. When the electronic bidding had been completed, the site published the rankings and the best price. If Mesotec was selected, an order form would be sent through a secure extranet. With other customers, including IBM and Bell Helicopter, Mesotec used Web-based EDI. When Web-based EDI was introduced, Mesotec was already using conventional EDI to receive order forms and schedule deliveries. However, Web-based EDI was cheaper and more efficient. For example, it required only an Internet connection to access a customer's secure extranet, rather than an expensive dedicated connection.

Since most of its customers were big companies, Mesotec understood that e-business was essential in meeting its need for speed and efficiency. Without electronic channels, the relationship with major accounts would be different, and the volumes probably much smaller. According to Mesotec's managers, the cost of implementing electronic business solutions was no more than that of software and an Internet connection. In fact, a good deal of the essential software was supplied by customers free of charge. In concrete terms, the company's sales increased by 40 percent within two years of the installation of electronic business tools. Electronic business may be the only means of reaching certain customers. However, e-business does not always mean having a Website. In this case, Mesotec could see no advantage in developing a public Website to pursue its EB strategy.

CAREER IMPLICATIONS

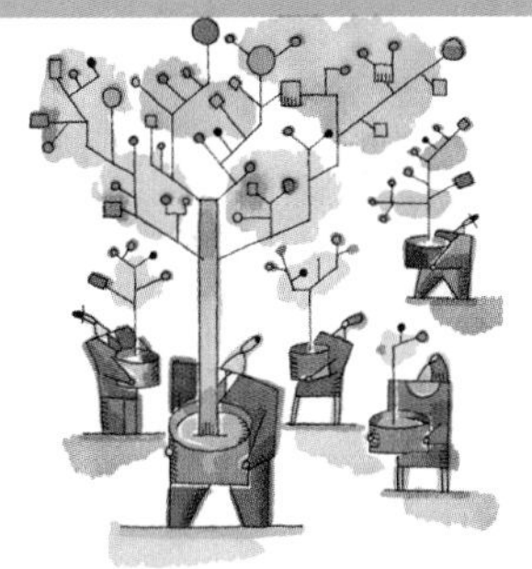

[Adapted from Strategis, **http://strategis.ic.gc.ca/epic/internet/inee-ef.nsf/vwGeneratedInterE/ee00596e.html** (February 9, 2004).]

price. These comparison shopping sites generate revenue by charging a small commission on transactions, by charging usage fees to sellers, and/or through advertising on their site.

Stages of Business-to-Consumer Electronic Business

With thousands of B2C-oriented Websites in existence, Websites range from passive to active. At one extreme are the relatively simple, passive Websites that provide only product information and the company address and phone number, much like a traditional brochure would do. At the other extreme are the relatively sophisticated, active Websites that enable customers to see products, services, and related real-time information and actually make purchases online. As shown in some early, pioneering research on EB (Kalakota, Olivia, and Donath, 1999; Quelch and Klein, 1996), companies usually start out with an electronic brochure and pass through a series of stages as depicted in Figure 5.19, adding additional capabilities as they become more comfortable with EB. These stages can be classified as ***e-information, e-integration,*** and ***e-transaction.***

E-information

One of the first ways corporations utilize the Web is to promote sales and marketing information via an electronic brochure, or ***e-brochure***. Figure 5.20 provides an example of an e-brochure developed by car manufacturer Ford (**www.ford.ca**). The e-information stage achieves the goal of global information dissemination, allowing potential customers to access information about the company and its products. The company can disseminate this information globally in the sense that e-information can be accessed by any Internet user with access to a Web browser. Furthermore, the information is available 24 hours a day, seven days a week, 365 days a year. No matter where on Earth the user is located and regardless of the time, the e-brochure is available for his or her review.

E-information is more flexible than traditional promotional methods such as hard-copy catalogues and print advertisements. When information needs to be updated, e-information can be modified and posted very quickly, whereas traditional methods require typesetting, printing, and/or distribution, depending on the medium. Eliminating these manual processes not only shortens cycle times but also reduces the associated labour expenses. In the process, users are provided with the timeliest information possible. E-information may ultimately lead to a purchase. However, the e-information stage is limited because it merely provides company and product information, not the capability to customize information dynamically, which leads to the next stage of B2C—e-integration.

E-integration

Once companies have mastered the e-information stage, they become more comfortable with EB and want to enhance their Websites by adding additional features and functionality. The e-information stage provides a mechanism to distribute information to the general public, yet cannot accommodate requests for customized information. Customized information is dynamic, meaning that Web pages are created on-the-fly to produce tailored information that addresses the particular needs of the consumer. For instance, a banking customer may want more than information related to the bank and its products. This customer would like to access information related to her accounts, such as the balance in her chequing account or the amount of interest credited to her savings account last month. In other words, customers may want information that is relevant to them rather than the general public.

In order to facilitate this type of customer request, Websites must be integrated with corporate databases to extract and display the appropriate information. This integration process characterizes the e-integration phase of B2C. The e-integration stage helps companies fulfill their goals of integration and mass customization. Firms such as the insurance and financial services company Allstate (**www.allstate.ca**) provide a useful example of the e-integration approach to EB. Customers register their identity through an online form to gain access to their account. Once registered, customers can access detailed, personalized information about their auto, home, and life insurance policies online. Allstate can also identify specific groups of customers, such as those holding home insur-

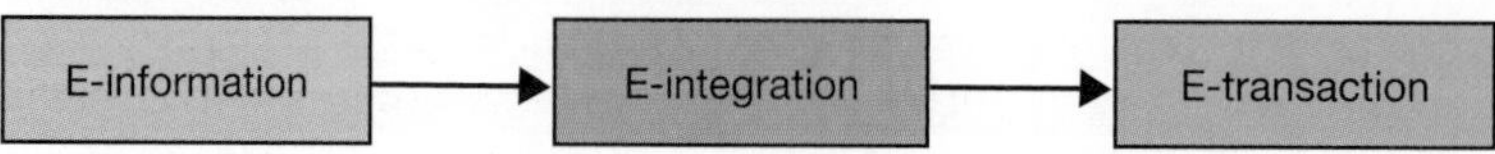

[**Figure 5.19** ➡ Stages of business-to-consumer electronic business.]

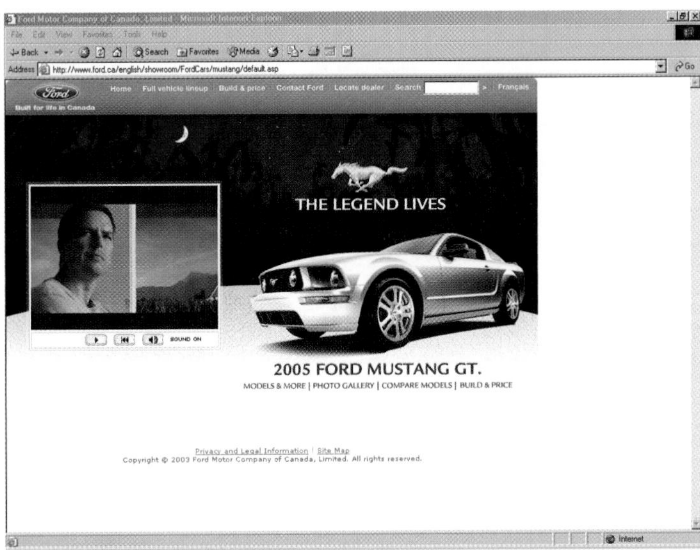

[Figure 5.20 ➥ An e-information Website operated by Ford.]

Source: Ford of Canada.

ance policies, and target marketing efforts to those individuals.

The Burlington Northern Santa Fe Railway (BNSF) (**www.bnsf.com**), one of North America's largest railroads, utilizes the e-integration approach to assist with transactional support. Using a Web-based application called Custom Tracing, customers enter their shipment number and receive information about the status of their shipment. In addition, customers can use the Website to calculate shipping rates by simply entering the source and destination locations. Companies that provide e-integration services have enabled customers to find the information they need when they want it, without having to call a customer service representative for assistance.

One drawback of the e-integration stage lies in its inability to accommodate online ordering. Although companies such as Allstate and Burlington Northern Santa Fe enable access to customized information, when customers want to conduct a transaction, they must resort to calling the company. For instance, when an Allstate customer needs to update his life insurance policy, he must contact his agent through other means. Similarly, BNSF customers must call the railroad to schedule shipments. In the cases of Allstate and BNSF, there are strategic business reasons not to enable online ordering, yet providing the ability to place orders online can prove beneficial in most cases. The ability to conduct transactions online leads us to the next stage of B2C—e-transaction.

E-transaction

E-transaction takes the e-integration stage one step further by adding the ability for customers to enter orders and payments online. The e-transaction stage helps companies fulfill their goals of collaboration, interactive communication, and transactional support. Many of the most well-known B2C Websites fall into the e-transaction category, such as the clicks-only e-tailer Amazon.ca (see Figure 5.21). Customers can not only find out product information but also make purchases, enter payments, and track the status of their orders once the sale has been made. The Amazon.ca Website has been so successful that the company has branched out from selling books to offering other products such as electronic equipment, home décor, apparel, pharmaceuticals, and even cars!

E-transaction can take many forms. Virtual companies such as Priceline.com and eBay have developed innovative ways of generating revenue. Priceline.com offers consumers discounts on airline tickets, hotel rooms, rental cars, new cars, home financing, and long-distance telephone service. The revolutionary aspect of the Priceline.com Website lies in its ***reverse pricing*** system called Name Your Own Price™. Customers specify the product they are looking for and how much they are willing to pay for it. This pricing scheme transcends traditional ***menu-driven pricing,*** in which companies set the prices that consumers pay for products. After a user enters the product and price, the system routes the information to appropriate brand-name companies such as

Web Search

WEB SEARCH OPPORTUNITY
Visit the Websites of Amazon.ca **www.amazon.ca** and Chapters.Indigo.ca **www.chapters.indigo.ca**. Compare and contrast them based on the EB factors that you are learning about here.

[Figure 5.21 ➥ Amazon.ca Website.]

Source: © 2004 Amazon.com, Inc. All Rights Reserved.

United Airlines and Avis Rent A Car, which either accept or reject the consumer's offer. Since Priceline.com opened its virtual doors in April 1998, it has sold more than seven million airline tickets, two million nights of hotel lodging, and two million days of rented cars.

eBay has transformed e-tailing into an ***electronic marketplace,*** which is similar to B2B trading exchanges except B2C electronic marketplaces service end consumers at retail prices. Unlike e-tailers such as Lands' End and Amazon.ca, where one seller services many buyers, an electronic marketplace services many buyers and sellers, who can come together to sell and purchase a wide variety of products. Items sold on eBay range from rare coins to antiques and fine art. Looking for that hard-to-find concert ticket? eBay may be the place to find it. However, you must outbid other consumers in an auction-style format to get what you want. The bidding starts at a price set by the seller and continues until a predetermined time, when the auction ends. If you are the top bidder, you are the proud owner of your prized concert ticket. But be careful, and know what you are purchasing and whom you are purchasing it from! A series of forged signatures on baseballs, bats, and pieces of paper have appeared on the eBay auction block. These included signed memorabilia from baseball greats Mickey Mantle, Joe DiMaggio, and Babe Ruth, all of whom attract high prices for their autographs. Although the authorities eventually caught the perpetrators, electronic marketplaces are not immune to improprieties.

The e-transaction stage can also include electronic distribution of products and services. If the product or service can be digitized, it can be delivered online, as in the case of information-based products, videos, and software. ***Digitization*** creates products without tangible features, which are commonly referred to as ***virtual products.*** Liquid Audio's Web-based music distribution system is changing how music is being purchased and delivered. The company's technology enables the music industry to use the Web as another distribution channel without fear of piracy. The system enables users to download CD-quality music that can be played only on the computer to which it was downloaded. The music is ***watermarked*** so that any illegal copy—even on cassette tapes—can be traced to the original purchaser. Electronic watermarking is similar in concept to watermarks placed on paper currency to prevent counterfeiting. Such technology works for the distribution of any type of information-based product. Orders of tangible products such as electronic equipment can be fulfilled by more traditional bricks-and-mortar or bricks-and-clicks methods, but any information-based components to these products or services—such as an owner's manual—can be digitized and delivered online. It is a certainty that you will see more and more virtual products such as music, art, video, and software delivered over the Web in the near future.

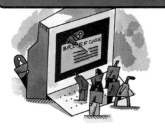

BRIEF CASE

Ottawa Plans Single e-Marketplace for Government Procurement

IBM Canada Ltd. and a consortium of five vendors are embarking on a $1.5-million, five-year project to build an electronic supply chain that will become the new Government of Canada Marketplace, an e-government initiative. The project to build a portal posting electronic catalogues and automating routine and mass purchases is the first electronic supply chain that works across departments in the Canadian government, said Kim Devooght, vice-president, federal public sector, IBM Canada in Ottawa.

Using this service, the government expects to save 10 percent on the cost of goods and services and 50 percent on administrative process costs associated with purchasing. The electronic marketplace will be piloted with Public Works and Government Services Canada, the RCMP, Transport Canada, and the Transportation Safety Board of Canada. Initially, the program will involve 1,300 users, potentially reaching 10,000 if it is expanded to all government branches. Once the team of vendors passes a first phase in which the concept is tested over five months, it will have to contend with hurdles like encouraging the government, made up of 157 departments and agencies, to "think as one," Devooght said. "We're taking existing business systems and converting them to automated forms. And generally speaking, when you have those kinds of projects, it's not the technology that gets in the way or causes concerns, it's issues of changes to business processes themselves. Departments are going to have to agree to use this solution as opposed to their roll-your-own solution or made-at-home kind of thing. And that means giving up a bit of control," he said.

Ottawa has been investigating the feasibility of marketplace services for two years. One question the government grappled with was how to make the marketplace financially viable because it's a self-funded project, said Marc Trépanier, director general of the electronic acquisitions program sector in the federal government. "The government is not putting money into this project other than funding the initial business case. After that, if the marketplace doesn't fund itself out of savings, it won't continue," he said. In building the supply chain, IBM Canada may take a page from partner AMS, which built eVA, a statewide e-procurement application for the state of Virginia. The service, linking public purchasers throughout the state with suppliers, began in 2001. It allows the government to post online vendor catalogues, handle bids, process payments, and give contract data. eVA has earned the Virginia government US$1.71 billion revenues on 219,263 orders.

Questions

1. How could the government make the e-marketplace initiative profitable?
2. Many online e-marketplaces have failed to meet expectations. Why do you think that this has been the case? Is the future brighter for these types of initiatives?

[Adapted from Fawzia Sheikh, "Feds Lay Groundwork for Inter-department E-marketplace," **http://www.itbusiness.ca/index.asp?theaction=61&sid=54595#**, ITBusiness.ca (February 9, 2004).]

THE FORMULA FOR ELECTRONIC BUSINESS SUCCESS

The basic rules of commerce are to offer valuable products and services at fair prices. These rules apply to EB as well as to any business endeavour. However, having a good product at a fair price may not be enough to compete in the EB arena. Companies that were traditionally successful in the old markets will not necessarily dominate the new electronic markets. Successful companies are found to follow a basic set of principles, or rules, related to Web-based EB.[2] These rules are:

Rule 1—The Website should offer something unique.
Rule 2—The Website must be aesthetically pleasing.
Rule 3—The Website must be easy to use and FAST!
Rule 4—The Website must motivate people to visit, to stay, and to return.
Rule 5—You must advertise your presence on the Web.
Rule 6—You should learn from your Website.

Rule 1. The Website should offer something unique. Providing visitors with information or products that they can find nowhere else leads to EB profitability. Many small firms have found success on the Web by offering hard-to-find goods to a global audience at reasonable prices. For example, Eastern Meat Farms (**www.salami.com**), an Italian market

[2]Note that these rules apply mainly to how to make a Website more successful. Realize that the underlying business model must be sound and that there are a host of similar rules that information systems personnel must follow to ensure that 1) the Website works well, 2) it interacts properly with back-end business information systems, and 3) the site is secure.

in New York, sells hard-to-find pasta, meats, cheeses, and breads over the Internet at its Website (see Figure 5.22). Their first order came in 1995 from a customer in Japan. Although the Japanese customer paid $69 in shipping costs for the $87 order of pasta, he did not mind; he was saving $150 by not buying the Italian delicacies locally (Rebello, 1996). Scantran, an online translation agency based in Ontario, offers localization services between English and the languages of Scandinavia and Finland. Competing sites may offer one or two of these languages, but not all of them together.

Rule 2. The Website must be aesthetically pleasing. Successful firms on the Web have sites that are nice to look at. People are more likely to visit, stay at, and return to a Website that looks good! Creating a unique look and feel can separate a Website from its competition. Aesthetics can include the use of colour schemes, backgrounds, and high-quality images (but not too many!). Furthermore, Websites should have a clear, concise, and consistent layout, taking care to avoid unnecessary clutter.

Rule 3. The Website must be easy to use and FAST! As with nearly all software, Websites that are easy to use are more popular. If Web surfers have trouble finding things at the site or navigating through the site's links, or have to wait for screens to download, they are not apt to stay at the site long or to return. In fact, some early studies suggest that the average length of time that a Web surfer will wait for a Web page to download on his screen is only a couple of seconds. Rather than presenting a lot of information on a single page, successful Websites present a brief summary of the information with hyperlinks, allowing users to "drill down" to locate the details they are interested in.

Rule 4. The Website must motivate people to visit, to stay, and to return. People visit Websites that provide useful information and links or free goods and services. One of the reasons that Microsoft's Website is popular is because users can download free software. Other firms motivate visitors to visit their Websites by enabling them to interact with other users who share common interests. These firms establish an online community where members can build relationships, help each other, and feel at home. For example, at GardenWeb (**www.gardenweb.com**), visitors can share suggestions and ideas with other gardeners, post requests for seeds and other items, and follow electronic links to other gardening resources. At this Website, the participants communicate and carry out transactions with one another, returning over and over for more (see Figure 5.23).

Rule 5. You must advertise your presence on the Web. Like any other business, a Website cannot be successful without customers. Companies must draw, or pull, visitors to their Websites. This strategy is known as ***pull marketing.*** Unlike ***push marketing,*** which actively pushes information at the consumer whether it is wanted or not (e.g.,

[Figure 5.22 ➥ The Salami.com Website.]

Source: **www.salami.com**.

CAREER IMPLICATIONS

Human Resource Management

According to Richard Dalzell (CIO of Amazon.com), one of the biggest challenges of an online retailer is taking care of the customers. The key success factors of such companies therefore lie in making their customers happy. Amazon, which is known as one of the most customer-friendly companies, realized this early on and has since focused on using technology innovatively to become known as the most customer-centric company in the world. Amazon has primarily focused on the development of a personalization technology that enables it to create a unique store that changes with every customer. The technology also helps Amazon build a real-time environment that knows who each customer is and what he or she wants to buy on the Internet. As a result, the tool deals with a lot of real-time data, including those data provided by their customers about their purchasing interests. The database is maintained by Oracle, while most of the tools and software that run on this database are created in-house. The company has also built 1-Click technology that provides customers with easy navigational capabilities and makes the site much more user-friendly.

Apart from the customer aspects, Dalzell argues that there are two other important factors that help in making a successful B2C e-business company. First, always look toward the future, and second, hire a world-class engineering team. Amazon so far has been successful in both. It is known as one of the most innovative companies, constantly reinventing the wheel in order to better align itself to the future. It also lays great importance on having world-class professionals in the company and spends a great deal of time and money on hiring. On its Website, Amazon claims that the top six reasons that you would want to choose to work for the company are to:

- Work with and learn from an unusually high proportion of smart, focused people who are passionate about their work.
- Work on challenging, interesting projects that have a huge impact on our success.
- Work in a casual but accountable environment in which hard work, initiative, and smart decisions are rewarded.
- Play an important part in continuing our leadership in e-commerce by bringing new ideas to the table and launching new businesses.
- Be rewarded with great career opportunities and the chance to participate financially in the company's long-term success.
- Have fun!

Indeed, Amazon sums it up very nicely by saying that its employees, "work hard, have fun, and make history."

[Adapted from Susannah Patton, "Talking to Richard Dalzell," **http://www.cio.com**; **www.amazon.com**.]

television commercials), pull marketing is a passive method used to attract visitors to your site and away from the thousands of other sites they could be visiting. The predominant method of pull marketing involves advertising the Website. The first way to advertise your firm's presence on the Web is to include the Website address on all company materials, from business cards and letterheads to advertising copy. It is now common to see a company's URL listed at the end of its television commercials.

Welcome to GardenWeb!
Search for:
Search
Quick Index:
Forums
Exchanges
Seeds
Plants
Members
Join Now!
Plants
HortiPlex
GardenWeb®
The Internet's Garden Community
Below you will find a listing of the many gardening resources available at GardenWeb.
If you would like to be added to our mailing list so you can hear about future updates to our gardening sites, simply fill in your email address below and click on the subscribe button.
Your Email Address:
Subscribe
The GardenWeb Forums
The GardenWeb Forums comprise the largest community of gardeners on the Internet. Covering more than 90 different plants, regions and topics, the forums allow you to tap the collective wisdom of the thousands of other users who visit GardenWeb each day. You can post queries on plant care, how to deal with a landscaping problem or perhaps initiate a

[**Figure 5.23** ➥ The GardenWeb Website.]

Source: **www.GardenWeb.com**.

Another strategy is to register the Website with the more popular search engines, such as Google and AltaVista. In most cases, registering with these sites is free and fast and can be done online. Many search engines provide context-sensitive advertising, meaning that your ad will be shown only when a related keyword is entered into the search engine. For example, if you are selling sporting goods, you can have your advertisement appear when certain terms like *baseball, football, basketball,* and so on are entered in the search.

In addition to registering with the many search engines, a firm can advertise its Website on other commerce sites or Websites containing related information. Given the cost of advertising on high-profile sites, such as Canada.com, and the fact that fewer and fewer Web surfers are paying attention to online ads, the trend in Web advertising is moving away from high, fixed monthly charges to a "pay by the click" scheme. Under this type of pricing scheme, known as ***hypermediation,*** the firm running the advertisement pays only when a Web surfer actually clicks on the advertisement.

Rule 6. You should learn from your Website. Smart companies learn from their Websites. A firm can track the path that visitors take through the many pages of its site and record the time of day, day of the week, or times throughout the year that people visit these sites. It can then use this information to improve its Website. If 75 percent of the visitors follow links to check the company's online posting of job opportunities within the firm, or check on current pricing for a particular product, then that firm can redesign its Website to provide that information quickly and easily for visitors. Similarly, pages that go unused can be eliminated from the site, reducing maintenance and upkeep.

BRIEF CASE

Steady Growth for Webview 360.com

Webview 360.com is a Manitoba-based company that provides a tool to view homes, condominiums, and commercial property through the Web. Webview 360 allows viewers to take a virtual tour of a property with the ability to zoom in and out of specific areas. Searching for a house can be done by location, style, size, or price, as well as numerous other searching preferences. Paul Schmitt, a real estate agent and Webview 360.com's founder, saw something in 1998 at a technical conference that caught his eye. An insurance company was using 360-degree digital imaging technology for insurance purchases. Schmitt returned to Winnipeg in February of 1999 to explore how this technology could be applied to the real estate industry.

Schmitt's goal was to provide listings of properties complete with 360-degree images of all important areas. Webview recognized the need to raise capital in order to get the business started. Initial thoughts were to go public; however, advice from close friends and business acquaintances encouraged Schmitt to obtain funds from private parties. In fact, Webview 360 experienced a lot of frustration as a result of the varied opinions and suggestions received from lawyers, accountants, financial advisers, and business people. However, after a few months, Schmitt met an interested "angel" from the U.S. who agreed to provide the company with sufficient funds to get started. He was then also encouraged to set up the company by way of franchises and offer franchise-licensing agreements to individuals across North America. It was at this time, Schmitt claims, that the stress started.

The guidelines for franchising law are extremely onerous and very time consuming. The legal fees for franchisee agreements alone amounted to thousands of dollars. Once again, Webview 360.com was faced with having to raise more money. Many people approached Schmitt with the intent to invest; however, he thought it would be best to have one to two large investors vs. numerous small ones. Schmitt approached a large investment fund and was successful in obtaining additional capital.

Lessons learned from the experience, according to Schmitt, were to listen carefully to what others tell you and always use a lawyer for any type of contract regardless of the size. Further, dot-coms should be ready for reluctance and hesitancy from the marketplace (initially for capital, later for product and service offerings). Be patient and persistent.

Questions

1. SMEs can use the Internet to "sell to the world," yet most small firms are merely needles in a giant haystack. How can small firms enhance their exposure on the Internet to increase sales?
2. The founder of Webview 360.com cautions Internet entrepreneurs to be "patient and persistent," yet others have claimed the key to success is to "go big, go fast, or go home." In your opinion, which of these strategies is the most correct?

[Adapted from Canada/Manitoba Business Service Centre, Document No. 6315 (2001).]

COMING ATTRACTIONS

Wireless Internet Access Coming to a Limo Near You

The term *ubiquitous commerce* or *u-commerce* is used to mean that business can be conducted at any time, from any place. The expansion of wireless networks is making u-commerce feasible in many urban settings. For example, the car was one of the few remaining places from which a weary business traveller could escape the tether to the office. However, a Vancouver technology company is trying to change that. Vancouver's In Motion Technology Inc. has an agreement with Rosedale Livery Ltd., a Toronto-based executive car service, to install wireless Internet access in the company's limousines.

Once installed, the service will allow Rosedale's customers to connect to the Internet with their Wi-Fi–enabled laptop or PDA during the drive to the airport or the next meeting to catch up with e-mails or connect to the head office. In Motion president Kirk Moir explained that the service, dubbed OnBoard Hotspot, involves installing a box into each vehicle that is monitored by In Motion's network operations centre. "We see ourselves in the business of enabling business professionals to be productive even while in transit by making wireless hotspots truly mobile," said Moir. "We're trying to allow (car services) to offer convenient, high-performance Internet connectivity, which we see increasingly being a new selection criteria for their passengers."

Moir said In Motion's service requires no special software, just a device running Windows with a Wi-Fi client installed. The car service also just needs to install the hardware; In Motion does the monitoring. "All the company is really required to do is install the hardware in their vehicles, and we look after it from there," said Moir. As far as connection speed, in Canada Moir said they're running on Telus Mobility's network, which theoretically can reach up to 144K. However, the typical connection speed seems to be around 80–90K. "It's equivalent to entry level DSL in the U.S. and Canada," said Moir.

Moir said they're focusing on the car service market for a number of reasons. It's a market where a 70–80K service speed is acceptable, with usually just one or two passengers sharing the connection, and with a clientele that values its time and needs to be connected. "Car services [are] also a particularly competitive segment of the transportation space; they understand the power and necessity of market differentiation," says Moir.

Rosedale Livery president Craig McCutcheon said Internet access from the vehicle has become an interesting perk to offer their customers. "We've found they're constantly asking the question, 'Hey, can I plug into your cell phone and get my e-mail?' That kind of stuff," said McCutcheon. "We've recognized that people are trying to get better Internet access between meetings, so it seemed like a nice fit. Customers think it's really neat; the first question they ask usually is, 'I wonder if my computer can do that.'"

[Adapted from Jeff Jedras, "Limo Company Drives Hotspots into Passengers' Laptops," *Computing Canada* (October 17, 2003).]

KEY POINTS REVIEW

1. **Describe electronic business and how it has evolved.** Electronic business is the online exchange of goods, services, and money between firms, and between firms and their customers. Although EB was being used as far back as 1948 during the Berlin Airlift, the emergence of the Internet and the World Wide Web has fuelled a revolution in the manner in which products and services are marketed and sold. Their far-reaching effects have led to the creation of an electronic marketplace that offers a virtually limitless array of new services, features, and functionality. As a result, a presence on the Internet and Web has become a strategic necessity for companies. The powerful combination of Internet and Web technologies has given rise to a global platform where firms from across the world can effectively compete for customers and gain access to new markets. EB has no geographical limitations. The global connectivity of the Internet provides a relatively economical medium for marketing products over vast distances. This increased geographical reach has been facilitated by storefronts located on every Web-enabled computer in the world. Unlike traditional storefronts, time limitations are not a factor, allowing firms to sell and service products seven days a week, 24 hours a day, 365 days a year to anyone, anywhere. A larger customer base creates increased sales volumes, which ultimately saves consumers money since firms can offer their products at lower prices. Companies are exploiting one or more of the capabilities of the Web to reach a wider customer base, offer a broader range of product offerings, and develop closer relationships with customers by striving to meet their unique needs. These wide-ranging capabilities include global information dissemination, integration, mass customization, interactive communication, collaboration, and transactional support.
2. **Describe the strategies that companies are adopting to compete in cyberspace.** The Web has transformed the traditional business operation into a hyper-competitive electronic marketplace. Companies must strategically position themselves to compete in the new EB environment. At one extreme, companies known as bricks-and-mortars choose to operate solely in the

traditional, physical markets. These companies approach business activities in a traditional manner by operating physical locations such as department stores, business offices, and manufacturing plants. In other words, the bricks-and-mortar business strategy does not include EB. In contrast, clicks-only (or virtual) companies conduct business electronically in cyberspace. These firms have no physical locations, allowing them to focus purely on EB. Other firms choose to straddle the two environments, operating in both physical and virtual arenas. These firms operate under the bricks-and-clicks business model.

3. **Explain the differences between intranets and extranets.** Intranet refers to the use of the Internet within an organization to support internal business processes and activities. Examples of the types of processes or activities that might be supported include things such as training, data storage, access to information, and employee collaboration. Extranet refers to the use of the Internet between firms for things such as supply chain management and inter-firm collaboration.

4. **Describe the difference between consumer-focused and business-focused electronic business.** Business-focused EB uses techniques such as electronic data interchange to enable the online exchange and sale of goods and services between firms. While EDI uses proprietary networks, the trend in business today is to use extranets (the public Internet and Web) as the vehicle for business-to-business EB. These portals are used to support distribution, procurement, and other activities. Consumer-focused EB refers to business use of the Internet, Web, and other platforms to reach customers. Companies usually start out with an electronic brochure and pass through a series of stages, including e-information, e-integration, and e-transaction, the latter including sales and service that are conducted online.

5. **Understand the keys to successful electronic business applications.** The basic rules of commerce are to offer valuable products and services at fair prices. These rules apply to EB as well as to any business endeavour. However, having a good product at a fair price may not be enough to compete in the EB arena. Companies that were traditionally successful in the old markets will not necessarily dominate the new electronic markets. Successful companies are found to follow a basic set of principles, or rules, related to Web-based EB. These rules include having a Website that offers something unique, is aesthetically pleasing, is easy to use, is fast, and that motivates people to visit, to stay, and to return. A company should also advertise its presence on the Web and should try to learn from its Website.

KEY TERMS

authentication 148
bricks-and-clicks 142
bricks-and-mortar 141
business-to-business 138
business-to-consumer 138
business-to-employee 138
clicks-only company 141
consumer-to-consumer 139
digitization 162
disintermediation 141
distribution portal 154
e-brochure 160
e-information 160
e-integration 160
e-tailing 158
e-transaction 160
electronic business 138
electronic commerce 138
electronic data interchange (EDI) 143
electronic marketplace 162
enterprise portal 152
extranet 144
firewall 146
hypermediation 166
Internet commerce 138
intranet 144
menu-driven pricing 161
portal 152
procurement portal 155
pull marketing 164
push marketing 164
reverse pricing 161
supply chain management 151
trading exchange 154, 156
tunnelling 151
value-added network (VAN) 143
virtual company 141
vertical market 154
virtual private network (VPN) 149
virtual product 162
watermarked 162
Web commerce 138

REVIEW QUESTIONS

1. What is electronic business (EB), and how has it evolved?
2. How have the Web and other technologies given rise to a global platform?
3. Compare and contrast two electronic business strategies.
4. Explain the differences between the Internet, an intranet, and an extranet. What is the common bond among all three?
5. Describe two types of portals and several applications.
6. Define trading exchanges, and give a couple of examples.
7. What are the three stages of business-to-consumer electronic business?
8. Compare and contrast reverse pricing and menu-driven pricing.
9. What is an electronic marketplace? Give an example.
10. List and describe six elements of or rules for a good Website.

SELF-STUDY QUESTIONS

Answers are at the end of the Problems and Exercises.

1. Electronic business is the online exchange of _________ between firms, and between firms and their customers.
   A. goods
   B. services
   C. money
   D. all of the above
2. _________ allow many buyers and many sellers to come together, offering firms access to real-time trading with other companies in their vertical markets.

A. Distribution portals
B. Procurement portals
C. Trading exchanges
D. E-exchanges

3. _________ companies are those that operate in the traditional, physical markets and do not conduct business electronically in cyberspace.

A. Bricks-and-mortar
B. Clicks-only
C. Both A and B
D. Dot-com

4. _________ automate the business processes involved in purchasing, or procuring, products between a single buyer and multiple suppliers.

A. Distribution portals
B. Procurement portals
C. Enterprise portals
D. Resource portals

5. According to the text, the three stages of Websites include all of the following **except** _________.

A. e-tailing
B. e-integration
C. e-transaction
D. e-information

6. The revolutionary aspect of the Priceline.com Website lies in its _________ system, called Name Your Own Price™. Customers specify the product they are looking for and how much they are willing to pay for it.

A. immediate pricing
B. menu-driven pricing
C. forward pricing
D. reverse pricing

7. Under this type of pricing scheme, known as _________, a firm running an advertisement pays only when a Web surfer actually clicks on the advertisement.

A. cost-effective
B. hypermediation
C. cost-plus
D. pay-plus

8. _________ creates electronic forms with which customers can register their identity and be assigned account numbers. Customer information is used as a tool for conducting market research, enabling the company to get to know its customers.

A. E-business
B. E-integration
C. E-transaction
D. E-information

9. A Website should _________.

A. be easy to use and fast
B. offer something unique and be aesthetically pleasing
C. motivate people to visit, to stay, and to return
D. do all of the above

PROBLEMS AND EXERCISES

1. Match the following terms with the appropriate definitions:

____ Electronic business
____ Hypermediation
____ Value-added networks
____ E-transaction
____ Electronic market
____ Electronic data interchange
____ Distribution portals
____ Vertical markets
____ E-integration
____ Digitization

a. Online exchange of goods, services, and money between firms, and between firms and their customers
b. Everything having to do with the application of information and communication technologies (ICT) to the conduct of business between organizations or from company to consumer
c. A process that creates products without tangible features, which are commonly referred to as virtual products
d. A class of extranets that automate the business processes involved in selling, or distributing, products from a single supplier to multiple buyers
e. A pricing scheme whereby a firm running an advertisement pays only when a Web surfer actually clicks on the advertisement
f. Telephone lines that are leased from telecommunications providers, creating a secure, dedicated circuit between a company and its business partners
g. Markets that service the needs of a specific sector, creating tremendous efficiencies for companies since they can take advantage of existing applications that already meet the requirements of other companies in their industry, eliminating the need to develop proprietary systems of their own
h. A stage that takes the e-integration stage one step further by adding the ability for customers to enter orders and payments online
i. A market that allows many buyers and many sellers to come together, offering firms access to real-time trading with other companies in their vertical markets
j. A stage in which Web pages are created on-the-fly to produce tailored information that addresses the particular needs of a consumer

2. Who is winning the battle between Amazon.ca (**www.amazon.ca**) and Chapters.Indigo.ca (**www.chapters.indigo.ca**)?

3. Visit Air Canada's Website (**www.aircanada.ca**) for real-time pricing, and test the clothing model at the clothing retailer Lands' End (**www.landsend.com**). How have Internet technologies improved over the years?

4. Search the World Wide Web for the Website of a company that is purely Web-based. Next, find the Website of a company that is a hybrid (i.e., they have a traditional "bricks-and-mortar" business plus a presence on the Web). What are the pros and cons of dealing with each type of company?

5. Do you feel that e-business will help or hurt shipping companies such as FedEx and UPS? Have you purchased anything over the Internet? If so, how was it delivered?
6. Do you receive advertisements through e-mail? Are they directed toward any specific audience or product category? Do you pay much attention or just delete them? How much work is it to get off an advertising list?
7. What is it about a company's Website that draws you to it, keeps you on the site longer, and keeps you coming back for more? If you could summarize these answers into a set of criteria for Websites, what would those criteria be?
8. Consider an organization with which you are familiar that maintains an e-business Website. Determine the types of information and processes available on the system. Do the employees make good use of the system and its capabilities? Why or why not?
9. As described in the Global Perspective in this chapter, "Cisco Systems Online—The World's Most Successful Distribution Portal," what makes the company successful? Visit **www.cisco.com** to find out why.
10. Visit the following services for comparison shopping: BestBookBuys.com, Bizrate (**www.bizrate.com**), and My Simon (**www.mysimon.com**). These companies focus on aggregating content for consumers. What are the advantages of these Websites?
11. Look at the list of your favourite bookmarks on the World Wide Web. Why have you saved these addresses? How often do you visit some of these Websites? Is it faster to bookmark an address than to look it up again?

ANSWERS TO THE SELF-STUDY QUESTIONS

1. D 2. C 3. A 4. B 5. A 6. D 7. B 8. B 9. D

Case 1: *BTO Auto: The Dell of Cars?*

Build-to-Order (BTO) Inc., based in Santa Monica, California, is the brainchild of CarsDirect.com founder Scott Painter. Painter plans to build custom cars to order starting at around US$35,000 by outsourcing most aspects of their construction to suppliers. He expects to obtain profit margins of 15–20 percent in an industry where the profit margins are typically less than 3 percent. Furthermore, he plans to do this with about 400 employees, not including suppliers. "We plan to be the Dell Computer of the auto industry, bypassing dealerships and delivering cars to consumers within days of their orders," says Painter.

The company's vision is " . . . to enable our customers to configure vehicle orders online or in person with pricing and availability information that is immediate, transparent, consistent and reliable, and to have that exact vehicle manufactured and delivered to their specific request in just a few short weeks." The concept is to use standardized parts that can be customized, allowing BTO to be largely an assembler. To make this work, an automobile is divided into about two dozen component modules or 12 major modules (e.g., door assemblies, dash assemblies, braking systems). BTO will provide buyers with the opportunity to go online and develop their ideal car from the available modules. Using just-in-time supply models, the parts will arrive at the assembly plant just as they are needed.

BTO CIO Sateesh Lele admits that the concept is not without risk, "A lot of CIOs probably wouldn't say, 'Let's create this car company and take on a huge industry. I know it's not going to be a walk in the park.'" Kevin Purty, research director of automotive strategies at AMR Research, doubts that a company planning to produce just 35,000 vehicles a year at $35,000 each can possibly make a profit, considering the high overhead costs associated with manufacturing and liability. "Automotive isn't about the Dell model," Purty argues. "The company will have to service vehicles, provide warranties, and do crash testing just like the big automotive companies."

Build-to-Order received $25 million in funding from partners such as Deloitte & Touche, AK Steele, and formula race-car maker TWR Group. Painter is convinced that the concept will appeal to those aged 28 to 35 making upwards of $70,000 a year who are tired of the dealership experience and want to have input in the development of their cars.

"The whole theory of mass production was that higher volume brings down the cost for everybody, but technology in the last five years changes all that," Painter says. "We're nimble, and we don't have to deal with legacy investments in obsolete tooling and manufacturing, legacy power trains, labour unions, or the franchise–dealer system."

Lele, who reports to Painter, is charged with putting in place the infrastructure to begin production in 2005. That includes the entire IT backbone, supply chain software, and a CRM system tuned to creating a constant dialogue with customers. "For the average CIO, maintenance makes up 80 percent of the budget," Lele says. "To have the opportunity to use 100 percent of the budget for a new development is a real high to a CIO."

[Adapted from Mary Hayes, "This CIO Likes Living On the Edge," *InformationWeek* (November 7, 2002).]

Discussion Questions

1. Do you think BTO Auto is likely to be successful? Why or why not?
2. Describe the IT infrastructure that BTO Auto will require in order to implement its strategy.
3. BTO Auto wants to apply the strategy of mass customization to the auto industry as Dell has done in the computer industry. Does this strategy fit this industry? Why or why not?

Case 2: *Can Canada Lead and Trail the World at the Same Time?*

A number of international studies have shown that Canada is among the global elite in terms of economic competitiveness and productivity. Canada has also ranked well internationally on factors relating to Internet infrastructure and e-business. Yet, while Canada is very strong on an aggregate level, it is not strong in all areas. In particular, the data suggests that Canadian businesses lag their counterparts in the U.S. and the EU in areas such as Net readiness and Internet commerce.

Canada has been an international leader in terms of information and communication technologies (ICT), Internet infrastructure, and innovation. One recently published example of Canada's high standing came from INSEAD, a French business school. The INSEAD study aggregated data from a wide variety of sources to come up with a measure of national new economy performance, which they named the Network Readiness Index (NRI). The NRI was used to rank 82 nations on a variety of variables including Internet usage, e-commerce, technology infrastructure, and regulatory structure, among others. Many of the variables were broken down into individual, business, and government categories. Overall, Canada ranked sixth among the 82 nations on the full 2002 NRI. This rank represented a jump from 12th place in 2001. Canada ranked second behind the U.S. among nations with populations greater than 10 million. The study made explicit mention of Canada's significant policy initiatives and public/private partnerships as contributing factors to its high ranking.

Data produced by the OECD showed Canada to be among global leaders in terms of investment in ICT. Canada lagged the U.S. on these dimensions, but was on par with the UK and ahead of other large European economies. Canada was also well positioned globally on a variety of measures of Internet infrastructure. Canada was second only to the U.S. in both Internet hosts per capita and Websites per capita. Canada led the U.S. and European nations in terms of broadband connectivity, reflecting perhaps the concerted effort by various levels of government in Canada to promote infrastructure development. Finally, Canada led the U.S. and Europe in the proportion of patents allocated to ICT. This suggests that Canada has pursued an innovation agenda in technologies relating to Net enablement and infrastructure development.

Despite these positive indicators, there is some evidence to suggest that, in the case of e-business, Canada has not attained the same level as the U.S. or some European nations. The evidence further shows that while Canadians and the Canadian government have embraced the Internet, the commercial sector has been slower to adopt e-business.

A closer examination of the Net Readiness study from INSEAD shows that while Canada had very advanced infrastructure and regulatory support for e-business, Net readiness in the business sectors lagged other nations. For example, while individual (fourth place) and government readiness (sixth place) were high, business readiness in Canada was relatively low (12th place). Figure 5.24 shows that Canada was first among key trading partners in both individual and government readiness, but second to last in business readiness. The opposite was found in the U.S., where individual readiness was seventh, while business readiness ranked first among nations.

Data from the OECD appears to corroborate this evidence. For example, Internet commerce as a percentage of total commerce in Canada, at 0.5 percent, lagged many other OECD nations (see Figure 5.25). Internet commerce in the U.S. was proportionally double that of Canada, and Canadian Internet commerce was only a quarter of that of Scandinavian countries. Other data suggests that Canadian businesses were less likely than their U.S. or European counterparts to buy and sell over the Internet, even though their connection rates were similar. The OECD data shows that despite having similarly high rates of connectivity, Canadian firms were less likely to purchase online and substantially less likely to sell online than European firms.

Another indication of Canada's global economic position came from the Growth Competitiveness Index (GCI), produced annually by the World Economic Forum. In 2002, Canada's GCI placed it in eighth place among the 74 nations measured, down from third place in 2001. Canada actually improved its placing for public institutions and macroeconomic environment categories (from 11th to ninth and 13th to 12th, respectively). However, Canada dropped from second to eighth place in the technology ranking category, causing the fall in the overall ranking. The drop in the technology rank appears to be linked to a slippage in national performance in innovation and ICT. Canada's fall in the rankings may also be due to another factor measured in the report: Canada's rank in government expenditure was 52nd among the 74 nations in the study. The results show that while Canada is still high among nations on measures of productivity and competitiveness, other nations are catching up, and in some cases passing Canada when it comes to e-business.

[Adapted from McClean, Johnston, and Wade, "Net Impact Canada: The International Experience," *The Canadian eBusiness Initiative* (May, 2003). **http://www.cebi.ca.**]

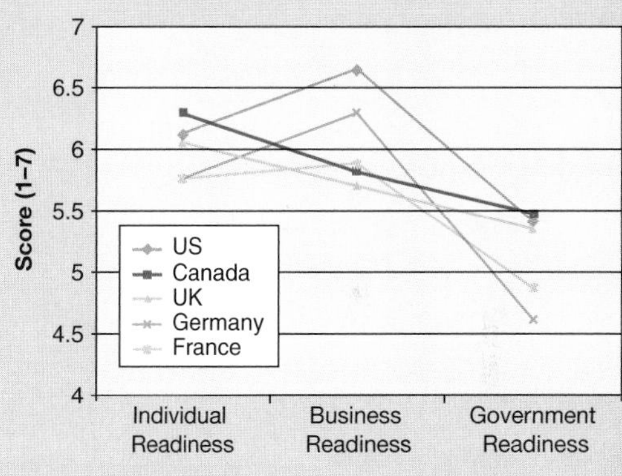

[Figure 5.24]

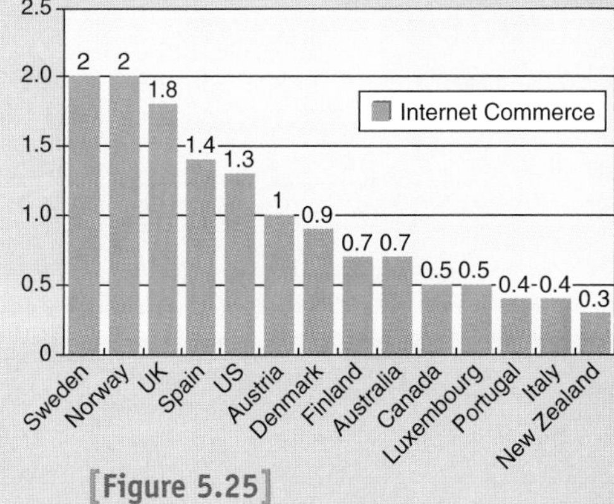

[Figure 5.25]

Discussion Questions

1. Why do you think Canada is falling behind some key trading partners in e-business?
2. Place yourself in the shoes of the Canadian federal government. What could you do to increase the adoption of e-business in Canada?
3. What do you see as the future of e-business in Canada?

Chapter 6

Preview

This chapter describes several types of information systems and where and how each is used in organizations. Some of the systems described are relatively new, while others have been mainstays in organizations since the 1960s.

After reading this chapter, you will be able to do the following:

1. Describe the characteristics that differentiate the operational, managerial, and executive levels of an organization.
2. Explain the characteristics of the three information systems designed to support each unique level of an organization: transaction processing systems, management information systems, and executive information systems.
3. Describe the characteristics of six information systems that span the organizational, managerial, and executive levels: decision support systems, expert systems, office automation systems, collaboration technologies, functional area information systems, and global information systems.

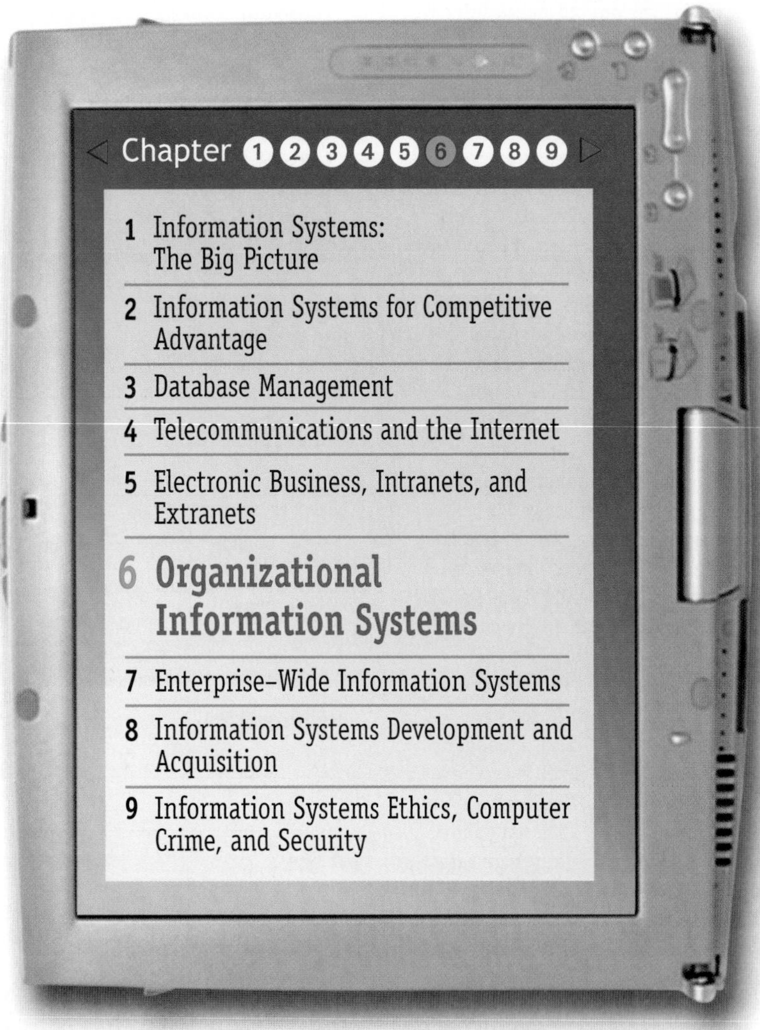

[**Figure 6.1** ➡ The Big Picture: focusing on organizational information systems.]

Organizational Information Systems

OPENING: The Beer Store Overhauls 10-Year-Old Transaction Processing Systems

Strategic systems and e-business are not the only means by which information systems can benefit organizations. Powerful but low-complexity back-office systems can also help firms by streamlining operations and increasing efficiencies. The Beer Store, Ontario's largest beer retailer, recently rolled out new transaction processing and order management systems to improve inventory control and enhance customer service.

The Beer Store's old system, which was created in-house about 10 years ago, could no longer scale to increasing demand. Brand selection alone had grown by 250 percent to more than 300 brands from 70 brewers. "It was time to upgrade," said Glenn Wood, Director of Information Services. "It's about having the right product at the right time and the right location," Wood said. "It's also about getting people in and out quickly. As brand proliferation continues, the longer that process takes." Beer Store employees had trouble maintaining inventory levels, particularly at peak times.

The Beer Store decided to implement a transaction processing system from Triversity Inc., based in Toronto, and an order management system from Yantra Corp., based in Massachusetts. "A lot of the application gaps we had as a business were predominantly around best practices, and the renewal was consistent with applying retail best practices," said Wood. "Execution, technology and point of sale is really part of that." Those elements involve both front of store selling and back-office inventory management—something critical in managing the supply chain. "We go through a lot of beer in the summer and it takes up a lot of space. People expect it to be cold, and that we'll always have their brand in stock," said Wood.

With the new point-of-sale transaction system, if the store clerk punches in an order for a 2-4 of Molson Canadian but that particular brand and package size is out of stock, the system will send a message to the Yantra store inventory application. It will then send back a message saying the 2-4 isn't available but two 12 packs are available. The POS does the substitution and discounts the price of the two 12 packs to match the price of the 2-4.

The Triversity system helps The Beer Store to manage marketing promotions. "Before, it took six months to a year for us to develop the capability to support a new marketing promotion," said Wood. "With the new system, we are able to get financial and inventory information updated across the entire chain of locations in real time—all of the kinds of things that can help us make decisions and measure effectiveness of promotions," Wood said.

[Adapted from Jennifer Brown, "The Beer Store Gets a Taste of J2EE Efficiency," *Computing Canada* (January 14, 2004).]

[**Figure 6.2** ➡ The Beer Store matches its new image with new information systems.]

Source: Marisa D'Andrea.

This chapter focuses on how organizations are using and applying information systems (see Figure 6.2). In the next chapter we discuss an additional class of organizational information system, the enterprise-wide information system. The next section describes the different types of information required at various levels of organizations. This is followed by a discussion of the general types of information systems used to span organizational boundaries.

DECISION-MAKING LEVELS OF AN ORGANIZATION

Every organization is composed of decision-making levels, as illustrated in Figure 6.3. Each level of an organization has different responsibilities and, therefore, different informational needs. In this section, we describe each of these levels.

Operational Level

At the ***operational level*** of a firm, the routine, day-to-day business processes and interactions with customers occur. Information systems at this level are designed to automate repetitive activities, such as sales transaction processing, and improve the efficiency of business processes and the customer interface. Managers at the operational level, such as site supervisors, make day-to-day decisions that are highly structured and recurring. ***Structured decisions*** are those in which the procedures to follow for a given situation can be specified in advance. For example, a supervisor may decide when to reorder supplies or how best to allocate personnel for the completion of a project. Because structured decisions are relatively straightforward, they can be programmed directly into operational information systems so that they can be made with little or no human intervention. For example, an inventory management system for a shoe store in the mall could keep track of inventory and issue an order for additional inventory when levels drop below a specified level. Operational managers within the store would simply need to confirm with the inventory management system that the order for additional shoes was needed. Information systems are extremely effective at processing transactions at the operational level. Figure 6.4 summarizes the general characteristics of the operational level.

Managerial Level

At the ***managerial level*** of the organization, functional managers (e.g., marketing managers, finance managers, manufacturing managers, and human resources managers) focus on monitoring and controlling operational-level activities and providing information to higher levels of the organization. Managers at this level, referred to as midlevel managers or functional managers, focus on effectively utilizing and deploying organizational resources to achieve the strategic objectives of the organization. Midlevel managers typically focus on problems within a specific business function, such as marketing or finance. Here, the scope of the decision usually is contained within the business function, is moderately complex, and has a time horizon of a few

[**Figure 6.3** ➥ Organizations are composed of levels, with each using information technology to automate activities or assist in decision making.]

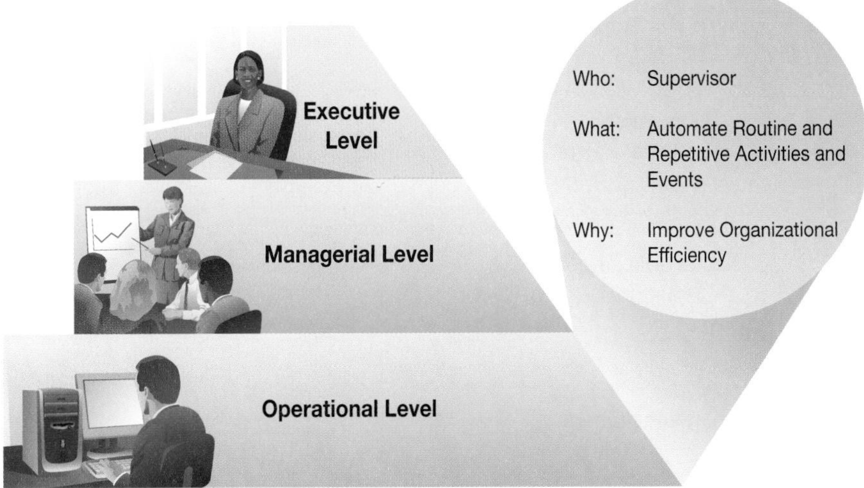

[**Figure 6.4** ➥ The operational level of an organization uses information systems to improve efficiency by automating routine and repetitive activities.]

days to a few months. For example, a marketing manager at Canadian Tire may decide how to allocate the advertising budget for the next business quarter or some fixed time period.

Managerial-level decision making is not nearly as structured or routine as operational-level decision making. Managerial-level decision making is referred to as semistructured decision making because solutions and problems are not clear-cut and often require judgment and expertise. For ***semistructured decisions***, some procedures to follow for a given situation can be specified in advance, but not to the extent where a specific recommendation can be made. For example, an information system could provide a production manager at Canadian Tire with summary information about sales forecasts for multiple product lines, inventory levels, and overall production capacity. The manager could use this information to create multiple production schedules. With these schedules, the manager could examine inventory levels and potential sales profitability, depending upon the order in which manufacturing resources were used to produce each type of product. Information systems are generally effective at supporting decision making at the managerial level. Figure 6.5 summarizes the general characteristics of the managerial level.

Executive Level

At the ***executive level*** of the organization, managers focus on long-term strategic issues facing the organization, such as which products to produce, which countries to compete

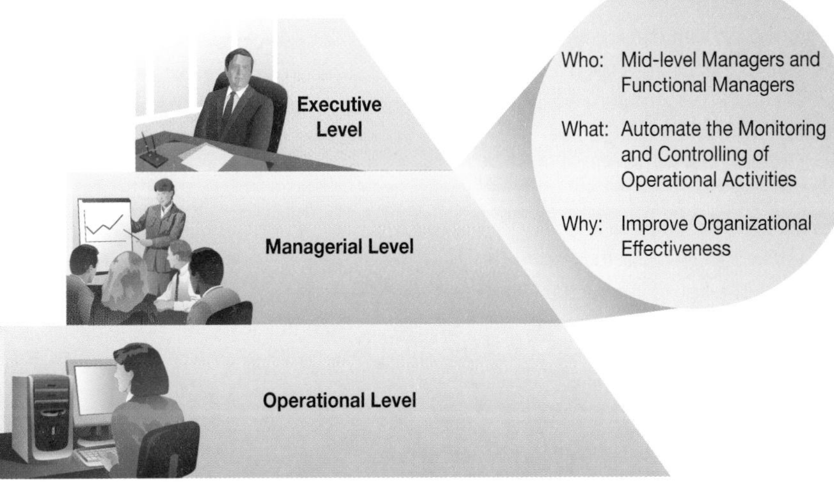

[**Figure 6.5** ➥ The managerial level of an organization uses information systems to improve effectiveness by automating the monitoring and control of organizational activities.]

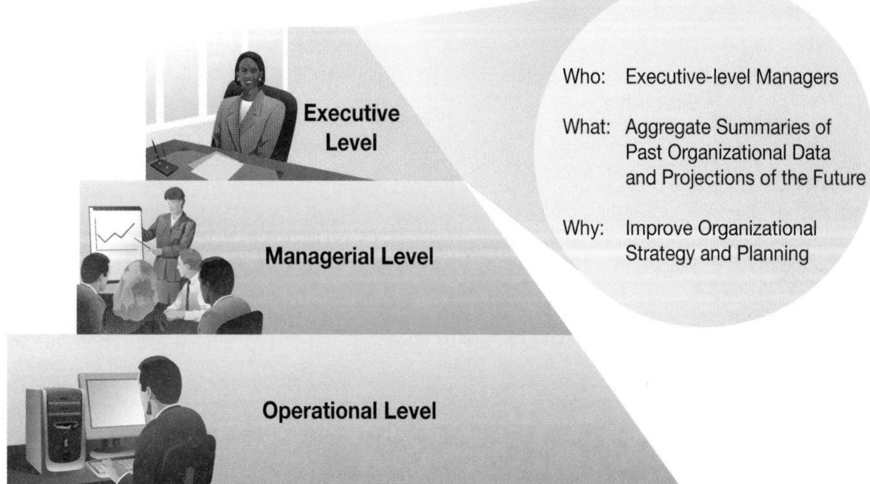

[**Figure 6.6** ➡ The executive level of an organization uses information systems to improve strategy and planning by providing summaries of past data and projections of the future.]

in, and what organizational strategy to follow. Managers at this level include the president and chief executive officer (CEO), vice-presidents, and possibly the board of directors, and are referred to as "executives." Executive-level decisions deal with complex problems with broad and long-term ramifications for the organization. Executive-level decisions are referred to as unstructured decision making because the problems are relatively complex and nonroutine. In addition, executives must consider the ramifications of their decisions in terms of the overall organization. For ***unstructured decisions,*** few or no procedures to follow for a given situation can be specified in advance. For example, top managers may decide to develop a new product or discontinue an existing one. Such a decision may have vast, long-term effects on the organization's levels of employment and profitability. To assist executive-level decision making, information systems are used to obtain aggregate summaries of trends and projections of the future. Since the decisions faced by executives are typically complex and unstructured, the ability of information systems to support decision making at this level is modest compared to operational and managerial levels. Figure 6.6 summarizes the general characteristics of the executive level.

In summary, most organizations have three general levels: operational, managerial,

WHEN THINGS GO WRONG

Online-Only Banks Struggle and Fail

Online banking is catching on with consumers, with nearly 64 percent of Canadian Internet users banking online in 2004, up 36 percent from 2003. For online-only banks, however, the number of visitors declined steadily over the same period. The vision for online-only banks was to have very low overhead costs relative to banks that had physical facilities and branches, in order to pass on savings to customers. The banks intended to offer low-interest credit cards and inexpensive online bill-payment services. Unfortunately, this vision has not proved to be a reality. In fact, in early 2002, Phoenix-based NextBank NA was the first Internet-only bank to fail when government regulators shut down the bank for having operated in an "unsafe and unsound manner." In Canada, the Bank of Montreal closed its online-only retail banking arm, mbanx, opting instead to pursue a multi-channel approach. Research has shown that as consumers get more comfortable with online commerce, they prefer banks that have both a physical and an online presence in order to have physical access to money and personal customer service. It remains to be seen what the final outcome will be for the online-only bank, but industry experts feel that as online banking becomes more of a commodity, with little or no charge for online services, the long-term prognosis for the online-only bank is not a good one.

[Adapted from L. Mearian, "Brick-and-Click Bank Sites Outpacing Online-Only Banks," **http://www.computerworld.com**, *Computerworld* (September 3, 2001); S. Machlis, "Feds Shut Down $700M Internet Bank," **http://www.computerworld.com**, *Computerworld* (February 8, 2002).]

and executive. Each level has unique activities, and each requires different types of information. The next section examines various types of information systems designed to support each organizational level.

GENERAL TYPES OF INFORMATION SYSTEMS

An easy way to understand how all information systems work is to use an input, process, and output model—the basic systems model (see Checkland, 1981, for a thorough discussion). Figure 6.7 shows the basic systems model that can be used to describe virtually all types of systems. As an example, Figure 6.8 shows elements of a payroll system decomposed into input, process, and output elements. The inputs to a payroll system include time cards and employee lists, as well as wage and salary information. Processing transforms the inputs into outputs that include paycheques, management reports, and updated account balances. The remainder of this section uses the basic systems model to describe various information systems.

Transaction Processing Systems

Many organizations deal with repetitive activities. Grocery stores scan groceries at the checkout counter. Banks process cheques drawn on customer accounts. Fast food restaurants process customer orders. All these repetitive activities are examples of ***transactions*** that occur as a regular part of a business's day-to-day operations. ***Transaction processing systems (TPSs)*** are a special class of information systems designed to process business events and transactions. Consequently, TPSs often reside close to customers at the operational level of the organization, as illustrated in Figure 6.9. The goal of transaction processing systems is to automate repetitive information-processing activities within organizations to increase speed and accuracy and to lower the cost of processing each transaction—that is, to make the organization more efficient. Because TPSs are used to process large volumes of information, organizations have spent considerable resources designing them. A TPS can reduce or eliminate people from the process, thereby reducing transaction costs and reducing the likelihood of data entry errors. Examples of the types of activities supported by TPS include:

- Payroll processing
- Sales and order processing
- Inventory management
- Product purchasing, receiving, and shipping
- Accounts payable and receivable

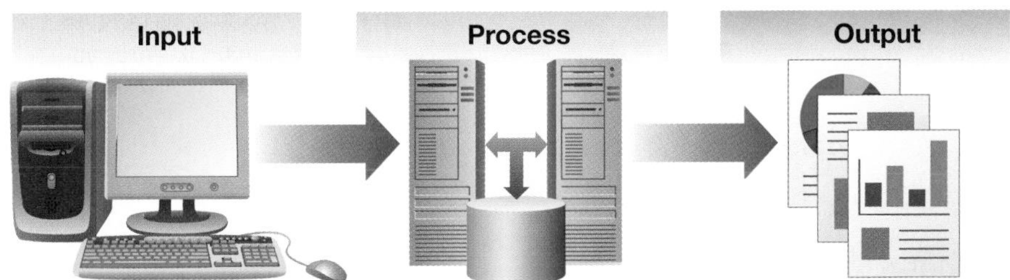

[Figure 6.7 ➥ The basic systems model can be used to describe all types of information systems.]

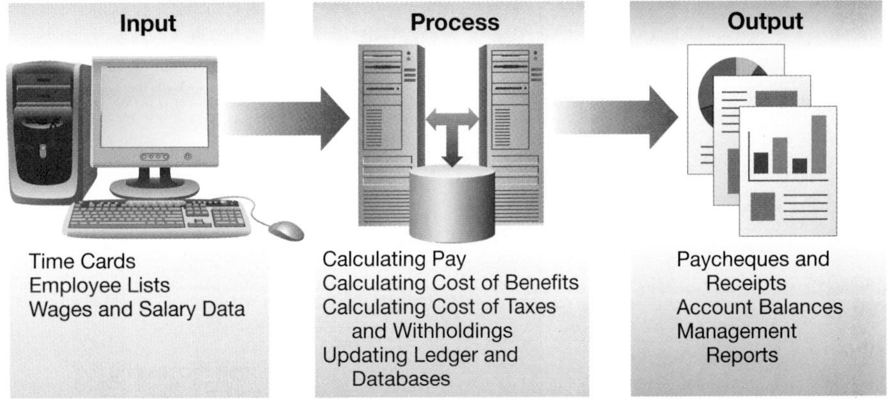

[Figure 6.8 ➥ A payroll system shown as an instance of the basic systems model.]

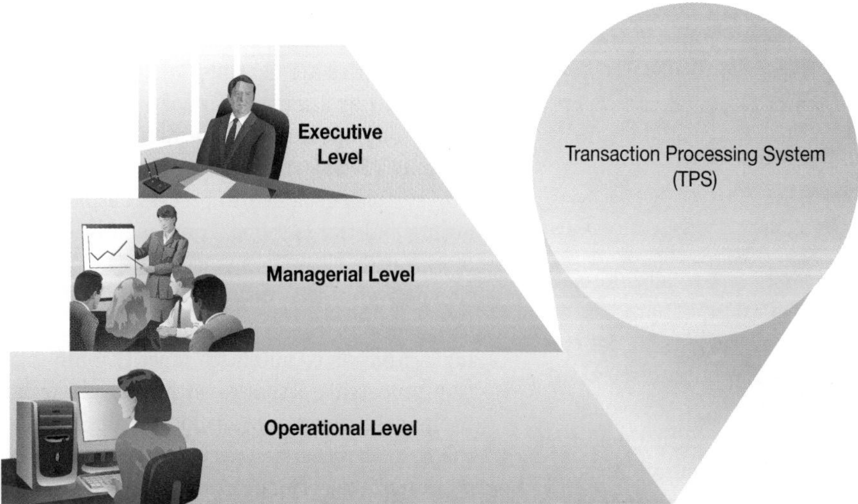

[**Figure 6.9** ➥ Transaction processing systems are used to improve operational-level decision making.]

Architecture of a Transaction Processing System

The basic model of a TPS is shown in Figure 6.10. When a business transaction occurs, source documents describing the transaction are created. ***Source documents,*** paper or electronic, serve as a stimulus to a TPS from some external source. For example, when you fill out a driver's licence application, it serves as a source document for a TPS that records and stores information on all licensed drivers in a province. Source documents can be processed as they are created—referred to as online processing—or they can be processed in batches—referred to as batch processing. ***Online processing*** of transactions provides immediate results to the system operator or customer. For example, an interactive class registration system that immediately notifies you of your success or failure to register for a class is an example of an online TPS. Note that online processing does not necessarily mean that results are presented on the Web (or another online medium); it merely implies that the results are available in real time. ***Batch processing*** of transactions occurs when transactions are collected and then processed together as a batch at some later time. Banks often use batch processing when reconciling cheques drawn on customer accounts. Likewise, your

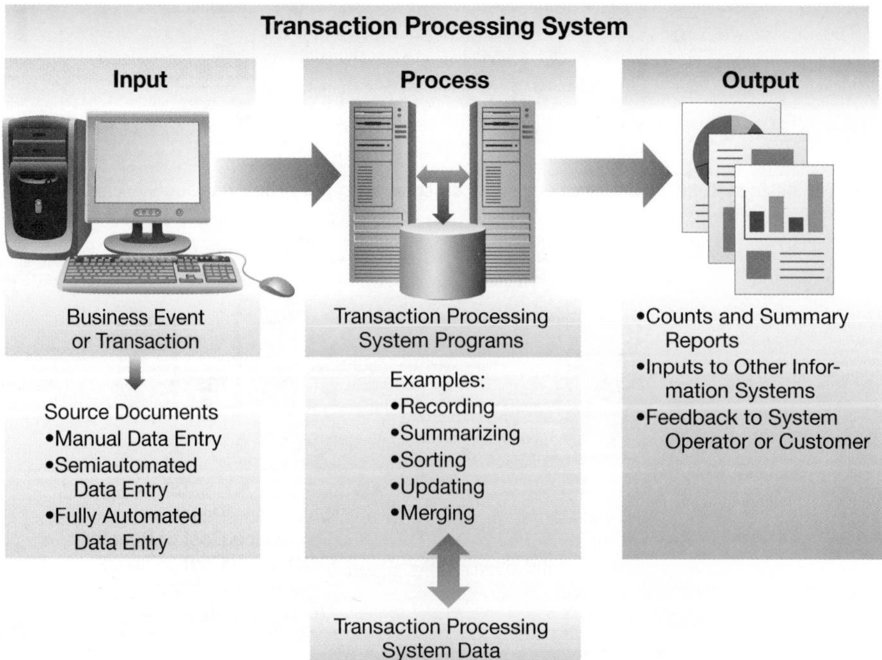

[**Figure 6.10** ➥ Architecture of a transaction processing system using the basic systems model.]

Online TPS	Batch TPS
University class registration processing	Students' final grade processing
Airline reservation processing	Payroll processing
Concert/sporting event ticket reservation processing	Customer order processing (for example, insurance forms)
Grocery store checkout processing	Bank cheque processing

[Table 6.1] ***Examples of online and batch transaction processing systems.***

university uses batch processing to process end-of-term grade reports—all inputs must be periodically processed in batches to calculate your grade point average. Online processing is used when customers need immediate notification of the success or failure of a transaction. Batch processing is used when immediate notification is not needed or is not practical. Table 6.1 lists several examples of online and batch transaction processing systems.

Information can be entered into a TPS in one of three ways: manually, semiautomated, or fully automated. ***Manual data entry*** refers to having a person enter the source document information by hand into the TPS. For example, when you apply for a new driver's licence, a clerk manually enters information about you into a driver's licence recording system, often copying the information from a form that you filled out.

BRIEF CASE

Shell Canada Adopts Radio Frequency ID Tags

Sometimes, the principal value of an information system is simply to reduce the time and effort it takes to complete an operation. Radio frequency identification (RFID) tags, for example, exemplify how new technologies create "time rebates" for customers. RFID tags transmit and receive radio signals over short distances, obviating the need to physically interact with a system. RFID tags are turning up in a diverse set of applications ranging from payment processing to baggage tracking. Even the times of runners in Quebec City's Marathon Des Deux Rives (as well as more than 120 other Canadian road races) are now tracked using RFID technology.

Shell Canada's easyPAY™ payment technology (see Figure 6.11) was first tested in the Calgary market in the fall of 2000 and subsequently rolled out in 2001 to other Shell retail sites in Vancouver, Edmonton, Toronto, Ottawa, and Montreal. The system embeds RFID technology in a tag that fits on a key ring. The tag communicates with a pump-mounted receiver to automatically bill fuel to a customer's chosen credit card.

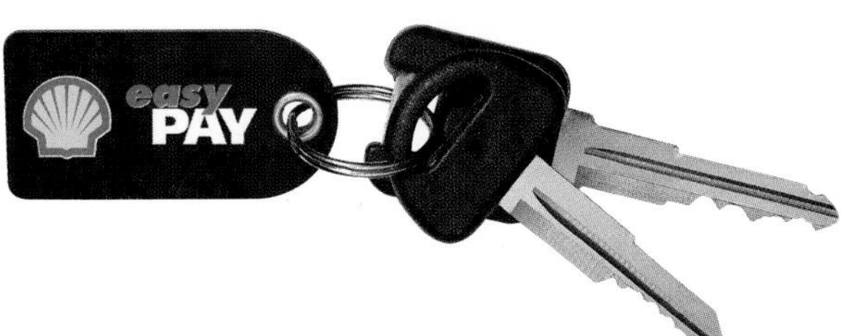

[Figure 6.11 ➡ Shell Canada's easyPAY™ Tag.]

Source: Courtesy of Shell Canada Products.

Shell conducted extensive research that revealed speed and convenience are becoming increasingly important factors for consumers purchasing gasoline. As a result, the company designed the system to meet the needs of consumers who want to have a simple, quick, and efficient experience when fuelling up. Shell Canada was initially reluctant to implement easyPAY™ since it allowed customers to bypass Shell's lucrative service station retail outlets. However, positive consumer reaction to the initiative outweighed any potential loss of in-store sales.

Shell has found that the customer is not the only beneficiary of the technology. The company is now able to quickly gather information about when and where its customers purchase gasoline in much the same way the marathon and other races can track precisely when runners have crossed the various kilometre markers.

Questions

1. Can Shell Canada use RFID technology to achieve a sustainable competitive advantage?
2. What other applications can you think of for RFID technologies?

[Adapted from Jonathan Copulsky and Mark Whitmore, "Giving Time Back to Your Customers," *IT World Canada* (November 1, 2002).]

[Table 6.2] ***Characteristics of a transaction processing system.***

Inputs	Business events and transactions
Processing	Recording, summarizing, sorting, updating, merging
Outputs	Counts and summary reports of activity inputs to other information systems; feedback to system operators or customers
Typical Users	Operational personnel and supervisors

In a ***semiautomated data entry*** system, a data capture device such as a grocery store checkout scanner speeds the entry and processing of the transaction. The checkout scanner speeds the checkout for the customer and also provides accurate and detailed data directly to many types of information systems. Another example of a semiautomated TPS is an electronic shopping mall on the Web. In this mall, customers enter their purchase requests, which go directly to an order fulfillment system without any additional human intervention.

Fully automated data entry does not require any human intervention. Two computers "talk" to each other via a computer network. For example, for automobiles built at Ford Motor Company, each part used in the manufacturing process represents a transaction in the inventory management system. When the inventory of windshields runs low, the inventory management system automatically contacts the supplier's computer system via a computer network to request more windshields. An electronic link between computers to share data related to business operations is referred to as electronic data interchange (EDI) and was discussed in detail in Chapter 4, "Telecommunications and the Internet." Many organizations spend considerable effort with their suppliers and customers working on EDI standards—both how to communicate over the network and how data is to be formatted—so that more and more information can be exchanged without human intervention.

The characteristics of a TPS are summarized in Table 6.2. Inputs to a TPS are business events or transactions. The processing activities of a TPS include recording, summarizing, sorting, updating, and merging transaction information with organizational databases. Outputs from a TPS include summary reports, inputs to other systems, and operator notification of processing completion. People who are very close to day-to-day operations most often use TPSs. For example, a checkout clerk at the grocery store uses a TPS to record your purchases. Supervisors may review transaction summary reports to control inventory, to manage operations personnel, or to provide customer service. Additionally, inventory management systems may monitor transaction activity and use this information to manage inventory reordering. This is an example of the output from a TPS being the input to another system.

Management Information Systems

Management information system (MIS) is a term with two meanings. It describes the field of study that encompasses the development, use, management, and study of computer-based information systems in organizations. It also refers to a specific type of organizational information system. A management information system is used to produce scheduled and ad hoc reports to support the ongoing, recurring decision-making activities associated with managing an entire business or a functional area within a business. Consequently, an MIS often resides at the managerial level of the organization, as shown in Figure 6.12. We will discuss the reports produced by an MIS later in this section.

Whereas transaction processing systems automate repetitive information-processing activities to increase efficiency, a management information system helps midlevel managers make more effective decisions. MISs are designed to get the right information to the right people in the right format at the right time to help them make better decisions. MISs can be found throughout the organization. For example, a marketing manager for Nike may have an MIS that contrasts sales revenue and marketing expenses by geographic region so that she can better understand how regional marketing for the "Tiger Woods Golf" promotions are performing. Examples of the types of activities supported by MISs include:

- Sales forecasting
- Financial management and forecasting
- Manufacturing planning and scheduling
- Inventory management and planning
- Advertising and product pricing

Information Systems

Cooking.com is an online marketer of housewares and has been doing good business for a long time. The company relied on the use of an application service provider (ASP) for online payment processing and credit card authorization. In addition, the system also provided the company with order confirmation, and it did not require heavy investment into IT resources. However, in recent times, before a holiday season, the company realized that its transactions had increased significantly, and the old ASP environment was falling short of handling the volume. The company was also concerned about security and reliability, in addition to speed. The company finally decided to buy server-based payment processing and authorization software from ClearCommerce, based in Austin, Texas. The software allowed the company to conduct real-time authorization and processing, even when the transaction volume was very high. The new software was installed on a new Sun Solaris server, at great expense to the company. There was a flat fee of US$75,000, as opposed to the nominal charges of the ASP. In addition, the company also had to set up a direct link to the credit card processor, First Data Merchant Service, using a Frame Relay line, to ensure a dedicated connection all the time. In spite of these additional costs, Cooking.com felt that its investment in this new transaction processing system was justified. According to the company, it was more important to ensure real-time processing and authorization, even in times of high volume, than reduction of costs.

CAREER IMPLICATIONS

[Adapted from L. Goff, "The Lowdown on . . . Payment Processing Systems," *Catalog Age* (February 2001).]

Architecture of a Management Information System

The basic architecture of an MIS is shown in Figure 6.13. At regular intervals, managers need to review summary information of some organizational activity. For example, a sales manager at a Ford dealership may review the weekly performance of all his sales staff. To aid his review, an MIS summarizes the total sales volume of each salesperson in a report. This report may provide a plethora of information about each person, including the following:

- What are this salesperson's year-to-date sales totals?
- How do this year's sales figures compare with last year's?
- What is the average amount per sale?
- How do sales change by the day of the week?

Imagine the difficulty of producing these weekly reports manually for an organization that has 50 salespeople, 500 salespeople, or even 5,000 salespeople! It would be very difficult, if not impossible, to create these detailed reports on each salesperson without an MIS.

An MIS combines information from multiple data sources into a structured report that allows managers to monitor and manage the

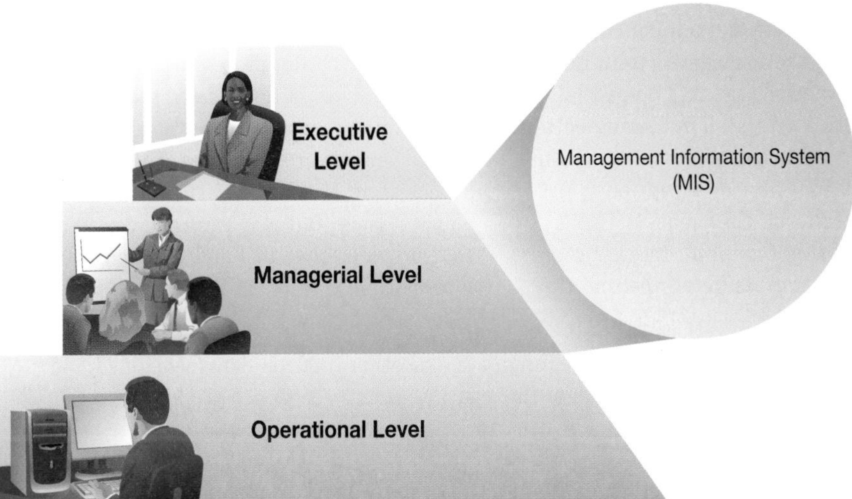

[**Figure 6.12** ➡ Management information systems are used to improve managerial-level decision making.]

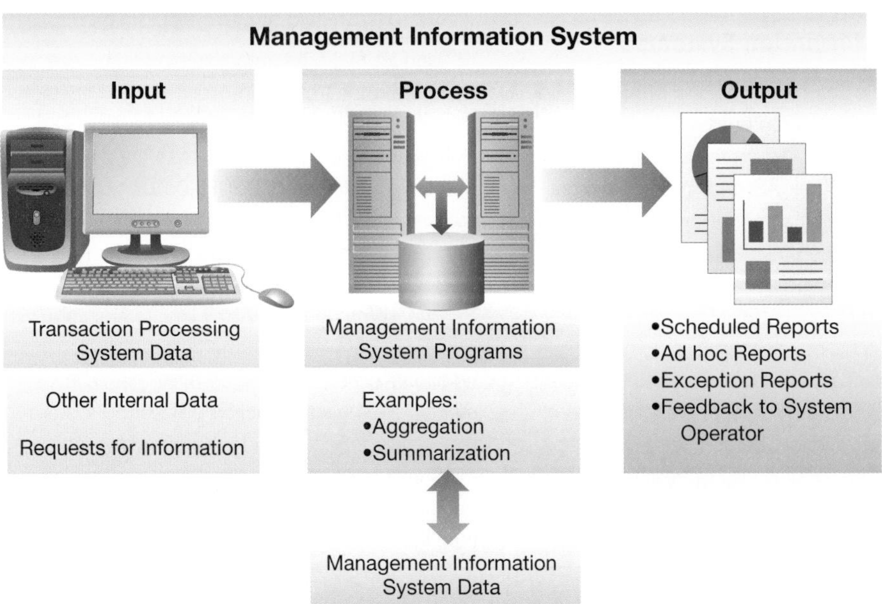

[Figure 6.13 ➥ Architecture of a management information system using the basic systems model.]

organization better. Reports produced at predefined intervals—daily, weekly, or monthly—to support the routine informational needs of managerial-level decision making are called ***scheduled reports*** (e.g., a weekly inventory level report). These reports can provide summaries of all types of information but most often provide information related to key indicators. A ***key-indicator report*** provides a summary of critical information on a recurring schedule. Key-indicator reports provide high-level summaries so that a manager can quickly see if all important activities are operating as planned. MISs can also be used to produce ***exception reports,*** which highlight situations that are out of the normal range. For example, a manager with a large number of sales personnel can produce an exception report highlighting those not achieving minimum sales goals. By focusing the manager's attention on specific information, the MIS helps the organization take a first step in making better decisions. When managers want greater detail as to why a key indicator or exception is not at an appropriate level, they request that a ***drill-down report*** be produced. In essence, drill-down reports provide details behind the summary values on a key-indicator or exception report.

Managers can also use an MIS to make ad hoc requests for information. ***Ad hoc reports*** refer to unplanned information requests in which information is gathered to support a nonroutine decision (e.g., world events precipitate an unforeseen demand for a product). For example, if a particular product at a car dealership, such as the Ford Mustang, is not selling as well as forecasts predicted, the manager can request a report showing which salespeople are selling the product effectively and which are not. The manager could use this information to examine reasons that this is occurring and investigate ways to intervene before the problem gets out of hand.

The characteristics of an MIS are summarized in Table 6.3. In general, inputs to an MIS are transaction processing data produced by a TPS; other internal data, such as sales promotion expenses; and ad hoc requests for special reports or summaries. The processing aspect of an MIS focuses on data aggregation and summary. Outputs are formatted reports that provide scheduled and nonrecurring information to a midlevel manager. For exam-

[Table 6.3] *Characteristics of a management information system.*

Inputs	Transaction processing data and other internal data; scheduled and ad hoc requests for information
Processing	Aggregation and summary of data
Outputs	Scheduled and exception reports; feedback to system operator
Typical Users	Midlevel managers

ple, a store manager can use an MIS to review sales information to identify products that are not selling and are in need of special promotion.

Executive Information Systems

In addition to operational personnel and midlevel managers, top-level managers or executives can use information technology to support day-to-day activities such as cash and investment management, resource allocation, or contract negotiation. Information systems designed to support the highest organizational managers are called ***executive information systems (EIS).*** An EIS (sometimes referred to as an executive support system—ES) consists

BRIEF CASE

The Canadian Breast Cancer Foundation Uses Transaction Processing System to Improve Efficiency at Annual Athletic Event

The largest fundraising event of the year for the Canadian Breast Cancer Foundation (CBCF) is the CIBC Run for the Cure, a five-kilometre race held annually in 36 cities across Canada. The event hosts over 150,000 runners and raises over $30 million annually.

Organizing such an event requires a highly coordinated effort among hundreds of volunteers, supported by a variety of information systems. The CBCF had been using a Web interface to allow people to register for the run online and make donations. Each volunteer leader was provided with a user authentication ID to log in to the site so they could pick up reports on a daily basis. The reports "let them know where they were in relation to registrations, donations, teams, how many T-shirts they needed to buy, etc., and they could compare that information to data from the previous year, so they knew where they stood on a day-to-day basis," explained the CBCF's national director for IT, Deborah Kroeger.

However, the event had become so large that when volunteers wanted to print out progress reports, the resulting documents were often 500 pages long or more. "It was just a nightmare for people," said Kroeger. "They were trying to come in Saturday night and Sunday morning and print off this information." Although the HTML-based system effectively managed the collection of donations and provided an appealing customer interface, it was not effective when it came to presenting the data to organizers.

[Figure 6.14 ➡ The Canadian Breast Cancer Foundation: CIBC Run for the Cure.]
Source: CP Photo/Toronto Star—Bernard Weil.

The CBCF decided to implement Crystal Reports software to help it coordinate the efforts of its volunteers and better understand its donors. Crystal Reports dramatically cut down the time and resources required by volunteers to process registrations and donations. Volunteers were spared hours of data entry, since the site moved over to an entirely self-service application. Runners could register online; supporters could donate money online and receive a .pdf tax receipt automatically. "That saved us all the mailing and the printing costs," said Kroeger.

Christine Tang, global references manager for Crystal Decisions, said that CBCF was different from many of its other customers in that it's a not-for-profit and a charity, but the organization still shared many of the same goals as Fortune 500 users. "At its core, it's really about performance metrics, because now, for the first time, their run directors are able to take a look and see how they're performing," she said. "If you think about it correlating to a business, it's the same type of data that you need to make sure that you're on track and performing and achieving your profit goals."

The next step for the CBCF is to understand more about its donors and how effective its pledge drives and direct mail campaigns have been, using data mining tools. "We want to be able to follow up with them and thank them," said Kroeger. "It will help us in our donor recognition and our stewardship."

Questions

1. As firms grow from small to medium to large in size, how do their IT requirements change?
2. Firms often underestimate the importance of scaleability when adopting an IT solution. What should firms do to manage this issue?

[Adapted from Neil Sutton, "Canadian Breast Cancer Foundation Runs for IT Cure," ITBusiness.ca (November 20, 2003).]

Web Search

WEB SEARCH OPPORTUNITY
Go to Globeinvestor, **www.globeinvestor.com**, Canada's most comprehensive investment research Website. The site contains investment news, stock quotes, and commentary from Canada and around the world.

of technology (hardware, software, data, and procedures) and the people needed to consolidate information and support users to assist executive-level decision making (see Figure 6.15). An EIS provides information to executives in a very highly aggregated form so that they can scan information quickly for trends and anomalies. For example, executives may track various market conditions—like the Dow Jones Industrial Average—to assist in making investment decisions. Although EISs are not as widely used as other types of information systems, this trend is rapidly changing because more and more executives are becoming comfortable with information technology and because an EIS can provide substantial benefits to the executive. Activities supported by an EIS include:

- Executive-level decision making
- Long-range and strategic planning
- Monitoring of internal and external events and resources
- Crisis management
- Staffing and labour relations

An EIS can deliver both "soft" and "hard" data to the executive decision maker. ***Soft data*** include textual news stories or other nonanalytical information. ***Hard data*** include facts and numbers. Lower-level TPSs and MISs generate much of the hard data provided by an EIS. Providing timely soft information to executive decision makers has been much more of a challenge. For example, deciding how to get the late-breaking news stories and information to the system in a format consistent with the EIS philosophy was a significant challenge to organizations. Many investment organizations, for example, subscribe to online services such as Dow Jones as a source for their stock market data. However, executives typically want to view only data that is aggregated and summarized in a user-friendly format. To get the right information into the hands of the executives, personnel or specially designed systems select appropriate information and translate the information into a user-friendly format.

The Internet has made it much easier to gather soft data to support executive decision making. Numerous Web-based news portals like **cnn.com**, **canada.com**, and **canoe.ca** allow users to easily customize news content so that information can be quickly summarized and evaluated by assistants for viewing by executives.

Architecture of an Executive Information System

The architecture of an EIS is shown in Figure 6.16. Inputs to an EIS are all internal data sources and systems; external data sources like Dow Jones and Bloomberg that contain information on competitors, financial markets, news (local, national, and international); and any other information deemed important by the executive in making day-to-day decisions. An EIS could "overload" the executive with too much information from too many sources. Systems designers use filtering software to customize the EIS so that only key information is provided in its most effective form to executives. Also, system designers provide output information to executives in a highly aggregated form, often using graphical icons to make selections and bar and line charts

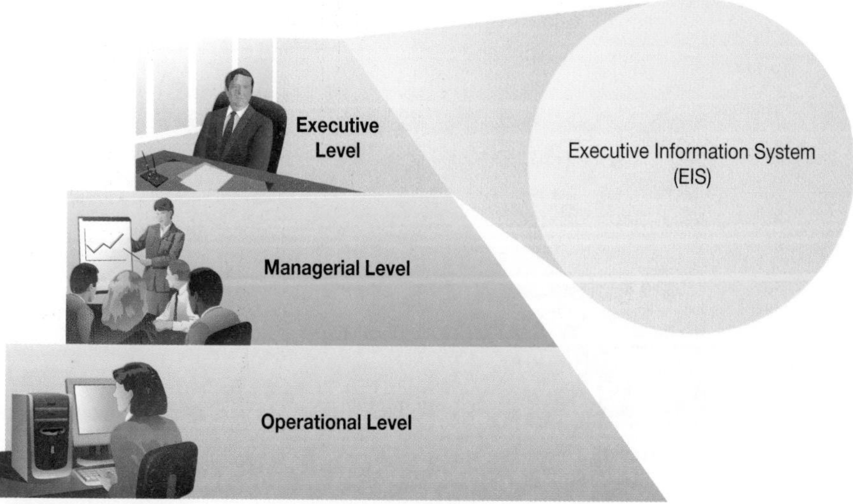

[**Figure 6.15** ➡ Executive information systems are used to improve executive-level decision making.]

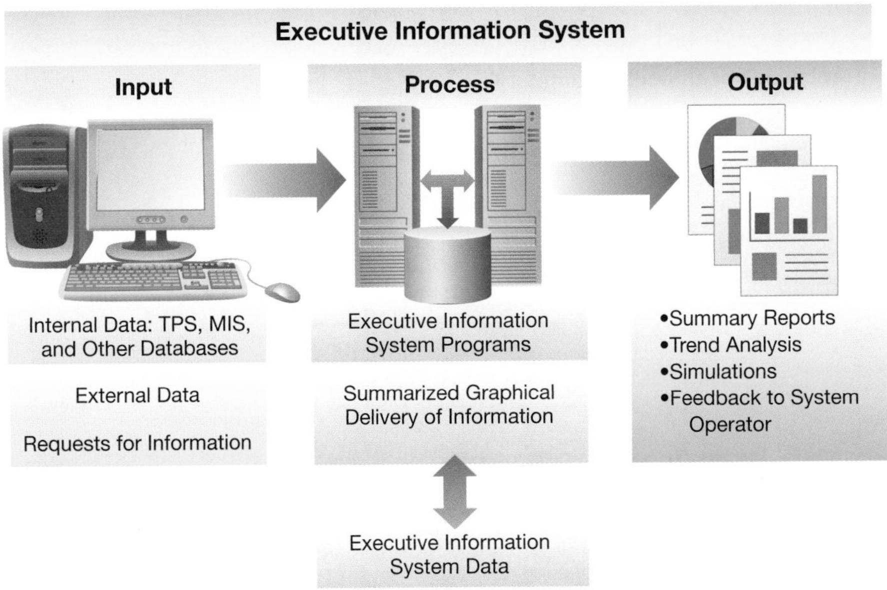

[Figure 6.16 ➥ Architecture of an executive information system using the basic systems model.]

to summarize data, trends, and simulations. Large monitors are often used to display the information so it is easier to view. The characteristics of an EIS are summarized in Table 6.4.

Although data are provided in a very highly aggregated form, the executive also has the capability to drill down and see the details if necessary. For example, suppose an EIS summarizes employee absenteeism and the system shows that today's numbers are significantly higher than normal. The executive can see this information in a running line chart, as illustrated in Figure 6.17. If the executive wants to understand why absenteeism is so high, a selection on the screen can provide the details behind the aggregate numbers, as shown in Figure 6.18. By drilling down into the data, the executive can see that the spike in absenteeism was centred in the manufacturing area. An EIS also can connect the data in the system to the organization's internal communication systems (e.g., electronic or voice mail) so the executive can quickly send a message to the appropriate managers to discuss solutions to the problem she discovered in the drill-down.

Figure 6.19 shows the relationship among operational, managerial, and executive levels of decision-making in the form of a pyramid. The operational level is shown at the base of the pyramid. Information systems at this level include transaction processing systems such as accounting and cash management systems. Transaction processing systems typically account for the largest and most costly component of an organization's IT infrastructure. The managerial level is shown in the middle of the pyramid. Information systems operating at this level analyze, aggregate, and summarize data from the operational level, and thus transform raw data into information useful for decision making. Management information systems include budgeting systems and production scheduling systems. The top of the pyramid is occupied by the executive level. Information systems at this level aggregate and present internal and external data, information, and knowledge in a format amenable to decision making by senior executives. Examples of executive information systems include strategic planning systems, R&D, and product development systems. As information systems move from the bottom to the top of

Inputs	Aggregate internal and external data
Processing	Summarizing, graphical interpreting
Outputs	Summary reports, trends, and simulations; feedback to system operator
Typical Users	Executive-level managers

[Table 6.4] ***Characteristics of an executive information system.***

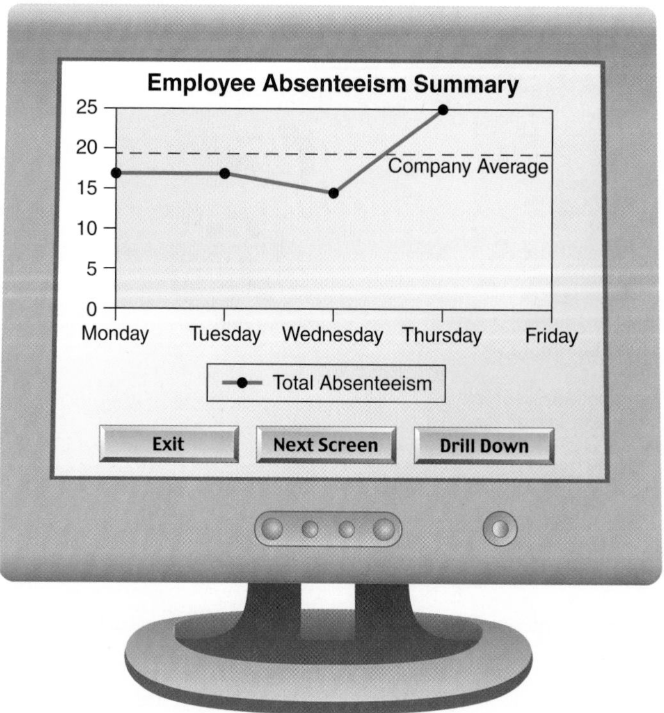

[Figure 6.17 ➥ Total employee absenteeism line chart.]

the pyramid, they become more sophisticated and complex. At the same time, however, the types of decisions that these systems support become more complicated and less structured. Because of this, and despite their sophistication, information systems at the executive level are comparatively less effective at supporting executive decisions than transaction processing systems are at supporting operational decisions.

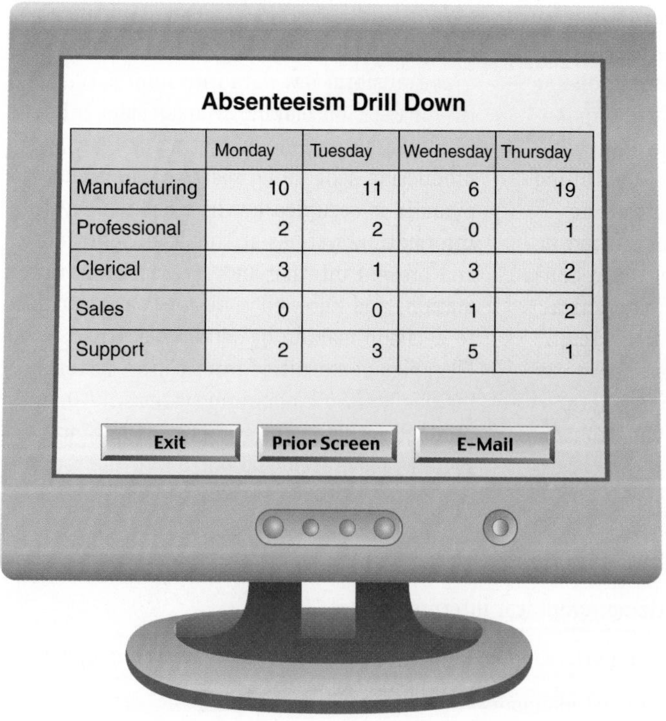

	Monday	Tuesday	Wednesday	Thursday
Manufacturing	10	11	6	19
Professional	2	2	0	1
Clerical	3	1	3	2
Sales	0	0	1	2
Support	2	3	5	1

[Figure 6.18 ➥ Drill-down numbers for employee absenteeism.]

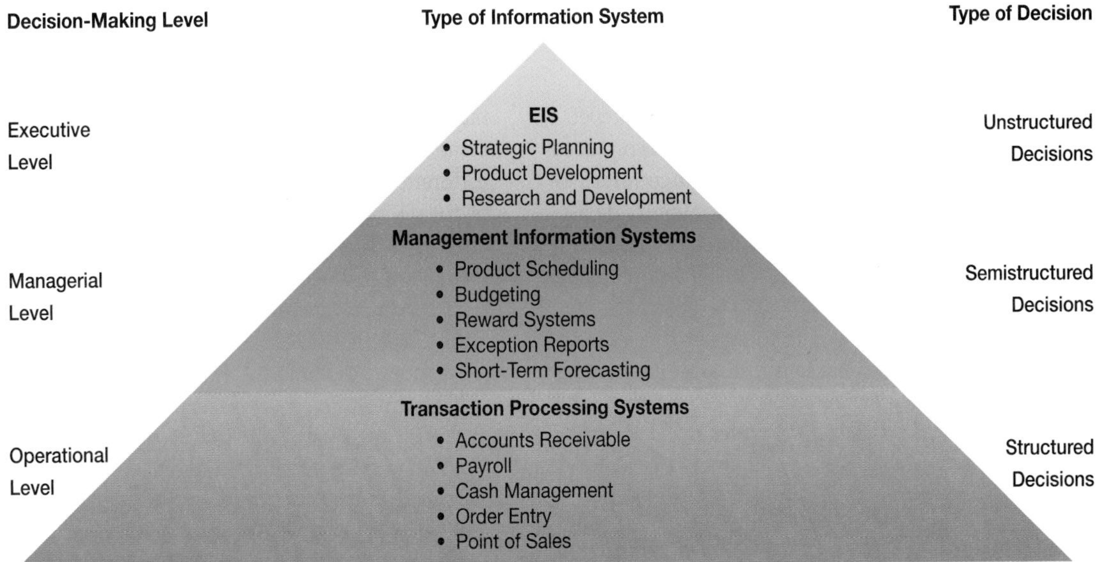

[Figure 6.19 ➥ Examples of information systems at each organizational level.]

INFORMATION SYSTEMS THAT SPAN ORGANIZATIONAL BOUNDARIES

The preceding section examined three general classes of information systems within specific hierarchical levels in the organization. There are also systems that span all levels of the organization (see Figure 6.20). Six types of boundary-spanning systems are:

- Decision support systems
- Expert systems
- Office automation systems
- Collaboration technologies
- Functional area information systems
- Global information systems

This section describes each of these in more detail. One additional form of organizational-spanning system, enterprise-wide information systems, is discussed in the following chapter.

Decision Support Systems

Decision support systems (DSS) are special-purpose information systems designed to support organizational decision making. A DSS is designed to support the decision making

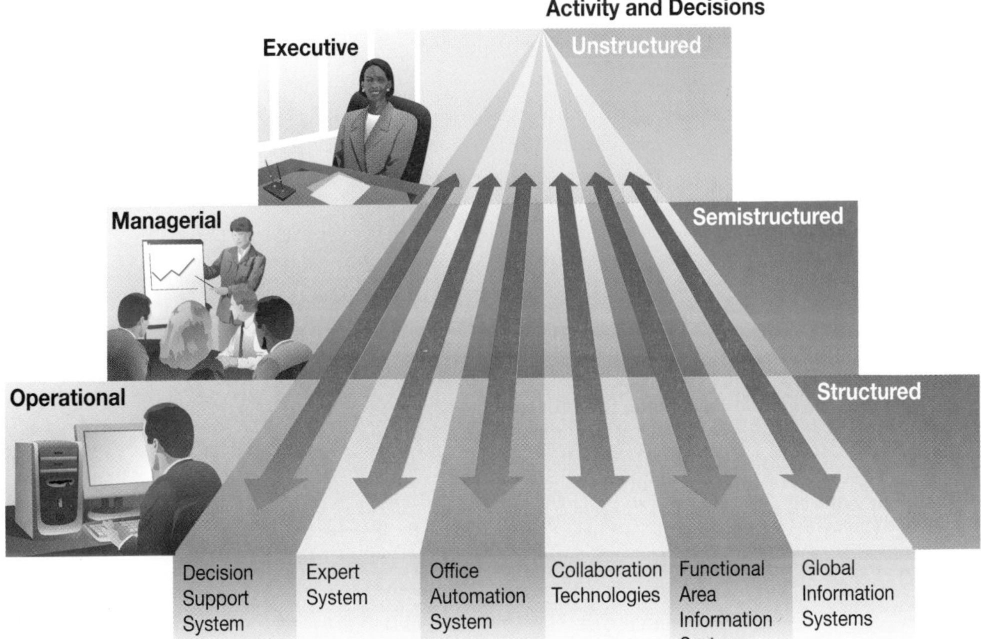

[Figure 6.20 ➥ Organizational boundary-spanning information systems.]

related to a particular recurring problem in the organization through the combination of hardware, software, data, and procedures. DSSs are typically used by managerial-level employees to help them solve semistructured problems such as sales and resource forecasting, yet a DSS can be used to support decisions at virtually all levels of the organization. With a DSS, the manager uses decision analysis tools such as Microsoft Excel—the most commonly used DSS environment—to either analyze or create meaningful data to support the decision making related to nonroutine problems. A DSS is designed to be an "interactive" decision aid, whereas people use the systems described previously—TPS, MIS, and EIS—primarily in a passive way by simply reviewing the output from the system.

A DSS augments human decision-making performance and problem solving by enabling users to examine alternative solutions to a problem via "what-if" analyses. ***What-if analysis*** allows you to make hypothetical changes to the data associated with a problem (e.g., loan duration, interest rate) and observe how these changes influence the results. For example, a cash manager for a bank could examine what-if scenarios of the effect of various interest rates on cash availability. Results are displayed in both textual and graphical formats.

Architecture of a Decision Support System

Like the architecture of all systems, a DSS consists of input, process, and output components as illustrated in Figure 6.21 (Sprague, 1980). Within the process component, models and data are utilized. The DSS uses ***models*** to manipulate data. For example, if you have some historical sales data, you can use many different types of models to create a forecast of future sales. One technique is to take an average of the past sales. The formula you would use to calculate the average is the model. A more complicated forecasting model might use time-series analysis or linear regression. See Table 6.5 for a summary of the models used to support decision making in organizations. Data for the DSS can come from many sources, including a TPS or MIS. The user interface is the way in which the DSS interacts with the user by collecting inputs and displaying output and results.

Table 6.6 summarizes the characteristics of a DSS. Inputs are data and models. Processing supports the merging of data with models so that decision makers can examine alternative solution scenarios. Outputs are graphs and textual reports. The next section discusses an example of a DSS that you might use at home.

Using a Decision Support System to Buy a Car

When you buy a new car, you must decide how to pay for it. Will you pay cash? Will you finance most or part of the purchase price? Organizations face the same decisions every day when purchasing supplies, raw materials, and capital equipment: should they pay cash

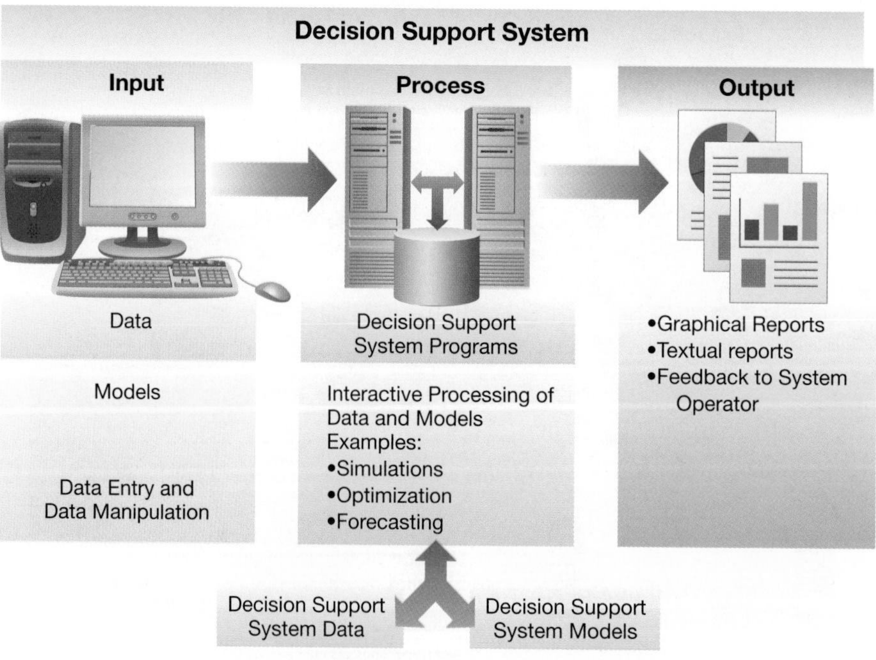

[**Figure 6.21** ➥ Architecture of a decision support system using the basic systems model.]

Area	Common DSS Models
Accounting	Cost analysis, discriminant analysis, break-even analysis, auditing, tax computation and analysis, depreciation methods, budgeting
Corporate Level	Corporate planning, venture analysis, mergers and acquisitions
Finance	Discounted cash flow analysis, return on investment, buy or lease, capital budgeting, bond refinancing, stock portfolio management, compound interest, after-tax yield, foreign exchange values
Marketing	Product demand forecast, advertising strategy analysis, pricing strategies, market share analysis, sales growth evaluation, sales performance
Personnel	Labour negotiations, labour market analysis, personnel skills assessment, employee business expense, fringe benefit computations, payroll and deductions
Production	Product design, production scheduling, transportation analysis, product-mix inventory level, quality control, learning curve, plant location, material allocation, maintenance analysis, machine replacement, job assignment, material requirement planning
Management Science	Linear programming, decision trees, simulation, project evaluation and planning, queuing, dynamic programming, network analysis
Statistics	Regression and correlation analysis, exponential smoothing, sampling, time-series analysis, hypothesis testing

[Table 6.5] ***Common DSS models for specific organizational areas.***

or finance these purchases? What information do they need to make this decision? The tools that organizations use are relatively simple and readily available to you. After going through the car-purchasing example, you will have a better understanding of how organizations use decision support technology to help their employees make day-to-day decisions.

Assume that the selling price of the car you decide to purchase is $20,000 and that you make a $2,500 down payment, leaving you with a monthly payment of about $400. You want to see how different financing options from your credit union might influence your monthly payments. As you can see from Table 6.7, interest rates vary depending upon the duration of your loan—lower rates for a shorter duration, higher rates for a longer duration. You now have all the information you need to analyze your financing options.

To conduct this analysis, you can use Microsoft Excel's loan analysis template (Excel uses the term *template* to refer to models). In this template, you enter the loan amount, annual interest rate, and length of the loan, as shown in Figure 6.22. With this information, the loan analysis DSS automatically calculates your monthly payment, the total amount paid, and the amount of interest paid over the life of the loan. You can change any of the input amounts to examine what-if scenarios—"What if I finance the loan over four years rather than five?" This is exactly how your college or university examines its financing options when it makes capital equipment purchases. Using this DSS tool, you decide to purchase your new vehicle over

Web Search

WEB SEARCH OPPORTUNITY

Auto insurance rates have risen steadily in Canada over the past five years. The Insurance Hotline uses a decision support system linked with external providers to calculate auto insurance quotes in eight provinces and two territories. Go to **www.insurancehotline.com/scripts/startquote.pl** to find out how much it would cost to insure your vehicle in a different area of Canada.

Inputs	Data and models; data entry and data manipulation commands (via user interface)
Processing	Interactive processing of data and models; simulations, optimization, forecasts
Outputs	Graphs and textual reports; feedback to system operator (via user interface)
Typical Users	Midlevel managers (although a DSS could be used at any level of the organization)

[Table 6.6] ***Characteristics of a decision support system.***

[Table 6.7] *Interest rates and loan duration.*

Interest Rate	Loan Duration
7% per year	3 years
10% per year	4 years
12% per year	5 years

five years (see Table 6.8 for a loan analysis summary). The next section discusses expert systems, a type of organizational information system that is closely related to decision support systems.

Expert Systems

An ***expert system (ES)*** is a special type of information system that uses reasoning methods based on knowledge about a specific problem domain in order to provide advice, much like a human expert. As the baby boom cohort enters retirement age, a vast amount of tacit knowledge will leave the workplace. Expert systems can be designed to capture that tacit knowledge, store it, and make it accessible to other members of the workforce. Expert systems are used to mimic human expertise by manipulating knowledge (understanding acquired through experience and extensive learning) rather than simply information (see Turban and Aronson, 2001, for more information). Human knowledge can be represented in an ES by facts and rules about a problem, coded in a form that can be manipulated by a computer. When you use an ES, the system asks you a series of questions, much as a human expert would. It continues to ask questions, and each new question is determined by your response to the preceding question. The ES matches the responses with the defined facts and rules until the responses point the system to a solution. A ***rule*** is a way of encoding knowledge, such as a recommendation, after collecting information from a user. Rules are typically expressed using an IF-THEN format. For example, a rule in an expert system for assisting with decisions related to the approval of automobile loans for individuals could be represented as follows:

> IF personal income is $50,000 or more,
> THEN approve the loan.

The most difficult part of building an ES is acquiring the knowledge from the expert and gathering and compiling it into a consistent and complete form capable of making recommendations. ESs are used when expertise for a particular problem is rare or expensive, such as in the case of a complex machine repair or medical diagnosis. ESs are also used when knowledge about a problem will be incomplete—in other words, when judgment will be used to make a decision with incomplete information, such as designing an investment portfolio or troubleshooting a computer system. Examples of the types of activities that can be supported by expert systems include the following:

- Medical diagnosis
- Mineral exploration

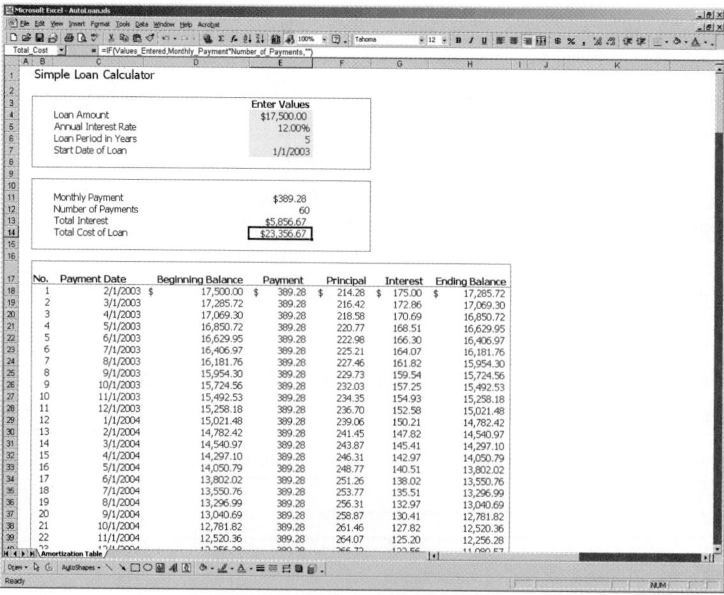

[Figure 6.22 ➡ Loan analysis template in Microsoft Excel.]

Source: Reprinted by permission from Microsoft Corporation.

Interest Rate	Loan Duration	Monthly Payment	Total Paid	Total Interest	Feasible Payment
7% per year	3 years	$540.35	$19,452.57	$1,952.57	No
10% per year	4 years	$443.85	$21,304.57	$3,804.57	No
12% per year	5 years	$389.28	$23,356.67	$5,856.67	Yes

[Table 6.8] ***Loan analysis summary.***

- Machine configuration
- Automobile diagnosis
- Financial planning
- Computer user help desk
- Software application assistance (for example, Microsoft Help "Wizards")

Architecture of an Expert System

As with other information systems, the architecture of an expert system can be described using the basic systems model (see Figure 6.23). Inputs to the system are questions and answers from the user. Processing is the matching of user questions and answers to information in the knowledge base. The processing in an expert system is called ***inferencing***, which consists of matching facts and rules, determining the sequence of questions presented to the user, and drawing a conclusion. The output from an expert system is a recommendation. The general

CAREER IMPLICATIONS

Marketing

According to a report by research firm IDC, 50 percent of large Canadian organizations say business analytics are something they're looking at and are considering a priority. Business analytics are sophisticated data analysis tools used by marketers to mine data and uncover useful information from large databases. Of those organizations that have invested in business analytics projects, 65 percent reported the experience as being positive. However, David Senf, IDC's manager of e-business operations, warned that figure isn't as impressive as it appears. "Take that with a grain of salt—the positive side was pretty broadly defined and the results were weighted more toward the middle," said Senf. Even those companies reporting a positive experience say there is still a need for improvement. Top challenges reported when dealing with business analytics projects included data quality, budgetary constraints, and managing expectations. "With 66 percent saying their warehoused data will be doubling over the next two years, data quality will become an increasingly important challenge," Senf said. "Good data can lead to better decision making, better alignment with stated business objectives, improved business intelligence, and improved visibility. However, there doesn't need to be 100 percent data quality, that's not achievable and not necessary," he said.

Intrawest, a Vancouver-based resort company operating ski and golf course resorts across North America, first started using business analytics three years ago and is reaping significant dividends. Kevin Konnar, director of data services for customer relationship management (CRM) at Intrawest, said the company looked to business analytics to increase its rate of return and grow revenues. The timing was right, with the company looking to leverage its existing customer base as it moves into new business areas. "We're seeing opportunity in the youth and the baby boomer markets, and we needed data to validate that perception," said Konnar. Intrawest, which is also expanding into areas like adventure travel, pulls customer data into its data warehouse from a variety of areas, from when someone buys a lift pass at a resort to when they e-mail a request for information through its Website. Konnar said the company is using those data to identify its top customers and give them a different level of service when they're contacted via e-mail, direct mail, or from the call centre. The company is also able to tailor any contact with a customer or a lead based on the customer's interests, matching them with the services the company offers. "It gives us a better idea of how to target the person with an offer that fits what they're looking for and are likely to be interested in," said Konnar. Since Intrawest started to use business analytics to support marketing, Konnar said campaign preparation time has dropped by 25 percent and campaign analysis time has dropped by 40 percent. As an example, should Intrawest see a large block of empty rooms coming up in the next month, it can mine the database to target people in the local region with last-minute offers to try and fill that space, he said.

[Adapted from Jeff Jedras, "IDC Study Shows Poor Data Quality in Business Analytics," *Computer Dealer News,* Vol. 19, No. 17 (November 21, 2003).]

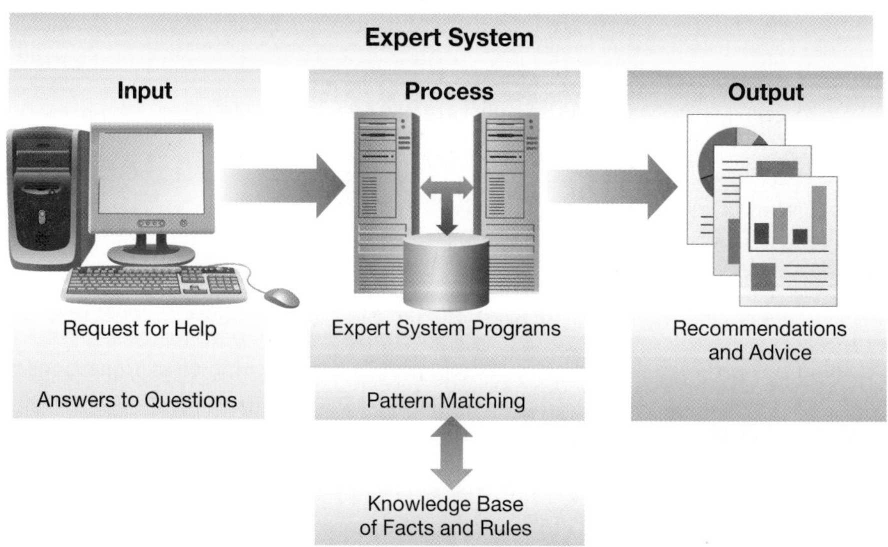

[Figure 6.23 ➡ Architecture of an expert system using the basic systems model.]

Web Search

WEB SEARCH OPPORTUNITY
Explore an online health expert system for common aliments at **http://easydiagnosis.com**.

characteristics of an expert system are summarized in Table 6.9.

An Expert System on the Web

Historically, expert systems have been standalone applications that ran on personal computers. With the advent of the Internet, EXSYS, a leading producer of expert system technology, provides an expert system development environment that allows expert systems to be delivered via the Web. At the EXSYS Website (**www.exsys.com**), you can test several demonstration expert systems. One system, for example, provides advice on selecting the right camcorder; another system that helps to troubleshoot and repair the Cessna Citation airplane—lighting and engine starting—is a particularly sophisticated example (see Figure 6.24). The system analyzes a user's response to several questions and presents specific repair or troubleshooting advice. This system also explains why it came to the conclusion that it did or why it is asking certain questions. This is a very powerful feature for training personnel and for helping users have confidence in the system's recommendation. Another site on the Web, called Expert System Builder (**www.esbuilder.com**), allows users to download software that can be used to develop customized expert systems.

Office Automation Systems

The ***office automation system (OAS)*** is the third type of system that spans organizational levels. OASs are a collection of software and hardware for developing documents, scheduling resources, and communicating. Document development tools include word processing and desktop publishing software, as well as the hardware for printing and producing documents. Scheduling tools include electronic calendars that help manage human and other resources, such as equipment and rooms. For example, "smart" electronic calendars can examine multiple schedules to find the first opportunity when all resources (people, rooms, equipment) are available. Communication technologies include electronic mail, voice mail, fax, videoconferencing, and groupware. Examples of the types of activities supported by an OAS include the following:

- Communication and scheduling
- Document preparation
- Analyzing and merging data
- Consolidating information

Architecture of an Office Automation System

The architecture of an OAS is shown in Figure 6.25. The inputs to an OAS are documents,

[Table 6.9] ***Characteristics of an expert system.***

Inputs	Request for help, answers to questions
Processing	Pattern matching
Outputs	Recommendation or advice
Typical Users	Midlevel managers (although an expert system could be used at any level of the organization)

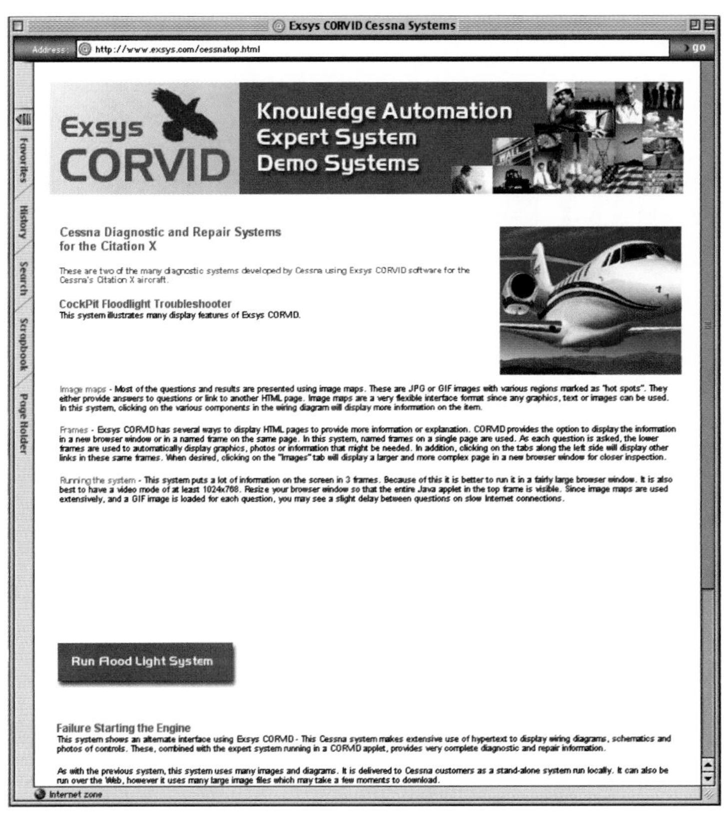

[**Figure 6.24** ➥ Web-based expert system for Cessna airplanes.]

Source: **www.exsys.com**.

schedules, and data. The processing of this information involves storing, merging, calculating, and transporting these data. Outputs include messages, reports, and schedules. The general characteristics of an OAS are summarized in Table 6.10.

BRIEF CASE

Expert System Used to Screen Graduate Program Applicants

Every year, graduate schools receive many applications; in the case of business schools, these applications can number in the thousands. A subset of these applications can be ruled out quickly if they fail to meet certain basic requirements. However, in most schools, all the applications must be dealt with by hand. The process of screening these applications is time consuming and resource intensive. In addition, annual turnover of committee members leads to a problem in establishing a consistent selection procedure. Acquired Intelligence Inc. (**www.aiinc.ca**), based in Victoria, B.C., developed an expert system for the University of Victoria's School of Public Administration to reduce the workload associated with graduate applications. The system was designed to screen applicants based on answers to a set of predefined questions. These questions were divided into three sections: university record, standard tests and rewards, and references. The system calculated a score based on the answers to these questions. This score was then used to compute a rating for the student. This rating was used to place the student into one of three categories: "accept," "discuss," or "reject." Since the number of applications was invariably greater than the number of available places, committee members only met to consider applications in the "accept" or "discuss" categories. This process saved committee members a substantial amount of time. A demo of this system is available at **www.aiinc.ca/demos/grad.shtml**.

Questions

1. As a student, what do you think about the system described above?
2. Are there limits to the use of expert systems? What types of decisions or situations are not appropriate for the use of expert systems?

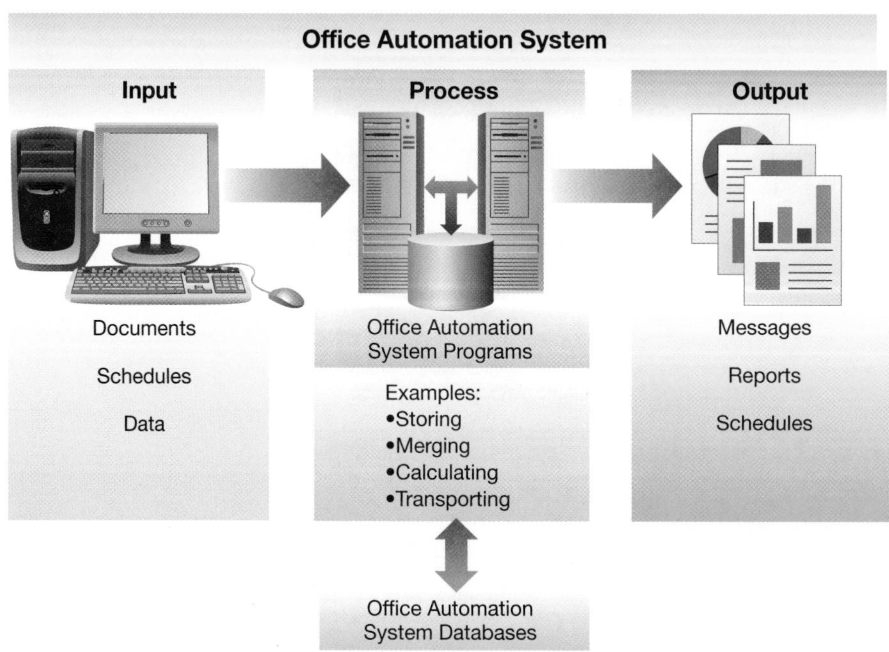

[**Figure 6.25** ➡ Architecture of an office automation system using the basic systems model.]

Automating Your Daily Calendar

A powerful tool for helping you get to class on time is Microsoft Outlook's Calendar. At the beginning of the semester, you can enter your class meeting times into the system. After they are entered, you can make these appointments recur automatically for as long as you like, as illustrated in Figure 6.26.

Additionally, you can set an alarm to notify you that class will begin in a few minutes. You can also use the alarm feature to remind you of meetings or appointments. Busy executives use this reminder feature to make sure they stay on schedule and do not miss any important meetings.

Collaboration Technologies

To be competitive, organizations constantly need to bring together the right combinations of people who, together, have the appropriate set of knowledge, skills, information, and authority to solve problems quickly and easily. Traditionally, organizations have used task forces, which are temporary work groups with a finite task and life cycle, to solve problems that cannot be solved well by existing work groups. Unfortunately, traditional task forces, like traditional organizational structures, cannot always solve problems quickly. Structure and logistical problems often get in the way of people trying to get things done quickly.

Organizations need flexible teams that can be assembled quickly and can solve problems effectively and efficiently. Time is of the essence. Membership on these ***virtual teams*** is fluid, with teams forming and disbanding as needed, with team size fluctuating as necessary, and with team members coming and going as they are needed. Employees may, at times, find themselves on multiple teams, and the life of a team may be very short. In addition, team members must have easy, flexible access to other team members, meeting contexts, and information. Think of these virtual teams as dynamic task forces.

Traditional office technologies, such as telephones and pagers, are of some use to members of virtual teams but are not well suited to support the types of collaboration described previously. Telephones and pagers are not useful for rich, rapid, multiple-person team collaboration. This technology is best suited for person-to-person communication. E-mail is a useful technology for teams, but it does not provide the structure needed for effective multiperson interactive problem solving. Companies need technologies that enable team members to interact through a

[Table 6.10]
Characteristics of an office automation system.

Inputs	Documents, schedules, data
Processing	Storing, merging, calculating, transporting
Outputs	Messages, reports, schedules
Typical Users	All organizational personnel

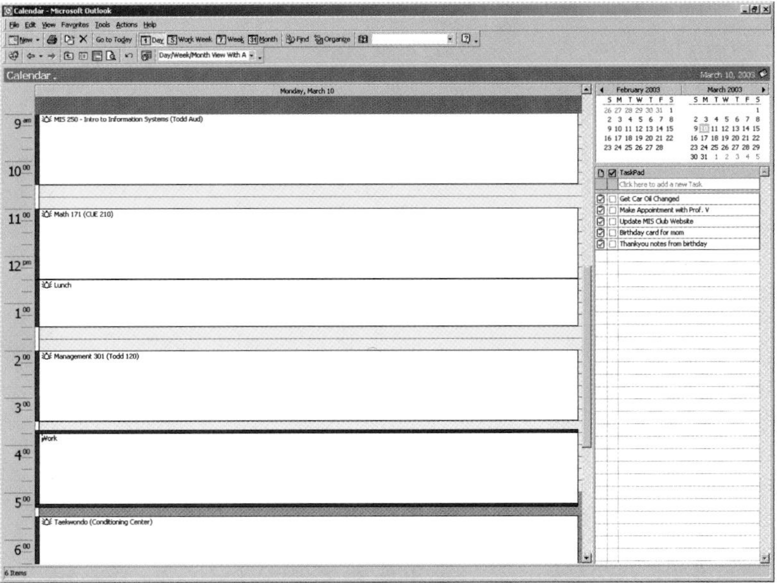

[**Figure 6.26** ➥ Coordinating a schedule in the Microsoft Outlook Calendar.]

Source: Reprinted by permission from Microsoft Corporation.

set of media either at the same place and time or at different times and in different locations, with structure to aid in interactive problem solving and access to software tools and information. A number of technologies, described in the following sections, fit the bill.

Videoconferencing

In the 1960s, at Disneyland and other theme parks and special events, the picturephone was first being demonstrated to large audiences. The phone company estimated that we would be able to see a live picture with our phone calls in the near future. It took another 30 years, but that prediction has come true within many organizations. Many organizations are conducting ***videoconferencing,*** and the demand for videoconferencing equipment is growing quickly. For example, sales for

CAREER IMPLICATIONS

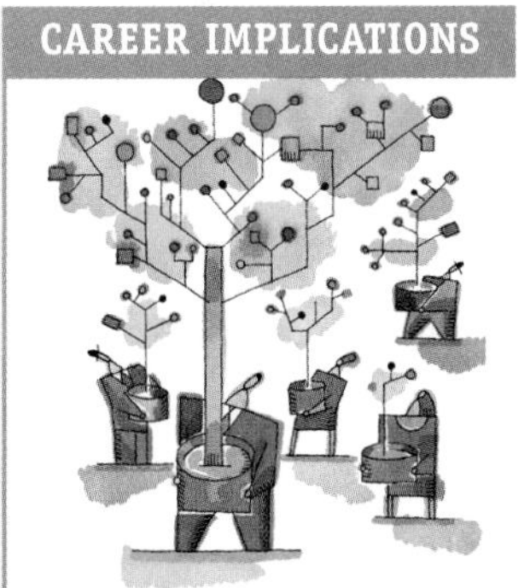

Operations Management

Expert systems were introduced in the mid-1980s and promised to "capture the expertise of skilled humans and then codify that expertise into a program." However, in spite of this hype, expert systems never reached their full potential and were often discarded after being implemented companywide. Incompatibility with a company's overall environment, along with requirements of experts to operate it, were cited as some of the primary reasons for an expert system's failure. However, after many years, expert systems are slowly growing in prominence. In the current age, expert systems are integrated into and embedded within many computer products. A new type of expert system, called online expert systems, is increasingly being used by organizations. Ebara Manufacturing is a Japanese pump manufacturer that specializes in several different kinds of pumps for a wide variety of industries. In the traditional system, the customers of Ebara would just request a pump, and the sales personnel in the company would have to figure out what kind of pump would be suitable for them. This system worked initially; however, as Ebara's product range increased and the products became more sophisticated, it became difficult for the company's employees to choose the most appropriate pump for a client. This caused problems for managing inventories and scheduling production. The company found the solution in an online expert system. The system now takes customers through a series of questions. Based on their responses to the questions (which primarily capture the customers' needs), the expert system decides on the appropriate product, often in less than a minute, cutting down on transaction time and increasing customer service. If you choose a career in operations management, you may find expert systems to be a valuable tool.

[Adapted from Fred Hapgood, "Embedded Logic: Overhyped, Then Much Maligned, Expert Systems Find Their Niche Inside Web Applications," *CIO Magazine* (May 1, 2000). **http://www.cio.com**.]

PictureTel, a leading videoconferencing company, grew from US$37 million in total revenue in 1990 to almost US$500 million in revenue in 2002. Figure 6.27 shows a videoconference system from PictureTel.

Stand-alone videoconferencing products are relatively large, expensive units (approximately US$20,000 and up) that have video quality similar to that of broadcast television and are used primarily to connect groups of people.

Desktop videoconferencing represents a second generation of video communication that has been enabled by the growing power of processors powering personal computers. A desktop system usually comprises a fast personal computer, a small camera (often with fixed focus, though zooming and panning features are available), a speaker telephone or separate microphone, videoconferencing software, and a special video board installed inside the computer. Using the Internet or a high-speed phone line, desktop videoconferencing is a much less expensive option than stand-alone videoconferencing, but the quality of the video and audio is not as good. For example, for under $150 you can purchase one of a number of cameras, such as a QuickCam, which plugs directly into the USB port on your personal computer (see Figure 6.28). You can then use desktop videoconferencing software, such as Microsoft's NetMeeting, available for free from Microsoft's Website, and conduct desktop videoconferencing sessions with friends, family, and colleagues through the Internet. For the audio portion, you need a multimedia PC with a sound card and speakers. You speak into the microphone plugged into your sound card and hear other people through the speakers that are plugged into your sound card.

Groupware

The term ***groupware*** refers to a class of software that enables people to work together more effectively. Lotus Development (now part of IBM) put groupware in the mainstream when it introduced the Notes software product in 1989. In recent years, many new groupware products have emerged, several of which work through or with the Internet. One industry sector that has come to rely on groupware products quite a bit is consulting. Chicago-based Accenture uses Notes as the basis for its internal information management system that enables consultants to exchange data with each other. With well over 30,000 people now working for the company all over the world in different time zones, it is very difficult to locate and contact the experts within the company for advice. All the large consulting firms are experiencing this problem and are using groupware like Lotus Notes or Livelink, from Canada's Open Text Corporation, to help solve this problem (see Figure 6.31 on page 198).

Electronic Meeting Software

Although many forms of groupware can be used to help groups work more effectively, one category of groupware focuses on helping groups have better meetings. These systems are commonly referred to as ***electronic meeting systems (EMSs)***. An EMS is essentially a collection of personal computers networked together with sophisticated software tools to help group members solve problems and make

[**Figure 6.27** ➥ PictureTel is a leading supplier of high-end videoconferencing technology.]

Source: © Steve Chenn/CORBIS.

[**Figure 6.28** ➥ Logitech's popular QuickCam.]

Source: Photo courtesy of Logitech.

COMING ATTRACTIONS

The Future of Desktop Videoconferencing

As computer components and fast connections to the Internet get less and less expensive, you can expect to see more desktop videoconferencing performed with personal computers. In fact, many notebook computers are now manufactured and sold with video cameras built in (see Figure 6.29). However, one of the most intriguing new technologies for desktop videoconferencing that we have seen is the omni-directional camera. Developed at Microsoft Research, the camera provides a 360-degree panoramic view, as well as motion- and sound-sensing capabilities (see Figure 6.30). This unit includes four tiny cameras and connects to a standard personal computer. Using a fast network connection, the unit can enable multiple people sitting around a table at one location to communicate with multiple people sitting around a table at another location. Each camera can sense sound and, if a person is talking, will focus on that person. The camera can also detect motion and can find and focus on moving people's faces, whether they are sitting at or standing around the table. This technology is in the research stage and is not currently being sold, although it works quite well. This type of videoconferencing unit opens up all kinds of possibilities and does so at a fraction of the cost of other videoconferencing units.

[Adapted from Rui, Gupta, and Cadiz, "Viewing Meetings Captured by an Omni-Directional Camera," Collaboration and Multimedia Systems Group, Microsoft Research, **http://www.research.microsoft.com/research/coet/Camera/chi2001/Omnidirectional/paper.doc**.]

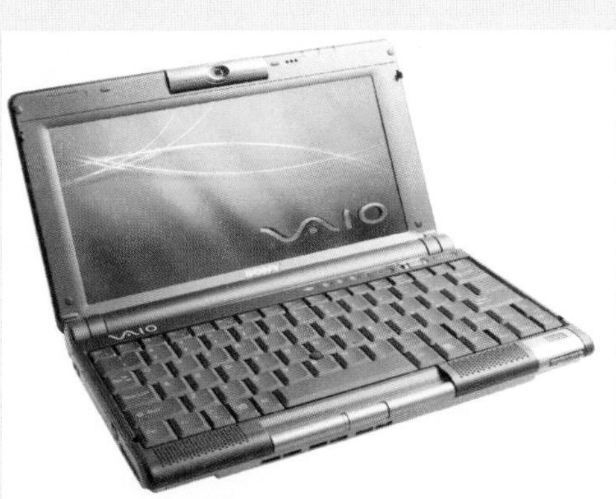

[Figure 6.29 ➥ The Sony Vaio Picturebook is one of many notebook computers that can be purchased with an integrated camera for both still pictures and video images.]

Source: © Sony Electronics.

[Figure 6.30 ➥ Microsoft Research has developed this omni-directional, motion- and sound-detecting camera for desktop videoconferencing in which multiple people are involved.]

decisions through interactive, electronic idea generation, evaluation, and voting. Some typical uses for an EMS include strategic planning sessions, marketing focus groups, brainstorming sessions for system requirements definition, business process reengineering, and quality improvement. EMSs have traditionally been housed within a dedicated meeting facility, as shown in Figure 6.32. However, EMSs are also being implemented with notebook computers so that the systems can be taken on the road. Additionally, Web-based implementations are supporting distributed meetings in which group members access the EMS software from their computers in their offices or from home. While EMS and related software have been around for quite some time, organizations are still discovering new and useful ways to use these tools to support e-meetings and other forms of group work.

Functional Area Information Systems

Functional area information systems are cross-organizational-level information systems designed to support a specific functional area (see Figure 6.33). These systems may be any of the types described previously—TPS, MIS, EIS, DSS, ES, and OAS. A functional area represents a discrete area of an organization that focuses on a specific set of activities. For example, people in the marketing function focus on the activities that promote the organization and its products in a way that attracts and retains customers. People in accounting and finance focus on managing

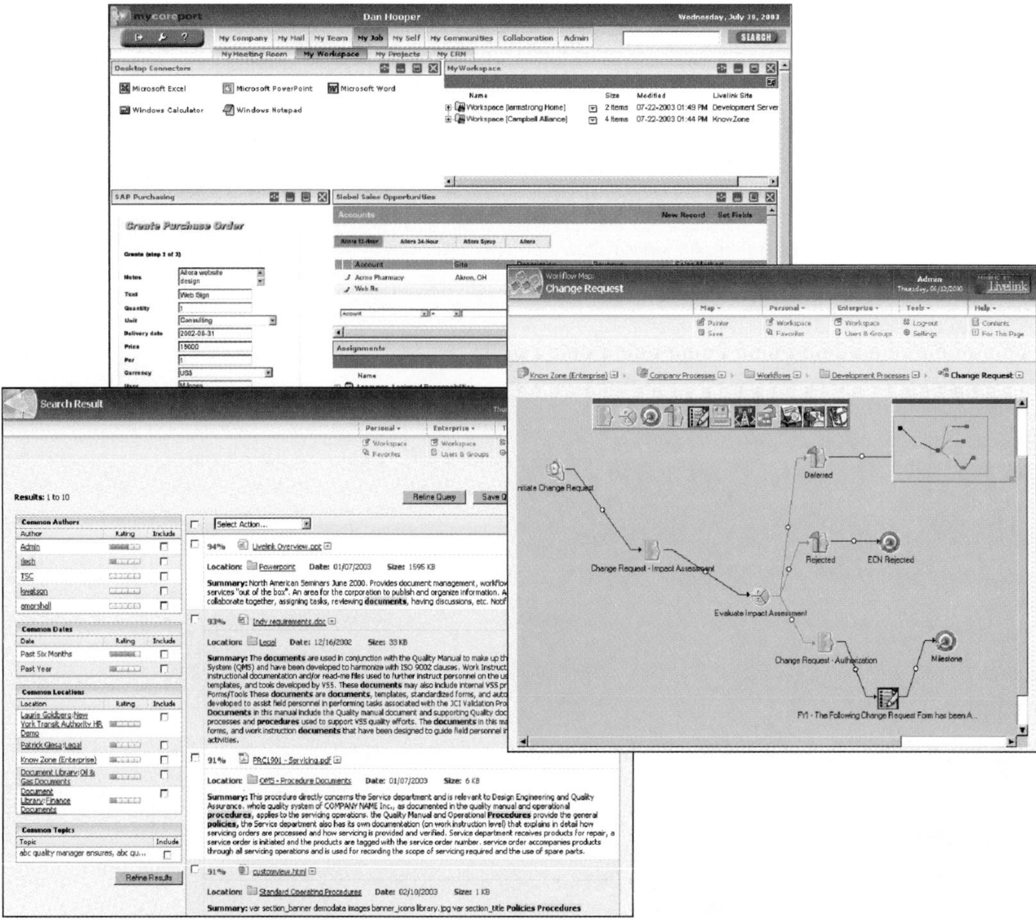

[Figure 6.31 ➥ Livelink Enterprise Server® is collaboration and content management software from Open Text Corp., based in Waterloo, Ontario.]

Source: Courtesy of Open Text.

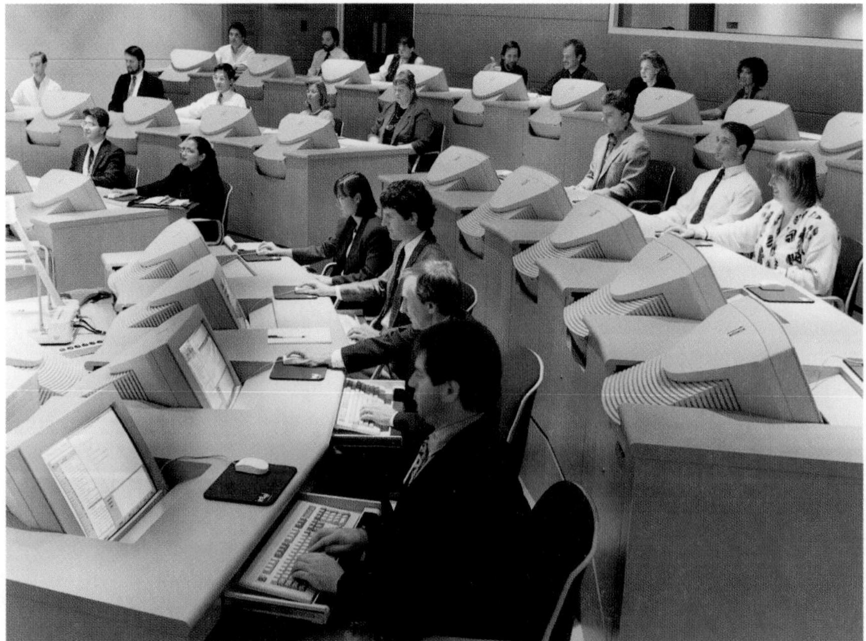

[Figure 6.32 ➥ A computer-supported meeting facility, complete with networked PCs and electronic meeting system software.]

Source: Courtesy of Ventanna Medical Systems Inc.

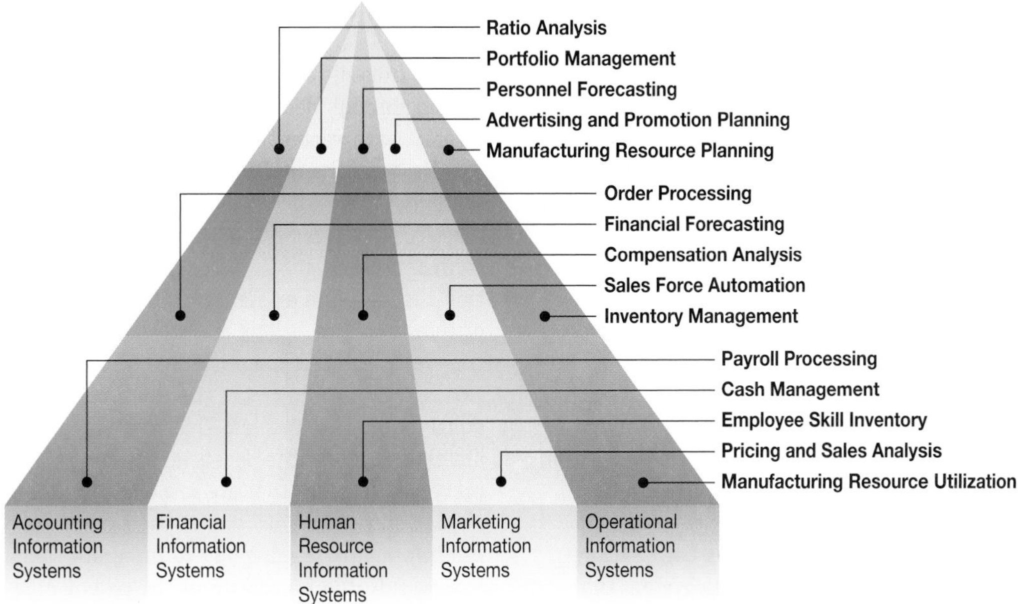

[Figure 6.33 ➥ Functional area information systems.]

and controlling the organization's capital assets and financial resources. Table 6.11 lists various organizational functions, describes the focus of each one, and lists examples of the types of information systems used in each functional area.

Global Information Systems

Organizations use a variety of system configurations in order to manage global operations more effectively. For example, Nestlé, one of the world's largest food producers, is considered one of the world's largest global companies,

[Table 6.11] ***Organizational functions and representative information systems.***

Functional Area	Information System	Examples of Typical Systems
Accounting and Finance	Systems used for managing, controlling, and auditing the financial resources of the organization	▮ Inventory management ▮ Accounts payable ▮ Expense accounts ▮ Cash management ▮ Payroll processing
Human Resources	Systems used for managing, controlling, and auditing the human resources of the organization	▮ Recruiting and hiring ▮ Education and training ▮ Benefits management ▮ Employee termination ▮ Workforce planning
Marketing	Systems used for managing new-product development, distribution, pricing, promotional effectiveness, and sales forecasting of the products and services offered by the organization	▮ Market research and analysis ▮ New product development ▮ Promotion and advertising ▮ Pricing and sales analysis ▮ Product location analysis
Production and Operations	Systems used for managing, controlling, and auditing the production and operations resources of the organization	▮ Inventory management ▮ Cost and quality tracking ▮ Materials and resource planning ▮ Customer service tracking ▮ Customer problem tracking ▮ Job costing ▮ Resource utilization

with over 500 factories and operations in more than 70 countries. According to Roche (1992), firms like Nestlé, which are operating in multiple nations, can have five distinct types of global information systems: 1) international information systems, 2) transnational information systems, 3) multinational information systems, 4) global information systems, and 5) collaborative information systems (see Table 6.12). We describe each in this section.

International information systems are a general class of information systems that support transactions that cross national boundaries. In other words, these systems support transactions that may originate in one nation and end in another nation. These types of systems can have either a centralized or a decentralized structure. Xerox Corporation uses a centralized information system that keeps track of all its copier machines that are placed in different customer locations around the world. This way, it maintains strong control over all maintenance and billing issues regarding its copier machines. ***Transnational information systems***, on the other hand, are not specific to any country or any particular organization. They exist as separate entities and as an international "transactional" space allowing people from different parts of the world to conduct transactions simultaneously. An example of such an information system is the foreign exchange systems that allow traders from different parts of the world (connected through decentralized networks) to interact with each other.

Next are the ***multinational information systems***, often used by multinational companies. These information systems act as a loose confederacy of various different local information systems. The existence of different types of rules and regulations on international data transfer and telecommunications has made this type of network very popular among multinational companies. This way, companies are able to retain the decentralized local data processing centres that are responsive to local needs and regulations, and at the same time use information technology to integrate them loosely into the framework of the parent organization. Up until a few years ago, Nestlé had such an information system structure. It had more than 140 financial systems that were being used around the world. However, the increasing globalization of the market and the recent advances in telecommunications and networks has caused a transition from multinational information systems to ***global information systems***. Such networks are used especially when a single transaction requires the input of data from multiple data centres

[Table 6.12] ***Types of global information systems.***

Type of Information System	Definition	Example
International Information System	System that supports transactions that may originate in one nation and end in another nation	Xerox's copier machine tracking system
Transnational Information System	International "transactional" space allowing people from different parts of the world to conduct transactions simultaneously	Foreign-exchange systems that allow traders from different parts of the world to interact with each other
Multinational Information System	A loose confederacy of various local information systems	Nestlé's 140 financial systems used at different locations in the world
Global Information System	Centralized network with an even distribution of integrated applications to all the nations	General Motors global inventory management system that consolidates all inventory information from around the world
Collaborative Information System	System that integrates different applications but is not specific to any given user	The international airline reservation systems funded jointly by many airline companies

CAREER IMPLICATIONS

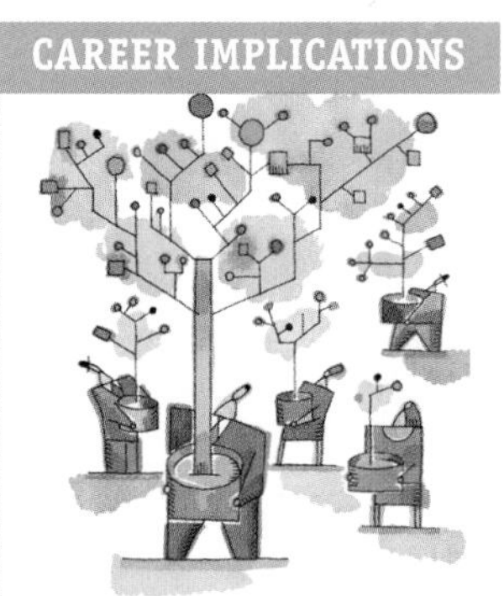

Human Resource Management

Organizations often use videoconferencing as a substitute for face-to-face interaction, especially where organizational members are not located in the same place. However, one of the primary problems most companies face related to videoconferencing is the time needed for system setup. Consequently, vendors of videoconferencing equipment are working on a new generation of products that are both easy to use and easy to set up. For example, new products from Sony have a built-in Ethernet port and software that enables users to connect to them from a remote computer. Additionally, the systems can be operated and maintained remotely through an Internet browser–based control centre. Once a meeting has been scheduled, meeting reminders are sent automatically to participants via e-mail. Also, before the start of the meeting, the videoconferencing system calls up the other participating devices. This way, the system is ready to start when the users arrive. The system also allows pictures and graphics to be integrated easily into the meeting. Ease of configuration and use is the trend for all types of information technology devices. As a result, videoconferencing is becoming very popular in a variety of human resource management contexts, including executive training and employee recruitment. In fact, no matter what career you pursue, it is likely that videoconferencing will be a valuable tool for you in all types of meeting situations. The good news is that you will be able to use videoconferencing easily, without frustration or the need for a technology guru.

[Adapted from **www.sel.sony.com/news**.]

located across more than one nation. These networks are usually centralized, and there is an even distribution of integrated applications to all the nations. As a result, data can be accessed irrespective of its location. After some major consolidation efforts, Nestlé has moved toward a global information system, namely through the implementation of an enterprise-wide information system (see Chapter 7). It has cut down its number of financial systems to just a few, with the objective of relying on just one in thefuture.

Finally, there are the ***collaborative information systems*** that integrate different applications but are not specific to any given user. For example, international airline reservation systems such as Galileo or Apollo have been funded by different airline companies and allow a multitude of airlines and travel agents to execute transactions, irrespective of their geographic location. These systems support the operational collaboration of major airline companies and travel agents.

GLOBAL PERSPECTIVE

Managing Human Resources in a Global Organization

There are several things you can do to improve the management of human resources in global organizations. First, it is important to hire individuals who are experienced in working in cross-cultural teams, who can speak different languages, and who have the necessary cultural sensitivity to empathize with other cultures. In addition to the general IS staff, it is also important to hire the proper IS leader or CIO. Global companies argue that the ideal quality required for a CIO is the ability to understand the global strategies of the company, and at the same time be able to collaborate successfully with the regional offices to implement those global strategies. Beyond personnel, the organizational reward system should be designed to reward individuals for their global initiatives, rather than base rewards solely on the local information systems' goals within the organization. Additionally, the organizational culture needs to be modified to fit the needs of local employees. For example, Fujitsu recently is making a breakthrough in the international market (especially in Internet and multimedia products) after years of overseas failure. To better deal with these new markets, it has changed its culture significantly to fit the local needs. There has been a relaxation in the strict Japanese standards of dress and conduct, introduction of flexible working hours, and the hiring of young, talented individuals representing a diverse set of cultures. Finally, the organization as a whole should also be extremely sensitive to the various cultural issues and political problems that exist between people from different countries when they are involved in cross-cultural IS operations. Such sensitivity and awareness can be developed through careful and in-depth research and also by having a diverse mix of employees representing different cultures.

CAREER IMPLICATIONS

Accounting and Finance

Avon Products was founded more than 100 years ago, and from the time of its initiation it focused on a direct-sales strategy whereby its sales force went from door to door in parts of the United States. However, in recent times, due to the emergence of new markets across the globe, the company has followed an expansion strategy. According to the company executives, the implementation of a globally integrated financial management system along with high-quality analysis and reporting tools has significantly helped in its expansion strategy. The company required an integrated and standardized financial management system that could serve as an operation management tool, not merely as a tool for reporting the company's profit and loss. At the same time, since the company was expanding into unknown markets, the tool had to be flexible enough to be easily customizable for local requirements. After evaluating many products, Avon chose Integrated Accounting System by CODA (based in Harrogate, England, and having U.S. headquarters in Manchester, New Hampshire) to build the Avon Standard Accounting System (ASAS), which is a global financial reporting system. Initially implemented at 40 sites around the globe, the tool helps to capture critical information that helps executives make strategic decisions. Later, the tool was connected to data warehouses to store financial and operational information, both at a global and at a local level. The global financial system allows the company to deal easily with the different tax and accounting requirements existing around the globe. At the same time, the system enables executives to develop standardized interfaces, which can be easily modified for the many overseas regional sites based on local needs and differences related to language, culture, currency rates, and tax and accounting regulations.

[Adapted from Peter Fabris, "Global Market Scents," *CIO Magazine* (September 1, 1995). **www.cio.com**.]

KEY POINTS REVIEW

1. **Describe the characteristics that differentiate the operational, managerial, and executive levels of an organization.** At the operational level of the firm, the routine day-to-day business processes and interactions with customers occur, and information systems are designed to automate repetitive activities, such as sales transaction processing. Operational-level managers such as site supervisors make day-to-day decisions that are highly structured and recurring. At the managerial level of the organization, functional managers focus on monitoring and controlling operational-level activities and providing information to higher levels of the organization. Midlevel or functional managers focus on effectively utilizing and deploying organizational resources to achieve the strategic objectives of the organization. At this level, the scope of the decision usually is contained within the business function, is moderately complex, and has a time horizon of a few days to a few months. At the executive level of the organization, decisions are often very complex problems with broad and long-term ramifications for the organization. Executive-level decisions are often referred to as being messy or ill-structured because executives must consider the ramifications on the overall organization.
2. **Explain the characteristics of the three information systems designed to support each unique level of an organization: transaction processing systems, management information systems, and executive information systems.** Transaction processing systems (TPSs) are designed to process business events and transactions and reside close to customers at the operational level of the organization. These systems are used to automate repetitive information-processing activities to increase speed and accuracy and to lower the cost of processing each transaction—that is, to make the organization more efficient. Management information systems (MISs) reside at the managerial level and are designed to produce regular and ad hoc reports to support the ongoing, recurring decision-making activities associated with managing an entire business or a functional area within a business. These systems are used to help midlevel managers make more effective decisions. Executive information systems (EISs) are used to provide information to executives in a highly aggregate form so that information can be scanned quickly for trends and anomalies. Executives use these systems to provide a one-stop shop for a lot of their informational needs.
3. **Describe the characteristics of six information systems that span the organizational, managerial, and executive levels: decision support systems, expert systems, office automation systems, collaboration technologies, functional area information systems, and global information systems.** Decision support systems (DSS) support organizational decision making and are typically designed to solve a particular recurring problem in the organization. DSSs are most commonly used to support semi-structured problems that are addressed by managerial-level employees. A DSS is designed to be an interactive decision aid. An expert system (ES) is a special type of information system that uses knowledge within some topic area to solve problems or provide advice. Expert systems are used to mimic human expertise by manipulating knowledge (understanding acquired through experience and extensive learning) rather than simply information. ESs are used when expertise for a particular problem is rare or expensive. In this way, organizations hope to replicate the

human expertise more easily and inexpensively. Office automation systems (OASs) are technologies for developing documents, scheduling resources, and communicating. Collaboration technologies such as videoconferencing, groupware, and electronic meeting systems are used to support the communication and teamwork of virtual teams. Functional areas represent discrete areas of organizations and typically include accounting and finance, human resource management, marketing, and production and operations management. Functional area information systems are designed to support the unique requirements of specific business functions. Finally, global information systems are used to support international activities of global organizations. There are five distinct types of global information systems: 1) international information systems, 2) transnational information systems, 3) multinational information systems, 4) global information systems, and 5) collaborative information systems. Each type of global information system has distinct characteristics to best support a given international information-processing situation.

KEY TERMS

ad hoc report 182
batch processing 178
collaborative information system 201
decision support system (DSS) 187
desktop videoconferencing 196
drill-down report 182
electronic meeting system (EMS) 196
exception report 182
executive information system (EIS) 183
executive level 175
expert system (ES) 190
fully automated data entry 180
functional area information system 197
global information system 200
groupware 196
hard data 184
inferencing 191
international information system 200
key-indicator report 182
management information system (MIS) 180
managerial level 174
manual data entry 179
models 188
multinational information system 200
office automation system (OAS) 192
online processing 178
operational level 174
rule 190
scheduled reports 182
semiautomated data entry 180
semistructured decisions 175
soft data 184
source documents 178
structured decisions 174
transactions 177
transaction processing system (TPS) 177
transnational information system 200
unstructured decisions 176
videoconferencing 195
virtual teams 194
what-if analysis 188

REVIEW QUESTIONS

1. Compare and contrast the characteristics of the operational, managerial, and executive levels of an organization.
2. What is the difference between "hard" and "soft" data?
3. Describe the differences between online processing and batch processing. Give examples of each.
4. What are the three methods used for inputting data into a transaction processing system? Provide examples of each.
5. List three different types of reports and where or how the information from each is used.
6. How does a management information system differ from a transaction processing system in terms of purpose, target users, capabilities, and so forth?
7. Describe and give examples of two types of data entry.
8. How does an executive information system "drill down" into the data?
9. What are the six types of information systems that traditionally span the boundaries of organizational levels?
10. Explain the purpose of a model within a decision support system.
11. What is the difference between a decision support system and an expert system?
12. What is groupware, and what are the different types?
13. Compare and contrast stand-alone videoconferencing and desktop videoconferencing.
14. Provide some examples of functionally specific information systems and needs within an organization.
15. Define and contrast five types of global information systems.

SELF-STUDY QUESTIONS

Answers are at the end of the Problems and Exercises.

1. At the ________ level of the organization, functional managers (e.g., marketing managers, finance managers, manufacturing managers, and human resources managers) focus on monitoring and controlling operational-level activities and providing information to higher levels of the organization.
   A. operational
   B. managerial
   C. organizational
   D. executive
2. Examples of the types of activities supported by management information systems include all of the following **except** ________.
   A. inventory management and planning
   B. manufacturing planning and scheduling
   C. financial management and forecasting
   D. sales and order processing

3. A(n) ________ report provides a summary of critical information on a recurring schedule.
   A. scheduled
   B. exception
   C. key-indicator
   D. drill-down

4. Examples of the types of activities that can be supported by expert systems include all of the following **except** ________.
   A. payroll calculations
   B. financial planning
   C. machine configuration
   D. medical diagnosis

5. A supervisor's decision when to reorder supplies or how best to allocate personnel for the completion of a project is an example of a(n) ________ decision.
   A. structured
   B. unstructured
   C. automated
   D. delegated

6. The types of boundary-spanning systems include all of the following except ________.
   A. decision support systems
   B. resource planning systems
   C. office automation systems
   D. expert systems

7. ________ processing of transactions provides immediate results to the system operator or customer.
   A. Online
   B. Batch
   C. Fully automated
   D. Semiautomated

8. A marketing manager for Nike may have a(n) ________ system that contrasts sales revenue and marketing expenses by geographic region so that she can better understand how regional marketing for the "Tiger Woods Golf" promotions are performing.
   A. transaction
   B. expert
   C. office automated
   D. management information

9. In a(n) ________ data entry system, a data capture device such as a grocery store checkout scanner speeds the entry and processing of the transaction.
   A. manual
   B. semiautomated
   C. fully automated
   D. expert

10. A(n) ________ information system is defined as a loose confederacy of various different local information systems.
   A. international
   B. multinational
   C. collaborative
   D. transnational

PROBLEMS AND EXERCISES

1. Match the following terms with the appropriate definitions:
   ____ Operational level
   ____ Transactions
   ____ Virtual teams
   ____ Source document
   ____ Online processing
   ____ Management information system
   ____ Expert system
   ____ Inferencing
   ____ Transaction processing system
   ____ Decision support system
   a. An information system designed to process day-to-day business event data at the operational level of an organization
   b. A special-purpose information system designed to mimic human expertise by manipulating knowledge (understanding acquired through experience and extensive learning) rather than simply information
   c. The bottom level of an organization, where the routine day-to-day interaction with customers occurs
   d. A special-purpose information system designed to support organizational decision making primarily at the managerial level of an organization
   e. Processing of information immediately as it occurs
   f. Repetitive events in organizations that occur as a regular part of conducting day-to-day operations
   g. An information system designed to support the management of organizational functions at the managerial level of the organization
   h. A document created when a business event or transaction occurs
   i. The matching of facts and rules, as well as determining the sequence of questions presented to the user, and drawing a conclusion
   j. Teams forming and disbanding as needed, with team size fluctuating as necessary, and with team members coming and going as they are needed

2. Do you feel that, as much as possible, transaction processing systems should replace human roles and activities within organizations? Why or why not? How much cost savings will there be if these humans are still needed to run the systems? What if you were the person being replaced? Will all errors necessarily be eliminated? Why or why not?

3. Imagine that your boss has asked you to build an inventory transaction system that would enable the receiving and shipping clerks to enter inventory amounts for purchases and sales, respectively. Discuss the pros and cons of building this system as an online processing system versus a batch processing system. Which would you recommend to your boss?

4. The national sales manager for ABC Corp. is interested in purchasing a software package that will be capable of providing

"accurate" sales forecasts for the short term and long term. She has asked you to recommend the best type of system for this purpose. What would you recommend? Do you have any reservations about such a system? Why or why not?

5. Visit **http://moneycentral.msn.com/investor/calcs/n_expect/main.asp** on the Web to determine your life expectancy using a decision support system. What did you learn? Is there a difference between life expectancies for different genders? If you browse MSN Money, what other interesting stuff do you find?

6. Interview a top-level executive within an organization with which you are familiar or within one of the companies from the Brief Cases. Determine the extent to which the organization utilizes executive information systems. Does this individual utilize an EIS in any way? Why or why not? Which executives do utilize an EIS?

7. Based on your experiences with transaction processing systems (in everyday life and/or in the workplace), which ones use online processing and which use batch processing? Do these choices fit the system, the information, and the environment? Would you make any adjustments? Why or why not?

8. Using any program you choose, or using the Website **www.moneycentral.com**, find or create a template that you could use in the future to determine monthly payments on car or home loans. Compare your template with the one at **http://en.autos.sympatico.msn.ca/loancalc/newloan.aspx?src=Home&pos=My2**. Would you have categorized the program you used to create this template as a decision support system before doing this exercise?

9. Go to Expert System Builder **www.esbuilder.com** and download a copy of the software. Use the esbuilder application to develop your own simple expert system. Perhaps design a system to predict hobbies or career choices. Note that the system will conform to the rules that you specify—it will assume that you are the expert.

10. Choose an organization with which you are familiar that utilizes office automation systems. Which systems does it use? Which functions have been automated, and which have not been? Why have some functions not been automated? Who decides which office automation system to implement?

11. Have you seen or used ad hoc, exception, key-indicator, and/or drill-down reports? What is the purpose of each report? Who produces and who uses the reports? Do any of these reports look or sound familiar from your work experience?

12. Interview an IS manager within an organization at a university or workplace. Of the three categories of information systems—transaction processing, management, and executive—which do people utilize most in this organization? Why? Have any of these areas experienced an increase or decrease in the last few years? What predictions does this manager have regarding the future of traditional information systems? Do you agree? Prepare a 10-minute presentation to the class on your findings.

13. Describe how various systems described in this chapter might enable workers to work from home rather than at the company's office. What technologies in particular might these workers utilize and how? Will companies look favourably on this use of technology? Why or why not?

14. Interview an IS professional, and ask about travel and assignments outside Canada. Do global assignments contribute to promotion? What is the length of an average assignment?

ANSWERS TO THE SELF-STUDY QUESTIONS

1. B 2. D 3. C 4. A 5. A 6. B 7. A 8. D 9. B 10. B

Case 1: *Canadian Specialty Photography Retailer Says It Will Develop a Clearer Picture of What's Going on in Its Stores through Business Intelligence Software*

Black Photo Corporation (Black's) is Canada's largest specialty photography retailer, with over 181 stores across the country. Most of these stores are small- or medium-sized retail outlets located in shopping malls. Each of these outlets generates sales data that must be aggregated and organized on a companywide basis. In order to facilitate the aggregation of this data across the company, Black's rolled out a series of online analytical processing (OLAP) tools developed by Cognos Incorporated. OLAP tools allow managers to access and analyze data in real time. In 2004, Black's implemented a series of OLAP cubes to facilitate basket analysis. OLAP cubes are multidimensional databases that hold data like a 3-D spreadsheet allowing different views of the data to be quickly displayed. Basket analysis is a process by which bundles of products purchased by customers (i.e., in a shopping basket) are analyzed for trends and patterns. This information can support decisions on product location, store layout, and shelf-space allocation. Basket analysis can also be used to help design in-store promotions. For example, if basket analysis shows that customers often purchase film and batteries together, then the two products might be bundled together at a special price or be placed near one another on a shelf.

The company was also hoping to track key performance indicators at the store level and roll out business intelligence for budgeting and planning to its finance department, according to Ron Short, Black's director of information systems and technology. Since it began using business intelligence to sort out its mass of data and provide more information to its vendor partners, Short said Black's has seen a 2,000-percent return on investment—an achievement that raised eyebrows among its senior managers. "No one believed our return on investment (ROI)," Short said, adding that deployment help from a consulting firm resulted in a 60-day turnaround on the project. "They were like, 'Yeah, right.'"

Part of that ROI can be attributed to a strategy whereby Black's charged the vendors who stocked its stores with product, like Pentax and Nikon, to access OLAP cubes containing a week's worth of sales data as a special service. Black's had originally only considered using the tools for internal forecasting analysis, but it soon became clear that vendors, too, might be interested in the data. "The vendors paid for this product," he said. Most of the photography vendors were surprised that Black's was willing to share its data, Short said, but the idea was to help all its business partners make better decisions in terms of product mix. Internally, Black's wanted to be able to offer its stores more timely access to reports, which previously took days or weeks to complete. There was also the issue of catering to individual report requests and customizing data, according to Short. The self-service capabilities of the OLAP cubes helped address that issue. Store managers could now access data at any time and organize it in any way they chose.

OLAP tools, basket analysis, and business intelligence software are all information systems designed to extract value from everyday transaction data. Transaction processing systems generate massive amounts of data, most of which is never used by management. These tools allow managers at different levels in the organization to access and perform analysis on this data in real time. "If you have 10 people sitting around a boardroom waiting for information, they all want it in 10 different ways," he said. "I don't even know what some of them do with the data, to be quite honest, but this puts it back on them." Short said Black's was focused on providing a "single view of the truth" by extracting the most reliable data from the company's mainframe computer. "You'd flip through some green screen to green screen," he said. "The data was there, but you just couldn't slice it down to what you needed."

[Adapted from Shane Schick, "Black's Takes Snapshot of Store Performance," *EDGE Magazine* (December 2003): 26–27.]

Discussion Questions:

1. What are some of the challenges that Black's faced in accessing and analyzing its transaction processing data?
2. What advantages did the new tools provide to Black's?
3. Of the different types of organizational information systems covered in this chapter, could any other type of information system solve Black's problems? Why or why not?
4. Which of the several advantages that the system provided was the most important? Why?

Case 2: *Ernst & Young Deploys Lotus Notes throughout Its Large, Global Enterprise*

Ernst & Young is one of the world's leading consulting organizations. Its mission is to help businesses around the world "identify and capitalize on business opportunities" (**www.ey.com**). It is a decentralized organization of some 130 national firms around the world that work together to provide seamless cross-border service to multinational businesses. It has over 70,000 employees in more than 650 locations. The company offers a wide range of solutions, including delivering leading-edge assurance, advisory, tax, and consulting services that help corporations achieve their business goals. Given the fact that it is such a large organization, one of the primary challenges the company faces is enabling the sharing of information and data among the company's tens of thousands of employees around the globe. The capability of its people to communicate, collaborate, and share knowledge—within local and multinational teams, within service lines, and across national boundaries—has become essential to maintaining and sharpening Ernst & Young's competitive edge in the global marketplace. In other words, the key to the success of this company lies in its ability to effectively manage and share information across the entire company. "We deliver our client solutions through multidisciplinary, and often multinational, teams working together in person or through connectivity to apply their combined skills and our organization's expertise to our clients' problems and needs. This is the core of our business," says John Whyte, CIO of Ernst & Young International.

The company began to search for a solution to take care of its information-sharing problem. The company's objective was to implement a stable infrastructure that would also provide quality service. After a lot of searching, the company finally decided to use a Lotus Notes infrastructure for messaging and sharing information and knowledge across the many member firms. Soon, Ernst & Young–member firms adopted Lotus Notes as their standard tool for collaborative working and knowledge management. This decision was made against a clean technology slate, so to speak; there were no legacy systems. Lotus Consulting helped the company in designing the internal Notes network and also provided system support, which included the assignment of a special Lotus Notes account manager, dedicated only to Ernst & Young. Within six months, member firms located in at least 12 countries in Asia-Pacific were making use of the Notes infrastructure and communicating and collaborating with each other through the system. These member firms were primarily connecting through the company's hub located in Singapore. Ernst & Young then introduced two new hubs, one in New Jersey and one in London. Within the next two years, there were over 100 Ernst & Young virtual teams communicating and interacting from locations around the world using their Domino/Notes Engagement Team Data Base to serve multinational clients. Even more teams were using Notes applications to manage projects and share work products and ideas within country boundaries. All but one country had migrated to Lotus Mail by the end of the second year—an outstanding achievement for a decentralized organization of Ernst & Young's size, geographical spread, and diversity. International e-mail traffic alone (that is, excluding in-country electronic messages, which, in fact, total even more) rose from 6,000 messages per month to 400,000 per month within a span of only one year. The number of e-mail messages rose to about 800,000 per month in three years. The effective implementation of the Notes infrastructure requirement was possible due to the excellent support of Lotus Consulting, which had taken the effort to satisfy the requirements of its client and help them at every step of the way.

"Notes enabled us to scale up to a global enterprise system that provides mission-critical connectivity among our people, within our teams, to our clients, and to internal and external knowledge stores," Whyte says.

Two years after Notes was implemented, Ernst & Young's worldwide revenues grew by 17 percent. Whyte says, "Some of that global growth is certainly due to being able to do work without barriers and have this high level of communication and knowledge-sharing capability."

Today, the company's focus is on making significant extensions to the existing system. The Notes infrastructure provides the company with the ability to build applications and add Internet/intranet capabilities without investing heavily in new software or hardware. Ernst & Young is now focusing on using the Internet along with the Notes/Domino messaging system and has already implemented the EYI InnerSpace, which is a global Domino-based intranet system.

[Adapted from "Success Story," **www.lotus.com/home.nsf/welcome/stories**; "Ernst and Young: Global Messaging and Knowledge Management Improve Consultancy Services," **www.lotus.com/home.nsf/welcome/stories**; and **www.ey.com**.

Discussion Questions

1. How are collaboration technologies and knowledge management useful to Ernst & Young?
2. How important is it to a firm such as Ernst & Young to use collaboration technologies such as Notes successfully? Why? How would it look if a leading IS/IT consultant were not deploying emerging technologies successfully?
3. Is the process of knowledge management using Notes useful only to consulting firms such as Ernst & Young? Why or why not?
4. What do you think is the role of the technology development and consulting firm in ensuring the successful implementation of an emerging technology within an organization?

Chapter 7

Preview

This chapter describes how companies are deploying enterprise-wide information systems to support and integrate their various business activities, to streamline and better manage interactions with customers, and to coordinate better with their suppliers in order to meet changing customer demands more efficiently and effectively.

After reading this chapter, you will be able to do the following:

1. Explain how organizations support business activities by using information technologies.
2. Describe what enterprise systems are and how they have evolved.
3. Explain the differences between internally and externally focused software applications.
4. Understand and utilize the keys to successfully implementing enterprise systems.

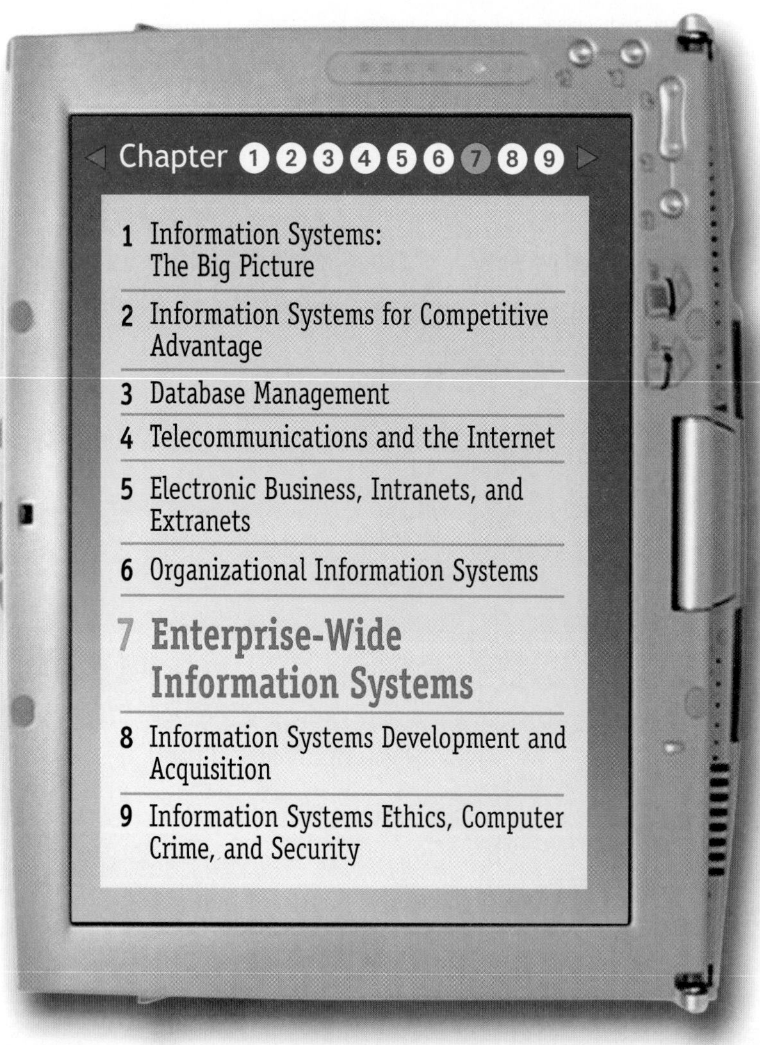

[Figure 7.1 ➥ The Big Picture: focusing on enterprise systems.]

Enterprise-Wide Information Systems

OPENING: SAP Switches Focus from Big to Small in Canada

With a reputation for offering complex and highly expensive enterprise software, SAP AG is faced with a daunting task: can the company appeal to the global small- and medium-sized enterprise (SME) market? Growth in SAP's core business is slowing as most of the world's largest companies have already implemented some form of enterprise resource planning (ERP) system.

"For SAP to really grow, they have to expand into the mid-market," said Alan Pelz-Sharpe, vice-president, North America, for Ovum Consultants Inc. in Boston.

"For most smaller companies, they are going to be interested in Oracle, Accpac, or Peoplesoft. SAP just looks like a big, scary option." Branding, Pelz-Sharpe said, is one element SAP must address to change the perception with SMEs that its solutions are pricey and complex. "They're very good at the technology, but when it comes to pure advertising and brand management, they're not very good at it and they'll have to do a lot of work to address that."

SAP Canada acknowledged an estimated 90 percent of business in Canada falls into the category of small- or medium-sized operations. To better address this market, SAP Canada will refocus its marketing efforts and enlist the assistance of regional partners. Companies with annual revenues of $20 million have the same problems to solve as companies with $100 million in revenues. To that end, SAP Canada has offered tailored versions of its mySAP All-in-One and SAP Business One solutions through its channel partners nationwide.

SAP America CEO Bill McDermott also sounded off on the company's performance north of the 49th parallel. "Our business in Canada is doing very well," he said. "We are the enterprise application market leader and we think we can better serve our Canadian customers with our Business Suite and our NetWeaver architecture." McDermott said Canada is a unique entity and will be treated as such. "Canada is a very special place, and we don't manage it as a region of the United States [the way] a lot of technology companies do. In fact, we believe it will be the growth engine of the North American market, if not all of SAP," he said.

Georgetown, Ontario–based Mold-Masters Limited™, one of the world's largest suppliers of products to the plastic injection moulding industry, turned to SAP in 1999 as part of its Y2K preparations, said president Jonathon Fischer. Since then, the company has completed a number of projects using SAP technology, most recently a means of automating the design of its orders. An SAP-based application allows customers to feed requests into Mold-Masters'™ online business tool, called Merlin™, which sends orders directly to its plants. Approximately 25 percent of the company's orders are now processed online, Fischer said, and the company aims to have 50 percent of all orders handled through design automation by the end of this year.

McDermott said 61 percent of all SAP projects are done in fewer than nine months, and Canadian customers have told him they managed to complete some projects in little more than two weeks. "Some of those projects [that went awry] were not managed very well, quite frankly," he said.

[Adapted from Liam Lahey, "Can SAP Rebrand to Penetrate Mid-Market?" *Computing Canada*, Vol. 29, No. 13 (July 4, 2003); and Shane Schick, "SAP Restructures Canadian Office at the Top Level," *Computing Canada*, Vol. 29, No. 21 (October 31, 2003).]

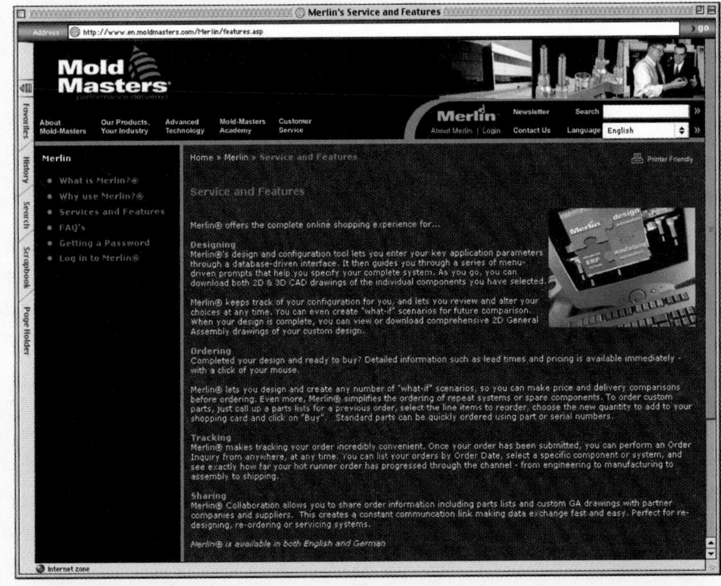

[**Figure 7.2** ➡ Georgetown, Ontario–based Mold-Masters Limited™ uses an application to facilitate online ordering, designed specifically for the SME market by ERP giant SAP.]

Source: Courtesy of Mold-Masters Limited™.

Figure 7.1 shows how this chapter fits within The Big Picture. An understanding of enterprise systems is critical to succeed in today's competitive and ever-changing world. Enterprise systems are now being implemented in firms of all sizes, across all industries. People with enterprise systems skills are in high demand and, therefore, the more you know about enterprise systems, the more you will be in demand in the employment marketplace!

ENTERPRISE SYSTEMS

Companies use information systems to support their various business processes and activities for internal operations such as manufacturing, order processing, and human resource management. Companies can also use information systems to support external interactions with customers, suppliers, and business partners. Businesses have leveraged information systems to support business processes and activities for decades, beginning with the installation of applications to assist companies with specific business tasks such as issuing paycheques. Oftentimes, these systems were built on different computing platforms such as mainframes and minicomputers, each operating in unique hardware and software environments. Applications running on different computing platforms are difficult to integrate, as custom interfaces are required for one system to communicate with another.

Running different applications on separate computing platforms can create tremendous inefficiencies within organizations because data cannot readily be shared between the systems. Information must be re-entered from one system to the next, and the same pieces of data may be stored in several versions throughout the organization. *Enterprise-wide information systems* (a.k.a. ***enterprise systems***), thus, are information systems that allow companies to integrate information across operations on a companywide basis. Rather than storing information in separate places throughout the organization, enterprise systems provide a central repository common to all corporate users. This, along with a common user interface, allows personnel to share information seamlessly no matter where the data are located or who is using the application.

The emergence of the Internet and Web has resulted in the globalization of customer and supplier networks, opening up new opportunities and methods to conduct business. Customers have an increasing number of options available to them, so they are demanding more sophisticated products that are customized to their unique needs. They also expect higher levels of customer service. If companies cannot keep their customers satisfied, the customers will not hesitate to do business with a competitor. Companies need to provide quality customer service and develop products faster and more efficiently to compete in global markets. Enterprise systems can be extended to streamline communications with customers and suppliers. Rather than focusing only on internal operations, these systems can also focus on business activities that occur outside organizational boundaries. Enterprise systems can help companies find innovative ways to increase accurate on-time shipments, avoid (or at least anticipate) surprises, minimize costs, and ultimately increase customer satisfaction and the overall profitability of the company.

Enterprise systems come in a variety of shapes and sizes, each providing a unique set of features and functionality. When deciding to implement enterprise solutions, there are a number of issues that managers need to be aware of. One of the most important factors involves selecting and implementing applications that meet the requirements of the business, as well as its customers and suppliers. In the following sections, we examine the ways in which information systems can be leveraged to support business activities. This is followed by an in-depth analysis of how enterprise systems have evolved and how companies are using these systems to support their internal and external operations.

Supporting Business Activities

As we talked about in Chapter 2, information systems can be used to increase competitive advantage by supporting and/or streamlining business activities (Porter and Millar, 1985). For example, an information system could be used to support a billing process in such a way that it helps to reduce the use of paper and, more important, the handling of paper, thus reducing material and labour costs. This same system can help managers keep track of that same billing process more effectively because they will have more accurate, up-to-date information about the billing process, enabling them to make smart, timely business decisions.

Information systems can be used to support either internally or externally focused business processes. Internally focused systems

CAREER IMPLICATIONS

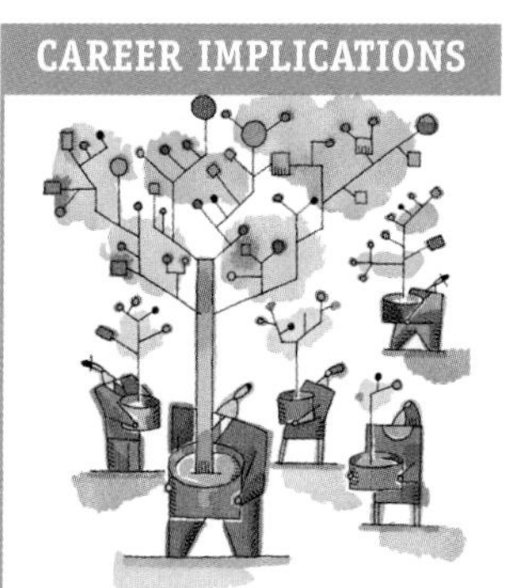

Accounting and Finance

Marius Bélanger, administrative director of Techmat, a soil and material engineering firm based in Saguenay, Quebec, can look back at a decade-old technology purchase and more than justify it. He estimates the accounting and project management system he chose for his company back in the early 1990s has allowed Techmat to save 50 percent on its administrative staff over the years. Techmat has doubled its revenue in the last 15 years, while the amount of resources it assigns to administrative work has stayed the same.

The company worked on a number of construction projects across Quebec, and its business was growing rapidly. It needed a way to manage the growth and so decided to look into acquiring an accounting and project management–based enterprise resource planning (ERP) system. It wanted to be able to track its employees and know when and on which projects they were spending their billable hours. It needed a real-time cost control system. "Because we invoice for resources that work on different projects, it is essential to keep rigorous tracking of the 'invoiceability' of our employees," Bélanger said. He looked into a few different solutions, and decided to opt for Jovaco Project Suite, from Montreal-based Jovaco Solutions Inc. "We had considered other systems, but Project Suite was the only one that met all of our needs. The quality-to-price ratio also constituted a determining factor in our decision," Bélanger said. "The main benefits provided by Project Suite are efficiency, connectivity, and versatility. Since the implementation of the system, the benefits have been evident."

Employees now spend less time on data entry, which allows them to spend more time on management activities, increasing the company's efficiency. Now timesheet and expense information only has to be entered once into the system. Less time spent on data entry has also increased the administrative staff's satisfaction. By having access to the information almost in real time, project managers can put more time into working on projects. By reducing the time spent on unbillable compilation of management data, it allows an increase in the percentage of billable time. Managers can view the data Techmat collects by customer and project type, which allows them to forecast trends in the market.

[Adapted from Poonam Khanna, "Techmat Stands Firm with 10-Year-Old ERP," **www.itbusiness.ca/index.asp?theaction=61&sid=54177#**, ITBusiness.ca (February 2, 2004).]

support functional areas, processes, or activities within the organization. These activities can be viewed as a series of links in a chain along which information flows within the organization. At each stage (or link) in the process, value is added in the form of the work performed by people associated with that process, and new, useful information is generated. Information begins to accumulate at the point of entry (i.e., a customer sends an order to the company) and flows through the various links, or processes, within the organization, progressing through the organization with new, useful information being added every step of the way. For example, when a customer places an order, the order is entered into an order entry application. The information containing the order is sent to the fulfillment department, which picks the items from inventory, packages them for distribution, and produces an additional piece of information called a packing list, which specifies the items contained within the package. The package, along with the packing list, is forwarded to the shipping department, which coordinates the shipment, produces an additional piece of information in the form of an invoice, and sends the package with its associated invoice to the customer. Each link in the process has a unique set of information inputs and outputs, as depicted in Figure 7.3.

In contrast with internally focused applications, which coordinate functions inside organizational boundaries, externally focused systems coordinate business activities with customers, suppliers, business partners, and others who operate outside the organization's boundaries. Systems that communicate across organizational boundaries are sometimes referred to as ***interorganizational systems (IOSs)*** (Kumar and Crook, 1999). The key purpose of an IOS is to streamline the flow of information from one company's operations to another's. This type of application could be used, for example, to coordinate the flow of information from a company to its potential or existing customers who exist outside the organization, and vice versa.

Competitive advantage can be accomplished here by integrating multiple business processes in ways that enable firms to meet a wide range of unique customer needs. Sharing information between organizations helps companies to adapt more quickly to changing

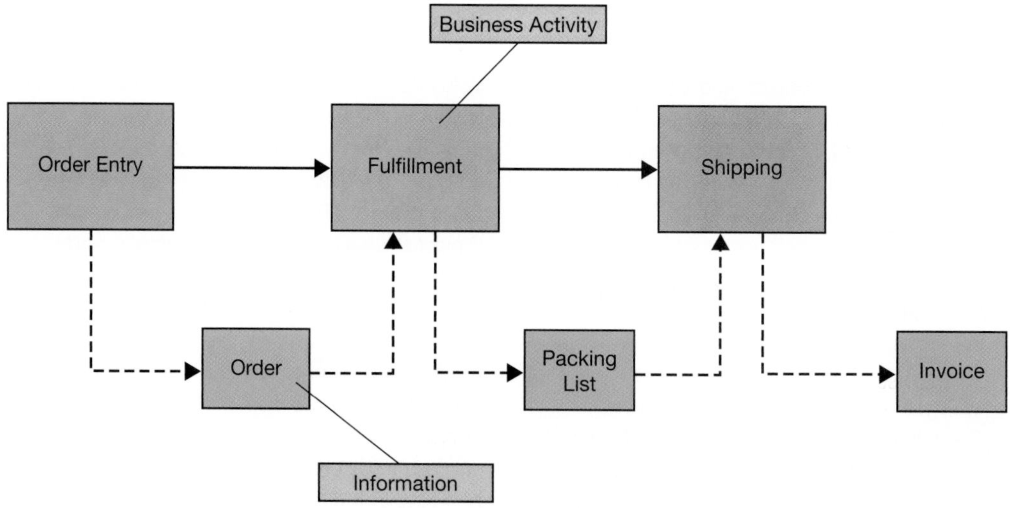

[**Figure 7.3** ➡ Information flow for a typical order.]

market conditions. For instance, should consumers demand an additional component be added to a product, a company can gain this information from its information systems that support sales and pass it along to its component suppliers in real time. Information allows the company and its suppliers to satisfy the needs of customers efficiently since changes can be identified and managed immediately, creating a competitive advantage for companies that can respond quickly.

We can view processes and information flows across organizations just as we previously viewed the processes and information flows within an organization. At each stage (or link) in the process, value is added by the work performed and new, useful information is generated and exchanged between organizations (see Figure 7.4). Using IOS, one company creates information and transmits it electronically to another company.

For example, when a company places an order for components with a supplier, the supplier processes the order as shown in Figure 7.4. The supplier performs the shipping activity, which results in the delivery of a physical package and the electronic transmission of the associated invoice to the customer. At this point, the information crosses corporate boundaries from the supplier's organization to the customer's (the organization that ordered the component from the supplier). The customer's receiving department takes delivery of the supplier's package and verifies

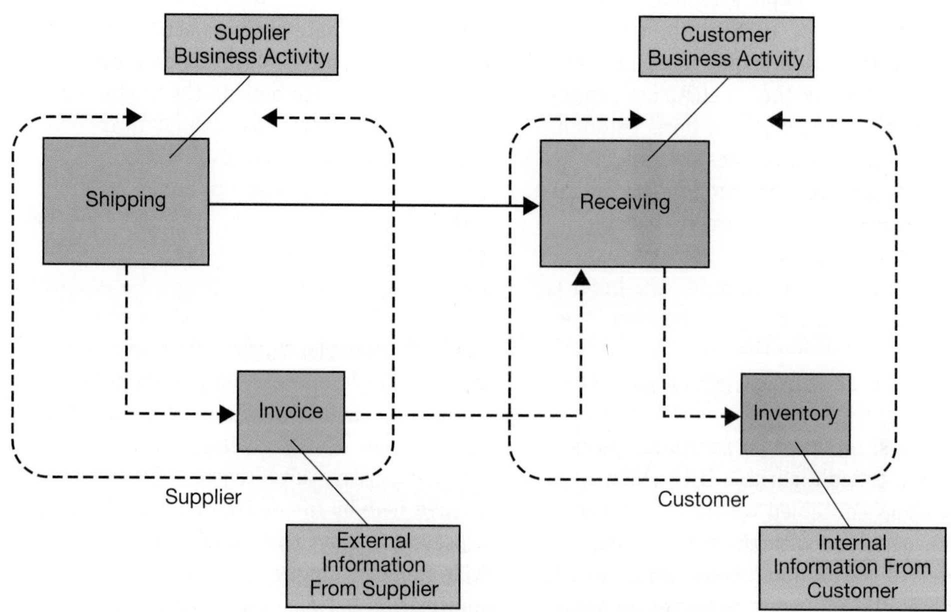

[**Figure 7.4** ➡ Information flow for a typical shipment across organizational boundaries.]

the invoice that was transmitted to ensure the order is complete. When the customer has accounted for the components, it stocks the items in inventory and updates inventory levels on its internal system accordingly.

Internally Focused Applications

Because companies within certain industries operate their businesses differently, one of the first challenges an organization must face is to understand how it can use information systems to support its unique internal business activities. Generally, the flow of information through a set of business activities is referred to as a ***value chain*** (Porter and Millar, 1985), in which information flows through functional areas that facilitate the internal activities of the business. Figure 7.5 depicts the value chain framework. In Chapter 2 we spoke of the strategic value of analyzing a value chain. We now show you how to use value chain analysis to implement enterprise systems.

Functional areas can be broken down into primary and support activities. Primary activities are functional areas within an organization that process inputs and produce outputs. Support activities are those activities that enable primary activities to take place. In the following sections, we focus on primary activities and then turn our attention to the support activities that make them possible.

Primary Activities

Primary activities include inbound logistics, operations and manufacturing, outbound logistics, marketing and sales, and customer service. These activities may differ widely based on the unique requirements of the industry in which a company operates, although the basic concepts hold in most organizations. Inbound logistics involve the business activities associated with receiving and stocking raw materials, parts, and products. For example, inbound logistics at Cisco Systems involve the receipt of electronic components that go into making their end products, such as routers. Shippers deliver electronic components to Cisco, at which time employees unwrap the packages and stock the components in the company's inventory. Cisco can automatically update inventory levels at the point of delivery, allowing purchasing managers to access real-time information related to inventory levels and reorder points.

Once the components have been stocked in inventory, the functional area of operations takes over. Operations can involve such activities as processing orders and/or manufacturing processes that transform raw materials and/or component parts into end products. As discussed in Chapter 5, Dell utilizes Web-based information systems to allow customers to enter orders online. This information is used to coordinate the manufacturing of a customized personal computer, in which the component parts are gathered and assembled to create the end product. During this process, inventory levels from inbound logistics are verified and, if the appropriate inventory exists, workers pick the components from existing supplies and build the product to the customer's specifications. When components are picked, items are deducted from inventory; once the product is assembled, inventory levels for the final product are updated. Canadian National Railways uses software from I2 Technologies to manage its vast inventory of rolling stock. The software forms the core of an information system used to forecast what will occur in the supply chain, then ensure that it has the appropriate assets in place to handle the situation.

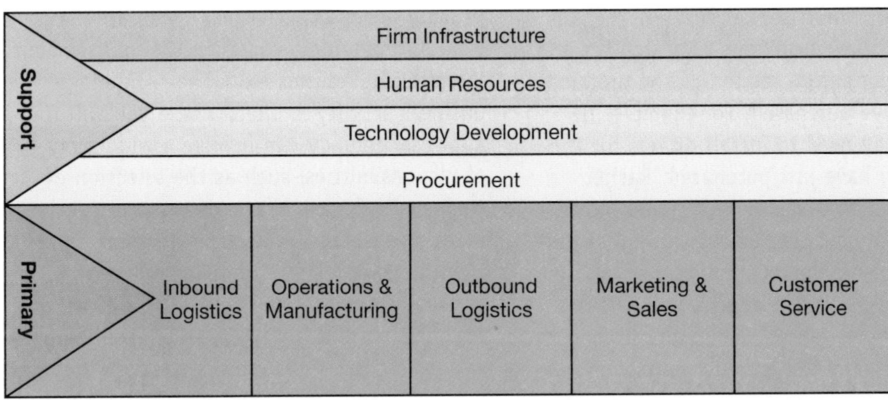

[**Figure 7.5** ➥ Value chain framework.]

Source: Porter and Millar, 1985.

The functional area of outbound logistics mirrors that of inbound logistics. Instead of involving the receipt of raw materials, parts, and products, outbound logistics focuses on the distribution of end products. For example, outbound logistics at Chapters.Indigo.ca involve the delivery of books that customers have ordered. Orders that have been processed by the operations area are forwarded to the department of outbound logistics, which picks the products from inventory and coordinates delivery to the customer. At that point, items are packaged and deducted from the company's inventory, and an invoice is created that will be sent to the customer. Chapters.indigo.ca can automatically update sales information at the point of distribution, allowing managers to view inventory and revenue information in real time.

The marketing and sales functional area facilitates the presales activities of the company. These include such things as the creation of marketing literature, communicating with potential and existing customers, and pricing goods and services. As discussed in Chapter 5, many companies support the business activity of marketing and sales by creating an e-brochure. Other companies, such as Via Rail, use information systems to update pricing information and schedules. This information is entered directly into the pricing and scheduling systems, which becomes immediately accessible throughout the organization and to end consumers through the corporation's Website.

Whereas marketing and sales focus on presales activities, the customer service functional area focuses on the postsales activities of the company. Customers may have questions and need help from a customer service representative. Many companies, such as Hewlett-Packard (HP), are utilizing information systems to provide customer service. These applications allow customers to search for and download information related to the products that they have purchased. For example, HP customers may need to install drivers for the printers they have just purchased. Rather than calling a customer service representative, customers can help themselves through a self-service customer support application.

Companies can use information systems to track service requests. When a customer calls in for repairs to a product, customer service representatives can access a bevy of information related to the customer. For instance, an agent can access technical information concerning the specific product, as well as review any problems the customer has encountered in the past. This enables customer service representatives to react quickly to customer concerns, improving the customer service experience.

Support Activities

Support activities are business activities that enable the primary activities to take place. Support activities include infrastructure, human resources, technology development, and procurement. Infrastructure refers to the hardware and software that must be implemented to support the applications that the primary activities use. An order entry application requires that employees who enter orders have a computer and the necessary software to accomplish their business objective. In turn, the computer must be connected via the network to a database containing the order information so that the order can be saved and recalled later for processing. Infrastructure provides the necessary components to facilitate the order entry process.

Human resources involve the business activities associated with employee management, such as hiring, interview scheduling, payroll, and benefits management. Human resources are classified as a support activity, since the primary activities cannot be accomplished without the employees to perform them. In other words, all the primary activities use the human resources business activity. For example, if a company needs a new customer service representative to serve the growing volume of customers, the request is processed through the human resources function, which creates the job description and locates the appropriate person to fill the job.

Technology includes the design and development of applications that support the primary business activities. If you are planning on pursuing a career in the management information systems field, the technology business activity is likely where you will find a job. Technology can involve a wide array of responsibilities, such as the selection of packaged software or the design and development of a custom application to meet a particular business need. Many companies are leveraging the technology business activity to build Internet, intranet, and extranet applications for these purposes. As seen in previous chapters, companies use these systems to support a wide variety of primary business activities.

Procurement refers to the purchasing of goods and services that are required as inputs to the primary activities. Allowing each functional area to send out purchase orders can create problems for companies, such as maintaining relationships with more suppliers than necessary and not taking advantage of volume discounts. The procurement business activity can leverage information systems by accumulating purchase orders from the different functional areas within the corporation. By having this information at their disposal, procurement personnel can combine multiple purchase orders containing the same item into a single purchase order. Ordering larger volumes from its suppliers means that the company can achieve dramatic cost savings through volume discounts. Procurement receives, approves, and processes requests for goods and services from the primary activities and coordinates the purchase of those items. This allows the primary activities to concentrate on running the business rather than adding to their workload.

Externally Focused Applications

The flow of information can be streamlined not only within a company but also outside organizational boundaries. A company can create additional value by integrating internal applications with suppliers, business partners, and customers. Companies accomplish this by connecting their internal value chains as a ***value system*** (Porter and Millar, 1985), in which information flows from one company's value chain to another company's value chain. Figure 7.6 depicts the value system framework. In this diagram, three companies are aligning their value chains to form a value system. First, company A processes information through its value chain and forwards the information along to its customer, company B, which processes the information through its value chain and sends the information along to its customer, company C, which processes the information through its value chain. Adding additional suppliers, business partners, and customers can create complex value systems. However, for our purposes, we simply view an organization's information systems as a value chain that interacts with the value chains of other organizations.

Externally focused systems can be used to coordinate a company's value chain with another company's value chain or with consumers (such as in business-to-consumer (B2C) electronic business). Any information that feeds into a company's value chain, whether its source is another company's value chain or an end consumer, is considered to be part of the value system. In other words, the value system for a particular organization acts like a vacuum cleaner, gathering information from the outside world.

The value system can be viewed as a river of information that flows from a source to an ultimate destination. Like a river, at any particular point there is a flow coming from upstream and progressing downstream. Value systems comprise ***upstream*** and ***downstream*** information flows. An upstream information flow consists of information that is received from another organization, whereas a downstream information flow relates to the information that is produced by a company and sent along to another organization. For instance, using the value system depicted in Figure 7.6 as an example, the upstream and downstream information flows for company B become quite evident. In this case, company B receives information from its upstream supplier, processes the information through its

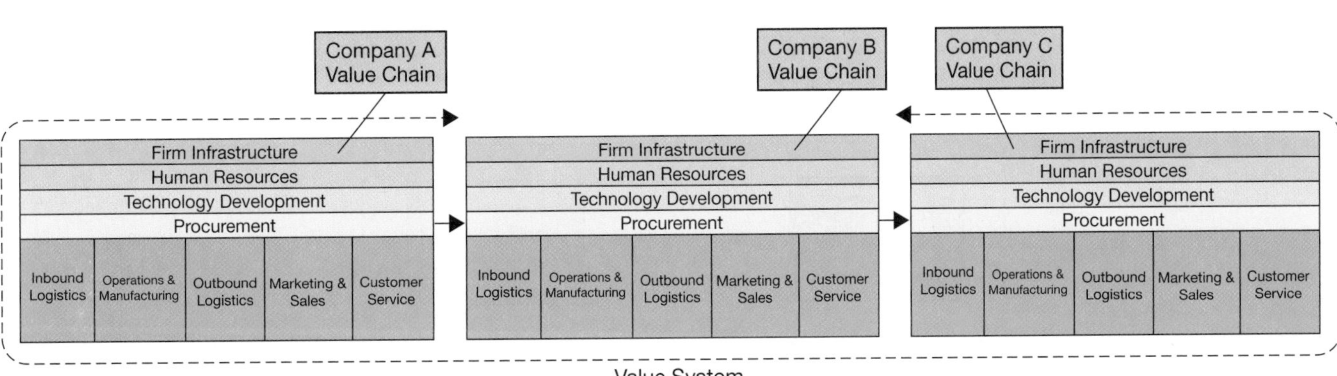

Figure 7.6 ➥ Value system framework.

Source: Porter and Millar, 1985.

internal value chain, and subsequently passes information downstream to its distributors and/or customers. It is these flows of external information into and from a company that can be leveraged to create additional value and competitive advantage. Next, we will look at the enterprise systems used to support the processes and information flows we have talked about so far.

TYPES OF ENTERPRISE SYSTEMS

Enterprise systems come in two forms—packaged and custom. ***Packaged applications*** are software programs written by third-party vendors, whereas ***custom applications*** are software programs that are designed and developed by company personnel. Packaged applications that you are likely familiar with are Microsoft Money and Quicken, which allow users to purchase software off-the-shelf to help them with their financial matters. Packaged systems are highly useful for standardized, repetitive tasks such as making entries in a cheque register. They can be quite cost-effective, since the vendor that builds the software application can spread out development costs through selling to a large number of users.

Yet packaged applications may not be well suited for tasks that are unique to a particular business. In these cases, companies may prefer to develop (or have developed for them) custom applications that can accommodate their particular business needs. The development costs of custom systems are much higher than packaged applications due to the time, money, and resources that are required to design and develop them. Furthermore, applications need to be maintained internally when changes are required. With packaged applications, the vendor makes the changes and distributes new versions to its customers. In all, there are trade-offs when choosing between the packaged and custom application routes. Managers must consider whether packaged applications can meet the business requirements and, if not, conduct a cost–benefit analysis to ensure that taking the custom application approach will prove worthwhile to the company.

Figure 7.7 provides a high-level overview of how enterprise systems typically evolve. As companies begin to leverage information systems applications, they typically start out by fulfilling the needs of particular business activities in a particular department within the organization. Systems that focus on the specific needs of individual departments are not designed to communicate with other systems in the organization and are, therefore, referred to as ***stand-alone applications.***

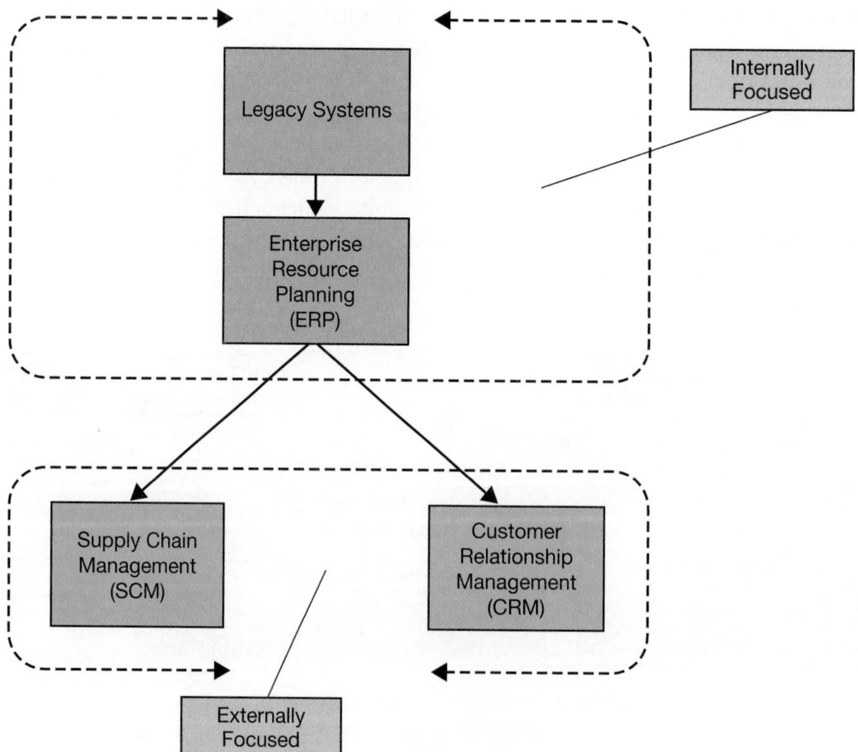

[**Figure 7.7** ➥ Stages of enterprise systems evolution.]

Stand-alone applications usually run on a variety of computing hardware platforms such as mainframes and minicomputers. Together, stand-alone applications and the computers they run on are often referred to as ***legacy systems***, given that they are typically older systems that are either fast approaching or beyond the end of their useful life within the organization. Legacy systems tend to require substantial resources to maintain them to accommodate emerging business needs.

Companies can gain several advantages by integrating and converting legacy systems so that information stored on separate computing platforms can be consolidated to provide a centralized point of access. The process of ***conversion*** transfers information stored on legacy systems to a new, integrated computing platform, which typically comes in the form of ***enterprise resource planning (ERP)*** applications. Although ERP applications do an excellent job of serving the needs of internal business operations on an organization-wide basis, they are not designed to completely accommodate the communication of information outside the organization's boundaries.

Systems that facilitate interorganizational communications focus on either the upstream or downstream information flows. Since these systems coordinate business activities across organizational boundaries, they are classified as externally focused applications. ***Supply chain management (SCM)*** applications operate on the upstream information flows, integrating the value chains of a company and its suppliers. In contrast, ***customer relationship management (CRM)*** applications concentrate on the downstream information flows, integrating the value chains of a company and its distributors. In some cases, companies deal directly with end consumers rather than selling products through distributors. CRM applications can also accommodate this scenario.

Legacy Systems

When companies first use information systems to support business activities, they usually begin by implementing systems in various departments rather than starting with a single application that can accommodate all aspects of the business. Each department implements applications to assist it with its daily business activities, which are optimized for its unique needs and the manner in which personnel in a particular unit accomplish job tasks. These applications tend to be infrastructure-specific, meaning that they run on particular hardware and software platforms. As a result, each department normally has its own computing system that runs its necessary

Information Systems

Micro Focus International Ltd. is a privately held company that provides solutions for developing and deploying COBOL (Common Business-Oriented Language) applications to help IT departments make the most of their existing enterprise application systems. The company has 470 employees worldwide, with principal offices in the United Kingdom, the United States, and Japan. Micro Focus helps firms to move legacy systems to Internet- and client/server-ready applications.

Ironically, fast-paced growth in the early 2000s meant that Micro Focus began to have trouble with its own legacy IT infrastructure. "As a company whose very purpose is to develop enterprise-wide solutions for our customers, we were in the strongest position to know what we wanted from our applications infrastructure," noted Sanjeev Garg, Micro Focus's director of worldwide business systems. For its marketing software, Micro Focus turned to Vancouver-based Pivotal Corp. Pivotal focuses on providing customer relationship management (CRM) software to mid-sized companies.

Firms may choose Pivotal over larger vendors like Siebel Systems or Oracle because the software is cheaper and easier to customize. Micro Focus's initial objective was on improving the way in which the company managed its customer information. Pivotal worked closely with the in-house Micro Focus developers to assist with both technical training and customization of the new system. "We needed to create a single, unified database of customer information to underpin all our business functions. We knew that this approach would enable us to take the new applications infrastructure beyond pure CRM and place us in the strongest possible position to enable Micro Focus to become a truly customer-focused organization."

For example, the worldwide technical support team is now able to capture, manage, and respond to support incidents more efficiently. This is achieved by linking serial numbers with customer licence and support histories. In so doing, the support team has all the necessary information immediately available to allow it to more effectively manage and resolve customer issues as they arise.

CAREER IMPLICATIONS

[Adapted from **www.pivotal.com/downloads/Case_Studies/ MicroFocusCaseStudy080304.pdf**.]

Web Search

WEB SEARCH OPPORTUNITY

Visit the ERP Jobs Website at **www.erp-jobs.com** and see what types of ERP-related career opportunities are currently available. Which packages and skills do companies appear to be looking for?

applications. Although departmental systems are greatly beneficial in enabling departments to conduct their daily business activities efficiently, these systems often are not very helpful when people from one part of the firm need information from another part of the firm (e.g., people in manufacturing need forecasts from sales).

As previously described, given that these older systems are not designed to communicate with other applications beyond departmental boundaries, they are classified as "legacy" systems, or systems that operate within the confines of a particular business need. Legacy systems and their associated stand-alone applications can prove problematic when information from multiple departmental systems is required to make business decisions (as is often the case). For example, if the applications for inbound logistics and operations are not integrated, companies will lose valuable time in accessing information related to inventory levels. When an order is placed through operations, personnel need to verify that the components are available in inventory before the order can be processed. If the inventory and order entry systems are not integrated, personnel must have access to two separate applications. Further, if these applications reside on different computing platforms, personnel must have two separate pieces of hardware on their desks to accomplish their duties. Figure 7.8 provides an example of how information flows through legacy systems within an organization.

As the diagram depicts, information is generated by the inbound logistics business activity, but it does not flow through to the next business activity, in this case operations. Since the inbound logistics and operations departments use different legacy systems, information cannot readily flow from one business activity to another. This problem was faced by the Société de transport de Montréal (STM), Montreal's public transit company. STM had already been using SAP products for finance, payroll, and human resources, but it wanted to integrate various disparate systems, especially those dealing with its operations. Understandably, a gap between inbound logistics and operations creates a highly inefficient process, where personnel must have access to two systems in order to get both the order entry and inventory information. For instance, if the inventory application is running on an IBM mainframe system and the order entry application is running on a UNIX-based minicomputer, operations personnel must have access to both the IBM mainframe and UNIX systems. This may mean installing two separate terminals at an employee's desk so the employee can view the information from both systems at the same time. In some cases, inventory information may be stored on both systems, creating the potential for inaccuracies. Should data be updated in one system but not the other, the data become outdated and inaccurate. In addition, there are further, unnecessary costs associated with entering, storing, and updating data redundantly.

Enterprise Resource Planning

When companies realize that legacy systems can create dramatic inefficiencies within their organizations, the next step is to integrate legacy information on a companywide basis. As previously described, applications that integrate business activities across depart-

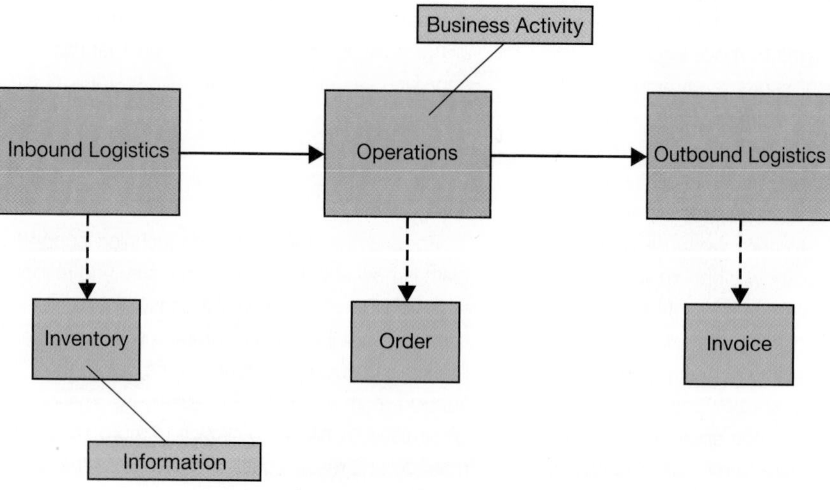

[Figure 7.8 ➥ Information flow using legacy systems.]

mental boundaries are often referred to as enterprise resource planning (ERP) systems. In the 1990s, there was a push by companies to implement integrated applications, as exhibited by ERP sales forecasts that are expected to reach approximately $50 billion annually. Readers should be cautioned that the terms *resource* and *planning* are misnomers, meaning that they do not accurately describe the purpose of ERP since these applications do very little in the way of planning or managing resources (Koch, Slater, and Baatz, 2000). The reason for the term *enterprise resource planning* is that these systems evolved in part during the 1990s from material requirements planning (a.k.a. MRP) packages. Do not get hung up on the words *resource* and *planning*. The key word to remember from the acronym ERP is *enterprise*.

ERP takes stand-alone applications a step further by providing a common data warehouse and similar application interfaces that service the entire enterprise rather than portions of it. Information stored on legacy systems is converted into large, centralized data repositories known as ***data warehouses.*** Data warehouses are databases that store information related to the various business activities of an organization. Data warehouses alleviate the problems associated with multiple computing platforms by providing a single place where all information relevant to the company and particular departments can be stored and accessed, as depicted in Figure 7.9.

In contrast to legacy systems, where it is difficult to share information between business activities, ERP applications make accessing information easier by providing a central information repository. By using an ERP solution, both inbound logistics and operations have access to inventory data since both business activities have access to the same pieces of information. Rather than having information flow from one department to the next, data can be accessed and updated at will, meaning that the next business activity can access information in the data warehouse whenever it needs to. This provides personnel access to accurate, real-time information. The beauty of ERP lies in the fact that information can be shared throughout the organization. For example, inventory information is accessible not only to inbound logistics and operations, but also to accounting and customer service personnel. If a customer calls in wondering about the status of an order, customer service representatives can find out by accessing the data warehouse through the ERP application. Prior to the emergence of ERP, customer service representatives may have had to retrieve information from two or more separate computing systems, making their job extremely difficult while potentially resulting in dissatisfied customers. Storing data in a single place

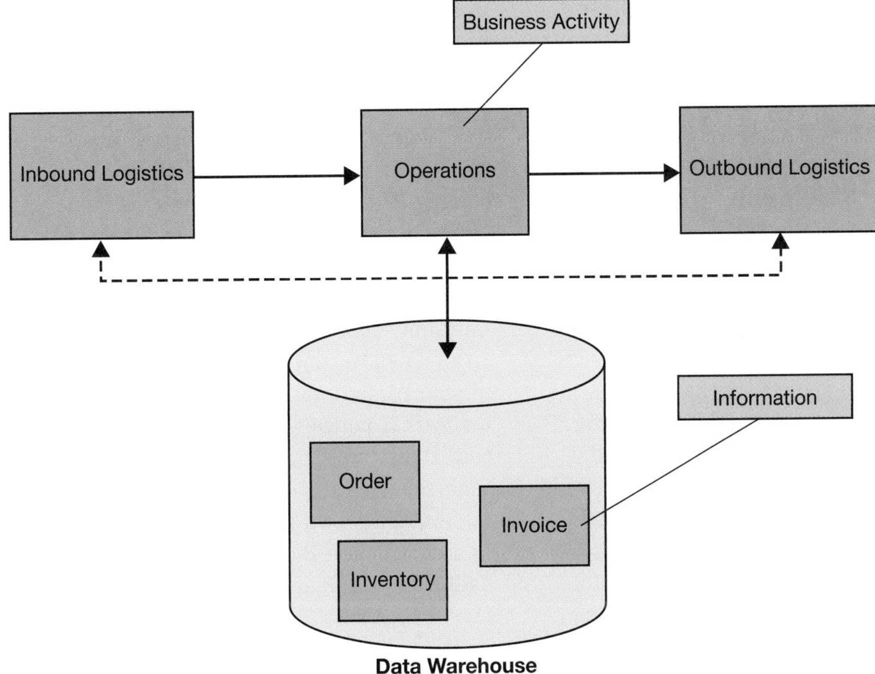

[**Figure 7.9** ➡ Information storage using an ERP solution.]

and making it available to everyone within the organization empowers everyone in the organization to be aware of the current state of business and to perform their jobs better.

ERP systems reside on servers and/or mainframes and can be accessed from desktops through client applications. They are designed to have a consistent look and feel, regardless of the unique needs of a particular department. In fact, to users they look very much like any other application. Inbound logistics and operations personnel will use a common user interface to access the same pieces of information from the data warehouse. Although the inbound logistics screens and the operations screens will have different features tailored to the unique needs of the business activity, the screens will look comparable, with similar designs, screen layouts, menu options, and so on. The Microsoft Office products provide a useful analogy. Microsoft Word and Microsoft Excel are designed to serve separate functions (word processing and spreadsheets, respectively), but overall the products look and feel very similar to one another. Word and Excel have similar user interfaces and simply differ in the features and functionality that each application offers. PeopleSoft, a large ERP company, offers a series of informative demos to illustrate what an ERP system does, and what it looks like. Examples are provided in the areas of finance (**www.peoplesoft.com/corp/en/products/ent/financial_mgmt/resource_library.jsp**), supply chain management (**www.peoplesoft.com/corp/en/products/ent_one/scm/resource_library.jsp**), CRM (**www.peoplesoft.com/corp/en/products/ent_one/crm/resource_library.jsp**), and human resources (**www.peoplesoft.com/corp/en/products/ent/hcm/hcm_resource_library.jsp**).

ERP systems are packaged applications that are purchased from software vendors. ERP vendors include SAP, Oracle, PeopleSoft, and SAGE, among others. SAP (see Figure 7.10) holds the largest market share with just over 25 percent of the market and has become the third largest software supplier in the world behind software behemoths Microsoft and Oracle. As of 2004, SAP had implemented over 67,500 copies of its ERP packages at 10,000 companies, with a total of 12 million users. Oracle started in 1977 as a database vendor and grew into an ERP vendor by developing integrated applications that access information stored in the data warehouse. Interestingly, Oracle not only sells ERP software, but also continues to sell its popular database management software, which serves as the database engine underlying many of the other ERP products. Oracle holds a 7-percent share of the ERP market with revenues from ERP sales in excess of US$2.4 billion. PeopleSoft and SAGE account for 6 percent and 5 percent of the ERP market, respectively. The wild card in this segment is Microsoft, currently in fifth place with 5 percent of the ERP market. Microsoft is aggressively developing enterprise systems software to complement its line of home and small business products.[1]

When selecting an appropriate ERP application for a company, management needs to take many factors into careful consideration. ERP applications come as packaged software, which means a one-size-fits-all strategy. However, businesses have unique needs even within their own industries. In other words, like snowflakes, no two companies are exactly alike. Management must carefully select an ERP application that will meet the unique requirements of their particular company. There are a number of factors that companies must consider in ERP selection. Among the most prevalent issues facing management are control, business requirements, and best practices (Ptak, 2000).

Control refers to the locus of control over the computing systems and decision making regarding these systems. Companies typically either opt for centralized control or allow particular business units to govern themselves. In the context of ERP, these decisions are based on the level of detail in the information that must be provided to management. Some corporations want to have as much detail as possible made available at the executive level, whereas other companies do not require such access. For instance, an accountant in one company may want the ability to view costs down to the level of individuals' transactions, while an accountant in another company may want only summary information. Another area related to control involves the consistency of policies and procedures. Some companies prefer that policies and procedures remain consistent throughout an organization. Other companies want to allow each business unit to develop its own policies and procedures to accommodate the unique ways that they do business. ERP applications vary widely in

[1]Percentages from **www4.gartner.com/5_about/press_releases/pr18june2003a.jsp**; additional information from **www.sap.com/canada/en/company/.**

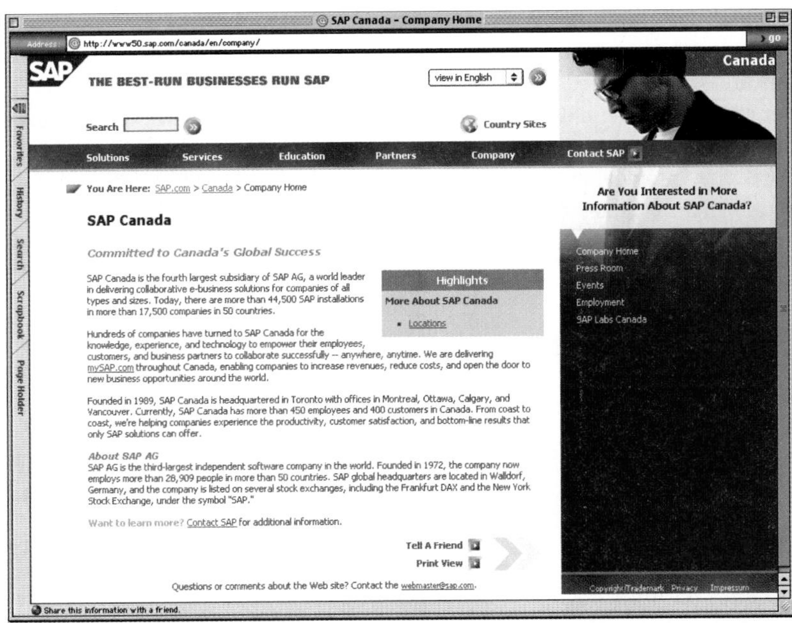

Figure 7.9 ➥ Information storage using an ERP solution.

Source: Courtesy of SAP Canada.

their allowance for control, typically assuming either a corporate or business-unit locus of control. Some ERP applications allow users to select or customize the locus of control. In either case, management must consider the ERP's stance on control to ensure it will meet the business requirements of the company.

Because all companies are different, no packaged software application will exactly fit the unique requirements of a particular business. ERP applications come in a variety of shapes and sizes, each designed to accommodate certain transaction volumes and business activities. As far as supporting various business activities is concerned, ERP systems can

CAREER IMPLICATIONS

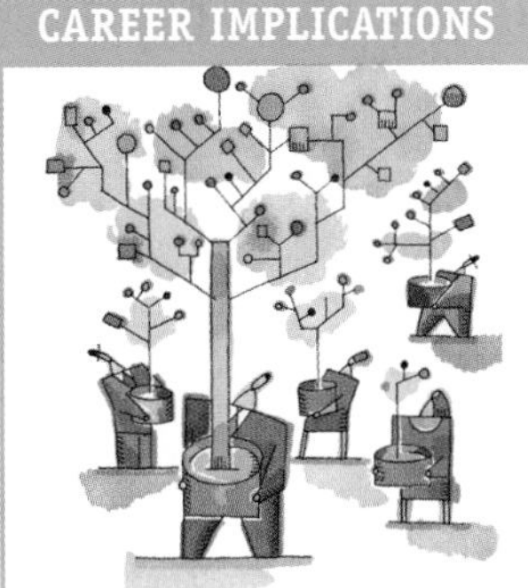

Human Resource Management

MDS Inc., a Toronto-based life sciences company, standardized its applications in HR, supply chain management, contract management, and other key areas using Oracle's E-Business Suite and IBM services. The technology behind MDS and its six subsidiaries was rebuilt from the ground up.

"They had too many disparate systems that didn't allow them to take advantage of economies of scale, share information between the companies," said Sal Causi, business development executive with IBM's life sciences division. "The flow of information was just very difficult for the parent company to understand what was going on at any one point in time."

All of MDS's operations across the world were reorganized to meet these goals, starting with its offices in Canada. MDS made it a priority to keep its suppliers and customers in the loop during the transformation. "A lot of them are used to it, because we're not the first business in the world to go through this," said David Poirier, MDS's CIO and president of shared services, "As a matter of fact, as companies get to certain sizes, we find they expect this and they're good at being able to deal with that. Nevertheless, communication is critical." MDS updated its key external partners throughout the implementation process.

In addition to streamlining operations, the new system helped MDS to comply with the *Personal Information Protection and Electronic Documents Act* (PIPEDA) in Canada and the *Sarbanes-Oxley Act* in the U.S. "This provides us with even better ability to meet the new standards because we have everything on one system. It's very auditable, it's trackable, and it's not as complex. It actually simplifies a lot of the procedures you'd want to have the ability to investigate or track," Poirier said.

[Adapted from Neil Sutton, "MDS Standardizes HR, Supply Chain Applications on Oracle and IBM," *Computing Canada*, Vol. 30, No. 1 (January 16, 2004).]

include a wide variety of features and functionality. Each function is classified as a component, and components are often bundled together to form software ***modules.*** The ERP modules provided by each ERP vendor vary in the specific functions that they provide, as well as in how they are referred to. Tables 7.1 and 7.2 provide a comparison between some of the ERP modules provided by SAP and Oracle.

As evidenced by Tables 7.1 and 7.2, it is critical for managers to understand the vendors' naming conventions and software modules to gain an understanding of how these features can be implemented to meet the requirements of the business's activities. The features and modules that the ERP comes with out of the box are referred to as the ***vanilla*** version. If the vanilla version does not support a certain business process, the software may require ***customizations*** to accommodate it. Customizations involve additional software that is integrated with the ERP or direct changes to the vanilla ERP application itself. SAP, for example, includes literally thousands of elements in its ERP software that can be customized, and also offers many industry-specific versions of its software that have already been customized for a particular industry based on SAP's perceptions of the best way to do things in that industry (i.e., best practices). Companies must take special care when dealing with customization issues. Customizations can be costly, and maintaining and upgrading customizations can be troublesome. For example, a customization made to the vanilla version will need to be reprogrammed when a new release of the ERP is implemented. This is due to the fact that subsequent releases of the ERP do not contain the necessary logic embedded in the customizations. In other words, new vanilla versions must be continually upgraded to accommodate the customization. This process can involve a substantial investment of time and resources.

One of the major hurdles posed to companies that implement ERP applications involves changing business processes to accommodate the manner in which the software works. ERP implementations are often used as a catalyst for overall improvement of underlying business processes. ERP applications are designed to operate according to industry-standard business processes, known as ***best practices.*** Many ERP vendors build best practices into their applications to provide guidelines for management to identify business activities within their organizations that need to be streamlined. Implementations will go more smoothly when companies change their business practices to fit the way the ERP software operates.

Altering the way in which business processes are conducted is known as

[Table 7.1] ***SAP R/3 modules.***

Module	Functionality
FI (financial accounting)	GL—General Ledger
	AR—Accounts Receivable
	AP—Accounts Payable
	LC—Legal Consolidations
HR (human resources)	PA—Personnel Administration
	PD—Planning and Development
MM (materials management)	IM—Inventory Management
	IV—Invoice Verification
	WM—Warehouse Management
PP (production planning)	SOP—Sales and Operations Planning
	MRP—Material Requirements Planning
	CRP—Capacity Requirements Planning
SD (sales and distribution)	OE—Order Entry
	FUL—Fulfillment
	SH—Shipping

[Table 7.2] ***Oracle ERP modules.***

Module	Functionality
Demand	Order Entry Accounts Receivable Inventory Management
Supply	Bill of Materials Materials Requirements Planning Work-in-process Management Purchasing
Finance	General Ledger Accounts Payable Cost Management

business process reengineering (BPR). Many organizations have spent many years developing business practices that provide them with a competitive advantage in the marketplace. Adopting their industry's best practices may force these companies to abandon their unique ways of doing business, putting them on par with their industry competitors. In other words, companies can potentially lose their competitive advantages by adapting the "best practices" within their industry. Best practices is an area that managers must carefully consider before selecting an ERP application. Some ERP vendors tightly integrate best practices into the software, and companies that reject best practices are in for a long and time-consuming implementation. Other vendors provide a series of options that companies select before implementing the software, allowing them some (but not complete) flexibility in reengineering their business processes to accommodate the ERP application.

There is also a growing, useful body of research evidence on ERP implementations that suggests that these business process reengineering and related organizational issues are just as important as the ERP technical implementation issues (Kumar and Van Hillegersberg, 2000; Markus and Tanis, 2000). Indeed, in order to be successful, in some situations managers must literally choose between either making the ERP system fit the organization or making the organization fit the ERP system (Soh, Sia, and Tay-Yap, 2000). Others have suggested that for the ERP system to help transform the organization and gain new competitive capabilities, a full organizational and operational change process is required (Willcocks and Sykes, 2000). Finally, there is some evidence that, in order to be successful, managers must first transform the organization and then implement the ERP system (Sarker and Lee, 2000). In any event, the evidence suggests that these organizational change issues are very important in implementations of ERP and other enterprise-wide information systems.

While ERP helps companies to integrate systems across the organization, ERP falls short in communicating across organizational boundaries (Larson and Rogers, 1998). Since ERP applications are designed to service internal business activities, they tend not to be well suited for managing value system activities. Companies wanting to integrate their value chains with the business activities of their suppliers, business partners, and customers typically choose to implement systems other than ERP to manage the upstream and/or downstream flow of information. These types of applications are designed to coordinate activities outside organizational boundaries and are discussed in the following sections.

Customer Relationship Management

With the changes introduced by the Web, in most industries a company's competition is simply a mouse click away. It is increasingly important for companies not only to generate new business, but also to attract repeat business. This means that companies must keep their customers satisfied to remain competitive. In today's highly competitive markets, customers hold the balance of power because if they become dissatisfied with the levels of customer service they are receiving, there are

BRIEF CASE

Vancouver Firm Adopts Business One

It took more than a year for SAP to sign on its first Canadian Business One customer. Vancouver-based Mini-Tankers provides on-site diesel refuelling services. The company began rolling out the ERP software for SMEs, starting with financials. First presented in the spring of 2002, Business One is targeted at companies with 10 to 150 employees, or revenues as low as $1 million. As noted in the opening case, this segment has become a target for enterprise system vendors like SAP. At launch time, SAP president Hasso Plattner said the software was for SMEs or the remote offices of large companies that would not typically have access to information held in a central location.

Mini-Tankers has 120 employees and more than 4,000 customers across Canada with revenues of $70 million in 2003. The company has experienced rapid growth in the last few years, and expects to pump 130 million litres of fuel in 2004 (compared to 1.8 million litres a year in 1995). Mini-Tankers currently processes more than one million transactions—on its sales side alone—each year. The multitude of transactions it processed in doing business prompted its chief financial officer, George Murray, to reconsider the company's business process systems. The product offers ERP on a smaller scale including sales-force automation, financial management with multicurrency functions, budgeting, inventory management, and a reporting module that allows access to all data.

"What we were finding was that our existing technologies were having difficulties keeping up with the pace of the growth and we didn't have an integrated platform," says Murray. "We were looking for something that could integrate all our business processes onto a common platform and provide for long-term scaleability. We were really impressed with the ability to integrate with third-party external users," he says. "Before we had Business One, there was no way a company of $10 million could think of becoming an SAP customer, except for rare circumstances. So the plan was to design a new product to go to market with something made specifically for their needs," says Michel Vincent, vice-president of SME for SAP Canada.

SAP Business One has 1,600 customers worldwide. Vincent says the company has taken its time making sure features in the software that are unique to the countries in the "second wave of the rollout"—such as Canada, France, Spain, and Italy—are all in place. "We needed to localize the product," he says. "Each country has its own requirements and we have to follow the tax requirements, accounting rules, and all of this." Instead of launching a product that doesn't fit anywhere the company decided to invest in localizing the product.

"I think SAP had some reservations about quickly rolling out Business One because they are so strong in the really big enterprise accounts but not in SMEs," says Warren Shiau, software analyst for IDC Canada. "In the past, they have never focused on building out the infrastructure in terms of channels to reach the customers below those really big enterprise-class customers. They [customers] need some sort of point of contact for service and implementation." Vincent agrees SAP needed time to set up a channel of resellers to handle the Business One product with national coverage. "Selling to companies of that size is new for us, so we need partners that have the experience of working with that kind of customer, that understand their needs, speak their language, understand their pain," he says. "What we needed was the complementary expertise of the people well-rooted in the SME space."

Questions

1. What challenges might Mini-Tankers face while implementing and using SAP Business One?
2. Why are ERP system vendors interested in the SME market? What particular challenges does this segment present to SAP?

[Adapted from Jennifer Brown, "Business One Finally Lands in Canada," *Computing Canada*, Vol. 29, No. 23 (November 28, 2003).]

many alternatives readily available to them. The global nature of the Web has affected companies worldwide and impacted a wide swath of industries. An economic transformation is taking place, shifting the emphasis from conducting business transactions to managing relationships. Vendors such as Siebel[2] argue that the cost of trying to get back customers that have gone elsewhere can be up to 50 to 100 times as much as keeping a current one satisfied. Companies are finding it imperative to develop and maintain customer satisfaction and develop

[2] See Siebel Systems, "CRM Case Studies," **www.siebel.com**.

Ready to Sever: Sobeys Dumps SAP

Canadian grocery giant Sobeys Inc. said it has no plans to reconsider its decision to pull the plug on its year-old, SAP-powered ERP system. The Stellarton, Nova Scotia–based company claims the system caused its database to crash in early December 2000, leaving it unable to process the transactions moving through the stores' systems. Bill McEwan, Sobeys' chief executive, said the problem created a five-week backlog just before the holiday shopping period.

The second largest supermarket chain in Canada, Sobeys has 400 company stores and 1,000 franchise stores including IGA, Foodland, and Price Chopper outlets. On January 24, 2001, McEwan announced the company was ditching the software because it couldn't handle its ordering and data processing needs for its stores in Ontario and Atlantic Canada. However, SAP officials said they only learned of the decision through a press release issued two days before a scheduled meeting with Sobeys brass.

"We're both surprised and disappointed by the announcement made by Sobeys," said William Wohl, spokesperson for SAP America in Philadelphia. "We've had such a good dialogue with Sobeys all along." Despite attempts by SAP to repair the relationship, Sobeys officials are adamant the ERP project will be dismantled.

"It was a situation where we had a business disruption. We looked at an evaluation of our enterprise-wide software and that resulted in the decision, so I would be surprised if there was a change in conclusion," said Stewart Mahoney, vice-president of treasury and investor relations for Empire Company Ltd., which owns 62 percent of Sobeys.

"We indicated we plan to move ahead without SAP, and Mr. McEwan and the Sobeys' board of directors were quite clear in terms of Sobeys coming to that conclusion," he said. Mahoney added the project will cost the company $89.1 million and Sobeys is predicting the interruption of business will cut its quarterly operating profit by 16 cents a share. "We're through with that period. But there was an opportunity cost there because that's a busy period for us leading up to the Christmas rush," Mahoney said.

SAP had been working with the company prior to this project, implementing a human resources and financial system. In fact, SAP and IBM were using Sobeys as an example of a satisfied customer. Sobeys has not said what they will use to replace the SAP system but will continue to use the software for its financial and human resource needs. In a statement issued after a meeting on January 26, SAP said it "agreed to continue discussions with Sobeys in private."

"Overall, SAP has a good record of getting sizing performance right. But within the retail sector there have been projects which run into problems due to the very high volumes and narrow time windows involved," said Derek Prior, SAP research director with Stamford, Connecticut–based Gartner Group Inc. "You don't hear of these failures frequently. The successes are much higher, but successes aren't news."

[Adapted from Jennifer Brown, "Sobeys Fires SAP over ERP Debacle," *Computing Canada,* Vol. 27, No. 3 (February 9, 2001).]

deeper relationships with their customers in order to compete effectively in their markets.

Applications focusing on downstream information flows have two main objectives in mind—to attract potential customers and to create customer loyalty. The process of attracting potential customers, or prospects, can be streamlined by implementing ***sales force automation (SFA)*** applications, which mainly focus on contact management and scheduling. SFA applications provide salespeople with computerized support tools to assist them in their daily routines. SFA focuses on presales marketing and sales functions, whereas ***customer relationship management (CRM)*** applications go beyond SFA by offering postsales support activities as well. CRM offers a completely integrated approach to customer management. CRM suites typically include SFA modules, as well as the ability to track activities related to customers throughout the entire organization. CRM helps close the loop once the sale has been made. For example, once a sale has been made, CRM can retrieve information related to a customer's order, such as identifying where the order is in the pipeline, whether it be in manufacturing, in the warehouse, or in the process of being shipped. CRM also integrates the multiple ways that companies interact with customers, such as electronic mail and call centres. By providing exactly the information the customer requests, CRM can help build customer loyalty through demonstrated responsiveness.

Web Search

WEB SEARCH OPPORTUNITY
Visit the Siebel Systems Website at **www.siebel.com** to see what the company is up to. What is it currently offering in the way of CRM capabilities? What other types of software and/or services does Siebel offer?

The appropriate CRM technology, combined with reengineering of sales-related business processes, can have a tremendous impact on a company's bottom line. Siebel Systems argues that improving customer satisfaction by 1 percent a year over a five-year period can result in increases of more than 10 percent in return on investment over the period. To pursue customer satisfaction as a basis for achieving competitive advantage, organizations must be able to access information and track customer interactions throughout the organization, regardless of where, when, or how the interaction occurs. This means that companies need to have an integrated system that captures information from retail stores, Websites, call centres, and various other ways that organizations communicate downstream within their value chain. More important, managers need the capability to monitor and analyze factors that drive customer satisfaction as changes occur according to prevailing market conditions.

CRM applications come in the form of packaged software that is purchased from software vendors. CRM applications are commonly integrated with ERP to leverage internal and external information to serve customers. Siebel Systems controls about 25 percent of the market, with the remainder split among a variety of vendors including Salesforce.com, E.Piphany, and FirePond. The market for CRM applications is expected to grow from $14 billion in 2002 to $17.7 billion in 2006. With billions of dollars at stake, ERP vendors such as Oracle, PeopleSoft, and SAP are entering the CRM fray, enhancing their ERP solutions to include CRM. SAP, for example, is now the number-two player in the CRM market with a 16-percent market share. Like ERP, CRM applications come with various features and modules. Management must carefully select a CRM application that will meet the unique requirements of their particular company. In general, CRM applications are modularized along two lines—sales and service. Sales modules include SFA functions, which are designed to assist companies with the presales (i.e., before the sale) aspects of the business activities, such as marketing and prospecting. Service modules help companies with the postsales (i.e., after the sale) customer service aspects of their business.

CAREER IMPLICATIONS

Marketing

Siebel Systems, the world's largest CRM company, needs to change the way it markets and sells its products. Like the SAP example in the opening case, Siebel wants to target the SME sector with an online customer relationship management service. Traditionally, Siebel had sold direct, leaving VARs to do only implementations. But Ken Rudin, the company's vice-president of product marketing and product management, said there are talks with unnamed resellers to join the new Siebel OnDemand CRM service it will host in partnership with IBM.

"I promise you we're doing everything we can to get a reseller signed up," he said. "I can't promise you that they will agree they want to do this right now. We've put together a pretty comprehensive plan in front of some of the most innovative resellers in these areas... We want to build a reseller channel." Siebel resellers include international consulting companies like Accenture, Cap Gemini, and Ernst & Young, as well as independent software vendors whose products link to Siebel's. Until resellers are signed up, the CRM OnDemand service will be sold through Siebel and IBM marketing staff who will share a Toronto telesales centre. It will also be among the offerings carried by IBM's SME field sales staff.

Two of Siebel's competitors in the SME market, Salesforce.com and Accpac International, doubt Siebel can quickly create a VAR channel. "I think it's going to be a huge challenge for them," said Ivan Macdonald, Accpac's senior vice-president of worldwide CRM operations. "They don't have a huge track record of partnering with the types of companies we do. It's very difficult to turn a ship that's got predominantly large direct sales to the enterprise." There is also an issue of channel conflict between Siebel and the resellers. When asked why Siebel resellers shouldn't be scared of the company competing directly against them, Siebel's Rudin replied: "VARs can still sell the company's other products, which is expected to be a healthy market. The only reason I think they should be scared is if they aren't the ones who figure out how to become a part of this and their competitors do. There will be a robust reseller channel. There has never been a successful business in the mid-market where it has only been sold direct."

[Adapted from Howard Solomon, "Siebel Wants VARs for eCRM," *Computer Dealer News,* Vol. 19, No. 15 (October 24, 2003).]

The National Basketball Association (NBA) uses E.Piphany's CRM application to gather information about basketball fans from around the world, including Canada, the United States, Europe, Asia, and Australia. This information allows the NBA to personalize promotions that are directly targeted to fan desires. By implementing CRM, the NBA can maximize overall value per customer and eliminate wasted marketing efforts, creating profits for both the league and its teams through one-to-one marketing. CRM products have helped organizations like the NBA identify who their customers are, gain an understanding of what they want, and provide products and services to meet their unique needs.

The service side of CRM brings with it many opportunities to gain competitive advantage by providing customized, individual attention to existing customers. However, facilitating premium customer service requires a great deal of coordination, since customers can interact with a company across multiple channels and through different personnel within the organization. MGM Mirage, which operates the Mirage, MGM Grand, Bellagio, Treasure Island, Golden Nugget, and Beau Rivage casinos and resorts, has deployed CRM to help it design marketing campaigns, such as seasonal promotions and special events, for its existing customers. With the gaming industry growing exponentially, the market has become highly competitive, and MGM Mirage needed an advantage. Customer information—including gambling activities, lodging preferences, and purchase histories—from all of its properties can be consolidated, providing management with a comprehensive, real-time view of market conditions. With accurate, real-time information, management can make decisions more efficiently than their competitors and design targeted marketing campaigns that work. Similarly, Air Canada uses CRM to personalize products and services for their most loyal frequent flyers by giving them rewards for their patronage and increasing repeat business with their most profitable customers.

Marriott International, one of the world's largest hotel and resort corporations, built its marketing philosophy around creating a superior experience for its customers. The company implemented Siebel Systems' CRM solution to accomplish just that. One way that Marriott achieved this goal was through the development of a program called Personal Planning Service, which allowed the company to create personalized vacation itineraries for guests at the time a reservation is made. When a customer returns for a visit to any one of Marriott's properties, an itinerary is built, based on customer requests and preference information stored in the CRM application. For example, when a customer arrives at one of Marriott's resorts, the company has scheduled client activities such as tee times, dinner reservations, and tours well in advance of the customer's stay. According to Marriott, the CRM system has resulted in higher customer satisfaction and an increase of $100 per visitor in service revenues beyond the room rate.

Companies that have successfully implemented CRM can experience greater customer satisfaction and increase productivity in their sales and service personnel, translating into enhancements to the company's profitability. CRM allows organizations to focus on driving revenue as well as streamlining costs, as opposed to emphasizing cost cutting alone. Cost cutting tends to have a lower limit because there are only so many costs that companies can streamline, whereas revenue generation strategies are bound only by the size of the market itself. The U.S. National Quality Research Center estimates that a 1-percent increase in customer satisfaction can lead to a threefold increase in a company's market capitalization. That is significant!

Supply Chain Management

In the previous section, we looked downstream at CRM applications. Now we turn our attention upstream. Getting the raw materials and components that a company uses in its daily operations is an important key to business success. When deliveries from suppliers are accurate and timely, companies can convert them to finished products more efficiently. Coordinating this effort with suppliers has become a central part of companies' overall business strategies, as it can help them reduce costs associated with inventory levels and get new products to market more quickly. Ultimately, this helps companies drive profitability and improve their customer service since they can react to changing market conditions swiftly. Collaborating, or sharing information, with suppliers has become a strategic necessity for business success. By developing and maintaining stronger, more integrated relationships with suppliers, companies can more effectively compete in their markets through cost reductions and responsiveness to market demands.

BRIEF CASE

Tim Hortons Installs ERP Web Portal

TDL Group Ltd. (Tim Hortons) needed a Web-based interface to its enterprise resource planning (ERP) system. The company wanted to eliminate the costly, time-consuming processes of transaction management and day-to-day ordering. In the past, Tim Hortons had to add staff at a higher rate than it could afford and was overtaxing district managers. The company reported a loss of $1 million for every 200 stores added before automation was in place. Tim Hortons spent about a year installing Movex, an ERP tool from Intentia. The software allowed the company to automate a slew of tasks including franchise agreement invoicing, electronic funds transfer, accounts receivable and payable, sales order management and purchasing, taxation control, inventory, and warehousing. Movex was also installed in a 250,000 sq. ft. production and distribution facility based on Brantford, Ontario operated by Maidstone Bakeries, a joint venture between TDL Group and Cuisine de France of Dublin, Ireland. Maidstone produces doughnuts, cookies, and other frozen baked goods for Cuisine de France and Tim Hortons outlets throughout North America. So far, TDL has more than 2,000 stores connected to the Internet portal, in most cases on a DSL line. The Movex system allows for automated collection from franchises and online reordering for stores. Another 300 "non-traditional" stores, such as those in food courts or gas stations, are yet to come online with the integrated portal. Industry analyst David Senf of IDC Canada said IT is playing a larger role in the restaurant industry, although it is largely happening behind the scenes. "Restaurants are challenged with managing inventory throughout a growing network of suppliers while optimizing profits through a greater understanding of buying patterns," Senf said.

Questions

1. Why do you think Tim Hortons chose Movex for its ERP system over more established vendors like SAP or PeopleSoft?
2. Is the ERP system described in the case a strategic system?

[Adapted from Liz Clayton, "Portal Energizes Tim Hortons Behind the Counter," *Computing Canada,* Vol. 29, No. 23 (November 28, 2003).]

GLOBAL PERSPECTIVE

CRM Sweeping Europe!

Customer relationship management software is sweeping across the continent as European companies look for ways to better understand and serve their customers. Europe has come relatively late to CRM. British consulting firm Hewson Group says that Europe accounted for just $1.7 billion of the $7.6-billion global CRM market last year, a small percentage compared with North America, which leads in CRM use. That is changing, however, Hewson founder Nick Hewson says. "CRM vendors are seeing a significantly increased proportion of their business out of Europe," he says. Europe is one of the fastest growing CRM markets, with the growth there expected to continue at 80 percent to 100 percent over the next three years, on par with or ahead of growth in the North American market.

It is not only a question of faster growth. According to some, European CRM implementations are typically more costly than those in North America. PricewaterhouseCoopers says the average implementation cost for its European clients is $7 million. That is significantly more than the $4 million its clients spend on CRM in North America, says Denis Collart, the consulting firm's CRM director for Europe. The difference, Collart says, is that Europeans tend to plan implementations more extensively and deploy them more broadly. "The major difference is that European companies get to CRM [by] starting with the business case," he says. "The [North American market] takes a tactical approach, but in Europe, it's more strategic." While North American projects often focus on a particular aspect of the business, Europeans tend to look at their CRM needs across the entire organization.

Europeans also often take their time on software deployments. An average European CRM project takes 12 to 15 months, while a North American CRM project takes six to nine months, according to PricewaterhouseCoopers. This approach may be grounded in a more reserved European business culture. "It's related to the speed of change in the marketplace," Collart says.

European organizations, less swayed by technology fads than their North American counterparts, may have been slower to adopt CRM. On the other hand, their ambitious, thorough CRM implementations—and the urgency with which deployments are made—indicate that Europe is waking up to the importance of the customer.

[Adapted from Jeff Sweat, "A New Appreciation for the Customer Is Sweeping Across Europe as More of the Continent's Businesses Invest Billions of Dollars in CRM Software," *InformationWeek* (May 21, 2001).]

The term ***supply chain*** is commonly used to refer to the producers of supplies that a company uses. Companies use many different suppliers to procure specific raw materials and components. These suppliers, in turn, work with their suppliers to obtain goods; their suppliers work with additional suppliers, and so forth. The further out in the supply chain one looks, the more and more suppliers are involved. As a result, the term *chain* becomes somewhat of a misnomer since it implies one-to-one relationships facilitating a chain of events flowing from the first supplier to the second to the third, and so on. A more descriptive term to describe the flow of materials from suppliers to a company is ***supply network,*** because multiple suppliers are involved in the process of servicing a single organization. Figure 7.11 depicts a hypothetical supply network.

Several problems can arise when firms within a supply network do not collaborate effectively. Information can easily become distorted as it moves from one company down through the supply network, causing a great deal of inefficiency. Problems such as excessive inventories, inaccurate manufacturing capacity plans, and missed production schedules can run rampant. These issues can lead to degradations in profitability and poor customer service. Implementing software applications to manage a company's activities with its supply network can help alleviate these barriers to competitiveness.

Applications focusing on upstream information flows have two main objectives in mind—to accelerate product development and to reduce costs associated with procuring raw materials, components, and services from suppliers. ***Supply chain management (SCM)*** applications are designed to assist companies in streamlining these areas. SCM applications are commonly integrated with ERP to leverage internal and external information to collaborate with suppliers. Most SCM applications come in the form of packaged software, which can be purchased from some of the leading SCM software vendors such as Agile Software,

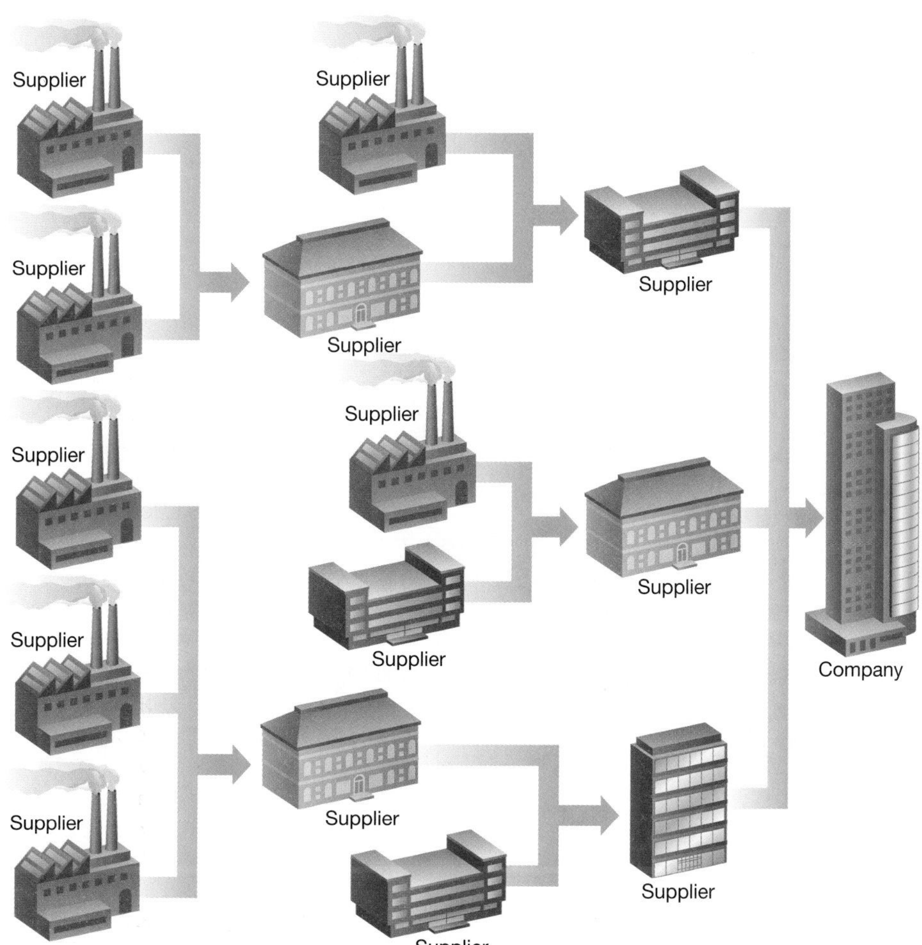

[**Figure 7.11** ➥ A typical supply network.]

Ariba (see Figure 7.12), i2 Technologies, and Manugistics. ERP vendors including BAAN, Oracle, and SAP also offer SCM solutions that are integrated with their ERP applications (Butler, 2001).

Like ERP and CRM applications, SCM packages are delivered in the form of modules (see Table 7.3), which companies select and implement according to their business requirements.

The appropriate SCM technology, combined with the coordination of business processes with the supply network, can provide substantial paybacks for companies. SCM solutions help streamline work flow and enhance employee productivity. Companies can more efficiently manage business travel, time, and expenses, and collaborate with suppliers in real time. Up to US$95 billion in operational savings is expected to be generated by implementing SCM in the U.S. manufacturing economy alone (Manugistics, 2001). To pursue supplier collaboration as a basis to achieve competitive advantage, organizations must be able to access information and track activities throughout the supply network. This means that companies need to have an integrated system that captures information from the various methods they use to communicate upstream with their suppliers. More important, managers need the capability to monitor and analyze factors that drive supplier productivity to ensure they can meet demands based on prevailing market conditions.

Many companies utilize SCM applications to accelerate product development. The ability to swiftly react to changing market conditions can provide companies with the competitive advantage of bringing products to market more quickly than their competition. The other major reason that SCM applications are becoming widely used is based on the fact that they can help companies streamline costs and create efficiencies across their supply networks. Dell uses Ariba's SCM application to automate its formerly paper-based purchasing process, shorten the time it takes to obtain goods and services from suppliers, and lower overall purchasing costs. Dell's SCM connected to its broad supplier network and integrated the company's purchasing activities with its

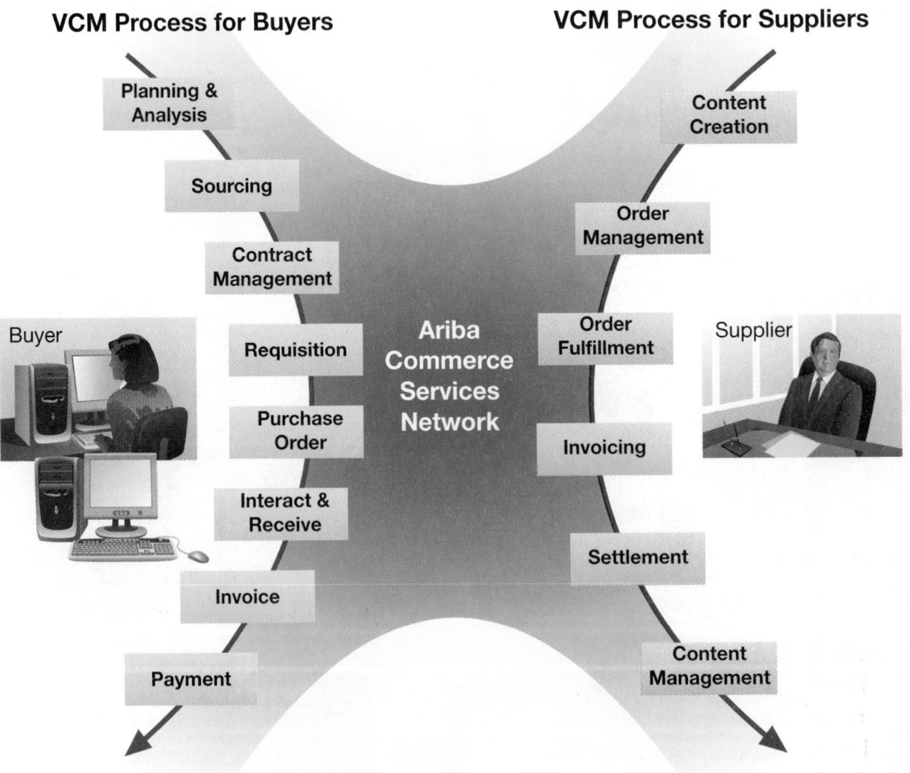

[**Figure 7.12** ➥ An overview of Ariba's value chain management solution—Commerce Services Network.]

Source: **www.ariba.com**.

[Table 7.3] *Functions that optimize the supply network.*[3]

Module	Key Uses
Supply chain collaboration	Share information and integrate processes up and down the supply chain Provide Internet-enabled processes such as collaborative planning, forecasting, and replenishment (CPFR) and vendor-managed inventory
Collaborative design	Streamline product design processes across supply chain partners to reduce time to market React quickly to changing market conditions, such as product launches and new customer segments
Collaborative fulfillment	Commit to delivery dates in real time Fulfill orders from channels on time with order management, transportation planning, and vehicle scheduling Support the entire logistics process, including picking, packing, shipping, and international activities
Collaborative demand and supply planning	Develop a one-number forecast of customer demand by sharing demand and supply forecasts instantaneously across multiple tiers Enable suppliers and vendors to use shared forecasts and real-time demand signals to replenish stock automatically
Collaborative procurement	Provide global visibility into direct material spending Allow partners to leverage buying clout and reduce ad hoc buying
Production planning	Support both discrete and process manufacturing Optimize plans and schedules while considering resource, material, and dependency constraints
Supply chain event management	Monitor every stage of the supply chain process, from price quotation to the moment the customer receives the product, and issue alerts when problems arise Capture data from carriers, vehicle on-board computers, GPS systems, and more
Supply chain exchange	Create an online supply chain community that enables partners to collaborate on design, procurement, demand and supply management, and other supply chain activities
Supply chain performance management	Report key measurements in the supply chain, such as filling rates, order cycle times, and capacity use Integrate planning and execution functions with competitive information and market trends

[3]See SAP's product literature at **www.sap.com**.

existing ERP solution. Ariba SCM provides Dell with data to identify inefficiencies within its supply network and negotiate key contracts for goods and services, resulting in significant volume purchasing discounts. Ariba showed that by automating and streamlining its procurement processes, Dell achieved over 60 percent reductions in procurement cycles and cost per purchase order. Canadian National Railways (CN) adopted an SCM package from i2 Technologies. CN executives had difficulty analyzing the information coming in from the marketplace and could not utilize the company's many assets—tens of thousands of railcars, 1,500 locomotives, and more than 25,000 kilometres of track—to meet customer demand. The company used the SCM application to forecast its business opportunities, as

Web Search

WEB SEARCH OPPORTUNITY

Visit the Manugistics Website at **www.manugistics.com** to see what the company is currently offering in the way of supply chain management capabilities. What other types of software and/or services does Manugistics offer?

BRIEF CASE

A Summer Meltdown for Canadian Banks

The summer of 2004 was a tough one for Canadian banks, at least as far as enterprise systems are concerned. Three Canadian financial institutions experienced full or partial system failures during this period. These glitches affected millions of customers across the country. For example, on May 31, 2004, a system crash during a routine software upgrade at the Royal Bank affected millions of standard transactions. One of the effects of the crash was the posting failure of direct payroll deposits; many people, including the premiers of Ontario and New Brunswick, did not get paid. The spill-over effect of this problem led to thousands of missed mortgage and loan payments. While the Royal Bank had the system up and running again in a couple of days, many users were inconvenienced.

On July 29, 2004, CIBC double-charged tens of thousands of loan accounts. If a customer withdrew $100, the record showed that he or she had withdrawn $200. Once again, the problem was fixed quickly, but in the critical eyes of the public, the damage was done. Finally, on August 24, 2004, TD Canada Trust failed to process transactions conducted with tellers at 500 branches in Ontario and British Columbia. Online banking systems and ATM machines also went offline. Direct costs of this error were computed to be $9 million; indirect costs, however, were predicted to be considerably higher.

In all three cases, the problems were traced to simple glitches that would not normally bring down a system. A confluence of factors led to each of the incidents. Enterprise systems are often so complex that occasional problems are inevitable. Organizations can reduce the incidence, or the effect, of problems by following a few simple steps. For example, system changes or software upgrades should be scheduled for off-peak periods. The Royal Bank decided to no longer schedule software maintenance or upgrades around the end of the month. It is also important to keep up-to-date documentation of all system changes, in case something needs to be corrected. Proposed system changes should be extensively tested for primary and secondary "spill-over" effects. Finally, backup and disaster recovery systems should be available in case something goes awry. Customers have come to expect fast, efficient service. The consequences of failure may take a very long time to forget.

Questions

1. Part of the blame for the system problems was placed not with the banks directly, but with IT outsourcing partners. How can firms, like banks, protect themselves from problems created by outsourcing firms?
2. Enterprise systems often require business process redesign. Is it better to change organizational processes to fit an enterprise system, or change the system to fit a firm's business processes?

well as to translate incoming market information. The solution allowed CN to recognize inconsistencies in its business system and find a solution to better manage its freight.

CAREER IMPLICATIONS

Operations Management

Grocery Gateway (GG) is Canada's largest online grocer, with approximately 125,000 registered customers. Shoppers can select from over 6,500 items on the company's Website, **www.grocerygateway.com**. Approximately 1,500 orders are delivered throughout the greater Toronto area—over 3,200 square kilometres—every day. Delivery represents a major component of GG's operating expenses. Even a small reduction in the cost of the average delivery results in a large improvement in operating results. GG decided to adopt a dynamic route optimization solution from Descartes Solutions, based in Waterloo, Ontario. The Descartes solution provided route delivery schedules generated from algorithms that took into account delivery windows, drive time, time of day, road type, and other factors. It was also integrated with GG's order processing system and warehouse control system. The system optimized current delivery routes, and suggested which routes were the most profitable. Based on this information, GG decided to restrict deliveries to some unprofitable locations.

THE FORMULA FOR ENTERPRISE SYSTEM SUCCESS

To summarize, the main objective of enterprise systems is to create competitive advantage by streamlining business activities within and outside a company. However, many implementations are more costly and time consuming than originally envisioned. It is not uncommon to have projects that run over budget, meaning that identifying common problems and devising methods for dealing with these issues can prove invaluable to management. One study found that 40 to 60 percent of companies that undertake enterprise system implementations do not fully realize the results that they had hoped (Langenwalter, 2000). Companies that have successfully installed enterprise systems are found to follow a basic set of recommendations related to enterprise system implementations (Koch, Slater, and Baatz, 2000). Although the following list is not meant to be comprehensive, these recommendations will provide an understanding of some of the challenges involved in implementing enterprise systems:

Recommendation 1—	Secure executive sponsorship
Recommendation 2—	Get help from outside experts
Recommendation 3—	Thoroughly train users
Recommendation 4—	Take a multidisciplinary approach to implementations

Secure executive sponsorship. The primary reason that enterprise system implementations fail is believed to be a direct result of a lack of top-level management support. According to SAP Canada, executive sponsorship is inextricably linked to employee involvement and motivation. Although executives do not necessarily need to make decisions concerning the enterprise system, it is critical that they buy into the decisions made by project managers. Many problems can arise if projects fail to grab the attention of top-level management. In most companies, executives have the ultimate authority regarding the availability and distribution of resources within the organization. If executives do not understand the importance of the enterprise system, this will likely result in delays or stoppages because the necessary resources may not be available when they are needed.

A second problem that may arise deals with top-level management's ability to authorize changes to the way the company does business. When business processes need to be changed to incorporate best practices, these modifications need to be completed. Otherwise the company will have a piece of software on its hands that does not fit the way people accomplish their business tasks. Lack of executive sponsorship can also have a trickle-down effect within the organization. If users and midlevel management perceive the enterprise system to be unimportant, they are not likely to view it as a priority. Enterprise systems require a concentrated effort, and executive sponsorship can propel or stifle the implementation. Executive management can obliterate any obstacles that arise.

Get help from outside experts. Enterprise systems are complex. Even the most talented information systems departments can struggle in coming to grips with ERP, CRM, and SCM applications. Most vendors have trained project managers and consultants to assist companies with installing enterprise systems. Vendors such as Siebel Systems work with consulting firms such as Accenture and IBM rather than maintaining a huge, internal implementation division. Consultants can give companies a head start since they are already trained on the package being implemented. They also have experience in helping other companies implement the software, making them keenly aware of potential problem areas that may arise during the implementation. Many consulting organizations have developed tried and trusted methodologies that help companies develop an appropriate project plan to guide them through the installation process.

Using consultants tends to move companies through the implementation more quickly and help companies train their personnel on the applications more effectively. However, companies should not rely too heavily on consultants and should plan for the consultants leaving once the implementation is complete. When consultants are physically present, company personnel tend to rely on them for assistance. Once the application goes live and the consultants are no longer there, users have to do the job themselves. A key focus should be facilitating user learning.

Thoroughly train users. Training is often the most overlooked, underestimated, and poorly budgeted expense involved in planning enterprise system implementations. Enterprise systems are much more complicated to learn than stand-alone systems. Learning a single application requires users to become accustomed to a new software interface, but enterprise system users regularly need to learn a new set of business processes as well. Once enterprise systems go live, many companies experience a dramatic drop-off in productivity. In a survey of 64 Fortune 500 companies that have implemented enterprise systems, 25 percent were shown to have experienced productivity problems after going live. The most common reason that performance problems arise is that the applications and processes are different from the previous system (Shah, 2001). Users that have not mastered the new system will not be able to perform effectively. This issue can potentially lead to heightened levels of dissatisfaction among users, as they prefer to accomplish their business activities in a familiar manner rather than doing things the new way. By training users before the system goes live and giving them sufficient opportunities to learn the new system, a company can allay fears and mitigate potential productivity issues.

Take a multidisciplinary approach to implementations. Enterprise systems affect the entire organization and, thus, companies should include personnel from different levels and departments in the implementation project (Kumar and Crook, 1999). In CRM and SCM environments in which other organizations are participating in the implementation, it is critical to enlist the support of personnel in their organizations as well. Project managers need to include in the implementation personnel from midlevel management, the information systems department, external consultants, and, most important, end users.

Failing to include the appropriate people in the day-to-day activities of the project can prove problematic in many respects. From a needs analysis standpoint, it is critical that all the business requirements be sufficiently captured before selecting an enterprise solution. Since end users are involved in every aspect of daily business activities, their insights can be invaluable. For instance, an end user might make salient a feature that no one on the project team had thought of. Having an application that does not meet all the business's requirements can result in poorly fitting software or customizations. Another peril in leaving out key personnel involves the threat of alienation. Departments and/or personnel that do not feel included may develop a sense of animosity toward the new system and view it in a negative light. In

COMING ATTRACTIONS

Can My ERP Talk to Your ERP?

SAP recently unveiled an upgrade to its business intelligence (BI) system that shows the company is slowly opening up the software used for collecting and analyzing customer, financial, and supply chain data to other vendors' business applications. The software maker said the latest version of mySAP Business Intelligence will include reporting software from Crystal Decisions that lets companies draw data from other business systems.

In addition, the company revealed at its Conference on Business Intelligence and Enterprise Portals, held recently in Leipzig, Germany, that mySAP BI will include the company's enterprise portal software and the option of integrating with tools from Ascential Software (formerly Informix) and linking to non-SAP data warehouses.

Crystal's reporting software will be embedded in the data warehouse component of mySAP, providing 1,800 predefined reports for analyzing customer data, such as sales opportunities and deal sizes, as well as human resources, supply chain, financial, and product life cycle data. Under the seller agreement, customers of SAP's Business Information Warehouse can generate up to 500 different reports. Those who want more report templates or want to customize reports will have to buy a separate licence.

While Crystal's software is capable of drawing data from non-SAP systems, only 20 of the 500 reports covered in the seller agreement can access other software, says Michael Schiff, an analyst at Current Analysis. "SAP is trying to move out of its closed environment and be perceived as open," he says. "But the real test will be to see if anyone not using SAP R/3 uses the business intelligence tools." SAP R/3 is the company's flagship enterprise resource planning system. "SAP has come a long way toward easing customer complaints that its ERP system, once referred to as an 'SAP jailhouse,' was too closed," Schiff says. In addition, the company has improved business intelligence tools with each release.

[Adapted from Antone Gonsalves, "SAP Takes Step toward More Open System," *InformationWeek* (January 30, 2002).]

extreme cases, users will refuse to use the new application, resulting in conflicts and inefficiencies within the organization.

Although these expansive enterprise system implementations are often cumbersome and difficult, the potential payoff is huge. As a result, organizations are compelled to implement these systems. Further, given the popularity and necessity of such systems, you are likely to find yourself involved in the implementation and/or use of such a system. We are confident that after reading this chapter, you will be better able to understand and help with the development and use of such systems.

KEY POINTS REVIEW

1. **Explain how organizations support business activities by using information technologies.** Organizations use information systems to better perform all of the various business processes (and activities within these processes) throughout each of the functional areas of the firm. Whether it be taking an order for a product, manufacturing a product, securing supplies from another firm, shipping a product to a customer, or providing service after the sale, companies can use information systems to make each of these processes and activities more effective and efficient. More important, companies can use information systems to integrate these processes and activities and to accumulate and use wisely the information that is generated each step of the way.
2. **Describe what enterprise systems are and how they have evolved.** Enterprise systems are information systems that span the entire organization and can be used to integrate business processes, activities, and information across all the functional areas of a firm. Enterprise systems can be either prepackaged software or custom-made applications. One popular, powerful type of enterprise system is the enterprise resource planning system, from vendors such as SAP and Oracle. These ERP packages evolved from "material requirements planning" systems during the 1990s and are, for the most part, used to support internal business processes.
3. **Explain the differences between internally and externally focused software applications.** Internally focused software applications are generally used to support business processes and activities that occur within the boundaries of a firm. Examples are the manufacturing of a product or the management of inventories. ERP packages are commonly used to support these types of processes and activities. External software applications are generally used to support business processes and activities that occur across organizational boundaries. Examples are taking product orders from customers and receiving supplies from other firms. Supply chain management packages, such as those from Manugistics, enable a firm to interact more effectively and efficiently with upstream business partners. Customer relationship management packages, such as those from Siebel Systems, enable a firm to interact more effectively and efficiently downstream with customers. ERP, CRM, and SCM applications are increasingly being targeted at SMEs.
4. **Understand and utilize the keys to successfully implementing enterprise systems.** Experience with enterprise system implementations suggest that there are some common problems that can be avoided and/or should be managed carefully. These include 1) securing executive sponsorship, 2) getting necessary help from outside experts (i.e., consultants such as Accenture), 3) thoroughly training users, and 4) taking a multidisciplinary approach to implementations.

KEY TERMS

REVIEW QUESTIONS

1. Describe what enterprise systems are and how they have evolved.
2. What are the advantages and disadvantages of enterprise systems?
3. What are the primary and support activities of a value chain?
4. Give an example of upstream and downstream information flows in a value system.
5. Compare and contrast customized and packaged applications.
6. How does customer relationship management differ from supply chain management?
7. Explain a data warehouse and the types of data that flow in and out of the warehouse.
8. Describe business process reengineering and give an example.
9. What are the four components of financial software modules?
10. What are the keys to successfully implementing an enterprise system?

SELF-STUDY QUESTIONS

Answers are at the end of the Problems and Exercises.

1. _______ are information systems that allow companies to integrate information support operations on a company-wide basis.
   A. Customer relationship management systems
   B. Enterprise systems
   C. WANs
   D. Interorganizational systems
2. Which of the following is a primary activity according to the value chain model?
   A. firm infrastructure
   B. customer service
   C. human resources
   D. procurement
3. According to the value chain model, which of the following is a support function?
   A. technology development
   B. marketing and sales
   C. inbound logistics
   D. operations and manufacturing
4. All of the following are true about legacy systems **except** _______.
   A. they are stand-alone systems
   B. they are older software systems
   C. they are enterprise resource planning systems
   D. they may be difficult to integrate into other systems
5. _______ is a component of the production planning module.
   A. Sales and operations planning
   B. Material requirements planning
   C. Capacity requirements planning
   D. All of the above
6. Which of the following companies produces ERP systems?
   A. Microsoft
   B. Oracle
   C. Computer Associates and SAP
   D. all of the above
7. All of the following are components of financial accounting software modules **except** _______.
   A. general ledger
   B. personnel administration
   C. accounts payable
   D. accounts receivable
8. Which of the following is commonly used to refer to the producers of supplies that a company uses?
   A. procurement
   B. sales force
   C. supply network
   D. customers
9. _______ is global visibility into direct material spending and allows partners to leverage buying clout and reduce ad hoc buying.
   A. Collaborative procurement
   B. Collaborative fulfillment
   C. Production planning
   D. Supply chain exchange
10. _______ are databases that store information related to the various business activities of an organization.
    A. Information stores
    B. Data warehouses
    C. Web marts
    D. Specialty databases

PROBLEMS AND EXERCISES

1. Match the following terms with the appropriate definitions:
   ____ Enterprise systems
   ____ Legacy systems
   ____ Data warehouses
   ____ Supply chain
   ____ Customer relationship management
   ____ Value chain
   ____ Supply chain management
   ____ Business process reengineering
   ____ Collaborative design
   ____ Upstream information flow

a. An information flow that consists of information received from another organization
b. Older systems that are not designed to communicate with other applications beyond departmental boundaries
c. Information systems that allow companies to integrate information support operations on a company-wide basis
d. Databases that store information related to the various business activities of an organization
e. Applications that concentrate on downstream information flows, integrating the value chains of a company and its distributors
f. Commonly used to refer to the producers of supplies that a company uses
g. Streamlining product design processes across supply chain partners to reduce time to market and react quickly to changing market conditions, such as product launches and new customer segments
h. The flow of information through a set of business activities
i. Applications that operate on upstream information flows, integrating the value chains of a company and its suppliers
j. Altering the way in which business processes are conducted

2. Find an organization that you are familiar with (or use one of the Brief Cases in the textbook), and determine how many software applications it is utilizing concurrently. Is the company's information system cohesive, or does it need updating and streamlining?
3. What part does training users in an ERP system play, and how important is it in software satisfaction? What productivity problems can result in an ERP implementation?
4. What are the payoffs in taking a multidisciplinary approach to an ERP implementation? What departments are affected, and what is the typical time frame? Research one of the Brief Cases in this chapter or find a company that has recently implemented an ERP system. What could the company have done better, and what did it do right?
5. Describe collaborative demand and supply planning, and find an example or two of companies applying this concept. What are the advantages and disadvantages? Is it cost-effective? What were some of the challenges of implementation? What improvements could be made?
6. A number of cases in this chapter discuss how major enterprise software firms are targeting the Canadian market. How does the Canadian market differ from other national markets? Do you think that differentiating between the Canadian market and other markets is the correct approach?
7. What companies are using data warehouses? Research this question, and determine the cost and size of a data warehouse. What are the advantages and disadvantages of data warehouses? What is the typical time frame for implementation?
8. Look on the World Wide Web and find Microsoft, Oracle, Computer Associates, PeopleSoft, and SAP. What are some of the different applications offered and their prices? What are the differences in Websites? What can you find out about software implementation?
9. Based on your own experiences with applications, have you used customized or off-the-shelf applications? What is the difference, and how good was the system documentation?
10. Some case examples in the chapter decided to adopt applications from large enterprise software vendors, while others chose niche products from smaller vendors. What are the advantages and disadvantages of choosing a large, global vendor versus a local or niche vendor for enterprise software?
11. Go through the job ads in the newspaper or on the Web and find a position that you would like to have in the future. Make an appointment to visit the company and ask questions of the human resources and information systems departments. Determine who hires for this position and what the qualifications are for the position. Find out exactly what the daily duties of the position are. You might even consider investigating an internship.
12. Choose an organization from one of the Brief Cases in the textbook or an organization with which you are familiar that utilizes customer relationship management. Who within the organization is most involved in this process, and who benefits?

ANSWERS TO THE SELF-STUDY QUESTIONS

1. B 2. B 3. A 4. C 5. D 6. D 7. B 8. C 9. A 10. B

Case 1: *ERP Implementation at MANCO*

Enterprise resource planning (ERP) systems are considered to be critical to the success of any business. However, many ERP implementations fail because certain social aspects are ignored. In this case, we narrate the experiences of a company named MANCO (a pseudonym), which realized that there was more to an ERP implementation than the technology itself. MANCO was founded in 1966 by two engineers who had seen the increasing demand for "high-quality air purification equipment worldwide." The company started off in the garage of one of the co-founders but had grown to be a large, well-established organization with worldwide sales of more than $25 million by the late 1990s. The company is headquartered in a large city located in the Midwest region of the United States but also has regional offices in other parts of the United States and a few subsidiary offices in the United Kingdom, Germany, and Australia. The company sells air purification equipment to commercial customers such as offices, bars, restaurants, bowling alleys, and so on, and also to industrial manufacturers of metal and chemical products. Most of the equipment is manufactured in its primary plant located in the Midwest. MANCO employs mixed-mode manufacturing strategies, including made-to-stock, assemble-to-order, and so on. Over a period of time, the company has earned considerable repute in the air purification equipment market, and the future seemed promising enough for MANCO.

However, in the recent past, things had not seemed to go as the CEO planned. There were growing problems in the organization, which threatened not only its stability but also its very existence. There were increasing customer complaints. The sales department was promising customers delivery dates that were unachievable. It was often booking orders without accurate specifications, which was delaying the engineering design and the actual production of the equipment. There were often errors and problems in the design and the design modifications, which led to a lot of wasted time. The problems often arose due to a lack of coordination between the mechanical and the electrical engineering groups within the organization, in addition to a lot of unnecessary paperwork and exchange of information between them. The lack of coordination, excessive information exchange, and other territorial disputes between the various departments were leading to unreasonable lead times, questionable product quality, and ultimately tremendous customer dissatisfaction. The information technology at MANCO was doing little to help ameliorate these increasing problems. MANCO's primary computer system was a Quantel minicomputer, acquired about 15 years ago, with a Quantel package QMRP 6.31 running on it that helped with inventory control, product structure, purchasing and receiving, order entry, invoice processing, Kanban replenishment, and so on. The minicomputer served 60 terminals and 20 printers, and supported flat files. It did not, however, have any relational DBMS capabilities, which affected the company's ability to produce any meaningful reports. Because production of a single piece of air purification equipment required incredible coordination and exchange of information (e.g., memos and reports between MANCO's various departments, from sales to engineering to manufacturing), the inability to run efficient reports was hindering the business significantly. In addition, MANCO had some IBM PC-compatible systems that were running CAD/CAM applications, supporting contact management, customer complaints tracking, human resource applications, and so on. In short, MANCO had several systems, each of which had little coordination or connectivity with the others. This led to a lot of redundant paperwork, ultimately slowing down the company's business processes. The CEO (in consultation with the MIS department) realized that a radical change was required in MANCO's information technology.

The company decided that the new system to be selected should have a Windows-based client-server platform that would support relational databases. This would enable users to make changes quickly to data and procedures being used by different departments. In addition, such a network would allow everyone to view information from other departments, tearing down some of the existing territorial barriers, and would also allow users to view real-time data as opposed to batch data. MANCO found the solution in a particular ERP package that was a fully integrated business management system designed especially for manufacturers. The system had several modules that handled financial analysis, capacity management, shop-floor control, order processing, and so on. In addition, the system supported CAD, EDI, external payroll, data collection, and generation of standard reports, query reports, custom reports, and executive reports (all of which were initially generated by separate systems, and often by hand). The system allowed the existing bills of materials (BOMs) to be quickly copied and modified. The CAD interface also automated the design processes and enabled BOM items to be fed directly into the system from other third-party CAD packages. All in all, it was a system that satisfied each of the information technology needs of the company.

However, before the system could be installed, the CEO realized that some critical organizational changes were required at MANCO. MANCO was struggling not only because of its archaic information technology, but (as discussed earlier) because of the lack of coordination and territorial attitudes between and within each of the company's departments, which, according to the CEO, had to be eliminated or at least reduced. The first step toward this goal was the dismissal of the three vice-presidents (sales, operations, and engineering) who were harbouring the territorial attitudes within the organization, and the appointment of a single senior VP of operations who would be in charge of all these departments (the coordination among these three departments was most critical to the organization's success). Next, there was an attempt to change the culture of the company by building the principles of quality into the employee psyche and also introducing a profit-sharing scheme. The company made a sincere effort to make employees put quality at the forefront of production. The profit-sharing scheme also helped employees realize that manufacturing the product and delivering it swiftly to the customer was critical to their own, and the company's, success. This speeded up the business processes, reduced redundancy, and opened up informal lines of communication.

After making the initial organizational changes, the company implemented the ERP package in six stages, which included some pilot implementations (to iron out any difficulties that might have arisen) and training sessions. After a few months, the system was fully functional at MANCO, and today it continues to handle most of the company's operations. In general, management is satisfied with the outcome, and MANCO has begun to regain some of its old glory.

[Adapted from S. Sarker and A. Lee, "Using a Case Study to Test the Role of Three Key Social Enablers in ERP Implementation," *Proceedings of International Conference on Information Systems* (Brisbane, Australia, 2000): 414–425.]

Discussion Questions

1. What were some of the information technology problems at MANCO?
2. From your knowledge of enterprise resource planning systems, do you think that the company was correct in selecting an ERP package to solve its IT problems?
3. What were some of the factors that led to the success of the ERP implementation at MANCO?
4. Would the ERP implementation at MANCO be successful even if it were not accompanied by some of the organizational structure and cultural changes?

Case 2: *2003 Blackout Prompts Firms to Think about Business Continuity and Disaster Recovery*

On August 14, 2003, the power grid supplying electricity to most of Ontario and the Eastern Seaboard went offline. More than 50 million homes and businesses lost power immediately, and some continued without electricity for three days or more. This event was a wake-up call for many businesses. Q9 Networks Inc., a Toronto-based Web hosting company, relied on diesel generators to supply its Toronto data centre with power during the blackout. However, it could not offer the level of service that its customers had come to expect. Q9 subsequently unveiled a new service that would guarantee uptime to its Web-hosting customers by drawing on the power of its main centre in Toronto, as well as a second site in Calgary. If one site were to go offline, then all the traffic would be routed through the second site.

Since information systems have become a strategic necessity for most organizations, business continuity and disaster recovery planning have become critical elements of the IS function. The Ontario blackout alerted many businesses to the fact that uptime isn't something that can be taken for granted. For example, there's a growing awareness of the need for multiple hosting sites, says Venky Srinivasan, director of technology for Toronto-based law firm Stikeman Elliott LLP. Stikeman currently uses Q9 for Web hosting and as its Internet gateway, but the firm is considering using a third-party host for more of its systems and data—particularly as Stikeman evolves into a 24/7 business. If Stikeman were to host more of its data or services outside of the firm, then the data centre would be "made redundant as much as possible," says Srinivasan. "For sure it should be in a totally different power grid, or maybe even outside of Canada. Maybe it should be in Europe."

"This sense of [urgency] has increased over the last seven or eight years," said Jay Grove, technical specialist with Hewlett-Packard Canada. "A lot of businesses are saying: 'We can't survive if we can't do business 24/7,' " Indeed, the "cycle times" for businesses are faster than ever before, adds Arthur Pelletier, director of client services for Export Development Canada. Extreme examples of today's 24/7 companies include Yahoo!, eBay, and Amazon, he said. Day traders are also heavily dependent on an impenetrable system to deal with all-important transactions. "If these [businesses] are not up, they don't exist... and they're out of business," said Pelletier. "If they're down for a long time, you might as well close the doors."

Particularly attuned to such scenarios are financial institutions, said Mike Ross, manager of IT service continuity management at TD Bank Financial Group. "We have plans in place, and we're moving toward looking at different options and implementing new solutions where necessary," Ross said. "TD is going down that road, as are other banks. I think quicker recovery times and no data loss is where large companies, especially financial institutions, will need to go." Consequently, some organizations are highly sensitive to disaster recovery and are willing to invest in high-end back-up systems capable of data mirroring and electronic vaulting. Such systems can instantly send back-up files on important transactions to a second site. Ideally, these systems ensure a seamless transition from the home site to the back-up site if ever there are unexpected problems prompted by such things as virus attacks, power outages, fires, or terror attacks. A second site also provides an audit trail option for firms that need to retrace the course of their operations following a disaster.

Solutions that support business continuity and disaster recovery are not cheap. "Businesses have to look at what the real risks are and they have to understand that it's an insurance they're doing, not an investment," said Pelletier. "If you think of it as 'I have to put money into something,' it's really wrong-headed. Companies have to ask themselves: 'What can I live with?' Sit down and examine your business elements.... How critical is this function really, and over what interval of time does that present itself?" Regardless of the back-up system an organization chooses, it should always expect the unexpected. There's only so much companies can do to prepare for the future, said Grove. "It's about going back to review previous incidents, like the blackout, and looking at how you could deal with them more effectively."

[Adapted from Neil Sutton, "Q9 Adds Global Redundancy Service in Wake of Blackout," *Computing Canada,* Vol. 29, No. 20 (October 17, 2003); and Scott Foster, "Companies Step Up Business Continuity Plans in Wake of Blackout," *Computing Canada,* Vol. 29, No. 20 (October 17, 2003).]

Discussion Questions

1. What are some important factors to take into consideration when formulating a disaster recovery plan?
2. Do you agree that disaster recovery planning is more like insurance than an investment?
3. How should disaster recovery and business continuity plans differ by industry, if at all? Provide examples.
4. Who should be included in a disaster recovery team?

Chapter 8

Preview

As you have read throughout this book and have experienced in your own life, information systems are of many different types, including decision support systems, executive information systems, group support systems, and Internet commerce systems. Just as there are different types of systems, different approaches have been found to be more appropriate for developing some types of systems and less appropriate for others. Learning all possible ways to develop or acquire a system and, more important, how to identify the optimal approach, takes years of study and experience. Toward this end, this chapter has several objectives.

After reading this chapter, you will be able to do the following:

1. Understand the process used by organizations to manage the development of information systems.
2. Describe each major phase of the systems development life cycle: system identification, selection, and planning; system analysis; system design; system implementation; and system maintenance.
3. Describe prototyping, rapid application development, and object-oriented analysis and design methods of systems development, along with each approach's strengths and weaknesses.
4. Understand the factors involved in building a system in-house, along with situations in which it is not feasible.
5. Explain three alternative systems development options: external acquisition, outsourcing, and end-user development.

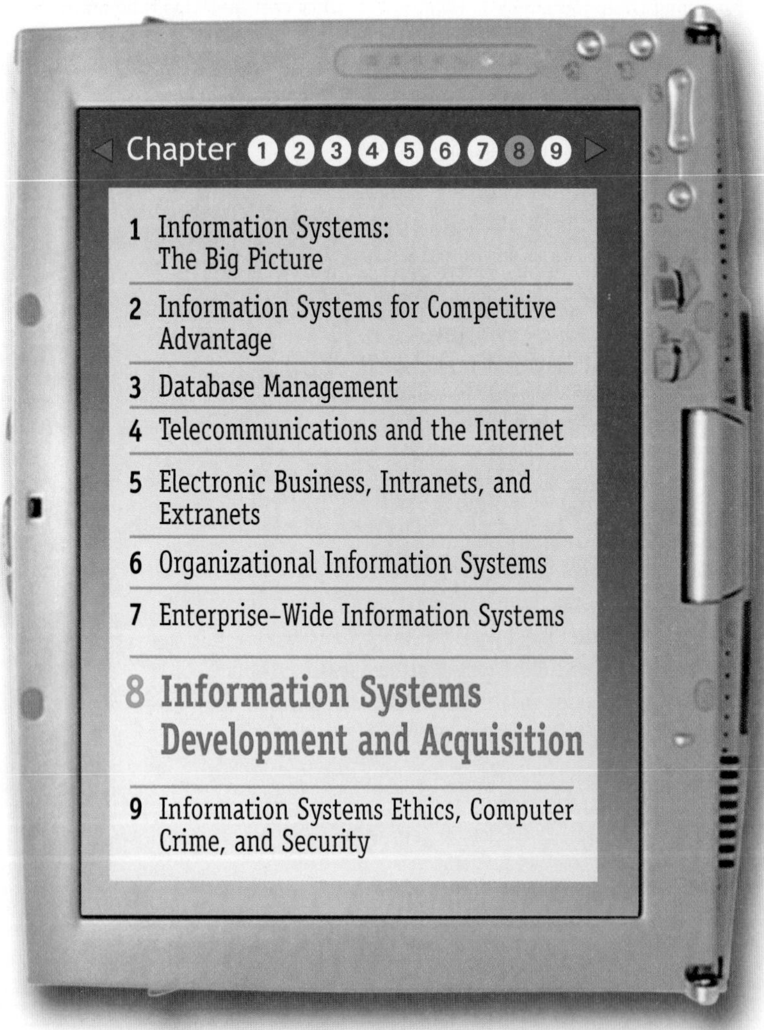

[**Figure 8.1** ➡ The Big Picture: focusing on information systems development and acquisition.]

Information Systems Development and Acquisition

OPENING: American Firm Chooses to "Nearsource" IT in Halifax

Outsourcing firm Keane Inc. agreed to fill 175 information technology jobs over three years at its Halifax Advanced Development Centre. Headquartered in Boston, Keane works with large firms and government agencies to plan, build, and manage application software, primarily through outsourcing agreements.

Keane will hire about 50 people in Halifax in 2004, says Alaisdar Graham, managing director of the Nova Scotia facility. The rest will probably be hired in 2005. Graham says the Halifax operation, which currently employs more than 300 people, has seen 30-percent annual growth recently and "there's no sign of it slacking off."

Keane's announcement is the latest example of nearshore outsourcing, in which U.S. companies shift IT work to Canada because of lower salary and infrastructure costs, proximity to the U.S., similarity of culture, and quality of service. Nearshore outsourcing has become a bright spot for the Canadian IT industry, with companies such as Montreal-based CGI Group Inc., RIS Resource Information Systems Inc. of Toronto, and others providing software development and services to U.S. clients. In late 2003, EDS Canada announced plans for a Global Centre of Excellence based on Microsoft Corp.'s .NET technology in Victoria. EDS said the centre would create 100 jobs.

Skills Keane needs include Java, Perl, and COBOL programming and expertise with Unix, Sybase, and WebSphere, Graham says. The company hopes to fill many jobs locally, but will also recruit from other provinces. The jobs will be of "huge" importance to the province, said Joe Gillis, a spokesman for Nova Scotia Business Inc., the provincial government agency that authorized the $1.5 million in rebates to Keane.

Nova Scotia's Economic Development Office recently gave Keane $2.5 million in funding to help it attain Capability Maturity Model Level 5 assessment from the Software Engineering Institute. Graham said his operation is the first Canadian nearshore outsourcing facility to obtain this designation for continuous process optimization, which he considers directly responsible for its growth. Graham says Keane originally located in Halifax because of Nova Scotia's low cost of living and proximity to New England, where many of Keane's clients are located. The company also received grants from the provincial and federal governments when it established the operation.

[Adapted from Grant Buckler, "American Outsourcing Firm Expands Halifax Operation," *Computing Canada*, Vol. 29, No. 23 (November 28, 2003).]

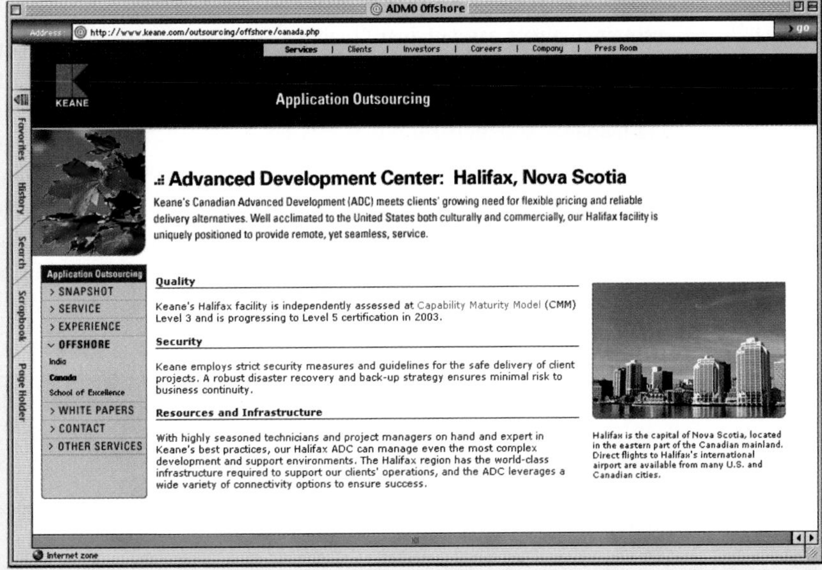

[**Figure 8.2** ➥ Boston-based Keane Inc. chooses "nearshore" outsourcing in Halifax over "offshore" outsourcing in Asia or Eastern Europe.]

Source: Keane Inc.

If you are a typical business student, you might be wondering why we have a chapter on building and acquiring information systems. The answer is simple: no matter what area of an organization you are in—such as marketing, finance, accounting, human resources, or operations—you will be involved in the systems development process. In fact, research indicates that the IS spending in most organizations is controlled by specific business functions. What this means is that even if your career interests are in something other than IS, it is very likely that you will be involved in the IS development process. Understanding all available options is important to your future success and an important part of your understanding of The Big Picture (see Figure 8.1).

THE NEED FOR STRUCTURED SYSTEMS DEVELOPMENT

The process of designing, building, and maintaining information systems is often referred to as ***systems analysis and design.*** Likewise, the individual who performs this task is referred to as a ***systems analyst.*** (This chapter uses *systems analyst* and *programmer* interchangeably.) Because few organizations can exist without effectively utilizing information and computing technology, the demand for systems analysts far outpaces the supply. Organizations want to hire systems analysts because they possess a unique blend of both managerial and technical expertise—systems analysts are not just "techies." In fact, systems analysts are in hot demand precisely due to their unique blend of technical and managerial expertise, but it was not always this way.

The Evolution of Information Systems Development

In the early days of computing, systems development and programming was considered an art that only a few technical "gurus" could master. Unfortunately, the techniques used to construct systems varied greatly from individual to individual. This variation made it difficult to integrate large organizational information systems. Furthermore, many systems were not easily maintainable after the original programmer left the organization. As a result, organizations were often left with systems that were very difficult and expensive to maintain. Many organizations, therefore, underutilized these technology investments and failed to realize all possible benefits from their systems.

To address this problem, information systems professionals concluded that system development needed to become an engineering-like discipline (Nunamaker, 1992). Common methods, techniques, and tools had to be developed to create a disciplined approach for constructing information systems. This evolution from an "art" to a "discipline" led to the use of the term ***software engineering*** to help define what systems analysts and programmers do. Transforming information systems development into a formal discipline would provide numerous benefits. First, it would be much easier to train programmers and analysts if common techniques were widely used. In essence, if all systems analysts had similar training, it would make them more interchangeable and more skilled at working on the systems developed by other analysts. Second, systems built with commonly used techniques would be more maintainable. Both industry and academic researchers have pursued the quest for new and better approaches for building information systems.

Options for Obtaining Information Systems

Organizations can obtain new information systems in many ways. One option, of course, is for the members of the organization to build the information system themselves. Organizations can also buy a prepackaged system from a software development company or consulting firm. Some information systems that are commonly used in many organizations can be purchased for much less money than what it would cost to build a new one. Purchasing a prepackaged system is a good option as long as its features meet the needs of the organization. For example, a payroll system is an example of a prepackaged system that is often purchased rather than developed by an organization because tax laws, wage calculations, cheque printing, and accounting activities are highly standardized. Figure 8.3 outlines several sources for information systems.

A third option is to have an outside organization or consultant custom build a system to an organization's specifications. This is generally referred to as having the development outsourced. This is a good option when an organization does not have

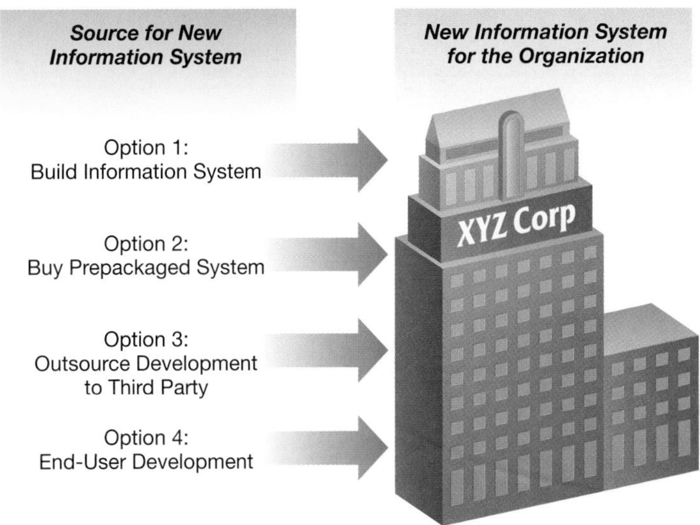

[Figure 8.3 ➡ There are a variety of sources for information systems.]

adequate systems development resources or expertise. A final option is to let individual users and departments build their own custom systems to support their individual needs. This is referred to as end-user development. Most organizations allow end users to construct only a limited range of systems. For example, systems that span organizational boundaries or perform complex changes to corporate databases are typically not candidates for end-user development. Alternatively, a common application that might be constructed with end-user development is a data analysis system using a spreadsheet application such as Microsoft Excel. Regardless of the source of the new information system, the primary role of managers and users in the organization is to make sure that any new system will meet the organization's business needs. This means that managers and users must understand the systems development process to ensure that the system will meet their needs.

Information Systems Development in Action

The tools and techniques used to develop information systems are continually evolving with the rapid changes in information systems hardware and software. As you will see, the information systems development approach is a very structured process that moves from step to step. Systems analysts become adept at decomposing large, complex problems into many small, simple problems. They can then easily solve each simple problem by writing a relatively short computer program. The goal of the systems analyst is to build the final system by piecing together the many small programs into one comprehensive system. This process of decomposing a problem is outlined in Figure 8.4. An easy way to think about this is to think about using Lego blocks for building a model house. When together, the blocks can create a large and very complex design. Apart, each block is a small, simple piece that has nothing without the others. When systems are built in this manner, they are much easier to design, program, and, most important, maintain.

The Role of Users in the Systems Development Process

Most organizations have a huge investment in transaction processing and management information systems. These systems are most often designed, constructed, and maintained by systems analysts and programmers within the organization, using a variety of methods. When building and maintaining information systems, systems analysts rely on information provided by system users, who are involved in all phases of the system's development process. To effectively participate in the process, it is important for all members of the organization to understand what is meant by systems development and what activities occur. A close and mutually respectful working relationship between analysts and users is a key to project success. Now that you understand the history and need for systems development, it is time to consider some of the relevant techniques that are used in systems development.

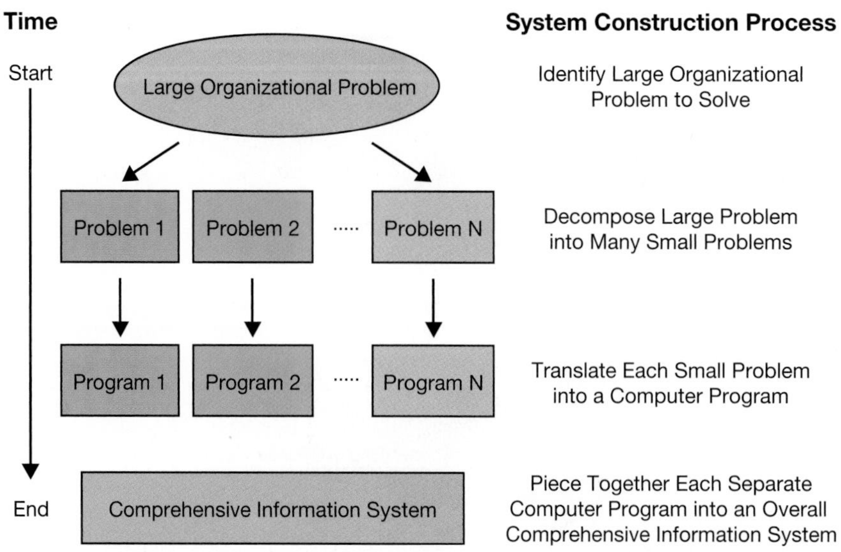

[**Figure 8.4** ➡ Problem decomposition makes solving big and complex problems easier.]

STEPS IN THE SYSTEMS DEVELOPMENT PROCESS

Just as the products that a firm produces and sells follow a life cycle, so do organizational information systems. For example, a new type of tennis shoe follows a life cycle of being introduced to the market, being accepted into the market, maturing, declining in popularity, and ultimately being retired. The term ***systems development life cycle (SDLC)*** is used to describe the life of an information system from conception to retirement (Hoffer, George, and Valacich, 2002). The SDLC has five primary phases:

1. System identification, selection, and planning
2. System analysis
3. System design
4. System implementation
5. System maintenance

Figure 8.5 is a graphical representation of the SDLC. The SDLC is represented as four boxes connected by arrows. Within the SDLC, arrows flow in both directions from the top box (system identification, selection, and planning) to the bottom box (system implementation). Arrows flowing down illustrate that the flow of information produced in one phase is being used to seed the activities of the next. Arrows flowing up represent the possibility of returning to a prior phase, if needed. The system maintenance arrow connecting the last phase to the first is what makes the SDLC a cycle.

Phase 1: System Identification, Selection, and Planning

The first phase of the systems development life cycle is ***system identification, selection, and planning***, as shown in Figure 8.7. Given that an organization can work on only a

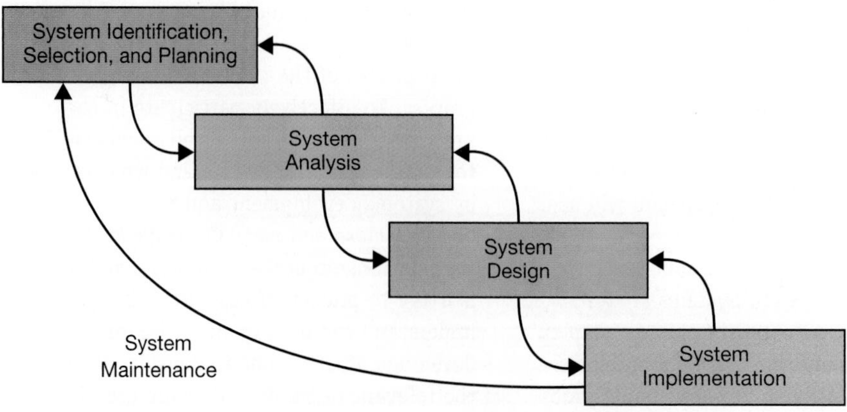

[**Figure 8.5** ➡ The systems development life cycle defines the typical process for building systems.]

BRIEF CASE

The SDLC at NASA

Organizations modify the basic SDLC slightly to fit their specific needs. For example, the National Aeronautics and Space Administration (NASA) follows an eight-step approach. High-quality software is a key component of NASA's success. The organization uses software to control countless Earth-based systems, such as those used to track, guide, and communicate with the space shuttles and space-based systems that control the functioning of orbiting satellites. It is easy to imagine that a system failure could have catastrophic results! Consequently, NASA, like many other organizations, has chosen to follow a formal SDLC to help ensure software and system quality and, more important, to help protect the lives and safety of its astronauts. The value of having standard procedures and steps such as the SDLC when building software not only speeds the development process, but it also ensures the creation of high-quality and reliable systems. As shown in Figure 8.6, the NASA SDLC comprises eight phases that are essentially the same as the five-step, generic process described in this chapter. Within every step of the NASA SDLC, guidelines have been developed for accepting and ensuring the quality of work products created. These guidelines are used to make sure that all work products meet specifications and are error-free before developers move to the next phase of the SDLC. The remainder of this section describes each phase of the SDLC.

Questions

1. What are the advantages and disadvantages of pursuing a formal SDLC, as NASA has done?
2. Many firms officially adhere to a formal SDLC, but in actual fact follow a much more ad hoc process. Why do you think that this is the case?

[Adapted from NASA, **http://www.nasa.gov**. Information verified February 2, 2004.]

limited number of projects at a given time due to limited resources, care must be taken so that only those projects that are critical to enabling the organization's mission, goals, and objectives are undertaken. Consequently, the goal of system identification and selection is simply to identify and select a development project from all possible projects that could be performed. Organizations differ in how they identify and select projects. Some organizations have a formal ***information systems planning*** process whereby a senior manager, a business group, an IS manager, or a steering committee identifies and assesses all possible systems development projects that an organization could undertake. Others follow a more ad hoc process for identifying potential projects, or in some cases avoid planning altogether (see Table 8.1). Nonetheless, after all possible projects are identified, those deemed most likely to yield significant organizational benefits,

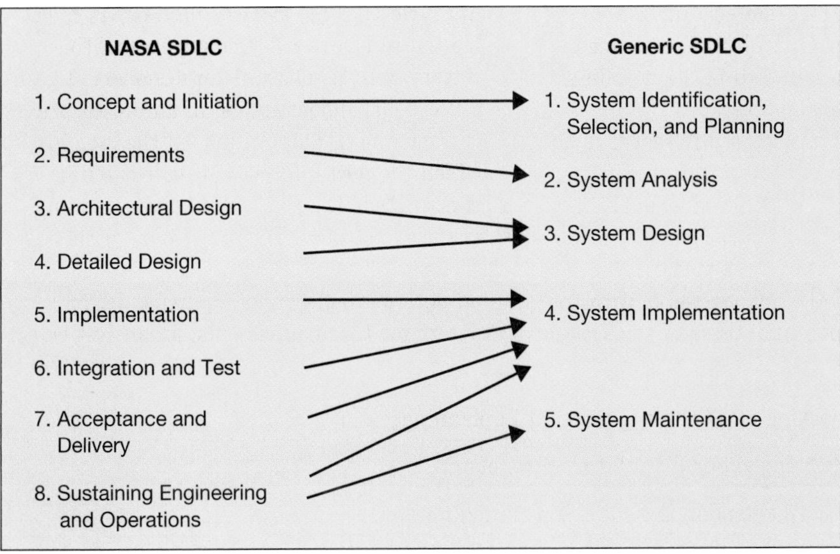

[**Figure 8.6** ➥ NASA's systems development life cycle as compared with the generic life cycle.]

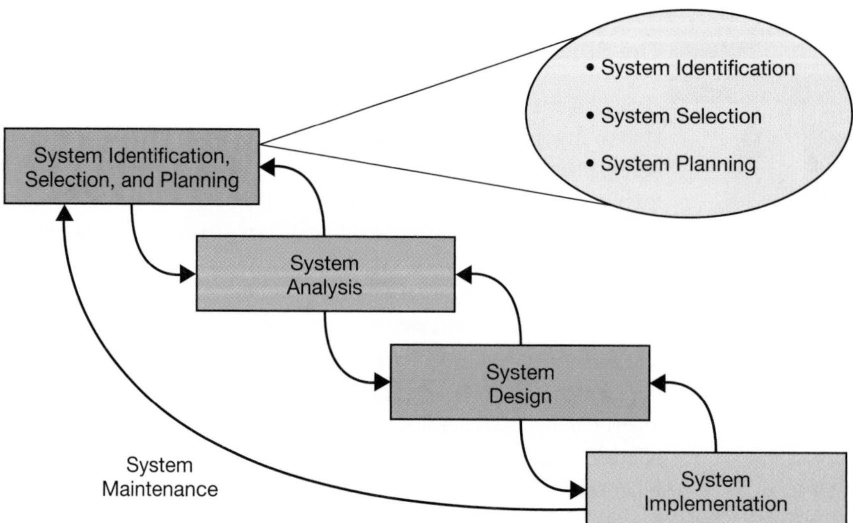

[**Figure 8.7** ➡ SDLC with Phase 1—System Identification, Selection, and Planning—highlighted.]

given available resources, are selected for subsequent development activities.

It is important to note that different approaches for identifying and selecting projects are likely to yield different organizational outcomes (see Table 8.2). For example, projects identified by top management more often have a strategic organizational focus, and projects identified by steering committees more often reflect the diversity of the committee and therefore have a cross-functional focus. Projects identified by individual departments or business units most often have a narrow, tactical focus. Finally, the typical focus of projects identified by the development group is the ease with which existing hardware and systems can be integrated with the proposed project. Other factors—such as project cost, duration, complexity, and risk—are also influenced by the source of a given project. The source of projects has been found to be a key indicator of project focus and success.

Just as there are often differences in the source of systems projects within organizations, there are often different evaluation criteria used within organizations when classifying and ranking potential projects. During project planning, the analyst works with the customers—the potential users of the system and their managers—to collect a broad range of information to gain an understanding of the project size, potential benefits and costs, and other relevant factors. After collecting and analyzing this information, the analyst can bring it together into a summary planning document that can be reviewed and compared with other possible projects. Table 8.3 provides a sample of the criteria often used by organizations. When reviewing a potential development project, organizations may focus on a single criterion, but most often examine multiple criteria to make a decision to accept or reject a project. If the organization accepts the project, system analysis begins.

Phase 2: System Analysis

The second phase of the systems development life cycle is called ***system analysis***, as highlighted in Figure 8.8. One purpose of the system analysis phase is for designers to gain a thorough understanding of an organization's current way of doing things in the area for which the new information system will be constructed. The process of conducting an analysis requires that many tasks, or subphases, be performed. The first subphase focuses on determining system requirements. To determine the requirements, an analyst works

[Table 8.1] ***Common excuses to avoid IS planning.***

I have so little to spend on IT there is no point in planning.
We don't know anything about IT, so how can we plan?
Once you have chosen a vendor, they do the planning for you.
I don't have the staff or the time for a big planning exercise.
I have a friend who operates a similar company, so I just acquire what she has.

Project Source	Primary Focus
Top management	Broad strategic focus
Steering committee	Cross-functional focus
Individual departments and business units	Narrow, tactical focus
Systems development group	Integration with existing information system focus

[Adapted from McKeen, Guimaraes, and Wetherbe. 1994.]

[Table 8.2] ***Sources of systems development projects and their likely focus.***

closely with users to determine what is needed from the proposed system. After collecting the requirements, analysts organize this information using data, process, and logic modelling tools. These elements will be illustrated and discussed later in the chapter (refer to Figure 8.12).

Collecting System Requirements

The collection and structuring of system requirements is arguably the most important activity in the systems development process because how well the information system requirements are defined influences all subsequent activities. The old saying "garbage in, garbage out" very much applies to the system-building process. Unfortunately, this stage of the SDLC is often given short shrift by systems development teams, who may be eager to move on to the design and development stages. ***Requirements collection*** is the process of gathering and organizing information from users, managers, business processes, and documents to understand how a proposed information system should function.

Systems analysts use a variety of techniques for collecting system requirements, including (Hoffer, George, and Valacich, 2002):

- *Interviews.* Analysts interview people informed about the operation and issues of the current or proposed system.
- *Questionnaires.* Analysts design and administer surveys to gather opinions from people informed about the operation and issues of the current or proposed system.
- *Observations.* Analysts observe workers at selected times to see how data are handled and what information people need to do their jobs.
- *Document analysis.* Analysts study business documents to discover issues, policies, and rules, as well as concrete examples of the use of data and information in the organization.

In addition to these techniques, there are contemporary approaches for collecting system requirements that include:

- *Critical success factors methodology.* A critical success factor, or CSF, is something that

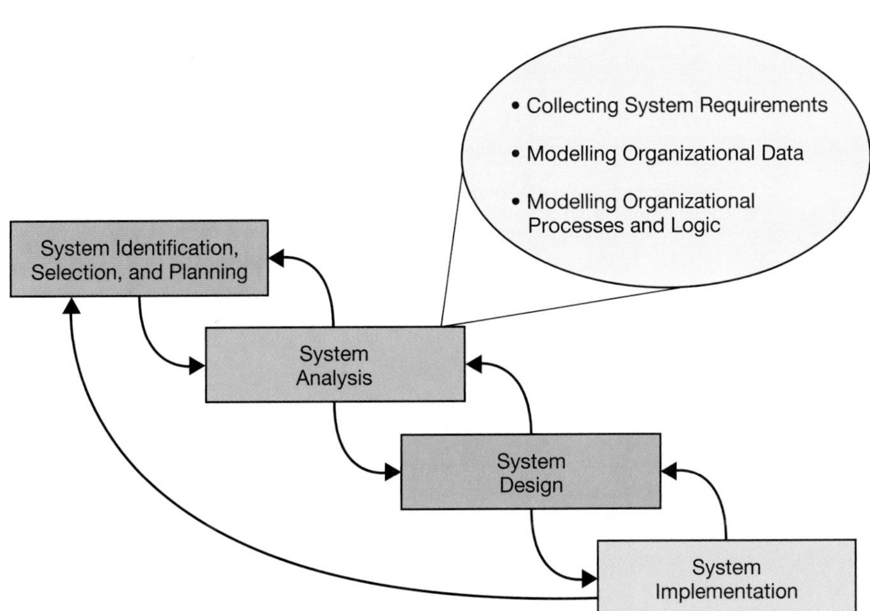

[Figure 8.8 ➡ SDLC with Phase 2—System Analysis—highlighted.]

[Table 8.3] *Possible evaluation criteria for classifying and ranking projects.*

Evaluation Criteria	Description
Strategic alignment	The extent to which the project is viewed as helping the organization achieve its strategic objectives and long-term goals
Potential benefits	The extent to which the project is viewed as improving profits, customer service, and so forth, and the duration of these benefits
Potential costs and resource availability	The number and types of resources the project requires and their availability
Project size/duration	The number of individuals and the length of time needed to complete the project
Technical difficulty/risks	The level of technical difficulty involved in successfully completing the project within a given time and resource constraint

[Source: Adapted from Hoffer, George, and Valacich. 2002. *Modern Systems Analysis and Design,* 3rd ed. Prentice Hall.]

must go well to ensure success for a manager, department, division, or organization. To understand an organization's CSFs, a systems analyst interviews people throughout the organization and asks each person to define her own personal CSFs. After the analyst collects these individual CSFs, she can merge, consolidate, and refine them to identify a broad set of organization-wide CSFs, as shown in Figure 8.9. Table 8.4 summarizes the strengths and weaknesses of the CSF approach.

- *Joint application design (JAD)*. A JAD is a special type of group meeting in which all (or most) users meet with the analyst at the same time. During this meeting, the users jointly define and agree upon system requirements or designs. This process has resulted in dramatic reductions in the length of time needed to collect requirements or specify designs. The JAD meeting can be held in a normal conference room or special-purpose JAD room (see Figure 8.10). Table 8.5 summarizes the strengths and weaknesses of the JAD approach.

Modelling Organizational Data

Data are facts that describe people, objects, or events. A lot of different facts can be used to describe a person: name, age, gender, race, and occupation. To construct an information system, systems analysts must understand

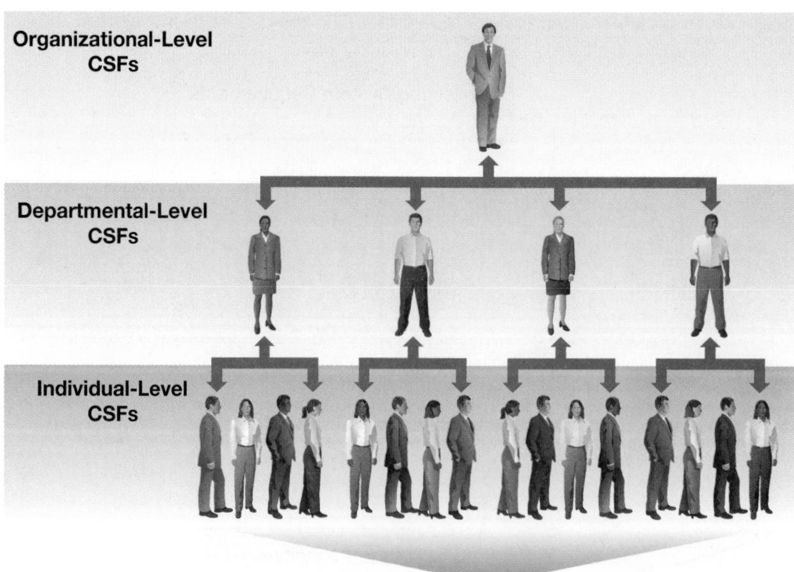

[Figure 8.9 ➥ Merging individual CSFs to represent organization-wide CSFs.]

Strengths	Weaknesses
Senior managers intuitively understand the approach and support its usage	High-level focus can lead to an oversimplification of a complex situation
Provides a method for understanding the information needs of the organization in order to make effective decisions	Difficulty in finding analysts trained to perform the CSF process that requires both understanding information systems and being able to communicate effectively with senior executives
	Method is not user-centred, but analyst-focused

[Table 8.4] *Strengths and weaknesses of the CSF approach (Boynton and Zmud, 1994).*

what data the information system needs in order to accomplish the intended tasks. To do this, they use data modelling tools to collect and describe the data to users, so as to confirm that all needed data are known and presented to users as useful information. Figure 8.11 shows an entity-relationship diagram (ERD), a type of data model, describing students, classes, majors, and classrooms at a university. Each box in the diagram is referred to as a data entity. Each data entity may have one or more attributes that describe it. For example, a "Student" entity may have attributes such as: ID, Name, and Local Address. Additionally, each data entity may be "related" to other data entities. For example, because students take classes, there is a relationship between students and classes: "Student Takes Class" and "Class Has Student." Relationships are represented in the diagram by lines drawn between related entities. Data modelling tools enable the systems analyst to represent data in a form that is easy for users to understand and critique. For more information on databases and data modelling, see Chapter 3, "Database Management."

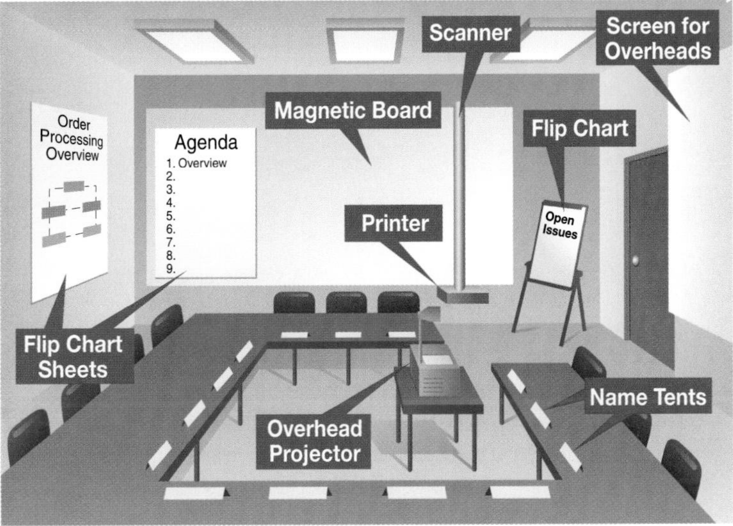

[Figure 8.10 ➡ A JAD room.]

Source: Adapted from J. Wood and D. Silver. *Joint Application Design*. John Wiley & Sons, 1989.

Modelling Organizational Processes and Logic

As the name implies, ***data flows*** represent the movement of data through an organization or within an information system. For example, your registration for a class may be captured in a registration form on paper or on a computer terminal. After it is filled out, this form probably *flows* through several processes to validate and record the class registration, as shown as "Data Flows" in Figure 8.12 on page 251. After all students have been registered, a repository of all registration information can be processed for developing class rosters or for generating student billing

Strengths	Weaknesses
Group-based process enables more people to be involved in the development effort without adversely slowing the process	Very difficult to get all relevant users to the same place at the same time to hold a JAD meeting
Group-based process can lead to higher levels of system acceptance and quality	Requires high-level executive sponsor to ensure that adequate resources are available to allow widespread participation
Group involvement in the design and development process helps to ease implementation, user training, and ongoing support	

[Table 8.5] *Strengths and weaknesses of the JAD approach.*

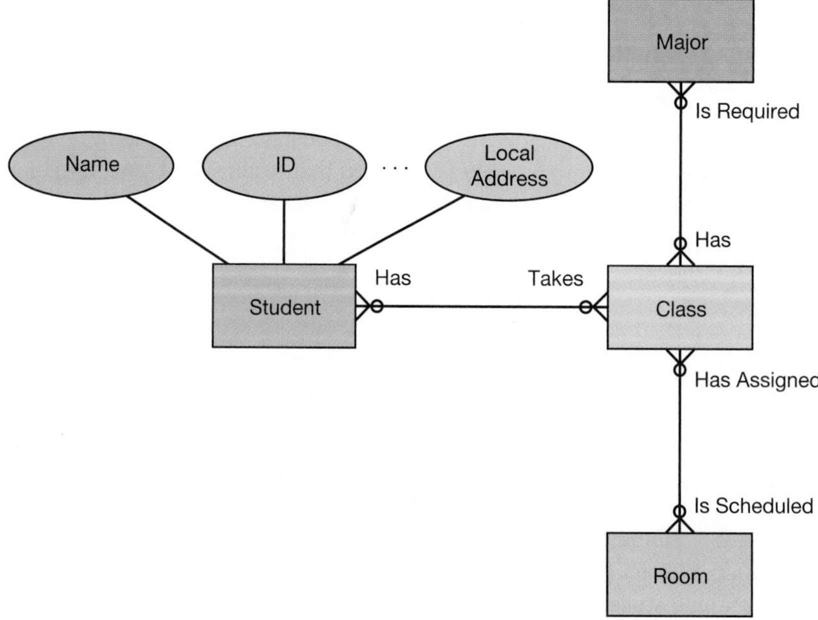

[Figure 8.11 ➥ A sample ERD for students.]

Web Search

WEB SEARCH OPPORTUNITY

Some Web-based forms are designed better than others. Go to the Web and critique a form from one of your favourite Websites, such as Sony (**www.sony.ca**) or Roots (**www.roots.ca**). Alternatively, an easy place to find such a form would be to go to any search engine—Google, or AltaVista (**www.google.ca**, **http://ca.altavista.com**)—and look at its "advanced" search form. Could any of these forms be improved? If so, how?

information, which is shown as "Data" in Figure 8.12. ***Processing logic*** represents the way in which data are transformed. For example, processing logic is used to calculate students' grade point averages at the conclusion of a term, as shown in the "Processing Logic" section in Figure 8.12.

After the data, data flow, and processing logic requirements for the proposed system have been identified, analysts develop one or many possible overall approaches—sometimes called *designs*—for the information system. For example, one approach for the system may possess only basic functionality but have the advantage of being relatively easy and inexpensive to build. An analyst might also propose a more elaborate approach for the system, but it may be more difficult and more costly to build. Analysts evaluate alternative system approaches with the knowledge that different solutions yield different benefits and different costs. After a system approach is selected, then details of that particular system approach can be defined.

Phase 3: System Design

The third phase of the systems development life cycle is ***system design,*** as shown in Figure 8.13. As its name implies, it is during this phase that the proposed system is designed; that is, the details of the chosen approach are developed. As with analysis, many different activities must occur during system design. The elements that must be designed when building an information system include:

- Forms and reports
- Interfaces and dialogues
- Databases and files
- Processing and logic

Designing Forms and Reports

A ***form*** is a business document containing some predefined data and often including some areas where additional data can be filled in. Figure 8.14 shows a computer-based form taken from a Website of the Government of the Northwest Territories. Using this form, users can search for a wide variety of service information.

A ***report*** is a business document containing only predefined data. In other words, reports are static documents that are used to summarize information for reading or viewing. For example, Figure 8.15 shows a report summarizing regional sales performance for several salespeople.

Designing Interfaces and Dialogues

Just as people have different ways of interacting with other people, information systems can have different ways of interacting with people. A system interface might be text-based, communicating with you through text and forcing you to communicate with it the same way. Alternatively, a system interface could use graphics and colour as a way to interact with you, providing you with colour-

Requirements

Data

Name	Year	GPA
Ric Munro	Fourth	3.7
Yolande Brohman	Grad	2.9
Malcolm Irving	First	3.2

Data Flows

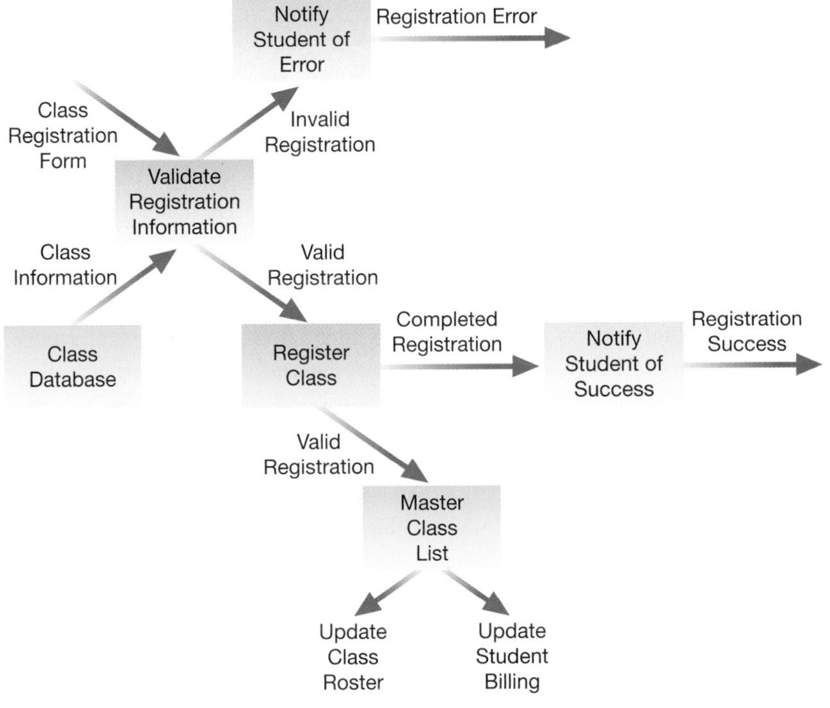

Processing Logic

```
i = read (number_of_classes)
total_hours = 0
total_grade = 0
total_gpa = 0
for j = 1 to i do
        begin
                read (course [ j ], hours [ j ], grade [ j ])
                total_hours = total_hours + hours [ j ]
                total_grade = total_grade + (hours [ j ] * grade [ j ])
        end
current_gpa = total_grade / total hours
```

[**Figure 8.12** ➥ Four key elements to development of a system: Requirements, Data, Data Flows, and Processing Logic.]

coded windows and special icons. A system dialogue could be developed such that it does nothing and waits for you to type in a command. Or it could ask you questions to which you respond by typing in commands, or present you with menus of choices from which you select your desired options. It could even do all these things. Over the past several

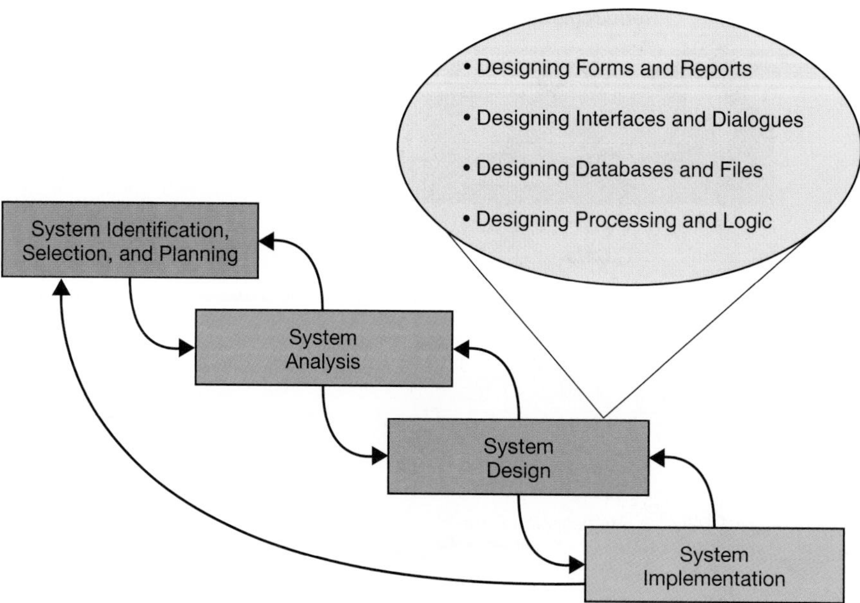

[Figure 8.13 ➥ SDLC with Phase 3—System Design—highlighted.]

years, standards for user interfaces and dialogues have emerged, making things easier for both designers and users. For example, both the Macintosh and Windows operating systems are standards that are generally referred to as being ***graphical user interfaces.*** (See Appendix B, "Information Systems Software," for more on GUIs.)

Designing Databases and Files

To design databases and files, a systems analyst must have a thorough understanding of an organization's data and informational needs. As described previously, a systems analyst often uses data modelling tools to first gain a comprehensive understanding of all the data used by a proposed system. After the conceptual data model has been completed, it can be easily translated into a physical data model in a database management system. For example, Figure 8.16 shows a physical data model to keep track of student information in Microsoft Access. The physical data model is more complete (shows more information about the student) and more detailed (shows how the information is formatted) than a conceptual data model. For example, contrast Figure 8.16 with the conceptual model in Figure 8.12 that contains student information.

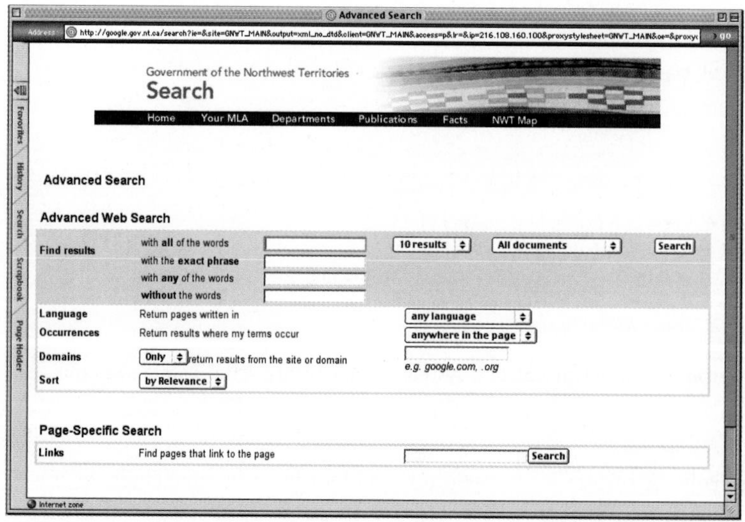

[Figure 8.14 ➥ Government of the Northwest Territories Website search form.]

Source: Courtesy of the Government of the Northwest Territories.

Ascend Systems Incorporated
SALESPERSON ANNUAL SUMMARY REPORT 2002

REGION	SALESPERSON	SIN	QUARTERLY ACTUAL SALES FIRST	SECOND	THIRD	FOURTH
Nova Scotia						
	Park	123 456 789	16,500	18,600	24,300	18,000
	Angellotti	123 456 789	22,000	15,500	17,300	19,800
	Irving	123 456 789	19,000	12,500	22,000	28,000
New Brunswick						
	Doucet	123 456 789	14,000	16,000	19,000	21,000
	Fleury	123 456 789	7,500	16,600	10,000	8,000
	Cook	123 456 789	12,000	19,800	17,000	19,000
PEI						
	Clark	123 456 789	18,000	18,000	20,000	27,000
	Yim	123 456 789	28,000	29,000	19,000	31,000

[**Figure 8.15** ➥ Sales summary report.]

C:\MSOFFICCE\ACCESS\STUDENT.MDB — Sunday, June 23, 2004
Table: Students — Page: 1

Properties

Date Created:	6/23/04 10:35:41 PM	Def. Updatable:	Yes
Last Updated:	6/23/04 10:35:43 PM	Record Count:	0

Columns

Name	Type	Size
StudentID	Number (Long)	4
FirstName	Text	50
MiddleName	Text	30
LastName	Text	50
ParentsNames	Text	255
Address	Text	255
City	Text	50
Province	Text	50
Region	Text	50
PostalCode	Text	20
PhoneNumber	Text	30
EmailName	Text	50
Major	Text	50
Note	Memo	–

[**Figure 8.16** ➥ An Access database that shows the physical data model for student information.]

Designing Processing and Logic

The processing and logic operations of an information system are the steps and procedures that transform raw data inputs into new or modified information. For example, when calculating your GPA, your school needs to perform the following steps:

1. Obtain the prior grade point average, credit hours earned, and list of prior courses
2. Obtain the list of each current course, final grade, and course credit hours
3. Combine the prior and current credit hours into aggregate sums
4. Calculate the new grade point average

The logic and steps needed to make this calculation can be represented many ways. One method, referred to as writing pseudocode—a textual notation for describing programming code—enables the systems analyst to describe the processing steps in a manner that is similar to how a programmer might implement the steps in an actual programming language. The "Processing Logic" in Figure 8.12 is an example of pseudocode. Other tools used by systems analysts during this activity include structure charts and decision trees. Converting pseudocode, structure charts, and decision trees into actual program code during system implementation is a very straightforward process.

COMING ATTRACTIONS

Web Services Revolutionize Application Development

Web services hold the potential to change many things about software, not the least of which is how it is developed. Despite vendors' claims that Web services are more evolutionary than revolutionary, the emerging programming paradigm requires a new mindset from both the technological and business perspectives.

In addition to creating a need for developers to learn how to use new tools—be it the new C++ or Web services–enabled versions of current languages—Web services by their nature are changing the way applications are built. Instead of traditional, monolithic stovepipe applications, developers must consider how to build more modular components, how to share data across otherwise disparate sources, and, ultimately, how to create applications out of those components and data sources. Furthermore, Web services are forcing programmers to consider how the application path they take can affect business. The big change that Web services bring, however, is that interoperability becomes a critical aspect that programmers plan for in the design stage rather than as an afterthought.

"In the short term, Web services are just another tool—like Java or COM [Component Object Model]—in the programmer's toolbox," said Frank Gillett, an analyst at Forrester Research Inc. in Cambridge, Massachusetts. "But in the longer term, people will start thinking from the Web services interfaces in, rather than building from the code out, which is how people do it today. Developers will have to think about the publishing and consuming of Web services from the beginning."

Aside from learning new technologies, such as how to implement Web services protocols, developers also need to consider how Web services applications will scale. "Analysis and design hasn't changed much when you develop a Web services app. What has changed severely is the development," said Roberto Torres, CTO and COO of CYDImex in Mexico City. Torres added that a few years ago developers built systems knowing that a specific number of users would access them; but with Web services' capability of opening systems more smoothly, it is difficult to know exactly how many users will access the software.

One of the areas where Web services will make application development more efficient is in the reuse of components or entire Web services. "Web services are reusable by definition. The question then becomes whether they do something people want to be able to reuse," said Rob Perry, an analyst at The Yankee Group in Boston. Perry explained that with Web services, reusability extends itself to other areas, such as connectors and integration services. Web services require highly componentized applications, so developers need to build those components with reusability in mind. Building Web services components also enables companies to share those services internally and with business partners.

However, there are a number of unresolved issues around Web services; namely, security, transactional integrity, management, provisioning, and trust. Companies such as Microsoft, IBM, Sun, and BEA are driving technology to solve these problems, in most cases with hopes of standardizing the technology with an independent organization such as the World Wide Web Consortium, but this work is still in a very early stage. Analysts are predicting that these issues will start to be addressed in a standard way beginning in 2004 and continuing at least through 2005. For developers, a big question remains the possibility of vendor lock-in: implementations of various Web services are not yet 100-percent interoperable. For now, Gillett said that Web services add an unknown element to the future of applications: "We've just scratched the surface. I don't think anyone understands where this will really go."

[Adapted from Tom Sullivan, "App Dev on the Web Services Path," *InfoWorld* (June 28, 2002).]

Phase 4: System Implementation

Many separate activities occur during ***system implementation***, the fourth phase of the systems development life cycle, as highlighted in Figure 8.17. One group of activities focuses on transforming the system design into a working information system that can be used by the organization. These activities include software programming and testing. A second group of activities focuses on preparing the organization for using the new information systems. These activities include system conversion, documentation, user training, and support. This section briefly describes what occurs during system implementation.

Software Programming and Testing

Programming is the process of transforming the system design into a working computer system. During this transformation, both processing and testing should occur in parallel.

GLOBAL PERSPECTIVE

The Difficulty of Managing International Development Teams

Obafemi Awolowo University (OAU) in Ile-Ife is a teaching hospital located in the southwestern region of Nigeria in Western Africa, which is inhabited primarily by the Yoruba people. A few years ago, Finland and Nigeria undertook a joint collaborative project to build a low-cost patient information system for the hospital. The project team, however, faced many challenges (related primarily to culture and the context in which Yorubaland was situated) that provided important lessons for IT developers as to the difficulties one may face when trying to develop and implement an information system in a foreign land. Politically, Yoruba had a kingship and a hierarchical model. Culturally, there was a significant gender difference in the society, and the traditional religion had a "pantheon of named gods." However, more than the culture, it was the context that caused significant problems for the IT developers. The climate in Yoruba was hot and humid, which led to technical problems with computers. There was a significant lack of infrastructure in terms of electrical supply, telecommunications availability, finance, and transportation. To add to this problem, there was a "lack of awareness" among the hospital staff as to the necessity of an information system. Moreover, the hardware and software vendors in the region had a "sell and run" strategy—it was difficult to find anyone to provide after-sales support and maintenance. The systems development team realized that in order to be successful in such an environment, it was important to be extremely sensitive to the cultural and contextual issues. Instead of adopting Western systems development methodologies and information systems to the context of Yoruba, they focused on building a new systems development methodology and information system that was fit for the Nigerian context—and so far have achieved success.

[Adapted from G. Walsham, *Making a World of Difference: IS in a Global Context* (Chichester: John Wiley & Sons, Ltd.), 2001; M. Korpela, "Traditional Culture or Political Economy? On the Root Causes of Organizational Obstacles of IT in Developing Countries," *Information Technology for Development* 7, No. 1 (1996): 29–42.]

As you might expect, a broad range of tests are conducted before a system is complete, including developmental, alpha, and beta testing (see Table 8.6).

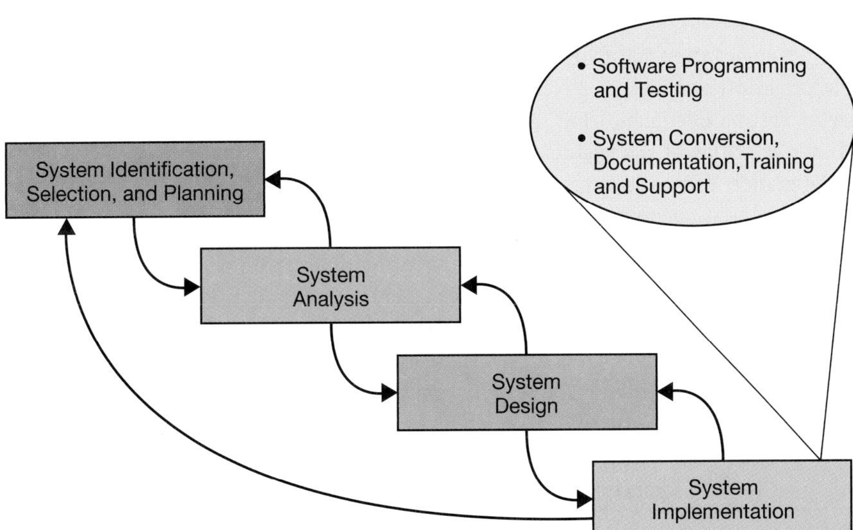

[Figure 8.17 ➥ SDLC with Phase 4—System Implementation—highlighted.]

[Table 8.6] *General testing types, their focus, and who performs them.*

Testing Type	Focus	Performed by
Developmental	Testing the correctness of individual modules and the integration of multiple modules	Programmer
Alpha	Testing of overall system to see whether it meets design requirements	Software tester
Beta	Testing of the capabilities of the system in the user environment with actual data	Actual system users

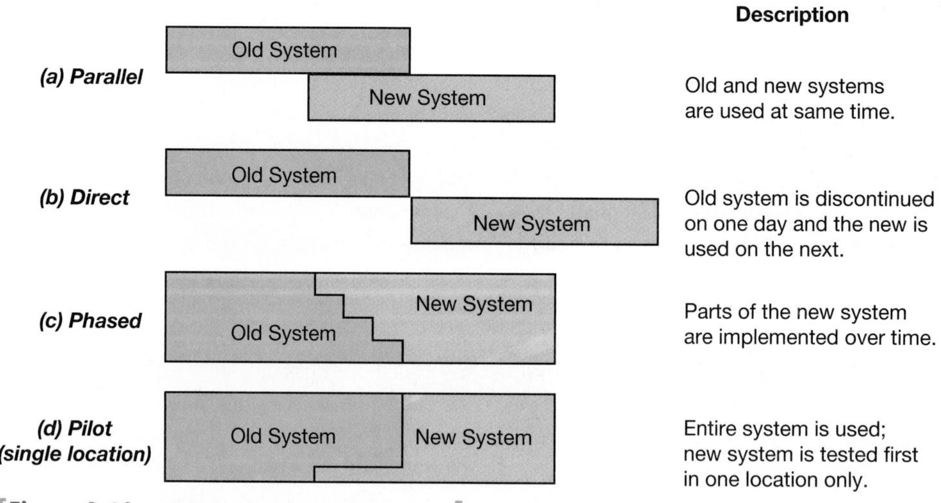
Description
(a) Parallel
Old System
New System
Old and new systems are used at same time.
(b) Direct
Old System
New System
Old system is discontinued on one day and the new is used on the next.
(c) Phased
New System
Old System
Parts of the new system are implemented over time.
(d) Pilot (single location)
Old System
New System
Entire system is used; new system is tested first in one location only.

[Figure 8.18 ➥ Software conversion strategies.]

System Conversion, Documentation, Training, and Support

System conversion is the process of decommissioning the current system (automated or manual) and installing the new system in the organization. Effective conversion of a system requires not only that the new software be installed, but also that users be effectively trained and supported. System conversion can be performed in at least four ways, as shown in Figure 8.18.

Many types of documentation must be produced for an information system. Programmers develop system documentation that details the inner workings of the system to ease future maintenance. A second type of documentation is user-related documentation, which is not typically written by programmers or analysts, but by users or professional technical writers. The range of documents can include the following:

- User and reference guides
- User training and tutorials
- Installation procedures and troubleshooting suggestions

In addition to documentation, users may also need training and ongoing support to use a new system effectively. Different types of training and support require different levels of investment by the organization. Self-paced training and tutorials are the least expensive options, and one-on-one training is the most expensive. Table 8.7 summarizes various user training options.

In addition to training, providing ongoing education and problem-solving assistance for users is also necessary. This is commonly referred to as system support, which is often provided by a special group of people in the organization who make up an information centre or help desk. Support personnel must have strong communication skills and be good problem solvers, in addition to being expert users of the system. An alternative option for a system not developed internally is to outsource support activities to a vendor special-

[Table 8.7] ***User training options.***

Training Option	Description
Tutorial	One person taught at one time by a human or by paper-based exercises
Course	Several people taught at one time
Computer-aided instruction	One person taught at one time by the computer system
Interactive training manuals	Combination of tutorials and computer-aided instruction
Resident expert	Expert on call to assist users as needed
Software help components	Built-in system components designed to train and troubleshoot problems
External sources	Vendors and training providers to provide tutorials, courses, and other training activities

BRIEF CASE

Benefits and Challenges of Working with Exceptional Software Developers

There is a profound difference between what many managers perceive software development to be and what it actually is. Some regard the profession as if developers were like construction workers. Once there is an architectural rendering of the system and a project schedule, all that needs to be done is the construction. The problem with this view is that there are few similarities between bricks and algorithms; bricks are commodities that are put together in predictable ways, while algorithms are products of intellect, each different from the other and requiring a different context in which to operate. Skill, to a software developer, is a function of the "elegance" of his or her product, a term that includes factors such as time efficiency, memory efficiency, succinctness, completeness, readability, reusability, and the appropriate allocation of effort to each of these. The difference between ordinary developers and exceptional developers is profound, not only in approach, but also in productivity. Some researchers have estimated up to a 20 to 1 difference in productivity between developer extremes. This means that what might take a mediocre programmer four weeks to complete, an exceptional developer could finish in a single day.

Future Vision Digital Services (a pseudonym), a medium-sized Web development firm based in Toronto, faced a problem with one of its most talented software architects. FVDS was in the final stages of implementing a solution for a client in Europe. The time difference between the two locations meant that normal business hours overlapped only during the morning in Toronto. The lead software architect, while brilliant, was unreliable, and often did not arrive at work until well after noon. Management ended up having to scramble to pull together alternative resources to complete the project, resulting in an inferior product.

Questions

1. What would you have done in the case of the project described above?
2. Software architects manage complex development products, but must themselves be managed. What key capability do IS managers require in order to channel the energies of talented software architects to match business requirements?

izing in technical system support and training. Regardless of how support is provided, it is an ongoing issue that must be managed effectively for the company to realize the maximum benefits of a system.

Phase 5: System Maintenance

After an information system is installed, it is essentially in the maintenance phase of the SDLC. In the maintenance phase, one person within the systems development group is responsible for collecting maintenance requests from system users. After they are collected, requests are analyzed so that the developer can better understand how the proposed change might alter the system and what business benefits and necessities might result from such a change. If the change request is approved, a system change is designed and then implemented. As with the initial development of the system, implemented changes are formally reviewed and tested before installation into operational systems. The ***system maintenance*** process parallels the process used for the initial development of the information system, as shown in Figure 8.19. Interestingly, it is during system maintenance that the largest part of the system development effort occurs.

The question must be, then, why does all this maintenance occur? It is not as if software wears out in the physical manner that cars, buildings, or other physical goods do. Correct? Yes, but software must still be maintained. The types of maintenance are summarized in Table 8.8 on page 259.

As with adaptive maintenance, both perfective and preventive maintenance are typically a much lower priority than corrective maintenance. Over the life of a system, corrective maintenance is most likely to occur after initial system installation or after major system changes. This means that adaptive, perfective, and preventive maintenance activities can lead to corrective maintenance activities if they are not carefully designed and implemented.

As you can see, there is more to system maintenance than you might think. Lots of time, effort, and money are spent in this final phase of a system's development, and it is important to follow prescribed, structured steps. In fact, the approach to systems development described in this chapter, from the

WHEN THINGS GO WRONG

Offshore Development Not Always User-Friendly

With offices in Toronto, Moscow, Brussels, Belgium, and the United States, Dmitri Buterin, president of Bonasource Inc., isn't a stranger to issues facing companies with offshore development projects. For several years, the Web development company has been involved in development projects around the globe with a focus on e-business applications such as information portals, employee intranets, and project management systems.

Touting the business benefits of offshore development, including quick access to the right skills, ROI, and turnover rates, Buterin said ensuring that the process remains user-friendly is an area that still faces some roadblocks. "Offshore development and usability are two major trends," Buterin said. "They are not easily reconciled, but they can and should be reconciled." Issues such as designing interfaces at a distance, working with individuals who don't speak English, cultural differences, and the fact that usability "isn't recognized as it should be around the world" are barriers that still face proponents of user-friendly software and offshore development projects, he said. By addressing the issues up front and building usability into the development process, "not only into the testing stage but also into the analysis and design phase," companies will be able to marry the trend of usability and offshore development, Buterin explained.

Daniel Ponech, information design instructor at the University of Toronto, said awareness of usability requirements has been somewhat lacking until now. "Finding out what the users need," learning functionality requirements, and simply asking what the users want can be as simple as ensuring that the user-interface contrast isn't hard on the user's eyes, Ponech said.

Providing a voice to the users and ensuring that both the on- and offshore development teams work together is the goal of the offshore development model used at Bonasource, Buterin explained. Having small, frequent releases of the software every few weeks is an important element in that model. "We get feedback as we go along and each release doesn't necessarily add more functionality," he said, adding that each release deals with usability issues in smaller portions. "A very important point is not to just describe what the system should do, but why the system should do it," Buterin said. Good recruitment methods and implementing visual prototyping are also ways to improve usability on offshore projects, he added.

Murray Sanders, managing partner at Mississauga, Ontario–based Interpix Design Inc., said there are endless cultural issues that still need to be overcome before usability and offshore software development will go hand in hand when working with projects that are sent offshore. "The industry is still immature," he said. "There may be lower costs involved, but it might also take four or five times to get it right."

[Adapted from Allison Taylor, "Offshoring Stumbles on Usability Issues," *ComputerWorld Canada* (December 31, 2003).]

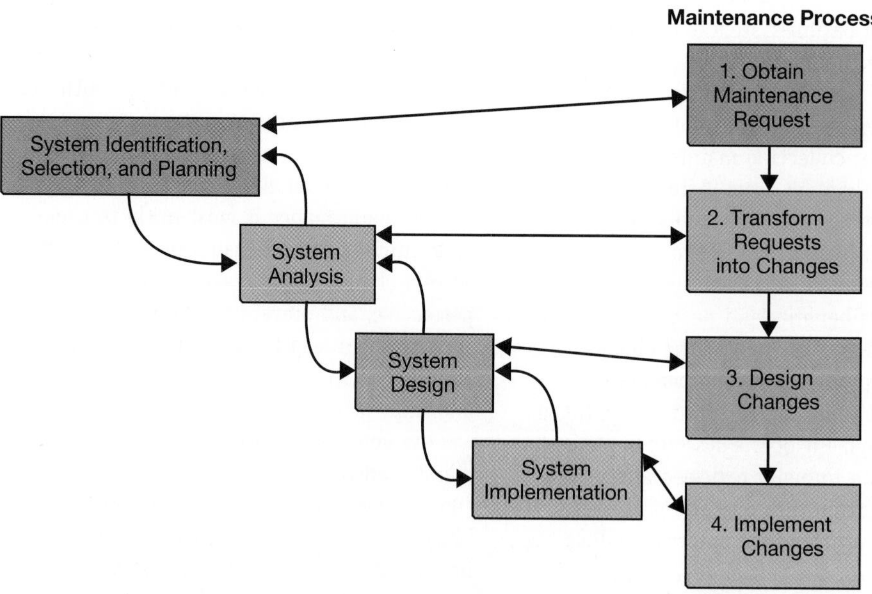

[**Figure 8.19** ➡ Mapping of maintenance to SDLC.]

Maintenance Type	Description
Corrective maintenance	Making changes to an information system to repair flaws in the design, coding, or implementation
Adaptive maintenance	Making changes to an information system to evolve its functionality to accommodate changing business needs or to migrate it to a different operating environment
Perfective maintenance	Making enhancements to improve processing performance or interface usability, or adding desired, but not necessarily required, system features (in other words, "bells and whistles")
Preventive maintenance	Making changes to a system to reduce the chance of future system failure

[Table 8.8] ***Types of software maintenance.***

CAREER IMPLICATIONS

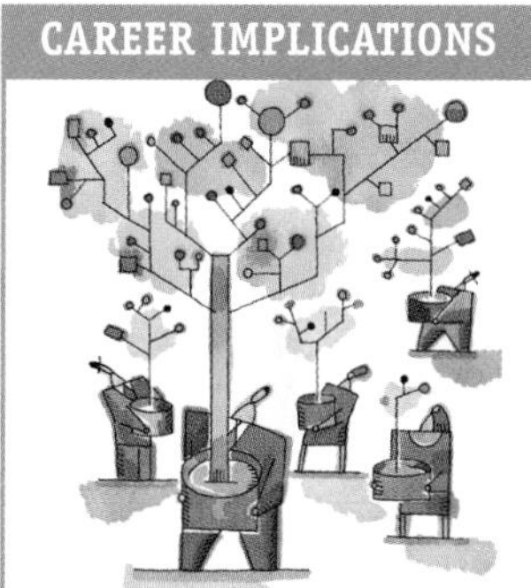

Human Resource Management

Once an information system has been implemented, many companies opt to outsource the support of the system to outside organizations. The reason for outsourcing is often to avoid the costs and complexities associated with hiring skilled IT professionals for supporting the information systems. Burger King recently outsourced its information systems support. The company announced that it had signed a contract with Perot Systems to provide IT services for its most critical business information systems. One of the primary responsibilities of Perot Systems is to provide help desk support, enterprise system management, data management, and global information system management for Burger King's many information systems. Perot Systems is involved in decentralizing Burger King's information systems from those of its parent company, Diageo, plc. As part of the contract, Perot Systems not only provides support, but also makes several enhancements to the company's existing information systems, which will significantly increase efficiency and flexibility within Burger King. By drawing on the technological innovations and expertise of Perot Systems, Burger King is able to optimize its IT environment and keep its operating costs down. At the same time, the company is able to keep its labour costs from rising. The efficiency and flexibility will enable Burger King to adapt smoothly to the changing and fast-paced business world of fast food.

[Adapted from "Burger King Corporation to Outsource Information Technology (IT) Support to Perot Systems: Latest Move toward Separation from Parent Company," **http://www.perotsystems.com/frmbase.asp?URL=/Content/newsandevents/news/Sept_5_2001.html** (September, 2001).]

initial phase of identifying, selecting, and planning for systems to the final phase of system maintenance, is a very structured and systematic process. Each phase is fairly well prescribed and requires active involvement by systems people, users, and managers.
It is likely that you will have numerous opportunities to participate in the acquisition or development of a new system for an organization for which you currently work or will work in the future. Now that you have an understanding of the process, you should be better equipped to make a positive contribution to the success of any systems development project.

OTHER APPROACHES TO DESIGNING AND BUILDING SYSTEMS

The systems development life cycle is one approach to managing the development process and is a very good approach to follow when the requirements for the information system are highly structured and straightforward—for example, for a payroll or inventory system. Today, organizations need a broad variety of information systems, not just payroll and inventory systems, for which requirements are either very hard to specify in advance or constantly changing. For example, an organization's Website is an information system with constantly changing requirements. How many Websites have you visited in which the content or layout seemed to change almost every day? For this type of system, the SDLC might work as a development approach, but it would not be optimal. In this section, we describe three approaches for developing flexible information systems: prototyping, rapid application development, and object-oriented analysis and design.

Prototyping

Prototyping is a systems development methodology that uses a "trial and error" approach for discovering how a system should operate. You may think that this does not sound like a process at all; however, you probably use prototyping all the time in many of your day-to-day activities, but you just do not know it! For example, when you buy new clothes you likely use prototyping—that is, trial and error—by trying on several shirts before making a selection.

Figure 8.20 diagrams the prototyping process when applied to identifying/determining system requirements. To begin the process, the system designer interviews one or several users of the system, either individually or as a group, using a JAD. After the designer gains a general understanding of what the users want, he develops a prototype of the new system as quickly as possible to share with the users. The users may like what they see or ask for changes. If the users request changes, the designer modifies the prototype and again shares it with them. This process of sharing and refinement continues until the users approve the functionality of the system.

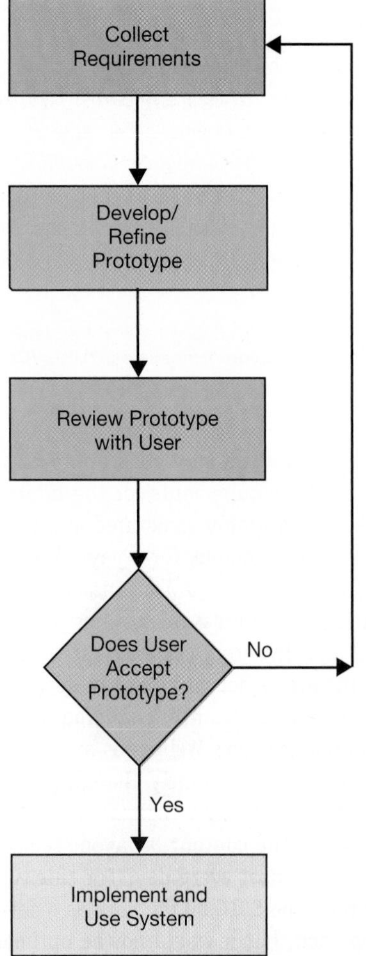

[**Figure 8.20** ➡ The prototyping process uses a trial-and-error approach to discovering how a system should operate.]

Rapid Application Development (RAD)

Rapid application development (RAD) is a four-phase systems development methodology that combines prototyping, computer-based development tools, special management practices, and close user involvement (Hoffer, George, and Valacich, 2002; McConnell, 1996; Martin, 1991). RAD has four phases: 1) requirements planning, 2) user design, 3) construction, and 4) the move to the new system. Phase 1, requirements planning, is similar to the first two phases of the SDLC, in which the system is planned and requirements are analyzed. To gain intensive user involvement, the RAD methodology encourages the use of JAD sessions to collect requirements. Where RAD becomes radical is during Phase 2, in which users of the information system become intensively involved in the design process. Computer-aided software engineering (CASE) and other advanced development tools (see Appendix B, "Information Systems Software") are used to structure requirements and develop prototypes quickly. As prototypes are developed and refined, they are continually reviewed with users in additional JAD sessions. Like prototyping, RAD is a process in which requirements, designs, and the system itself are developed via iterative refinement, as shown in Figure 8.21. In a sense, with the RAD approach, the people building the system and the users of that system keep cycling back and forth between Phase 2 (user design) and Phase 3 (construction) until the system is finished. As a result, RAD requires close cooperation between users and designers to be successful. This means that management must actively support the development project and make it a priority for everyone involved.

Object-Oriented Analysis and Design

Object-oriented analysis and design (OOA&D) is very similar to other analysis and design approaches (Booch, 1990; Coad and Yourdon, 1991; Halladay and Wiebel, 1993; Hoffer, George, and Valacich, 2002). For example, when using the SDLC approach, systems analysts primarily follow a top-down process in which the system requirements are broken

CAREER IMPLICATIONS

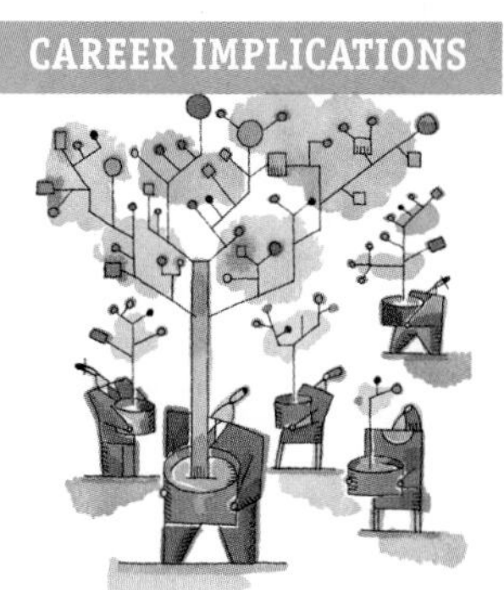

Accounting and Finance

"Leasing sounds really good to finance people, but it gives asset management people headaches," said Nikki Cule, the plans and controls manager for Zurich North America Canada. Cule has painstakingly gone through every line of every invoice, licence agreement, and contract Zurich has ever received from an IT or telecom vendor. She says most companies would be hard pressed to answer questions such as: do you know where your contracts are for IT products and services? Do you know what they say and what they cost the company? Do you compare invoices to contracts to make sure the amounts are correct?

Often a change in business, such as selling off portions of the company, can raise a lot of issues when it comes to asset management. Five years ago, Zurich North America Canada had about 2,100 employees in 14 cities across the country. But when the company sold its lines of personal insurance operations to ING in 2002, it moved its mainframe operations to Schaumburg, Illinois. Later Zurich sold its life insurance business to Manulife (2001 and 2002). Today, there are 600 employees in Zurich's commercial operations only, across eight cities. Cule's work on lease management and procurement centralizing started before all the changes, but the real efforts on invoice management and contract management began after.

A few years ago, Cule discovered errors that were costing the company tens of thousands of dollars and no one was noticing. Her secret? Centralizing procurement and invoice management, and making one group responsible for managing the assets. "It's not that I'm down on leasing companies, but in the last two years we've had four different frontline people from a leasing company working with us and the only thing I had were my records," she says. "I have found instances where invoices and contracts don't match," she says. During an extensive audit of Zurich's telco system, it was discovered the company had 135 1-800 lines not in use. Cutting those off reduced the bill by 20 percent. Her advice for those looking to get a better grip on asset management is to review invoices and look for products and services that are no longer needed or being used. "I've been able to prove we sent equipment back to the reseller, but the leasing company still puts it on the lease. We were really paying the price," she says.

[Adapted from Jennifer Brown, "Keeping an Eye on Asset Management," *Computing Canada,* Vol. 29, No. 23 (November 28, 2003).]

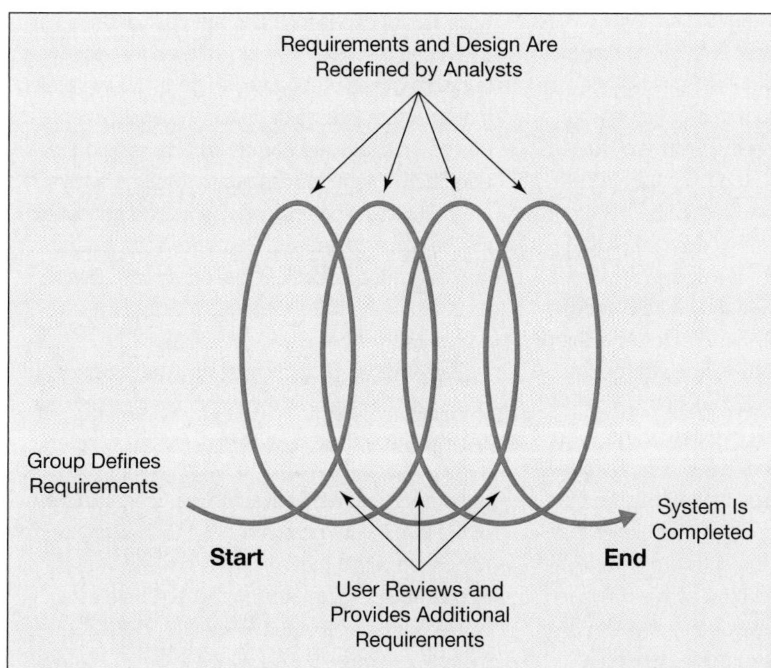

[**Figure 8.21** ➥ Iterative refinement is a key to the success of RAD.]

[Table 8.9] *Strengths and weaknesses of prototyping, RAD, and OOA&D approaches.*

Approach	Strengths	Weaknesses
Prototyping	Develops close working relationship between designer and users; works well for messy and hard-to-define problems	Not practical with a large number of users; system may be built too quickly, which could result in lower quality
Rapid Application Development	Active user involvement in design process; easier implementation due to user involvement	Systems are often narrowly focused—limits future evolution; system may be built too quickly, which could result in lower quality
Object-Oriented Analysis and Design	Integration of data and processing during design should lead to higher-quality systems; reuse of common modules makes development and maintenance easier	Very difficult to train analysts and programmers on the object-oriented approach; limited use of common modules

down into smaller and smaller pieces until specific programming modules can be defined, programmed, and pieced together to yield a system. Similarly, data and their interrelationships are modelled by the analysts, and these conceptual models are turned over to a programmer who actually implements these data models in a database management system. In most instances, a systems analyst develops a high-level design for the data and the processing and provides this design to programmers, who actually implement the design in programming code and databases. The analyst often never does any coding. This is different

CAREER IMPLICATIONS

Information Systems

While overall salaries in IT are expected to drop in 2004/2005, a recent study found that salaries of highly skilled software developers in Canada specializing in fields such as customization and embedded software will command salary increases of 13 to 15 percent in 2004. The study (titled IT/Software Salaries: False Sense of Complacency?) was conducted by Personnel Systems in conjunction with the Software Human Resource Council (SHRC). Approximately 300 Canadian IT companies took part in the comparison of salaries for IT employees from 2001 to 2003. "Software developers are seen as having a higher level of skill sets within the entire IT industry range of jobs. They are still in more demand than many other jobs, like Web developers or help desk analysts," said Janice Schellenberger, partner with Personnel Systems in Ottawa. "As such, what we see reflected in their salaries is that they continue to receive increases that are higher than the rest of the technology sector, and higher than the rest of the jobs within the software IT marketplace." Schellenberger attributed some of this to the fact that specialized developers require a combination of skills. For example, embedded software specialists need to have knowledge of software and hardware.

Since the onset of the industry downturn, software developers with advanced skills are also being required to take on more responsibilities, said Ian Germaise, a consultant who has worked in the embedded software stream. "Embedded development is getting hotter, and people who have lots of experience and are specialists in certain areas can get very high salaries, especially because they are expected to do their own project management," he said. "Often the analysis and design functions are combined, whereas in the past there might be a separate systems analyst on the team." The additional workload accounts for the salary increases, Germaise said, but he noted that top software developers can usually write their own ticket because their skills are so crucial to their employer's strategy.

Schellenberger said the study was conducted because of the perception within the industry that job shortages have disappeared due to the economic climate. "What we're saying is that you need to be careful with that assumption," she said. Many of the layoffs that occurred in the technology sector happened within the telecom and related industries, Schellenberger said, adding that software as a whole was not impacted as greatly. "Certainly, these shortages still exist. Once the market starts to improve, you're going to see the pressure for those kinds of skills build quickly again," she said.

[Adapted from Allison Taylor, "Pay Hikes Seen for Select Developers," *ComputerWorld Canada* (May 30, 2003).]

with the OOA&D approach, due to the tight coupling between the methods and data and between the conceptual model of the system and its actual implementation. OOA&D can turn every programmer into an analyst and every analyst into a programmer. What this means is that the analyst using an OOA&D approach can be thinking simultaneously right from the start about the "what" (the data) and the "how" (the operations to be performed) as he defines all the relevant objects that the system entails. Furthermore, if an object-oriented programming language is being used, it enables the design and implementation of the objects to happen quickly and simultaneously. In sum, OOA&D is a more integrative prototyping process than the SDLC approach, in which data and operations on the data are modelled separately and at a conceptual level and are later implemented and brought together in a subsequent phase of the systems development process.

This section has described other popular information systems development approaches beyond the SDLC. Although each of these approaches has been discussed separately, the wise organization and skilled analyst often utilizes multiple methods when developing a single system. What should be clear to you is that no approach is perfect and that all have strengths and weaknesses (see Table 8.9). To put this another way, a skilled systems developer is much like a skilled craftsman, with many tools at his disposal. The skilled craftsman chooses the most appropriate tool and approach for the task at hand. Using one systems development approach or tool for all systems and problems is akin to using only a hammer to build a house. Building a house with just a hammer might be possible, but it would probably be a strange-looking house!

NEED FOR ALTERNATIVES TO BUILDING SYSTEMS YOURSELF

Building systems in-house with the IS staff is always an option to consider. Many times, however, this is not a feasible solution. The following are four situations in which you might need to consider alternative development strategies.

Situation 1: Limited IS Staff

Often, an organization does not have the capability to build a system itself. Perhaps its IS staff is small or deployed on other activities, such as maintaining a small network and helping users with problems on a day-to-day basis. This limited staff may simply not have the capability to take on an in-house development project without hiring several analysts or programmers, which is very expensive in today's labour market.

Situation 2: IS Staff Has Limited Skill Set

In other situations, the IS staff may not have the skills needed to develop a particular kind of system. This has been especially true with the explosion of the Web; many organizations are having outside groups manage their sites. For example, Walt Disney contracted the development and management of its Website and the sites of many of its subsidiaries, including ABC News and ESPN, to a company called Starwave.com. Starwave was founded by Paul Allen, one of Bill Gates' initial partners at Microsoft and owner of the Portland Trailblazers, Seattle Seahawks, and numerous other companies (**www.paulallen.com**). This relationship continued until 1998, when Disney purchased Starwave and transformed it into the Walt Disney Internet Group (Court, 1998). In essence, Disney did not initially have the right set of skills to move onto the Internet, so it had an outside organization develop and manage its Websites. Once it realized the strategic importance of the Internet, Disney purchased this expertise by buying Starwave. In short, although the existing IS staff at Disney was highly skilled at producing and managing traditional applications, the sudden call for Web-based systems required that Disney seek outside help. It is not as if the IS director can tell Mr. Eisner—the CEO of Walt Disney—that Disney cannot build a new Website because the IS staff does not have the necessary skills to build it! Fortunately, there are alternatives to having the IS staff build the system; the IS director can simply tap into specialized skills not present within the existing IS staff that are available on the open market.

Situation 3: IS Staff Is Overworked

In some organizations, the IS staff may simply not have the time to work on all the systems that are required or desired by the organization. Obviously, the number of people dedicated to new development is not infinite. Therefore, you must have ways to prioritize development projects. In most cases, systems that are of strategic importance or that affect the whole organization are likely to receive a higher priority than those that offer only minor benefits or affect only one department or a couple of people in a department. Nonetheless, the IS manager must find a way to support all users, even when the IS staff may be tied up with other "higher-priority" projects.

Situation 4: Problems with Performance of IS Staff

Earlier in this book we discussed how and why systems development projects could sometimes be risky. Often the efforts of IS departments are derailed due to staff turnover, changing requirements, shifts in technology, or budget constraints. Regardless of the reason, the result is the same: another failed (or flawed) system. Given the large expenditures in staff time and training, as well as the high risk associated with systems development efforts, the prudent manager tries to limit the risk of any project as much as possible. What if it were possible to see the completed system to know what it looked like before development began? Being able to see into the future would certainly help you learn more about the system and whether it would meet your needs, and it would help to lower the risk of a project. When building a system in-house, it is obviously not possible to see into the future. However, using some of the alternative methods described in this chapter, you can, in fact, see what a completed system might look like. These methods will enable you to know what you are buying, which greatly lowers the risk of a project.

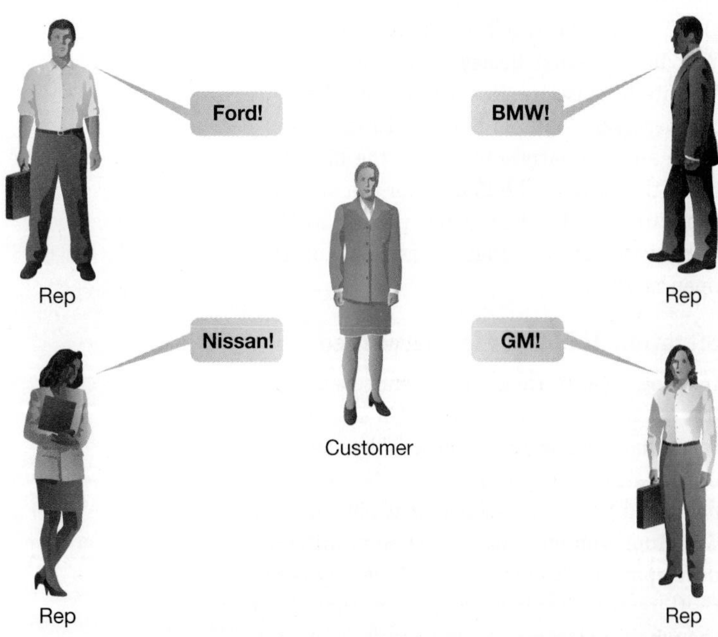

[Figure 8.22 ➥ A prospective car buyer with a "wish list."]

COMMON ALTERNATIVES TO IN-HOUSE SYSTEMS DEVELOPMENT

Any project has at least four different systems development options. Previously, we discussed the first option: building the system in-house with your IS staff. The other options are:

- External acquisition
- Outsourcing
- End-user development

The following sections examine each of these options in closer detail to see how one or more of them might fit the four situations described in the preceding section.

External Acquisition

Purchasing an existing system from an outside vendor such as IBM, EDS, or Accenture is referred to as ***external acquisition.*** How does external acquisition of an information system work? Think about the process that you might use when buying a car. Do you simply walk into the first dealership you see, tell them you need a car, and see what they try to sell you? You had better not. Probably you have done some up-front analysis and know how much money you can afford to spend and what your needs are. If you have done your homework, you probably have an idea of what you want and which dealership can provide the type of car you desire (see Figure 8.22).

This up-front analysis of your needs can be extremely helpful in narrowing your options and can save you a lot of time. Understanding your needs can also help you sift through the sales hype that you are likely to encounter from one dealer to the next as each tries to sell you on why his model is perfect for you. After getting some information, you may want to take a couple of promising models for a test drive, whereby you actually get behind the wheel and see how well the car fits you and your driving habits. You might even talk to other people who have owned this type of car to see how they feel about it. Ultimately, you are the one who has to evaluate all the different cars to see which one is best for you. They may all be good cars; however, one may fit your needs just a little better than the others.

The external acquisition of an information system is very similar to the purchase of a car. When you acquire an IS, you should do some analysis of your specific needs. For example, how much can you afford to spend, what basic functionality is required, and approximately how many people will use the system?

Next, you can begin to "shop" for the new system by asking potential vendors to provide information about the systems that they have to offer. After evaluating this information, it may become clear that several vendors have systems that are worth considering. You may ask those vendors to come to your organization and set up their systems so that you and your colleagues are able to "test drive" them. Seeing how people react to the systems and seeing how each system performs in the organizational environment can help you "see" exactly what you are buying. By seeing the actual system and how it performs with real users, with real or simulated data, you can get a much clearer idea of whether that system fits your needs. When you take a car for a test drive, you learn how the car meets your needs. By seeing how the system meets your needs before you buy, you can greatly reduce the risk associated with acquiring that system.

Steps in External Acquisition

In many cases, your organization will use a competitive bid process for making an external acquisition. In the competitive bid process, vendors are given an opportunity to propose systems that meet the organization's needs. The goal of the competitive process is to help the organization ensure that it gets the best system at the lowest possible price. Most competitive external acquisition processes have at least five general steps:

1. System identification, selection, and planning
2. System analysis
3. Development of a Request for Proposal (RFP)
4. Proposal evaluation
5. Vendor selection

You have already learned about the first two steps because they apply when you build a system yourself, as well as when you purchase a system through an external vendor. Step 3, development of a Request for Proposal, is where the external acquisition process differs significantly from in-house development.

Development of a Request for Proposal (RFP)

A ***Request for Proposal,*** or RFP, is simply a report that is used to tell vendors what your requirements are and to invite them to provide information about how they might be able to meet those requirements (see Figure 8.23). An RFP is sent to vendors who might potentially be interested in providing hardware and/or software for the system.

[**Figure 8.23** ➥ Sample RFP document for an information systems project.]

Among the areas that may be covered in an RFP are:

- A summary of existing systems and applications
- Reliability, back-up, and service requirements
- Requirements for system performance and features
- The criteria that will be used to evaluate proposals
- Timetable and budget constraints (how much you can spend)

The RFP is then sent to prospective vendors along with an invitation to present their bids for the project. Eventually, you will likely receive a number of proposals to evaluate. If, on the other hand, you do not receive many proposals, it may be necessary to rethink the requirements—perhaps the requirements are greater than the budget limitations, or the timetable is too short. In some situations, you may first need to send out a preliminary Request for Information simply to gather information from prospective vendors. This will help you determine whether, indeed, the desired system is feasible or even possible. If you determine that it is, you can then send out an RFP.

Proposal Evaluation

The fourth step in external acquisition is to evaluate proposals received from vendors. This evaluation may include viewing system demonstrations, evaluating the performance of those systems, and examining criteria important to the organization and judging how the proposed systems "stack up" to those criteria. Demonstrations are a good way to get a feel for the different systems' capabilities. Just as you can go to the showroom to look over a new car and get a feel for whether it meets your needs, it is also possible to screen various systems through a demonstration from the vendor. During a demonstration, a sales team from the vendor presents an oral presentation about their system, its features, and cost, followed by a demonstration of the actual system. In some cases, this may take place at your location; other times, it may take place at the vendor's facility or at one of the vendor's clients, particularly when the system is not easily transportable. Although such demonstrations are often useful in helping you understand the features of different systems being proposed, they are rarely enough in and of themselves to warrant purchasing the system without further evaluation.

One of the ways you can better evaluate a proposed system is through ***systems benchmarking.*** Benchmark programs are sample programs or jobs that simulate your computer workload. You can have benchmarks designed to test portions of the system that are most critical to your needs based on your systems analysis. A benchmark might test how long it takes to calculate a set of numbers, how long it takes to access a set of records in a database, or how long it would take to access certain information given a certain number of concurrent users. Some common system benchmarks include:

- Response time given a specified number of users
- Time to sort records
- Time to retrieve a set of records
- Time to produce a given report
- Time to read in a set of data

In addition, vendors may also supply benchmarks that you can use, although you should not rely solely on vendor information. For popular systems, you may be able to rely on system benchmarks published in computer trade journals such as *PC Magazine* or *PC Week*. However, in most cases, demos and benchmarks alone do not provide all the information you need to make a purchase. The systems analysis phase should have revealed some specific requirements for the new system. These requirements may be listed as criteria that the organization can use to further evaluate vendor proposals. Depending upon what you are purchasing—hardware, software, or both—the criteria you use will change. Table 8.10 provides examples of commonly used evaluation criteria.

Vendor Selection

In most cases, more than one system will meet your needs, just as more than one car will usually meet your needs. However, some probably "fit" better than others. In these cases, you should have a way of prioritizing or ranking competing proposals. One way of doing this is by devising a scoring system for each of the criteria and benchmarking results. For example, an organization might create a scoring system in which benchmarking results might be worth 100 total points, while online help features are worth only 50 points. All the points for each criterion are then summed to give an overall score for each system. Then the system with the highest score (or one of the systems among several with the highest scores) is selected. Figure 8.24 shows an example of a form that could be used to evaluate systems and choose a vendor by using this method.

In the example shown in Figure 8.24, System A looks like the best solution because it scored highest. Using such an evaluation method, it is possible that scoring low on a given criterion might exclude otherwise outstanding systems from being purchased. You can see that Systems B and C fared very poorly on the Vendor Support criterion. It is possible that those systems do not have very good vendor support. However, it is also possible that the vendor did not adequately communicate its commitment to support, perhaps because it did not realize it was such an important issue. Therefore, it is very impor-

[Table 8.10] ***Commonly used evaluation criteria for computer systems.***

Hardware Criteria	Software Criteria	Other Criteria
Clock speed of CPU	Memory requirements	Installation
Memory requirements	Help features	Testing
Secondary storage (including capacity, access time, and so on)	Usability	Price
Video display size	Learnability	
Printer speed	Number of features supported	
	Training and documentation	
	Maintenance and repair	

tant for you to communicate with vendors about the evaluation process and which criteria you value most highly.

Companies may use other, less formalized approaches to evaluate vendors. Sometimes they use simple checklists; other times they use a more subjective process. Regardless of the mechanism, eventually a company completes the evaluation stage and selects a vendor, ending the external acquisition process.

Criterion	Max Points (or Weight)	Systems Being Evaluated (Score)		
		A	B	C
Disk Capacity	20	10	17	12
Compatibility	50	45	30	25
Usability	30	12	30	20
Vendor Support	35	27	16	5
Benchmark Results	50	40	28	30
(add as needed...)				
Total	185	134	121	92

[**Figure 8.24** ➥ Sample system evaluation form with subset of criteria.]

Outsourcing

A related, but different, alternative to purchasing an existing system is outsourcing. With the external acquisition option, an organization typically purchases a single system from an outside vendor. ***Outsourcing*** is the practice of turning over responsibility of some to all of an organization's information systems development and operations to an outside firm. Outsourcing includes a variety of working relationships. The outside firm, or service provider, may develop your information systems applications and house them within its organization, it may run your applications on its computers, or it may develop systems to run on existing computers within your organization. Anything is fair game in an outsourcing arrangement.

In recent years, outsourcing has become a very popular option for organizations. Canadian firms have entered into IT outsourcing contracts worth well over $1 billion per year over the last four years (see Table 8.11). For example, in 2002, CIBC entered into a seven-year agreement with HP worth $2 billion. Large outsourcing agreements of this sort often involve asset transfers between a firm and its outsourcing partner. IT staff may also become employees of the outsourcing firm. For example, 175 employees of National Bank Financial transferred to IBM upon signing their outsourcing agreement, and 550 Caisses Desjardins staff moved to CGI as part of their agreement. The volume of IT outsourcing in Canada compares favourably with amounts in the United States (see Table 8.11).

Why Outsourcing?

There are many reasons that a firm might outsource some (or all) of its information systems services. Some of these are old reasons, but some are new to today's environment (Applegate and McFarlan, 1999):

- *Cost and quality concerns*: In many cases, it is possible to achieve higher-quality systems at a lower price through economies of scale, better management of hardware, lower labour costs, and better software licences on the part of a service provider.
- *Problems in IS performance*: IS departments may have problems meeting acceptable service standards due to cost overruns, delayed systems, underutilized systems, or poorly performing systems. In such cases, organizational management may attempt to increase reliability through outsourcing.
- *Supplier pressures*: Perhaps not surprisingly, some of the largest service providers are also the largest suppliers of computer equipment (e.g., IBM and Hewlett-Packard). In some cases, the aggressive sales forces of these suppliers are able to convince senior managers at other organizations to outsource their IS functions.
- *Simplifying, downsizing, and reengineering*: Organizations under competitive pressure often attempt to focus on only their "core competencies." In many cases, organizations simply decide that running information systems is not one of their "core competencies" and decide to outsource this function to companies such as IBM and EDS, whose primary competency is developing and maintaining information systems.
- *Financial factors*: When firms turn over their information systems to a service provider, they can sometimes strengthen their balance sheets by liquefying their IT assets. Also, if users perceive that they are actually paying for their IT services rather than simply having them provided by an in-house staff, they may use those services more wisely and perceive them to be of greater value.
- *Organizational culture*: Political or organizational problems are often difficult for an IS group to overcome. However, an external service provider often brings enough clout, devoid of any organizational or functional ties, to streamline IS operations as needed.

[Table 8.11] *Selected outsourcing agreements in Canada and the United States.*

Company	Outsourcing Partner	Value of Outsourcing Contract	Year Contract Signed	Duration of Contract
CANADA				
CIBC	HP	$2B	2002	7 years
Caisses Desjardins	CGI	$1B	2000	10 years
B.C. Hydro	Accenture	$1B	2001	10 years
Hydro One	Cap Gemini	$1B	2001	10 years
Air Canada	IBM	$908M	2001	7 years
Scotiabank	IBM	$900M	2001	7 years
TD Bank	IBM	$720M	2003	7 years
National Bank	Cognicase	$600M	2000	10 years
MDS	IBM	$293M	2003	7 years
CP Rail	IBM	$200M	2003	7 years
National Bank Financial	IBM	$200M	2003	9 years
ATB Financial	IBM	$90M	2003	5 years
UNITED STATES				
J. P. Morgan Chase	IBM	US$5B	2002	7 years
Bank of America	EDS	US$4.5B	2002	10 years
American Express	IBM	US$4B	2002	7 years
Procter & Gamble	HP	US$3B	2003	10 years
Visteon	IBM	US$2B	2003	10 years

[Adapted in part from Larry Dignan, "Outsmarting Outsourcers," *Baseline Magazine,* 20 (July 2003).]

CAREER IMPLICATIONS

Marketing

BP Fuels, one of Canada's biggest natural gas producers, stands behind a new trend in IT: business transformation outsourcing (BTO). BTO is a merger of business process outsourcing and business process reengineering touted by giant international technology and consulting companies such as IBM, Accenture, and Cap Gemini Ernst & Young. Called by one Meta Group analyst an "appealing, albeit somewhat nebulous concept," the providers go beyond traditional outsourcing of a service, such as hosting a call centre, to offer guarantees of improving a customer's business processes. So far it's a young field, but one which Don Brilz, a vice-president of BP Canada Energy who oversees the company's business transformation outsourcing arrangement with IBM, says could have a huge impact on the multinational company. "In terms of efficiency, it could be monstrous," he said in an interview. "Radical is a better word."

The arrangement started out three years ago as a traditional outsourcing deal with British-based BP plc for services, with IBM operating a three-floor data centre in BP's Calgary office. Since then, the relationship has turned what Brilz called a "journey" into business transformation. "We are beginning to discover areas of opportunity where IBM can add value by doing things differently," he said. Getting a handle on BTO can be a challenge. "You don't write a business transformation outsourcing contract," said Brilz. "You write a relationship contract for a provision of service which has an incentivization business." BTO is not without its risks, he adds. BP has realized contract management could have been done better, and it lost some skills needed to keep an eye on IBM's work. "We lost expertise maybe deeper than we should have," he said. "The economies of scale haven't materialized to the level we expect," he said. "I buy into the concept," he added, "but there's a lot IBM and others have to learn about what is process excellence. They're going in the right direction, but the marketing and messaging is running far ahead of the actual capabilities."

[Adapted from Howard Solomon, "BP Fuels Business Transformation Outsourcing Market," **www.itbusiness.ca/index.asp?theaction=61&sid=54316#**, ITBusiness.ca (February 2, 2004).]

- *Internal irritants*: Tension between end users and the IS staff is sometimes difficult to eliminate. At times, this tension can intrude on the daily operations of the organization, and the idea of a remote, external, relatively neutral IS group can be appealing. Whether or not the tension between users and the IS staff (or service provider) is really eliminated is open to question; however, simply having the IS group external to the organization can remove a lingering thorn in management's side.

Managing the IS Outsourcing Relationship

There are many hidden costs of outsourcing. In fact, according to a study by the Gartner Group, half of all outsourcing contracts are labelled "losers" by senior executives. The total cost of an outsourcing relationship does not consist only of the cost on the contract. For example, vendor search and contract preparation costs typically add about 3 percent to the total cost of an outsourcing project. It is often complicated and time consuming to transition internal operations to an outsourcing partner. Ongoing management of the outsourcing relationship can add 8 percent to the cost of a contract, or more if the outsourcing partner is located overseas. If unchecked, poor language skills, time zone differences, visa difficulties, high employee turnover, cultural differences, lack of domain knowledge, and internal conflict can all conspire to reduce the effectiveness of an outsourcing relationship. Finally, transitioning operations from the outsourcing partner back into the firm once the contract is complete can be costly and time consuming.

McFarlan and Nolan (1995) argue that the ongoing management of an outsourcing alliance is the single most important aspect of the outsourcing project's success. Their recommendations for the best management are:

1. A strong, active CIO and staff should continually manage the legal and professional relationship with the outsourcing firm.
2. Clear, realistic performance measurements of the systems and of the outsourcing arrangement, such as tangible and intangible costs, benefits and service levels, should be developed.
3. The interface between the customer and the outsourcer should have multiple levels (for example, links to deal with policy and relationship issues, and links to deal with operational and tactical issues).

Managing outsourcing alliances in this way has important implications for the success of the relationship. For example, in addition to making sure a firm has a strong CIO and staff, McFarlan and Nolan recommend that firms assign full-time relationship managers and coordinating groups lower in the organization to "manage" the IS outsourcing project. This means that as people within the IS function are pulled away from traditional IS tasks such as systems development, they are moved toward new roles and organized into new groups. The structure and nature of the internal IS activities change from exclusively building and managing systems to including managing relationships with outside firms that build and manage systems under service-level agreements or other legal contracts.

Not All Outsourcing Relationships Are the Same

Most organizations no longer enter into a strictly legal contract with an outsourcing vendor, but into a mutually beneficial relationship with a strategic partner. In such a relationship, the firm and the vendor are each concerned with, and perhaps have a direct stake in, the success of the other. Yet other types of relationships exist, which means that not all outsourcing agreements need to be structured the same way (Fryer, 1994). In fact, at least three different types of outsourcing relationships can be identified:

- Basic relationship
- Preferred relationship
- Strategic relationship

A basic relationship can best be thought of as a "cash and carry" relationship, in which you buy products and services on the basis of price and convenience. Organizations should try to have a few preferred relationships, in which the buyer and supplier set preferences and prices to the benefit of the other. For example, a supplier can provide preferred pricing to customers that do a specified volume of business. Most organizations have just a few strategic relationships, in which both sides share risks and rewards.

We have now discussed two systems development alternatives that rely on external organizations to alleviate either completely or partially the burden of managing IS development projects in-house. In some cases, however, it may not be possible or convenient to rely on agencies outside the organization for development. In these cases, organizations

Web Search

WEB SEARCH OPPORTUNITY

Outsourcing has become very popular. Many observers believe that outsourcing will continue to grow as a way for organizations to develop and operate their information systems. Search the Websites of some popular information systems trade magazines to find out the latest news and predictions about outsourcing. Start with **www.computerworld.com** and **www.itworldcanada.com**. Then you might want to look at **www.outsourcing-center.com** for a host of materials on outsourcing.

BRIEF CASE

CP Rail Overhauls IT Infrastructure Spending with $200M Outsourcing Deal

The Canadian Pacific Railway, Canada's second largest railway company, has taken the ongoing overhaul of its IT infrastructure to the next level through a seven-year, $200-million outsourcing agreement with IBM Canada. About 100 employees in CP Rail's IT department had been offered positions at IBM at the same level of compensation and benefits, and would be given an enhanced career path in IT, IBM said. CP Rail said it would move its mainframe and data facilities in Calgary and Toronto to IBM facilities in the same cities. CP Rail vice-president of information services, Allen Borak, said the IBM deal will include management of the servers, storage, and emergency recovery planning at CP Rail. This will free the company's remaining in-house IT staff to continue development work on application development to better forecast, track, and map the delivery of goods. CP Rail said some 2.5 trillion bytes of data move through its systems every day.

"Cost was a major driver—we had done a lot of good things to try and achieve cost take-out, but we had reached a point where we could not take it much lower in-house," Borak said. Some of CP Rail's major application development work will be aimed at improving the management of its intermodal trains, locomotives that carry steel containers filled primarily with consumer goods from Asia, which also move on ships and trucks. "We want to speed [the] flow of our IT architecture and broaden the access to it," Borak said. The company will continue to develop customer-facing applications in-house.

CP Rail began a major revamp of its IT strategy almost seven years ago, when it committed $350 million to a suite of more than 20 projects. This included the implementation of SAP enterprise resource planning technology, electronic data interchange to automate train planning, and an HR system linked to the corporate intranet.

IBM Canada president Ed Kilroy said the agreement would see CP Rail work with IBM's Center for Transportation Innovation in Boulder, Colorado. The two companies will study the interconnections of freight cars, locomotives, facilities, track, and train crews, and develop IT-enabled business processes to make it easier to transport goods and services over railways. "This agreement goes beyond traditional outsourcing," he said. "It reflects a trend in Canada and elsewhere where we see customers want more than just an outsourcing company but a business partner with deep industry knowledge."

Questions

1. What challenges might CP Rail face in its IT outsourcing deal with IBM?
2. CP Rail may have been able to negotiate a better deal with an offshore outsourcer. Why do you think the company decided instead to enter into an outsourcing agreement with a local provider?

[Adapted from Shane Schick, "CP Rail Unloads Systems to IBM," *Computing Canada,* Vol. 29, No. 24 (December 12, 2003).]

may rely on another option for systems development projects.

End-User Development

In many organizations, the growing sophistication of users within the organization offers IS managers a fourth alternative for systems development. This fourth alternative is ***end-user development***—having users develop their own applications. This means that the people who are actually going to use the systems are also those who will develop those systems. End-user development, then, is one way IS departments can speed up application development without relying on external entities such as vendors or service providers. However, end-user development also has risks associated with it. This section outlines the benefits of having end users develop their own applications, as well as some of the drawbacks of this approach.

Benefits of End-User Development

To help you better understand the benefits of end-user development, you should quickly review some of the problems with conventional development that are suggested by the four situations presented earlier in this chapter:

- *Cost of labour*: Conventional systems development is labour-intensive. Over the past several decades, software costs have increased while hardware costs have declined, as shown in Figure 8.25. As you can see from the figure, it becomes much cheaper for IS managers to substitute hardware for labour by giving users their own equipment. An IS manager can significantly reduce the cost of application development

Operations Management

A panel of Canadian companies insist their operations are running more efficiently after implementing product lifecycle management (PLM) technologies. PLM is "about people, process, and technology," explained Joanne Friedman, CEO of ConneKted Minds Inc., a consultancy in Richmond Hill, Ontario. "It's not about managing technology anymore." PLM, which may involve software, hardware, and technical support, allows manufacturing companies to share product data across all functions, customers, and suppliers. Friedman predicted the North American market for the technology could grow to $90 billion by the end of the decade.

In the past, the decision about introducing PLM was made by an organization's engineers, until it gravitated to the domain of an executive team. It is now handled by C-level executives because it's considered a business decision, she said. In North America, 28 to 32 percent of mid-sized to large enterprises use some version of PLM, and the number will grow substantially over the next few years, Friedman estimated. Recently, Volvo Motor Graders rolled out IBM's PLM technologies in its Goderich, Ontario, operation. One of the incentives for the purchase was a problem organizing workflow, said Dave Ross, vice-president of engineering at Volvo Motor Graders. "The pressure we had was trying to make the engineering change notice process more efficient and try to free up designer time to do design, as opposed to keystrokes to make change notes."

Smaller businesses are starting to play in the PLM arena because "they see the value of time to market, cost efficiency, increased cash flow," said Friedman. She said these companies have a broader strategic perspective, but shun the "big bang of cost," preferring to add pieces of the PLM system over time in a tactical approach. Smaller players can expect to pay $150,000 to $2 million for a PLM solution, whereas large multinationals will fork over $10 million to $20 million.

[Adapted from Fawzia Sheikh, "Volvo Revs Design Efficiency Engine," *Computing Canada,* Vol. 29, No. 24 (December 12, 2003).]

simply by giving end users the tools they need and enabling them to develop their own applications. Better yet, the various departments within the organization can purchase their own equipment, and the IS staff can simply provide guidance and other services.

- *Long development time*: New systems can take months or even years to develop, depending on the scale and scope of the new system and the backlog of systems waiting to be developed. As a result, users' needs may significantly change between when a system is initially proposed and when it is actually implemented. In these cases, the system may be virtually obsolete before it has even been implemented! End user-developed systems can "skip" the queue of systems waiting to be developed by the IS organization, resulting in more rapidly developed systems.
- *Slow modification or updates of existing systems*: Related to the time it takes to develop new systems is the problem of maintaining existing systems. Often, updates to existing systems are given a lower priority than developing new systems. Unfortunately, this can result in systems that are unable to keep pace with changing business needs, becoming antiquated and underused.

When end users develop their own systems, the users have the responsibility of maintaining and updating applications as needed. Also, when systems are implemented, they often cause changes to the underlying business processes. These changes may necessitate further change or modification to the application, as highlighted in Figure 8.26. Rather than rely on IS to make these changes, users are able to modify the application in a timely manner to reflect the changed business process.

- *Work overload*: One reason for long development times and slow modifications is that IS departments are often overloaded with work. When you leverage the talents of end-user developers, you can, in effect,

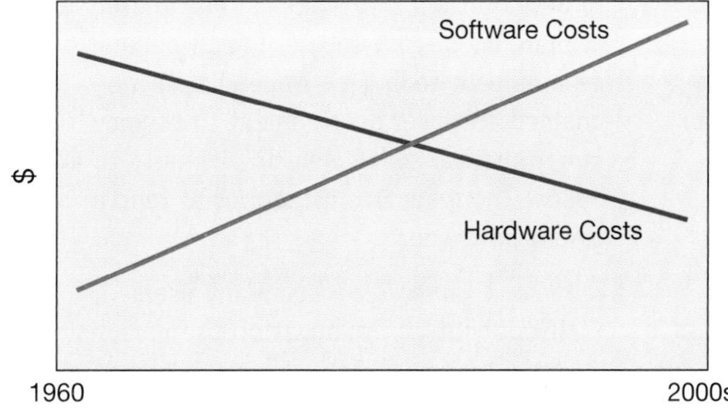

[**Figure 8.25** ➥ Rising software costs versus declining hardware costs.]

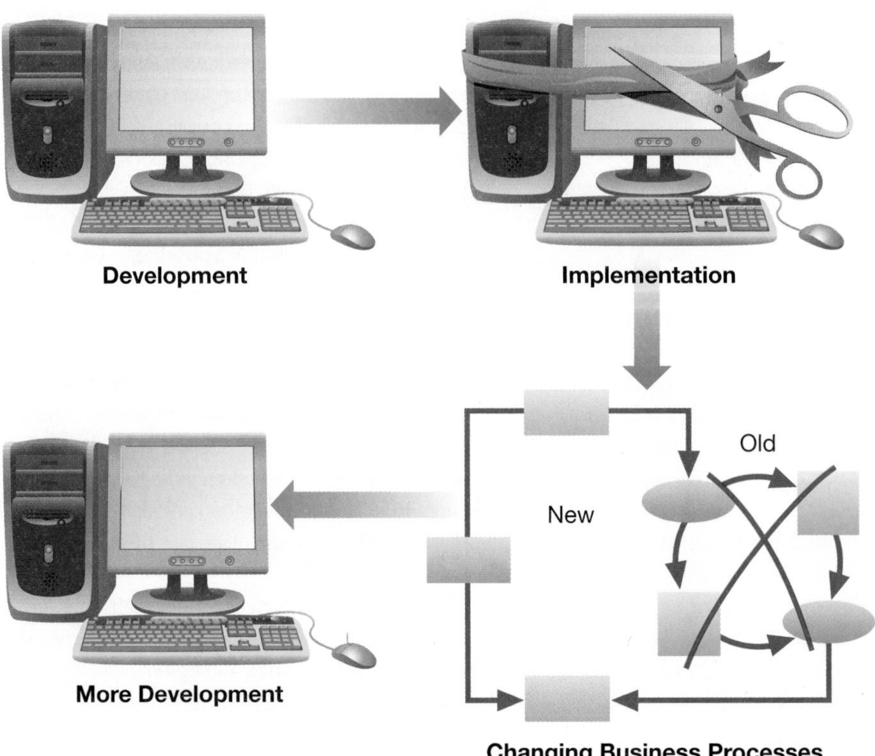

[**Figure 8.26** ➡ Continuous cycle of development: a system is developed and implemented. However, it eventually becomes inadequate, and new development takes place.]

increase the size of the development staff by shifting some of the workload normally handled by IS professionals to end users.

End-user development can radically decrease the development workload in the IS department. However, such a shift may cause other areas within IS, such as a help desk, for example, to become flooded with requests for assistance. Nonetheless, end-user development can be an excellent option for organizations faced with some of the problems previously described.

Encouraging End-User Development

End-user development sounds great, but how can organizations encourage and enable users to develop their own systems? Fortunately, the availability of easy-to-use, fourth-generation development tools (see Appendix B) has enabled end-user development to become more practical today than in the early to mid-1980s. There are five categories of fourth-generation tools:

- *Personal computer tools*: Many users throughout an organization use personal computer tools, including spreadsheets, database management systems, and graphics programs. Frequently, these tools enable users to build their own applications using macro languages or embedded tools within the software designed to enable users to customize their own systems.
- *Query languages/report generators*: These tools are usually associated with database systems and enable you to search a database by entering various search criteria. Structured Query Language, or SQL, is the most common query language for this purpose. Although users often use query languages independently, report generators may require some assistance from IS staff.
- *Graphics generators*: People can use these tools to extract relevant information from databases and convert that data to a graphic such as a pie chart, a line graph, or an area plot.
- *Decision support or modelling tools*: Although spreadsheets can be used as decision support aids, dedicated decision support tools are often available for more complex, multidimensional models that may be too complicated to be handled easily in a spreadsheet.
- *Application generators*: Application generators are designed to automate much of the relatively tedious programming work associated with systems development. With these tools, you can specify what you want done,

then the application generator decides how to accomplish that task and generates the program code. Computer-aided software engineering (CASE) tools often include an application generator that end users or IS professionals can use.

End-User Development Pitfalls

This chapter has painted a pretty rosy picture of end-user development so far. However, it is important to understand that along with the benefits come some drawbacks, as depicted in Figure 8.27. The information systems and computer science professions have established software development standards and generally accepted practices that are used throughout different organizations and across different types of systems. Unfortunately, users may not be aware of these standards, such as the need for adequate documentation, built-in error checking, and testing procedures. In small, personal applications, not adhering to the standards may not present a problem. However, if the system manages or interconnects with important business data, then lack of adherence to sound principles can quickly become a *big* problem if data becomes corrupted or is not secure.

Another problem for end user–developed systems is a potential lack of continuity. Suppose James develops a new system that meets his needs perfectly. James understands the system and uses it every day. However, one day James is transferred and is replaced by Jordan, a new hire to the company. The system that was intuitive for James to use may not be so intuitive for Jordan. Jordan may quickly abandon James's system or may be forced to develop her own system. This example shows how end-user development can easily result in a lack of continuity among applications, leading to redundant development efforts and a lot of wasted productivity in the organization. In organizations where turnover is frequent, a lot of time can be lost "reinventing the wheel" simply because systems that are in place are undocumented and cannot easily be used by new employees.

Related to the continuity problem is the question of whether users and managers should be spending their time on IS development. That is, the organization has hired individuals to be financial managers, production managers, marketers, or salespeople. The organization expects these employees to add

The 5th Wave
By Rich Tennant
©RICHTENNANT
"OK, TECHNICALLY THIS SHOULD WORK. JUDY, TYPE THE WORD, 'GOODYEAR' ALL CAPS, BOLDFACE, AT 700-POINT TYPE SIZE."

[**Figure 8.27** ➡ End-user development can sometimes be problematic.]

Source: The 5th Wave by Rich Tennant.

value to the organization based on the skills that they have to offer. If the time and energy of these individuals are diverted to developing new systems, then the organization loses out on the potential productivity these individuals have to offer in other ways. Also, individual motivation, morale, and performance might suffer if the employee is unable to concentrate on her area of expertise and instead spends too much of her time worrying about developing new systems.

KEY POINTS REVIEW

1. **Understand the process used by organizations to manage the development of information systems.** The development of information systems follows a process called the systems development life cycle (SDLC). The SDLC is a process that first identifies the need for a system and then defines the processes for designing, developing, and maintaining an information system. The process is very structured and formal and requires the active involvement of managers and users.
2. **Describe each major phase of the systems development life cycle: system identification, selection, and planning; system analysis; system design; system implementation; and system maintenance.** The SDLC has five phases: system identification, selection, and planning; system analysis; system design; system implementation; and system maintenance. Systems identification, selection, and planning is the first phase of the SDLC, in which potential projects are identified, selected, and planned. System analysis is the second phase of the SDLC, in which the current ways of doing business are studied and alternative replacement systems are proposed. System design is the third phase of the SDLC, in which all features of the proposed system are described. System implementation is the fourth phase of the SDLC, in which the information system is programmed, tested, installed, and supported. System maintenance is the fifth and final phase of the SDLC, in which an information system is systematically repaired and improved.
3. **Describe prototyping, rapid application development, and object-oriented analysis and design methods of systems development, along with each approach's strengths and weaknesses.** Prototyping is an iterative systems development process in which requirements are converted into a working system that is continually revised through a close working relationship between analysts and users. The strengths of prototyping are that it helps develop a close working relationship between designers and users and that it is a good approach for hard-to-define problems. Its weaknesses are that it is not a practical approach for a large number of users and that it can at times lead to a lower-quality system if the system is built too quickly. Rapid application development (RAD) is a systems development methodology that combines prototyping, computer-based development tools, special management practices, and close user involvement. The strength of RAD is that users are actively involved in the design process, which makes system implementation much easier. The weaknesses of RAD are that systems are sometimes narrowly focused—which might limit future evolution—and that quality problems might result if a system is designed and built too quickly (as is the case with prototyping). Object-oriented analysis and design (OOA&D) is a systems development approach that focuses on modelling objects—data and operations bundled together—rather than on modelling these separately. The strengths of OOA&D are the integration of data and processing during the design phase, which should lead to higher-quality systems, and the reuse of common modules, which should make development and maintenance easier. The weaknesses of OOA&D are that it is very difficult to train analysts and programmers in the object-oriented approach and that analysts often recreate common modules.
4. **Understand the factors involved in building a system in-house, along with situations in which it is not feasible.** It is not feasible for an organization to build a system in-house in at least four situations. First, some organizations have limited IS staffing and, therefore, do not have the capability to build a system themselves. Second, an organization may have IS staff with a limited skill set. Existing IS staff may be highly skilled at producing traditional applications but not have the skills to build new types of systems or systems that require emerging development tools. Third, in many organizations, the IS staff does not have the time to work on all the systems that the organization desires. Fourth, some organizations have performance problems with their IS staff, whereby staff turnover, changing requirements, shifts in technology, or budget constraints have resulted in poor results. In any of these situations, it may be advantageous to an organization to consider an alternative to in-house systems development.
5. **Explain three alternative systems development options: external acquisition, outsourcing, and end-user development.** External acquisition is the process of purchasing an existing information system from an external organization or vendor. External acquisition is a five-step process. Step 1 is system identification, selection, and planning, which focuses on determining whether a proposed system is feasible. Step 2 is system analysis, which focuses on determining the requirements for the system. Step 3 is the development of a Request for Proposal (RFP). An RFP is a communication tool indicating an organization's requirements for a given system and requesting information from potential vendors on their ability to deliver such a system. Step 4 is proposal evaluation, which focuses on evaluating proposals received from vendors. This evaluation may include viewing system demonstrations, evaluating the performance of those systems, and examining criteria important to the organization and how the proposed systems meet those criteria. Step 5 is vendor selection, which focuses on choosing the vendor to provide the system. Outsourcing refers to the turning over of partial or entire responsibility for information systems development and management to an outside organization. End-user development is a systems development method whereby users in the organization develop, test, and maintain their own applications.

KEY TERMS

REVIEW QUESTIONS

1. What are the five phases of the systems development life cycle?
2. List and describe six techniques used in requirements collection.
3. What are the four major components or tasks of the system design phase of the SDLC?
4. What are the four options for system conversion? How do they differ from each other?
5. Compare and contrast the four types of system maintenance.
6. What are three alternative approaches to the SDLC for designing and building systems?
7. What are the advantages and disadvantages of prototyping?
8. List and define the four phases of rapid application development.
9. What is object-oriented analysis and design, and what are its strengths and weaknesses?
10. Define outsourcing, and list three major types.
11. What is system benchmarking, and what are some common benchmarks?
12. What are some of the reasons why outsourcing is more popular than ever?
13. What are the three recommendations made in this chapter for managing an outsourcing IS relationship?
14. Describe five categories of fourth-generation tools.
15. End-user developers have what advantages and disadvantages?

SELF-STUDY QUESTIONS

Answers are at the end of the Problems and Exercises.

1. Which of the following is **not** one of the five phases of the systems development life cycle?
   A. system analysis
   B. system implementation
   C. system design
   D. systems resource acquisition
2. ________ is the process of gathering and organizing information from users, managers, business processes, and documents to understand how a proposed information system should function.
   A. Requirements collection
   B. Systems collection
   C. Systems analysis
   D. Records archiving
3. Which of the following is the correct order of phases in the systems development life cycle?
   A. maintenance, analysis, planning, design, implementation
   B. analysis, planning, design, implementation, maintenance
   C. planning, analysis, design, implementation, maintenance
   D. maintenance, planning, analysis, design, implementation
4. In the systems design phase, the elements that must be designed when building an information system include all of the following **except** ________.
   A. reports and forms
   B. questionnaires
   C. databases and files
   D. interfaces and dialogues
5. ________ maintenance involves making enhancements to improve processing performance or interface usability, or adding desired, but not necessarily required, system features (in other words, "bells and whistles").
   A. Preventive
   B. Perfective
   C. Corrective
   D. Adaptive
6. Which of the following is an alternative to building a system in-house?
   A. external acquisition
   B. end-user development
   C. outsourcing
   D. all of the above

7. A ________ is a report that an organization uses to tell vendors what its requirements are and to invite them to provide information about how they might be able to meet those requirements.
   A. request letter
   B. vendor request
   C. Request for Proposal
   D. payables request
8. Which of the following is **not** a type of outsourcing?
   A. basic
   B. elite
   C. strategic
   D. preferred
9. Which of the following factors is a good reason to outsource?
   A. problems in IS performance
   B. supplier pressures
   C. financial factors
   D. all of the above
10. Most competitive external acquisition processes have at least five general steps. Which of the following is **not** one of those steps?
   A. vendor selection
   B. proposal evaluation
   C. development of a Request for Proposal
   D. implementation

PROBLEMS AND EXERCISES

1. Match the following terms with the appropriate definitions:

____ Request for Proposal	____ Systems benchmarking
____ Alpha testing	____ Systems development life cycle
____ End-user development	____ Prototyping
____ Pilot conversion	____ Systems analysis
____ Outsourcing	____ External acquisition
____ Data flows	____ Requirements collection

   a. The movement of data through an organization or within an information system
   b. Term that describes the life of an information system from conception to retirement
   c. The second phase of the systems development life cycle
   d. The process of gathering and organizing information from users, managers, business processes and documents to understand how a proposed information system should function
   e. Performed by software testers to assess whether the entire system meets the design requirements of the users
   f. When the entire system is used in one location, but not in the entire organization
   g. A systems development methodology that uses a trial-and-error approach for discovering how a system should operate
   h. The practice of turning over responsibility of some to all of an organization's information systems development and operations to an outside firm
   i. Users developing their own applications
   j. Purchasing an existing system from an outside vendor
   k. A way to evaluate a proposed system by testing a portion of it with the system workload
   l. A report that is used to tell vendors what your requirements are and to invite them to provide information about how they might be able to meet those requirements
2. Explain the differences between data and data flows. How might systems analysts obtain the information they need to generate the data flows of a system? How are these data flows and the accompanying processing logic used in the system design phase of the life cycle? What happens when the data and data flows are modelled incorrectly?
3. When Microsoft posts a new version of Internet Explorer on the Microsoft Website and states that this is a beta version, what does it mean? Is this a final working version of the software, or is it still being tested? Who is doing the testing? Search the World Wide Web to find other companies that have beta versions of their products available to the public. You might try Corel at **www.corel.com**. What other companies did you find?
4. Why is the system documentation of a new information system so important? What information does it contain? For whom is this information intended? When will the system documentation most likely be used?
5. Conduct a search on the World Wide Web for "systems development life cycle," using any browser. Check out some of the hits. Compare them with the SDLC outlined in this chapter. Do all these life cycles follow the same general path? How many phases do the ones you found on the Web contain? Is the terminology the same or different? Prepare a 10-minute presentation to the class on your findings.
6. Choose an organization with which you are familiar that develops its own information systems. Does this organization follow a systems development life cycle? If not, why not? If so, how many phases does it have? Who developed this life cycle? Was it someone within the company, or was the information system adopted from somewhere else?
7. Describe your experiences with information systems that were undergoing changes or updates. What kind of conversion procedure was being used? How did this affect your interaction with the system as a user? Who else was affected? If the system was down altogether, for how long was it down? Do you or any of your classmates have horror stories, or were the situations not that bad?
8. Compare and contrast RAD and object-oriented methodologies. What are the strengths and weaknesses of each? Visit Object Group at **www.objectconsulting.com.au** or Object FAQ at **www.objectfaq.com/oofaq2**.
9. Conduct a search on the World Wide Web for "object-oriented analysis and design" using any browser you wish. (Hint: Because people write differently, search using both "object-oriented" and "object oriented.") Check out some of the hits. You should have found numerous articles regarding OOA&D's use by IS departments. Are these articles positive or negative regarding OOA&D? Do you agree with the articles? Prepare a 10-minute presentation to the class on your findings.
10. Interview an IS manager within an organization with which you are familiar. Determine whether the organization uses methodologies such as prototyping, RAD, and/or OOA&D for system pro-

jects. Who chooses the methodology? If the organization has not used a methodology, is it due to choice, or is it due to a lack of need, understanding, or capability of using the methodology?

11. Choose an organization with which you are familiar, and determine whether it builds its applications in-house. How many IS staff members does the organization have, and how large is the organization they support?

12. Think about the requirements of a career in IS. Do IS positions generally require people to work 40 hours a week, or more if a project has a deadline? Do positions in the IS department require people skills? To find these answers, visit the IS department at your university, a local business, or **www.monster.ca**.

13. Find an organization that outsources work, either on the Internet at **www.itbusiness.ca** or **www.infoworld.com** or a company you may want to work for in the future. What are the managerial challenges of outsourcing, and why is this a popular alternative to hiring additional staff?

ANSWERS TO THE SELF-STUDY QUESTIONS

1. D 2. A 3. C 4. B 5. B 6. D 7. C 8. B 9. D 10. D

Case 1: *IT Outsourcing: A Mixed Blessing for Canada*

The offshore outsourcing of technology jobs will have a negative impact on the viability of the IT industry in Canada, according to a majority of professionals surveyed by the Canadian Information Processing Society. Of the 111 senior IT professionals polled, more than half told CIPS they have outsourced some IT functions or are considering it; 69.4 percent said they believed the trend does not bode well for the sector's overall health. Only 33 percent said they believed offshore outsourcing would help the Canadian economy.

The research reflects the growing fear among Canadian IT workers that their skills may be obsolete if lower-level programming work is be moved to India, China, Romania, or elsewhere (see Table 8.12). From the employer's perspective, however, offshore outsourcing is simply a matter of dollars and sense. "What is the difference between sourcing a product offshore? We all have radios here, and I doubt many of them were made in Canada," said Gabor Takach, a lawyer who leads the technology group at Torys LLP. "This trend (offshore outsourcing) represents a concentration of expertise and a new and efficient way of delivering a service." Paul Harrington, a consultant to retail, small business, and marketing companies, said some IT workers may have reason to feel paranoid. "When an industry disappears—like buggy whips—they just disappear," he said. "Everybody in every industry has to take a look at what's happening in their industry. This is an industry that's in a great deal of turmoil at the moment."

Kevin Yan, CEO of global software development services firm Arackal Digital Solutions, said he looks at offshore outsourcing as a productivity tool because it allows companies to eliminate low-value coding tasks. "If you have a better way of doing business out there, why wouldn't you do it?" John Chettleburgh, a staffing industry consultant and former vice-president at CNC Global, pointed out that most offshore outsourcing is done by Canada's largest firms, which means some of the jobs may not disappear entirely. "It could mean a renaissance for these kinds of jobs in the SME market in Canada," he said.

While CIPS found that coding, testing, call centre work, and some back-office banking activities were the primary candidates for offshore outsourcing, Yan warned that some skill sets are best kept at home. "Business knowledge is not easily replicable," he said, adding that the ability to analyze processes can be a strong complement to an IT background. "You're bound to introduce risk into projects if you don't also integrate some onshore resources. If you don't do that, I would say you're bound to fail."

Country or Region	Outsource Industry Revenue (Millions)	Number of Outsource IT Professionals	IT Employee Cost per Year	Charge Rate per Hour
Canada	$3,780	45,000	$36,000	$42
India	$8,955	137,500	$8,000	$15
Ireland	$1,920	30,000	$28,000	$32
China	$1,040	26,000	$9,600	$20
Eastern Europe	$360	12,000	$7,000	$15
Russia	$165	5,500	$7,000	$15
Mexico	$120	4,000	$7,000	$15

[Adapted from "Will Work for Rupees," *Wired Magazine* (February 2004).]

[Table 8.12] *Canada compared to other outsourcing destinations.*

Chettleburgh agreed, adding that corporate enterprises have to do a better job of retraining employees potentially affected by offshore outsourcing and better capturing the knowledge they have learned about their organization.

Takach described himself as part of a "last generation" of students who graduated with an engineering degree who might have qualified for a management position. Today, he said, the situation is greatly changed. "You can still study computer science, but not with a view to just turning out code," he said. "We're culturally indoctrinated [in North America] to want to advance and move ahead to bigger projects," added Yan. "In India, it's different. They like doing the same thing. They appreciate the stability of the job." Although some firms, like EDS, are creating "nearshore" outsourcing operations in Canada, Chettleburgh said the rising Canadian dollar could "obliterate" the economic benefits of that model.

[Adapted from Shane Schick, "The Opportunity Cost of Offshore," **www.itbusiness.ca/index.asp?theaction=61&sid=54499#**, ITBusiness.ca (February 2, 2004).]

Discussion Questions

1. Compare this case to the chapter's opening case. Drawing on these opposing opinions, what impact do you think the global trend toward IT outsourcing will have on Canada?
2. How does offshore IT outsourcing affect how information systems is taught at Canadian colleges and universities?
3. What elements of IT management can be outsourced, and what elements should be kept in-house?
4. Should the Canadian government step in to stem the flow of IT jobs going offshore? If so, how?

Case 2: *Information Systems Failure at Integrated Solutions*

Integrated Solutions is an industrial services provider with a large global presence. The company is primarily headquartered in the United States but has large-scale operations (including offices and personnel) in Canada as well as most nations in Europe, Asia, South America, and Africa. The company is considered to be the market leader in its industry. In the glory days of the company, it was considered the most technologically sophisticated in its industry and had an excellent technological infrastructure. However, over time, the inability to keep up with the immense changes in technology had resulted in some old legacy systems, more than half of which were not properly integrated. The company's problems related to IT started in the latter half of 1996. Around that time, a lot of customers would call to check on the status of their orders. It took Integrated Solutions days to respond to most of these queries. On the other hand, some of its competitors would take only minutes to respond to such requests. Due to the global nature of the company, some of its customers would place multiple orders in different countries. Because the company's information systems were not properly integrated, such services would take even longer. Employees prepared most of these reports by hand, leading to delays and a higher risk of errors than if the process were automated. The company's pricing structure was also very complex, often requiring tremendous customization, and the existing information systems helped little in this matter as well.

Frustrated with the state of the company, Integrated Solutions decided to turn to a consulting firm to turn things around and finally contacted a consulting group to develop a long-term IT plan and to replace the existing systems. The consulting firm proposed the development and implementation of a globally integrated information system, which it believed would be the perfect solution for the company's situation. The plan received a "go ahead" signal from the chairman, and the CIO was immediately given the responsibility to execute it. The plan also had the active involvement of the president, the CFO, and other personnel from some of its overseas regional offices. The estimated cost of the new information system was approximately $36 million.

Unfortunately, after three years very little had been accomplished on this project. Some of the regional personnel had objected to the development of the new system, and that had been the beginning of the problems associated with the project. Initially, there was a lot of debate and controversy over the choice of the development software. The consulting firm had proposed the use of Visual Basic; however, many key members of the company did not welcome this. One European executive had proposed the use of a certain tool that had met with a lot of success in Europe. Another member from another part of the world proposed yet another warehouse management tool, which he believed would fit the requirements of the firm. After some time, the European tool was selected. However, the developers in the United States were not familiar with this tool. As a result, a team was gathered in Europe and was flown to the United States to work on the development of this new system. The European team first developed a prototype of the new system. However, when the team started building the actual system, it started taking much longer than was expected. After a while, people realized that the prototype had very little functionality, and it was impossible to understand exactly what the actual global system would look like just by looking at the prototype. The company executives soon became convinced that the new system would not be the solution for the problem, and they started focusing their attention elsewhere.

The company made the decision to acquire an outside vendor package instead of building the system in-house and selected a vendor from Britain for this purpose. The vendor chosen was small, however, and people could put little faith in its ability to provide solutions to all the company's IT-related problems. Thus, even after many years, Integrated Solutions was unable to develop its own global information system and had to turn to a packaged solution from an outside vendor. It cost the company approximately $50 million ($14 million more than the original budget), apart from a significant delay in the completion of the project. In addition, the company suffered tremendously in the stock market (its stock price fell by 50 percent) and lost a lot of its existing market share, thus losing its position as the market leader.

Many factors led to the failure of the development and implementation of the global information system at Integrated Solutions. More than the technology, the company's management was responsible for some of the problems with the project. Many of the overseas regional managers pushed products of their own choice and refused to accept the system as developed on a different platform. The CIO's inability to take control of the situation, along with the lack of trust and respect between the CIO and the chairman, led to the chaos surrounding the choice of the development tool. The lack of strong leadership thus led to the choice of an inappropriate development tool and a packaged solution of lower quality.

Today, the company is trying to recover its position. It is now focusing on developing a new system based on the modules of its existing information systems and is hoping that, in due time, it will be able to recover its original position as the most technologically advanced market leader in the area of industrial services.

[Adapted from James M. Spitze, "Inside a Global Systems Failure," **www.cio.com/research/global/**, *CIO Magazine* (February 1, 2001).]

Discussion Questions

1. What were some of the information systems–related problems that Integrated Solutions faced?
2. Why did the global information systems implementation at Integrated Solutions fail?
3. What could Integrated Solutions have done differently to achieve a more favourable outcome?
4. Do you think Integrated Systems followed a good approach for building and acquiring the global information system? If so, why, and what did it do that was good? If not, why not, and what do you think the company could have done differently?

Chapter 9

Preview

Given that computers and information systems are now a fundamental part of doing business, opportunities for misusing and abusing information, computers, and systems now abound. This new wired world we live in causes us to ask some important new ethical questions. Who owns information, particularly information about us? Who is responsible for the accuracy of information? Should guidelines be set for how business organizations and business professionals use information, computers, and information systems, and if so, what should these guidelines be? What penalties should be assessed for computer crime and abuses? How can we secure our computers and information?

After reading this chapter, you will be able to:

1. Describe the advent of the Information Age and how computer ethics impact the use of information systems.
2. Discuss the ethical concerns associated with information privacy, accuracy, property, and accessibility.
3. Define computer crime and list several types of computer crime.
4. Contrast what the terms *computer virus*, *worm*, *Trojan horse*, and *logic* or *time bomb* mean.
5. Explain what is meant by computer security and describe various methods for providing computer security.

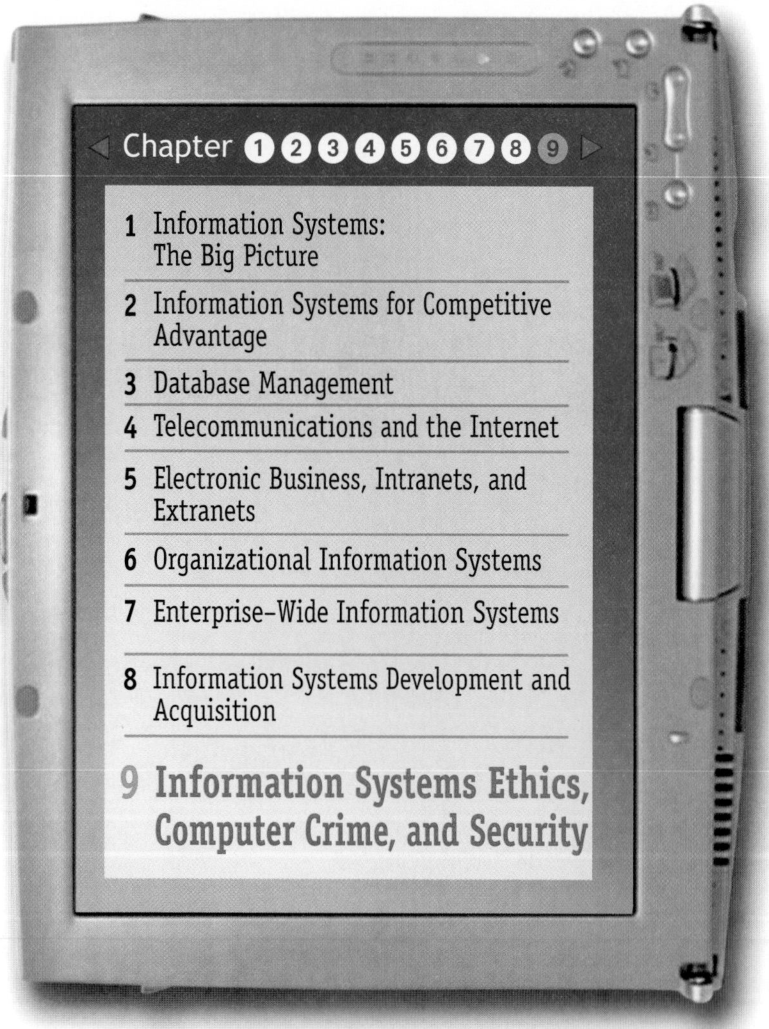

[**Figure 9.1** ➡ The Big Picture: focusing on information systems ethics, computer crime, and security.]

Information Systems Ethics, Computer Crime, and Security

OPENING: Canada Customs and Revenue Agency Audits Security Policy

Canadian security experts lambasted the Canada Customs and Revenue Agency (CCRA; now known as the Canada Revenue Agency) over the lack of encryption to protect the personal data of more than 120,000 individuals that was lost when a server was stolen from a regional office. The CCRA eventually admitted the breach weeks after its Quebec Tax Service office was broken into. One of the four stolen laptops, which acted as a server, contained a database with unencrypted information including names, dates of birth, social insurance numbers, and home addresses, but not personal income tax information, according to the CCRA. In unscrupulous hands, this data could be used to apply for a driver's licence, credit card, or passport.

The database spanned records from 1999 to 2001. Approximately 94,000 of those affected were in the construction industry. The rest of the records contained information on employment insurance and Canada Pension Plan rulings on contract and independent workers. CCRA spokesman Dominique McNeely says it did not want to make the information public until it had contacted those affected by letter. "We had to check to make sure we were contacting the right clients," he says. "It did take us a while, but we had to make literally millions of calls and checks within our system."

McNeely says the servers were not contained in their usual locked room at the time of the theft. "They were in our office, which is protected by an alarm system, but most police agencies will concur it is practically impossible to stop a determined thief," he says. "We could talk about human error, but it's not like we left them on the front lawn." The CCRA has put a 24-hour security guard on patrol at the office since the incident, McNeely says, and bars are being installed on the ground floor where a window was smashed. "Our servers aren't encrypted," he says. "They're only password-protected, because if our servers were encrypted, it would slow down our operations to a point where it just wouldn't be workable. That's why we keep them locked in a more secure room." Critics say there is no excuse in today's environment for claiming that reasonable encryption has a performance problem on IT equipment. "That's utter, unmitigated nonsense," says Mich Kabay, associate professor in the department of computer information systems at Norwich University in Northfield, Virginia. "You can use perfectly reasonable key lengths with off-the-shelf encryption software and do a reasonable job of interfering with all but a systematic, government-sponsored cracking attempt."

Paul K. Wing, a Toronto-based independent security consultant and the former head of IT at Scotiabank, says there are known techniques using digital certificates that enable organizations to separate the personal data and transactional history onto different servers. "The government hasn't shown enough leadership around how to protect data that's stored and how to [make] data [anonymous]," he argues. "You don't have to have files of data sitting on a database that have my name and address and the things that link to me." The incident marked the second time that a CCRA office lost confidential information. In February 2003, a server, along with eight laptops containing information on 538 income assistance clients, was stolen from a two-storey Coquitlam, B.C., location.

[Adapted from Shane Schick, "CCRA Loses Data in Server Theft," *Computing Canada*, Vol. 29, No. 20 (October 27, 2003).]

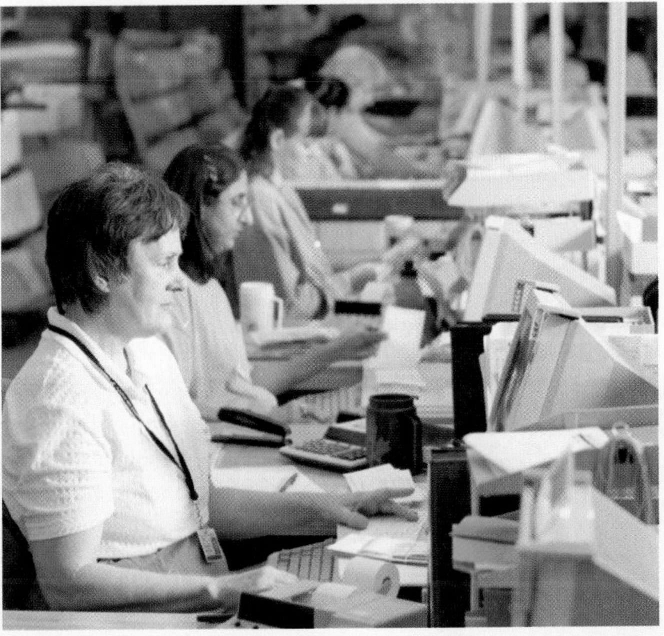

[**Figure 9.2** ➥ Security audit leads to new policies at the Canada Revenue Agency.]

Source: Canada Customs and Revenue Agency. Reproduced with permission of the Minister of Public Works and Government Services Canada, 2004.

This chapter focuses on the last puzzle piece for seeing The Big Picture, the issues associated with information systems ethics, computer crime, and security (see Figure 9.1). The chapter is partitioned into three major sections that focus on each topic. These topics are becoming increasingly important to successfully managing information systems and living our daily lives.

INFORMATION SYSTEMS ETHICS

In his book *The Third Wave*, futurist Alvin Toffler describes three distinct phases or "waves of change" that have taken place in the past or are currently taking place within the world's civilizations (see Figure 9.3). The First Wave—a civilization based upon agriculture and handwork—was a comparatively primitive stage that began as civilizations formed, and it lasted for hundreds of years. The Second Wave of change—the Industrial Revolution—overlapped the First Wave. The Industrial Revolution began in Great Britain toward the end of the eighteenth century and continued over the next 150 years, moving society from a predominantly agrarian culture to the urbanized machine age. Where once families supported themselves by working the land or handcrafting items for sale or trade, now mothers, fathers, and children left home to work in factories. Steel mills, textile factories, and eventually automobile assembly lines replaced farming and handwork as the principal source of family income.

Not only did occupations change as the Industrial Revolution progressed, but so did educational, business, and social and religious institutions evolve to accommodate the mechanized society. On an individual level, punctuality, obedience, and the ability to perform repetitive tasks were qualities to be instilled and valued in children in public schools and, ultimately, in workers.

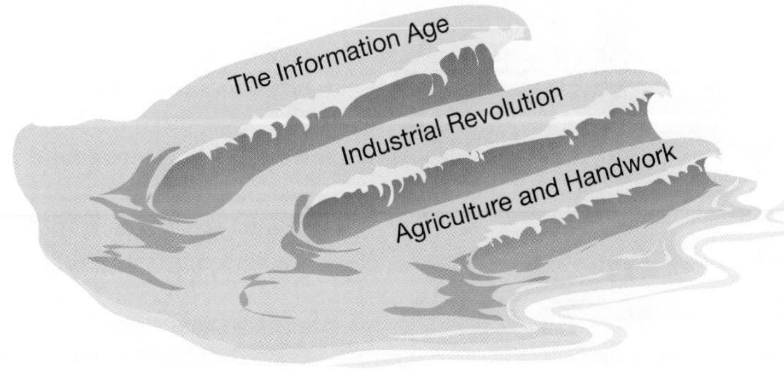

[**Figure 9.3** ➡ The Information Age is the biggest wave of change.]

The Information Age Arrives

In a much shorter period of time than it took for civilization to progress past the First Wave, societies worldwide moved from the machine age into the ***Information Age***—a period of change Toffler has dubbed the "Third Wave." As the Third Wave gained speed, information became the currency of the realm. For thousands of years, from primitive times through the Middle Ages, information, or the body of knowledge known to that point, was limited. It was transmitted verbally, within families, clans, and villages, from person to person, generation to generation. Then came Johann Gutenberg's invention of the printing press with movable type in 1455, and a tremendous acceleration occurred in the amount and kind of information available to populations. Now knowledge could be imparted in written form, and sometimes came from distant locations. Information could be saved, absorbed, debated, and written about in publications, thus adding to the exploding data pool.

Computer Literacy and the Digital Divide

Most modern-day high-school and university students grow up in a computerized world. If by some chance they do not know how to operate a computer by the time they graduate from high school, they soon acquire computer skills, because in today's work world, knowing how to use a computer—called ***computer literacy***—can mean the difference between being employed or unemployed. Knowing how to use a computer can also open up myriad sources of information to those who have learned how to use the computer as a device to gather, store, organize, and otherwise process information. In fact, some fear that the Information Age will not provide the same advantages to the computer literate and the computer illiterate—those whose computer skills are limited. It is worth noting that computer literacy is not the same thing as information literacy. Those with advanced computer skills are not necessarily better informed than those with limited computer skills, although the computer literate are likely to have much better access to information.

The first computer-related occupations have evolved as computers have become more sophisticated and more widely used. Where once we thought of computer workers primarily as programmers, data entry clerks, systems analysts, or computer repairpersons, today many more job categories in virtually all industries (see Figure 9.4) involve the use of computers. In fact, today there are few occupations where computers are not somehow in use. Computers manage air traffic, perform medical tests, monitor patients during surgery, help surgeons perform operations, and more. Since they are especially adept at processing large amounts of data, they are used extensively by universities and public schools, businesses of all sizes, and in all levels and departments of government. Engineers, architects, interior designers, and artists use special computer-aided design (CAD) programs. Musicians play computerized instruments, and songs are written and recorded with the help of computers. Not only do we use computers at work, we also use them in our personal lives. We teach our children on them, manage our finances, do our taxes, compose letters and term papers, create greeting cards, send and receive electronic mail, surf the Internet, and play games on them.

Unfortunately, there are still many people in our society who are being left behind in the Information Age. The gap between those individuals in our society who are computer literate and have access to information resources like the Internet and those who do not is referred to as the ***digital divide.*** The digital divide is one of the major ethical challenges facing society today, when you consider the strong linkage between computer literacy and a person's ability to compete in the Information Age. For example, access to raw materials and money fuelled the Industrial Revolution, "but in the informational society, the fuel, the power, is knowledge," emphasizes John Kenneth Galbraith, a Canadian-born economist specializing in emerging trends in the world economy. "One has now come to see a new class structure divided by those who have information and those who must function out of ignorance. This new class has its power not from money, not from land, but from knowledge."

The good news is that as the price of computing equipment and Internet access has fallen in North America, the digital divide has become less pronounced, but there are still major challenges to overcome. In particular, people in rural communities, the elderly, people with disabilities, and minorities lag national averages for Internet access and computer literacy. Outside North America, the gap gets even wider and the obstacles much more difficult to overcome, particularly in the third world, where infrastructure and financial resources are lacking. Clearly, the digital divide is a major ethical concern facing the Information Age.

Ethics is the science of human duty that encompasses a system of principles and rules concerning duty. There is a broad range of ethical issues that have emerged through the use and proliferation of computers. ***Computer ethics*** is used to describe the issues and standards of conduct as they pertain to the use of information systems. In 1986, Richard O. Mason wrote a classic article on the issues central to this debate—information privacy, accuracy, property, and accessibility—and these issues are still at the forefront of most ethical debates related to how information systems store and process information (see Figure 9.5). Next, we examine each of these issues.

Information Privacy

If you use the Internet regularly, sending e-mail messages and visiting Websites, you may have felt that your personal privacy is at risk. Several Websites where you like to shop greet you by name and seem to know which products you are most likely to buy. Every day,

[**Figure 9.4** ➥ Computers are used in countless types of jobs and industries.]

Sources: (9.4a) ©Getty Images, Inc. (9.4b) ©Getty Images, Inc. (9.4c) ©Getty Images, Inc. (9.4d) ©Getty Images/Eye Wire, Inc.

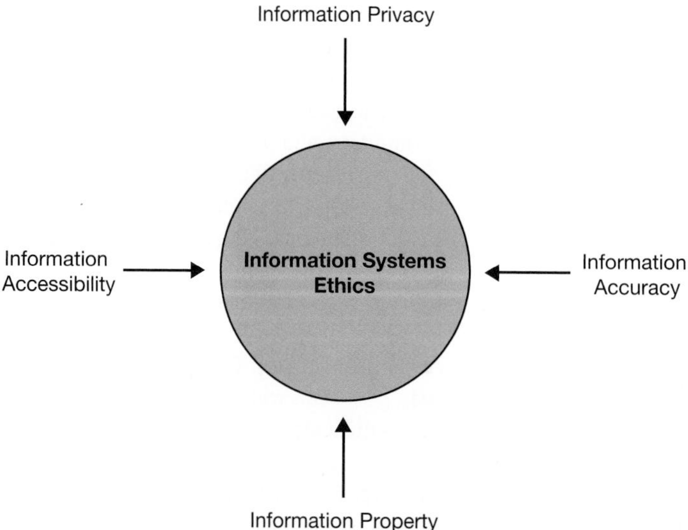

[**Figure 9.5** ➥ Information privacy, accuracy, property, and accessibility are central to most ethical concerns about information technology.]

the inbox in your browser's mail program is full to overflowing with messages urging you to buy something. As a result, you may feel as though eyes are upon you every time you surf the Web. ***Information privacy*** is concerned with what information an individual should have to reveal to others through the course of employment or through other transactions such as online shopping.

The widespread use of computers and the advent of the Internet have produced new concerns about privacy in Canada. The ease with which electronic information can be acquired, stored, searched, replicated and transmitted has enormous implications for consumers who give personal information to a business. Even if the personal information is not given online, most businesses will still store information about their clients electronically. Why should governments, businesses, and consumers care about the trading of personal information? One reason is that personal information databases can become targets of illegal activity. Software can be hacked and hardware can be stolen. This means that sensitive information stored in databases could potentially fall into the wrong hands, with disastrous results for consumers (for example, this chapter's opening case). Another reason is that personal information, which an individual might find embarrassing, could be disclosed to others. Finally, many people believe that the continuing acquisition of personal information, particularly unauthorized acquisition, infringes on human dignity. In many parts of the world, the private sector has been largely unregulated. This has changed recently as governments responded to these new concerns about privacy.

Privacy Legislation in Canada

In Canada, the federal government enacted the ***Personal Information Protection and Electronic Documents Act (PIPEDA)***, which became fully operative January 1, 2004. The objective of PIPEDA is to balance "the right of privacy of individuals with respect to their personal information and the need of organizations to collect, use or disclose personal information for purposes that a reasonable person would consider appropriate in the circumstances." The legislation applies to any organization in Canada that engages in "commercial activity." Not only does this include businesses in the private sector, but it may also include nonprofit organizations to the extent that they engage in commercial activities (e.g., fundraising). Any personal information that a business collects, uses, or discloses from its customers will fall under PIPEDA. In short, private-sector IS managers in Canada must be familiar with the main principles and rules of PIPEDA. The full legislation and accompanying commentary be found at **www.privcom.gc.ca/legislation/02_06_01_e.asp.**

The portion of PIPEDA that deals with privacy was the result of negotiations among consumer advocates, businesses, and government during the mid-1990s. The result of these negotiations was the Canadian Standards Association's Model Code for the Protection of Personal Information, produced in 1996. The code stated that a balance must be struck between the desires of businesses to acquire personal information and the rights of consumers to the protection of their privacy. It set out 10 principles to guide businesses in the handling of personal information. This code was later adopted by Parliament when it drafted PIPEDA.

The following is a brief overview of the 10 principles found in PIPEDA:

- *Principle 1—Accountability:* The main point of this principle is that an organization is responsible for the personal information under its control and is obligated to comply with all of the rules set out by PIPEDA. It also states that the organization shall designate an individual to ensure that the organization complies with these regulations. Compliance includes implementing procedures to protect personal information, establishing procedures to handle complaints, training staff, and developing information that will explain the organization's policies and practices. In addition, organizations must ensure that third parties who come into contact with personal information under the care of the organization provide comparable levels of protection for that information. This is especially important for businesses that outsource to third parties.
- *Principle 2—Identifying Purposes:* This principle requires that organizations identify the purpose for which personal information is collected. This information should be communicated to the individual when the information is collected. This principle is designed to operate in conjunction with the Consent, Limiting Collection, Openness, and Access principles noted below.
- *Principle 3—Consent:* This is perhaps the most important principle underlying PIPEDA. Quite simply, personal information should not be collected, used, or disclosed without the knowledge and consent of the individual. Parliament's view was that consent without knowledge (e.g., knowing the purpose of the collection) would be no consent at all. There are certain limited circumstances in which organizations may collect personal information without consent. For the IS manager, the relevant exception is when the collection of the information is clearly in the best interests of the individual and consent cannot be obtained in a timely fashion. An organization may also use or disclose personal information in the case of an emergency that threatens the life, health, or security of an individual. If the organization identifies new purposes for the personal information in their possession, they must seek the consent of those individuals to use that information in that new way. Consent may be obtained in many ways: oral, written, a checkoff box, or even the signing of an application form that details the collection, use, and disclosure of personal information. Finally, consent may be withdrawn at any time.
- *Principle 4—Limiting Collection:* This principle requires that organizations limit their collection of personal information to that which has been identified as necessary for its purposes. Personal information should not be collected indiscriminately. This is why identifying the purpose for which personal information is collected is so crucial. Without having identified the purpose for which personal information is collected, organizations can be in contravention of the act.
- *Principle 5—Limiting Use, Disclosure, and Retention:* This principle is similar to Limiting Collection in that it restricts the use and disclosure of personal information to that which has been identified as necessary for its purposes. However, there is a crucial addition that every IS manager needs to be aware of. Personal information that is no longer required to fulfill the organization's identified purpose must be destroyed, erased, or made anonymous. Furthermore, organizations must develop guidelines for this process.
- *Principle 6—Accuracy:* This principle has two components. The first is that personal information must be as accurate and up-to-date as is necessary for the purposes identified by the organization. The second is that an organization shall not routinely update personal information, unless it is necessary for the purposes identified for collecting the information.
- *Principle 7—Safeguards:* This principle is especially important for IS managers, even if they are not in charge of privacy protection at their organizations. This principle stipulates that organizations must safeguard the personal information that they collect. The more sensitive the personal information, the greater the safeguards required to protect it. Safeguards include physical measures (e.g., restricted offices), organizational measures (e.g., security clearances), and technological measures (e.g., passwords).

- *Principle 8—Openness:* This principle requires organizations to make information about their privacy procedures available to individuals. Specifically, individuals should not have to wait an unreasonable amount of time to receive this information. This is another reason why it is important for an organization to develop policies and procedures before they collect personal information.
- *Principle 9—Individual Access:* This principle, along with consent, represents the foundation of most modern privacy law. This principle stipulates that not only do individuals have a right to access their own personal information, but that they also have the right to challenge the accuracy of that information. For IS managers, this is important because they will need to arrange to store personal information in such a way that it can be readily accessed to accommodate this requirement. They will also have to provide information about third parties who have had access to this information. They will have 30 days from the receipt of the request to provide this information. This information is to be presented to the individual in such a way that it is easy to understand (e.g., no abbreviations or codes). One of the few exceptions to this principle is if access to an individual's personal information would in some way compromise the personal information of another.
- *Principle 10—Challenging Compliance:* This principle stipulates that an individual has a right to challenge an organization's compliance with these principles.

Many companies in Canada now post privacy policies in their offices, stores, and online (see Figure 9.6 for an information privacy statement from Penguin Group). Others are going a step further, requiring customers and employees to sign a privacy document or contract. If individuals are not satisfied with the handling of their personal information, PIPEDA stipulates that they may file a complaint with the Privacy Commissioner or go before the Federal Court to seek redress. Depending upon the size and seriousness of the violation, organizations could face steep fines for failing to protect personal information in their possession.

For example, the Privacy Commissioner recently released a decision involving data collection on the Internet. The case focused on whether a protocol called NETBIOS (Network Basic Input/Output System), which Microsoft uses to facilitate the sharing of printers and files on a local area network, could be considered personal information. Not only may NETBIOS contain personal information (e.g., username), but it may also compromise the security of Internet users. The commissioner found that NETBIOS constituted personal information under PIPEDA, because it could potentially contain personal informa-

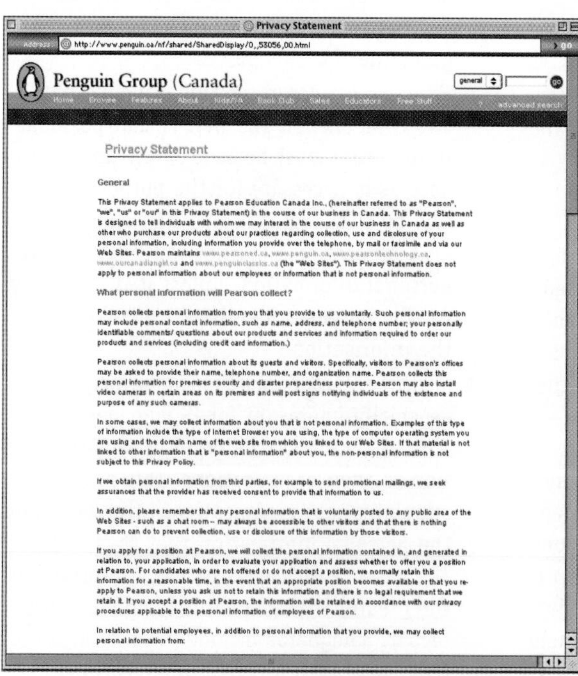

Privacy Statement

General

This Privacy Statement applies to Pearson Education Canada Inc., (hereinafter referred to as "Pearson", "we", "us" or "our" in this Privacy Statement) in the course of our business in Canada. This Privacy Statement is designed to tell individuals with whom we may interact in the course of our business in Canada as well as other who purchase our products about our practices regarding collection, use and disclosure of your personal information, including information you provide over the telephone, by mail or facsimile and via our Web Sites. Pearson maintains www.pearsoned.ca, www.penguin.ca, www.pearsontechnology.ca, www.ourcanadiangirl.ca and www.penguinclassics.ca (the "Web Sites"). This Privacy Statement does not apply to personal information about our employees or information that is not personal information.

What personal information will Pearson collect?

Pearson collects personal information from you that you provide to us voluntarily. Such personal information may include personal contact information, such as name, address, and telephone number; your personally identifiable comments/ questions about our products and services and information required to order our products and services (including credit card information.)

Pearson collects personal information about its guests and visitors. Specifically, visitors to Pearson's offices may be asked to provide their name, telephone number, and organization name. Pearson collects this personal information for premises security and disaster preparedness purposes. Pearson may also install video cameras in certain areas on its premises and will post signs notifying individuals of the existence and purpose of any such cameras.

In some cases, we may collect information about you that is not personal information. Examples of this type of information include the type of Internet Browser you are using, the type of computer operating system you are using and the domain name of the web site from which you linked to our Web Sites. If that material is not linked to other information that is "personal information" about you, the non-personal information is not subject to this Privacy Policy.

If we obtain personal information from third parties, for example to send promotional mailings, we seek assurances that the provider has received consent to provide that information to us.

In addition, please remember that any personal information that is voluntarily posted to any public area of the Web Sites - such as a chat room -- may always be accessible to other visitors and that there is nothing Pearson can do to prevent collection, use or disclosure of this information by those visitors.

If you apply for a position at Pearson, we will collect the personal information contained in, and generated in relation to, your application, in order to evaluate your application and assess whether to offer you a position at Pearson. For candidates who are not offered or do not accept a position, we normally retain this information for a reasonable time, in the event that an appropriate position becomes available or that you re-apply to Pearson, unless you ask us not to retain this information and there is no legal requirement that we retain it. If you accept a position at Pearson, the information will be retained in accordance with our privacy procedures applicable to the personal information of employees of Pearson.

In relation to potential employees, in addition to personal information that you provide, we may collect personal information from:

[Figure 9.6 ➥ Information privacy statement from Penguin Group.]

Source: Copyright © 2002–2004. (Canada), a division of Pearson Penguin Canada Inc.

tion (although it normally would not). Because of the ruling, IS managers will have to consider all electronic interactions as falling under the act.

As we can see, PIPEDA does not set out hard and fast rules for the protection of personal information. Rather it sets out a series of general principles. It is important to understand that circumstances will dictate the type of actions necessary to comply with the law. The policies and procedures of a small business dealing with relatively general personal information will be very different from those of a larger organization dealing with very sensitive personal information. IS managers must be prepared to match their privacy procedures with their business's circumstances.

Over the last few years, several provinces have begun working on privacy legislation. Quebec has had legislation regulating personal information in the private sector since 1994. On January 1, 2004, the *Personal Information Protection Act* (British Columbia) and the *Personal Information Protection Act* (Alberta) came into force. In addition, some provinces have freedom of information and protection (FOIP) acts that govern how Canadians can access information held by public bodies.

How do IS managers deal with many different privacy laws? Fortunately, the trend thus far seems to be that the provinces are passing legislation that is similar to PIPEDA, with the intent of producing similar regulatory regimes. The Privacy Commissioner of Canada has stated that if the provincial legislation is "substantively similar" to PIPEDA, then the provincial legislation will be applied to businesses that operate in that province. This was the case with the Quebec legislation, which the commissioner held was substantively similar to PIPEDA. "Substantively similar" means that the provincial law must contain, at a minimum, the 10 principles set out in PIPEDA. IS managers will have to follow both the federal and the provincial legislation.

Privacy Legislation in the United States

The United States lacks a comprehensive statute, such as PIPEDA, that regulates personal information in the private sector. Rather, the trend at the federal level is toward targeting particular consumers or certain types of personal information. One example of this is the *Children's Online Privacy Protection Act* (COPPA), which became fully operative in 2000. The legislation aims at protecting the personal information of children. IS managers operating in the U.S. will have to be familiar with COPPA because it applies not just to Websites targeting children, but also to Websites that receive visits from children. The Federal Trade Commission, which enforces COPPA, has developed guidelines for compliance. Firms must provide information on their Websites about their collection polices, obtain "verifiable consent" from parents, provide a means for allowing parents to view their child's personal information, and establish internal security controls. Many of the FTC's guidelines are similar to the principles found in PIPEDA. Other legislation, like the *Gramm-Leach-Bliley Act* (financial regulation), the *Patriot Act,* the *Digital Millennium Copyright Act,* and the *Health Insurance Portability and Accountability Act* (insurance regulation) have privacy components.

Privacy Legislation in Europe

The regulation of personal information in the private sector in Europe is complex for two reasons. The first is that the European Union and its member states have a complex constitutional relationship. The second is that personal data protection in Europe is considered a fundamental human right ("Everyone has the right to the protection of personal data concerning him or her," Article 8 of the Charter of Fundamental Rights of the European Union).

The European Union implemented the General Data Protection directive (General Directive) in 1998. The directive applies to all member states, as well as to some non–EU members (Iceland, Liechtenstein, Norway), who make up the European Free Trade Association. The General Directive has two aims: to ease information flow within the EU, and to provide a minimum level of data protection. Like PIPEDA, the General Directive has a series of guiding principles: legitimacy, finality, transparency, proportionality, confidentiality and security, and control. In addition to regulating member states, the General Directive also forbids transferring personal data to third parties (i.e., countries that have not adopted the General Directive) that do not have a similar level of data protection. This means that companies based outside of Europe that wish to deal with the personal data of European citizens must reside in a country with comparable privacy laws. With PIPEDA, Canada qualifies for this standard, but many countries, including the U.S., do not.

Not only does each member state have its own method of administering the General Directive, but each may also have its own additional laws and regulatory schemes for personal information in the private sector. It is beyond the scope of this book to review data protection legislation in each of the EU member states. However, more information about privacy laws in the EU and around the world can be found at **www.privacyknowledgebase.com/document.jsp?docid=REFDP000**.

Information Accuracy

The issue of information accuracy has become highly charged in today's wired world. ***Information accuracy*** is concerned with the authenticity and fidelity of information, as well as identifying who is responsible for informational errors that harm people. With all the computerization that has taken place, people have come to expect to receive and retrieve information more easily and quickly than ever before. In addition, because computers "never make mistakes," we have come to expect this information to be accurate. A case in point is the bank. The combination of automated teller machines, computerized record systems, and large, electronic client and transaction databases should provide customers with quick and accurate access to their account information. However, we continue to hear about and experience record-keeping errors at banks.

An error of a few dollars in your banking records does not seem significant. However, what if it were an error in the bank's favour of hundreds or thousands of dollars? What if the error caused one of your important payments (such as a home mortgage payment) to bounce, as was the case for many customers of the Royal Bank of Canada in May 2004? Bank errors can be quite important.

BRIEF CASE

PIPEDA Creates Confusion for Businesses

Months after federal privacy legislation came into effect, experts point to a startling number of Canadian companies that don't know how to comply with it. The *Personal Information Protection and Electronic Documents Act* (PIPEDA), which became official for private firms on January 1, 2004, is a minefield for companies that don't understand the difference between the confidentiality of personal data and the collection of that data. "People are not aware of the depth, the breadth, the magnitude of it," said Ian Turnbull, executive director of the Canadian Privacy Institute, a consultancy that helps companies with privacy compliance. "A lot of people are turning to their lawyers, and their lawyers are giving them legal advice as opposed to practical advice.... They're not getting enough [information] and what they're getting is confusing."

A privacy tool developed by the Enterprise-Wide Privacy Task Force of the Canadian Institute of Chartered Accountants (CICA) and the American Institute of Certified Public Accountants (AICPA) aims to furnish Canadians with privacy information and put it in context. The 70-page best practices guide is designed to help companies comply with PIPEDA, as well as any relevant provincial and international privacy legislation. "It gives you the baseline best practices and then tells you where you have to supplement those to address unique specific requirements of one or more pieces of legislation," said Robert Parker, a partner with Deloitte's enterprise risk practice and one of the guide's contributors. Even companies that believe they are compliant with PIPEDA may only be paying it lip service, said Parker. There is a difference between writing a corporate-wide privacy policy and having not just your employees but also your back-office systems adhere to it.

Ontario's Information and Privacy Commissioner, Ann Cavoukian, has endorsed the CICA guide. "One thing that the commissioner has found as she's spoken to businesses is that [they] are looking for ways to help them comply with PIPEDA," said Brian Beamish, director of policy and compliance in the commissioner's office. "PIPEDA sets down some general principles for managing personal information, and it's sometimes difficult to transfer those general principles in what can be a complex business situation," added Beamish. Turnbull emphasized the need for more practical solutions. "Organizations just don't have a good handle on the information they have," he said. "When the second hand swept by midnight on December 31, 2003, it started privacy for the whole country, and privacy is not going to go away," said Turnbull.

Questions

1. What implications does PIPEDA have for a firm's IT function?
2. Do you think that PIPEDA is good for Canadian businesses? Why, or why not?

[Adapted from Neil Sutton, "PIPEDA Confusion Sets In," **www.itbusiness.ca/index.asp?theaction=61&sid=55160#**, ITBusiness.ca (March 29, 2004).]

Now imagine how significant a data accuracy error might be in other settings. Hospitals use similar automation and computer-intensive record keeping. Imagine what would happen if prescription information appeared incorrectly on a patient's chart and the patient became deathly ill as a result of the medicine that was mistakenly dispensed to him. The significance of such a data accuracy error could be tremendous. Furthermore, it would not be clear who was to blame. Would this be the fault of the doctor, the pharmacist, the programmer, the data entry clerk, or maybe some combination of errors by the system designer, the system analyst, the system programmer, the database administrator, and the vendor? It would be too easy simply to blame the computer.

Computer-based information systems, and the data within those systems, are only as accurate and as useful as they have been made to be. The now-infamous quote that "Computers make mistakes. Banks make mistakes, too" would be better restated as, "Computers never make mistakes; only humans make mistakes" (Mason, 1986). This reflects the need for better precautions and greater scrutiny when modern information systems are designed, built, and used. This means that everyone must be concerned with data integrity, from the design of the system, to the building of the system, to the person who actually enters data into the system, to the people who use and manage the system. Perhaps more important, when data errors are found, people should not blame the computer. After all, people designed and built it, and entered data into it in the first place.

Information Property

It happens to all of us. Nearly every day, we receive unwanted solicitations in the mail from credit card companies, department stores, magazines, or charitable organizations. Many of these envelopes are never opened. We ask the same question over and over again: "How did I get on another mailing list?" Your name, address, and other personal information were most likely sold from one company to another for use in mass mailings. ***Information property*** focuses on who owns information about individuals and how information can be sold and exchanged. ***Intellectual property (IP)*** refers to property that is subject to copyright, trademark, or patent legislation. IP law has been around for centuries. The advent of personal computers and the Internet, however, has posed new challenges to IP law in industrialized countries. For instance, any copyrighted material that exists in digital form can be endlessly replicated and transmitted. This is a double-edged sword for holders of copyright. On the one hand, it means that replication and distribution costs are low. But on the other hand, it makes it easy for others to violate that copyright.

Canada's *Copyright Act* grants a series of rights to the author of a work upon its completion. There are actually very few formal requirements for establishing ***copyright*** in Canada. One is that the author (whether a person or a corporation) must be a resident of Canada or a resident of a "treaty country"—which includes more than 150 countries around the world. The work must also be original and fall under the class of a literary, dramatic, musical, or artistic work. The courts will protect works in any form, including electronic. In Canada, computer software falls under the category of literary work. The most important right granted to the copyright holder is the right to reproduce a work and, by extension, the right to prevent others from reproducing it. Copyright issues have been thrust onto the world stage recently, primarily due to the ease with which digital information can be copied and distributed. Students may be familiar with copyright issues that have arisen from the extensive use of file-sharing networks. These networks became popular as a means to share digital music files, but now are being used to distribute other digital products, including movies and software.

The legal implications of copyright for IS managers are extensive. The most common issue is dealing with software purchased from other companies. When a software program is purchased, most likely the company will not "own" that copy (as one might "own" a copy of a book that could be resold to a third party), but rather the company will have a licence to use that software program. That licence will be governed by the contract agreed to between the vendor and the purchaser. The contract may restrict or limit the ways in which the IS manager can use or modify the program. Another copyright issue that IS managers may have to deal with relates to compiling databases. Courts in Canada and the United States have stated that the legitimate use of copyrighted material in one context does not necessarily mean that use in the compilation of a database will be legitimate.

Linking (through hyperlinks on one's Website) to copyrighted material is another contentious issue. Copyright holders believe that such linking impairs the value of their work by making it easer for individuals to violate their copyright. In the United States, copyright holders have been aided by the passage of the *Digital Millennium Copyright Act*. The statute forbids offering, providing, or otherwise trading in copyrighted technology. Courts in the U.S. have used this legislation to force Websites that provide links to copyrighted material to stop doing so. In Canada, the courts have drawn a distinction between hyperlinks that link to Websites that offer copyrighted material (permissible), and embedded hyperlinks that automatically begin a transfer of information from another Website (forbidden).

A ***trademark*** is a mark used by a firm for the purposes of distinguishing its goods and services from those of another firm. It therefore protects both firms and consumers. A trademark may be a design, word, phrase, slogan, colour, or sound. Since the purpose of the trademark is to distinguish one firm's goods and services from another's, it is imperative that the trademark be distinctive. The greater the distinctiveness of the trademark, the greater the protection it is afforded by the court. A trade name, which is used to identify a particular business, may be a trademark if it is also used to distinguish goods and services. For instance, "Apple" is both a trade name and a trademark because it distinguishes the products and services of Apple Computers from those of its competitors. In Canada, trademarks are established in one of two ways. The most common way is simply through the adoption and use of a trademark within Canada. The other way is registering the trademark under the federal *Trade-marks Act*.

For IS managers, the most pressing trademark issue is domain names. Domain names are unique alphanumeric words that function as a stand-in for an Internet protocol address. In Canada and the United States, domain names are registered through approved registrars on a first-come, first-served basis. During the mid-1990s, many companies were slow to appreciate the economic potential of the Internet and failed to register appropriate domain names. This led to a phenomenon known as "cybersquatting," in which individuals and businesses essentially engaged in a kind of domain name arbitrage by registering the names of well-known companies and products. Rather than pay for those domain names, many companies decided to sue the holders of the domain name and the registrar for trademark violations.

It is important to note that domain name registration does not necessarily trump trademark law. In Canada, companies have had success in wresting away domain names on the basis of trademark violation. In the United States, trademark holders have been aided by the passage of the *Anticybersquatting Consumer Protection Act* in 1999. The act targets those who deliberately register a trademark as a domain name and allows the court to transfer the domain name to the trademark holder.

There are some other problems with current trademark law in the Information Age. Trademarks are generally considered in territorial terms. This means that trademarks are enforceable only in regions in which they are used. In other jurisdictions, it is possible for another company to use a similar trademark. Furthermore, it is possible for two different users to employ the same trademark in the same region so long as there is no risk of confusing consumers. For years, Canadian Airlines, an airline company, and Molson Canadian, a brewery, shared the trademark "Canadian." The problem is that domain names are unique. Different users simply cannot share them. Whose trademark takes precedence in such a circumstance? So far, there does not seem to be any clear guide.

A ***patent*** is a right to exclusively manufacture an invention for a specified time. In the United States, though not in Canada, patents have recently been extended to cover business methods. A business method patent can be gained by inventing a special technique for doing business. Most of these business methods relate to e-business. For instance, Priceline.com patented its reverse auction process. While Canadian companies have not been able to patent these business methods in Canada, they have registered patents in the U.S. For instance, Royal Bank, a Canadian company, patented its automobile financing buy-back program in the U.S. IS managers should be aware that opportunities exist in the U.S. to patent such business methods and that pitfalls exist as well. Patent holders in the U.S. have shown that they are very much willing to sue those who they believe have infringed their patent.

Information Accessibility

With the rapid increase in online databases containing personal information and the influx of computer-based communication between individuals, who has the right to access and monitor this information has raised many ethical concerns. ***Information accessibility*** focuses on defining what information a person or organization has the right to obtain about others and how this information can be accessed and used.

For example, e-mail is one of the most popular software applications of all time, and projections are that its use will only continue to increase. That is why e-mail aficionados and privacy groups were chilled when under the Clinton administration the FBI demonstrated a software application named Carnivore to telecommunications industry representatives. Carnivore was designed to be connected to Internet service providers' computers, where it would lurk undetected by ISP subscribers, eavesdropping on all communications delivered by the ISP, including e-mail, instant messaging, chat rooms, and visits to Internet sites. If the FBI detected communications that it decided were threatening, as in, for example, the activities of terrorists, members of organized crime groups, and hackers, they could unleash Carnivore (see Figure 9.7).

Carnivore provides the "surgical ability" to intercept and collect only those communications that are the subject of lawful wiretaps, explained FBI spokesman Paul Bresson in a *TechWeb* article (Mosquera, 2000). "There's a minimization factor built in [that] actually limits messages viewable to human eyes," he said. Despite built-in "minimization factors," Carnivore would sniff through a large percentage of ISP subscribers' activities on the Internet. "This is about the most intrusive form of search there is," countered Marc Rotenberg, director of the Electronic Privacy Information Center (EPIC). Unlike police searches of cars and houses for drugs, Rotenberg claimed, Carnivore would allow "dragnet fishing" while sifting through all traffic on an ISP.

After September 11, 2001, government officials requested more leeway in deploying Carnivore in its ongoing fight against terrorism. Privacy groups are concerned that personal privacy might be eroded in a quest to provide heightened homeland security. Clearly, Carnivore and other eavesdropping technologies will be central to numerous ethical discussions.

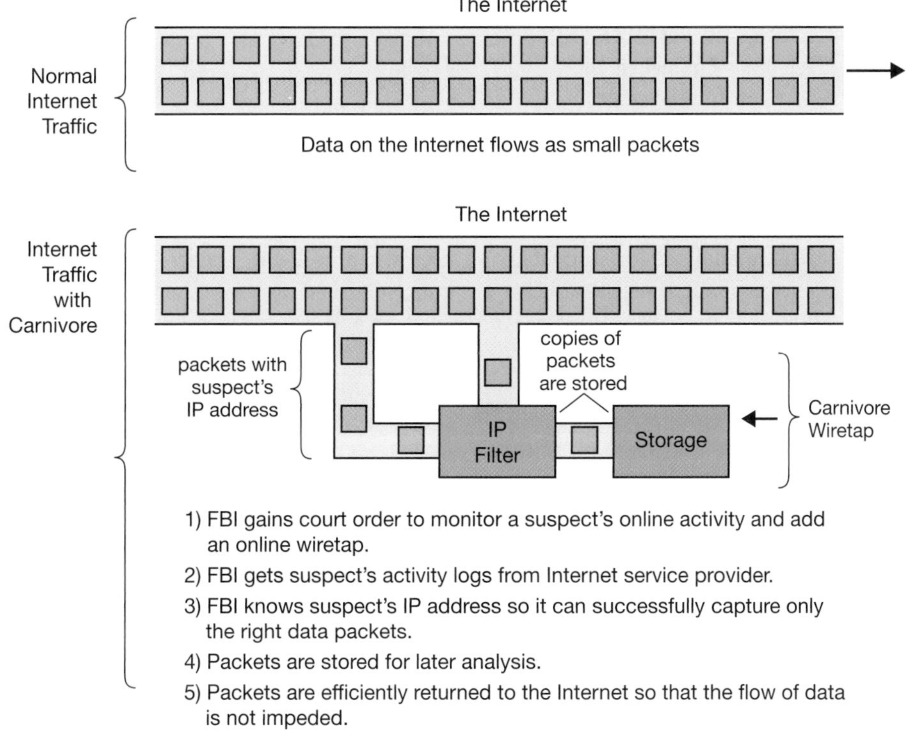
The Internet
Normal Internet Traffic
Data on the Internet flows as small packets
The Internet
Internet Traffic with Carnivore
packets with suspect's IP address
copies of packets are stored
IP Filter
Storage
Carnivore Wiretap
1) FBI gains court order to monitor a suspect's online activity and add an online wiretap.
2) FBI gets suspect's activity logs from Internet service provider.
3) FBI knows suspect's IP address so it can successfully capture only the right data packets.
4) Packets are stored for later analysis.
5) Packets are efficiently returned to the Internet so that the flow of data is not impeded.

[Figure 9.7 ➥ How Carnivore works.]

Web Search

WEB SEARCH OPPORTUNITY
Cybersquatting is an ethical dilemma facing many famous people and companies. Use a search engine to investigate a popular entertainer who has an "official" Website, and provide a list of domain names that are similar to those of the official site.

The Need for a Code of Ethical Conduct

The Internet Age not only has found governments playing catch-up to pass legislation pertaining to computer crime, privacy, and security, but has also created an ethical conundrum. For instance, the technology exists to rearrange and otherwise change photographs, but is the practice ethical? After all, if photographs no longer reflect absolute reality, how can we trust published images? It may not be illegal for you to "steal" computer time from your school or place of employment to do personal business, but most people would consider this unethical. Should guidelines be in place to dictate how businesses and others use information and computers? If so, what should the guidelines include, and who should write them? Should there be penalties imposed for those who violate established guidelines? If so, who should enforce such penalties?

Many businesses have devised guidelines for the ethical use of information technology and computer systems, and many computer-related professional groups have also published guidelines for their members. Such organizations include the Assistive Devices Industry Association of Canada, the Association for Computing Machinery, the Australian Computer Society, the Canadian Information Processing Society, the Data Processing Management Association, the Hong Kong Computer Society, the Institute of Electrical and Electronics Engineers, the International Federation for Information Processing, the International Programmers Guild, and the National Society of Professional Engineers.

Most universities and many public school systems have written guidelines for students, faculty, and employees about the ethical use of computers. EDUCOM, a nonprofit organization of colleges and universities, has developed a policy for ethics in information technology that many universities endorse. In part, the EDUCOM statement concerning software and intellectual rights says: "Because electronic information is volatile and easily reproduced, respect for the work and personal expression of others is especially critical in computer environments. Violations of authorial integrity, including plagiarism, invasion of privacy, unauthorized access, and trade secret and copyright violations, may be grounds for sanctions against members of the academic community."

Most organization and school guidelines encourage all system users to act responsibly, ethically, and legally when using computers, and to follow accepted rules of online etiquette, as well as federal and provincial laws.

Responsible Computer Use

The Computer Ethics Institute is a research, education, and policy study organization with members from the IT professions and from academic, corporate, and public policy communities. The group studies how advances in information technology have impacted ethics and corporate and public policy, and has issued widely quoted guidelines for the ethical use of computers. The guidelines prohibit:

- Using a computer to harm others
- Interfering with other people's computer work
- Snooping in other people's files
- Using a computer to steal
- Using a computer to bear false witness
- Copying or using proprietary software without paying for it
- Using other people's computer resources without authorization or compensation
- Appropriating other people's intellectual output

The guidelines recommend:

- Thinking about social consequences of programs you write and systems you design
- Using a computer in ways that show consideration and respect for others

Responsible computer use in the Information Age includes avoiding the types of behaviour mentioned above. As a computer user, when in doubt, review the ethical guidelines published by your school, place of employment, and/or professional organization.

Some users bent on illegal or unethical behaviour are attracted by the anonymity they believe the Internet affords. But the fact is that we leave electronic tracks as we wander through the Web, and some perpetrators have been traced and successfully prosecuted when they thought they had hidden their trail. Mafiaboy, the architect of a number of high-profile attacks, for example, was traced to a suburb of Montreal. The fact is, too, that if you post objectionable material on the Internet and people complain about it, your ISP can ask you to remove the material or remove yourself from the service.

Human Resource Management

A McGill University student successfully challenged the administration's requirement that students submit assignments to Turnitin.com, a California Website monitoring plagiarism, or risk a zero grade. The second-year international development student had "an ethical and political problem" with Montreal-based McGill's policy and refused to turn in his work, said Ian Boyko, national chairperson of the Canadian Federation of Students in Ottawa. "After some deliberation, the university realized it was on thin ice and agreed to mark his paper and not give him a zero."

The university student association noted several issues emerging from the incident. For one thing, many of its members are concerned that the decision to run papers through the site was made without consulting an "academic senate or university board of governors or department council," said Boyko. "But I think when a student writes an assignment, it's an original piece of work. It's the student's copyright, his or her intellectual property. For a student to have to submit that, without being compensated, so a Website based in California can get richer, I think he took objection to that. Human beings have been detecting plagiarism for years. I don't see why that needs to all of a sudden come to an end right now."

Dave Chan, president of the Graduate Business Council at York University, disagrees. "We discussed Turnitin with our students and they loved it. Plagiarism is a large and growing problem, and anything that can put a stop to it, or at least slow it down, is a good thing," he noted. "If a student has nothing to hide, then what's the problem?" he added.

The McGill student's reluctance to participate in the program was the first such incident in the six-year history of San Francisco–based Turnitin.com, said CEO Dr. John Barrie. The company said it has clients in more than 50 countries, receives more than 20,000 student term papers every day, and has never been sued. "If you just look at the odds, it was bound to happen at some point," he added. He said McGill has indicated no interest in cancelling its subscription.

Barrie seems unfazed by the episode at McGill. His company is on the verge of releasing a Canadian legal opinion stating it's "100 percent in compliance with Canadian intellectual property and privacy laws. I have always thought that the claims by that particular student were without merit." Turnitin.com takes seriously the privacy rights of students and gives access to papers only to their instructors, he said.

CAREER IMPLICATIONS

[Adapted from Fawzia Sheikh, "Student Group Questions Ethics of Anti-Plagiarism Site," **www.itbusiness.ca/index.asp?theaction=61&sid=54546#**, ITBusiness.ca (January 15, 2004).]

COMPUTER CRIME

The CCRA incident mentioned in the chapter opening is an example of computer crime. ***Computer crime*** is defined as the act of using a computer to commit an illegal act. This broad definition of computer crime can include:

- Targeting a computer while committing an offence. For example, someone gains unauthorized entry to a computer system in order to cause damage to the computer system or to the data it contains.
- Using a computer to commit an offence. In such cases, computer users may steal credit card numbers from Websites or a company's database, skim money from bank accounts, or make unauthorized electronic fund transfers from financial institutions.
- Using computers to support a criminal activity, despite the fact that computers are not actually targeted. For example, drug dealers and other professional criminals may use computers to store records of their illegal transactions.

One of the fastest growing "information" crimes in recent years has been ***identity theft.*** Identity theft is the stealing of another person's social insurance number, credit card number, and other personal information for the purpose of using the victim's good financial credit history to borrow money, buy merchandise, and otherwise run up debts that are never repaid. In some cases, thieves even withdraw money directly from victims' bank accounts. Since many government and private organizations keep information about individuals in accessible databases, opportunities abound for thieves to retrieve it. Reclaiming one's identity and restoring a good credit rating can be frustrating and time consuming for victims.

One solution to identity theft lies in the government and private sector working together to change practices used to verify a person's identity. For example, a mother's maiden name and an individual's social insurance number are too easily obtained. Other methods of personal identification, such as biometrics and encryption, may need to be used if the problem is to be solved. Methods of information security—including biometrics and encryption—will be discussed later in the chapter.

Before moving on, it is important to distinguish between unethical behaviour and a crime. Identity theft is clearly a crime. However, many "misuses" of computers and information may not be crimes but would be considered unethical by most people. As technology moves forward and allows humans to do things not possible before, existing laws often do not apply to these emerging situations. One of the ongoing debates regarding technological innovations revolves around the question: "Just because it is not a crime, does that make it okay to do it?"

The Issue of Computer Access

Traditionally, there have been two sides to the issue of computer access. On one side were liberal civil rights champions, the information industry, communications service providers, and expert computer users called hackers. This side supported the prosecution of computer criminals under the law, but sought to protect the free exchange of information.

On the opposing side of the computer access issue were privacy advocates, government agencies, law enforcement officials, and businesses that depend on the data stored in computers. Their point of view was much stricter, advocating the free exchange of information only among those with authorization for access. Anyone who breaks into a computer is trespassing, they said, and all intruders should be subject to penalties under the law.

In today's Information Age, however, the debate has expanded, and lines between the two sides may not be as clearly drawn. The global reach of computer networks has raised concern over copyrights, privacy, and security among all user groups. Most computer users now agree that ownership rights of those who create software and other copyrighted materials disseminated over networks must be protected. And when financial or health data—typically the most sensitive of all data—are collected about individuals and stored on computers, that information should not be freely available to anyone who can retrieve it. Both sides of the information access argument agree that one of the major challenges of the Internet Age will be to protect privacy and security, while at the same time allowing authorized access to digital information.

"Did they have to add a sound file?"

[Figure 9.8 ➥ Unauthorized computer access is a crime.]

Source: © Ted Goff.

Unauthorized Computer Access

A person who gains unauthorized access to a computer system has committed a computer crime. ***Unauthorized access*** means that the person who has gained entry to a computer system has no authority to use such access (Figure 9.8). Here are a few examples from media reports:

- Employees steal time on company computers to do personal business.
- Intruders break into government Websites and change the information displayed.
- Thieves steal credit card numbers and social insurance numbers from electronic databases, then use the stolen information to charge thousands of dollars in merchandise to victims.

Because computer crime has increased with the increasing use of computers, there are now federal and provincial laws in place that expressly prohibit these crimes.

Hacking and Cracking

Those individuals who are knowledgeable enough to gain access to computer systems without authorization have long been referred to as ***hackers.*** The name was first used in the 1960s to describe expert computer users and

GLOBAL PERSPECTIVE

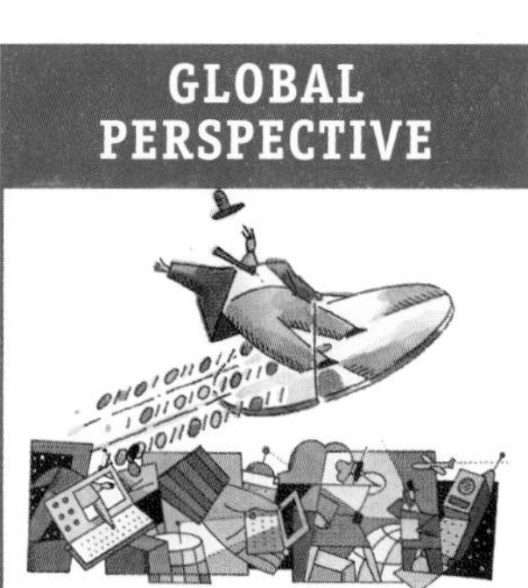

Controlling Global Cybercrime

It's a war on terror you don't hear about on the nightly news, and the base from which these special ops work is a quiet suburb. But stopping crackers and viruses in their tracks is the mission of the analysts and engineers at Symantec's Security Operation Center (SOC) in Alexandria, Virginia. Located in an unassuming industrial park 25 minutes from Washington, D.C., Symantec's SOC analysts hunt down crackers, violations, and malicious activities as they occur around the world. Beside the flat-screen TV beaming CNN into the SOC, a map of the world appears in front of the analysts, showing where on the globe attacks are originating. At that time, Canada was No. 2 in terms of the number of unique IP addresses attacking, with 4,570 attacks.

The centre provides its clients with around-the-clock security analysis, early warning detection, and the ability to act on suspected acts immediately. Customers can view this activity as Symantec tracks it on its network through a secure portal. With the increase of blended threats such as Nimda and CodeRed, IT organizations are looking for help in the war on digital terror, says Brian Dunphy, senior manager, analysis operations with Symantec. "We aren't the end all, be all solution for security for an enterprise. It's the enterprise's responsibility to make sure their network is secure, but at least they know they don't need people on 24/7," said Dunphy. Managed services at Symantec include monitored and managed firewall and virtual private network (VPN) services to detect and respond to cracker attacks, intrusion detection, Internet vulnerability assessment, managed virus protection, and gateway service.

Symantec's 1,000-square-metre security operation centre is one of five SOCs the company operates around the world. Customers can contract for round-the-clock surveillance. To date, the SOC protects 600 companies worldwide—companies ranging in size from Fortune 500 companies to mid-size enterprises—is capable of managing 12,500 customer devices such as firewalls and intrusion detection systems, and is expandable to 50,000 devices. Entrance to the facility is protected by biometric authentication including hand geometry (palm scanner), an access card, and a PIN code. Inside the SOC, a team of 15 security analysts and customer engineers keep an eye on their clients' systems, watching not only for immediate incidents, but trends as they happen around the world.

IDC Canada Ltd. analyst Dan McLean says it's too early to know what the market will be for managed security services in Canada. Security services (consulting, implementation, and management) for 2003 is estimated to be about a $450-million market in Canada. Security software spending in Canada in 2003 hit $145 million—not a lot relative to what other investments companies make in IT.

[Adapted from Jennifer Brown, "Going Deep Inside the SOC," *Computing Canada*, Vol. 30, No. 1 (January 16, 2004).]

programmers who were students at the Massachusetts Institute of Technology (MIT). They wrote programs for the mainframes they used and freely exchanged information, but they followed unwritten rules against damaging or stealing information belonging to others. They claimed that their motives for roaming freely through computer systems were based entirely on curiosity and the desire to learn as much as possible about computers.

As computer crime became more prevalent and damaging, true hackers—those motivated by curiosity and not by a desire to do harm—objected to use of the term to describe computer criminals. Today, those who break into computer systems with the intention of doing damage or committing a crime are usually called ***crackers.***

Types of Computer Criminals and Crimes

Computer crimes are almost as varied as the users who commit them (see Figure 9.9).

"Sure, you can fire me, but I'll just hack into the HR computer and hire myself again. That's how I got this job to begin with."

[**Figure 9.9** ➡ Computer crimes are as varied as the individuals who commit them.]

Source: © Ted Goff.

Web Search

WEB SEARCH OPPORTUNITY
The article at **www.cnn.com/TECH/specials/hackers/primer/** describes three types of computer hackers. Review this article, and prepare a short report that defines each of the three types.

Some involve the use of a computer to steal money or other assets, or to perpetrate a deception for money, such as advertising merchandise for sale on a Web auction site, collecting orders and payment, then sending either inferior merchandise or no merchandise at all. Other computer crimes involve stealing or altering information. Some of those thieves who steal information or disrupt a computer system have demanded a ransom from victims in exchange for returning the information or repairing the damage. Techno-terrorists have planted destructive programs in computer systems, then threatened to activate them if a ransom is not paid. Crimes in the form of electronic vandalism cause damage when offenders plant viruses, cause computer systems to crash, or deny service on a Website.

Use of the Internet has fostered other types of criminal activity, such as the stalking of minors and others by sexual predators through newsgroups and chat rooms.

Who Commits Computer Crimes?

When you hear the term *computer cracker*, you might imagine a techno-geek, someone who sits in front of her computer all day and night attempting to break the ultrasuper secret security code of one of the most sophisticated computer systems in the world, perhaps a computer for the RCMP, a Swiss bank, or the CIA. While this fits the traditional profile for a computer cracker, there is no clear profile today. More and more people have the skills, tools, and the motive to hack into a computer system. A modern-day cracker could be a disgruntled, middle-aged, white-collar worker sitting at a nice desk on the fourteenth floor of the headquarters building of a billion-dollar software manufacturer. Computer crackers have been around for decades. For the most part, we associate crackers with their pranks and crimes involving security systems and viruses. Crackers have caused the loss of billions of dollars' worth of stolen goods, repair bills, and lost goodwill with customers.

Surveys have shown that when businesses and other organizations are victimized, the perpetrators are most often employees or others inside the organization. For example, in a 1998 survey of 1,600 companies in 50 countries, co-sponsored by PricewaterhouseCoopers and *InformationWeek*, 73 percent of the respondents reported some security breach or corporate espionage during a one-year period. Intrusions reported by survey respondents came from these groups (Figure 9.10), in order of frequency:

- Authorized employees—58 percent
- Employees who were not authorized to use a computer system—24 percent
- Outside computer users or terrorists—13 percent
- An organization's competitors—3 percent
- Other—2 percent

Data Diddling, Salami Slicing, and Other Techno-Crimes

As long as computers and the data they contain are an integral part of our daily lives, criminals will devise ways to take illegal advantage of the technology. Such crimes cost society billions of dollars annually. (The exact amount can only be estimated, since many businesses do not report crimes for fear of losing customers if the offences became public.) Over the years, colourful jargon has evolved to label the many types of computer crime, as summarized in Table 9.1.

Software Piracy

Software developers and marketers want you to buy as many copies of their products as you want, of course. But commercial software vendors do not want you (or anyone else) to buy one copy, then bootleg additional copies to sell or to give to others. Vendors also take a dim view of companies that buy one copy of a software application, then make many copies to distribute to employees. In fact, the practice is called ***software piracy***, and it is illegal.

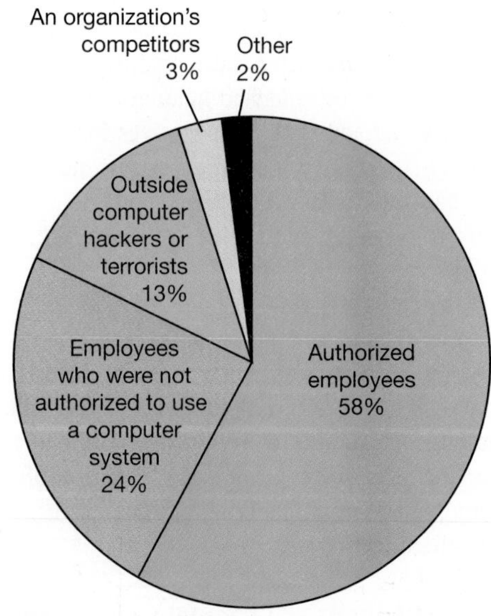

[**Figure 9.10** ➡ Who makes unlawful intrusions into computer systems.]

[Table 9.1] ***Types of computer crimes.***

Computer Crime	Description
Data diddling	The changing of data going into or out of a computer. For example, a student breaks into his university's grade-recording system and changes the grades he earned in last semester's classes.
Salami slicing	A form of data diddling that occurs when a person shaves small amounts from financial accounts and deposits them in a personal account. For example, a bank employee deposits a few pennies from each of thousands of accounts into an account set up in a fictitious name. The amounts are too small to raise flags, but over time the thief collects a substantial sum.
Phreaking	Crimes committed against telephone company computers with the goal of making free long-distance calls, impersonating directory assistance or other operator services, diverting calls to numbers of the perpetrator's choice, or otherwise disrupting telephone service for subscribers.
Cloning	Cellular phone fraud in which scanners are used to steal the electronic serial numbers of cellular phones, which are used for billing purposes and are broadcast as calls are made. With stolen serial numbers, clones can be made to make "free" calls that are billed to the owner of the original cell phone.
Carding	Refers to the practice of stealing credit card numbers online, to be resold or used to charge merchandise against victims' accounts.
Piggybacking or shoulder-surfing	The act of simply standing in line behind a card user at an automated teller machine (ATM), looking over that person's shoulder, and memorizing the card's personal identification number (PIN). With the right equipment, the stolen numbers can then be placed on counterfeit access cards and used to withdraw cash from the victim's account.
Social engineering	Gaining information needed to access computers by means of tricking company employees by posing as a magazine journalist, telephone company employee, or forgetful co-worker in order to persuade honest employees to reveal passwords and other information. The information is then used to break into a computer system or to steal company equipment and other contraband.
Dumpster diving	This approach requires no technical expertise, since it consists simply of going through dumpsters and garbage cans for company documents, credit card receipts, and other papers containing information that might be useful.
Spoofing/phishing	A scam used to steal passwords for legitimate accounts on computers in which the "spoofer" uses a program that duplicates an organization's log-in screen. When legitimate users log on to the system, the counterfeit screen responds with an error message but secretly captures the user's ID and password. The swindle lets intruders pass as legitimate users, thus allowing them to steal computer time and resources.

When you buy commercial software, it is legal for you to make one back-up copy for your own use. It is also legal to offer shareware or public-domain software for free through bulletin boards and other Websites. But *warez peddling*—offering stolen proprietary software for free over the Internet—is a crime. (*Warez* is the slang term for such stolen software.)

Software piracy has become a problem because it is so widespread, costing the commercial software industry billions of dollars a year. The crime is difficult to trace, but some individuals and companies have been successfully prosecuted for pirating software (see Case 2 at the end of this chapter).

Software Piracy Is a Global Business

A major international issue businesses deal with is the willingness (or unwillingness) of governments and individuals to recognize and enforce the ownership of intellectual

[Table 9.2] ***Software piracy levels and dollar losses by region.***

Region	Piracy Levels	Dollar Loss
North America	25%	$2,937,437,000
Western Europe	34%	$3,079,256,000
Asia/Pacific	51%	$4,084,061,000
Latin America	58%	$869,777,000
Middle East/Africa	55%	$376,344,000
Eastern Europe	63%	$404,491,000

Source: BSA, 2001.

property—in particular, software copyright. Piracy of software and other technologies is widespread internationally. The Business Software Alliance (BSA) points to countries such as Vietnam, China, Indonesia, Ukraine, and Russia as those with the highest percentages of illegal software (BSA, 2001). In these countries, more than 85 percent of the software used consists of illegal copies. Worldwide losses due to piracy were nearly $12 billion in 2000! Because technology usage varies significantly by region, average piracy levels and dollar losses greatly differ across regions (see Table 9.2).

Is this an ethical problem? Perhaps in part, but there are other perspectives that businesspeople must acknowledge and deal with as well. In part, the problem stems from countries' differing concepts of ownership. Many of the ideas about intellectual property

BRIEF CASE

Computer Criminal Hall of Fame

A few individuals with expertise in cracking and phreaking have used their skills to become well-known computer criminals:

John Draper, a.k.a. "Cap'n Crunch," was a notorious phone phreak who operated in the late 1960s and early 1970s. Draper discovered that the whistle that came as a prize in boxes of Cap'n Crunch cereal perfectly duplicated the 2,600-hertz tone used by the telephone company's switching system. He could blow the whistle into a telephone receiver and activate switches that allowed him to make free long-distance calls. Draper was caught by the FBI and served a year and four months in prison in two separate convictions for wire fraud. Once released, Draper did not return to his old habits.

Throughout his career as a phreak and cracker in the 1980s, Kevin Lee Poulsen's crimes ranged from setting up his own telephone wiretaps, to posing as a telephone directory assistance operator, to using computers to win cash and cars in radio giveaway contests. Poulsen served nearly five years in prison. After his release in 1996, he became a computer security consultant.

By 1995, Kevin Mitnick had been convicted five times of various telecommunications and computer crimes. He served time in a juvenile detention centre and in federal prison in California for stealing long-distance telephone service, breaking into Pentagon computers, stealing software online, and other techno-crimes. Mitnick violated terms of his probation and in 1992 was again on the run from the law. He continued to ply his trade, was captured in 1995, and was again sentenced to prison. Mitnick was released early in 2000 but was forbidden to use computers for four years after his release.

The most famous Canadian hacker is probably Mafiaboy (his real name is protected by legislation covering young offenders), who admitted to 56 charges of mischief in January 2001. Mafiaboy was apparently responsible for initiating denial-of-service attacks that shut down a number of high-profile Websites, including Yahoo!, CNN.com, Amazon.com, and eBay. For his crimes, Mafiaboy was sentenced to eight months in a juvenile detention centre and fined $160. Estimates of the damage caused by Mafiaboy's actions range from US$7.5 million to US$1.7 billion.

Questions

1. How serious do you consider crimes such as cracking? Phreaking? Software piracy? Virus writing?
2. What can governments and organizations do to protect themselves and their citizens and employees from cyber attacks?

ownership stem from long-standing cultural traditions. For example, the concept of individual ownership of knowledge is traditionally a strange one in many Middle Eastern countries, where knowledge is meant to be shared. Plagiarism does not exist in a country where words belong to everyone. By the same token, piracy does not exist either. This view is gradually changing; the Saudi Arabia Patent Office granted its first patents several years ago, and their piracy rates have plummeted from 79 percent in 1996 to 59 percent in 2000.

In other cases, there are political, social, and economic reasons for piracy. In many other countries, software publishers are simply not catering to the needs of consumers, who often just do not have the funds to purchase software legitimately. This is true in many areas of South America and other regions with low per capita income. It is particularly true of students and other members of university communities, whose needs are critical in some areas.

Other factors leading to piracy or infringement of intellectual property agreements throughout the world include lack of public awareness about the issue, lack of an industrial infrastructure that can produce legitimate software, and the increasingly high demand for computer and other technology products. The United States has repeatedly pressured and threatened other countries accused of pirating. It is interesting to note, however, that despite the fact that few of these cultural and economic explanations are valid in the United States, it leads the world in the sheer volume of illegal software in use.

Computer Viruses and Other Destructive Code

Recently, one of the popular antivirus Websites reported that 500 new computer viruses were unleashed on computer users each month. ***Viruses*** are destructive programs that disrupt the normal functioning of computer systems. They differ from other types of malicious code in that they can reproduce themselves. Some viruses are intended to be harmless pranks, but more often they do damage to a computer system by erasing files on the hard drive or by slowing computer processing or otherwise compromising the system.

Viruses are planted in host computers in a number of ways (Figure 9.11). Boot sector viruses attach themselves to that section of a hard or floppy disk that lets the user boot up or start the computer. They are most often spread through use of an infected floppy disk. File infector viruses attach themselves to files with certain extensions, such as .doc or .exe.

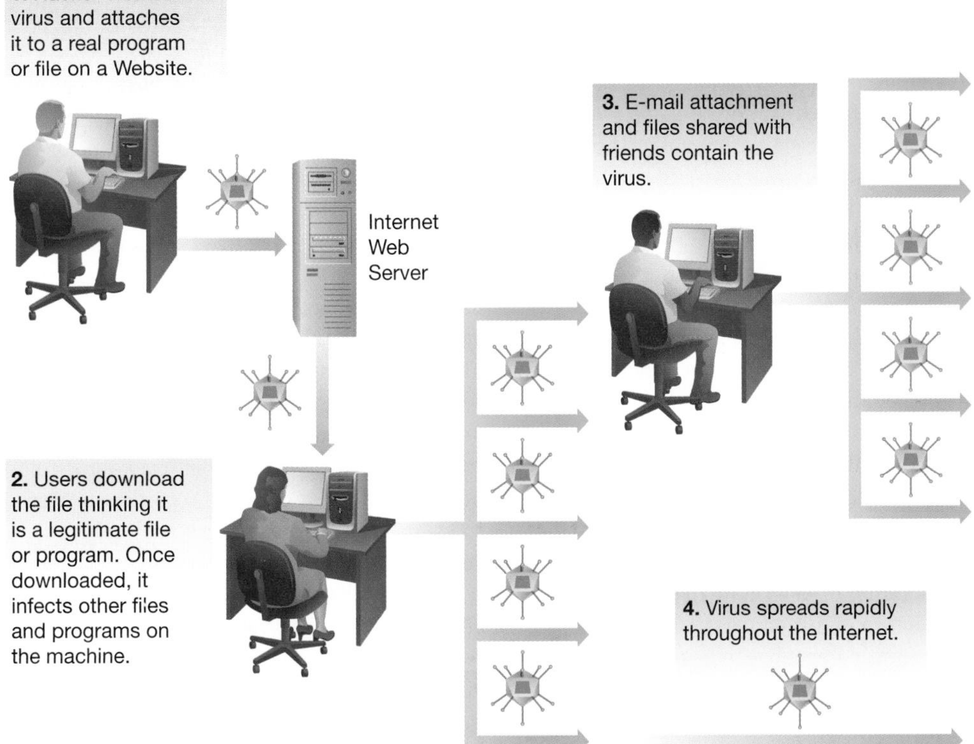
1. Hacker creates a virus and attaches it to a real program or file on a Website.
Internet Web Server
2. Users download the file thinking it is a legitimate file or program. Once downloaded, it infects other files and programs on the machine.
3. E-mail attachment and files shared with friends contain the virus.
4. Virus spreads rapidly throughout the Internet.

[Figure 9.11 ➡ How a computer virus is spread.]

Some viruses are a combination of boot sector and file infector viruses, and many of these can change in order to fool antivirus programs. Viruses transmitted through e-mail messages became popular in the late 1990s. When an unsuspecting recipient of an e-mail message opens the message or an attachment to the message, the virus is activated. Usually such e-mail viruses can then send copies of themselves to everyone in the victim's address book, thus spreading throughout networked computers at an alarming rate.

Worms, Trojan Horses, and Other Sinister Programs

Viruses are among the most virulent forms of computer infections, but other destructive code can also be damaging. A ***worm,*** for example, usually does not destroy files, but, like a virus, it is designed to copy and send itself, spreading rapidly throughout networked computers. It eventually brings computers to a halt simply by clogging memory space with the outlaw code, thus preventing normal function.

Another destructive program is the ***Trojan horse.*** Unlike a virus, the Trojan horse does not copy itself, but like viruses it can do much damage. When a Trojan horse is planted in a computer, its instructions remain hidden. The computer appears to function normally, but in fact it is performing underlying functions dictated by the intrusive code. For example, under the pretext of playing chess with an unsuspecting systems operator, a cracker group installed a Trojan horse in a Canadian mainframe. While the game appeared to be proceeding normally, the Trojan horse program was sneakily establishing a powerful unauthorized account for the future use of the intruders.

Logic or time bombs are variations of Trojan horses. They also do not reproduce themselves and are designed to operate without disrupting normal computer function. Instead, they lie in wait for unsuspecting computer users to perform a triggering operation. Time bombs are set off by specific dates, such as the birthday of a famous person. Logic bombs are set off by certain types of operations, such as entering a specific password, or adding or deleting names and other information to and from certain computer files. Disgruntled employees have planted logic and time bombs upon being fired, intending for the program to activate after they have left the company. In at least one instance in recent history, a former employee in Minnesota demanded money to deactivate the time bomb he had planted in company computers before it destroyed employee payroll records.

COMPUTER SECURITY

The general rule for deciding whether computer security is at risk is simple: All computers connected to networks are vulnerable to security violations from outsiders as well as insiders, and to virus infections and other forms of computer crime. ***Computer security*** refers to precautions taken to keep computers and the information they contain safe from unauthorized access. Here are a few safeguards that can help organizations maintain a high level of computer security.

Organizations should decide which computer operations are most vulnerable to break-ins by unauthorized users. They should then implement a security plan to protect those areas diligently. The information technology department is usually responsible for instituting security measures. Once an organization assesses its risks, it should formulate a plan that details what action will be taken if security is breached. Making back-up copies of important files on a regular basis can help with reconstruction if a damaging security breach should occur.

Organizations can prevent unauthorized access to computers by keeping stored information safe and allowing access only to those employees who need it to do their jobs. Passwords are effective only if chosen carefully and changed frequently. Besides passwords, employees may be asked to provide an ID combination, a security code sequence, or personal data such as a mother's maiden name. Employees authorized to use computer systems may also be issued keys to physically unlock a computer, photo ID cards, smart cards with digital ID, and other forms of physical devices allowing computer access.

Organizations can use special software to help keep stored information secure. Access-control software, for example, may allow computer users access only to those files related to their work, and may allow read-only access, which means the user can read files but cannot change them. Organizations may also use antivirus software. It does not restrict a user's access but scans files for viruses and, in many cases, eradicates them.

Organizations may also use a form of security called ***biometrics*** to grant or deny access to a computer system. With biometrics,

CAREER IMPLICATIONS

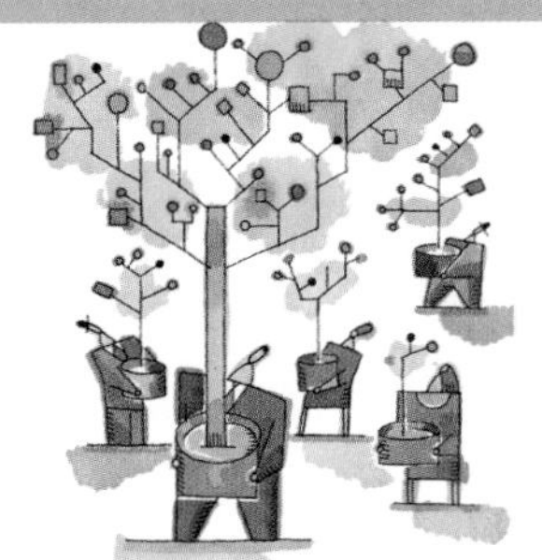

Information Systems

When you're the head of security for the Bank of Montreal, you had better know your stuff. Robert Garigue's professional life has been devoted to the protection of information systems: first as an information warfare expert in the Canadian military, then as a chief technology officer for the province of Manitoba, and finally as BMO's chief information security officer. Garigue's attitude toward security is somewhat unconventional. "The job of security is more of a social work job," he explains. "It's an issue that involves the whole community—from software developers to vendors to business units to suppliers. A lot of the work we do is around education and best practices." Each year is successively more challenging for anyone in charge of information protection. For example, BMO recently faced an embarrassing incident when a pair of recycled BMO servers that "had client information that could have potentially been disclosed" turned up on eBay. "It was a painful experience," Garigue admits, "but more than anything else, everyone learned from it. I'm proud of how the organization dealt with these issues in an accountable way." His philosophy is that firewalls, antivirus software, intrusion detection, and patches are a given; the challenge is getting people who own the risk to recognize it. "It's okay if they choose not to address it, as long as it's done consciously as a trade-off between risk and benefit."

[Adapted from Patricia MacInnis, "A Security Officer to Bank On in Tough Times," *Computing Canada*, Vol. 29, No. 24 (December 12, 2003).]

employees may be identified by fingerprints, retinal patterns in the eye, or other bodily characteristics before being granted access to use a computer (see Figure 9.12). After September 11, 2001, the use of better security methods became a high priority for airports, large corporate buildings, and computers. Biometrics have the promise of providing very high security, so governments and many companies are investigating how best to use this technology.

Another way for organizations to ensure computer security is to make every effort to hire trustworthy employees. Trustworthy employees are less likely to commit offences associated with unauthorized access.

[**Figure 9.12** ➥ Biometric devices are used to verify a person's identity.]

Source: © AP/Wide World Photos.

Encryption

In any discussion of privacy and security of digitized data, the problem of unauthorized eavesdroppers arises. Organizations can use secure channels not available to computer users outside their LANs and intranets, but the Internet and public telephone lines and airwaves are not subject to the same restricted use. Most of us send e-mail around the globe; call friends, family, and colleagues on wireless telephones; and trust our desktop and mainframe computers with all manner of personal, financial, and corporate secrets. Until recent years, we may have felt secure in our activities. Now, however, news stories about corporate spies, malicious hackers, curious neighbours and co-workers, and suspicious government agencies have us wondering if every transfer of information is somehow subject to unseen eavesdroppers (see the Video Case at the end of the chapter for a closer examination of this issue).

When you do not have access to a secure channel for sending information, encryption is the best bet for keeping snoopers out. ***Encryption*** is the process of encoding messages before they enter the network or airwaves, then decoding them at the receiving end of the transfer so that recipients can read or hear them (see Figure 9.13). The process works because, if you scramble messages before you send them, eavesdroppers who might intercept them cannot decipher them without the decoding key.

We now have access to encryption software that scrambles text and voice messages and also allows us to send digital signatures that guarantee we are who we say we are when we send a message. You can activate the encryption function from your browser.

```
Ciphertext letters:
JOGPSNBUJPO TZTUFNT UPEBZ
Equivalent plaintext letters:
INFORMATION SYSTEMS TODAY
```

[**Figure 9.13** ➡ Encryption is used to encode information so that unauthorized people cannot understand it.]

How Encryption Works

All encryption systems use a key—the code that scrambles, then decodes, messages. When both sender and recipient use the same key, this is called a ***symmetric secret key system.*** This method of encrypting messages was used for centuries. One problem with symmetric secret key encryption is that, since both sender and recipient must keep their key secret from others, key management can be a problem. If too many people use the same key, the system can soon become ineffective. If different keys are used for sending messages to different people, the number of keys can become unmanageable.

Key management problems of secret key encryption systems were eliminated with the development of ***public key*** technology. Public key encryption is asymmetric, since it uses two keys—a private key and a public key (see Figure 9.14). (An eccentric former MIT hacker and researcher named Whit Diffie is credited with first envisioning the possibility of using two keys—public and private—to encrypt and decode messages. He and two co-workers published their concept in 1976.) Each person has his own key pair, a public key that is freely distributed and a private key that is kept secret. Say you want to send a message to Jane using this encryption system. First, you get Jane's public key, which is widely available, and you use it to scramble your message. Now even you cannot decode the encrypted message. When Jane receives the message, she uses her private key, known only to her, to unscramble it. Public key systems also allow you to authenticate messages. If you encrypt a message using your private key, you have "signed" it. A recipient can verify that the message came from you by using your public key to decode it.

CAREER IMPLICATIONS

Accounting and Finance

The Visa Canada Association and banks that issue Visa cards hope Canadian consumers will feel more secure about shopping online thanks to Verified by Visa. The service is a global Visa security initiative that was introduced to the Canadian market in late 2003. Verified by Visa—which many cardholders will find they must sign up for in order to buy online from participating merchants—assigns passwords that cardholders enter to complete online transactions. Being asked for the password online is "basically like being asked to sign for your credit card being used at a regular merchant," says Sean Amato-Gauci, senior manager of business and product development for credit cards at RBC Royal Bank in Toronto.

"It almost acts like a face-to-face transaction," says Visa Canada's director of emerging channels, Zack Fuerstenberg. Visa Canada and the banks are promoting the program to consumers as a way they can feel more secure about using their cards online. Fuerstenberg acknowledged that, in fact, merchants selling goods online have more to fear from credit card fraud than consumers, since the merchant does not obtain the cardholder's signature in an online transaction and therefore has no proof the transaction was legitimate if the consumer denies it. "Because it's a card-not-present transaction," Fuerstenberg says, "traditionally the merchant bears the responsibility." However, he says, "A lot of the research we've done indicates that there's a perception issue that's a barrier to online shopping."

Jack Nolan is director of operations at Motorola Canada, which was among the first Canadian merchants to sign on with Verified by Visa. He hopes the program will help alleviate the fears many consumers still have about online shopping. "It is more the merchant who is at risk for sure," Nolan says, but he added that Motorola has had very few instances of online credit card fraud and has software filters that pick up most attempts at fraud. Concern about consumer confidence in online shopping was Motorola's main motivation for signing on with the program, he says.

Canadian financial institutions offering Verified by Visa include CIBC, Citizens Bank of Canada, Laurentian Bank, Royal Bank, Scotiabank, TD Canada Trust, and Vancouver City Savings Credit Union.

[Adapted from Grant Buckler, "Visa Launches Verification System for Holidays," *Computing Canada,* Vol. 29, No. 24 (December 12, 2003).]

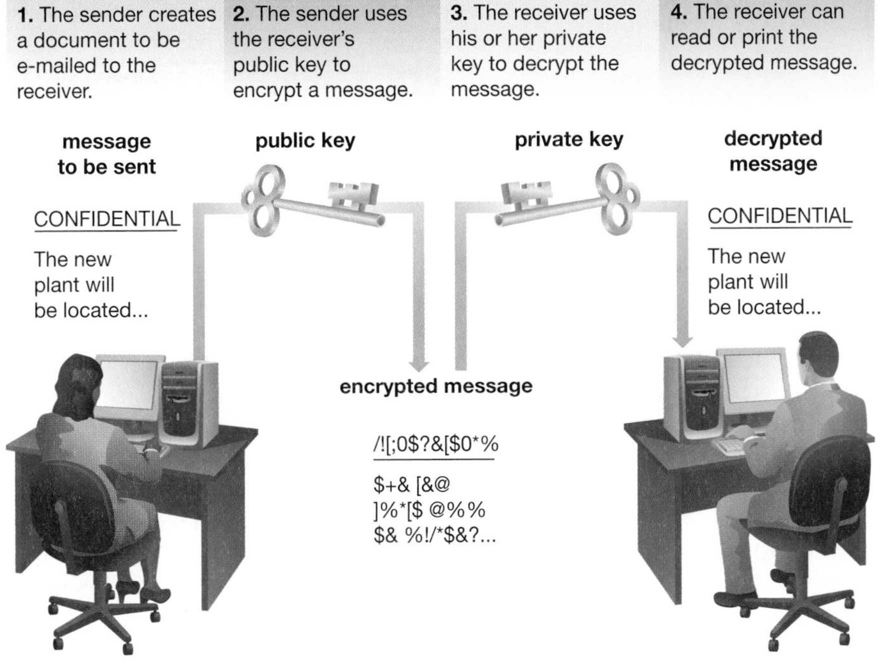
1. The sender creates a document to be e-mailed to the receiver.
2. The sender uses the receiver's public key to encrypt a message.
3. The receiver uses his or her private key to decrypt the message.
4. The receiver can read or print the decrypted message.
message to be sent
public key
private key
decrypted message
CONFIDENTIAL
The new plant will be located...
encrypted message
/![;0$?&[$0*%
$+& [&@
]%*[$ @%%
$& %!/*$&?...
CONFIDENTIAL
The new plant will be located...

[**Figure 9.14** ➡ How keys are used to encrypt and decrypt information.]

To implement public key encryption on a large scale, such as on a busy Website, requires a more sophisticated solution. Here, a third party, called a ***certificate authority***, is used. The certificate authority acts as a trusted intermediary between computers and verifies that a Website is a trusted site. The certificate authority knows that each computer is what it says it is and provides the public keys to each computer. ***Secure sockets layer (SSL)***, developed by Netscape, is a popular public key encryption method used on the Internet.

Other Encryption Approaches

Other encryption breakthroughs followed Diffie's public–private key revelation. In 1977, three MIT professors, Ron Rivest, Adi Shamir, and Len Adleman, created RSA (named for the surname initials of the inventors), a system based on the public–private key idea. They licensed the technology to several companies, including Lotus and Microsoft, but federal laws against exporting encryption technology kept companies from incorporating RSA into their software. In 1991, Phil Zimmermann devised Pretty Good Privacy (PGP), a versatile encryption program that he gave away free to anyone who wanted to try it. It soon became the global favourite for encrypting messages.

While innovative encryption aficionados were mainstreaming the encryption concept, the government fought to keep control over keys that would allow its agents to decode communications deemed suspicious. In 1993, then–U.S. President Bill Clinton endorsed the Clipper Chip, a chip that could generate uncrackable codes. The catch was that only the government would have the key to decode any messages scrambled via the Clipper Chip. Opponents criticized the idea as a threat to personal liberty. But when a flaw was found in the chip that under certain conditions would allow users to take advantage of the chip's strong encryption capabilities without giving the government the key, the Clipper Chip idea was scrapped before it could become reality.

Internet Security

Cases like these frequently make the news: someone breaks into a government Website and scrambles the message displayed, adding profanity. A popular search engine's Website is hacked and service is denied to users for several hours while the problem is corrected. Crackers add personal messages to a commercial service provider's Webpage about a sports celebrity. Clearly, if you plan to publish a Website you will want to make the site secure.

Businesses and ISPs use firewalls to keep LANs and WANs secure. A ***firewall*** consists of software and hardware designed to keep unauthorized users out of network systems. Firewall software can filter incoming and outgoing information and block unauthorized users and has thus become very popular. In fact, many individuals who have high-speed Internet access at home often purchase a personal

Operations Management

From the invention of the safety fuse in 1831 to Alfred Nobel's discovery of smokeless powder, the blasting cap, and dynamite in the late 1800s, Dyno Nobel ASA of Oslo, Norway, has long been a leader in the field of explosives. However, the company has not always been as innovative with data security as it has been with blast security.

Since Dyno is a global business with operations spanning 13 countries (including Canada), the corporate network must be able to provide real-time access to the company's worldwide locations, provide a high level of security, and ensure business continuity. Managing the data communications network on such a vast global level poses a key challenge, says information technology/information systems manager Steve Hall. "Obviously you can't make explosives in metropolitan areas, so we have some unique challenges as far as the remoteness of the sites that we have to hook up to," says Hall. "In some of the really remote sites you really don't have a choice as to who the local provider is, and they don't all work at the same speed."

In an effort to consolidate its network, Dyno Nobel signed a four-year contract valued at more than US$6 million with AT&T to deploy an Internet protocol virtual private network (IP VPN). An IP VPN is a corporate network system that allows branch offices to connect directly with one another across an IP network rather than travelling through a central location. Because of this, IP VPN systems are typically faster and more efficient than the standard hub and spoke systems. One problem with IP VPN systems, however, is with data security. Since there is no central clearinghouse to scan the data, the corporate network is prone to virus attacks and spam. To address this problem, AT&T installed filtering and virus-detection gear at the perimeter of its VPN.

[Adapted from Dianne Daniel, "Explosives Manufacturer Uses VPN to Connect Remote Sites Worldwide," *Communications & Networking,* Vol. 7, No. 5 (May 2004).]

firewall using products from providers such as Network Associates, Zone Labs, or Symantec.

Virus Prevention

Viruses that are spread via e-mail transmitted over the Internet are also frequently in the news. Despite their colourful names—Melissa, I Love You, HappyTime—viruses can be deadly infections once contracted by your computer. Here are some precautions you can take to ensure that your computer is protected:

- Purchase and install antivirus software, then update frequently to be sure you

Marketing

Tourism British Columbia has tapped the services of T4G Ltd., a Toronto-based IT consulting firm, to update its tourism management information technology platform and provide better links among the province's 18,000 tourism operators. T4G implemented a Web services–enabled product to run Tourism BC's marketing operations for travellers and suppliers like owners of bed and breakfasts or kayaking operations, said Dave Hyndman, director of tourism solutions at T4G. The reason behind implementing this new technology was to give the responsibility of providing and maintaining content to the people who are closest to the information, Hyndman said. So regional destination marketing organizations or suppliers will have secure access to an industry extranet that they can use to alert Tourism BC about changes to their community or business. Tourism BC staff, however, will likely review the information before it is put online.

It's a timely announcement as the province gears up to host the 2010 Olympics, an event that is considered "a fantastic opportunity for tourism before, during, and after the actual games," said Ray LeBlond, director of corporate communications for Tourism BC. LeBlond said he couldn't estimate the increased traffic that will occur on the organization's Website as a result of the Olympics.

Changes to B.C.'s official travel Website underscore a trend that T4G is observing throughout the tourism sector. He said, in large part, the whole exercise of gathering content for most of these tourism operations has been driven by the production of the annual printed visitors' guide. But this method has flaws, he explained, since a B&B that decides to add a swimming pool following the deadline for visitors' guide materials cannot tell travellers about the new amenity via one of the most popular tourism communications tools.

[Adapted from Fawzia Sheikh, "Tourism BC Turns to Web-based Management System," **www.itbusiness.ca/index.asp?theaction=61&sid=55066#**, ITBusiness.ca (March 18, 2004).]

BRIEF CASE

Security or Privacy: Which Takes Precedence?

Concerns are being raised that the confidential medical data of British Columbians could wind up in the hands of U.S. authorities if the provincial government proceeds with plans to outsource the administration of the province's Medical Services Plan to an American company. The B.C. government has short-listed two companies, IBM Canada and Virginia-based Maximus, to take over administration services of the Medical Services Plan (MSP) and the PharmaCare program. A legal opinion obtained by the B.C. Government and Service Employees' Union (BCGEU) says Canadian subsidiaries of U.S. companies are subject to the *Patriot Act.* Passed in the U.S. after the September 11, 2001, terrorist attacks, the act requires a company with access to documents sought by the FBI to turn them over, without informing the owner of the information of the release. BCGEU President George Heyman said the union has filed a judicial review seeking to stop the privatization from proceeding, arguing that it is unacceptable to let a private company have access to sensitive medical information. "In addition to worries about how this will affect our health-care system, there are serious issues of personal privacy," said Heyman. "Putting an American company or even an affiliate in charge of our health-care system will give it access to private information about every British Columbian."

The outsourcing is being handled by the Ministry of Management Services, which also has responsibility for privacy. Minister Joyce Murray said the government is taking the concerns raised by the BCGEU seriously. After contacting the B.C. Privacy Commissioner and other privacy offices across Canada, Murray said it became clear the *Patriot Act* wasn't on the radar screen and they decided to seek an expert legal opinion. Two potential experts have been short-listed, and Murray said they expect to have an opinion within one month. "We've been very clear from the beginning that the protection of individuals' information is a high priority for this government," said Murray, noting BC already had strong privacy legislation in place. "We'll make sure that any concerns we receive with respect to this opinion about the *Patriot Act* are incorporated within the structure of the final contract." Murray said any concerns raised in the legal opinion will be worked into the structure of the contract to ensure Canadian information stays inside Canada. "It's a fundamental issue that the information of Canadians on Canadian soil is not accessible to other organizations from other countries," said Murray. "We're going to ensure that contracts are structured such that we have that protection in place."

John Beardwood, treasurer of the Canadian IT law association, doubts that the answer will be so simple. Beardwood said believing privacy concerns raised by the *Patriot Act* could be overcome in the contract would be "misstated and misthought," and such a solution likely wouldn't be accepted by the vendor. "If I'm the vendor, I'm going to say to the customer there's nothing I can do about this, I have to follow the law," said Beardwood. "It's a bit of a hard sell to expect a vendor to indemnify the customer for any problems that might arise under Canadian law, given the fact they're following American law." The issue for a U.S.–based IT company operating in Canada is the potential conflict between the U.S. *Patriot Act,* which requires it to hand over the data without consent, and Canada's *Personal Information Protection and Electronic Documents Act* (PIPEDA), which requires consent. Beardwood said there are exceptions to PIPEDA's consent provisions. For example, if a government institution can show reasonable grounds the information relates to a contravention of the laws of Canada or a foreign jurisdiction, then consent may be waived. But that requires the FBI to work through Canadian authorities, and Beardwood said, in his view, the vendor would still have to inform the customer.

With outsourcing becoming a major business for IT companies, the Information Technology Association of Canada is following the case closely, and policy director Bill Munson said they're eagerly awaiting the legal opinion being sought by B.C. government. Munson said companies doing business across borders with conflicting legislation is part of global business, but this case appears to be different. Usually, he said, the laws of country A may be tight but there may be some laxness in country B's laws, creating some wiggle room. That may not be the case here.

Questions

1. Which do you think should be accorded the highest priority: security or privacy? Is it possible for both to coexist?
2. Should firms operating in Canada be subject to foreign legislation? Why or why not?

[Adapted from Jeff Jedras, "B.C. Outsourcing Plan Sparks Privacy Fears," *Computing Canada,* Vol. 30, No. 4 (March 26, 2004).]

Web Search

WEB SEARCH OPPORTUNITY
Visit the Privacy Rights Clearinghouse at **www.privacyrights.org** to learn more about how to protect your privacy. Review one of the site's numerous "fact sheets" on how to protect your privacy, and prepare a one-page report summarizing the fact sheet. Also, visit the site of the Privacy Commissioner of Canada, **www.privcom.gc.ca/index_e.asp**, to see the latest news on privacy issues in Canada.

are protected against new viruses. These programs can locate viruses, inform you of their presence, and, in many cases, destroy them before they do their damage. Update downloads are available, usually for a fee, at the vendor's Website.

- Make a back-up disk of important applications stored on your hardware, so in worst-case scenarios you can replace destroyed programs. To protect work in progress, back up files regularly.
- Do not use disks or shareware from unknown or suspect sources, and be equally careful when downloading material from the Internet, making sure that the source is reputable.
- Delete without opening any e-mail message received from an unknown source. Be especially wary of opening attachments. It is better to delete a legitimate message than to infect your computer system with a destructive germ.

If your computer system contracts a virus, report the infection to your school or company's IT department so that appropriate measures can be taken, and inform people listed in your address book, in case the virus has sent itself to everyone on your e-mail list. If forewarned, individuals listed in your address book can often delete the infectious message before it infects their computers.

How to Maintain Your Privacy Online

When you make Web purchases in Canada, vendors are required by law to respect your privacy. However, the same levels of privacy protection do not exist in all jurisdictions. In the United States, for example, a vendor can track what pages you look at, what products you examine in detail, which products you choose to buy, what method of payment you choose to use, and where you have the product delivered. After collecting all that information, unscrupulous vendors can sell it to others, resulting in more direct-mail advertising, electronic spam in your e-mail inbox, or calls from telemarketers.

When surveyed about concerns related to online shopping, most consumers list issues of information privacy as a top concern. As a result, governments have pressured vendors to post their privacy policies on their Websites. Unfortunately, these polices do not often protect the privacy of consumers, particularly as you move outside of Canada. To protect yourself, you should always review the privacy policy of all companies you do business with and refuse to do business with those that do not have a clear policy. According to the

COMING ATTRACTIONS

Nanotechnology Aims to Revolutionize IT Manufacturing

A more cost-effective method of manufacturing microchips will gradually replace multi-billion-dollar foundries, predicts nanotechnology expert Douglas Mulhall. "We now see hundreds of companies around the world manufacturing products by printing them three-dimensionally. It looks like this technology will become as common as bubble-jet printing technology is now." Bubble-jet printing occurs at billionths of a metre—every page has literally tens of millions of ink drops on it, said Mulhall. When the same concept is applied to the manufacturing process using nanotechnology as a catalyst, it "allows us to accurately translate CAD drawings, for example, into something that actually functions."

A key example of this ability is the printing of microchips, he said. "We're already printing chips on a board in a box. So you can imagine the disruptive influence if you replace a $4-billion factory with boxes that sit on a tabletop and cost anywhere from $75,000 to $750,000." Such boxes are already being used to manufacture some types of programmable chips, surgical models, and car parts, resulting in "tremendous cost savings" for those that are taking advantage, said Mulhall.

"Nanotechnology is breaking out all over the planet. South Korea, India, and China are leaders in the nanotechnology field, and they're the ones that Canadians have to compete against." Jay Myers, chief economist of the Canadian Manufacturers & Exporters, agreed that "nanotechnology is a huge, disruptive technology that will replace the existing manufacturing process. Soon to come will be the end of the silicon era, marked by a move to alternatives such as diamonds, he added. Silicon runs too hot for the "tremendous increase in [production] speeds that we'll start to see," he said. "Diamonds can run 100 times faster at a tenth of the heat. And there's a quantum leap in the capability of diamond materials to carry signals compared to silicon."

Possible barriers to the development of nanotechnology include pollution from nanoscale materials, which could have a deleterious impact on the environment, said Mulhall.

[Adapted from Scott Foster, "Nanotechnology Expert Predicts Death of Chip Foundries," **www.itbusiness.ca/index.asp?theaction=61&sid=55097#**, ITBusiness.ca (March 24, 2004).]

consumer watch group at **safeshopping.org**, a seller's privacy policy should at least indicate:

- What information the seller is gathering from you
- How the seller will use this information
- Whether and how you can "opt out" of these practices

To make sure your shopping experience is a good one, you can take a few additional steps to maintain your privacy.

- **Choose Websites that are monitored by independent organizations.** There are several independent organizations that monitor the privacy and business practices of Websites. Organizations such as **www.epubliceye.com** and **www.bbb.org** provide a valuable service for consumers by monitoring the business practices of sellers and requiring conformance to standard guidelines or providing consumers a rating of a seller's practices. Choosing sites that are independently evaluated by a reputable rating company is a good way to increase your privacy.
- **Avoid having "cookies" left on your machine.** Many commercial Websites are designed to leave a small file on your hard drive so that the owner of the site can monitor where you go and what you do on the site. It is possible that the site owner could obtain your e-mail address from the visit, potentially sending you unsolicited e-mail spam. Fortunately, most Web browsers provide the ability to turn off cookies or to warn you that the site is trying to deposit a cookie on your hard drive; when configured to warn you, your browser will prompt you with a notification and ask you if you want to accept the cookie. A problem with this approach is that online activity can slow down considerably, as so many Websites use cookies. In addition to using settings within your Web browser, you can get special "cookie management" software to help better maintain your privacy (go to **www.cookiecentral.com** for more on cookie management options).
- **Visit sites anonymously.** There are ways to visit Websites anonymously. Using services provided by companies such as Anonymizer.com, you have total privacy from marketers, identity thieves, or even co-workers when surfing the Web. The software blocks cookies, Java, and other tracking methods from being left on your computer; for Websites that require cookies to be left on your machine in order for you to visit, the software allows cookies to be encrypted so that no one can trace your activity. Similarly, URL addresses are also encrypted so that anyone monitoring your activity cannot log a meaningful address.
- **Use caution when requesting confirming e-mail.** When you buy products online, many companies will send you a confirming e-mail message to let you know that the order was received correctly. If you use a shared computer or buy online with a computer at work where your online activity can be monitored, you should take care to protect the privacy of your purchases. A good strategy is to have a separate e-mail account, such as one that is available for viewing via a Web browser, that you use when making online purchases. For example, Hotmail, Yahoo!, Excite, and countless other Web portals provide free e-mail services that can be accessed using a standard Web browser. This allows you to keep your primary e-mail address private from unscrupulous sellers and keeps your correspondence private from anyone who has access to your computer.

Of course, there are no guarantees that all your online experiences will be problem-free, but if you follow the advice provided here, you are likely to survive and thrive in the world of online electronic commerce.

Avoid Getting Conned in Cyberspace

Con artists and other lawbreakers have gone high-tech and are using the Internet to cheat consumers in a number of clever ways. The U.S. Federal Trade Commission has compiled advice on how not to get taken by crafty con artists on the Internet (**www.ftc.gov/bcp/conline/pubs/online/dotcons.htm**). Among the listed "dot-cons" were auction cheats, charges for a "free" Website appearing on telephone bills, and various investment, travel and vacation, business, and health-care products scams. Table 9.3 summarizes the top 10 cybercons being perpetrated on consumers using the Internet. Review this table so that you better understand what techniques con artists are using to separate you from your money. What can businesses, particularly small businesses that may not have the resources to hire full-time security consultants, do to protect themselves from data security threats? Microsoft has provided a security checklist for small businesses, shown in Table 9.4. The best advice for doing business on the Internet is to follow the adage, "If it's too good to be true, then it probably is."

[Table 9.3] ***Top 10 list of dot-cons from the Federal Trade Commission and advice on how not to get conned.***

The Con	The Bait	The Switch	Advice
Internet auctions	Great deals on great products.	After sending money, consumers receive inferior item or nothing at all.	Investigate the seller carefully. Use a credit card or escrow service to pay.
Internet access service	Free money, simply for cashing a cheque.	After cashing "free" cheque, consumers are locked into long-term Web service with steep penalties for early cancellation.	Read both sides of the cheque, the fine print, or any documentation that comes with the cheque.
Credit card fraud	View online adult images for free, just for sharing your credit card number to "prove" you are over 18.	Fraudulent promoters run up unauthorized charges on consumers' cards.	Share your credit card numbers only when you are buying from a company you trust. Dispute unauthorized charges (federal law limits your liability to $50).
International modem dialing	Free access to adult material by downloading "viewer" or "dialler."	Exorbitant long-distance phone bills as the viewer or dialler reconnects to an international carrier.	Do not download programs providing "free" access without carefully reading all the fine print. Dispute unauthorized charges to your account.
Web cramming	Free custom-designed Website for 30-day trial.	Telephone is billed even when consumers do not accept offer or agree to continue service.	Review phone bill carefully, and challenge all charges you do not recognize.
Multilevel marketing plans/ pyramids	Make money selling products you sell, as well as those sold by people you recruit to sell.	Consumers are required to recruit other distributors, but products sold to distributors do not qualify for commissions.	Avoid programs that require you to recruit distributors, buy expensive inventory, or commit to a minimum sales volume.
Travel/ vacations	Great trips for bargain prices.	Low-quality accommodations and services, often with hidden charges.	Get references and the details of the trip in writing.
Business opportunities	Be your own boss, and earn a high salary.	Consumers invest in unproven or insecure ventures.	Talk with others who have made the same investment; get all promises in writing, and study the contract carefully. Consult with a lawyer or accountant.
Investments	Realize huge investment returns.	Big profits always mean big risks.	Check with provincial and federal securities and commodities regulators; insist on talking with other investors.
Health-care products/ services	Cure serious illness or fatal health problems.	Consumers put faith in unproven solutions and put off pursuing needed health care.	Consult with health professionals to evaluate cure-alls or promises to provide fast or easy cures.

Source: **www.ftc.gov/bcp/conline/pubs/online/dotcons.htm.**

[Table 9.4] ***Small business computer security checklist.***

Action	Explanation
1. Update your software	If there's a patch available, install it. It's a simple way to avoid serious problems, yet many fail to do so.
2. Protect against viruses	Companies large and small can be crippled by viruses. Make sure every company PC, server, and laptop is fully protected.
3. Set up a firewall	This isn't as intimidating as it sounds, and it's the most important thing you can do to thwart hackers.
4. Tighten in-house security	Not all threats are high-tech. A casual break-in or disgruntled employee can cause serious damage too.
5. Strengthen passwords	If you or your employees use simple passwords and/or fail to change them regularly, your company is vulnerable.
6. Back up critical data	If the thought of losing everything stored in your computers terrifies you, there's a simple solution. Schedule regular back-ups.
7. Embrace smart Web browsing	Unscrupulous sites, as well as pop-ups and animations, can be dangerous. So can browsing from a server.
8. Safeguard wireless networks	Wireless networks are more vulnerable than cabled networks. Do all you can to reduce your exposure.
9. Connect remote users securely	Remote access to your network may be a business necessity, but it's also a security risk you need to closely monitor.
10. Lock down servers	Your servers are your network's command centre. If your servers are compromised, your entire network is at risk.
11. Lock down clients	A lack of stringent administrative procedures could sabotage all of the security safeguards you've just instigated.

Source: **www.microsoft.com/smallbusiness/gtm/securityguidance/hub.mspx**.

WHEN THINGS GO WRONG

Watch Out for Wednesdays!

The number of serious Internet security incidents is rising, and for some reason more attacks are launched on Wednesdays than any other day of the week. Those conclusions are contained in the Q2 Internet Risk Impact Summary Report from Internet Security Systems of Atlanta. The number of serious security incidents increased by 13.7 percent between 2002 and 2003, the report said.

Especially at risk are users who make use of wireless technologies, broadband access from a home office, and file-sharing and messaging applications. This increased risk is also a result of corporate laptops and workstations being used on home-based broadband networks. Wednesday showed the highest rate of security events, registering an average of 1,809,222 during the second quarter of 2003.

What's really important about these numbers, Internet Security Systems said, is that attacks are increasingly targeting known vulnerabilities, meaning that if companies simply stayed up to date with current patches and software updates, they would be unaffected by most of the nefarious activity going on. The problem is that companies cannot keep up with the rate at which new patches are released, and even if a patch is obtained, ensuring that it is installed on every single vulnerable machine is a huge headache in large companies. Microsoft used to issue security patches when vulnerabilities were found, sometimes many times in a month, but the company found that users were ignoring the updates. The company then moved to a system of regular monthly updates to aggregate all fixes into one patch. This approach led to concern from some users that security updates may not be released for up to 30 days. Ironically, the day of the week on which Microsoft releases most of its security patches is . . . Wednesday.

[Adapted from Peter Wolchak, "Watch Out for Wednesdays, the Worst Hack Day," *Backbone* (January/February 2004).]

KEY POINTS REVIEW

1. **Describe the advent of the Information Age and how computer ethics impact the use of information systems.** The Information Age refers to a time in the history of civilization when information became the currency of the realm. To be successful in many careers today requires that people be computer literate, since the ability to access and effectively operate computing technology is a key part of many careers. A digital divide is said to exist between people who are computer literate and those who are not. Because computer literacy is so critical in the Information Age, a major ethical concern for society centres on who is computer literate and who is not.
2. **Discuss the ethical concerns associated with information privacy, accuracy, property, and accessibility.** Information privacy is concerned with what information an individual should have to reveal to others through the course of employment or through other transactions such as online shopping. Canada has enacted the *Personal Information Protection and Electronic Documents Act* to protect the rights of consumers in this country. Information accuracy is concerned with the authenticity and fidelity of information, as well as identifying who is responsible for informational errors that harm people. Information property focuses on who owns information about individuals and how information can be sold and exchanged. Information accessibility focuses on defining what information a person or organization has the right to obtain about others and how this information can be accessed and used. While the Information Age has brought widespread access to information, the downside is that others may now have access to your personal information that you would prefer to keep private. Because there are few safeguards for ensuring the accuracy of information, individuals and companies can be damaged by informational errors. Additionally, because information is so easy to exchange and modify, information ownership violations readily occur. Likewise, with the rapid increase in online databases containing personal information and the increase in the use of computer-based communication between individuals, who has the right to access and monitor this information has raised many ethical concerns.
3. **Define computer crime, and list several types of computer crime.** Computer crime is defined as the act of using a computer to commit an illegal act, such as targeting a computer while committing an offence, using a computer to commit an offence, or using computers in the course of a criminal activity. A person who gains unauthorized access to a computer system has also committed a computer crime. Those individuals who are knowledgeable enough to gain access to computer systems without authorization have long been referred to as hackers. Today, those who break into computer systems with the intention of doing damage or committing a crime are usually called crackers. Hackers and crackers can commit a wide variety of computer crimes, including data diddling, salami slicing, phreaking, cloning, carding, piggybacking or shoulder-surfing, social engineering, dumpster diving, and spoofing. Crackers are also associated with the making and distributing of computer viruses and other destructive codes. Finally, making illegal copies of software, a worldwide computer crime, is called software piracy.
4. **Contrast what the terms *computer virus, worm, Trojan horse,* and *logic* or *time bomb* mean.** Viruses are destructive programs that disrupt the normal functioning of computer systems. They differ from other types of malicious code in that they can reproduce themselves. Some viruses are intended to be harmless pranks, but more often they do damage to a computer system by erasing files on the hard drive or by slowing computer processing or otherwise compromising the system. A worm usually does not destroy files, but, like a virus, it is designed to copy and send itself, spreading rapidly throughout networked computers. It eventually brings computers to a halt simply by clogging memory space with the outlaw code, thus preventing normal functioning. Unlike a virus, the Trojan horse does not copy itself, but like viruses it can do much damage. When a Trojan horse is planted in a computer, its instructions remain hidden. The computer appears to function normally, but in fact it is performing underlying functions dictated by the intrusive code. Finally, logic or time bombs are variations of Trojan horses. They also do not reproduce themselves and are designed to operate without disrupting normal computer function. Instead, they lie in wait for unsuspecting computer users to perform a triggering operation. Time bombs are set off by specific dates, such as the birthday of a famous person, whereas logic bombs are set off by certain types of operations, such as entering a specific password, or adding or deleting names and other information to and from certain computer files.
5. **Explain what is meant by computer security and describe various methods for providing computer security.** Computer security refers to precautions taken to keep computers and the information they contain safe from unauthorized access. Computer security can be enhanced by keeping computers in a secure location, by keeping information stored in password-protected areas, by using special software to keep stored information secure, by using biometrics to authenticate users, and by hiring trustworthy employees. Encryption—the process of encoding messages before they enter the network or airwaves—is the best bet for keeping information secure when you do not have access to a secure channel. Firewalls can be used to keep LANs and WANs secure. Viruses can be reduced or eliminated (or at least the damage mitigated) if several steps are followed, including installing antivirus software; backing up critical information; refusing to use disks, data, or software from unknown sources; refusing to open e-mail attachments from unknown sources; and reporting virus infections immediately to your company or school's IT department. When on the Internet, you can better maintain your privacy by using only reputable Websites, controlling the use of cookies, surfing anonymously, and being careful about who has access to your e-mail.

KEY TERMS

biometrics 300
carding 297
certificate authority 303
cloning 297
computer crime 293
computer ethics 283
computer literacy 282
computer security 300
copyright 289

REVIEW QUESTIONS

1. Describe the advent of the Information Age and how computer ethics impact the use of information systems.
2. What is the difference between the digital divide and computer literacy?
3. Compare and contrast information accuracy, information privacy, and information property.
4. Define computer crime, and list several types of computer crime.
5. Explain the purpose of PIPEDA.
6. List and describe five security precautions organizations can implement to secure their computer networks.
7. Define unauthorized access, and give several examples from recent media reports.
8. Viruses that are spread via e-mail transmitted over the Internet are also frequently in the news. What are five ways to prevent these viruses?
9. What is identity theft, and what is the solution, according to this chapter?
10. What are the differences in privacy laws among Canada, the U.S., and the EU?
11. Compare and contrast a worm, a virus, a Trojan horse, and a logic or time bomb.
12. List five dot-cons that you find interesting, and give the advice suggested for avoiding these traps.

SELF-STUDY QUESTIONS

Answers are at the end of the Problems and Exercises.

1. Being ________, or knowing how to use the computer as a device to gather, store, organize, and process information, can open up myriad sources of information.
   A. technology illiterate
   B. digitally divided
   C. computer literate
   D. computer illiterate
2. A broad definition of computer crime includes all of the following **except** ________.
   A. targeting a computer while committing an offence
   B. using computers in the course of a criminal activity, despite the fact the computers are not actually targeted
   C. the act of using a computer to commit a legal act
   D. using a computer to commit an offence
3. ________ focuses on defining what information a person or organization has the right to obtain about others and how this information can be accessed and used.
   A. Information accessibility
   B. Information accuracy
   C. Information privacy
   D. Information property
4. The Computer Ethics Institute is a research, education, and policy study organization with members from the IT professions and from academic, corporate, and public policy communities. The guidelines prohibit all of the following **except** ________.
   A. using a computer to harm others
   B. using a computer to bear false witness
   C. copying or using proprietary software without paying for it
   D. using computer resources with authorization
5. In Canada, the federal law to protect privacy rights is called ________.
   A. the *Computer Fraud and Abuse Act*
   B. the *Electronic Communications Privacy Act*
   C. the *Personal Information Protection and Electronic Documents Act*
   D. the General Privacy Directive
6. Those individuals who break into computer systems with the intention of doing damage or committing a crime are usually called ________.
   A. hackers
   B. crackers
   C. computer geniuses
   D. computer operatives
7. Computer security refers to precautions taken to keep computers and the information they contain safe from unauthorized access. Which of the following is **not** a safeguard that can help organizations maintain a high level of computer security?
   A. keeping stored information safe with passwords and allowing access only to those employees who need it to do their jobs
   B. using biometrics that may include fingerprints and retinal scans or other bodily characteristics

C. making every effort to hire employees on parole
D. utilizing special software to help keep stored information secure

8. A(n) ________ consists of hardware or software designed to keep unauthorized users out of network systems.

A. encryption system
B. firewall
C. alarm system
D. logic bomb

9. Crimes committed against telephone company computers with the goal of making free long-distance calls, impersonating directory assistance or other operator services, diverting calls to numbers of the perpetrator's choice, or otherwise disrupting telephone service for subscribers is called ________.

A. phreaking
B. cloning
C. carding
D. data diddling

PROBLEMS AND EXERCISES

1. Match the following terms with the appropriate definitions:

____ Digital divide
____ Biometrics
____ Information privacy
____ Encryption
____ Information accuracy
____ Shoulder-surfing
____ Identity theft
____ Information accessibility
____ Worm
____ Computer security
____ Computer ethics
____ Social engineering

a. The stealing of another person's social insurance number, credit card number, and other personal information for the purpose of using the victim's credit rating to borrow money, buy merchandise, and otherwise run up debts that are never repaid
b. An area concerned with what information an individual should have to reveal to others through the course of employment or through other transactions such as online shopping
c. The gap between those individuals in our society who are computer literate and have access to information resources such as the Internet and those who do not
d. Code that usually does not destroy files, but, like a virus, is designed to copy and send itself, spreading rapidly throughout networked computers and eventually bringing computers to a halt simply by clogging memory space with the outlaw code, thus preventing normal functioning
e. An area concerned with the authenticity and fidelity of information, as well as identifying who is responsible for informational errors that harm people
f. Refers to precautions taken to keep computers and the information they contain safe from unauthorized access
g. Focuses on defining what information a person or organization has the right to obtain about others and how this information can be accessed and used
h. The process of encoding messages before they enter the network or airwaves, then decoding them at the receiving end of the transfer, so that recipients can read or hear them
i. The identification of employees by fingerprints, retinal patterns, or other bodily characteristics before granting them access to use a computer
j. The issues and standards of conduct as they pertain to the use of information systems
k. Gaining information needed to access computers by tricking company employees by means of posing as magazine journalists, telephone company employees, and forgetful co-workers in order to persuade honest employees to reveal passwords and other information
l. The act of simply standing in line behind a card user at an automated teller machine (ATM), looking over that person's shoulder, and memorizing the card's personal identification number (PIN), then placing the stolen number on a counterfeit access card and using it to withdraw cash from the victim's account

2. The Electronic Frontier Foundation, **www.eff.org**, has a mission of protecting rights and promoting freedom in the "electronic frontier." The organization provides additional advice on how to protect your online privacy. Review its suggestions, and provide a summary of what you can do to protect yourself.

3. Do you consider yourself computer literate? Do you know of any friends or relatives who are not computer literate? What can you do to improve your computer literacy? Is computer literacy necessary in today's job market? Why or why not?

4. Look at the following Websites for tips and articles on identity theft: **www.consumer.gov/idtheft** and **www.identitytheft.org**. Did you find anything that you think might help you in the future?

5. Complete the computer ethics quiz at **http://web.cs.bgsu.edu/maner/xxicee/html/welcome.htm**. Do ethical codes apply to all professions?

6. Find your school's guidelines for ethical computer use on the Internet and answer the following questions: are there limitations as to the type of Websites and material that can be viewed (i.e., pornography, etc.)? Are students allowed to change the programs on the hard drives of the lab computers or download software for their own use? Are there rules governing personal use of computers and e-mail?

7. Do you believe that there is a need for a unified information systems code of ethics? Visit **www.fau.edu/netiquette/net/ten.html**. What do you think of this code? Should it be expanded, or is it too general? Search the Internet for additional codes for programmers or Web developers. What did you find?

8. Visit the Consumer Sentinel, **www.consumer.gov/sentinel**, to learn about how law enforcement agencies around the world work together to fight consumer fraud. The site contains statistics on consumer complaints and sorts this data in many interesting ways. Prepare a report using the most current data on the top five complaint categories.

9. Choose an organization with which you are familiar. Determine what the company's computer ethics policy is by obtaining a written copy and reviewing it. In addition, asking questions and observing several employees may provide insight into the actual application. Does this organization adhere to a strict or casual ethics policy? Prepare a 10-minute presentation to the rest of the class on your findings.

10. Visit **www.safeshopping.org** and prepare a summary of its top 10 safe online shopping tips. Did you find these tips useful enough to share with a friend or classmate? Did you bookmark the site or e-mail it to a friend?

11. To learn more about protecting your privacy, visit **www.cookiecentral.com**, **www.privcom.gc.ca/index_e.asp**, and **www.ipc.on.ca**. Did you learn something that will help protect your privacy? Why is privacy more important than ever?

12. When you make a withdrawal or a deposit of funds at an ATM machine, do people stand back enough so they cannot watch you, or have you had someone hover over you? Are you careful to take any receipts with you and not leave any evidence of your access code and account number?

13. Do you feel the media generates too much hype regarding hackers and crackers? Since companies such as Microsoft have been hacked into, are you concerned about your bank account or other sensitive information?

14. Review Table 9.3's list of dot-cons from the U.S. Federal Trade Commission. Have any suspicious groups contacted you or any of your friends or classmates?

15. Search the Internet for information about the damaging effects of software piracy, and/or look at the following Website: **www.microsoft.com/piracy**. Is software piracy a global problem? What can you do to mitigate the problem? Give a short presentation to the class.

16. There are many brands of software firewalls, with Zone Labs' ZoneAlarm (**www.zonealarm.com**), Norton's Personal Firewall (**www.symantec.com**), McAfee's Firewall (**www.networkassociates.com**), and BlackICE Defender (**http://blackice.iss.net**) being four of the most popular. Visit one of these sites and learn more about how a firewall works and what it costs to give you this needed protection; prepare a one-page report that outlines what you have learned.

ANSWERS TO THE SELF-STUDY QUESTIONS

1. C 2. C 3. A 4. D 5. C 6. B 7. C 8. B 9. A

Case 1: *The Ethics of IS Consulting*

Thousands of businesses, large and small, are actively participating in one of the fastest growing industry sectors of the modern world: information systems consulting services. Many large organizations, such as IBM, EDS, and Accenture, have long been successful in providing IS consulting services. New companies enter this industry on a daily basis.

As with other business endeavours, IS consulting services is an area of business that puts people into situations that test their ethics. One potentially problematic area that applies to all consulting—not just IS consulting—is the fundamental conflict between needing to secure consulting contracts to bring revenue into the consulting firm and needing not to overpromise what can be delivered and/or when it can be delivered. The pressure to bring in business to generate revenue is great. New business is, after all, the lifeblood of the consulting firm. There is natural pressure to secure a consulting contract even though it may not be absolutely clear that the firm can deliver exactly what the client wants or needs by the exact deadlines that the client has set. For IS consultants, the pressure is great to promise that the job can be done quickly using "rapid" methodologies, especially given that these methodologies are in vogue. Of course, it is in the consulting firm's long-term interests not to overpromise, but the pressure is there nonetheless.

One other potential ethical dilemma facing IS consultants is the question of whom they work for and where their loyalties lie. With joint application design and the use of systems development teams in which IS consultants work closely with business users, it is sometimes difficult for consultants to determine exactly for whom they work—the client or the consulting firm. On the one hand, they are serving the client and must satisfy the client's needs. On the other hand, they work for the consulting firm. They may get pulled in two different directions, especially if the relationship between the client and the consulting firm deteriorates. The consulting firm might want the consultant to stick with the letter of the contract, to withhold certain services, or to keep her time with the client to a minimum. On the other hand, the consultant may want to go the extra distance to please the client. After all, with contemporary systems development approaches, the consultant probably spends more time with the client organization's personnel than with the consulting firm's personnel, and the client organization is likely to be doing the primary evaluation of the consultant's performance. In fact, in some cases, the consultants may be housed physically and semipermanently within the client organization, may be paid directly by the client, and may enjoy other employee benefits provided by the client organization.

With increased use of joint application design and other approaches to partnering with business users comes one final, fundamental ethical dilemma that all consultants face daily. This dilemma is whether to solve problems for clients in such a way that the client learns how to solve the problems itself or to solve problems for clients in such a way that the client needs to call the consultant back in again to solve similar problems in the future. There is a natural pressure to do the latter to ensure future business.

A useful analogy for this ethical dilemma is the way that a barber cuts your hair. A barber who wants to ensure that you will have to come back to him again would give you the best possible haircut. In addition, he would have no mirrors in the shop so that you could not see what he was doing, and he would not answer any of your questions about how he was cutting and styling your hair. On the other hand, a barber who wanted you to become self-sustaining and empowered to take care of yourself would not only give you a good haircut, but he would have mirrors all around so that you could see exactly what he was doing. He would explain exactly what he was doing at all times and answer any of your questions. Now, you would not necessarily be able to cut your own hair, but you would know how to do so and could explain this to another person who could then cut your hair. You would not necessarily have to come back to that same barber. Good consultants do not try to generate more business for themselves in this way. They want you to ask them back because you want to have them back, not because you need to have them back.

Discussion Questions

1. How would you deal with an IS manager who was pushing you to develop a system in a time frame that was too rapid to enable you to do a good job? What if it was the client who was pushing you?
2. To whom should an IS consultant ultimately be loyal, the client or the consulting firm? Why?
3. Should IS consultants not only strive to solve clients' problems, but also help to teach and enable them to solve their own problems in the future? Why or why not?
4. What, in your opinion, are some of the characteristics of a good consultant? How do you think a good consultant will ensure that a client will return in the future?

Case 2: *Canada Starts to Get Tough on Software Piracy*

Groups leading the charge against software piracy say eight companies in Ontario and Alberta have agreed to pay a combined total of $330,300 for using unlicensed software, but some are concerned that illegal copying in Canada remains higher than in the U.S. "I think it's the most settlements we've ever announced in a single day in Canada," said Bob Kruger, vice-president of enforcement for the Business Software Alliance (BSA) in Washington, D.C., which worked with the Toronto-based Canadian Alliance Against Software Theft (CAAST) to bring about charges against the eight firms.

Meanwhile, Jacqueline Famulak, CAAST president and regional legal counsel (Canada) for Apple Computer Inc. in Markham, Ontario, is pleased that CAAST and BSA were able to resolve the cases. "I couldn't tell you exactly how many we [settled] last year, but it was definitely not more than a dozen," said Famulak. CAAST attributed the success of settling these cases to asking the organizations suspected of piracy to conduct a software audit and submit a report to the software-piracy watchdog. "They were all cooperative. They all agreed not only to delete the unlicensed software and purchase new software, but also to establish compliance policies in the workplace," said Famulak.

An August study conducted by International Planning & Research Corp. of West Chester, Pennsylvania, concluded 39 percent of all software installed in Canada in 2002 was pirated, up 1 percent from 2001. The corresponding U.S. figure is 23 percent, which has dropped incrementally over the past few years, according to BSA figures. Kruger attributed the rate discrepancy to a number of issues, particularly that U.S. laws are "more strict and comprehensive." In fact, companies found to have wilfully infringed someone's copyright can be held liable for up to US$150,000 in the U.S. for each work copied, compared to a $20,000 charge for similar suits in Canada, he said. This may all be rooted in different perceptions in the two countries about the seriousness of software piracy, with some in Canada ranking it among crimes such as "petty shoplifting—taking a towel from a hotel room," Kruger added.

BSA's efforts to stem piracy include offering companies free software-auditing tools and other resources to better manage software. CAAST's awareness efforts, which consist of radio ads and information mail-outs, are helping to better educate companies about what constitutes illegal software use, Famulak explained. Famulak said CAAST follows up on every lead, whether it's by phone, anonymous letter, or e-mail, and pursues a company when it feels it has enough evidence. This may mean writing a "semi-friendly letter" that wins the cooperation of the organization or going so far as obtaining a search order to enter the premises with the help of police.

The study International Planning & Research undertook also found that software piracy costs Canada $342 million each year in federal and provincial tax losses and inhibits growth of a strong software sector. Furthermore, direct and indirect job losses add up to 32,112 and direct and indirect wage and salary losses weigh in at more than $1.4 billion.

[Adapted from Fawzia Sheikh, "Piracy Watchdogs Fine Eight Firms for Unlicensed Software," *Computing Canada,* Vol. 30, No. 1 (January 16, 2004).]

Discussion Questions

1. Do you believe that all software piracy is wrong? Or is it acceptable in certain circumstances?
2. Do you own, or have you ever owned, pirated software?
3. Based on the article above, what do you think Canada should do to reduce the level of software piracy by organizations?
4. If you were in charge of a large corporation, what would be in your computer and software usage policy?

Digital Employee Privacy at the Canadian Imperial Bank of Commerce

CBC

"We could have a lively situation on our hands if some of these e-mail privacy scenarios come true," remarked Bob Jones, manager, compliance, at Canadian Imperial Bank of Commerce (CIBC). Jones was aware that Toronto-based CIBC had implemented word recognition software in its U.S. broker to comb e-mail messages sent by employees for specified business words. Now he wondered about the implications of installing the software in Canada. What if these routine searches flagged an e-mail message that also contained personal information about an employee? In the wake of various legislation, as well as e-mail worms that have crippled corporate networks, the use of e-mail at work has become a hot topic of discussion in management circles.

As of May 2004, the Canadian Imperial Bank of Commerce had 37,000 employees worldwide serving six million individual customers, 350,000 small businesses, and 7,000 corporate and investment banking customers. The bank had total assets of $277 billion, and a net income of $2 billion in 2003. Formed out of a 1961 merger between the Canadian Bank of Commerce and Imperial Bank of Canada, CIBC was one of North America's leading financial institutions, offering retail and wholesale products and services through its electronic banking network, branches, and offices around the world.

Privacy practices in the banking industry could be traced back to the landmark 1924 Tournier case (*Tournier v. the National Provincial and Union Bank of England*). Common law and guidelines resulted from that decision, and thus the case had become necessary background for management employees in the banking industry.

The Tournier case concerned a bank customer with a £10 overdraft who, having no fixed address, gave his bank branch manager the name and address of his new employers. When he defaulted on repayments, the branch manager telephoned those employers to ask if they knew his customer's address; in the course of doing so, he disclosed the overdraft and default, and expressed his opinion that his customer was betting heavily. As a result, Tournier lost his job, sued the bank, and won his case upon appeal.

Since the Tournier decision, banks have become extremely sensitive about protecting customer information. Strict privacy policies have been put in place, and systems containing personal information have been protected from unauthorized use and manipulation. In Canada, PIPEDA has enshrined many of these practices into law.

Employee privacy was somewhat different from customer privacy. By design, in most banks, customers are provided with the best level of privacy protection available. However, there are legitimate reasons why banks might want to monitor what employees are doing on company time and with company equipment.

For banks like CIBC, providing employees with access to company e-mail has become a strategic necessity. However, with e-mail access comes the possibility of unwittingly receiving or transmitting an e-mail worm or virus. Computer Economics Inc., a research firm based in Carlsbad, California, reported that the ILOVEYOU virus alone had infected three million computers around the world, causing US$2 billion in direct economic losses and a further US$6.7 billion in lost productivity. Insurer Lloyd's of London has predicted that computer viruses will prove to be the biggest insurance risk in upcoming years, prompting business analysts to call for a widespread change in company e-mail policies.

In addition to protecting company systems from viruses, employers like CIBC have obligations to ensure that employees do not act illegally, for example in perpetrating frauds or by acting immorally. E-mail could be used by employees to make inappropriate or defamatory comments. It could also be used to transmit sensitive corporate information without appropriate security.

CIBC's Electronic Communication Policy

E-mail and voice mail were both included in Section 4.6 of CIBC's Principles of Business Conduct. CIBC recognized that occasional personal use could not be avoided. "E-mail and voice mail are essential ways to communicate with employees, customers, suppliers, and other parties. Although all e-mail and voice mail facilities supplied by CIBC are its property, CIBC recognizes that incidental or occasional personal use of both is unavoidable."

CIBC reserves the right to access and monitor both internal and external e-mail and voice mail, including stored messages, and to restrict the use of both without prior notice. The company also reserves the right to produce all office communications in legal proceedings.

Assentor Software

To ensure that its U.S. brokerage employees are not acting inappropriately in their dealings with customers through e-mail communications, CIBC relies on software to screen and archive e-mail messages in a central database. The software, called Assentor, has the ability to screen not only key words, but also combinations of words and sentences (so-called natural language technology). The software allows CIBC to "flag" and hold potentially inappropriate e-mail communications, such as high-pressure sales tactics, insider information, and other potentially litigious issues, such as sexual harassment. These flagged e-mails are then held for human analysis and review before being sent.

The Tower Group, a technology research firm, predicts that natural language functionality will become the technology of choice for e-mail compliance tools. Companies in the financial services industry that use Assentor include CIBC, A.G. Edwards, BancBoston, Southwest Securities, and the National Association of Securities Dealers. Additional firms use other, often less powerful, e-mail screening methods.

Call centres typically tape conversations for quality control, and most organizations announce to the customer at the beginning of the call that the conversation will be taped. Employees working at call centres know when they arrive at work that their conversations will be taped due to the possibility of disputes—for example, replaying a taped call would confirm if the customer requested a "buy order" of 500 shares instead of a "sell order" for 5,000 shares of the same stock. It is much easier, on the other hand, to forget that e-mail use could be monitored.

CIBC had recently developed an Electronic Mail Policy, which went into more detail than the previous Principles of Business Conduct document. This policy outlined appropriate and inappropriate use of this company resource. A short summary of the policy read:

> Electronic mail (e-mail) systems provided by the CIBC Group of Companies (CIBC Group) are its property. Employees are to use these systems for company business primarily within the boundaries of this policy and its standards. Business information, and the ability to freely communicate it, are valuable assets that play a significant role in CIBC's success. The protection and appropriate use of these assets is everyone's responsibility.
>
> All messages sent or received by electronic mail are CIBC records and must be handled in a manner consistent with CIBC record management policies and practices. Caution and discretion should be used in the nature and content of all messages sent, stored or distributed.
>
> CIBC recognizes that incidental or occasional use of e-mail for personal communications is unavoidable. However, all users with access to CIBC e-mail systems should be aware that the CIBC reserves the right to access, to monitor and to archive all e-mail messages, transmitted, received or stored on its systems, without further prior notice.

"E-mail use is often similar to casual conversations rather than formal written communications," stated Jones, "because employees forget that it is recorded and can be monitored." Jones went on to stress that e-mail is a business resource covered by a separate e-mail policy. He concluded by asking, "How should employees be discouraged from inappropriate language, content, and usage?"

Jones knew that these were not easy questions to answer. Recent court cases, as well as articles in newspapers and trade journals, had brought the issue of e-mail privacy to CIBC's attention once more. For example, high-profile cases against Microsoft, Merrill Lynch, Enron, WorldCom, *The Wall Street Journal, The New York Times,* and Martha Stewart had all turned on incriminating e-mail messages.

Some corporations used e-mail screening to catch e-mail misuse, but since these filters tended to slow down network traffic, the practice was not universal. Other firms put in place policies that banned certain types of attachments. Many firms archive e-mail, but access it only in the event of a complaint.

What Should CIBC Do?

Jones found that making the decision to implement the Assentor software was a lot easier than deciding what to do in the event that the software found something improper.

"What if an employee sends a personal message using a business 'word' flagged by Assentor and his or her direct manager finds out about a private situation?" wondered Jones. "What are the legal ramifications if the employee is reassigned or fired and subsequently claims bias on the part of the manager? What about the question of company ethics? Should we be reading personal e-mail from employees?"

Jones was wondering how to best reinforce the e-mail policy at CIBC. "The employee should know that e-mail is a business resource that *could* be monitored by the employer. But how would we enforce it?

"If we were to cease monitoring e-mail, it might seem to be a viable solution, but remember that we have a responsibility to our customers, shareholders, and the regulatory agencies to ensure proper records are kept and to monitor business e-mail use. It is also a regulatory requirement in the securities industry. Should we consider taking that risk and not having an e-mail screen? Probably not. There are things that an employee legally can't say, and some things they shouldn't say. Assentor 'sniffs' this out for us, and our employees should understand this.

"I believe it is all about how we present it to our employees. To best implement our Principles of Business Conduct, clear communication and upfront understanding from our employees will go far to prevent negative impressions. We want to be as upfront and clear as possible to them. How best, then, to do that? Should we inform our employees once? Inform them once per year? Have them sign a code of conduct? Or inform the employee every time he or she logs on to a company computer?"

Questions

1. What are the main arguments for and against installing the Assentor software?
2. Assuming the bank decides to install the software, what other decisions then have to be made?
3. Should e-mail be considered any differently from other forms of corporate communication?
4. Suggest a detailed employee monitoring plan for the bank. Include in your plan how employees are monitored, how they are notified or informed, what the monitored information can and can not be used for, how the monitored information is dealt with by the bank, and what sanctions should be in place in cases where various types of infractions are uncovered.
5. Explore the trade-off between honouring employees' rights to privacy and corporate interests.
6. As an employee, how do you feel about your communications being monitored? What could you do about it?
7. If, as an employer, you discovered through routine monitoring of e-mail that sexually inappropriate messages were being exchanged by some employees about another employee, what would you do?
8. Suggest ways that you might educate employees on proper e-mail procedure. How can employees be discouraged from inappropriate language, content, and usage?

Video Resource: "E-Mail Alert," *Venture* (October 27, 2002).

Source: Based on K. Mark and M. Wade, "Canadian Imperial Bank of Commerce: Digital Employee Privacy," Ivey Management Services, 2000.

Preview

If you want to purchase a computer, you have a broad range of options. Over the years, hardware has become less expensive, making it possible for individuals and organizations of all sizes to take advantage of computer-based technologies. However, large computer systems can still cost more than a million dollars. Organizations must select the right hardware or risk making a costly mistake. To make an informed decision about IS hardware, you must understand what IS hardware is and how it works.

After reading this appendix, you will be able to do the following:

1. Describe key elements of information systems hardware.
2. List and describe the types of computers that are being used in organizations today.

Our approach in this appendix is not to bog you down with hardware facts and jargon but to provide you with an overview.

KEY ELEMENTS OF INFORMATION SYSTEMS HARDWARE

Information systems hardware is classified into three types: input, processing, and output devices (see Figure A.1). ***Input devices*** are used to enter information into a computer. ***Processing devices*** transform inputs into outputs. The ***central processing unit (CPU)***, with the help of several other closely related devices that store and recall information, is the most important processing element of a computer. We will discuss this in detail in this appendix. Finally, ***output devices***, such as a computer monitor and printer, deliver information to you in a usable format. This section describes each of these three key elements of information systems hardware: input, processing, and output devices (for a more detailed discussion, see Keogh, 2002).

[**Figure A.1** ➡ Input devices include the mouse and keyboard; output devices include the printer and monitor; the central processing unit transforms input into output.]

Source: Courtesy of Dell Computer Corporation.

Input Devices

For information systems hardware to perform a task, data must be input into the system. Certain types of data can be entered more easily using one type of input device than another. For example, keyboards are currently the primary means to enter text and numbers. Alternatively, architects and engineers can use scanners to enter their designs and drawings into computers. Graphics tablets simulate the process of drawing or sketching on a sheet of paper. A great deal of research and development is conducted to identify optimal ways to input various types of information and to build and sell new input devices. To organize our discussion of input devices, we classify them into four general categories by the type of information being entered: entering text and numbers, pointing and selecting information, entering batch data, and entering audio and video. Table A.1 summarizes the fundamental characteristics of each category.

Entering Text and Numbers

The primary device used to support the entry of text and numbers into a computer is the ***keyboard***. Used first as the input method on typewriters, keyboard data entry is a mainstay of the computer industry.

Ergonomics One advance in keyboard technology is the ergonomically correct keyboard, which is designed to reduce the stress placed on the wrists, hands, and arms when typing. Figure A.2 shows a normal keyboard and the Microsoft Natural keyboard.

[Table A.1] ***Methods of providing input to an information system.***

Information Category	Representative Device(s)
Entering original text/numbers	Keyboard
Selecting and pointing	Mouse Trackball and joysticks Touch screen Light pen Touch pad
Entering batch data	Scanners Bar code/optical character readers
Entering audio and video	Microphones and speakers Video and digital cameras MIDI

When typing for long periods, some normal keyboard users develop aching, numbing, and tingling in their arms, wrists, or hands. These injuries are generally referred to as repetitive stress injuries. The broadened use of computers in the workplace and the associated injuries to workers, resulting in more sick days and insurance claims, has made the ***ergonomics***—the design of computer hardware and work environments that minimize health risks such as repetitive stress injuries—of keyboards and employees' workstations much more important to organizations. Other ways to reduce repetitive stress injuries include:

- Have an ergonomically designed workplace—desk, chair, monitor size and angle, keyboard height and position.
- Take frequent breaks from typing. When your wrists and fingers start to ache, take a break.
- Maintain a straight wrist position when typing. Do not let your wrists bend up/down or left/right.
- Avoid resting on your wrists while typing. Keep your wrists elevated off the desk.
- Use a light touch on the keys. Do not press harder than you need to on the keyboard to enter information.
- Maintain good health habits and exercise your arms, wrists, and hands.

Other Keyboard Innovations

Standard keyboards connect to the back of the system unit with a cord, but you can elect to purchase a cordless keyboard. Like television remote controls, some battery-operated cordless keyboards use infrared waves to send signals to the computer. One drawback of infrared keyboards is that the device must be proximate to the receiver at all times for signals to be read correctly. Alternatively, Bluetooth-enabled wireless keyboards are not affected by line-of-sight limitations.

(a)

(b)

[**Figure A.2** ➥ Normal keyboard (a) versus the Microsoft Natural keyboard (b).]

Sources: [A.2a] Courtesy Apple Computer, Inc. [A2b] Courtesy Microsoft Corporation.

Pointing and Selecting Information

In addition to entering text and numbers, computer users use ***pointing devices*** to select items from menus, to point, and to sketch or draw (see Figure A.3). You probably have used a pointing device, such as a mouse, when using a graphical operating environment (such as Microsoft Windows) or when playing a video game. Several of the most popular types of pointing devices are listed in Table A.2.

Entering Batch Data

Another category of computer-based input is batch input. ***Batch input*** is used when a great deal of routine information needs to be entered into the computer. ***Scanners*** convert printed text and images into digital data. Scanners range from a small handheld device that looks like a mouse to a large desktop box that resembles a personal photocopier, both of which are shown in Figure A.4. Rather than duplicating the image on another piece of paper, the computer translates the image into digital information that can be stored or manipulated by the computer. Special ***text recognition software*** can convert handwritten text into the computer-based characters that form the original letters and words. Insurance companies, universities, and other organizations that routinely process large batches of forms and documents have applied scanner technology to increase employee productivity.

When the keyboard, mouse, and typical scanner cannot handle the job of transferring data to the computer, specialized scanners may be called for. These devices include optical mark recognition (OMR) devices, optical character recognition (OCR) devices, bar-code readers, and magnetic ink character readers and are summarized in Table A.3.

Smart Cards

Used in many European and Asian countries, as well as at many colleges and universities, ***smart cards*** are a special type of credit card with a magnetic strip, a microprocessor chip, and memory circuits. When issued by a school, smart cards are photo-identification cards that can also be used to unlock dormitory doors, make telephone calls, do laundry, make purchases from vending machines or student cafeterias and snack bars, and more. For making purchases, the cards are backed by funds deposited in a student account. Each time a user makes a purchase,

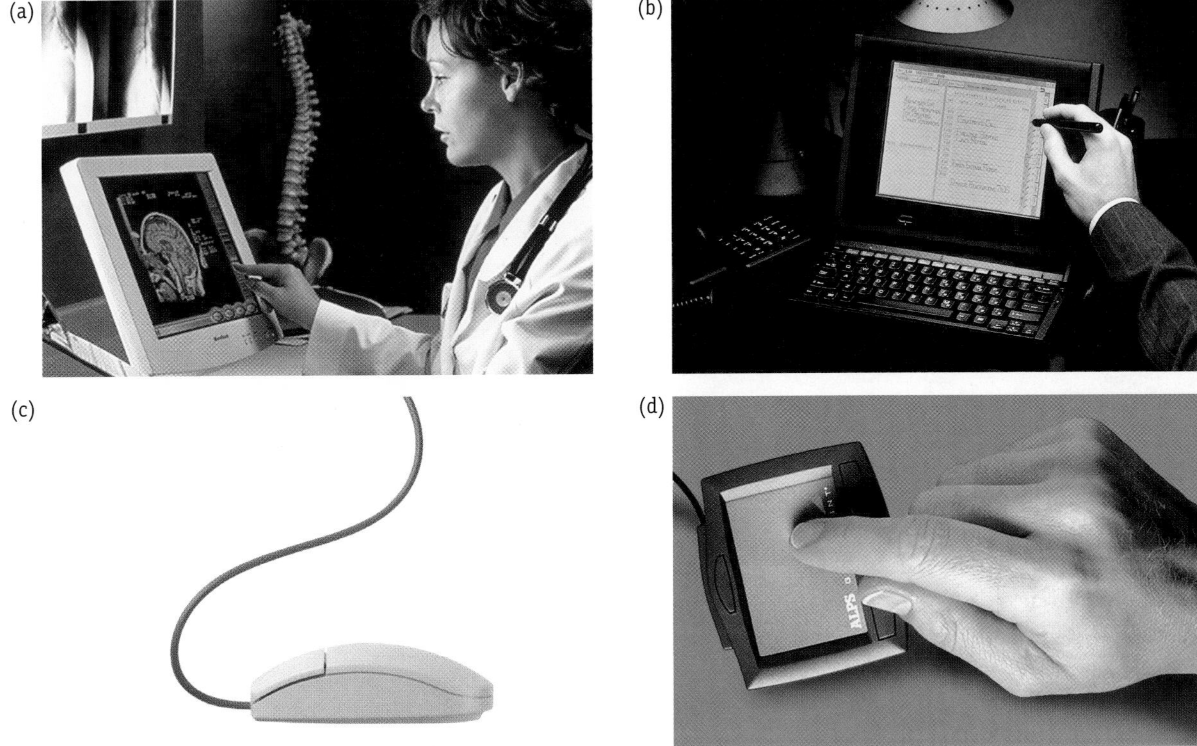

[Figure A.3 ➥ Pointing devices: a touch screen (a), a light pen (b), a mouse (c), and a touch pad (d).]

Sources: [A.3a] Getty Images, Inc. [A.3b] Courtesy Grid Systems Coroporation. [A.3c] Getty Images, Inc. [A.3d] Apple Computer, Inc.

the card keeps track of the balance remaining. Because of the microprocessor embedded in the smart card, it is much more resistant to tampering than current credit cards with magnetic strips.

Entering Audio and Video

Audio refers to sound that has been digitized for storage and replay on the computer. Audio input is helpful when a user's hands need to be free to do other tasks; it can be entered into computers via a microphone, radio, CD, or other audio device. ***Video*** refers to still and moving images that can be recorded, manipulated, and displayed. Video has become popular for assisting in security-related applications, such as room monitoring and employee verification. It has also gained popularity for video-conferencing and chatting on the Internet using your PC and very inexpensive video cameras.

Voice input Perhaps one of the easiest ways to enter data into a computer is simply to speak into a microphone. With the increased interest in such applications as Internet-based telephone calls and videoconferencing, microphones have become an

[Table A.2] ***Selecting and pointing devices.***

Device	Description
Mouse	Pointing device that works by sliding a small box-like device on a flat surface; selections are made by pressing buttons on the mouse.
Trackball	Pointing device that works by rolling a ball that sits in a holder; selections are made by pressing buttons located near or on the holder.
Joystick	Pointing device that works by moving a small stick that sits in a holder; selections are made by pressing buttons located near or on the holder.
Touch screen	A method of input for which you use your finger; selections are made by touching the computer display.
Light pen	Pointing device that works by placing a pen-like device near a computer screen; selections are made by pressing the pen to the screen.

(a)

(b)

[Figure A.4 ➥ Handheld (a) and flatbed (b) scanners are a type of batch input device.]

Sources: [A.4a] Intermec Technologies Corporation. [A.4b] Courtesy of Epson America, Inc.

important component of computer systems. A process called ***speech recognition*** also makes it possible for your computer to understand speech. The two-step process works like this: First, you speak into a microphone connected to a speech recognition board installed in the system unit of your computer. Then special speech recognition software digitizes your spoken words and displays them on the monitor screen. Speech recognition technology is especially helpful for physicians and other medical professionals, people with disabilities, airplane cockpit personnel, factory workers whose hands get too dirty to use keyboards, and computer users who cannot type and do not want to learn. Drawbacks are that users must pause after each word, and computers do not always hear spoken words correctly (see Figure A.5).

Other audio input Audio input devices let users enter sounds into the computer for processing. They can then analyze and manipulate the sounds via sound editing software for output to audiotapes, CDs, or other media. Here are a few examples of how audio input, other than spoken words, might be used:

- A musician may connect an electronic keyboard to the computer, in order to compose or manipulate music. Electronic keyboards or synthesizers are connected via a ***musical instrument digital interface (MIDI)*** port, which can also transfer sound to the computer. MIDI is a standard for connections and communications between your computer and digital musical instruments.
- A scientist studying the sounds made by whales may enter those sounds into a computer to analyze pitch, volume, tone, and other patterns.
- Audiologists and other medical personnel may enter sounds to be played back to patients during hearing tests or therapy.
- Forensic scientists may use a computer to analyze a voice on a tape recorder for identification by a crime victim or witnesses.

[Table A.3] ***Specialized scanners for inputting information.***

Scanner	Description
Optical mark recognition (OMR)	Used to scan questionnaires and test-answer forms where answer choices are circled or blocked in, using pencil or pen
Optical character recognition (OCR)	Used to read and digitize typewritten, computer-printed, and even hand-printed characters such as on sales tags on department store merchandise or patient information in hospitals
Bar-code/optical character readers	Used in grocery stores and other retail businesses to record prices at the checkout counter; also used by libraries, banks, hospitals, utility companies, and so on
Magnetic ink character recognition (MICR)	Used by the banking industry to read data, account numbers, bank codes, and check numbers on preprinted cheques

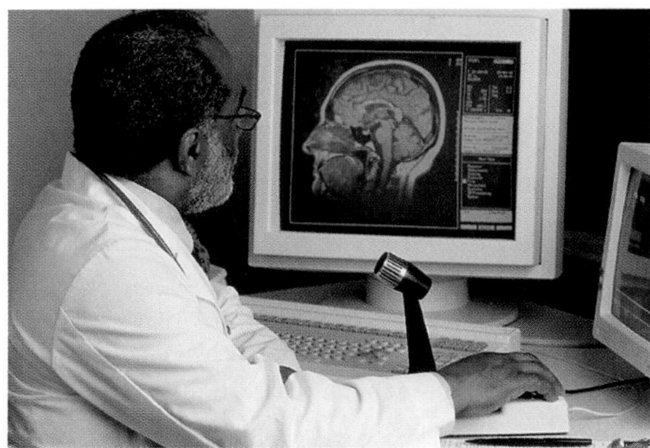

[**Figure A.5** ➥ Voice input is becoming an important way for many to interact with a computer.]

Source: Peter Beck/Corbis/Stock Market.

- Filmmakers may manipulate sounds to serve specific story purposes.

Video input A final way in which information can be entered into a computer is through video input. Digital cameras record images, in digital form, on small, removable memory cards, rather than on film. Most cards can hold more than 100 images. Card capacity depends upon the resolution you select and the preset capacity of the card you buy. When the camera's memory card is full, you can connect it to a port on a PC for downloading to the computer's memory (described below). Accompanying software lets you clear the memory card for later use. Most digital cameras are portable and can be used at any location. Stationary digital cameras are attached to a video board inside the PC. They allow you to record digital photos of yourself and others, documents, or products and other items. High-quality digital cameras are generally more expensive than film-based cameras, ranging in price from $300 to $10,000 or more. However, they offer two main advantages. You can store digital images without using a scanner, and you can take photographs without having film developed. Photos taken with digital cameras are suitable for family albums, but for professional-quality photos, traditional cameras are still the best choice, although the gap in quality between the two camera types is narrowing.

Video cameras, VCRs, televisions, DVDs, and other video devices can provide video input to a computer. Since huge digital files are created when video clips are put into the computer, storage requirements are demanding. That is why video segments run on PCs are usually short. A high-quality digital video camera is typically more expensive than a comparable nondigital video recorder. These high-quality digital cameras are starting to be used in the motion picture industry and by manufacturing companies when performing quality control. For example, Ford Motor Company uses high-resolution video cameras to evaluate the quality of parts by comparing images of newly manufactured items with images stored in a database. If the images match, the part passes a quality control inspection. If the images do not match, the part can be rejected without human intervention.

However, there are also lower-quality cameras that are priced from $50 to $200 (see Figure A.6). These devices, often referred to as *cams,* have become very popular with people wanting to use the Internet for chatting with friends and family, using a program like Microsoft's NetMeeting (**www.microsoft.com/windows/netmeeting**). Unlike high-quality digital video cameras (see Figure A.7), these cams use ***streaming video***, in which the camera sends a sequence of moving images in a compressed form over the Internet and the images are displayed on the receiver's screen as they arrive. ***Streaming media*** is streaming video with sound. With streaming video or streaming media, a Web user does not have to wait for the entire file to be downloaded before seeing the video or hearing the sound. Instead, the media are sent in a continuous stream that is played as it arrives. This is why *streaming* has become popular for real-time chatting and it is how live broadcasts, like the news on CBC displayed on a computer (**www.cbc.ca/newscast.html**), can be viewed on the Internet.

Both audio and video are expected to increase in popularity as common input options. We have described numerous options for providing input to a computer. After information is entered into a computer, it can be processed, stored, and manipulated.

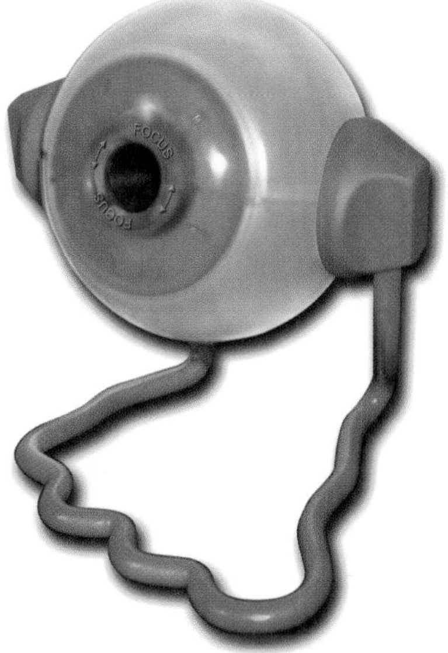

[**Figure A.6** ➥ Low-priced Web cams are popular with people who like to chat over the Internet.]

Source: © Orange Micro, Inc.

[Figure A.7 ➥ High-quality digital video cameras can be connected directly to a computer for storing information, as well as for editing and adding special effects.]

Source: Courtesy of Sony Electronics, Inc.

In the next section, we describe the processing aspects of information systems hardware.

Processing: Transforming Inputs into Outputs

In this section we provide a brief overview of computer processing. To begin, we describe how data and information are represented within a computer. Next, we briefly describe the internal processing components of a desktop computer, focusing primarily on the central processing unit (CPU) and data storage technologies.

Binary Code

Your brain can readily process written words, photographs, music, an instructor's lecture (at least some of the time), videos, and much more. If you grew up speaking English, your brain will process incoming information in that language only. Similarly, computers can process incoming data, but only after the words, photos, music, and other information have been translated into a language they can understand. The language computers understand is called digital data or ***binary code***, which simply means that all incoming data must be translated into the 1s and 0s of binary math. Binary, or base-2, math (2, 4, 8, 16, 32, and so on) is used by computers instead of the more familiar base 10, because it simplifies the way a computer's hardware works.

Binary codes make up ***machine language***, the only language computers understand. The individual 1s and 0s that make up the code are called ***bits***—short for binary digits. Eight bits equal a ***byte***, or about one typed character, such as the letter "A" or the number "6" on the keyboard. You will often see computer storage and memory measurement terms. Table A.4 will help you make sense of them.

Future memory and storage capacities will also include petabytes (one quadrillion bytes), exabytes (one quintillion bytes), and brontobytes (one sextillion bytes).

The bits in the binary code are the basic instruction units for all the work the computer does. The bits represent on/off commands for tiny electric switches inside the computer's processor, called transistors. When a low-voltage current is applied to a switch, it is read as a 0 and the switch is closed. A high-voltage current is read as a 1 and the switch is opened. Similarly, positive and negative magnetized locations used to store data are represented in binary notation as 0s or 1s.

One of the biggest challenges for the computer industry has been to determine how to translate all the different types of information into digital data that a computer can understand. Early computers could not translate incoming data at all. They used paper cards on which strings of 1s and 0s were represented by punched holes. Later, computers received information from a keyboard, which was the

[Table A.4] ***Elements of computer storage.***

Measurement	No. of Bits	No. of Bytes	No. of Kilobytes	No. of Megabytes	No. of Gigabytes
Byte	8	1			
Kilobyte* (K)	8,192	1,024	1		
Megabyte (MB)	8,388,608	1,048,576	1,024	1	
Gigabyte (GB)	8,589,934,592	1,073,741,824	1,048,576	1,024	1
Terabyte (TB)	8,796,093,022,208	1,099,511,627,776	1,073,741,824	1,048,576	1,024

*A kilobyte equals a little more than 1,000 bytes, but the number is usually rounded to 1,000. The same is true for the number of kilobytes in a megabyte, and so on.

first time a translation was made to 1s and 0s from text that computer users could understand. Today's computers can translate many types of data, including words, photos, sound, and video, to binary code, then manipulate and store it. One of the main reasons why computers become so quickly outdated is that newer models keep coming out that can process more and more types of information.

Programs (applications) you run on your computer contain instructions. (This is *software,* covered in Appendix B.) Programs may tell the computer to open a specific file, move data from one location to another, open a new window on the monitor screen, add a column of figures, and so on. Before the computer can follow program instructions, however, those instructions must be converted to machine language. The central processing unit (described below) uses a special built-in program called a language translator to translate incoming data into binary code called machine language. After the processor converts incoming data to machine language, it organizes the bits into groups—for instance, 32-bit instructions—that represent specific operations and storage locations.

Once the computer receives instructions from a program, it processes the information into a form you, the computer user, can understand. In a word processing program, for example, the letters and numbers you type are displayed on the monitor, just as they would appear on a sheet of paper if you were using an old-fashioned typewriter. But, unlike the typewriter, when you press the "L" key, for example, on the computer keyboard, the computer is actually receiving the information as a series of 1s and 0s, specifically "01001100." As you type a letter or a term paper, the data is processed, then displayed on the monitor in a form that makes sense to you. The binary code the computer actually uses is hidden from your view (see Figure A.8). You see words, lines, and paragraphs. After you write a document, you can then print it out on paper, store it on the computer's hard disk, or even post it to an Internet Website.

Other binary codes are used to relay data and instructions to and from the central processing unit (CPU). For example, fixed-length binary codes such as ***ASCII*** (American Standard Code for Information Interchange) and ***EBCDIC*** (Extended Binary-Coded Decimal Interchange Code) are used to represent numbers, letters, and other characters in binary form. ASCII is the standard binary code adopted for data communications systems and is used by most microcomputers (see Table A.5). EBCDIC, developed by IBM, is used primarily on IBM mainframe computers. Both ASCII and EBCDIC use various eight-bit combinations to represent characters in the English language. Software translators are used to convert

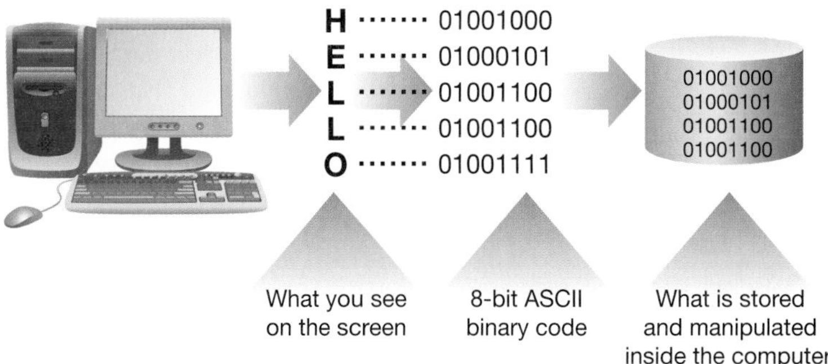

[**Figure A.8** ➥ How computers translate information into binary code so that the computer can store and manipulate the information.]

English characters in ASCII to characters in other languages such as French, Spanish, or German.

A third binary code, called ***Unicode***, is better suited than either ASCII or EBCDIC for representing the letters and characters in languages other than English. This is because Unicode uses 16 bits, instead of the eight bits used by ASCII and EBCDIC to represent characters. By using 16 bits, Unicode can represent more characters than ASCII and EBCDIC and can, therefore, encode most languages.

[Table A.5] ***ASCII codes for alphabet and numbers.***

Character	ASCII-8 Binary Code	Character	ASCII-8 Binary Code
A	0100 0001	S	0101 0011
B	0100 0010	T	0101 0100
C	0100 0011	U	0101 0101
D	0100 0100	V	0101 0110
E	0100 0101	W	0101 0111
F	0100 0110	X	0101 1000
G	0100 0111	Y	0101 1001
H	0100 1000	Z	0101 1010
I	0100 1001	0	0011 0000
J	0100 1010	1	0011 0001
K	0100 1011	2	0011 0010
L	0100 1100	3	0011 0011
M	0100 1101	4	0011 0100
N	0100 1110	5	0011 0101
O	0100 1111	6	0011 0110
P	0101 0000	7	0011 0111
Q	0101 0001	8	0011 1000
R	0101 0010	9	0011 1001

System Unit

A computer's ***system unit*** is the physical box that houses all of the electronic components that do the work of the computer (see Figure A.9). Buttons on the outside, front surface of the system unit turn the machine on and off and reset the machine without turning the power off. Most PC system units include a hard drive and a CD/DVD drive. Through ports at the back of the system unit, you can connect peripheral hardware, such as a keyboard, a mouse, speakers, printers, and scanners.

The system unit contains the following:

- Motherboard, power supply, and fan
- Central processing unit (CPU)
- RAM and ROM
- Hard drive, diskette drive, CD-ROM, or DVD-ROM drive
- Ports for plugging in peripherals and add-in slots for sound, video, internal modem, and other cards

In all types and models of computers, the main circuit board or system board, most often called the motherboard, is the heart of the system unit.

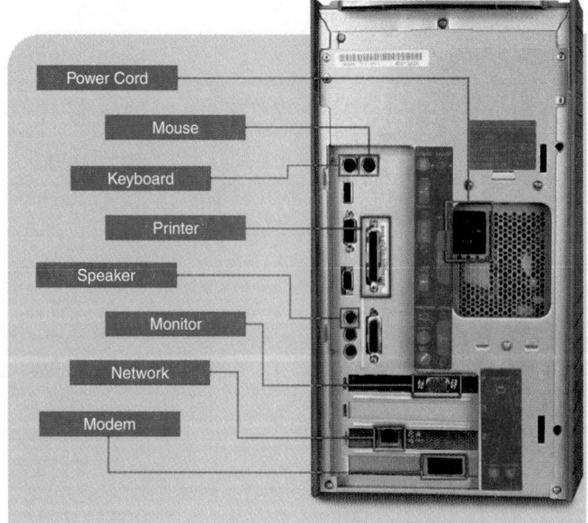

[**Figure A.9** ➡ The system unit houses all of the electronic components that do the work of the computer.]

Source: Courtesy of Toshiba America Information Systems, Inc.

Motherboard

The ***motherboard*** is aptly named because it contains all of the components that do the actual processing work of the computer (see Figure A.10). It is a large printed plastic or fibreglass circuit board that holds or connects to all of the computer's electronic components. Plugged into or otherwise connected to the motherboard are the central processing unit (often referred to as the computer's brain), RAM and ROM (memory), hard disk, diskette, and CD-ROM drives, all expansion slots, ports for printers and other external devices, and the power supply. All of these devices are described below.

The computer's ***power supply*** converts electricity from the wall socket to a lower voltage. Power can vary from 110 to 240 volts, depending upon where you are in the world, to lower voltages—5 to 12 volts DC—and the power supply adjusts voltage to prevent damage to the computer's components. The power supply also regulates the voltage to eliminate spikes and surges common in most electrical systems. For added protection against external power surges, many PC owners opt to connect their systems to a separately purchased voltage surge suppressor. The power supply includes a fan for air-cooling the electronic components inside the system unit. That low humming noise you hear while the computer is running is the fan.

Central Processing Unit

The ***central processing unit (CPU)*** is often called the computer's brain. It is also called a microprocessor, processor, or chip and is responsible for performing all of the operations of the computer. Its job includes loading the operating system (e.g., Windows) when the machine is first turned on and performing, coordinating, and managing all the calculations and instructions relayed to the CPU while the computer is running.

The CPU consists of two main sections: the ***arithmetic logic unit (ALU)*** and the ***control unit***. The ALU performs mathematics, including all forms of addition, subtraction, multiplication, and division. It also performs logical operations, which involve comparing packets of data, then executing appropriate instructions. Combined in various ways, these functions allow the computer to perform complicated operations rapidly. The control unit works closely with the ALU by performing four primary functions:

1. *Fetching* the next program instruction from the computer's memory.
2. *Decoding* instructions, so that the computer knows what to do next. The control unit uses separate ***registers*** (temporary storage locations inside the CPU) to store the instructions and to store information about storage location in memory.

[Figure A.10 ➥ A computer's motherboard holds or connects to all of the computer's electronic components.]

3. *Retrieving* the necessary data from memory and telling the ALU to *execute* the required instructions. The control unit again uses registers to store retrieved data and the action performed.
4. *Storing* results of its computations in a register or in memory.

Both the ALU and the control unit use registers because they can access them more quickly than they can access main memory (RAM), thus adding to processing efficiency.

The CPU is composed of millions of tiny transistors arranged in complex patterns that allow it to interpret and manipulate data. The inner workings of a CPU are very complex. For most of us, it is easiest to think of a CPU as being a "black box" where all the processing occurs. The CPU is a small device made of silicon. For example, the Intel Pentium® 4 CPU packs more than 42 million transistors into an area about the size of a dime! The Pentium 4 is packaged in a container that is bigger than a dime, of course (see Figure A.11), because additional wiring is used to connect all of these transistors of the CPU to the motherboard.

The general trend in computing is toward smaller, faster, and cheaper devices. But for how long can this trend continue? In the 1970s, Dr. Gordon Moore, then a researcher at Intel, hypothesized that computer processing performance would double every 18 months. When Moore made this bold prediction, he did not limit it to any specified period of time. This prediction became known as ***Moore's Law***. Interestingly, Dr. Moore has been basically correct so far. Feature size—the size of lines on the chip through which signals pass—has been reduced from about the width of a human hair (20 microns—a micron is equal to one millionth of a metre) in the 1960s to the size of a bacterium in the 1970s (5 microns), to smaller than a virus (.13 micron—the feature size on an Intel Pentium 4) today.

As feature size is reduced, a greater number and variety of circuits can be packed increasingly closer together. Both feature density and complexity has facilitated the continued performance increases that microprocessors have realized. Figure A.12 shows this trend. For more on Moore's Law, visit Intel's Website (**www.intel.com/research/silicon/mooreslaw.htm**) or search on the Web using the phrase "Moore's Law," and you will get numerous interesting pages to review.

The number of transistors that can be packed into a modern CPU and the speed at which processing and other activities occur are remarkable. For example, the Intel Pentium 4 can complete hundreds of millions of operations every second. To achieve these incredible speeds, the CPU must execute instructions very rapidly. In addition to the number of transistors on the CPU, three other factors greatly influence its speed—its system clock speed, registers, and cache memory—and these are described next.

[Figure A.11 ➥ The Intel Pentium 4 microprocessor contains more than 42 million transistors.]

Source: © Intel Corporation.

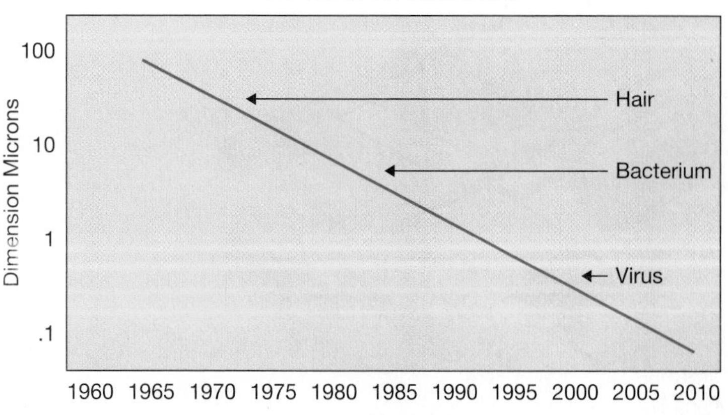

[**Figure A.12** ➡ Moore's Law predicted that computer processing performance would double every 18 months. To increase performance, feature size has had to shrink.]

Clock speed Within the computer, an electronic circuit generates pulses at a rapid rate, setting the pace for processing events to take place, rather like a metronome marks time for a musician. This circuit is called the ***system clock***. A single pulse is a ***clock tick***, and in microcomputers the processor's ***clock speed*** is measured in hertz (Hz). One MHz is one million clock ticks, or instruction cycles, per second. Microprocessor speeds are measured in different units, depending upon the type of computer. Personal computer speeds are most often measured in GHz (gigahertz, or one billion hertz). Microprocessor speeds improve so quickly that faster chips are on the market about every six months. Today, most new PCs operate at faster than 3 GHz. To give you an idea of how things have changed, the original IBM PC had a clock speed of 4.77 MHz.

See Table A.6 for a description of computer speeds. It takes a permanent storage device such as a hard disk (described below) about 10 milliseconds to access information. Within a CPU, however, a single transistor can be changed from a 0 to a 1 in about 10 picoseconds (one trillionth of a second). Changes inside the CPU occur about one billion times faster than they do in a fixed disk because the CPU operates only on electronic impulses, whereas the fixed disks perform both electronic and mechanical activities, such as spinning the disk and moving the read/write head (described below). Mechanical activities are extremely slow relative to electronic activities.

Registers Within the CPU itself, there are ***registers*** that provide temporary storage locations where data must reside while it is being processed or manipulated. For example, if two numbers are to be added together, both must reside in registers, with the result placed in a register. Consequently, one factor influencing the speed and power of a CPU is the number and size of the registers.

Cache memory A ***cache*** (pronounced "cash") is a small block of memory used by processors to store those instructions most recently or most often used. Just as you might keep file folders you use most in a handy location on your desktop, cache memory is located within or close to the CPU. Thanks to cache memory, before performing an operation the processor does not have to go directly to main memory, which is farther from the microprocessor and takes longer to reach. Instead, it can check first to see if needed data is contained in the cache. Cache memory is another way computer engineers have increased processing speed.

[Table A.6] ***Elements of computer time.***

Name	Fraction of a Second	Description	Example
Millisecond	1/1000	One thousandth of a second	Fixed disks access information in about 10–20 milliseconds.
Microsecond	1/1,000,000	One millionth of a second	A 2 GHz CPU executes approximately two billion operations in a second—or about 2000 operations every microsecond.
Nanosecond	1/1,000,000,000	One billionth of a second	Most types of RAM used in PCs have access times (the time needed to read information from the RAM to the CPU) of from 5–70 nanoseconds (lower is better). Most cache memory has access times of less than 20 nanoseconds.
Picosecond	1/1,000,000,000,000	One trillionth of a second	Inside a CPU, the time it takes to switch a circuit from one state to another is in the range of 5–20 picoseconds.

Cache may be located inside the microprocessor—similar to registers—or outside of, but close to, the microprocessor. Special high-speed cache memory, called ***internal cache***, is incorporated into the microprocessor's design. ***External or secondary cache*** is usually not built into the CPU, but is located within easy reach of the CPU on the motherboard. The more cache available to a CPU, the better the overall system performs because more information is readily available.

The CPU translates input into binary data and binary data into information that can be understood by humans. To be used by the CPU, data must be stored either temporarily or permanently. We describe this next.

Primary Storage

Primary storage is for current information. Computers need temporary storage space for current calculations, and this type of memory, measured in bytes, provides it. In addition to registers and cache, described above, examples of primary storage are random access memory (RAM) and read-only memory (ROM). RAM and ROM are made up of chips containing thousands of electronic circuits etched on silicon wafers. These memory chips are monolithic. That is, all the circuits found on one chip make up one inseparable unit of storage. Each circuit or switch is either conducting an electrical current (on) or not conducting an electrical current (off).

Random Access Memory (RAM)

Random access memory (RAM) is the computer's main or ***primary memory***. It consists of several chips mounted on a small circuit board called a ***single in-line memory module (SIMM)*** that plugs into the motherboard (see Figure A.13). RAM stores the programs and data currently in use. Random access memory is so named because data stored here can easily and quickly be accessed randomly by the CPU. RAM provides temporary storage of data for the CPU; because information is stored temporarily, it is referred to as ***volatile***. That is, instructions and work stored in RAM are lost when the power to the computer is turned off or when new data is placed there. So if you have been working at your computer for hours on a research paper, do not trip over the power cord or otherwise accidentally turn off the power! If you do, unless you have saved your work in progress to your computer's hard disk or to a diskette (secondary storage), you will lose all your diligent work.

For the most efficient and speedy processing, the more RAM a computer has, the better. Today, the amount of RAM in most microcomputers is measured in megabytes. When this book went to print, most PC users considered 256 MB of RAM essential to run available software, and many routinely opted for 1 GB of RAM or more! Tomorrow's PC users will undoubtedly have some number of gigabytes, or even terabytes, of RAM as an option.

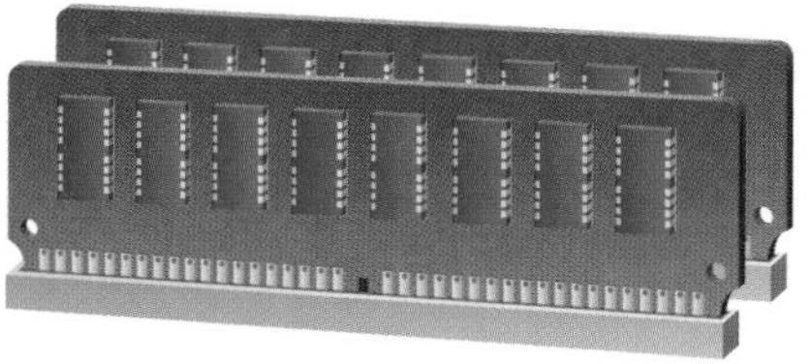

[**Figure A.13** ➡ Random access memory (RAM) consists of several chips mounted on a small circuit board called a SIMM.]

Source: Beekman, *Computer Confluence*, 5e, Prentice Hall, 2003.

Read-Only Memory (ROM)

Read-only memory (ROM) exists as a chip on the motherboard that can be read from but cannot be written to. That is, the CPU can read the information stored in ROM, but the computer user cannot change it. ROM is nonvolatile, which means that it does not lose its instructions when the power to the computer is shut off. ROM stores programs as instructions that are automatically loaded when the computer is turned on, such as the basic input/output system (BIOS). The amount of ROM in most computers is tiny compared to the amount of RAM.

A variation of ROM is erasable ROM, referred to as EEPROM (electrically erasable programmable read-only memory). You may have heard of EEPROM referred to by a more user-friendly term, ***flash memory***. This type of memory can be repeatedly written to and erased like RAM, but, unlike RAM, it retains its information after power is turned off. Flash memory comes in a variety of forms, and is the storage technology behind many popular consumer devices like digital cameras and MP3 players.

Secondary Storage

Secondary, nonvolatile storage is for permanently storing data to a large-capacity storage component, such as a hard disk, diskette, CD-ROM disk, or tape (see Table A.7). Nonvolatile means that data is not lost from secondary storage when the computer's power is shut off. Hard disks and diskettes are magnetic media. That is, diskettes and the disks inside a hard disk drive are coated with a magnetic material. Reading data from the disks involves converting magnetized data to electrical impulses that can be understood by the processor. Writing to the disks is the reverse—converting electrical impulses to magnetized spots representing data.

Hard disk drives, diskette drives, and tapes are secondary storage devices with ***read/write heads*** that inscribe data to or retrieve data from hard disks, diskettes, and tapes. Hard disk, diskette, and tape drives are usually installed internally, but may

[Table A.7] *Comparing methods of secondary storage.*

Type	Speed	Method of Data Access	Relative Cost/MB
Magnetic tape	Slow	Sequential	Low
Floppy disks	Slow	Direct	Low
Fixed disks	Fast	Direct	High
Compact discs	Medium	Direct	Medium
Optical disks	Fast	Direct	Medium

be externally located and attached via cables to ports on the back of the system unit. Diskettes and tapes are removable secondary storage media. That is, they must be inserted into the appropriate drive (or tape reader) to be read from or written to, and are removed when these tasks are accomplished.

Hard Drives

Most of the software run on a computer, including the operating system, is stored on the ***hard drive*** or ***hard disk***. The hard drive is a peripheral device usually located inside the system unit of a computer. It writes data and programs to a fixed disk. The storage capacity of the hard drives for today's microcomputers is measured in gigabytes (GB), or billions of bytes. It is not unusual for PCs currently on the market to come equipped with hard drives with 80 GB to 160 GB storage capacities. Modern supercomputers can have millions of gigabytes of storage. Most microcomputers have one hard drive, but additional drives can usually be added, either internally or externally. To make sure critical data is not lost, some computers employ ***RAID (redundant array of independent disks)*** technology to store redundant copies of data on two or more hard drives. RAID is not typically used on an individual's computer, but is very common for Web servers and many business applications.

Hard drives consist of several disks, or platters, stacked on top of one another so that they do not touch (see Figure A.14). Each disk within a disk pack has an access arm with two read/write heads—one positioned close to the top surface of the disk and another positioned close to the bottom surface of the disk. (Both surfaces of each disk are used for data storage, usually with the exception of the top surface of the top disk and the bottom surface of the bottom disk.) The read/write heads do not actually touch either surface of the disks. In fact, a ***head crash*** occurs if the read/write head for some reason touches the disk. When this happens, data is lost.

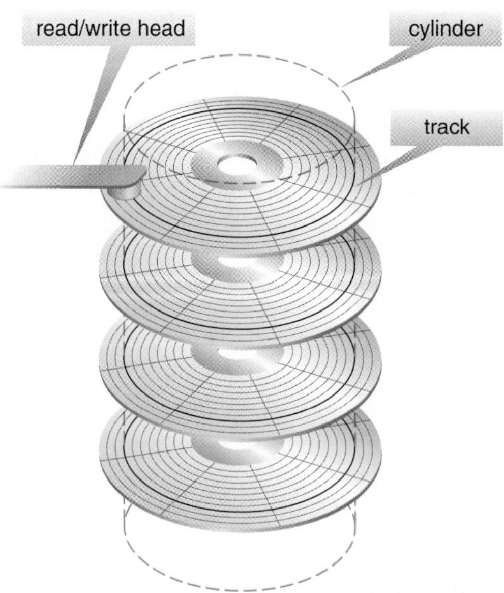

[Figure A.14 ➥ A hard drive consists of several disks that are stacked on top of one another and read/write heads to read and write information.]

Source: Pfaffenberger, CIYF Brief 2003, Prentice Hall, 2003.

The disks inside the hard drive rotate as data is written to or read from them.

Diskette Drives and Diskettes

Many personal computers also contain diskette drives. They are separate from the hard drive, and the port for inserting diskettes is located on the outside of the system unit.

Diskettes (also called floppy disks) are $3\frac{1}{2}$-inch, round, flexible Mylar devices that record data as magnetized spots on tracks on the disk surface (see Figure A.15). The actual diskette is enclosed in a nonflexible plastic jacket that fits into the diskette drive on the computer so the diskette can be read or written to. Diskettes are small enough to be easily carried home in a purse or a pocket and can be used by more than one computer. The disadvantage to using diskettes for storage is that they may not have sufficient capacity to store large amounts of data. Typically, one diskette can store 1.4 MB of data, although higher-capacity diskettes are available. For this reason, many new systems, particularly note-

[Figure A.15 ➥ Diskettes provide low-capacity storage.]

book computers, are being shipped without diskette drives.

In addition to the standard internal hard disk, some microcomputers may also have a ***Zip® drive***, which is a high-capacity, removable diskette drive that uses 100 MB or 250 MB Zip disks or cartridges. Zip® drives offer computer users easy-to-use additional data storage that is handy for backing up information and sharing stored data with other computers.

Optical Disk Storage

Optical disks, or those using laser beam technology, have become popular as storage requirements have increased. An ***optical disk***, coated with a metallic substance, is written to when a laser beam passing over the surface of the disk burns small spots into the disk surface, each one representing a data package. The data can be read when a laser scans the surface of the disk and a lens picks up various light reflections from the data spots. Some optical disks are read-only. That is, information is entered on them by a manufacturer and cannot be changed by the computer user. Nor can new information be written to the disk by the computer user. One advantage to using optical disks for storage is that they can hold much more information than diskettes: One optical disk can record the information from hundreds of diskettes. Optical disks have made possible the huge growth in multimedia software applications for PCs.

CD-ROM Disks

The most popular type of optical disk storage is the ***CD-ROM (compact disc–read-only memory)***. A CD-ROM drive is now standard equipment with most computer systems. As the name implies, CD-ROM disks can only be read; they cannot be written to. Since the typical CD-ROM disk can store up to 660 MB, which is equal to about 400 diskettes, they can easily hold entire encyclopedias, plus audio and video clips, and more (see Figure A.16).

CD-R and CD-RW

A type of optical disk that data can be written to is the ***CD-R (compact disc–recordable)*** disk. Using these disks requires special software and a CD-R disk drive, distinct from a CD-ROM drive. Once written to, however, CD-R disks can be read by any CD-ROM drive.

One of the problems with a CD-R disk is that information can only be written onto it once. A ***CD-RW*** disk (RW stands for rewritable) allows the disk to be written onto multiple times. Most new computers come with a CD-RW drive so that users can store and back up large amounts of information on a reusable disk.

DVD-ROM

Currently, ***digital video disks (DVD-ROM)*** have more storage space than CD-ROM disks, because DVD-ROM drives use a shorter-wavelength laser beam, which allows more optical pits to be deposited on the disk. Single-layered disks hold about 4.7 GB of information, and double-layered disks increase storage capacity to 8.5 GB. The huge storage capacity of DVD-ROM disks makes them ideal for movie-quality videos with state-of-the-art sound. Experts predict that the DVD will eventually replace the CD-ROM because of its increased storage capacity. Recordable and rewritable DVD systems are now standard on many new computers.

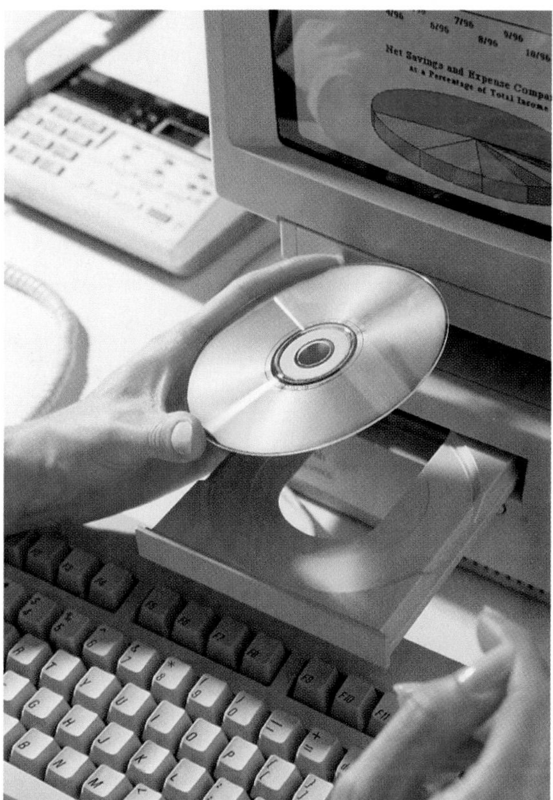

[**Figure A.16** ➥ CD-ROM is a popular storage method because it is inexpensive, is reliable, and provides abundant storage capacity.]

Source: © Corbis/Stock Market.

Tapes

Magnetic tapes used for storage of computer information consist of narrow plastic tape coated with a magnetic substance. Storage tapes range from one-half-inch–wide wound on a reel, to one-fourth-inch–wide, wound into a plastic cassette that looks much like a music cassette tape. Like on other forms of magnetic storage, data are stored in tiny magnetic spots. Storage capacity of tape is expressed as ***density***, which equals the number of ***characters per inch (CPI)*** or ***bytes per inch (BPI)*** that can be stored on the tape. Mainframe computers use tape drives called stackers that wind tape from a supply reel to a take-up reel as data are read.

Magnetic tape is still used for storing large amounts of computer information, but it is gradually being replaced by high-capacity disk storage, since disk storage is equally reliable. In fact, information stored on disks is easier to locate, because computers must scan an entire tape to find a specific data file.

Now that you understand how information is input into a computer and how it is processed, we can turn our attention to the third category of hardware—output technologies.

Output Devices

After information is input and processed, it must be presented to the user. Computers can display information on a screen, print it, or emit sound. The sections that follow discuss details about how each of these output devices operates.

Video Output

Monitors are used to display information from a computer. They consist of a cathode ray tube (CRT), which is similar to a television, but with much higher resolution. Monitors can be colour, black and white, or monochrome (meaning all one colour, usually green or amber). Notebooks and other portable computers use ***liquid crystal display (LCD)*** or plasma screens because a CRT is too bulky for a portable device, which needs a thin, lightweight monitor. The research and development of monitor technologies focuses on creating lightweight, low-cost, high-resolution devices. Because display monitors are embedded into a broad range of products and devices, such as automobiles, to display global positioning, route maps, and other relevant information, they must be sturdy, reliable, lightweight, and low in cost (see Figure A.17).

Printers and Plotters

Information can be printed in several different ways, as shown in Figure A.18. A plotter (Figure A.18a) is used for transferring engineering designs from the computer to drafting paper, which is often as big as 86 × 110 cm. The plotter uses several pens as it draws each of the lines individually. ***Dot matrix printers*** (Figure A.18b) are older, electric typewriter–based technology for printing information on paper. Letters are formed using a series of small dots. Once the most commonly used type of printer, dot matrix printers are now mostly found printing voluminous batch information, such as periodic reports and forms. ***Inkjet printers*** use a small cartridge to transfer ink onto paper. This process creates a typewriter-like image that can initially smear because the ink is wet when it is sprayed onto the paper. Inkjet printers (Figure A.18c) can be designed to print both black and white and colour. ***Laser printers*** use an electrostatic process to force ink onto the paper, literally "burning" the image onto the paper. The resulting high quality is considered necessary for almost all business letters and documents. Laser printers (Figure A.18d) can also produce colour images, but high-end colour laser printers can cost thousands of dollars.

Audio Output

In addition to transmitting text as output, a computer can also transmit audio as output. With the use of small specialized speakers and a ***sound card,*** a computer can produce high-quality sound. The computer translates digits into sound by sending data to a sound card that interprets these data into tones. The tones are then sent to the speakers for output. Musicians and composers often use this output to

(a)

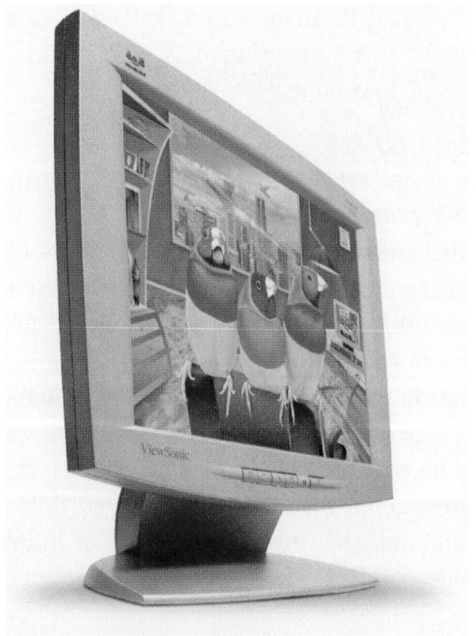

(b)

[**Figure A.17** ➥ Monitors display information from a computer: a CRT-type display (a) and an LCD-type display (b).]

Source: Courtesy of ViewSonic Corporation.

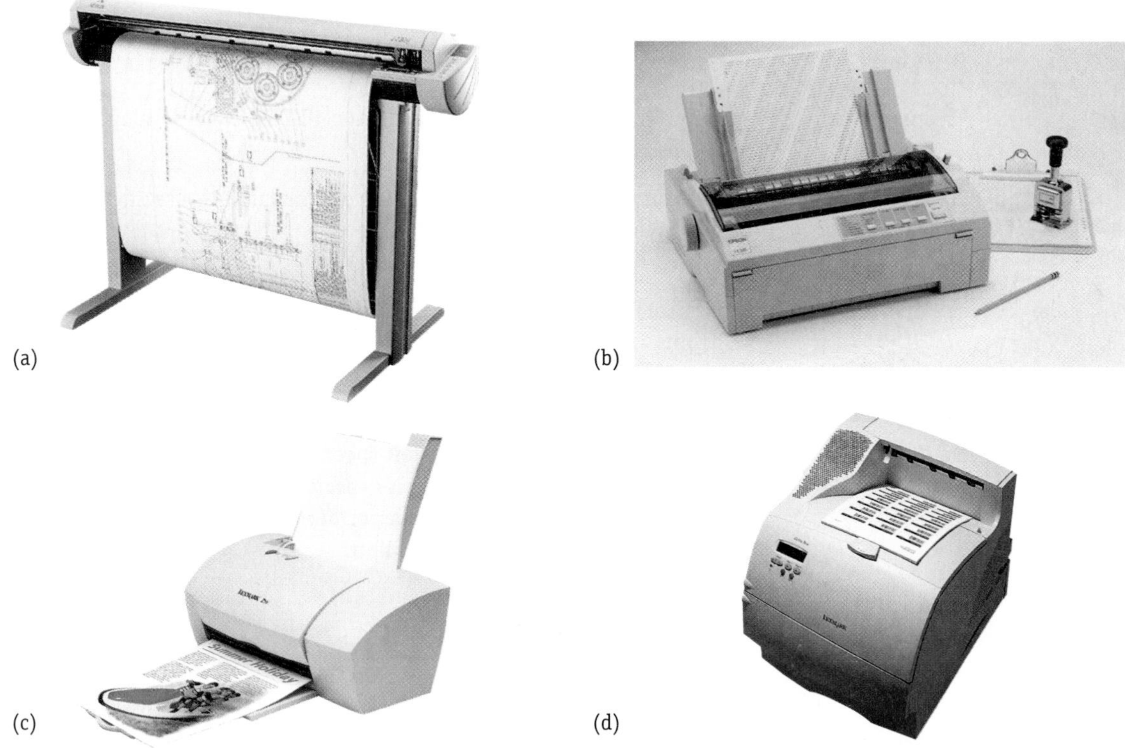

(a) (b) (c) (d)

[Figure A.18 ➥ A plotter (a), a dot matrix printer (b), an inkjet printer (c), and a laser printer (d).]

Sources: [A.18a] Courtesy of Xerox Corporation. [A.18b] Courtesy of Epson, America, Inc. [A.18c] Lexmark International, Inc. [A.18d] Lexmark International, Inc.

simulate a full orchestra when working on new or unfamiliar pieces of music.

Now that you understand how computer hardware works, we can discuss the types of computers that people and organizations typically use.

TYPES OF COMPUTERS

Over the last 60 years, information systems hardware has gone through many radical changes. In the 1940s, almost all business and government information systems consisted of file folders, filing cabinets, and document repositories. Huge rooms were dedicated to the storage of these records. Information was often difficult to find, and corporate knowledge and history were difficult to maintain. Only certain employees knew specific information. If or when these employees left the firm, so did all their corporate knowledge. The computer provided the solution to the information storage and retrieval problems facing organizations of the 1940s. Shifts in computing eras were facilitated by fundamental changes in the way computing technologies worked. Each of these fundamental changes is referred to as a distinct generation of computing. Table A.8 highlights the technology that defined the four generations of computing. We conclude by briefly describing the five general types of computers currently being used in organizations (see Table A.9).

Supercomputers

The most powerful and expensive computers that exist today are called ***supercomputers***. Supercomputers are often used for scientific applications, solving massive computational problems that require large amounts of data. They can cost many millions of dollars. For example, Sandia National Laboratories uses a supercomputer to model the physics of nuclear explosions. This particular machine has several gigabytes of RAM and the computational horsepower of more than 9,000 Pentium processors. Pharmaceutical companies, such as Eli Lilly and Dow Chemical, use supercomputers to design and evaluate new combinations of chemical elements in order to quickly identify promising prescription drugs and treatments. IBM's "Blue Pacific" supercomputer operates 15,000 times faster than an average personal computer, with more than 5,800 processors and 2.6 trillion bytes of memory. To achieve this incredible speed, supercomputers are equipped with numerous fast processors that work in parallel to execute several instructions simultaneously. An extensive staff is usually required to operate and maintain supercomputers and to support the researchers and scientists using them. Supercomputers often run only one application at a time in order to dedicate all processing capabilities to a single massive application. Figure A.19 shows a Cray supercomputer, one

[Table A.8] ***Generations of computing (Freed, 1995).***

Generation	Defining Event	Computing Era	Major Characteristics/Events
1 (1946–1958)	Vacuum tubes	Mainframe era begins	ENIAC and UNIVAC were developed
2 (1958–1964)	Transistors	Mainframe era continues	UNIVAC was updated to use transistors
3 (1964–1990s)	Integrated circuits	Mainframe era ends; minicomputer era begins and ends; personal computer era begins	IBM 360—integrated circuits and general-purpose operating system; microprocessor revolution: Intel, Apple Macintosh, IBM PC, MS-DOS
4 (1990s–present)	Multimedia	Personal computer era ends; interpersonal computing era begins; internetworking era begins	High-speed microprocessor and networks; high-capacity secondary storage; low cost, high performance integrating video, audio, and data

Source: L. Freed, *The History of Computing* (Emeryville, CA: Ziff-Davis Press, 1995).

of the more popular computers in this class. In addition to Cray and IBM, Hitachi, NEC, and Fujitsu are leading producers of supercomputers.

Mainframes

The backbone of large corporate computing has historically been large, high-powered computers called ***mainframes***. These machines can be the size of a large refrigerator (and even larger), and they often cost several million dollars to purchase. Organizations normally use mainframe computers for processing large amounts of business data, and the machines are designed to support hundreds, or even thousands, of users simultaneously. In addition to businesses, many federal and provincial governments use mainframe computers to manage the massive amount of data generated by day-to-day governmental activities. Federal agencies, such as the Canada Revenue Agency (CRA), have several mainframe computers to handle the massive databases related to individual and corporate payroll and tax information. Large corporations, such as Avis, Air Canada, and Fairmont

[Table A.9] ***Characteristics of computers currently being used in organizations.***

Type of Computer	Number of Simultaneous Users	Physical Size	Typical Use	Memory	Typical Cost Range
Supercomputer	1–several	Like an automobile	Scientific research	2,000+ GB	$1,000,000 to more than $20,000,000
Mainframe	1000+	Like a refrigerator	Large general-purpose business and government	Up to 100+ GB	$1,000,000 to more than $10,000,000
Midrange	4–200	Like a file cabinet	Midsize general-purpose business	Up to 10 GB	$10,000 to more than $100,000
Workstation	1	Fits on a desktop	Engineering design	512 to 2,048 MB	$5,000 to more than $50,000
Microcomputer	1	Handheld to fitting on a desktop	Personal productivity	256 to 1024 MB	$500 to more than $5,000

[Figure A.19 ➥ The Cray supercomputer.]

Source: Cray, Inc.

[Figure A.20 IBM mainframe computer.]

Source: Courtesy of IBM Corporate Archives.

Hotels, use mainframes to perform repetitive tasks, such as processing reservations. Unisys and IBM are the largest producers of mainframes (see Figure A.20).

Midrange Computers

Midrange computers, often referred to as minicomputers, are scaled-down versions of mainframes that were created for companies that did not have the budgets for mainframes and did not need that amount of computing power. In the past few years, the distinction between large midrange computers and small mainframes has blurred in both performance and price. Nonetheless, midrange computers have become integral to many smaller and midsized organizations and typically cost tens to hundreds of thousands of dollars, supporting from four to 200 users simultaneously. As with mainframes, IBM is a leader in the midrange computer market, with its AS/400 model. Manufacturers such as Hewlett-Packard and Dell also service this market. Previously in decline, the midrange market has seen an upsurge as firms have adopted servers to manage and disseminate information.

Workstations

Workstations are a special class of microcomputer (as in your PC) designed for individuals. Many have the power of some midrange computers, but they fit on a desktop. Computer hardware companies such as Silicon Graphics, Sun Microsystems, and Hewlett-Packard are leaders in this market. Workstations have an extremely fast CPU (or multiple CPUs), large capacities of RAM and secondary storage, and high-quality video displays, and cost between $5,000 and $50,000. Figure A.21 shows a Sun Sparcstation, one of the more popular computers in this class. Workstations are often used by engineers to design new products using processing-intensive applications, such as computer-aided design (CAD); by financial analysts modelling stock market fluctuations; and by researchers working with large, complex, computationally intensive applications. For example, researchers at NASA are using workstations to study the effects of global warming on ocean surface temperatures.

Microcomputers

Microcomputers, also referred to as ***personal computers (PCs)***, fit on desktops, generally cost between $1,000 and $5,000, and are used in homes and offices

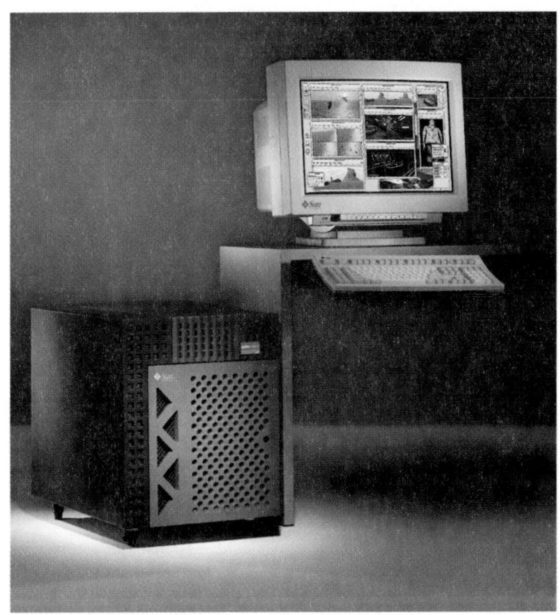

[Figure A.21 ➥ A Sun workstation is typically used by engineers.]

Source: © Getty Images, Inc.

(see Figure A.22). Microcomputers can be relatively stationary desktop models or portable, notebook-sized computers that weigh about 2.5 kg (5 lb.) or less. High-end microcomputers can cost more than $5,000 and rival the power and speed of low-end workstations. High-end microcomputers are often used as network and Web servers that manage shared resources such as printers or large databases, or deliver content over the Internet. In the last few years, the popularity of microcomputers has exploded. Within organizations, microcomputers are the most commonly used computing technology for knowledge workers and have become as commonplace as the telephone. In fact, more microcomputers than televisions are now sold in Canada each year. Let us delve a bit deeper into the development of microcomputers.

Network Computers

A ***network computer*** is a microcomputer with minimal memory and storage designed to connect to networks, especially the Internet, to use the resources provided by servers. The concept of network computing is to reduce the obsolescence and maintenance of personal computers by allowing inexpensive machines to access servers that deploy resources—software programs, printers, and so on—to all machines on the network. Many feel that network computing is the wave of the future because the machines are less expensive than typical PCs and because they can be administered and updated from a central network server. Despite this optimism, sales of network computers have largely fallen short of expectations. Oracle and Sun Microsystems are two companies aggressively pushing the network-computing concept (see Figure A.23).

Portable Computers

When computers appeared that could fit on a desktop, users considered them the ultimate in lighter, smaller, handier machines. Then came laptop computers you could carry, but the first models were heavy and bulky. Next on the portable computer scene were notebook computers that could fit in a backpack or briefcase. Today battery-powered laptop and notebook computers are popular both for business and personal use (see Table A.10 for a summary of trade-offs between desktop and portable computers). The computers are equipped with a flat display panel, fold into a small, convenient carry case, and can weigh as little as 2.5 kg or less. With a portable computer, you can use a keyboard and a mouse as well as a trackball, touch pad, or other built-in pointing device. Most portable computers come equipped with internal modems and USB ports and can connect to printers, scanners, or other peripherals. Many students, employees, and others now use a portable computer as their only PC, rather than buying both a desktop and a portable machine. The two most popular forms of portable computers—notebooks and handhelds—are described below.

Notebook computers Mobile computers once weighed 9 kg (20 lb.) and were portable only in the sense that they could be moved—with difficulty—from one location to another. A few years ago, machines evolved to what was referred to as a *laptop,* which weighed around 4.5 kg (10 lb.), and could be folded up and carried like a briefcase. The trend has been toward smaller, lighter, yet ever more powerful ***notebook computers*** that weigh 2.5 kg (5 lb.) or less and can be easily carried in a briefcase or backpack (see Figure A.24).

Handheld computers The first handheld computers were introduced around 1994, but they failed to live up to expectations, perhaps because consumers had expected that they would replace PCs. Then, in 1996, Palm introduced a handheld computer that was never intended to replace the PC but performed some essential computing tasks so well that users

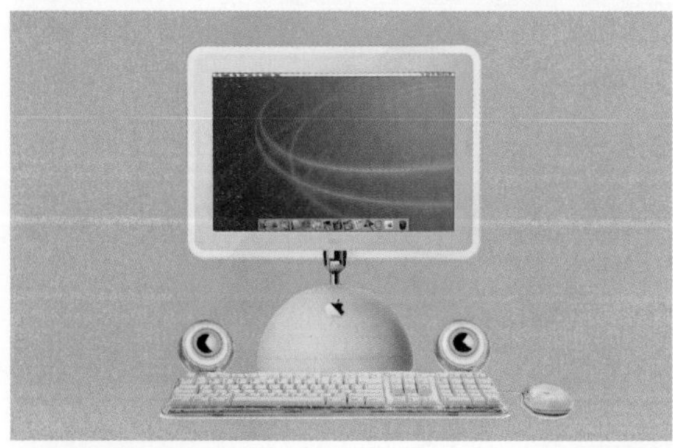

[**Figure A.22** ➥ A personal computer.]

Source: Apple Computer, Inc.

[**Figure A.23** ➥ A Sun Microsystems network computer.]

Source: Sun Microsystems.

[Table A.10] ***Trade-offs between desktop and portable computers.***

Desktop Computer	Portable Computer
One location for use	Mobile—any location for use
Lower price	Higher price
Expandable	Very limited expandability
Better ergonomics—full size/high-resolution color screen, large key-board, and so on	Cramped ergonomics—small screen, limited colour quality, small keyboard, awkward pointing device, and so on
Relatively easy to service/repair	Hard to service/repair

[Figure A.24 ➡ Notebook computers are very portable and typically weigh less than 3 kilograms.]

Sources: [A.24a] Courtesy of Dell Computer Corporation, [A.24b] Courtesy of Sony Electronics, [A.24c] Courtesy IBM Corporation.

could often leave their laptop and notebook computers at home. Since then, billed first as information appliances, then as ***personal digital assistants (PDAs)***, handheld computers have filled a niche in the portable computer market. Today, the capabilities of many PDAs are beginning to rival the functionality of desktop PCs. For example, Compaq's "Pocket PC," which runs using Microsoft's CE operating system, allows users to send and receive e-mail, work on documents and spreadsheets, surf the Web, and perform countless other activities (see Figure A.25).

As you can see, things have really evolved since the early mainframe days. In most organizations today, IS encompasses a diverse range of computing technologies, from supercomputers, mainframes, and midrange computers to workstations, personal computers, and personal digital assistants. For individuals, computers have become commonplace, with many families having several computers. Using history as a guide, it is a good bet that computing hardware will continue to evolve at a rapid pace, with intended and unforeseen consequences for all of us.

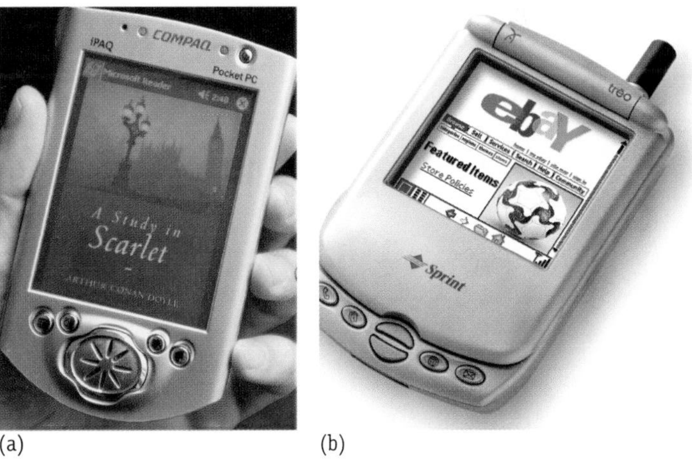

[Figure A.25 ➡ Personal digital assistants allow you to have a very powerful computer in the palm of your hand.]

Sources: [A.25a] © AP/Wide World Photos [A.25b] Courtesy of Handspring, Inc.

KEY POINTS REVIEW

1. **Describe key elements of information systems hardware.** Information systems hardware is classified into three types: input, processing, and output technologies. Input hardware consists of devices used to enter information into a computer. Processing hardware transforms inputs into outputs. The central processing unit (CPU) is the device that performs this transformation with the help of several other closely related devices that store and recall information. Finally, output-related hardware focuses on delivering information in a usable format to users.

2. **List and describe the types of computers that are being used in organizations today.** Computers come in all shapes, sizes, degrees of power, and prices. The five general classes of computers are supercomputer, mainframe, midrange, workstation, and microcomputer. A supercomputer is the most expensive and most powerful kind of computer; it is primarily used to assist in solving massive research and scientific problems. A mainframe is a very large computer that is the main, central computing system for major corporations and governmental

agencies. A midrange computer offers lower performance than mainframes but higher performance than microcomputers. Minicomputers are typically used for engineering and midsized business applications. A workstation is a very high-performance microcomputer, typically used to support individual engineers and analysts in solving highly computational problems. A microcomputer is used for personal computing, small business computing, and as a workstation attached to large computers or to other small computers on a network.

KEY TERMS

arithmetic logic unit (ALU) 326
ASCII (American Standard Code for Information Interchange) 325
audio 321
batch input 320
binary code 324
bits 324
byte 324
bytes per inch (BPI) 331
cache 328
CD-R (compact disc—recordable) 331
CD-ROM (compact disc—read-only memory) 331
CD-RW (compact disc—rewritable) 331
central processing unit (CPU) 319, 326
characters per inch (CPI) 331
clock speed 328
clock tick 328
control unit 326
density 331
diskette 330
dot matrix printer 332
DVD-ROM (digital video disk—read-only memory) 331
EBCDIC (Extended Binary-Coded Decimal Interchange Code) 325
ergonomics 320
external or secondary cache 329
flash memory 329
hard drive or hard disk 330
head crash 330
inkjet printer 332
input devices 319
internal cache 329
keyboard 319
laser printer 332
liquid crystal display (LCD) 332
machine language 324
magnetic tape 331
mainframe computer 334
microcomputer 335
midrange computer 335
monitors 332
Moore's Law 327
motherboard 326
musical instrument digital interface (MIDI) 322
network computer 336
notebook computer 336
optical disk 331
output devices 319
personal computer (PC) 335
personal digital assistant (PDA) 337
pointing devices 320
power supply 326
primary memory 329
primary storage 329
processing devices 319
RAID (redundant array of independent disks) 330
random access memory (RAM) 329
read-only memory (ROM) 329
read/write heads 329
registers 326, 328
scanners 320
secondary, nonvolatile storage 329
single in-line memory module (SIMM) 329
smart card 320
sound card 332
speech recognition 322
streaming media 323
streaming video 323
supercomputer 333
system clock 328
system unit 326
text recognition software 320
Unicode 325
video 321
volatile 329
workstation 335
Zip drive 331

REVIEW QUESTIONS

1. Information systems hardware is classified into what three major types?
2. Describe various methods for entering data into and interacting with a computer.
3. Define ergonomics, and give examples of how repetitive stress injuries could be reduced.
4. How do computers represent internal information, and how is this different from the ways in which humans typically communicate information to each other?

5. Describe the system unit and its key components.
6. What determines the speed of a CPU?
7. How do a computer's primary storage, secondary storage, ROM, and RAM interact?
8. Compare and contrast the different types of secondary data storage.
9. What are output devices? Describe various methods for providing computer output.
10. Describe the different types of computers and their key distinguishing characteristics.

SELF-STUDY QUESTIONS

Answers are at the end of the Problems and Exercises.

1. A system unit contains all of the following **except** _______.
   A. CD-ROM
   B. central processing unit
   C. power supply
   D. monitor
2. Which of the following is **not** an input device?
   A. touch pad
   B. touch screen
   C. sound board
   D. light pen
3. Which of the following is an example of hardware?
   A. an operating system
   B. Microsoft Suite
   C. system software
   D. central processing unit
4. Which of the following is an output device?
   A. laser printer
   B. touch screen
   C. video camera
   D. keyboard
5. Which of the following could be ergonomically designed?
   A. keyboard
   B. chair
   C. monitor
   D. all of the above
6. _______ can convert handwritten text into computer-based characters.
   A. Scanners
   B. Bar-code/optical character readers
   C. Text recognition software
   D. Audio video
7. A _______ card is a special credit card with a microprocessor chip and memory circuits.
   A. smart
   B. master
   C. universal
   D. proprietary
8. Which of the following has the largest storage, along with video capacity?
   A. CD-ROM
   B. floppy disk
   C. DVD-ROM
   D. cache memory
9. Which of the following type of computer is used for personal and small business usage?
   A. supercomputer
   B. microcomputer
   C. workstation
   D. mainframe
10. A _______ is the most powerful and expensive computer today.
   A. HAL
   B. mainframe
   C. personal digital assistant
   D. supercomputer

PROBLEMS AND EXERCISES

1. Match the following terms with the appropriate definitions:

____ Cache memory	____ DVD-ROM
____ Batch input	____ Motherboard
____ Smart card	____ Streaming video
____ Ergonomics	____ Network computer
____ Audio	____ Flash memory

   a. A special type of credit card with a magnetic strip that includes a microprocessor chip and memory circuits
   b. A small block of memory used by the central processor to store those instructions most recently or most often used
   c. An optical storage device that has more storage space than a diskette or CD-ROM disk and uses a shorter-wavelength laser beam, which allows more optical pits to be deposited on the disk
   d. A sequence of moving images, sent in a compressed form over the Internet and displayed on the receiver's screen as the images arrive
   e. The design of computer hardware and work environments that minimize health risks such as repetitive stress injuries
   f. A large printed plastic or fibreglass circuit board that contains all of the components that do the actual

processing work of the computer, and holds or connects to all of the computer's electronic components

g. A type of input for large amounts of routine information

h. A microcomputer with minimal memory and storage designed to connect to networks to use the resources provided by servers

i. Memory that can be repeatedly written to and erased like RAM, but unlike RAM it retains its information after power is turned off

j. Sound that has been digitized for storage and replay on the computer

2. Imagine that you have decided it is time to purchase a new computer. Analyze your purchase options with regard to using this computer for personal productivity versus business productivity. What differences might your potential usage make on your hardware choices? Why?

3. Imagine that you have just informed your supervisor that you will need to purchase new computers for yourself and three fellow employees. Your supervisor states that she has heard in the news that computer prices are dropping constantly, and she feels that you should wait a bit before making this purchase. She adds that you can still be 100-percent effective with your current computer and software. Develop a counterargument explaining why you should make the purchase now instead of waiting. Will this be a hard sell? Why or why not?

4. Go visit a computer shop or look on the Web for mice or touch pads. What is new about how these input devices look or how they are used? What are some of the advantages and disadvantages of each device?

5. What types of printers are most common today? What is the cost of a colour printer versus a black and white one? Compare and contrast laser and inkjet printers in terms of speed, cost, and quality output. What kind of printer would you buy or have you bought?

6. What happens when a computer runs out of RAM? Can more RAM be added? Is there a limit? How does cache memory relate to RAM? Why is RAM so important in today's modern information systems world? Search the Web for RAM retailers. Compare their prices and options.

7. Do you feel that floppy disks are obsolete? Why or why not? What storage and retrieval options are available in addition to CD-ROMs and floppy disks? What are you currently using, and what would you like to purchase?

8. Back in the 1970s, rockets were sent to the moon with the amount of computing power found in today's microcomputers. Now, these microcomputers seem to be outdating themselves every two years. Will this era of continuous improvement end? Why or why not? If so, when?

9. Do you have a Palm handheld or some other type of PDA (personal digital assistant), or know of someone who does? What functions do PDAs offer? Look on the Web or go to the mall to shop for one. Are the prices decreasing? At what point do you plan to purchase one?

10. Interview an IS manager within an organization that you are familiar with. Determine what issues played a role in the latest information systems hardware purchase this person made. Other than budget, what issues do you think should be considered?

11. Based on your experiences with different input devices, which do you like the best and least? Why? Are your preferences due to the devices' design or usability, or are they based on the integration of the device with the entire information system?

12. Visit a company that utilizes several different types of computers. Which types do they use? What categories of computers are used at this company (e.g., workstations)? Does the company have any plans to expand its computer usage to another category? Why or why not?

13. In simple language, explain what happens with the keystrokes that you type into a computer using a keyboard. Be sure to discuss memory, processing, and inputs. Draw any diagrams that may help you with this explanation.

14. Check the Web for information on different types of Apple computers. What is new? What brands of IBM-compatible computers have you used or purchased? What are you currently using? What influences your computer purchasing decisions?

15. Choose a few of the computer hardware vendors that sell computers to the general public. These include Dell, Compaq, IBM, Gateway, Apple, and many lesser-known brands. Using each company's home page on the Web, determine what options these vendors provide for input devices, processing devices, and output devices. Does it seem that this company has a broad range of choices for its customers? Is there something that you did not find available from this company? Present your findings in a 10-minute presentation to the rest of the class.

ANSWERS TO THE SELF-STUDY QUESTIONS

1. D 2. C 3. D 4. A 5. D 6. C 7. A 8. C 9. B 10. D

Preview

Software directs the functions of all computer hardware. Without software, the biggest, fastest, most powerful computer in the world is nothing more than a fancy paperweight. After reading this appendix, you will be able to do the following:

1. Describe the common functions of system software.
2. Describe the various types of application software.
3. Describe the characteristics of various types of programming languages and application development environments.

If you use an ATM to withdraw money, a word processor to prepare papers, or e-mail to communicate with your classmates and professors, you rely on software to execute instructions. Software is also intertwined with all types of products and services—toys, music, appliances, health care, and countless other products. As a result, the term ***software*** can be confusing because it is used in many different ways. We will unravel this confusion in the next section by describing the different types of software that are used in today's organizations.

KEY INFORMATION SYSTEMS SOFTWARE COMPONENTS

Software consists of programs, or sets of instructions, that tell the computer to perform certain processing functions. Software's job is to provide instructions that allow all the hardware components in your computer system to speak to each other. The two basic types of information systems software are system software and application software. In the next section, we discuss system software and how it supports the overall operation of the computer hardware.

System Software/Operating System

System software is the collection of programs that controls the basic operations of computer hardware. System software, or the ***operating system***, as it is sometimes called, coordinates the interaction between hardware devices (for example, the CPU and the monitor), peripherals (for example, printers), application software (for example, a word processing program), and users, as shown in Figure B.1.

Operating systems are often written in assembly language, a very low-level computer programming language that allows the computer to operate quickly and efficiently. The operating system is designed to insulate you from this low-level language and make computer operations unobtrusive. The operating system performs all of the day-to-day operations that we often take for granted when using a computer, such as updating the system clock, printing documents, or saving information to a disk. Just as our brain and nervous system control our bodies' breathing, heartbeat, and senses without our conscious

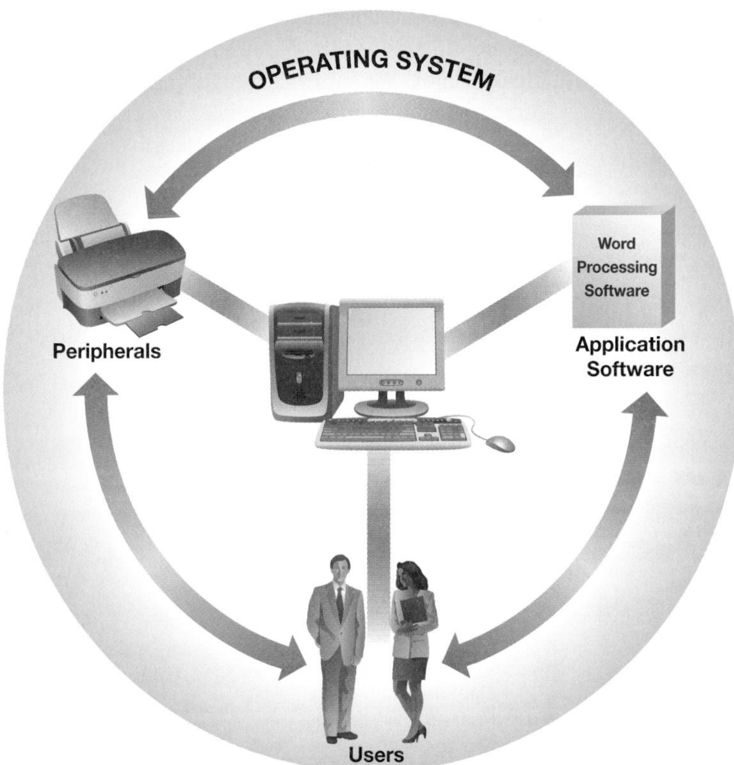

[**Figure B.1** ➥ Operating systems coordinate the interaction between users, application software, hardware, and peripherals.]

realization, the system software controls the computer's basic operations transparently.

Common System Software Functions

Many tasks are common to almost all computers. These include getting input from a keyboard or mouse, reading and/or writing data from a storage device (such as a hard disk drive), and presenting information to you via a monitor. Each of these tasks is performed by the operating system, just as a manager of a firm oversees people and processes (as depicted in Figure B.2).

For example, if you want to copy a word processing file from a floppy disk onto your computer, operating systems make this very easy for you. Using an operating system like Microsoft Windows, you simply use the mouse to point at a graphic icon of the word processing file, then click and drag it onto an icon of your hard disk. That is all it takes to copy the file on the floppy disk to your hard drive. The operating system makes this process appear easy. However, underlying the icons and simple dragging operations is a complex set of coded instructions that tells the electronic components of the computer that you are transferring a set of bits and bytes located on the floppy disk to a location on your internal hard disk. Imagine if you had to program those sets of instructions every time you wanted to copy a file from one place to another. The operating system manages and executes these types of system operations so that you can spend your time on more important tasks.

The operating system performs many different tasks, including the following:

- Booting (or starting) your computer
- Reading programs into memory and managing memory allocation
- Managing where programs and files are located in secondary storage
- Maintaining the structure of directories and subdirectories
- Managing multitasking and multithreading
- Managing security and fault tolerance
- Formatting disks
- Controlling the computer monitor
- Sending documents to the printer

Interfaces: Command versus GUI

The operating system is stored on disk, and a portion of it is transferred into temporary memory when the computer boots up. After the operating system is in memory, it begins to manage the computer and provide an ***interface***. Different operating systems and application programs use different types of user interfaces, with the most typical being command, menu, or GUI. It is through this interface that you interact with the computer. The ***command-based interface*** requires that you type text commands into the computer to perform basic operations. You could type the command "DELETE File1" to erase the file with the name "File1." MS-DOS (Microsoft Disk Operating System) is an example of an operating system that uses a command-based user interface.

The most common type of interface for the PC is called a ***graphical user interface (GUI)*** (see Figure B.3). The GUI uses pictures, icons, and menus to send instructions from the user to the computer system. GUIs eliminate the need for users to input arcane commands into the computer and are, therefore, a popular interface. Examples of system software using a GUI are the Windows and Macintosh operating systems.

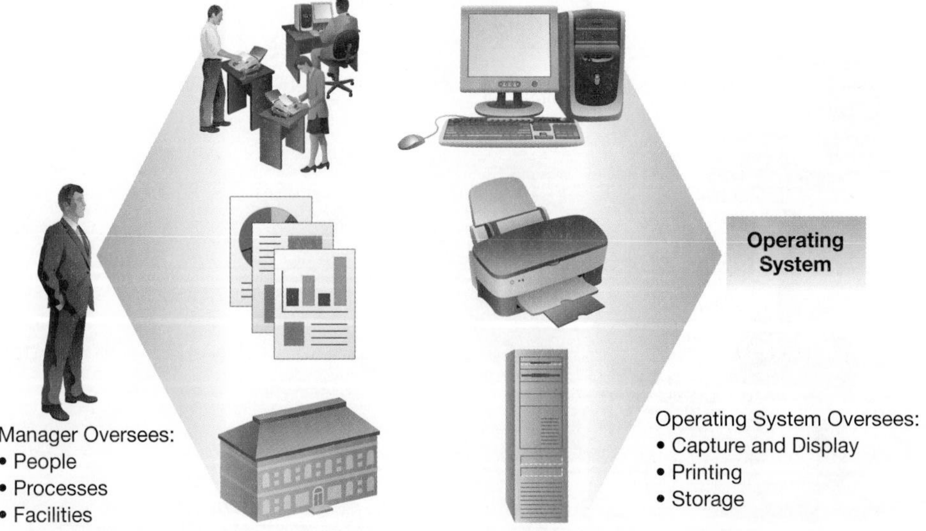

Figure B.2 ➥ A manager oversees organizational resources, whereas an operating system oversees computer resources.

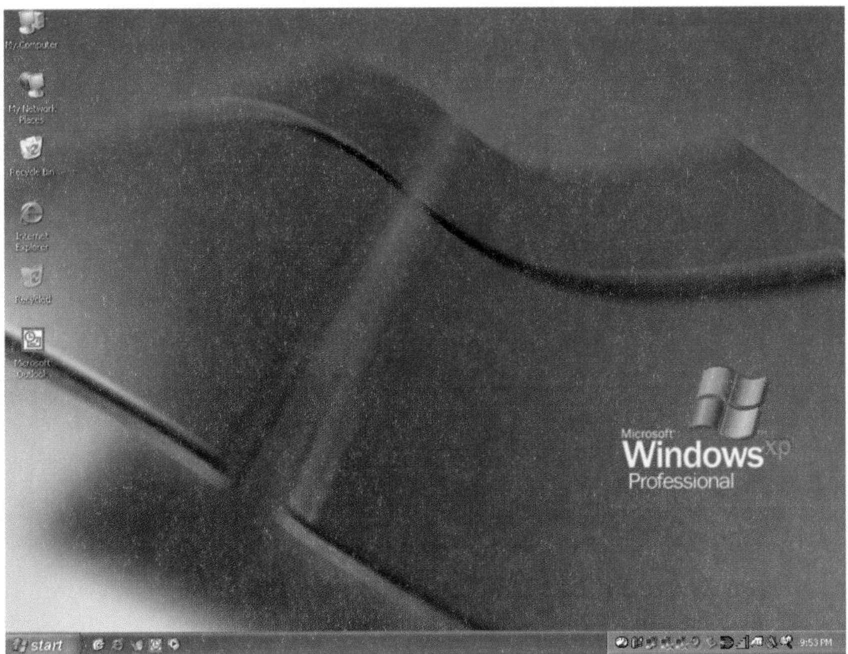

[Figure B.3 ➡ The Windows operating environment uses a graphical user interface.]

Popular Operating Systems

Just as there are many kinds of computers, there are many different kinds of operating systems (see Table B.1). In general, operating systems—whether for large mainframe computers or for small notebook computers—perform similar operations. Obviously, large multiuser supercomputers are more complex than small desktop systems; therefore, the operating system must account for and manage that complexity. However, the basic purpose of all operating systems is the same.

Utilities

Utilities, or ***utility programs,*** are designed to manage computer resources and files. Some are included in operating system software. Others must be purchased

[Table B.1] *Common operating systems.*

Operating System	Description
MVS/ESA (Multiple Virtual Storage/Enterprise Systems Architecture)	A highly reliable proprietary operating system used on large IBM mainframe computers that is being rapidly superseded by IBM's newer mainframe operating system, OS/390
UNIX	A multiuser, multitasking operating system that is available for a wide varity of computer platforms from vendors such as Sun Microsystems, Hewlett-Packard, and Silicon Graphics
MS-DOS (Microsoft Disk Operating System)	A command-based operating system used on IBM-compatible PCs that was first introduced in 1981
Windows	The most popular operating system in the world, operating on network servers, desktop PCs, notebooks, and handheld computers
OS/2	An operating system developed in 1988 by IBM for powerful PCs; can run applications written for OS/2, MS-DOS, Java, or Windows
Mac OS	The first commercially popular graphical-based operating system, making its debut in 1984, running on Apple Macintosh personal computers
Linux	An operating system designed in 1991 by the Finnish university student, Linus Torvalds, and it is known for its security, low price, and adaptability; by 2000, Linux powered 31% of all Web servers

separately and installed on your computer. Table B.2 provides a sample of a few utility programs that are considered essential.

As mentioned earlier, system software (or the operating system) is only one type of software that is used to run a computer. In the next section, we discuss the second type, application software, that is used in today's information systems.

Application Software

Unlike system software, which manages the operation of the computer, ***application software*** lets a user perform a specific task, such as writing a business letter, processing the payroll, managing a stock portfolio, or manipulating a series of forecasts to come up with the most efficient allocation of resources for a project. The application program interacts with the system software, which, in turn, interacts with the computer hardware.

The two basic types of application software are:

- Customized, or proprietary, software—developed specifically by or for a particular organization
- Commercial software—purchased off-the-shelf and used by a variety of people and/or organizations to meet their specific needs.

These two types of software will be discussed next.

Customized Application Software

Customized application software is developed to meet the specifications of an organization. This software may be developed in-house by the company's own IS staff or it may be contracted, or outsourced, to a specialized vendor charged with developing the software to the company's contractual specifications. Customized application software has two primary advantages over commercial software:

1. Customizability—It can be tailored to meet unique user requirements. For example, suppose a retailer needs a kiosk in its store to help shoppers locate specific products. Many shoppers may not be familiar with computers and may be intimidated by operating a keyboard or a mouse. With customized software, the company could develop a touch screen input interface, with which users could simply point at objects in a catalogue. The computer could then process this information and tell the user that, for example, women's shoes are located on the first floor in the southeast corner and provide a map of the store.
2. Problem specificity—The company pays only for the features specifically required for its users. For example, company- or industry-specific terms or acronyms can be included in the program, as can unique types of required reports. Such specificity is not possible in off-the-shelf programs that are targeted to a general audience.

Off-the-Shelf Application Software

Although customized software has advantages, it is not automatically the best choice for an organization. ***Off-the-shelf application software*** is typically used to support common business processes that do not require any specific tailoring. Table B.3 summarizes advantages of the off-the-shelf application software.

Combining Customized and Off-the-Shelf Application Software

It is possible to combine the advantages of customized and off-the-shelf software. Companies can purchase off-the-shelf software and then modify it for their own use. For example, a retailer may want to purchase an off-the-shelf inventory management program and then modify it to account for the specific products, outlets, and reports it needs to

[Table B.2] ***Common types of computer software utilities.***

Utility	Description
Backup	Archives files from the hard disk to a diskette or to tapes
File defragmentation	Converts a fragmented file stored on your hard disk (one not stored contiguously) into one that will load and be manipulated more rapidly
Disk and data recovery	Allows the recovery of damaged or erased information from hard and floppy disks
Data compression	Compresses data by substituting a short code for frequently repeated patterns of data, much like the machine shorthand used by court reporters, allowing more data to be stored on a disk
Antivirus	Monitors and removes viruses—lines of code designed to disrupt the computer's operation and make your life miserable
File conversion	Translates a file from one format to another, so it can be used by an application other than the one used to create it
Device drivers	Allows new hardware added to your computer system, such as a game controller, printer, scanner, and so on, to function with your operating system

[Table B.3] ***Advantages of off-the-shelf application software.***

Advantage	Description
Low cost	Because off-the-shelf applications are developed for general markets, development costs are distributed across a large customer base
Faster procurement	Customized software takes a notoriously long time to develop, whereas users can simply purchase off-the-shelf software and install it
High quality	Because off-the-shelf software typically has a large customer base, developers continuously invest in refinement and testing
Low risk	Off-the-shelf application software is relatively easy to evaluate through in-house testing, customer feedback, or software reviews in the popular and trade press

conduct its day-to-day business. In some cases, the company selling the off-the-shelf software makes these customized changes for a fee. Other vendors, however, do not allow their software to be modified.

Examples of Information Systems Application Software

Application software is categorized according to its design and by the type of application or task it supports. The task-oriented categories for application software are: (1) large business systems and office automation, and (2) personal productivity tools. Applications in the business category are purchased or developed by the organization to support the central, organization-wide operations of the company. Those in the office automation or personal productivity category are tools used to support the daily work activities of individuals and small groups. We will describe and provide examples of each type of application software in the following sections.

Business Information Systems

Business information systems are applications developed to perform organization-wide operations. For example, most organizations have payroll applications to process their payrolls. A payroll application may take as inputs individual time sheets. These time sheets can be fed through an optical scanner to create a file of time sheet data, organized by employee social insurance numbers. The application software can look at each employee's pay rate and hours worked to calculate a gross pay figure. The application software can also calculate the federal, provincial, and local taxes that must be deducted from the employee's gross pay. After calculating all deductions, the application arrives at a net pay owed each employee.

Once the application has taken all time sheets, organized and sorted them by employee, and calculated gross pay, deductions, and net pay for each employee, the figures form a payroll master file. The payroll application creates the payroll master file and backs it up, perhaps on a tape drive on a mainframe computer. To process cheques, the payroll application creates a cheque and register file that includes the date, the employee's name, the social insurance number, and the employee's net pay. The register file contains all of the previous elements, along with the time period, gross pay, and deductions for that time period for the employee's records. The cheque file is sorted by department, and cheques are printed. Registers (a record of the cheques printed) are also sorted and printed for distribution to employees.

This payroll process may not seem to be complex to conduct for only two or three employees. However, consider a large governmental organization, such as the RCMP, which must process and account for tens of thousands of employees' cheques. Suddenly, a relatively simple process becomes a potential information-processing nightmare. Application software easily manages these very large, data-intensive operations.

Mega-retailers such as Sears and Lands' End must manage millions of pieces of merchandise and millions of transactions on a daily basis (Figure B.4). These businesses rely on inventory management, order processing, billing, and shipping applications to conduct their operations. Without sophisticated, large-scale business application software, these businesses could not survive.

Office Automation/Personal Productivity Application Software

The second category of application software is called ***office automation*** or ***personal productivity software***. Individuals or groups who want to accomplish a wide range of tasks from word processing to graphics to e-mail use this type of software. Many of the large, well-known software companies, including Microsoft, Corel, Netscape, and IBM, produce office automation software. Table B.4 outlines several popular personal productivity tools. See Chapter 6 for more information on this topic.

[Figure B.4 ➥ Large retailers manage millions of transactions per day.]

Source: **www.landsend.com.**

[Table B.4] ***Some examples of popular personal productivity tools.***

Tool	Examples
Word processor	Microsoft Word, Corel WordPerfect, Lotus AmiPro
Spreadsheet	Microsoft Excel, Lotus 1-2-3
Database management system	Borland Paradox, Microsoft Access, Borland dbase, Microsoft FoxPro
Presentation software	Microsoft PowerPoint, Software Publishing Corporation Harvard Graphics
PC-based e-mail	Lotus cc:Mail, Microsoft Mail, Novell Groupwise
Web browser	Netscape Navigator, Microsoft Internet Explorer

PROGRAMMING LANGUAGES AND DEVELOPMENT ENVIRONMENTS

Each piece of application software we have discussed in this chapter is based on some programming language. A programming language is the computer language used by the software vendor to write application programs. For application software such as spreadsheets or database management systems, the underlying programming language is invisible to the user. However, programmers in an organization's information systems group and, in some instances, end users can use programming languages to develop their own specialized applications. Many different types of programming languages exist, each with its own strengths and weaknesses. Popular languages used in businesses and industry today are summarized in Table B.5.

Compilers and Interpreters

Programs created using programming languages must be translated into code—called assembly or ***machine language***—that the hardware can understand. Most programming languages are translated into machine languages through a program called a ***compiler***, as depicted in Figure B.5. The compiler takes an entire program written in a programming language, such as C, and converts it into a completely new program in machine language that can be read and executed directly by the computer. Use of a compiler is a two-stage process. First, the compiler translates the computer program into machine language, and then the CPU executes the machine language program.

Some programming environments do not compile the entire program into machine language. Instead, each statement of the program is converted into machine language and executed one statement at a time, as depicted in Figure B.6. The type of program that does the conversion and execution is called an ***interpreter***. Programming languages can be either compiled or interpreted.

Programming Languages

Over the past few decades, software has evolved. In the early days of computing, programming languages were quite crude by today's standards. Initially used in the 1940s, the first generation of programming languages was called machine languages. Programmers wrote in binary code to instruct the computer exactly which circuits to turn on and which to turn off. As you might guess, machine language is very unsophisticated and therefore very difficult to write. Because it is so difficult, very few programs are actually written in machine language. Instead, programmers rely on higher-level languages. In the early 1950s, a more sophisticated method for programming was developed, in which the binary codes used in machine language were replaced by symbols, called symbolic languages, that were a lot easier for humans to understand. Programs written in symbolic language, or any higher-level language, still need to be converted into machine language in order to run.

In the mid-1950s, the first high-level programming language, called FORTRAN, was developed by IBM. The big innovation of high-level languages was that they used English-like words to instruct the

[Table B.5] *Popular programming languages.*

Language	Application	Description
BASIC	General purpose	**B**eginner's **A**ll-Purpose **S**ymbolic **I**nteraction **C**ode. An easy-to-learn language, BASIC works well on most PCs.
C/C++	General purpose	C++ is a newer version of C. Developed at AT&T Bell Labs. Complex languages used for a wide range of system and application programming.
COBOL	Business	**Co**mmon **B**usiness-**O**riented **L**anguage. Developed in 1960. It was the first language for developing business software. COBOL is used for most business transaction processing applications on mainframes.
FORTRAN	Scientific	**FOR**mula **TRAN**slator. The first commercial high-level language, developed by IBM in the 1950s. Designed for scientific, mathematical, and engineering applications.
Pascal	Teaching structured programming	Named after mathematician Blaise Pascal. Uses a building block approach to programming. Useful in developing large programs.
HTML	World Wide Web	**H**ype**rt**ext **M**arkup **L**anguage. The most widely used language for developing Web pages. Markup languages simplify pages for transmission by using symbols that tell what document elements should look like when displayed.
Java	World Wide Web	An object-oriented programming language developed at Sun Microsystems in the early 1990s. It is a popular programming language for the Internet because it is highly transportable from one make of computer to another.
LISP	Artificial intelligence	**LIS**t **P**rocessor. Dates from the late 1950s. One of the main languages used to develop applications in artificial intelligence. Also the language for high-speed arcade graphics games.

computer. Consequently, high-level languages are much easier to program in than lower-level languages. Table B.5 shows that some high-level languages are better suited for different applications. Programmers must fully understand the tasks that are to be accomplished when writing a new application in order to choose the best programming language for those tasks.

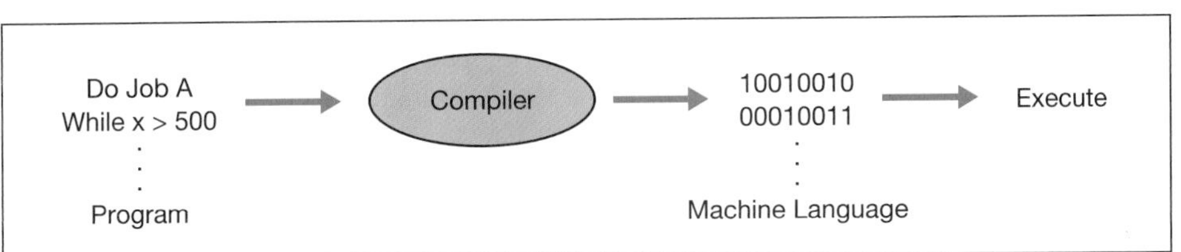

[Figure B.5 ➥ A compiler translates the entire computer program into machine language, and then the CPU executes the machine language program.]

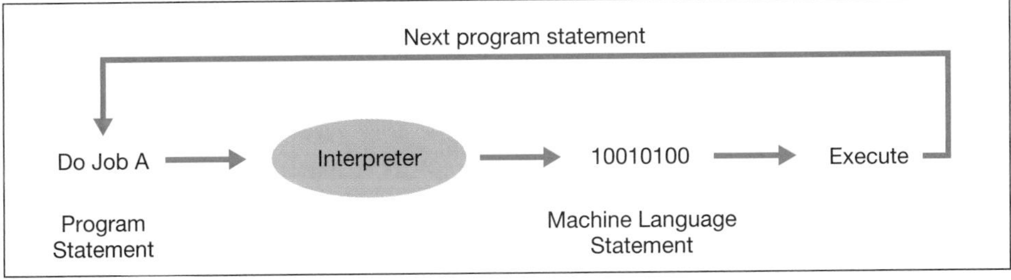

[Figure B.6 ➥ Interpreters read, translate, and execute one line of source code at a time.]

In the 1970s, several user-oriented languages called fourth-generation languages were created. These languages are more like English than third-generation languages in that they focus on the desired output instead of the procedures required to get that output. Fourth-generation languages (4GLs), also called outcome-oriented languages, are commonly used to write and execute queries of a database. For example, the widely used database query language called Structured Query Language (SQL) is a fourth-generation language. See Figure B.7 for several lines of SQL displayed in a sentence-like statement requesting that the LAST and FIRST names of people in a database called CUSTOMER with credit limits equal to $100 be displayed.

More recently, fifth-generation languages (5GLs) have been developed for application within some expert system or artificial intelligence applications. 5GLs are called natural languages because they allow the user to communicate with the computer using true English sentences. For example, Hewlett-Packard and other software vendors have developed tools for document search and retrieval and database queries that let the user query the documents or database with English-like sentences. These sentences are then automatically converted into the appropriate commands (in some cases SQL) needed to query the documents or database and produce the result for the user. If the system does not understand exactly what the user wants, it can ask for clarification. The same code shown in Figure B.7 might appear as shown in Figure B.8 if a natural language were used. Although 5GL languages are not common and are still being further developed, they have been used to forecast the performance of financial portfolios, help diagnose medical problems, and estimate weather patterns.

Of course, programming languages continue to evolve. One new characteristic for describing programming languages is whether or not they are object-oriented. In addition, visual programming languages and Web development languages are rapidly gaining popularity. We discuss these next.

Object-Oriented Languages

Object-oriented languages are the most recent in the progression of high-level programming languages. These languages allow programmers to group data and program instructions together into modules, or ***objects,*** that can be manipulated by the programmer. For example, an object might be student majors and grade point averages and a set of corresponding rules for calculating credits needed for graduation. The process of grouping pieces of data together is called ***encapsulation***. When pieces of data are encapsulated, they can be isolated from other parts of the program. The programmer can then make changes in various parts of the program without having to rewrite the entire code.

A second key characteristic of object-oriented languages is ***inheritance***. This means that when one class of objects is defined, all other objects with the same characteristics are automatically defined by the same terms. For example, if "student majors" is defined as an object for a search, then through inheritance, objects such as "English major," or "mathematics major" would fall under the same definition. Therefore, once an object is created, it can be plugged into several different applications. Programmers using object-oriented programming (OOP) can save time because they do not have to repeatedly write many lines of code to define the same or related objects.

In addition to being object-oriented, programs and programming languages can also be ***event-driven***. Unlike a program written in a procedural programming language, a program written with the event-driven approach does not follow a sequential logic. The programmer does not determine the sequence of execution for the program. The user can press certain keys and click on various buttons and boxes presented to her. Each of these user actions can cause *events* to occur, which triggers a program procedure that the programmer has written. Object-oriented programming languages tend to be useful for designing event-driven applications. An example of an object-oriented environment that supports

```
SELECT LAST FIRST
FROM CUSTOMER
WHERE CREDIT_LIMIT = 100
```

NEVO LIV
BROHMAN DAVID
BJERKAN HEIDI
JESSUP JAMIE
VALACICH JAMES
WADE CHRISTOPHER

[**Figure B.7** ➥ A 4GL query using SQL that requests that the LAST and FIRST name of those that have a CREDIT_LIMIT equal to $100 be displayed from a database called CUSTOMER.]

BEGINNING WITH THE LAST NAME ON THE FOLLOWING LIST OF CUSTOMERS, FIND CUSTOMERS WHO HAVE A CREDIT LIMIT OF $100.

NEVO LIV
BROMHMAN DAVID
BJERKAN HEIDI
JESSUP JAMIE
VALACICH JAMES
WADE CHRISTOPHER

[**Figure B.8** ➥ A 5GL query using natural language to request the same information as the SQL query in Figure B.7.]

the development of event-driven applications is Microsoft Visual Basic. In addition, Visual Basic is also a visual programming language, which we will discuss next.

Visual Programming Languages

Just as you may have found it easier to use a computer operating system with a graphical user interface, like Windows or Mac OS, programmers using ***visual programming languages*** may also take advantage of the GUI. For instance, programmers can easily add a command button to a screen with a few clicks of a mouse (see Figure B.9) instead of explaining pixel-by-pixel and using many lines of code. Visual Basic and Visual C++ are two popular examples of visual programming languages.

Web Development Languages

If you have been surfing the Web for a while, you probably either already have a personal Web page or you have thought of posting one. In that event, you have some experience with using a programming language. The language you used to create your Web page is called ***hypertext markup language (HTML)***. HTML is a text-based file format that uses a series of codes, or tags, to set up a document. Because HTML editing programs are visually oriented and easy to use, you do not need to memorize the language to set up a Web page. The programs for creating Web pages are called ***Web page builders*** or ***HTML editors***, and there are many on the market, including Microsoft FrontPage, most Web browsers, and word processing programs such as Word and WordPerfect.

In HTML, the tags used to identify different elements on a page and to format the page are set apart from the text with angle brackets (< >). The "a href" command sets up a hyperlink from a word or image on the page to another HTML document. Tags also denote document formatting commands, such as text to be used as a title, sizes of text in headings, the ends of paragraphs, underlining, italics, bolding, and where to insert pictures and sound (see Table B.6).

A good way to learn HTML is to find a Web page you like, then use the "View Source" command on your browser to see the hypertext that created the page (see Figure B.10). Once you have created your Web page and saved it to disk, you can upload it to an Internet account you have created through your ISP.

XML

Extensible markup language (XML) was designed both to be used as a Web page construction tool, when users want to create their own markup tags, and to build database queries. XML is a powerful language that lets users create database fields for a number of different applications. XML makes it easy for Web users to request and receive information from a variety of databases. To view documents created in XML, you need a browser that supports the language, commonly called an XML parser. The latest versions of Microsoft's Internet Explorer and Netscape Navigator can fill the bill.

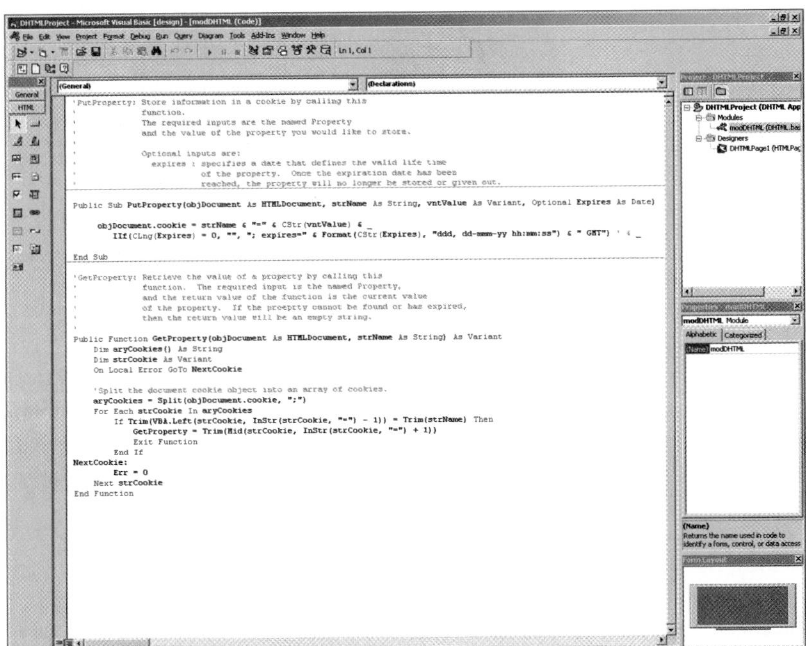

[**Figure B.9** ➥ Visual Basic, a visual programming language, is used to create standard business forms.]

Source: Microsoft Visual Basic.

[Table B.6] ***Common HTML tags.***

Tag	Description
<html> ... </html>	Creates an HTML document
<head> . . . </head>	Sets off the title and other information that is not displayed on the Web page itself
<body> . . . </body>	Sets off the visible portion of the document
<b> . . . </b>	Creates bold text
<a href="URL"> . . . </a>	Creates a hyperlink
<a href="mailto:EMAIL"> . . . </a>	Creates a mailto link
<p> . . . </p>	Creates a new paragraph
<table> . . . </table>	Creates a table

Adding Dynamic Content to a Web Page

Markup languages such as HTML are for laying out or formatting Web pages. If you want to add animated cartoons or other dynamic content, or have users interact with your Web page other than by clicking on hypertext links, then you will need access to tools such as XML, Java, ActiveX, or a scripting language.

Java ***Java*** is a programming language that was developed at Sun Microsystems in the early 1990s. It lets you spice up your Web page by adding active content such as circles that whirl and change colours, hamsters marching to a tune, forms to help users calculate car payments at various interest rates, or any other such dynamic content (see Figure B.11). You can do this in one of two ways: by learning Java or a similar language and programming the content you want, or by downloading free general-purpose ***applets*** from the Web. Applets are small programs that you can choose from to provide the content you want on your Web page. When a user accesses your Web page, the applets you inserted are downloaded from the server with your Web page to a Java-enabled browser running on a PC. Later, when the user leaves your Web page, the Web page and the applets disappear from his computer.

ActiveX ***ActiveX*** was developed by Microsoft Corporation to perform the same function as Java. It, too, lets users program in or insert objects from any ActiveX-supported application or ActiveX-enabled Web page. ActiveX differs from Java in that it was designed to run on Windows computers and is not always supported by other platforms.

Scripting languages ***Scripting languages*** can also be used to supply interactive components to a Web page. These languages let you build programs or scripts directly into HTML page code. Web page designers frequently use them to check the accuracy of user-entered information, such as names, addresses, and credit card numbers. You can also use them to connect freestanding applets to your HTML-created Web page. Two common scripting languages are Microsoft's VBScript and Netscape's JavaScript.

JavaScript ***JavaScript,*** created by Netscape, bears little resemblance to Java. Both, however, are useful component software tools for creating Web pages. That is, both allow users to add or create applets that lend dynamic content to Web pages. Both are also cross-platform programs, meaning that they can typically be used by computers running Windows, Linux, Mac OS, and other operating systems.

The development of programming languages is an ongoing process of change and innovation. These changes often result in more capable and complex systems for the user. The popularity of the Internet has spurred the creation of innovative and evolving software. From the pace of change that is occurring, it is clear that many more innovations are on the horizon.

Automated Development Environments

Over the years, the tools for developing information systems have increased both in variety and in power. In the early days of systems development, a developer was left to use a pencil and paper to sketch out design ideas and program code. Computers were cumbersome to use and slow to program, and most designers worked out on paper as much of the system design as they could before moving to the computer. Today, system developers have a vast array of powerful computer-based tools at their disposal. These tools have changed forever the ways in which systems are developed. ***Computer-aided software engineering (CASE)*** refers to automated software tools used by

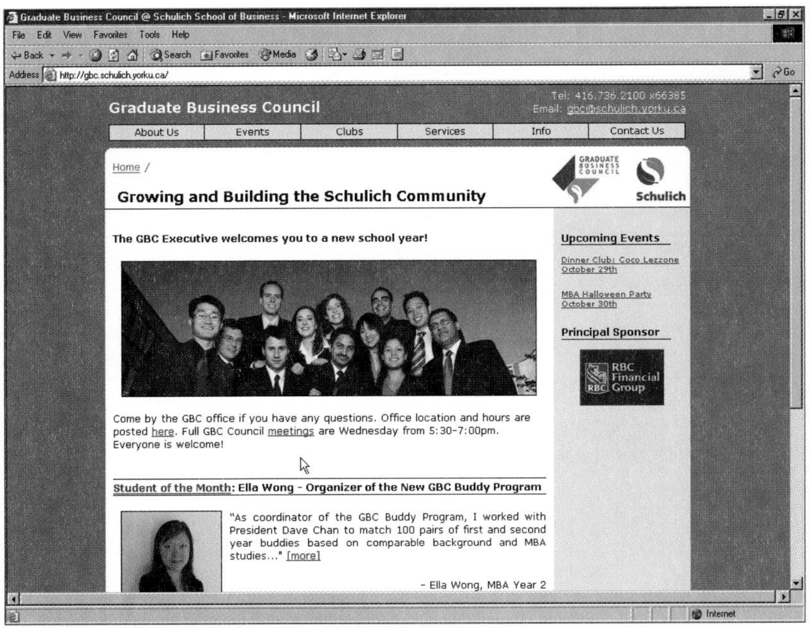


```
<!DOCTYPE HTML PUBLIC "-//W3C//DTD HTML 4.01 Transitional//EN">
<html><!-- InstanceBegin template="/Templates/gbc_template.dwt" codeOutsideHTMLIsLocked="false" -->
<head>
<!-- InstanceBeginEditable name="doctitle" -->
<title>Graduate Business Council @ Schulich School of Business</title>
<!-- InstanceEndEditable -->
<meta http-equiv="Content-Type" content="text/html; charset=iso-8859-1">
<!-- InstanceBeginEditable name="head" -->
<meta name="Description" content="Graduate Business Council, Schulich School of Business, York University">
<meta name="Keywords" content="Graduate Business Council, Schulich School of Business, York University">
<!-- InstanceEndEditable -->
</head>

<body bgcolor="#787878" link="#0C3D91" vlink="#0C3D91" alink="#0C3D91" topmargin="0" marginwidth="0" marginheight="0">
<!-- configure drop down menu -->
<!--     vqm__database='http://www.gbc.schulich.yorku.ca/gbc/gbc_new.nsf/';-->
  <script language="JavaScript1.2" vqm_id="http://www.paulfriesen.com/gbc_website.js">
        vqm__notice='Visual QuickMenu Pro, (c) 2004 OpenCube Inc., All Rights Reserved, Visit - www.opencube.com';
        vqm__codebase='http://gbc.schulich.yorku.ca/';
        vqm__database='http://gbc.schulich.yorku.ca/';
</script>
  <script language="JavaScript1.2" src="http://gbc.schulich.yorku.ca/gbc_website.js"></script>
  <script language="JavaScript1.2" src="http://gbc.schulich.yorku.ca/tdqm_loader.js"></script>
  <!--
<script language="JavaScript1.2" vqm_id="gbc_website.js">
        vqm__notice='Visual QuickMenu Pro, (c) 2004 OpenCube Inc., All Rights Reserved, Visit - www.opencube.com';
        vqm__codebase='/Backup/not%20encrypted/Academic/York/GBC%20Exec/Web%20Master/GBC%20Website/';
        vqm__database='/Backup/not%20encrypted/Academic/York/GBC%20Exec/Web%20Master/GBC%20Website/';
</script>

  <script language="JavaScript1.2" src="/Backup/not%20encrypted/Academic/York/GBC%20Exec/Web%20Master/GBC%20Website/gbc_website.js"></script>
  <script language="JavaScript1.2" src="/Backup/not%20encrypted/Academic/York/GBC%20Exec/Web%20Master/GBC%20Website/tdqm_loader.js"></script>
-->
<div align="center">
  <table width="750" border="0" cellspacing="5" cellpadding="0">
    <tr valign="bottom">
      <td width="50%" align="left"><font color="#FFFFFF" size="4" face="Verdana, Arial, Helvetica, sans-serif"><strong>Graduate
        Business Council</strong></font></td>
      <td width="50%" align="right"><font color="#FFFFFF" size="2" face="Verdana, Arial, Helvetica, sans-serif">Tel:
        416.736.2100 x66385<br>
        Email: </font><a href="mailto:gbc@schulich.yorku.ca"><font color="#FFFFFF" size="2" face="Verdana, Arial, Helvetica,
sans-serif">gbc@schulich.yorku.ca</font></a></td>
    </tr>
  </table>
  <table width="750" border="0" cellspacing="5" cellpadding="0">
    <tr>
      <td>
        <!-- insert drop down menu -->
        <script id="vqp_generate_mainitems" language="javascript1.2">generate_mainitems()</script>
      </td>
    </tr>
  </table>
  <table width="750" border="0" cellpadding="0" cellspacing="0" bgcolor="#FFFFFF">
    <tr>
      <td valign="top"> <table width="750" border="0" cellspacing="0" cellpadding="0">
          <tr>
            <td align="left" valign="top"><img src="imgs/tl_curve_white.gif" width="6" height="6"></td>
            <td align="right" valign="top"><img src="imgs/tr_curve_white.gif" width="6" height="6"></td>
          </tr>
          <tr>
            <td colspan="2" valign="top"> <table width="750" height="61" border="0" cellpadding="2" cellspacing="2">
                <tr>
```

[Figure B.10 ➡ A Web page (a) and the HTML commands used to create it (b).]

Source: Courtesy of the Schulich School of Business, Graduate Business Council.

systems developers to design and implement information systems. Developers can use these tools to automate or support activities throughout the systems development process, with the objective of increasing productivity and improving the overall quality of systems. The capabilities of CASE tools are continually evolving and being integrated into a variety of development environments. In what follows, we briefly review some of the interesting characteristics of CASE.

Types of CASE Tools

Two of the primary activities when developing large-scale information systems are the creation of design documents and the management of information. Over the life of a project, thousands of documents need to be created—from screen prototypes, to database content and structure, to layouts of sample forms and reports. At the heart of all CASE environments is a repository for managing information.

CASE also helps developers represent business processes and information flows using graphical diagramming tools. By providing standard symbols to represent business processes, information flows between processes, data storage, and the organizational entities that interact with the business process, CASE eases a very tedious and error-prone

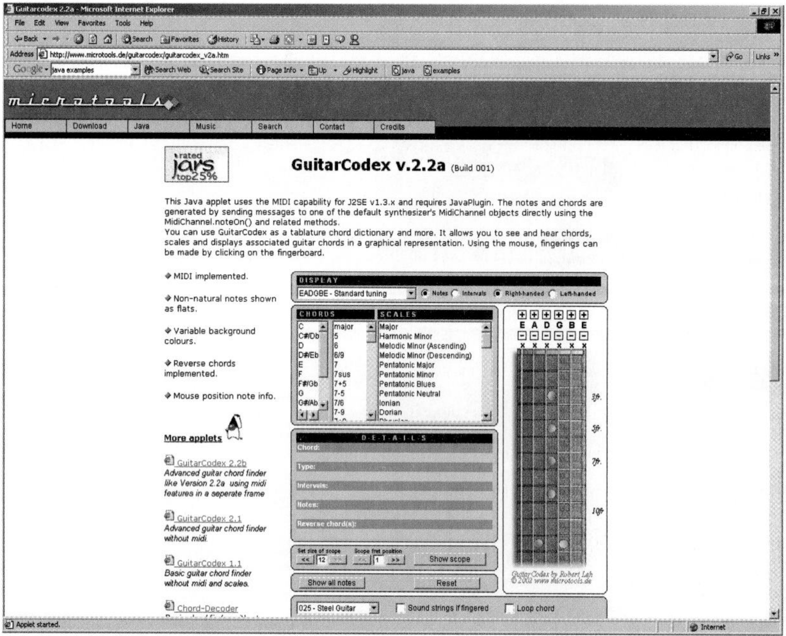

[Figure B.11 ➥ Java helps to provide dynamic content to Web pages.]

Source: Adapted from Hoffer, George, and Valacich, *Modern Systems Analysis and Design* (Reading, MA: Addison Wesley Longman, 1999).

activity (see Figure B.12). The tools not only ease the drawing process but also ensure that the drawing conforms to development standards and is consistent with other design documents developed by other developers.

Another powerful capability of CASE is its ability to generate program source code automatically. CASE tools keep pace with contemporary programming languages and can automatically produce programming code directly from high-level designs in languages such as Java, COBOL, BASIC, and C. In addition to diagramming tools and code generators, a broad range of other tools assists in the systems development process. The general types of CASE tools used throughout the development process are summarized in Table B.7.

The Influence of CASE on Individuals

CASE can be used to dramatically increase the speed of development and maintenance of a system, not

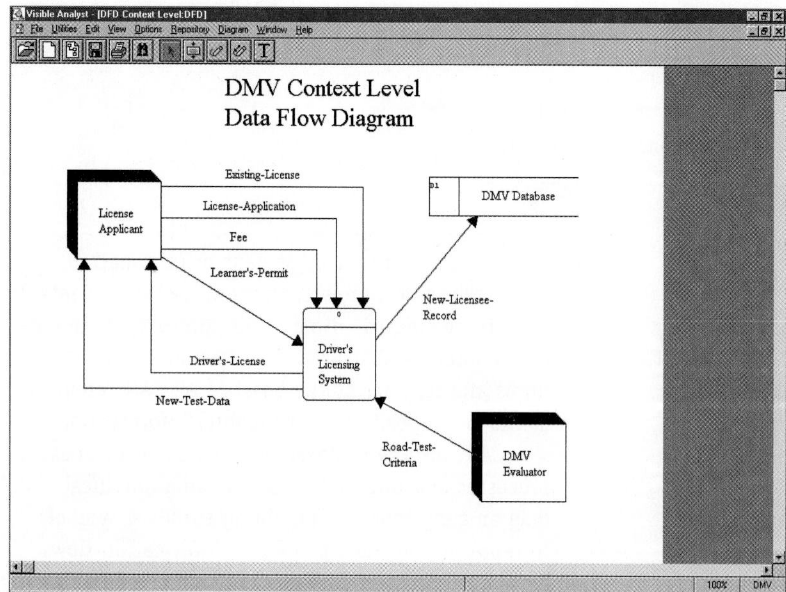

[Figure B.12 High-level system design diagram from a CASE tool.]

Source: Visible Systems (Visible Analyst product).

[Table B.7] *General types of CASE tools.*

CASE Tool	Description
Diagramming tools	Tools that enable system process, data, and control structures to be represented graphically.
Screen and report generators	Tools that help model how systems look and feel to users. Screen and report generators also make it easier for the systems analyst to identify data requirements and relationships.
Analysis tools	Tools that automatically check for incomplete, inconsistent, or incorrect specifications in diagrams, screens, and reports.
Repository	A tool that enables the integrated storage of specifications, diagrams, reports, and project management information.
Documentation generators	Tools that help produce both technical and user documentation in standard formats.
Code generators	Tools that enable the automatic generation of program and database definition code directly from the design documents, diagrams, screens, and reports.

Source: Adapted from Hoffer, George, and Valacich, *Modern Systems Analysis and Design* (Reading, MA: Addison Wesley Longman, 1999).

to mention increase the quality of the system. CASE also influences the culture of an organization in many significant ways. In fact, researchers have found that people with different career orientations have different attitudes toward CASE (Orlikowski, 1989). For example, those within the development group with a managerial orientation welcome CASE because they believe it helps reduce the risk and uncertainty in managing development projects. On the other hand, people with a more technical orientation tend to resist the use of CASE because they feel threatened by the technology's capability to replace some skills they have taken years to master. Table B.8 lists several possible impacts of CASE on the roles of individuals within organizations. CASE is clearly a powerful technology that can have numerous and widespread impacts. Its adoption should be a well-thought-out and highly orchestrated activity.

[Table B.8] *Common impacts of CASE on individuals within organizations.*

Individuals	Common Impact
Systems analysts	CASE automates many routine tasks of the analyst, making the communication skills (rather than analytical skills) of the analyst most critical.
Programmers	Will piece together objects created by code generators and fourth-generation languages. Their role will become more of maintaining designs than maintaining source code.
Users	Will be much more active in the systems development process through the use of upper CASE tools.
Top managers	Will play a more active role in setting priorities and strategic directions for IS by using CASE-based planning and through user-oriented system development methods.
Functional managers	Will play a greater role in leading development projects by using CASE to re-engineer their business processes.
IS project managers	Will have greater control over development projects and resources.

Source: Adapted from 1992, Chen and Norman.

KEY POINTS REVIEW

1. **Describe the common functions of system software.** System software is the collection of programs that form the foundation for the basic operations of the computer hardware. System software, or the operating system, performs many different tasks. Some of these tasks include booting your computer, reading programs into memory, managing memory allocation to those programs,

managing where programs and files are located in secondary storage, maintaining the structure of directories and subdirectories, formatting disks, controlling the computer monitor, and sending objects to the printer. The system software manages the dialogue you can have with a computer using either a command-based or graphical interface. A command-based interface requires that text commands be typed into the computer, whereas a graphical user interface (GUI) uses pictures and icons, as well as menus, to send instructions back and forth between the user and the computer system.

2. **Describe the various types of application software.** You can find a large number of computer software applications. Customized application software is developed specifically for a single organization. This kind of software is tailored to an organization's unique requirements. Off-the-shelf application software is not customized to the unique needs of one organization but is written to operate within many organizations. In general, off-the-shelf software is less costly, faster to procure, of higher quality, and less risky than customized software. Business information systems are applications developed to perform a firm's organization-wide operations, such as payroll or inventory management. Office automation or personal productivity software is designed to support activities such as word processing and electronic mail.
3. **Describe the characteristics of various types of programming languages and application development environments.** A programming language is the computer language used by programmers to write application programs. In order to run on a computer, programs must be translated into binary machine language. Programming languages are translated into machine languages through special types of programs, which are called compilers and interpreters. Over the past several decades, software has evolved. Early software used machine language, which told the computer exactly which circuits to turn on and which to turn off. Next, symbolic languages used "symbols" to represent a series of binary statements. This was followed by the development of high-level languages, such as FORTRAN, COBOL, C, and Java. The difference between these high-level languages and earlier languages is that the high-level languages use English-like words and commands, making it easier to write programs. Fourth-generation languages are called outcome-oriented languages because they contain even more English-like commands and tend to focus on what output is desired instead of the procedures required to get that output. Again, these languages made it even easier to program. Fifth-generation languages are called natural languages because they allow the user to communicate with the computer using true English sentences. In addition to this generational evolution, object-oriented programming, visual programming, and Web development languages are relatively new enhancements to programming languages. Object-oriented languages group together data and their corresponding instructions into manipulable objects. Visual programming languages use a graphical interface to build graphical interfaces for other programs. Web development languages are a rapidly evolving set of tools designed for constructing Internet applications and Web content. Together, object-oriented, visual programming, and Web development languages are making it easier for programmers to develop today's complex software systems, especially for modern Internet-based systems. Finally, computer-aided software engineering environments help systems developers construct large-scale systems more rapidly and with higher quality.

KEY TERMS

REVIEW QUESTIONS

1. Define the term *software,* and name several software packages and their uses.
2. Describe at least four different tasks performed by an operating system.
3. What is the difference between a command-based interface and a graphical user interface?
4. Describe the similarities and differences between at least two major operating systems in use today.
5. Name and describe four functions of utility programs.
6. Contrast the use of off-the-shelf application software and customized application software.
7. Describe the evolution of programming languages, as well as various contemporary programming languages in use today.
8. What is HTML, and why is it important?
9. Describe various options for adding dynamic content to a Web page.
10. What is CASE, and how can it influence individuals within organizations?

SELF-STUDY QUESTIONS

Answers are at the end of the Problems and Exercises.

1. Which of the following is an example of an operating system?
   A. Microsoft Access
   B. Microsoft Excel
   C. Microsoft Word
   D. Microsoft Windows
2. An operating system performs which of the following tasks?
   A. booting the computer
   B. managing where programs and files are stored
   C. sending documents to the printer
   D. all of the above
3. Which of the following is a popular operating system?
   A. Noodle
   B. Linux
   C. FORTRAN
   D. PowerEdge
4. Which is **not** an advantage of off-the-shelf application software?
   A. lower cost
   B. faster to obtain
   C. easier to use
   D. higher quality due to large customer base
5. Which is **not** an example of office automation or personal productivity software?
   A. payroll system
   B. database management system
   C. Web browser
   D. word processing
6. Which of the following is **not** a tool for adding dynamic content to a Web page?
   A. Hot Coffee
   B. ActiveX
   C. scripting languages
   D. Java
7. Automated software tools used to develop information systems that can improve the overall system quality and increase programmer productivity are called ________.
   A. computerized programming
   B. automated development
   C. computer-aided programming
   D. none of the above
8. A utility program may provide ________.
   A. antivirus protection
   B. file conversion capability
   C. file compression and defragmentation
   D. all of the above
9. Fifth-generation languages are also referred to as ________ languages.
   A. assembly
   B. natural
   C. high-level
   D. low-level
10. What were first-generation programming languages called?
    A. natural language
    B. assembly language
    C. machine language
    D. none of the above

PROBLEMS AND EXERCISES

1. Match the following terms with the appropriate definitions:

   ____ Operating system
   ____ Applets
   ____ Visual programming languages
   ____ Graphical user interface
   ____ Customized application software
   ____ Scripting language
   ____ Interpreter
   ____ Business information systems
   ____ Compiler
   ____ Object-oriented programming languages

   a. Translates a computer program into machine language, which is then executed by the computer

b. An interface that enables the user to use pictures, icons, and menus in order to send instructions to the computer

c. Coordinates the interaction between users, applications, and hardware

d. Applications developed to perform the organization-wide operations of a firm

e. Programming languages that provide a graphical user interface and are generally easier to use than non–GUI languages

f. Small software programs that can be used to provide special features to a Website

g. Programming languages that group together data and their corresponding instructions into manipulable objects

h. Software developed based on specifications provided by a particular organization

i. Translates the computer program into machine language one statement at a time

j. Used to supply interactive components to a Web page by building programs or scripts directly into HTML page code

2. How do software programs affect your life? Give examples of software from areas other than desktop computers. Are the uses for software increasing over time?

3. In what situations would customized software be utilized? How does the cost compare with the benefit?

4. What are the implications for an organization of having more than one operating system? What might be the advantages? What are some of the disadvantages? Would you recommend such a situation? Can you find organizations using the World Wide Web that specifically mention their utilization of multiple operating systems in their information system architecture? Do these organizations comment on this arrangement or simply mention its existence? Prepare a 10-minute presentation to the rest of the class on your findings.

5. Imagine that you are in charge of procuring software applications for your division of a company. You are in need of a powerful business information systems software application that will control most of the accounting and bookkeeping functions. Based on your current knowledge of the intricacies of the accounting profession and its practices, would you be more likely to purchase this application as a customized software application or an off-the-shelf software application? Why did you select this choice? What would make you choose the other option?

6. What is a business information system, and what types of processing does it do? Many companies' business systems track what besides inventory? Why?

7. Based on the information within this appendix and within the chapters of this textbook, discuss the importance of a single decision to purchase one software application over another—for example, purchasing Microsoft Excel instead of Lotus 1-2-3. Who will be affected? How will they be affected? What changes might occur because of the purchase?

8. Based on your own experiences with computers and computer systems, what do you like and dislike about different operating systems that you have used? Were these used on a professional or a personal level, or both? Who made the decision to purchase that particular operating system? Did you have any say in the purchase decision?

9. Choose an organization that utilizes a variety of different software applications. Are these software applications customized applications, off-the-shelf applications, or a combination of the two? Talk with some of the employees to determine how they feel about using customized versus off-the-shelf software applications.

10. Search the Web for organizations that specialize in creating customized software applications for their clients. What specific product categories do these organizations specialize in, if any? Were you able to find any pricing information directly from their Websites?

11. Have the off-the-shelf software applications you have used met your requirements? Were you able to perform the functions and routines that you needed? Did the software meet your expectations? Would you have bought this type of software if you knew then what you know today?

12. Find an organization that does a lot of in-house programming and utilizes a variety of different programming languages. Determine the generation level of these languages. Are the same personnel programming in most (or all) of the languages, or are different personnel programming in each of the languages? Is this assignment of programmers intentional or unintentional?

13. Imagine that you and a friend are at an ATM getting some cash from your account to pay for a movie. The ATM does not seem to be working. It is giving you an error message every time you press any button. Is this most likely a software-related problem or a hardware-related problem? Why? Use the information in this appendix and in the previous appendix to help you make your decision.

14. Describe how you would handle the resistance to implementing CASE tools by those who feel they will be replaced by technology. From whom is this resistance most likely to come? Is this fear legitimate? Why or why not?

ANSWERS TO THE SELF-STUDY QUESTIONS

1. D 2. D 3. B 4. C 5. A 6. A 7. D 8. D 9. B 10. C

Appendix C Networking

Preview

The purpose of this appendix is to introduce key networking concepts, technologies, and applications. This discussion provides you with a solid foundation for understanding how computers are connected across a room or across the world.

After reading this appendix, you will be able to do the following:

1. Understand networking fundamentals, including network services and transmission media
2. Describe network software and hardware, including media access control, network topologies, and protocols, as well as connectivity hardware for both local area and wide area networks

Telecommunications and networking technologies, like those described throughout this book, are taking on more and more importance as organizations rely more on computer-based information systems. Understanding how the underlying networking technologies work and where these technologies are heading will help to complete your understanding of the "essential" elements of information systems. In this appendix we describe the enabling technologies underlying computer networks, how they are used together to form networks, and how these networks are used. The discussion begins with a description of the fundamental elements of computer networking.

NETWORKING FUNDAMENTALS

Telecommunications advances have enabled individual computer networks—constructed with a variety of hardware and software—to connect together in what appears to be a single network. Networks are increasingly being used to dynamically exchange relevant, value-adding knowledge and information throughout global organizations and institutions. The following sections take a closer look at the fundamental building blocks of these complex networks and the services they provide.

Servers, Clients, and Peers

A ***network*** consists of three separate components: servers, clients, and peers, as depicted in Figure C.1. A ***server*** is any computer on the network that makes access to files, printing, communications, and other services available to users of the network. Servers only provide services. A server typically has a more advanced microprocessor, more memory, a larger cache, and more disk storage than a single-user workstation. A ***client*** is any computer, such as a user's workstation or PC on the network, or any software application, such as a word processing application, that uses the services provided by the server. Clients only request services. A client usually has only one user, whereas many different users share the server. A ***peer*** is any computer that may both request and provide services. Whether a particular computer or device on the network is considered a server, client, or peer depends on the operating system that is running. The trend in business is to use ***server-centric networks***, in which servers and clients have defined roles. However, ***peer-to-peer networks*** that enable any computer or device on the network to provide and request services can be found in small offices and homes.

[**Figure C.1** ➥ A server is a computer on the network that enables multiple computers (or "clients") to access data. A peer is a computer that may both request and provide services.]

Network Services

Network services are the capabilities that networked computers share through the multiple combinations of hardware and software. The most common network services are file services, print services, message services, and application services. ***File services*** are used to store, retrieve, and move data files in an efficient manner, as shown in Figure C.2a. An individual can use the file services of the network to move a customer file electronically to multiple recipients across the network. ***Print services*** are used to control and manage users' access to network printers and fax equipment, as shown in Figure C.2b. Sharing printers on a network reduces the number of printers an organization needs. ***Message services*** include the storing, accessing, and delivering of text, binary, graphic, digitized video, and audio data. These services are similar to file services, but they also deal with communication interactions between users and applications. Message services include electronic mail or the transfer of messages between two or more networked computers, as shown in Figure C.2c.

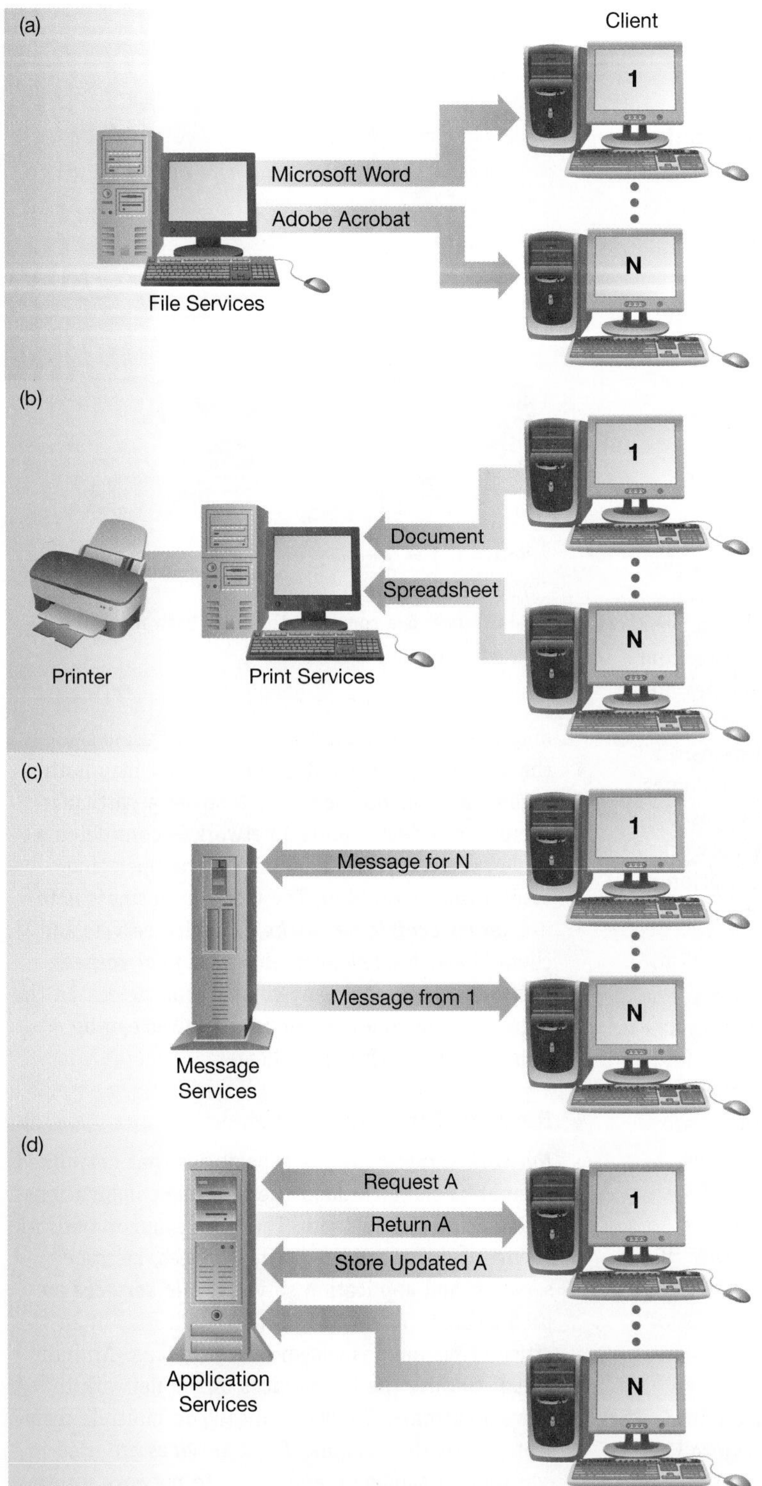

[**Figure C.2** ➥ Networks can provide file, print, message, and application services.]

Application services run software for network clients and enable computers to share processing power, as shown in Figure C.2d. Application services highlight the concept of client-server computing, in which processing is distributed between the client and server. Clients request information or services from the servers. The servers store data and application programs. For example, the physical search of database records may take place on the server, while a much smaller database application that handles the user-interface functions runs on the client.

When an organization decides to network its computers and devices, it must decide what services will be provided and whether these services will be

[Table C.1] *Key benefits and drawbacks of different cable media.*

Medium	Key Benefit(s)	Drawback(s)
Twisted pair	Inexpensive; easy to install and reconfigure	Highly susceptible to EMI, eavesdropping, and attenuation; unsuitable for high speeds
Coaxial	Higher bandwidth than twisted pair; lower susceptibility to EMI, eavesdropping, and attenuation than twisted pair	More expensive than twisted pair; more difficult to install, reconfigure, and manage attenuation than twisted pair; bulky
Fibre-optic	Very high bandwidth; low attenuation and immune to EMI and eavesdropping	Expensive cable and hardware; complex installation and maintenance

centralized (a server-centric approach), distributed (a peer-to-peer approach), or some combination of both. These decisions ultimately affect the choice of the network operating system. The ***network operating system (NOS)*** is system software that controls the network and enables computers to communicate with each other. In other words, the NOS enables network services. In most local area network (LAN) environments, the NOS consists of two parts. The first and most complex part is the system software that runs on the file server. The system software coordinates many functions, including user accounts, access information, security, and resource sharing. The second and much smaller part of the NOS runs on each workstation connected to the network. In peer-to-peer networks, usually a piece of the NOS is installed on each attached workstation and runs on top of the local operating system. A recent trend is to integrate the NOS into the workstation operating system itself. Recent versions of Windows use this approach. Examples of NOSs are Banyan Vines, Novell NetWare, Microsoft LAN Manager, and LANtastic.

Transmission Media

Every network uses some type of ***transmission medium***—the physical pathway to send data and information between two or more entities on a network. To send messages, computers send energy-based signals—electric currents using electromagnetic waves—to contact each other. These electromagnetic waves can be altered by semiconductor materials and are represented in two discrete, or binary, states—the 0s and 1s of a computer, known as bits. These bits are transmitted over physical pathways, or media, as computers communicate with each other.

When deciding which type of medium to use in a network, an organization should consider bandwidth, attenuation, immunity from electromagnetic interference (EMI) and eavesdropping, the cost of the cable, and ease of installation (as summarized in Table C.1). Recall that ***bandwidth*** is the transmission capacity of a computer or communications channel, measured in megabits per second (Mbps), and represents how much binary data can be reliably transmitted over the medium in one second. Some networks have a bandwidth of 10 Mbps; others have 100 Mbps or more. To appreciate the importance of bandwidth for speed, consider how long it would take to transmit a document the length of this book (about two million characters, or 16 million bits). It would take about 1.6 seconds at 10 Mbps and .16 seconds at 100 Mbps. In contrast, using a standard PC modem that transmits data at a rate of 56 kilobits per second (kbps), it would take nearly five minutes to transmit the same document. In addition to bandwidth, a second key issue to consider is transmission media's vulnerability to attenuation. ***Attenuation*** results when the power of an electric signal weakens as it is sent over increasing distance, as shown in Figure C.3. In a network, an important concern is how far a signal can travel and still maintain its original properties or meaning. ***EMI (electromagnetic interference)*** occurs when fluorescent lights, weather, or other electronic signals interfere with the original signal being sent. All media differ as to how immune they are to EMI, as we will see in the next sections.

Two forms of media are used in networks: cable and wireless media. The following sections describe the characteristics of both cable and wireless media.

Cable Media

Cable media physically link computers and other devices in a network. The most common forms of cable media are twisted pair, coaxial, and fibre-optic.

Twisted Pair Cable

Twisted pair (TP) cable is made of two or more pairs of insulated copper wires twisted together (see

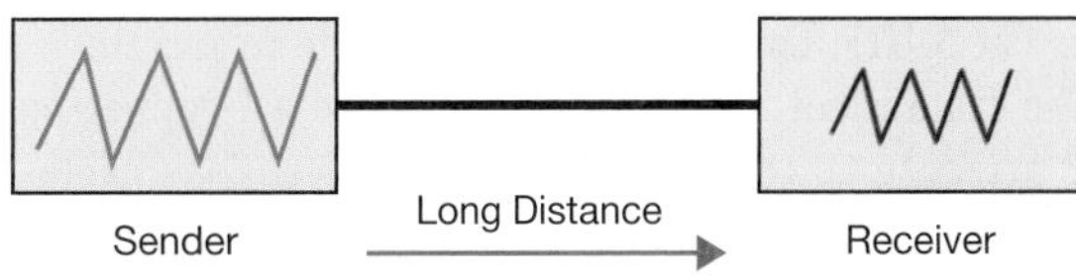

[**Figure C.3** ➥ Signals weaken when sent over increasing distances.]

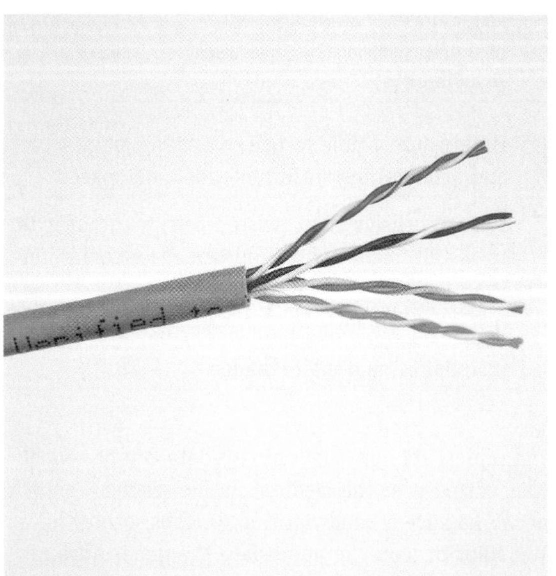

(a)

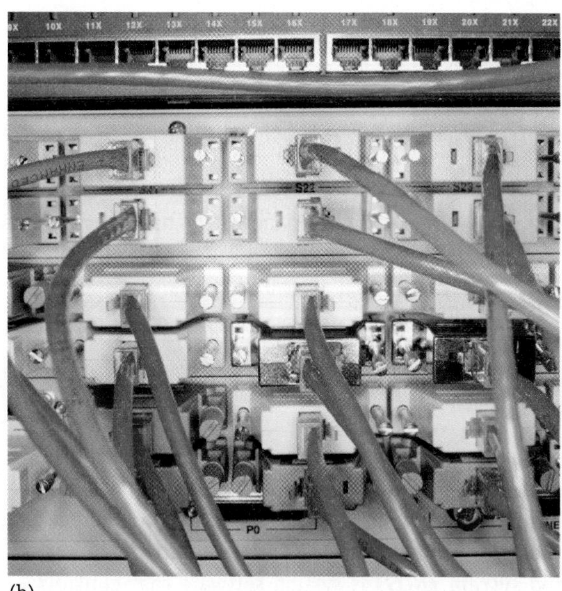

(b)

[Figure C.4 ➥ On the left is a cable spliced open showing several twisted pairs, and on the right is a sample network installation that utilizes many twisted pair cables at once.]

Sources: [A.3a] ©Belkin Components, [A.3b] © Getty Images, Inc.

Figure C.4). The cable may be unshielded (UTP) or shielded (STP). Telephone wire installations use UTP cabling. UTP is rated according to its quality; category 3 (Cat 3) and Cat 5 UTP are often used in network installations. Unshielded cable is cheap, easy to install, and has a capacity of from 1 to 100 Mbps at distances up to 100 metres. However, like all copper wiring, it has rapid attenuation and is very sensitive to EMI and eavesdropping—the undetected capturing of network information. Shielded twisted cable is cable wrapped in an insulation that makes it less prone to EMI and eavesdropping. Shielded twisted cable is more expensive than unshielded twisted cable, and it is more difficult to install because it requires special grounding connectors to drain EMI. STP can support bandwidths up to 500 Mbps at distances up to 100 metres. However, it is most commonly used to support networks running at 16 Mbps.

Coaxial Cable

Coaxial (or ***"coax"***) ***cable*** contains a solid inner copper conductor, surrounded by plastic insulation and an outer braided copper or foil shield (see Figure C.5). Coax cable comes in a variety of thicknesses—thinnet coax and thicknet coax—based on resistance to EMI. Thinnet coax is less costly than STP or Cat 5 UTP; thicknet coax, however, is more expensive than STP or Cat 3 UTP. Coax is the simplest cable to install. The cable is cut, and a connector, called a T-connector, is attached to the cable and each device. Coax cable is most commonly used for cable television installations and for networks operating at 10 Mbps. Its attenuation is lower than twisted pair cable, and it is moderately susceptible to EMI and eavesdropping.

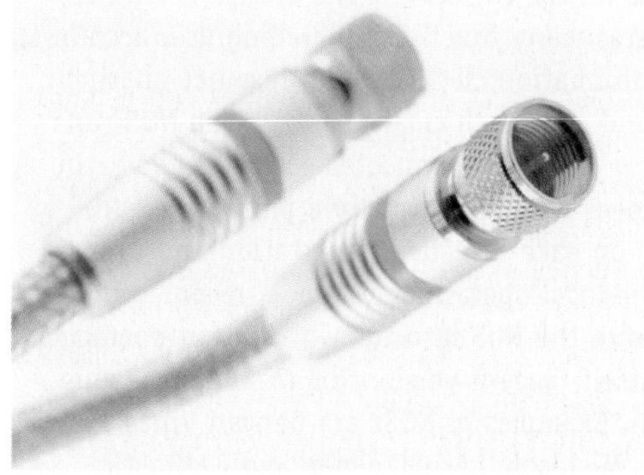

[Figure C.5 ➥ These sample coaxial cables are ready to be connected to a computer or other device.]

Source: © Getty Images, Inc.

Fibre-Optic Cable

Fibre-optic cable is made of a light-conducting glass or plastic core, surrounded by more glass, called cladding, and a tough outer sheath (see Figure C.6). The sheath protects the fibre from changes in temperature, as well as from bending or breaking. This technology uses pulses of light sent along the optical cable to transmit data. Fibre-optic cable transmits clear and secure data because it is immune to EMI and eavesdropping. Transmission signals do not break up because fibre-optic cable has low attenuation. It can support bandwidths from 100 Mbps to greater than 2 Gbps (gigabits per second) and distances from 2 to 25 kilometres. It can transmit video and sound. Fibre-optic cable is more expensive than copper wire, due to the cost and difficulties of installation and repair. Fibre-optic cables are used

[Figure C.6 ➥ Fibre-optic cable consists of a light-conducting glass or plastic core, surrounded by more glass, called cladding, and a tough outer sheath.]

Source: © Getty Images, Inc.

for high-speed ***backbones***—the high-speed central networks to which many smaller networks can be connected. A backbone may connect, for example, several different buildings in which other, smaller LANs reside.

Wireless Media

With the popularity of cellular phones and pagers, wireless media are rapidly gaining popularity. ***Wireless media*** transmit and receive electromagnetic signals using methods such as infrared line of sight, high-frequency radio, and microwave systems. Many home and corporate networks now use wireless media. In fact, networks based on wireless media are growing faster than all other types of networks put together. Unfortunately, the protocols and terminology surrounding wireless media can be confusing. Table C.2 compares some current and future wireless data transmission protocols.

Infrared Line of Sight

Infrared line of sight uses high-frequency light waves to transmit data on an unobstructed path between nodes—computers or some other device such as a printer—on a network, at a distance of up to 24.4 metres. The remote controls for most audio/visual equipment (such as your TV, stereo, and other consumer electronics equipment) use infrared light. Infrared systems may be configured as either point-to-point or broadcast. For example, when you use your TV remote control, you have to be in front of the TV to have successful communication. This is an example of point-to-point infrared. Many new printers and notebooks have the capability to transmit data using infrared communication, allowing these devices to be easily connected. With broadcast infrared communication, devices do not need to be positioned directly in front of each other, but simply have to be located within some distance of each other. Infrared equipment is relatively inexpensive, but point-to-point systems require strict line-of-sight positioning. Installation and maintenance focus on ensuring proper optical alignment between nodes on the network. Point-to-point infrared systems can support up to 16 Mbps at 1 km, whereas broadcast systems support less than 1 Mbps. Attenuation and susceptibility to EMI and eavesdropping are problematic, particularly when objects obstruct the light path, or when other environmental conditions such as smoke or high-intensity light are prevalent.

High-Frequency Radio

High-frequency radio signals can transmit data at rates of up to 11 Mbps to network nodes from 12.2 up to approximately 40 kilometres apart, depending on the nature of any obstructions between them. The flexibility of the signal path makes high-frequency radio ideal for mobile transmissions. For example, most police departments use high-frequency radio signals that enable police vehicles to communicate with each other as well as with the dispatch office. This medium is expensive due to the cost of antenna towers and high-output transceivers. Installation is complex and often dangerous due to the high voltages. Although attenuation is fairly low, this medium is very susceptible to EMI and eavesdropping.

[Table C.2] ***Wireless protocols for data transmission***

Protocol	Frequency	Bandwidth	Range	Typical Uses
Bluetooth	2.4 Ghz	1 Mbps	10 m	Headphones, keyboards, phones
Infrared	~100 Hz	~115 Kbps	5 m	Remote controls, PDAs
802.11b (Wi-Fi)	2.4 Ghz	11 Mbps	50 m	Office, home networks, laptops
802.11a	5 Ghz	54 Mbps	35 m	Office, home networks, laptops
802.11g	2.5 Ghz	22 Mbps	50 m	Office, home networks, laptops
Others: 802.11e (designed to support data streaming), 802.11i (includes advanced security features), 802.16e (mobile broadband), 802.20 (large area broadband)				

[Table C.3] *Types of pagers.*

Pager Type	Description	Advantages
Tone-only	User is alerted with an audible tone to call a predetermined phone number for a message	Simple
Numeric display	User is alerted and number to call is displayed	Can use any phone number; phone number is stored; less chance of error or missing message
Alphanumeric display	User is alerted and reads alphanumeric message	Same as numeric display, plus complete, accurate text message
Tone and voice	User is alerted and receives a short voice message	User gets notification and message in single event; easier for caller and user

Three common applications of high-frequency radio communication are pagers, cellular phones, and wireless networks. A ***pager*** is a one-way, wireless messaging system. (See Table C.3 for a summary of types of pagers and their advantages.) In a business setting, there are countless uses for a pager. If you travel, your boss can easily contact you when you are away from the office. If you are on vacation, you can learn the outcome of an important business deal. Pagers are also popular with families for notifying others of changes in plans, notifying parents when kids need to be picked up from school, or notifying teenagers when it is time to come home!

Unlike pagers, a ***cellular phone*** provides two-way wireless communication. In a cellular system, for example, a city is divided into ***cells*** with a low-powered radio antenna/receiver in each cell; these cells are monitored and controlled by a central computer (see Figure C.7). Any given cellular network has a fixed number of radio frequencies. When a user initiates or receives a call, a unique frequency is assigned to the caller by the mobile telephone switching office for the duration of the call. As a person travels within the network, the central computer at the switching office monitors the quality of the signal and automatically assigns the call to the closest cellular antenna.

High-frequency radio-wave technology is increasingly being used to support ***wireless local area networks (WLANs)***. The ease of installation has made WLANs popular for business and for home use. For example, many homes have multiple computers and have a need to share Internet access, files, or peripheral devices. Unfortunately, many older homes do not have a wired infrastructure to connect computers and devices, making wireless networking, often referred to as Wi-Fi, particularly attractive. As discussed previously, personal area networks (PANs) use low-powered Bluetooth radio-wave technology.

Microwave

Microwave transmission is a high-frequency radio signal that is sent through the air using either

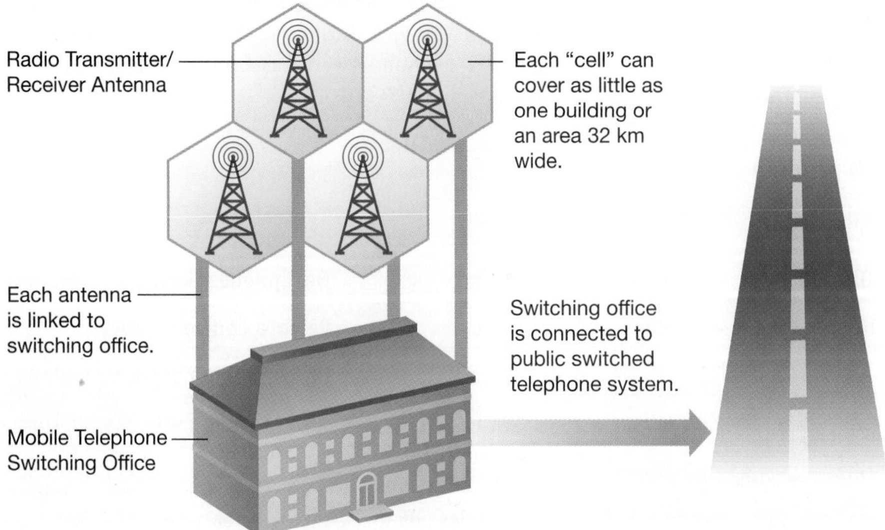
Radio Transmitter/
Receiver Antenna
Each "cell" can
cover as little as
one building or
an area 32 km
wide.
Each antenna
is linked to
switching office.
Switching office
is connected to
public switched
telephone system.
Mobile Telephone
Switching Office

[Figure C.7 ➡ A cellular network divides a geographic region into cells.]

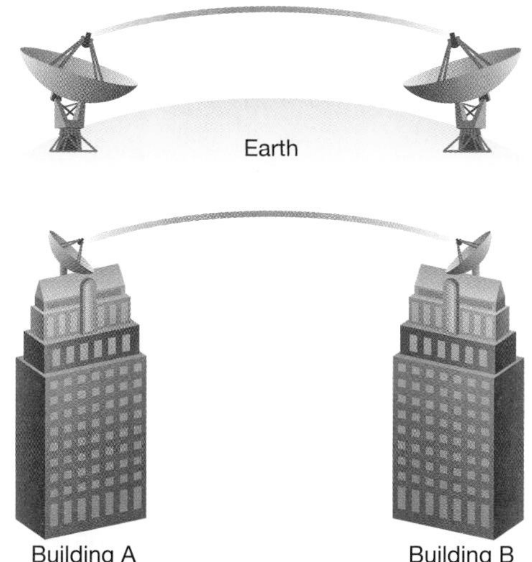

[Figure C.8 ➥ Terrestrial microwave requires a line-of-sight path between a sender and a receiver.]

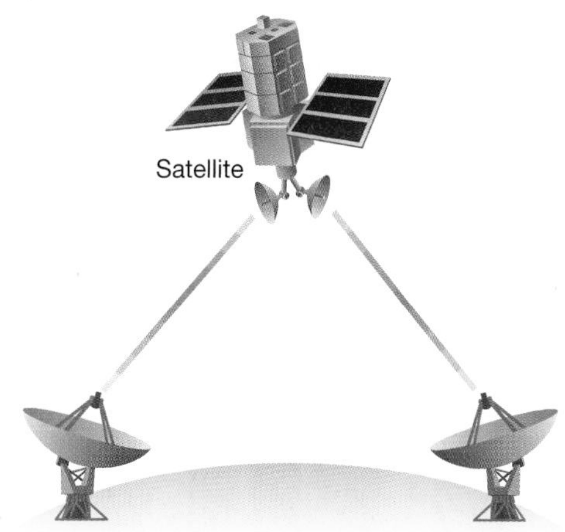

[Figure C.9 ➥ Communications satellites are relay stations that receive signals from one earth station and rebroadcast them to another.]

terrestrial (Earth-based) systems or satellite systems. Both terrestrial and satellite microwave transmission require line-of-sight communications between the signal sender and the signal receiver. ***Terrestrial microwave***, shown in Figure C.8, uses antennas that require an unobstructed path, or line of sight, between nodes. Terrestrial microwave systems are used to cross inaccessible terrain or to connect buildings where cable installation would be expensive. The cost of a terrestrial microwave system depends on the distance to be covered. Typically, businesses lease access to these microwave systems from service providers rather than invest in antenna equipment. Data may be transmitted at up to 274 Mbps. Over short distances, attenuation is not a problem, but signals can be obstructed over longer distances by environmental conditions such as high winds and heavy rain. EMI and eavesdropping are significant problems with microwave communications.

Satellite microwave, shown in Figure C.9, uses a relay station that transfers signals between antennas located on Earth and satellites orbiting the Earth. In other words, a ***satellite*** is a microwave station located in outer space. Satellite transmissions are delayed because of the distance signals must travel. Satellite communication's greatest strength is that it can be used to access very remote and undeveloped locations on the Earth. Such systems are extremely costly because their use and installation depends on space technology. Companies such as AT&T sell satellite services with typical transmission rates ranging from <1 to 10 Mbps, but the rates can be as high as 90 Mbps. Like terrestrial microwave, satellite systems are prone to attenuation and susceptible to EMI and eavesdropping.

As with cable media, there are key differences among the types of wireless media. Table C.4 summarizes the key benefits and drawbacks of each wireless

[Table C.4] ***Key benefits and drawbacks of different wireless media.***

Medium	Key Benefit(s)	Drawback(s)
Infrared line of sight	Easy to install and configure; inexpensive	Very limited bandwidth; line of sight required; environmental factors influence signal quality
High-frequency radio	Mobile stations; low attenuation	Frequency licensing; complex installation
Terrestrial microwave	Can access remote locations or congested areas; high bandwidth; low attenuation	Frequency licensing; complex installation; environmental factors influence signal quality
Satellite microwave	Can access remote locations; high bandwidth; Earth stations can be fixed or mobile	Frequency licensing; complex installation; environmental factors influence signal quality; propagation delays

[Table C.5] *Relative comparison of wireless media.*

Medium	Expense	Speed	Attenuation	EMI	Eavesdropping
Infrared line of sight	Low	Up to 16 Mbps	High	High	High
High-frequency radio	Moderate	Up to 11 Mbps	Low	High	High
Terrestrial microwave	Moderate	Up to 274 Mbps	Low	High	High
Satellite microwave	High	Up to 90 Mbps	Moderate	High	High

medium. Table C.5 compares wireless media across several criteria.

NETWORK SOFTWARE AND HARDWARE

Standards play a key role in creating networks. The physical elements of networks—adapters, cables, and connectors—are defined by a set of standards that have evolved since the early 1970s. Standards ensure the interoperability and compatibility of network devices. The Institute of Electrical and Electronics Engineers (IEEE) has established a number of telecommunications standards. The three major standards for LAN cabling and media access control are Ethernet, token ring, and ARCnet. (See Table C.6 for a summary of LAN standards.) Each standard combines a media access control technique, network topology, and media in different ways. Software is blended with hardware to implement protocols that allow different types of computers and networks to communicate successfully. Protocols are often implemented within a computer's operating system or within a special piece of software called a network operating system. Each of these topics is described more thoroughly below.

Media Access Control

Media access control are the rules that govern how a given node or workstation gains access to the network to send or receive information. There are two general types of access control: distributed and random access. With distributed control, only a single workstation at a time has authorization to transmit its data. This authorization is transferred sequentially from workstation to workstation. Under random control, any workstation can transmit its data by checking whether the medium is available. No specific permission is required. The following sections describe each type in more detail.

Distributed Access Control

The most commonly used method of distributed access control is called token passing. ***Token passing*** is an access method that uses a constantly circulating electronic token, a small packet of data, to prevent collisions and give all workstations equal access to the network. A collision occurs when two or more workstations simultaneously transmit messages onto the network. A workstation must possess the token before it can transmit a message onto the network.

A workstation that receives the token and wants to send a message marks the token as busy, appends a message to it, and transmits both. The message and token are passed around the ring, as depicted in Figure C.10. Each workstation copies the message and retransmits the token/message combination. When it is received back at the originating workstation, the message is removed, the token is marked as free, and it is transmitted to the next workstation on the network.

Random Access Control

The most commonly used method of random access control is called ***CSMA/CD—carrier sense multiple access/collision detect***. In CSMA/CD, each workstation "listens" to the network to determine whether a message is being transmitted. If the network is quiet, the workstation sends its message; otherwise, it waits. When a workstation gains access to the medium and sends information onto the network, messages are sent to all workstations on the network; however, only the destination with the proper address is able to "open" the message. If two or more workstations try to send a message simultaneously, all workstations detect that a collision has

[Table C.6] *Summary of major LAN standards.*

Network Standards	Access Control	Topology	Typical Media	Speed
Ethernet	CSMA/CD	Bus	Coax or twisted pair	10–100 Mbps
Token ring	Token passing	Ring	Twisted pair	4–100 Mbps
ARCnet	Token passing	Star or bus	Coax or twisted pair	2.5–20 Mbps

occurred, and all sending is ceased. After a short, random period of time, the workstations again try to send their messages. When network traffic is light, there are few collisions and data is quickly transmitted. However, the speed of transmission deteriorates rapidly under heavy traffic conditions.

Network Topologies

Network topology refers to the shape of a network. The three common network topologies are star, ring, and bus.

Star Network

A ***star network*** is configured, as you might expect, in the shape of a star, as shown in Figure C.11a. That is, all nodes or workstations are connected to a central hub or concentrator through which all messages pass. Active hubs amplify transmission signals so long cable lengths may be used. The workstations represent the points of the star. Star topologies are easy to lay out and modify. However, they are also the most costly because they require the largest amount of cabling. Although it is easy to diagnose problems at individual workstations, star networks are susceptible to a single point of failure at the hub that would result in all workstations losing network access.

Ring Network

A ***ring network*** is configured in the shape of a closed loop or circle, with each node connecting to the next node, as shown in Figure C.11b. In ring networks, messages move in one direction around the circle. As a message moves around the circle, each workstation examines it to see whether the message is for that workstation. If not, the message is regenerated and passed on to the next node. This regeneration process enables ring networks to cover much larger distances than star or bus networks can. Relatively little cabling is required, but a failure of any node on the ring network can cause complete network failure. It is difficult to modify and reconfigure the network. Ring networks normally use some form of token-passing media access control method to regulate network traffic.

Bus Network

A ***bus network*** is in the shape of an open-ended line, as shown in Figure C.11c, and, as a result, is the easiest network to extend and has the simplest wiring layout. This topology enables all network nodes to receive the same message through the network cable at the same time. However, it is difficult to diagnose and isolate network faults. Bus networks use CSMA/CD for media access control.

Protocols

In addition to media access control and network topologies, all networks employ protocols to make sure communication between computers is successful. ***Protocols*** are agreed-upon formats for transmitting data between connected computers. They specify how computers should be connected to the network, how errors will be checked, what data compression method will be used, how a sending computer will signal that it has finished sending a message, and how a receiving computer will signal that it has received a message. Protocols allow packets to be

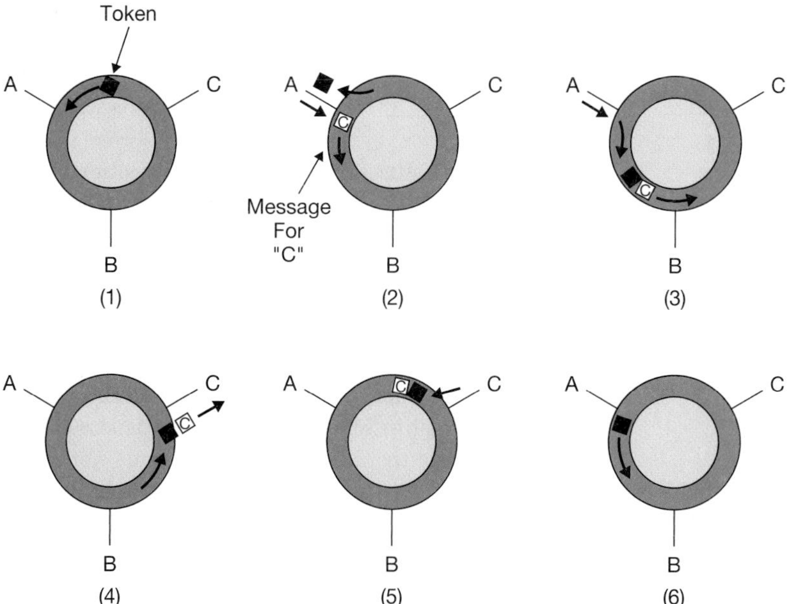

Figure C.10 ➡ Station A receives the token and adds a message for station C; C receives the message and token, then forwards both back to station A; station A removes the message and forwards the empty token on to the next station on the network.

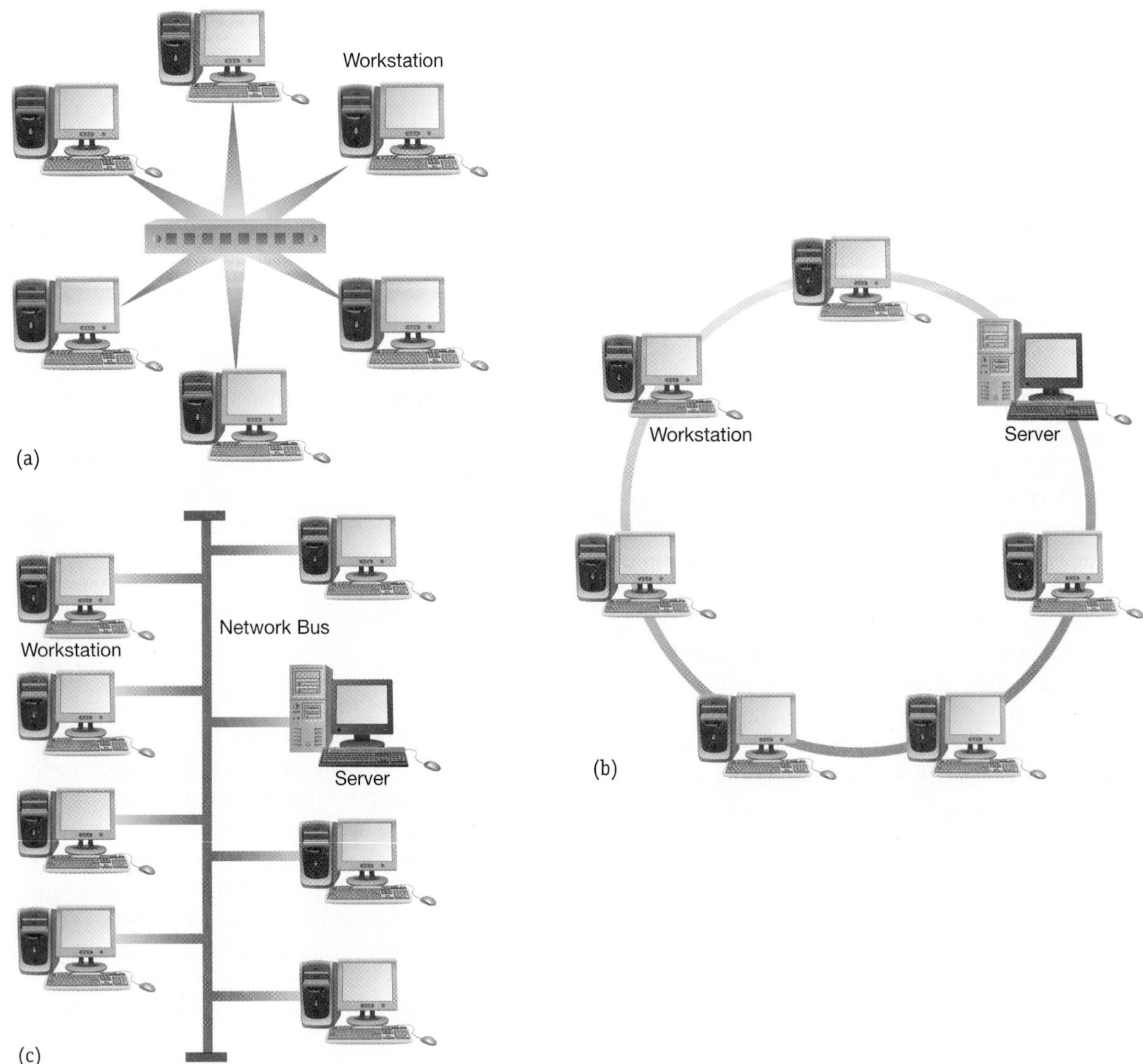

[**Figure C.11** ➡ (a) The star network has several workstations connected to a central hub. (b) The ring network is configured in a closed loop, with each workstation connected to another workstation. (c) The bus network is configured in the shape of an open-ended line where each workstation receives the same message simultaneously.]

correctly routed to and from their destinations. There are literally thousands of protocols for programmers to use, but a few are a lot more important than the others. In this section, we will first review the worldwide standard, called the OSI model, for implementing protocols. Next, we briefly review two of the more important network protocols: Ethernet and TCP/IP.

The OSI Model

The need of organizations to interconnect computers and networks that use different protocols has driven the industry to an open system architecture, in which different protocols can communicate with each other. The International Organization for Standardization (ISO) defined a networking model called the Open Systems Interconnection (OSI) that divides computer-to-computer communications into seven connected layers. The ***OSI model*** is a protocol that represents a group of specific tasks, represented in Figure C.12 as successive layers, which enable computers to communicate data. Each successively higher layer builds on the functions of the layers below. For example, suppose you are using a PC running Windows and are connected to the Internet, and you want to send a message to a friend who is connected to the Internet through a large workstation computer running UNIX—two different computers and two different operating systems. When you transmit your message, it is passed down from layer to layer in the Windows protocol environment of your system. At each layer, special bookkeeping information specific to the layer, called a header, is added to the data. Eventually, the data and headers

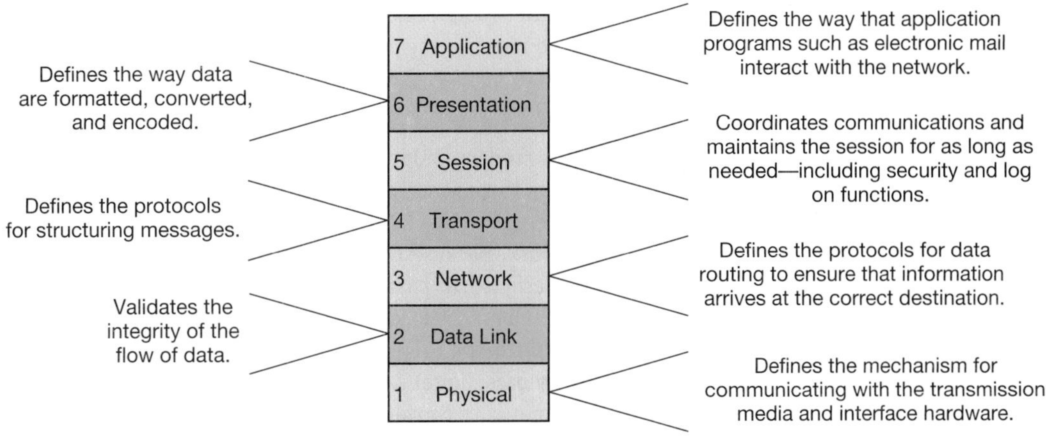

[**Figure C.12** ➡ The Open Systems Interconnection (OSI) model has seven layers and provides a framework for connecting different computers with different operating systems to a network.]

are transferred from the Windows Layer 1 to UNIX's Layer 1 over some physical medium. Upon receipt, the message is passed up through the layers in the UNIX application. At each layer, the corresponding header information is stripped away, the requested task is performed, and the remaining data package is passed on until your message arrives as you sent it, as shown in Figure C.13. In other words, protocols represent an agreement between different parts of the network about how data is to be transferred.

Ethernet

Ethernet is a local area network protocol developed by Xerox Corporation in 1976. It uses a bus or star network topology and uses random access control to send data. The original Ethernet supports data transfer rates of 10 Mbps. A later version, called 100Base T or Fast Ethernet, supports transfer rates of 100 Mbps, and the latest version, called Gigabit Ethernet, supports transfer rates of 1 gigabit, or 1,000 megabits, per second. You need some type of Ethernet card installed in your computer to use this type of network connection.

TCP/IP

The Internet was based on the idea that individual networks could be separately designed and developed, yet still connect their users to the Internet by

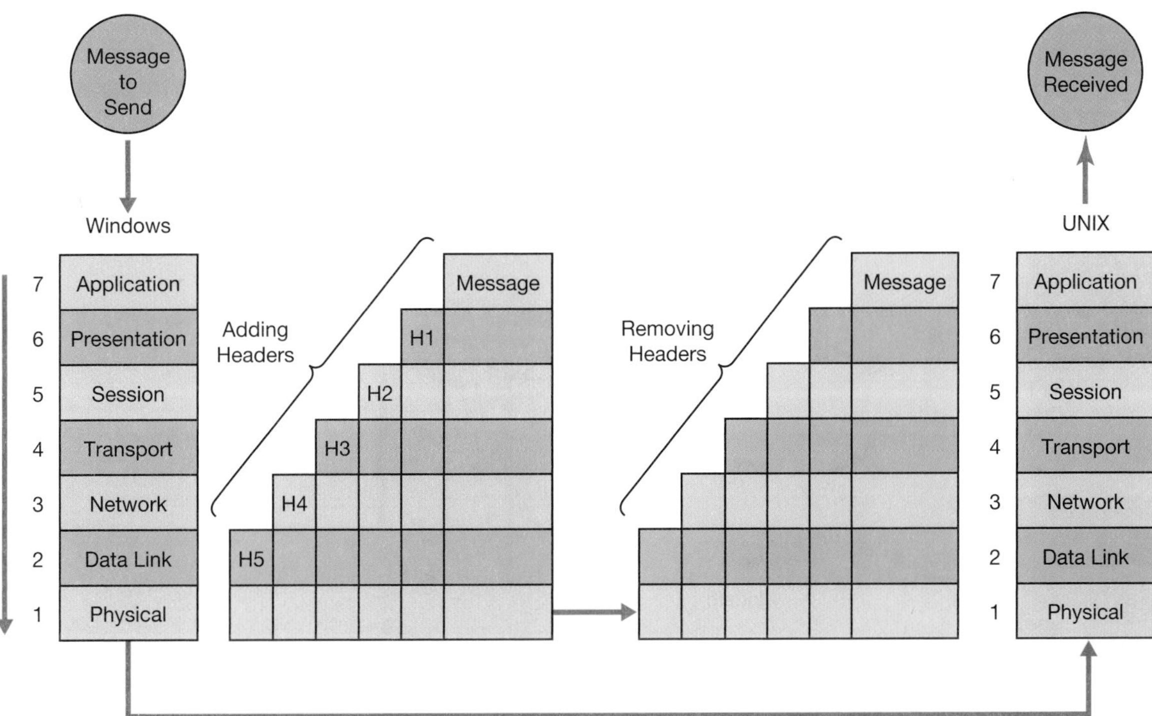

[**Figure C.13** ➡ Message passing between two different computers.]

using their own unique interfaces. ***Transmission control protocol/Internet protocol (TCP/IP)***, the protocol of the Internet, allows different interconnected networks to communicate using the same language. For example, TCP/IP allows IBM, Macintosh, and Dell users to communicate despite any system differences. Computer scientist Vinton Cerf and engineer Robert Kahn defined the Internet protocol (IP), by which packets are sent from one computer to another on their way to a destination, as part of the DARPA project. TCP/IP was discussed more thoroughly in Chapter 4.

Connectivity Hardware

Stand-alone computers can be physically connected to create different types of networks. Transmission media connectors, network interface cards, and modems are used to connect computers or devices in a network. After individual devices are connected to the network, multiple segments of transmission media can be connected to form one large network. Repeaters, hubs, bridges, and multiplexers are used to extend the range and size of the network. These devices are described below.

Transmission Media Connectors

Transmission media connectors, or simply ***connectors***, are used to terminate cable in order to be plugged into a network interface card or into other network components. Connectors include T-connectors for coax cable and RJ-45 connectors (similar to a phone jack) for twisted pair cable.

Network Interface Cards

A ***network interface card (NIC)*** is a PC expansion board that plugs into a computer so that it can be connected to a network. Each NIC has a unique identifier (determined by the manufacturer) that is used to identify the address of the computer on the network.

Modems

A ***modem*** (MOdulator/DEModulator) enables computers to transmit data over telephone lines and thereby connect your PC with other PCs in a computer network. Because the dial-up telephone system was designed to pass the sound of voices in the form of analog signals, it cannot pass the electrical pulses—***digital signals***—that computers use. The only way to pass digital data over conventional voice telephone lines is to convert it to audio tones—***analog signals***—that the telephone lines can carry. Hence, a modem converts digital signals from a computer into analog signals so that telephone lines may be used as a transmission medium to send and receive electronic information. If you send an e-mail message through a phone line from your university through the Internet to a friend at another university, the modem attached to your PC converts your digital message into audio tones. The message is transmitted over the telephone lines to your university, then travels through the Internet from your university to your friend's university. Your friend also uses a modem to dial in to her university to read your message, as shown in Figure C.14. Most university and corporate networks now support high-speed Internet access, and therefore dial-up access using modems is quickly becoming a thing of the past.

Repeaters

A ***repeater*** is a network device used to regenerate or replicate a signal as it weakens when travelling on a network. A repeater also moves data from one media segment to another and effectively extends the size of the network.

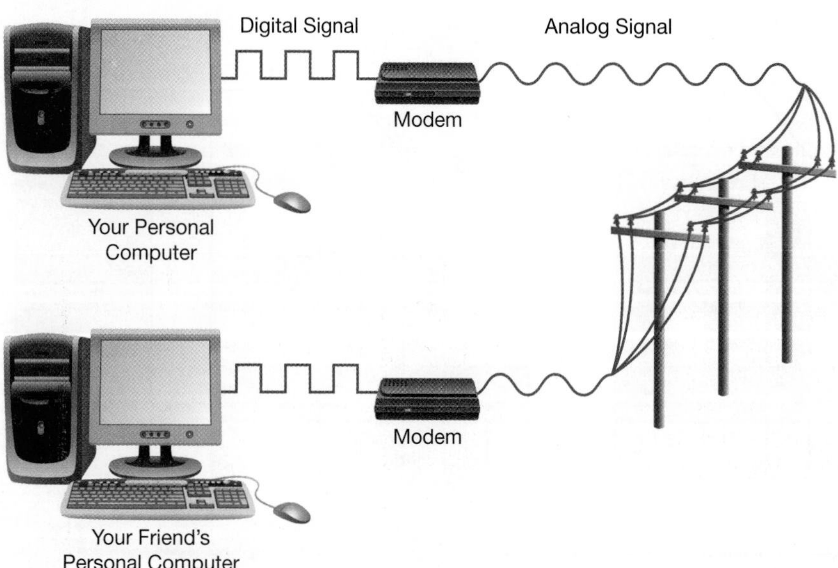

[**Figure C.14** ➡ Modems convert digital signals into analog and analog signals into digital.]

Hubs

A ***hub*** is used as a central point of connection between media segments. Like repeaters, hubs enable the network to be extended to accommodate additional workstations. Hubs are commonly used in 10Base-T networks.

Bridges

A ***bridge*** is used to connect two different LANs or two segments of the same LAN by forwarding network traffic between network segments. However, unlike repeaters, bridges determine the physical location of the source and destination computers. They are typically used to divide an overloaded network into separate segments, helping to minimize intersegment traffic. Bridges are also used to connect segments that use different wiring or network protocols.

Multiplexers

A ***multiplexer (MUX)*** is used to share a communications line or medium among a number of users. Sometimes the transmission medium provides more capacity than a single signal can occupy. To use the entire media bandwidth effectively, multiplexers are used to transmit several signals over a single channel. Multiplexers convert and combine signals from multiple users for simultaneous transmission over a single line or medium.

Organizations use these components to construct a LAN by attaching individual computers and media segments into one network. Organizations today also want to connect users and/or networks in different geographical areas. Distributed LANs, interconnected by WANs, are needed to exchange data and information across an organization. The WAN, however, appears transparent to the user because information stored in a computer at another location appears to be locally available. ***Internetworking*** connectivity hardware—switches, routers, brouters, CSUs (channel service units), and gateways—provides businesses with the freedom to locate their operations in different cities or countries, while at the same time running them as integrated units. These technologies are briefly described below.

Switches

A ***switch*** is a device that channels incoming data from any of multiple input ports to the specific output port that will take the data toward its intended destination.

Routers

A ***router*** is an intelligent device used to connect two or more individual networks. When a router receives a signal, it looks at the network address and passes the signal or message on to the appropriate network. Unlike most switches, routers use software to predict the most efficient path through a large network, like the Internet.

Brouters

A ***brouter*** (pronounced brau-ter) is short for *bridge router* and provides the capabilities of both a bridge and a router.

Channel Service Units

A ***channel service unit (CSU)*** is a device that acts as a "buffer" between a LAN and a public carrier's WAN. CSUs ensure that all signals placed on the public lines from the LAN are appropriately timed and formed for the public network.

Gateways

A ***gateway*** performs protocol conversion so that different networks can communicate even though they "speak" different languages. For example, communications between a LAN and a large system, such as a mainframe, whose protocols are different, require a gateway.

KEY POINTS REVIEW

1. **Understand networking fundamentals, including network services and transmission media.** In networking, a distinction is made between servers, clients, and peers. A server is a computer that stores information (programs and data) and provides services to users through a network. A client is any device or software application that makes use of the information or services provided by a server. Peers are two separate computers or devices on a network that request and provide services to each other. Servers and clients are combined to create server-centric networks. Peers are combined to create peer-to-peer networks. Networks provide file, print, message, and application services that extend the capabilities of stand-alone computers. The network operating system (NOS) is the major piece of software that controls the network. In a typical LAN, the NOS consists of two parts. The first and most complex is the system software that runs on the server. The NOS software coordinates many functions, including user accounts, access information, security, and resource sharing. The second and much smaller part of the NOS runs on each workstation connected to the LAN. Networks exchange information by using cable or wireless transmission media. Cable media include twisted pair, coaxial, and fibre-optic. Wireless media include infrared line of sight, high-frequency radio, and microwave.

2. **Describe network software and hardware, including media access control, network topologies, and protocols, as well as connectivity hardware for both local area and wide area networks.** Network access control refers to the rules that govern how a given workstation gains access to the network. There are two general types: distributed and random access. With distributed access, only a single workstation at a time has authorization to transmit its data. Under random access control, any workstation can transmit its data by checking whether the medium is available. The shape of a network can vary; the three most common topologies are star, ring, and bus configurations. Protocols are agreed-upon formats for transmitting data between connected computers. The need of organizations to interconnect devices that use different protocols has driven the industry to an open system architecture, in which different protocols can communicate with each other. The International Organization for Standardization (ISO) defined a networking model called the Open Systems Interconnection (OSI) that divides computer-to-computer communications into seven connected layers. Each successively higher layer builds on the functions of the layers below. Hardware and software vendors can use networking standards such as OSI to build devices that can be more easily interconnected. Ethernet is an important protocol for local area networks, whereas TCP/IP (transmission control protocol/Internet protocol) is most widely used for the world's largest WAN, the Internet. In a network, each device or computer must be connected to the medium or cable segment. To accomplish this, transmission media connectors, network interface cards, and modems are used. After individual devices are connected to the network, multiple segments of transmission media can be connected to form one large network. Repeaters, hubs, bridges, and multiplexers are used to extend the range and size of the network. Switches, routers, brouters, CSUs (channel service units), and gateways are used to interconnect wide area networks.

KEY TERMS

analog signals 368
application services 358
attenuation 359
backbone 361
bandwidth 359
bridge 369
brouter 369
bus network 365
cell 362
cellular phone 362
channel service unit (CSU) 369
client 357
coaxial cable 360
connectors 368
CSMA/CD (carrier sense multiple access/ collision detect) 364
digital signals 368
EMI (electromagnetic interference) 359
Ethernet 367
fibre-optic cable 360
file services 357
gateway 369
high-frequency radio 361
hub 369
infrared line of sight 361
internetworking 369
media access control 364
message services 357
microwave transmission 362
modem 368
multiplexer (MUX) 369
network 357
network interface card (NIC) 368
network operating system (NOS) 359
network services 357
network topology 365
OSI model 366
pager 362
peer 357
peer-to-peer networks 357
print services 357
protocols 365
repeater 368
ring network 365
router 369
satellite 363
satellite microwave 363
server 357
server-centric networks 357
star network 365
switch 369
terrestrial microwave 363
token passing 364
transmission control protocol/ Internet protocol (TCP/IP) 368
transmission medium 359
twisted pair cable 359
wireless local area network (WLAN) 362
wireless media 361

REVIEW QUESTIONS

1. Explain the difference between servers, clients, and peers.
2. What are the major types of network services available?
3. What are three common types of transmission media that use cabling?
4. What are four common methods of wireless transmission media for networking, and how do they differ from each other?
5. What is a network topology? Describe the three common topologies that are used today.
6. What is the purpose of the OSI model?
7. What is Ethernet, and why is it so popular?
8. What is TCP/IP, and what roles does it play in the use of the Internet?
9. What are the various types of hardware used to connect computers together into networks?
10. What is a modem used for, and how does one work?

SELF-STUDY QUESTIONS

Answers are at the end of the Problems and Exercises.

1. Which of the following is a type of computer on a network that makes access to files, printing, communications, and other services available to users of the network?
   A. server
   B. client
   C. peer
   D. pager
2. Which of the following is **not** a type of cable medium?
   A. twisted pair
   B. coaxial
   C. fibre-optic
   D. tertiary groups
3. Which of the following is a type of wireless medium?
   A. fibre-optic
   B. TCP/IP
   C. infrared
   D. microterminal
4. Which of the following are types of networks?
   A. star, ring, bus
   B. star, box, ring
   C. star, ring, triangle
   D. ring, bus, rectangle
5. All of the following are common applications of high-frequency radio communication **except** ________.
   A. pagers
   B. cellular phones
   C. wireless networks
   D. facsimiles
6. The International Organization for Standardization (ISO) defined a networking model called the ________ that divides computer-to-computer communications into seven connected layers.
   A. Network Allocation System (NAS)
   B. Open Systems Network (OSN)
   C. Open Systems Interconnection (OSI)
   D. Network Transfer System (NTS)
7. Which of the following is a type of local area network protocol developed by Xerox Corporation in 1976 that typically uses a bus or star network topology and uses random access control to send data?
   A. Ethernet
   B. bridge
   C. star
   D. gateway
8. Which of the following is the protocol of the Internet, allowing different interconnected networks to communicate using the same language?
   A. Ethernet
   B. C++
   C. transmission control protocol/Internet protocol (TCP/IP)
   D. router
9. After individual devices are connected to a network, multiple segments of transmission media can be connected to form one large network. All of the following **except** ________ are used to extend the range and size of the network.
   A. bridges
   B. repeaters
   C. modems
   D. hubs
10. A ________ performs protocol conversion so that different networks can communicate even though they "speak" different languages.
    A. gateway
    B. channel service unit
    C. modem
    D. brouter

PROBLEMS AND EXERCISES

1. Match the following terms with the appropriate definitions:

    ____ Pager
    ____ Token passing
    ____ Network operating system
    ____ Router
    ____ Bus network
    ____ Peer-to-peer network
    ____ Attenuation

    a. A decrease in the power of an electrical signal as it is sent over a distance
    b. A one-way, wireless messaging system
    c. A network access control method in which a token circulates around a ring topology and stations can transmit messages onto the network only when a nonbusy token arrives at a station
    d. A network topology in which all stations are connected to a single open-ended line
    e. A group of software programs that manages and provides network services
    f. An intelligent device used to connect two or more individual networks
    g. A network that enables any computer or device on the network to provide and request services

2. Using terms such as *digital, analog, dial-up telephone lines*, and *modem*, explain how a file is sent from your computer to your friend's computer through the regular phone system. What happens when and where?

3. Compare and contrast client-server and peer-to-peer networks. How do the computers and devices interact with each other in these networks? How does the term *client* relate to a peer-to-peer network? Under what circumstances is one type of network better than the other? Why?

4. Describe one of your experiences with a computer network. What type of topology was being used? What was the network operating system? Was the network connected to any other networks? How?

5. Scan the popular press and/or the World Wide Web for clues concerning emerging technologies for computer networking. This may include new uses for current technologies or new technologies altogether. Discuss as a group the "hot" issues. Do you feel they will become a reality in the near future? Why or why not? Prepare a 10-minute presentation of your findings to be given to the class.

6. Working in a group, have everyone describe what type of network would be most appropriate for a small office with about 10 computers, one printer, and one scanner, all within one floor in one building, and relatively close to one another. Be sure to talk about transmission media, network topology, hardware, and software. Did all group members come up with the same option? Why or why not? What else would you need to know to make a good recommendation?

7. Investigate the popular press, Web, or people you know working in companies to see to what extent firms are using twisted pair versus coaxial cable versus fibre-optic cabling. Under which circumstances is each being used, and what appear to be the trends in the use of cabling types?

8. Perform the same analysis as in Question 7, but this time check into uses of wireless networking. Which forms of wireless networking appear to be most popular and why?

9. Do some shopping on the Web and/or at a local computer store to determine what you would need, and what it would cost, to set up a wireless local area network in your home.

10. Ask questions of IS personnel at your place of work or at your school and determine which types of networks are being used in your office or classroom and how these local area networks are connected to the broader backbone network for this organization.

11. Search the Web for background information on the origin and uses of the Ethernet protocol. How did it begin, and how popular is it today?

12. Search the Web for background information on the origin and uses of the TCP/IP protocol. Why has it become so popular and powerful?

13. Investigate Cisco's Website and determine what types of networking products the company produces and sells. Why are its products so popular, and who are its competitors?

14. Investigate the options for high-speed, broadband Internet access into your home. What options are available to you, and how much do they cost?

ANSWERS TO THE SELF-STUDY QUESTIONS

1. A 2. D 3. C 4. A 5. D 6. C 7. A 8. C 9. C 10. A

Abilene network backbone: The network that connects Internet2 universities by using regional network aggregation points called **gigaPoPs** and very high-speed network equipment and facilities.

ActiveX: Software components developed by Microsoft that provide dynamic content to a Web page in a manner similar to a Java applet.

Ad hoc reports: Reports created due to unplanned information requests in which information is gathered to support a nonroutine decision.

Adaptive maintenance: Making changes to an information system to make its functionality meet changing business needs or to migrate it to a different operating system.

Alpha testing: Testing performed by the development organization to assess whether the entire system meets the design requirements of the users.

Analog signals: Audio tones used to transmit data over conventional voice telephone lines.

Applet: A program designed to be executed within another application such as a Web page.

Application services: Processes that run software for network clients and enable computers to share processing power.

Application software: Software used to perform a specific task that the user needs to accomplish, such as writing a business letter, processing the payroll, managing a stock portfolio, or manipulating a series of forecasts to come up with the most efficient allocation of resources for a project.

Arithmetic logic unit (ALU): Part of the central processing unit (CPU) that performs mathematics, including all forms of addition, subtraction, multiplication, and division.

ARPANET: The Advanced Research Projects Agency Network, a large, wide area network that linked many universities and research centres.

ASCII (American Standard Code for Information Interchange): An eight-bit code for representing numbers, letters, and other characters in binary form.

Asymmetric digital subscriber line (ADSL): A data transfer format that enables large amounts of data to be sent relatively quickly over existing copper telephone lines with speeds ranging from 1.5 to 9 Mbps downstream and from 16 to 640 Kbps upstream.

Asynchronous transfer mode (ATM): A method of transmitting voice, video, and data over high-speed LANs at speeds of up to 2.2 Gbps.

Attenuation: The result when the power of an electric signal weakens as it is sent over increasing distance.

Attribute: Each record typically consists of many attributes, which are individual pieces of information. For example, a name and social insurance number are attributes about a person.

Audio: Sound that has been digitized for storage and replay on a computer.

Authentication: The process of confirming the identity of a user who is attempting to access a system or Website.

Automating: Using information systems to do an activity faster or cheaper.

Backbone: A network that manages the bulk of network traffic and typically uses a higher-speed protocol than the individual LAN segments connected to it.

Backbone network: A network that manages the bulk of network traffic and typically uses a higher-speed protocol than the individual LAN segments connected to it.

Bandwidth: The transmission capacity of a computer or communications channel, often measured in megabits per second (Mbps); it represents how much binary data can be reliably transmitted over the medium in one second.

Batch input: Methods for rapidly entering large amounts of data into a computer.

Batch processing: The processing of transactions after some quantity of transactions are collected and then processed together as a "batch" at some later time.

Best-cost provider: An organization offering products or services of reasonably good quality at competitive prices.

Best practices: Procedures and processes from business organizations that are widely accepted as being among the most effective and/or efficient.

Beta testing: Testing performed by actual system users, who test the capabilities of the system with actual data in their work environment.

Binary code: Methods for representing digital data and information using sequences of zeros and ones.

Biometrics: A type of security that grants or denies access to a computer system through the analysis of fingerprints, retinal patterns in the eye, or other bodily characteristics.

Bits: The individual 1s and 0s that make up a byte.

Bluetooth: A wireless specification for personal area networking (PAN) of desktop computers, peripheral devices, mobile phones, pagers, portable stereos, and other handheld devices.

Bricks-and-mortar: Term used to identify traditional firms doing business the old-fashioned way, from a physical storefront.

Bridge: Device used to connect two different LANs or two segments of the same LAN by forwarding network traffic between network segments; unlike repeaters, bridges determine the physical location of the source and destination computers.

Brouter: Short for ***bridge router*** (pronounced brau-ter); provides the capabilities of both a bridge and a router for managing network traffic.

Bus network: Network in the shape of an open-ended line; it is the easiest network to extend and has the simplest wiring layout.

Business information systems: Software applications that are developed to perform organization-wide operations.

Business process reengineering: Significant organizational change designed to improve the functioning of an organization as opposed to merely dropping in an information system with no attempts at changing and improving the organization.

Business rules: Rules included in data dictionaries to prevent illegal or illogical entries from entering the database.

Business-to-business: Electronic commerce that is used to conduct business with business partners such as suppliers and intermediaries.

Business-to-consumer: EC used to conduct transactions between businesses and consumers.

Business-to-employee: EC that occurs between businesses and their employees.

Byte: Typically eight bits, or about one typed character.

Bytes per inch (BPI): The number of bytes that can be stored on one inch of magnetic tape.

CA*net 4: Canada's a high-speed network, similar to Internet2, that connects provincial research networks, universities, research centres, government research laboratories, schools, and other eligible sites.

Cable modem: A specialized piece of equipment that enables a computer to access Internet service designed to operate over cable TV lines.

Cache: Pronounced "cash," it is a small block of memory used by processors to store those instructions most recently or most often used.

Carding: Refers to the practice of stealing credit card numbers online, to be resold or used to charge merchandise against victims' accounts.

CD-R (compact disc—recordable): A type of optical disk that data can be written to.

CD-ROM (compact disc—read-only memory): A type of optical disk that cannot be written to, but can only be read.

CD-RW (compact disc—rewritable): A type of optical disk that be written onto multiple times.

Cell: A geographical area containing a low-powered radio antenna/receiver for transmitting telecommunications signals within that area; monitored and controlled by a central computer.

Cellular phone: Mobile phone that uses a communications system that divides a geographic region into sections, called **cells**.

Central processing unit (CPU): Also called a microprocessor, processor, or chip, it is responsible for performing all of the operations of the computer.

Centralized computing: A system of large centralized computers, called mainframes, used to process and store data.

Certificate authority: A trusted intermediary between computers that verifies that a Website is a trusted site and is used when implementing public key encryption on a large scale.

Channel service unit (CSU): A device that acts as a "buffer" between a LAN and a public carrier's WAN. CSUs ensure that all signals placed on the public lines from the LAN are appropriately timed and formed for the public network.

Characters per inch (CPI): The number of characters that can be stored on one inch of magnetic tape.

Chief information officer: Title given to executive-level individuals who are responsible for leading the overall information systems component within their organizations and integrating new technologies into the organization's business strategy.

Clicks-and-mortar: Term used to identify firms doing traditional, physical business and doing business on the Internet as well.

Clicks-only: Term used to identify firms doing business solely on the Internet, with no physical storefront.

Client: Any computer, such as a user's workstation or PC on the network, or any software application, such as a word processing application, that requests and uses the services provided by the server.

Clock speed: The speed of the system clock, typically measured in hertz (Hz).

Clock tick: A single pulse of the system clock.

Cloning: Cellular phone fraud in which scanners are used to steal the electronic serial numbers of cellular phones as calls are made.

Coaxial cable (or "coax cable"): Contains a solid inner copper conductor surrounded by plastic insulation and an outer braided copper or foil shield and is most commonly used for cable television installations and for networks operating at 10 Mbps. Its attenuation is lower than twisted pair cable, and it is moderately susceptible to EMI and eavesdropping.

Collaboration system: An information system that enables people to communicate electronically with each other in order to solve problems, make decisions, and perform other forms of joint work.

Collaborative computing: A synergistic form of distributed computing, in which two or more networked computers are used to accomplish a common processing task.

Collaborative information system: A type of international information system that integrates different applications and data that can be shared by different companies in different countries.

Combination primary key: A combination of two or more attributes used to uniquely identify a row in an entity in a database.

Command-based interface: Computer interface that requires the user to enter text-based commands to instruct the computer to perform specific operations.

Competitive advantage: A firm's ability to do something better, faster, more cheaply, or uniquely when compared with rival firms in the market.

Compiler: A software program that translates a programming language into machine language.

Computer-aided design (CAD): Using high-powered computers to design very state-of-the-art, high-quality products.

Computer-aided software engineering (CASE): Software tools that provide automated support for some portion of the systems development process.

Computer-based information system: A combination of hardware, software, and telecommunications networks that people build and use to collect, create, and distribute data.

Computer crime: The act of using a computer to commit an illegal act.

Computer ethics: A broad range of issues and standards of conduct that have emerged through the use and proliferation of information systems.

Computer literacy: The knowledge of how to operate a computer.

Computer security: Precautions taken to keep computers and the information they contain safe from unauthorized access.

Connectors: Also called transmission media connectors; used to terminate cable in order to be plugged into a network interface card or into other network components. Connectors include T-connectors for coax cable and RJ-45 connectors (similar to a phone jack) for twisted pair cable.

Consumer-to-consumer: A form of EC that does not even involve business firms, such as an online textbook exchange service for students at a university or an online trading Website such as eBay.com.

Control unit: Part of the central processing unit (CPU) that works closely with the ALU (arithmetic logic unit) by fetching and decoding instructions, as well as retrieving and storing data.

Conversion: The process of transferring information from a legacy system to a new computing platform.

Copyright: A series of rights granted to an author of a work under the *Copyright Act*.

Corrective maintenance: Making changes to an information system to repair flaws in its design, coding, or implementation.

Cracker: An individual who breaks into computer systems with the intention of doing damage or committing a crime.

CSMA/CD (carrier sense multiple access/collision detect): A format in which each workstation "listens" to the network to determine whether a message is being transmitted. If the network is quiet, the workstation sends its message; otherwise, it waits. When a workstation gains access to the medium and sends information onto the network, messages are sent to all workstations on the network; however, only the destination with the proper address is able to "open" the message.

Custom applications: Software programs that are designed and developed by company personnel as opposed to being bought off-the-shelf.

Customer relationship management (CRM): The process of managing all aspects of the relationship with customers including finding them, marketing and selling to them, servicing their needs after the sale, and so on.

Customer relationship management system (CRMS): Information system to support interaction between the firm and its customers.

Customization: Modifying software so that it better suits user needs.

Customized application software: Software that is developed based on specifications provided by a particular organization.

Data: Recorded, unformatted information, such as words and numbers, that often has no meaning in and of itself.

Data dictionary: A document prepared by the database designers to describe the characteristics of all items in a database.

Data diddling: A type of computer crime where the data going into or out of a computer is altered.

Data flows: Data moving through an organization or within an information system.

Data mart: A data warehouse that is limited in scope and customized for the decision support applications of a particular end-user group.

Data mining: A method used by companies to sort and analyze information to better understand their customers, products, markets, or any other phase of their business for which data have been captured.

Data model: A map or diagram that represents the entities of a database and their relationships.

Data type: Each attribute in the database is a particular type such as text, number, or date.

Data warehouse: An integration of multiple, large databases and other information sources into a single repository or access point that is suitable for direct querying, analysis, or processing.

Database: A collection of related data organized in a way to facilitate data searches.

Database administrator: A person responsible for the development and management of the organization's databases.

Database management system (DBMS): A software application with which you create, store, organize, and retrieve data from a single database or several databases.

Decision support system (DSS): A special-purpose information system designed to support organizational decision making.

Defense Advanced Research Projects Agency (DARPA): A U.S. governmental agency that began to study ways to interconnect networks of various kinds, which led to the development of the ARPANET (Advanced Research Projects Agency Network).

Density: The storage capacity of magnetic tape that is typically referred in either characters per inch (CPI) or bytes per inch (BPI).

Desktop videoconferencing: The use of integrated computer, telephone, video recording, and playback technologies—typically by two people—to interact with each other using their desktop computers from remote sites.

Developmental testing: Testing performed by programmers to ensure that each module is error-free.

Differentiation strategy: An organization's stratagy of providing better products or services than its competitors.

Digital divide: The gap between those individuals in our society who are computer literate and have access to information resources like the Internet and those who do not.

Digital signals: The electrical pulses that computers use to send bits of information.

Digital subscriber line (DSL): Uses special modulation schemes to fit more data onto traditional copper phone wires; referred to as "last-mile" solutions because they are used only for connections from a telephone switching station to a home or office, and they generally are not used between telephone switching stations.

Digitization: A process that creates products without tangible features, which are commonly referred to as *virtual products.*

Digitizing: The process of converting a photograph or a song into digital information, or bits, which then can travel across a network.

Direct conversion: Changing from an old to a new system by beginning the new system and discontinuing the old system at the same time.

Disintermediation: The phenomenon of cutting out the intermediary and reaching customers more directly and efficiently.

Diskettes: Also called floppy disks, are $3\frac{1}{2}$-inch, round, flexible Mylar devices that record data as magnetized spots on tracks on the disk surface.

Distance learning: The process of providing instruction to students who are physically separated from instructors through the use of some sort of communication technologies including videoconferencing, Internet chatting, and various Web-based tools.

Distributed computing: A model of using separate computers to work on subsets of tasks and then pooling their results by communicating over a network.

Distribution portals: Enterprise portals that automate the business processes involved in selling, or distributing, products from a single supplier to multiple buyers.

Domain name: Used in uniform resource locators (URLs) to identify a source or host entity on the Internet.

Domain name system: A database used to associate Internet host names with their Internet IP addresses.

Dot matrix printer: A printing technology where characters and images are formed using a series of small dots; most commonly found in printing voluminous batch information, such as periodic reports and forms.

Downsizing: When companies slash costs, streamline operations, and/or let employees go.

Downstream: An information flow that relates to the information that is produced by a company and sent along to another organization such as a distributor.

Drill-down reports: Reports that provide details behind the summary values on a key-indicator or exception report.

Dumpster diving: A type of computer crime where individuals go through dumpsters and garbage cans for company documents, credit card receipts, and other papers containing information that might be useful.

DVD-ROM (digital video disk—read-only memory): A type of optical disk that uses a shorter-wavelength laser beam that allows more information to be stored on a disk than a standard CD-ROM.

E-brochure: A Web tool used to promote sales and marketing information.

E-business: Term used to refer to the use of a variety of types of information technologies and systems to support every part of the business.

E-business innovation cycle: The time period and to what extent an organization derives value from a particular information technology.

E-information: The first stage of a Website, in which information about a company and its product is disseminated globally to potential customers who have access to the Internet and a Web browser.

E-integration: The second stage of a Website, in which sites containing general information about a company and its product must be integrated with corporate databases to extract and display personal customer information necessary to achieve mass customization.

E-tailing: Electronic retailing.

E-transaction: This third stage of a Website takes the e-integration stage one step further by adding the ability for customers to enter orders and payments online.

EBCDIC (Extended Binary-Coded Decimal Interchange Code): An eight-bit code for representing numbers, letters, and other characters in binary form; typically used on mainframe computers.

Economic opportunities: Opportunities that a firm finds for making more money and/or making money in new ways.

Electronic brochure: Using the Web to disseminate sales and marketing information.

Electronic commerce: Exchanges of goods and services via the Internet among and between customers, firms, employees, business partners, suppliers, etc.

Electronic data interchange (EDI): The digital, or electronic, transmission of business documents and related data between organizations via telecommunications networks that enables the online exchange and sale of goods and services between firms.

Electronic fund transfer: The process of transferring funds from one financial account to another via computer.

Electronic mail (e-mail): The transmission of messages over computer networks.

Electronic marketplace: Also called a trading exchange. A Website built by a third party that allows buyers and sellers to come together, offering firms access to real-time trading with other companies in their vertical markets.

Electronic meeting system (EMS): A collection of personal computers networked together with sophisticated software tools to help group members solve problems and make decisions through interactive, electronic idea generation, evaluation, and voting.

EMI (electromagnetic interference): Occurs when fluorescent lights, weather, or other electronic signals interfere with the original signal being sent.

Enabling technologies: Information technologies that enable a firm to accomplish a task or goal or to gain or sustain competitive advantage in some way.

Encapsulation: The grouping of data and instructions into a single object in object-oriented programming languages.

Encryption: The process of encoding messages before they enter the network or airwaves, then decoding them at the receiving end of the transfer so that recipients can read or hear them.

End-user development: A systems development method whereby users in the organization develop, test, and maintain their own applications.

Enterprise network: A WAN that is the result of connecting disparate networks of a single organization into a single network.

Enterprise portal: Information system that provides a single point of access to secured, proprietary information, which may be dispersed throughout an organization.

Enterprise resource planning (ERP): Information system that supports and integrates all facets of the business, including planning, manufacturing, sales, marketing, and so on.

Enterprise resource planning system (ERPS): Information system that supports and integrates all facets of the business, including planning, manufacturing, sales, marketing, and so on.

Enterprise systems: Information systems that support many or all of the various parts of the firm.

Entity: Things about which we collect data, such as people or classes.

Entity-relationship diagram (ERD): A diagramming technique that is commonly used when designing databases, especially when showing associations between entities.

Ergonomics: The design of computer hardware and work environments that minimize health risks.

Ethernet: A local area network protocol developed by Xerox Corporation in 1976. It uses a bus or star network topology and uses random access control to send data. The original Ethernet supports data transfer rates of 10 Mbps. A later version, called 100Base-T or Fast Ethernet, supports transfer rates of 100 Mbps, and the latest version, called Gigabit Ethernet, supports transfer rates of 1 gigabit, or 1,000 megabits, per second. You need some type of Ethernet card installed in your computer to use this type of network connection.

Ethics: The science of human duty that encompasses a system of principles and rules concerning duty. A broad range of ethical issues have emerged through the use and proliferation of computers.

Event-driven: Programming language characteristic that allows the development of programs to execute based on user-requested events rather than on a linear sequence through the program.

Exception report: Reports that highlight situations that are out of the normal operating range.

Executive information system (EIS): An information system designed to provide information in a very aggregate form so that managers at the executive level of the organization can quickly scan it for trends and anomalies.

Executive level: The top level of the organization, where executives focus on long-term strategic issues facing the organization.

Expert system (ES): A special-purpose information system designed to mimic human expertise by manipulating knowledge—understanding acquired through experience and extensive learning—rather than simply information.

Extensible markup language (XML): A Web programming language that allows designers to create customized features that enable data to be more easily shared between applications and organizations.

External acquisition: The process of purchasing an existing information system from an external organization or vendor.

External or secondary cache: Special high-speed cache memory that is usually not built into the CPU, but is located within easy reach of the CPU on the motherboard.

Extranet: The use of the Internet by firms and companies for business-to-business interactions.

Facsimile, or fax, machine: Machines that digitize images, such as letters, memos, newspaper and magazine articles, photos, contracts, even handwritten notes, so that they can be transmitted to other fax machines over telephone lines.

Fibre-optic cable: Made of a light-conducting glass or plastic core, surrounded by more glass, called cladding, and a tough outer sheath that protects the fibre from changes in temperature, as well as from bending or breaking; uses pulses of light sent along the optical cable to transmit video or sound data clearly and securely because it is immune to EMI and eavesdropping; has low attenuation; can support bandwidths from 100 Mbps to greater than 2 Gbps (gigabits per second) and distances from 2 to 25 kilometres.

File services: Processes used to store, retrieve, and move data files in an efficient manner; individuals can use the file services of the network to move a customer file electronically to multiple recipients across the network.

File transfer: The process of connecting to a remote computer in order to either upload (sending to the remote machine) or download (obtaining from the remote machine) files and data.

Firewall: Hardware or software designed to keep unauthorized users out of network systems.

Fixed wireless: A wireless solution requiring that the user's computer be stationary rather than mobile.

Flash memory: A variation of ROM that can be repeatedly written to and erased like RAM, but, unlike RAM, it retains its information after power is turned off.

Foreign key: An attribute that appears as a nonprimary key attribute in one entity and as a primary key attribute (or part of a primary key) in another entity.

Form: 1. A collection of blank entry boxes, each representing a field, that is used to enter information into a database. 2. A business document that contains some predefined data and may include some areas where additional data is to be filled in, typically for a single record.

Fully automated data entry: Data entry into an information system that does not require any human intervention.

Functional area information system: A cross-organizational-level information system designed to support a specific functional area.

Gateway: A connection between the internal computer systems and networks of a company and the Internet, enabling people to send electronic mail and other data or files over the Internet to and from nearly anywhere in the world.

Geostationary: A system of satellites that are placed in fixed positions above the Earth's surface and orbit along with the Earth (also called a geosynchronous orbit).

Geosynchronous: A system of satellites that are placed in fixed positions above the Earth's surface and orbit along with the Earth (also called a geostationary orbit).

GigaPoP: Regional network aggregation points used in connecting different systems within a network backbone, such as the Abilene network backbone.

Global information system: A type of international information system that is used when a single transaction requires the input of data from multiple centres located in more than one nation.

Global network: Spans multiple countries and may include the networks of several organizations. The Internet is an example of a global network.

Gopher: A text-based, menu-driven interface that enables users to access a large number of varied Internet resources as if they were in folders and menus on their own computers.

Graphical user interface (GUI): Computer interface that enables the user to select pictures, icons, and menus to send instructions to the computer.

Groupware: Software that enables people to work together more effectively.

Hacker: An individual who gains unauthorized access to computer systems.

Hard data: Facts and numbers that are typically generated by transaction processing systems and management information systems.

Hard drive or hard disk: A secondary storage device for storing data, usually located inside the system unit of a computer.

Hardware: Physical computer equipment, such as the computer monitor, central processing unit, or keyboard.

Head crash: A failure inside a hard disk when the read/write head touches the disk and results in the loss of the data and/or the operation of the hard disk.

High-frequency radio: Signals can transmit data at rates of up to 11 Mbps to network nodes from 12.2 to 39.6 kilometres apart.

Hub: Used as a central point of connection between media segments; like repeaters, hubs enable the network to be extended to accommodate additional workstations; commonly used in 10Base-T networks.

Hyperlink: A reference or link on a Web page to other documents that contain related information.

Hypermediation: A "pay by the click" pricing scheme in which the firm running the advertisement pays only when a Web surfer actually clicks on the advertisement.

Hypertext: Text in a Web document that is highlighted and, when clicked on by the user, evokes an embedded command that goes to another specified file or location and brings up that file or location on the user's screen.

Hypertext markup language (HTML): The standard method of specifying the format of Web pages. Specific content within each Web page is enclosed within codes, or markup tags, which stipulate how the content should appear to the user.

Hypertext transfer protocol (HTTP): The process by which servers process user requests for Web pages.

Identity theft: Stealing another person's social insurance number, credit card number, and other personal information for the purpose of using the victim's credit rating to borrow money, buy merchandise, and otherwise run up debts that are never repaid.

Inferencing: The matching of user questions and answers to information in a knowledge base within an expert system in order to make a recommendation.

Informating: The ability of information technology to provide information about the operation within a firm and/or about the underlying work process that the system supports.

Information: Data that has been formatted and/or organized in some way as to be useful to people.

Information accessibility: An ethical issue that focuses on defining what information a person or organization has the right to obtain about others and how this information can be accessed and used.

Information accuracy: An ethical issue concerned with the authenticity and fidelity of information, as well as identifying who is responsible for informational errors that harm people.

Information Age: A period of time in society where information has become a valuable or dominant currency of the realm.

Information privacy: An ethical issue that is concerned with what information an individual should have to reveal to others through the course of employment or through other transactions such as online shopping.

Information property: An ethical issue that focuses on who owns information about individuals and how information can be sold and exchanged.

Information systems: Assumed to mean computer-based information systems, which are combinations of hardware, software, and telecommunications networks that people build and use to collect, create, and distribute useful data; this term is also used to represent the field in which people develop, use, manage, and study computer-based information systems in organizations.

Information systems planning: 1. A formal organizational process for assessing the information needs of an organization in which the systems, databases, and technologies for meeting those needs are identified. 2. Planning for the investment in the deployment of information systems. This planning helps people meet organizational strategies and objectives given the organization's resource constraints.

Information technology: Refers to machine technology that is controlled by or uses information.

Informational system: The systems designed to support decision making based on stable point-in-time or historical data.

Infrared line of sight: Uses high-frequency light waves to transmit data on an unobstructed path between nodes—computers or some other device such as a printer—on a network, at a distance of up to 24.4 metres.

Inheritance: A characteristic of object-oriented programming languages that requires lower-level objects, or children, to inherit the characteristics of higher-level, or parent, objects.

Inkjet printer: A printing technology where characters and images are formed by transferring ink onto paper.

Input devices: Hardware that is used to enter information into a computer.

Instant messaging (IM): Having conversations with others in real time on the Internet.

Intangible benefits: A benefit of using a particular system or technology that is difficult to quantify. Examples of intangible benefits include faster turnaround on fulfilling orders and resulting improvements in customer service.

Intangible costs: A cost of using a particular system or technology that is difficult to quantify. Examples include the costs of reducing traditional sales, losing some customers that are not "Web ready," or losing customers if the Web application is poorly designed or not on par with competitors' sites.

Integrated Services Digital Network (ISDN): A standard for worldwide digital communications that is intended to replace analog systems and uses existing twisted pair telephone wires to provide high speed data service.

Interface: The way in which the user interacts with the computer.

Internal cache: Special high-speed cache memory that is incorporated into the microprocessor's design.

International information system: A general class of information systems that support transactions that cross national boundaries.

Internet: A term derived from the concept of internetworking, which means connecting host computers and their networks together to form even larger networks. The Internet is a large worldwide collection of networks that use a common protocol to communicate with each other.

Internet2: Developed in 1996 by leading universities as a faster, private alternative to the public Internet to be a testing-ground network to develop advanced Internet technologies and applications.

Internet backbone: The collection of main network connections and telecommunications lines that make up the Internet.

Internet Corporation for Assigned Names and Numbers: Also called ICANN, a nonprofit corporation that assumed responsibility from InterNIC for managing IP addresses, domain names, and root server system management.

Internet over Satellite (IoS): Technologies that allow users to access the Internet via satellites that are placed in fixed positions above the Earth's surface in what is known as a geostationary or geosynchronous orbit (i.e., the satellite moves along with the Earth).

Internet Registry: A central repository for Internet-related information that provides central allocation of network system identifiers.

Internet service provider (ISP): An individual or organization that enables other individuals and organizations to connect to the Internet.

Internetworking: Connecting host computers and their networks together to form even larger networks.

InterNIC: A government–industry collaboration created by the NSF in 1993 to manage directory and database services, domain registration services, and other information services on the Internet.

InterNIC Registration Service: A service offered by InterNIC for assigning Internet addresses.

Interorganizational systems: Systems that communicate across organizational boundaries.

Interpreter: A software program that translates a programming language into machine language one statement at a time.

Intranet: An internal, private network using Web technologies to facilitate the secured transmission of proprietary information within an organization, thereby limiting the viewing access to authorized users within the organization.

IP address: An Internet protocol address assigned to every computer and router to connect to the Internet; it serves as the destination address of that computer or device and enables the network to route messages to the proper destination.

IP datagram: A data packet that conforms to the IP specification.

IPv6: The latest version of the Internet protocol, also referred to as IPng, for IP next generation.

Java: An object-oriented programming language that was developed at Sun Microsystems in the early 1990s that is used in developing applications on the Web and other environments.

JavaScript: A scripting language, created by Netscape, that allows developers to add dynamic content to Websites.

Key-indicator report: Reports that provide a summary of critical information on a recurring schedule.

Keyboard: Input device for entering text and numbers into a computer.

Knowledge: A body of governing procedures, such as guidelines or rules, which are used to organize or manipulate data to make it suitable for a given task.

Knowledge society: Term coined by Peter Drucker to refer to a society in which there is a relatively high proportion of knowledge workers, where these types of people have risen in importance and leadership, and where education is the cornerstone of the society.

Knowledge worker: Term coined by Peter Drucker to refer to professionals who are relatively well educated and who create, modify, and/or synthesize knowledge as a fundamental part of their jobs.

Laser printer: A printing technology where characters and images are formed by using a laser beam.

Learning organization: Described by David Garvin as an organization that is "skilled at creating, acquiring, and transferring knowledge, and at modifying its behaviour to reflect new knowledge and insights."

Legacy system: An older stand-alone computer system within an organization with older versions of applications that are either fast approaching or beyond the end of their useful life within the organization.

Liquid crystal display (LCD): A type of computer monitor that is most commonly used on notebook and portable computers.

Listserv: A mailing list that allows individual users to participate in group discussions via e-mail.

Local area network (LAN): A computer network that spans a relatively small area, allowing all computer users to connect with each other to share information and peripheral devices, such as a printer.

Logic or time bomb: A type of computer virus that lies in wait for unsuspecting computer users to perform a triggering operation or for a specific date before executing its instructions.

Low-cost leadership strategy: Strategy by which an organization offers the best prices in its industry on its goods and/or services.

Machine language: A binary-level computer language that computer hardware understands.

Magnetic tape: A secondary storage method that consists of narrow plastic tape coated with a magnetic substance.

Mailing lists: Also known as listservs; let you use e-mail to participate in discussion groups on topics of special interest to you.

Mainframe computer: A very large computer that is used as the main, central computing system for many major corporations and governmental agencies.

Making the business case: The process of identifying, quantifying, and presenting the value provided by an information system.

Management information system (MIS): 1. A field of study that encompasses the development, use, management, and study of computer-based information systems in organizations. 2. An information system designed to support the management of organizational functions at the managerial level of the organization.

Managerial level: The mid level of the organization, where functional managers focus on monitoring and controlling operational-level activities and providing information to higher levels of the organization.

Manual data entry: Having a person enter information by hand into an information system.

Media access control: The rules that govern how a given node or workstation gains access to the network to send or receive information; there are two general types of access control: distributed and random access.

Menu-driven pricing: A pricing system in which companies set and present the prices that consumers pay for products; these prices are non-negotiable.

Message services: The storing, accessing, and delivering of text, binary, graphic, digitized video, and audio data; similar to file services, but they also deal with communication interactions between users and applications; include electronic mail or the transfer of messages between two or more networked computers.

Metropolitan area network (MAN): A computer network of limited geographic scope, typically a city-wide area, that combines both LAN and high-speed fibre-optic technologies. MANs are attractive to organizations that need high-speed data transmission within a limited geographic area.

Microcomputer: A category of computer that is generally used for personal computing, for small business computing, and as a workstation attached to large computers or to other small computers on a network.

Microwave transmission: A high-frequency radio signal sent through the air using either terrestrial (Earth-based) systems or satellite systems.

Midrange computers: Often referred to as minicomputers, these are computers whose performance is lower than that of mainframes, but higher than microcomputers.

Mobile wireless: Wireless approaches for connecting to the Internet where the computer or handheld device can be moved and will continue to connect.

Models: Conceptual, mathematical, logical, and analytical formulas used to represent or project business events or trends.

Modem: Short for modulator/demodulator; a modem is a device or program that enables a computer to transmit data over telephone lines.

Modules: In a software application, components (classified software functions) that are bundled together.

Monitor: A computer display screen.

Moore's Law: The general trend in computing is toward smaller, faster, and cheaper devices; specifically that computer processing performance would double every 18 months.

Motherboard: A large printed plastic or fibreglass circuit board that holds or connects to all of the computer's electronic components.

Multinational information system: A type of international information system that consists of a loose confederacy of various different local information systems.

Multiplexer: Used to share a communications line or medium among a number of users.

Musical Instrument Digital Interface (MIDI): A standard adopted by the electronic music industry for controlling and interconnecting musical devices and computers.

National Science Foundation: The organization in the U.S. that initiated the development of the NSFNET (National Science Foundation Network), which became a major component of the Internet.

National Science Foundation Network (NSFNET): A network developed by the U.S. in 1986 that became a major component of the Internet.

Network: A group of computers and associated peripheral devices connected by a communication channel capable of sharing information and other resources (e.g., a printer) among users.

Network access points: Serve as access points for ISPs and are an exchange point for Internet traffic; these access points determine how traffic is routed and are often the points of most Internet congestion.

Network computer: A microcomputer with minimal memory and storage designed to connect to networks, especially the Internet, to use the resources provided by servers.

Network interface card (NIC): An expansion board that plugs into a computer so that it can be connected to a network.

Network operating system (NOS): System software that controls the network and enables computers to communicate with each other.

Network services: Capabilities of networked computers that enable them to share files, print, send, and receive messages, and to use shared software applications.

Network topology: The shape of a network; the three common network topologies are star, ring, and bus.

New economy: An economy in which information technology plays a significant role and that enables producers of both the tangible (computers, shoes, etc.) and intangible (services, ideas, etc.) to compete efficiently in global markets.

Newsgroups: Also called computer-based discussion groups; allow individuals and organizations to participate in discussions on almost any subject.

Nonrecurring costs: One-time costs that are not expected to continue after the system is implemented.

Normalization: A technique for converting complex databases into ones that are simple and clear.

Notebook computer: A mobile microcomputer that weighs five pounds or less.

Object-oriented analysis and design: Systems development methodologies and techniques based on objects rather than on data and processes.

Object-oriented languages: Programming languages that group together data and its corresponding instructions into manipulatable objects.

Objects: The bundling of data and programming instructions for manipulating that data into a single module.

Off-the-shelf application software: Software designed and used to support general business processes that does not require any specific tailoring to meet the organization's needs.

Office automation or personal productivity software: Information systems that span organizational levels and are used for developing documents, scheduling resources, and communicating.

Office automation system (OAS): A collection of software and hardware for developing documents, scheduling resources, and communicating.

OLAP server: The chief component of an OLAP system that understands how data is organized in the database and has special functions for analyzing the data.

Online analytical processing (OLAP): Graphical software tools that provide complex analysis of data stored in a database.

Online customer service: Assistance for customers offered over the Internet.

Online ordering: Customers visiting a company's Website to order and, in many cases, actually pay for products and services over the Internet.

Online processing: Processing of information as that information occurs.

Online transaction processing (OLTP): Immediate automated responses to the requests from multiple concurrent transactions from customers.

Operational level: The bottom level of an organization, where the routine, day-to-day business processes and interaction with customers occur.

Operational systems: The systems that are used to interact with customers and run a business in real time.

Operating system: Software that coordinates the interaction among hardware devices, peripherals, application software, and users.

Optical disk: A storage disk coated with a metallic substance that is written to (or read from) when a laser beam passes over the surface of the disk.

Organizational learning: The ability of an organization to learn from past behaviour and information and improve as a result.

Organizational strategy: A firm's plan to accomplish its mission and goals and to gain or sustain competitive advantage over rivals.

OSI model: Open Systems Interconnection; a protocol that represents a group of specific, successive tasks that enable computers to communicate with one another.

Output devices: Hardware devices that deliver information in a usable form.

Outsourcing: Turning over partial or entire responsibility for information systems development and management to an outside organization.

Packaged application: A software program written by third-party vendors.

Packet switching: The process of breaking information into small chunks called data packets and then managing the transfer of those packets from computer to computer via the Internet.

Pager: A one-way, wireless messaging system.

Parallel conversion: Changing over from the old to a new system by running both at the same time until the organization is sure that the new system is error-free, that the users are adequately trained, and that the support procedures are in place.

Patent: A right to exclusively manufacture an invention for a specified time.

Peer: Any computer that may both request and provide services.

Peer-to-peer networks: Networks that enable any computer or device on the network to provide and request services.

Perfective maintenance: Making enhancements to improve processing performance, to improve interface usability, or to add desired, but not necessarily required, system features.

Personal area network (PAN): An emerging technology that uses wireless communication to exchange data between computing devices using short-range radio communication, typically within an area of 10 metres.

Personal computer (PC): A class of computers that fit on desktops and are used in homes and offices.

Personal digital assistant (PDA): A handheld microcomputer that has somewhat limited processing and storage capabilities.

Phased conversion: Change over from the old to a new system by utilizing parts of the new system and adding new modules and features to that new system as each part is validated as working properly. This process continues until the entire system is operating and the old system is replaced.

Phreaking: Crimes committed against telephone company computers with the goal of making free long-distance calls, impersonating directory assistance or other operator services, diverting calls to numbers of the perpetrator's choice, or otherwise disrupting telephone service for subscribers.

Piggybacking or shoulder-surfing: The act of simply standing in line behind a card user at an automated teller machine (ATM), looking over that person's shoulder, and memorizing the card's personal identification number (PIN).

Pilot conversion: Changing over from the old to a new system by running the entire system in one location until it is validated as operating properly and then diffusing the system into the entire organization.

Plain old telephone service (POTS): Standard telephone lines with a speed, or bandwidth, that is generally about 52 Kbps (52,000 bits per second); also called the public switched telephone network (PSTN).

Pointing devices: Input devices for pointing at items and selecting menu items on a computer.

Portals: In the context of B2B EC, defined as access points (or front doors) through which a business partner accesses secured, proprietary information from an organization.

Power supply: A device that converts electricity from the wall socket to a lower voltage appropriate for computer components and regulates the voltage to eliminate surges common in most electrical systems.

Preventive maintenance: Making changes to a system to reduce the chance of future system failure.

Primary key: A field included in a database that ensures that each instance of an entity is stored or retrieved accurately.

Primary memory: The computer's main or random access memory (RAM).

Primary storage: Temporary storage that is also referred to as random access memory (RAM) and read-only memory (ROM).

Print services: Used to control and manage users' access to network printers and fax equipment.

Private branch exchange (PBX): A telephone system that serves a particular location, such as a business, connecting one telephone extension to another within the system and connecting the PBX to the outside telephone network.

Processing devices: Computer hardware that transforms inputs into outputs.

Processing logic: The steps by which data is transformed or moved, as well as a description of the events that trigger these steps.

Procurement portals: Enterprise portals that automate the business processes involved in purchasing, or procuring, products between a single buyer and multiple suppliers.

Protocols: Rules dictating communication between senders and receivers within a network.

Prototyping: An iterative systems development process in which requirements are converted into a working system that is continually revised through close work between analysts and users.

Proxy variables: A measurement of changes as a result of systems implementation in terms of their perceived value to the organization, particularly where it is difficult to determine and measure direct effects from a system.

Public key: A data encryption technique that uses two keys—a private key and a public key—to encrypt and decode messages.

Public switched telephone network (PSTN): Also called plain old telephone service (POTS), it is a network of standard telephone lines with a speed, or bandwidth, that is generally about 52 Kbps (52,000 bits per second).

Pull marketing: A strategy by which companies must draw, or pull, visitors to their Websites.

Push marketing: An active strategy in which the company pushes its information at the consumer whether it is wanted or not (e.g., television commercials).

Query: Method used to request information from a database.

Query by example (QBE): A capability of a DBMS that enables data to be requested by providing a sample or a description of the types of data we would like to see.

RAID (redundant array of independent disks): A secondary storage technology that makes redundant copies of data on two or more hard drives.

Random access memory (RAM): A type of primary storage that is volatile and can be accessed randomly by the CPU.

Rapid application development: A systems development methodology that combines prototyping, computer-based development tools, special management practices, and close user involvement.

Read-only memory (ROM): A type of primary storage on which data has been prerecorded and is nonvolatile.

Read/write heads: Components that inscribe data to or retrieve data from hard disks, diskettes, and tapes.

Record: A collection of related attributes about a single entity.

Recurring costs: Ongoing costs that occur throughout the life cycle of systems development, implementation, and maintenance.

Registers: Temporary storage locations inside the CPU where data must reside while it is being processed or manipulated.

Relational database model: The most common DBMS approach in which entities are presented as two-dimensional tables, with records as rows and attributes as columns.

Repeater: A network device used to regenerate or replicate a signal as it weakens when travelling on a network; also moves data from one media segment to another and effectively extends the size of the network.

Report: 1. A compilation of data from the database that is organized and produced in printed format. 2. A business document that contains only predefined data used for reading and viewing, typically for multiple records.

Report generators: Software tools for retrieving data from a database and manipulating (aggregate, transform, or group) and displaying it in a useful format.

Request for Proposal: A communication tool indicating buyer requirements for a given system and requesting information from potential vendors.

Requirements collection: The process of gathering and organizing information from users, managers, business processes, and documents to understand how a proposed information system should function.

Reverse pricing: A pricing system in which customers specify the product they are looking for and how much they are willing to pay for it; this information is routed to appropriate companies, which either accept or reject the consumer's offer.

Ring network: A network that is configured in the shape of a closed loop or circle, with each node connecting to the next node.

Router: An intelligent device used to connect and route data traffic across two or more individual networks.

Rule: A way of encoding knowledge, typically expressed using an IF-THEN format, within an expert system.

Salami slicing: A form of data diddling that occurs when a person shaves small amounts from financial accounts and deposits them in a personal account.

Sales force automation (SFA): The system of applications that mainly focus on contact management and scheduling.

Satellite: A device launched to orbit Earth and enable network communication.

Satellite microwave: The process of using relay stations that transfer high-frequency radio signals between antennas located on Earth and satellites orbiting the Earth.

Scanners: Input devices that convert printed text and images into digital data.

Scheduled reports: Reports produced at predefined intervals—daily, weekly, or monthly—to support the routine informational needs of managerial-level decision making.

Scripting languages: A programming technique for providing interactive components to a Web page.

Secondary key: Attributes not used as the primary key that can be used to identify one or more records within a table that share a common value.

Secondary nonvolatile storage: Methods for permanently storing data to a large-capacity storage component, such as a hard disk, diskette, CD-ROM disk, or tape.

Secure sockets layer (SSL): A popular public key encryption method used on the Internet.

Semiautomated data entry: Data entry into an information system using some type of data capture device such as a grocery store checkout scanner.

Semistructured decisions: Managerial-level decision making where solutions and problems are not clear-cut and often require judgment and expertise.

Server: Any computer on the network that enables access to files, printing, communications, and other services available to users of the network; it typically has a more advanced microprocessor, more memory, a larger cache, and more disk storage than a single-user workstation.

Server-centric networks: Networks in which servers and clients have defined roles.

Service mentality: The belief among information systems personnel that their chief goal is satisfying their systems customers within the firm while fundamentally believing that the customers, not the systems personnel, own the technology and the information.

Single in-line memory module (SIMM): A small circuit board that can hold RAM chips.

Smart card: A special type of credit card with a magnetic strip, a microprocessor chip, and memory circuits.

Social engineering: Gaining information needed to access computers by means of tricking company employees by posing as a magazine journalist, telephone company employee, or forgetful co-worker in order to persuade honest employees to reveal passwords and other information.

Soft data: Textual news stories or other nonanalytical information.

Software: A program or set of programs that tell the computer to perform certain processing functions.

Software engineering: A disciplined approach for constructing information systems through the use of common methods, techniques, or tools.

Software piracy: A type of computer crime where individuals make illegal copies of software protected by copyright laws.

Sound card: A specialized circuit board that supports the ability to convert digital information into sounds that can be listened to on speakers or headphones plugged into the card; a microphone can also be plugged into the card for capturing audio for storage or processing.

Source documents: Documents describing a transaction that serve as a stimulus to a transaction processing system from some external source.

Speech recognition: Software and hardware used to convert spoken words into commands and data.

Spoofing: A scam used to steal passwords from legitimate accounts by using phony login screens.

Stand-alone application: Systems that focus on the specific needs of individual departments and are not designed to communicate with other systems in the organization.

Star network: A network with several workstations connected to a central hub.

Strategic planning: The process of forming a vision of where the organization needs to head, converting that vision into measurable objectives and performance targets, and crafting a plan to achieve the desired results.

Streaming media: Streaming video with sound.

Streaming video: A sequence of compressed moving images that are sent over the Internet.

Structured decisions: Decisions where the procedures to follow for a given situation can be specified in advance.

Structured Query Language (SQL): The most common language used to interface with databases.

Supercomputer: The most expensive and most powerful category of computers. It is primarily used to assist in solving massive research and scientific problems.

Supply chain: The network producers of supplies that a company uses.

Supply chain management: Management of the network of suppliers and subsuppliers that a company interacts with.

Supply network: The flow of materials from multiple suppliers involved in the process of servicing a single organization.

Switch: A device that channels incoming data from any of multiple input ports to the specific output port that will take the data toward its intended destination.

Symmetric digital subscriber line (SDSL): A data transfer format that enables large amounts of data to be sent relatively quickly over existing copper telephone lines; said to be symmetric because it supports the same data rates (up to 3 Mbps) for upstream and downstream traffic; works by sending digital pulses in the high-frequency area of telephone wires.

Symmetric secret key system: An encryption system where both the sender and recipient use the same key for encoding (scrambling) and decoding the message.

System analysis: The second phase of the systems development life cycle, in which the current ways of doing business are studied and alternative replacement systems are proposed.

Systems analysis and design: The process of designing, building, and maintaining information systems.

Systems analyst: The primary person responsible for performing systems analysis and design activities.

Systems benchmarking: A standardized set of performance tests designed to facilitate comparison between systems.

System clock: An electronic circuit inside a computer that generates pulses at a rapid rate for setting the pace of processing events.

System conversion: The process of decommissioning the current system and installing a new system into the organization.

System design: The third phase of the systems development life cycle, in which all features of the proposed system are described.

Systems development life cycle (SDLC): The process of identifying the need for, as well as designing, developing, and maintaining contemporary types of information systems.

System effectiveness: The extent to which a system enables people and/or the firm to accomplish goals or tasks well.

System efficiency: The extent to which a system enables people and/or the firm to do things faster, at lower cost, or with relatively little time and effort.

System identification, selection, and planning: The first phase of the systems development life cycle, in which potential projects are identified, selected, and planned.

System implementation: The fourth phase of the systems development life cycle, in which the information system is programmed, tested, installed, and supported.

Systems integration: Making it so that two information systems can work together better and/or can exchange data more seamlessly with each other.

System maintenance: The fifth (and final) phase of the systems development life cycle, in which an information system is systematically repaired and/or improved.

System software: The collection of programs that controls the basic operations of computer hardware.

System unit: The physical box that houses all of the electronic components that do the work of the computer.

T1 line: Developed by AT&T as a dedicated digital transmission line that can carry 1.544 Mbps of information.

T3 line: A digital transmission line that provides about 45 Mbps of service at about 10 times the cost of leasing a T1 line.

Table: A collection of related records where each row is a record and each column is an attribute.

Tangible benefit: A benefit of using a particular system or technology that can be quantified.

Tangible cost: A cost of using a particular system of technology that is quantifiable.

Technology: Any mechanical and/or electrical means to supplement, extend, or replace human, manual operations or devices.

Telecommunications: Refers to the transmission of all forms of information, including digital data, voice, fax, sound, and video, from one location to another over some type of network.

Telecommunications network: A group of two or more computer systems linked together with communications equipment.

Telecommuting: The process of working at home or at another remote location and "commuting" to the office via computing and networking technologies.

Telemedicine: The exchange of medical information from one location to another via a computer network.

Telnet: Enables users to connect, or log in, to any computer on the Internet.

Terminals: Local input devices used to enter data onto mainframes in centralized computing systems.

Terrestrial microwave: The process of using Earth-based antennas that require an unobstructed path or line of sight between nodes; often used to cross inaccessible terrain or to connect buildings where cable installation would be expensive.

Text recognition software: Software designed to convert handwritten text into computer-based characters.

Token passing: An access method that uses a constantly circulating electronic token, a small packet of data, to prevent collisions and give all workstations equal access to the network.

Top-level domain: Categories of Internet domain names as indicated by their suffix (e.g., .com, .edu, or .org).

Total quality management: A management system in which people within the organization are constantly monitoring what they do to find ways to improve the quality of operations, products, services, and everything else about the firm.

Trading exchange: A Website where multiple buyers and sellers come together to conduct business; also called an electronic marketplace.

Transaction processing system (TPS): An information system designed to process day-to-day business event data at the operational level of the organization.

Transactions: Repetitive events in organizations that occur as a regular part of conducting day-to-day operations.

Transmission control protocol/ Internet protocol (TCP/IP): The protocol of the Internet, which allows different interconnected networks to communicate using the same language.

Transmission media: The physical pathway to send data and information between two or more entities on a network.

Transnational information system: A type of international information system that is not specific to any country or any particular organization.

Trojan horse: A destructive computer code whose instructions remain hidden to the user because the computer appears to function normally, but in fact it is performing underlying functions dictated by the intrusive code.

Tunnelling: A technology used by VPNs to encapsulate, encrypt, and transmit data over the Internet infrastructure, enabling business partners to exchange information in a secured, private manner between organizational firewalls.

Twisted pair cable: Cable made of two or more pairs of insulated copper wires twisted together.

Unauthorized access: Occurs when a person gains access to a computer system who does not have authority to do so.

Unicode: A 16-bit code used for representing numbers, letters, and other characters in binary form.

Uniform resource locator: The unique Internet address for a Website and specific Web pages within sites.

Unstructured decisions: Decisions for which few or no procedures to follow for a given situation can be specified in advance.

Upstream: An information flow consisting of information received from another organization, such as from a supplier.

Usenet: Enables groups of people with common interests to send messages or other binary information to each other. Unlike listserv, Usenet has no master list of subscribers. Rather, anyone with access to Usenet may use a newsreader program to post and read articles from the group.

Utilities or utility programs: Software designed to manage computer resources and files.

Value-added network (VAN): Medium-speed WANs that are private, third-party-managed networks and are economical because they are shared by multiple organizations.

Value chain: The process of adding value throughout each of the functions within the organization.

Value chain analysis: The process of analyzing an organization's activities to determine where value is added to products and/or services and the costs that are incurred in doing so.

Value system: A collection of interlocking company value chains.

Vanilla: The features and modules that the ERP comes with out of the box.

Vertical market: A market comprising firms within a specific industry sector.

Video: Still and moving images that can be recorded, manipulated, and displayed on a computer.

Videoconferencing: The use of integrated telephone, video recording, and playback technologies by two or more people to interact with each other from remote sites.

Virtual company: A firm that exists either on paper or on the Internet but has few or no physical components or attributes.

Virtual private network: A secure network that utilizes telecommunications lines from a telephone service provider and enables a connection to be created when a transmission needs to take place and terminated once the transmission has been completed, and enables the user to scale bandwidth up and down as needed.

Virtual product: A product without tangible features created through the process of digitization.

Virtual teams: Work teams that are composed of members that may be from different organizations and different locations that form and disband as needed.

Viruses: Destructive programs that disrupt the normal functioning of computer systems.

Visual programming languages: Programming languages that have a graphical user interface (GUI) for the programmer and are designed for programming applications that will have a GUI.

Voice mail: Telecommunication technology that allows callers to leave voice messages in a voice mailbox, much like leaving a message on an answering machine.

Voice over IP (VoIP): A collection of hardware and software that enables the use of the Internet as the transmission medium for telephone calls.

Volatile: Memory that loses its contents when the power is turned off.

WAIS (wide area information server): Internet tool that enables users to locate information by indexing electronic data using standard keywords.

Watermarked: The process of marking products so that they can be traced to the original purchaser.

Web browser: A software application that can be used to locate and display Web pages including text, graphics, and multimedia content.

Web commerce: The component of Internet commerce conducted strictly over the World Wide Web.

Web page: A hypertext document that contains not only information, but also references or links to other documents that contain related information.

Web page builders or HTML editors: Programs for assisting in the creation and maintenance of Web pages.

Web server: A computer used to host Websites.

Website: A collection of interlinked Web pages created by the same author.

What-if analysis: A capability of some information systems (e.g., a decision support system) that allows a user to make hypothetical changes to the data associated with a problem and to observe how these changes influence the results.

Wide area network (WAN): A computer network that spans a relatively large geographical area; typically used to connect two or more LANs.

Wireless local area network (WLAN): Local area network using a wireless transmission protocol.

Wireless media: The tools used to transmit and receive electromagnetic signals using methods such as infrared line of sight, high-frequency radio, and microwave systems.

Wisdom: Accumulated knowledge, gained through a combination of academic study and personal experience, that goes beyond knowledge by representing broader, more generalized rules and schemas for understanding a specific domain or domains; wisdom allows you to understand how to apply concepts from one domain to new situations or problems.

Work profile matrix: A chart that consists of job categories and work categories and shows how much time is spent on each of the job categories and each of the different types of work.

Workstation: A special class of microcomputer designed for individuals that has the power of some midrange computers but fits on a desktop.

World Wide Web (Web): A system of Internet servers that support documents formatted in HTML, which supports links to other documents, as well as graphics, audio, and video files.

Worm: Destructive computer code that is designed to copy and send itself throughout networked computers.

Zip drive: A high-capacity, removable diskette drive that typically uses 100 MB Zip disks or cartridges.

References

CHAPTER 1

Farrell, C., A. T. Palmer, and S. Browder. 1998. "A Rising Tide for Workers," *BusinessWeek* (August 31). **www.businessweek.com/1998/35/b3593010.htm.**

Koch, C. 1998. "Can Federalism Fly?" *CIO* 11(12): 46–50.

Porter, M. 1985. "Technology and Competitive Advantage," *Journal of Business Strategy* 5(3): 60–78.

Porter, M. and V. Millar. 1985. "How Information Gives You Competitive Advantage," *Harvard Business Review* 63(4): 149–161.

Rothfeder, J. and L. Driscoll. 1990. "CIO Is Starting to Stand for 'Career Is Over': Once Deemed Indispensable, the Chief Information Officer Has Become an Endangered Species," *BusinessWeek* (February 26, 1990): 78.

Stevens, D. 1994. "Reinvent IS or Jane Will." *Datamation* (December 15, 1994): 84.

Todd, P., J. McKeen, and R. Gallupe. 1995. "The Evolution of IS Job Skills: A Content Analysis of IS Jobs," *MIS Quarterly* 19(1): 1–27.

Wade, M. and M. Parent. 2002. "Relationships between Job Skills and Performance: A Study of Webmasters," *Journal of Management Information Systems* 18(3): 71–98.

CHAPTER 2

Bakos, J. Y. and M. E. Treacy. 1986. "Information Technology and Corporate Strategy: A Research Perspective," *MIS Quarterly* 10(2): 107–120.

Belcher, L. W. and H. J. Watson. 1993. "Assessing the Value of Conoco's EIS," *MIS Quarterly* 17(3): 239–254.

Brynjolfsson, E. 1993. "The Productivity Paradox of Information Technology," *Communications of the ACM* 36(12): 66–76.

Hagendorf, J. 1998. "Trying to Keep Pace—IS Spending Climbs, Along with Needs, Costs," *Computer Reseller News*. Information from: **www.techweb.com**. Information verified: April 29, 1998.

Harris, S. E. and J. L. Katz. 1991. "Organizational Performance and Information Technology Investment Intensity in the Insurance Industry." *Organization Science* 2(3): 263–295.

Leibs, S. and K. M. Carrillo. 1997. "Research Productivity—Replacing Workers with IS Doesn't Guarantee Maximum Gains, Finds a New Study from Harvard: What Does? You May Be Surprised," *InformationWeek*. Information from: **www.techweb.com**. Information verified: April 29, 1998.

Porter, M. E. 1979. "How Competitive Forces Shape Strategy." *Harvard Business Review* 57 (March–April 1979): 137–145.

Porter, M. E. 1985. *Competitive Advantage: Creating and Sustaining Superior Performance*. New York: The Free Press.

Porter, M. E. 2001. "Strategy and the Internet," *Harvard Business Review* 79(3): 62–78.

Sassone, P. G., and A. P. Schwartz. 1986. "Cost-Justifying OA," *Datamation* (February 15): 83–88.

Shank, J. and V. Govindarajan. 1993. *Strategic Cost Management: Three Key Themes for Managing Costs Effectively*. New York: The Free Press.

Wheeler, B. C. 2002a. "Making the Business Case for IT Investments Through Facts, Faith, and Fear," ISWorld.net Online Teaching Case and Teaching Note. **www.coba.usf.edu/departments/isds/faculty/abhatt/cases/TN-ITInvestments.doc**.

Wheeler, B. C. 2002b. "NeBIC: A Dynamic Capabilities Theory for Assessing Net-Enablement." *Information Systems Research* 13(2).

Zuboff, S. 1988. *In the Age of the Smart Machine: The Future of Work and Power*. New York: Basic Books.

CHAPTER 3

Boar, B. 1998. "Understanding Data Warehousing Strategically." White paper, NCR. **www.ncr.com**.

Date, C. J. 1995. *An Introduction to Database Systems*. New York: Addison-Wesley.

Hoffer, J. A., M. B. Prescott, and F. R. McFadden, 2002. *Modern Database Management*, 6th ed. Upper Saddle River, NJ: Pearson Education.

CHAPTER 4

Sarker, Suprateek and Saonee Sarker. 2000. "Implementation Failure of an Integrated Software Package: A Case Study from the Far East," *Annals of Cases on Information Technology Applications and Management in Organizations* 2: 169–186.

CHAPTER 5

Alexander, M. 2001. "IBM Web Site to Drive ASIC Design Collaboration," Information from: **www.internetweek. com/story/INW20010308S0004**. Information verified: July 27, 2001.

Chatterjee, D. and V. Sambamurthy. 1999. "Business Implications of Web Technology: An Insight into Usage of the World Wide Web by U.S. Companies," *Electronic Markets—International Journal of Electronic Commerce & Business Media* 9(2) (Spring 1999).

Christensen, C. M. and R. S. Tedlow. 2000. "Patterns of Disruption in Retailing," *Harvard Business Review* (January–February 2000): 6–9.

Dell 2001. "Welcome to Business Center," Information from: **www.dell.com/us/en/biz/default.htm**. Information verified: August 1, 2001.

Kalakota, R., R. A. Oliva, and E. Donath. 1999. "Move Over, E-Commerce," *Marketing Management* 8(3) (Fall 1999): 23–32.

Looney, C. A. and D. Chatterjee. 2002. "Web-Enabled Transformation of the Brokerage Industry: An Analysis of Emerging Business Models," *Communications of the ACM 45(8): 75–81.*

McDougall, P. 2000. "Dell: Beyond the Box?" *InformationWeek* 787 (May 22, 2000): 48–57.

Microsoft Corporation. 2001. "Microsoft Business Case Studies," **Web.microsoft.com/business/casestudies/default.asp** (June 2001).

Quelch, J. A. and L. R. Klein. 1996. "The Internet and Internal Marketing," *Sloan Management Review* 63 (Spring): 60–75.

Rebello, K. 1996. "Italian Sausage that Sizzles in Cyberspace," *BusinessWeek* (September 23, 1996): 118.

SciQuest. 2001. "SciQuest Corporate Page," Information from: **www.sciquest.com**. Information verified: August 1, 2001.

Sullivan, K. B. 1999. "Boeing Achieves Internet Liftoff," ZDNet eWeek, **Web.zdnet.com/eweek** (May 10, 1999).

Szuprowicz, B. 1998. *Extranet and Intranet: E-commerce Business Strategies for the Future.* Charleston, SC: Computer Technology Research Corporation.

Tempest, N. 1999. "Charles Schwab Corporation (B)," *Harvard Business School Press* (September 13, 1999).

Turban, E., J. Lee, D. King, and H. M. Chung. 2000. *Electronic Commerce: A Managerial Perspective.* Upper Saddle River, NJ: Prentice Hall.

CHAPTER 6

Checkland, P. B. 1981. *Systems Thinking, Systems Practice.* Chichester, UK: John Wiley.

Roche, E. M. 1992. *Managing Information Technology in Multinational Corporations.* New York: Macmillan.

Sprague, R. H., Jr. 1980. "A Framework for the Development of Decision Support Systems," *MIS Quarterly* 4(4): 1–26.

Turban, E. and J. E. Aronson. 2001. *Decision Support Systems and Intelligent Systems*, 6th ed. Englewood Cliffs, NJ: Prentice Hall.

CHAPTER 7

Butler, S. 2001. "From B2B to SCM," *Entrepreneur.com.* Information from: **www.entrepreneur.com.** Information verified: August 16, 2001.

Koch, C., D. Slater, and E. Baatz. 2000. "The ABCs of ERP," *CIO Magazine.* Information from: **www.cio.com.** Information verified: August 6, 2001.

Kumar, K. and J. Van Hillegersberg. 2000. "ERP Experiences and Evolution," *Communications of the ACM* 43(4): 23–26.

Kumar, R. L. and C. W. Crook. 1999. "A Multi-Disciplinary Framework for the Management of Interorganizational Systems," *The DATA BASE for Advances in Information Systems* 30(1): 22–36.

Langenwalter, G. A. 2000. *Enterprise Resources Planning and Beyond.* Boca Raton, FL: St. Lucie Press.

Larson, P. D. and D. S. Rogers. 1998. "Supply Chain Management: Definition, Growth, and Approaches," *Journal of Marketing Theory and Practice* 6(4): 1–5.

Manugistics. 2001. "Enterprise Profit Optimization," Information from: **www.manugistics.com.** Information verified: August 16, 2001.

Markus, M. L. and D. Tanis. 2000. "The Enterprise Systems Experience—From Adoption to Success." In *Framing the Domains of IT Research: Glimpsing the Future Through the Past*, edited by R. W. Zmud. Cincinnati, OH: Pinnaflex Educational Resources.

Porter, M. E. and V. E. Millar. 1985. "How Information Gives You Competitive Advantage," *Harvard Business Review* (July–August): 149–160.

Ptak, C. A. 2000. *ERP Tools, Techniques, and Applications for Integrating the Supply Chain.* Boca Raton, FL: St. Lucie Press.

Sarker, S. and A. S. Lee. 2000. "Using a Case Study to Test the Role of Three Key Social Enablers in ERP Implementation," *Proceedings of the International Conference on Information Systems*, Brisbane, Australia: 414–425.

Shah, J. B. 2001. "ERP Losing Favor as Businesses Reevaluate What to Target—SCM, CRM Software Now More in Demand," *Ebn* 1265 (June 4): 4–5.

Soh, C., S. K. Sia, and J. Tay-Yap. 2000. "Cultural Fits and Misfits: Is ERP a Universal Solution?" *Communications of the ACM* 43(4): 47–51.

Willcocks, L. and R. Sykes. 2000. "The Role of the CIO and IT Function in ERP," *Communications of the ACM* 43(4): 32–38.

CHAPTER 8

Applegate, L. M. and F. W. McFarlan. 1999. *Corporate Information Systems Management: Text and Cases*, 5th ed. Chicago, IL: Irwin.

Booch, G. 1990. *Object Oriented Design with Applications.* Redwood City, CA: Benjamin/Cummings.

Boynton, A. C. and R. W. Zmud. 1994. "An Assessment of Critical Success Factors." In *Management Information Systems*, 2nd ed., edited by Gray, King, McLean, and Watson. Fort Worth, TX: The Dryden Press.

Coad, P. and E. Yourdon. 1991. *Object-Oriented Design.* Englewood Cliffs, NJ: Prentice Hall.

Court, R. 1998. "Disney Buys Out Starwave," **www.wired.com**, *Wired Magazine* (April 30, 1991).

Fryer, B. 1994. "Outsourcing Support: Kudos and Caveats," **www.computerworld.com**, *Computerworld* (April 11, 1994).

Halladay, S. and M. Wiebel. 1993. *Object Oriented Software Engineering.* Englewood Cliffs, NJ: Prentice Hall.

Hoffer, J. A., J. F. George, and J. S. Valacich. 2002. *Modern Systems Analysis and Design*, 3rd ed. Englewood Cliffs, NJ: Prentice Hall.

Martin, J. 1991. *Rapid Application Development.* New York: Macmillan.

McConnell, S. 1996. *Rapid Development.* Redmond, WA: Microsoft Press.

McFarlan, F. W. and R. L. Nolan. 1995. "How to Manage an IT Outsourcing Alliance," *Sloan Management Review* 36(2): 9–24.

Nunamaker, J. F., Jr. 1992. "Build and Learn, Evaluate and Learn," *Informatica* 1(1): 1–6.

CHAPTER 9

BSA. 2001. "Sixth Annual BSA Global Software Piracy Study," *Business Software Alliance* (May). **www.bsa.org.**

Mason, R. O. 1986. "Four Ethical Issues for the Information Age," *MIS Quarterly* (16): 423–433.

Mosquera, M. 2000. "FBI E-Mail Surveillance Raises Privacy Concerns." **www.techweb.com/wire/story/TWB20000713S0013.**

APPENDIX A

Freed, L. 1995. *The History of Computing.* Emeryville, CA: Ziff-Davis Press.

Keogh, J. 2002. *The Essential Guide to Computer Hardware.* Ridgefield Park, NJ: Prentice Hall.

APPENDIX B

Chen, M. and R. J. Norman. 1992. "Integrated Computer-Aided Software Engineering (CASE): Adoption, Implementation, and Impacts." In *Proceedings of the Hawaii International Conference on System Sciences* 3, ed. J. F. Nunamaker, Jr. Los Alamitos, CA: IEEE Computer Society Press: 362–373.

Hoffer, J. A., J. F. George, and J. S. Valacich. 2002. *Modern Systems Analysis and Design*, 3rd ed. Upper Saddle River, NJ: Prentice Hall.

Orlikowski, W. J. 1989. "Division Among the Ranks: The Social Implications of CASE Tools for Systems Developers." In *Proceedings of the Tenth International Conference on Information Systems:* 199–210.

Name Index

Organization Index

Subject Index

Note: Key terms and the page(s) on which they are defined appear in boldface.

O

P

Q

R